T·H·E
BEDSIDE
BOOK OF
COLONIAL
DOINGS

T·H·E
BEDSIDE
BOOK OF
COLONIAL
DOINGS

A marvellous Australian miscellany
of fascinating events, facts and figures.

J. H. HEATON

CORNSTALK PUBLISHING
an imprint of Angus & Robertson Publishers

Unit 4, Eden Park, 31 Waterloo Road,
North Ryde, NSW, Australia 2113, and
16 Golden Square, London W1R 4BN,
United Kingdom

First published as part of Australian Dictionary
of Dates and Men of the Time
by George Robertson in 1879
This presentation first published in Australia
by Angus & Robertson Publishers in 1984
This edition 1986
Reprinted 1987

National Library of Australia
Cataloguing-in-publication data.

Heaton, J.H. (John Henniker), 1848-1914.
  The bedside book of colonial doings.

  ISBN 0 207 15447 3.

  1. Australia — History — Dictionaries.
  1. Title.

994

Printed in Singapore

A

ABORIGINAL CRICKETERS.

The aboriginal team of cricketers, trained and taught the game by Mr. Wills, arrived in Sydney from Victoria, February 16, 1867; on the 21st they commenced a three-days' match against eleven of the Albert Club, which resulted in a win for the latter, Feb. 21, 22, 23, 1867. The scores were :—Albert, 1st innings, 135, 2nd innings, 163, total, 298 ; aboriginal team scoring but 72 and 92, making their total only 164. The team was captained by Mr. Wills, and the names of the aboriginal players were as follows :—Rose, Bullocky, Cuzens, Mullagh, Jellico, Peter, Tarpot, Paddy, Dick-a-Dick, Watty, and Twopenny.

ABORIGINAL CRICKETERS TEAM OF 1866
A & R Archives

ABORIGINAL CRICKETERS IN ENGLAND. A team of aboriginal cricketers visited England for the purpose of contesting the game with renowned English clubs. The team was captained by Lawrence, and consisted of the following aboriginal players :—Bullocky, Cuzens, Dick-a-Dick, King Cole, Mullagh, Peter, Shepherd, Mosquito, Jim Crow, Charley, Tiger, Twopenny, Red-Cap; February 8, 1868. First match played at the Oval, Kennington, London, against eleven gentlemen of the Surrey Club, in the presence of 7,000 spectators. Surrey Club : 1st innings, 222. Aboriginals : 1st innings, 83, 2nd innings, 132. The aboriginals scored their first victory over an English team at Ladywell, against eleven gentlemen of Lewisham. The attendance was upwards of 4,000. A handsome silver cup was presented to Red-Cap by the Captain of the Lewisham team as the highest scorer on the Australian side. Gentlemen : 1st innings, 60, 2nd, 53, total, 113. Aboriginals : 1st innings, 42, 2nd 72, total, 114.—June 10, 1868. v. Marylebone. Played at Lords' ground, Marylebone; upwards of 3,000 present. M.C.C. : 1st innings, 164, 2nd innings, 121, total, 285. Aboriginals : 1st innings, 185, 2nd innings, 45, total, 230.—June 12 and 13, 1868. v. Gentlemen of Kent. Played on Kent County ground, Gravesend. The gentlemen won in one innings by 69 runs.—June 2, 1868. v. Richmond Club. Played at the old deer park, Richmond. There was a very large attendance. This match was not played out, but so far as it proceeded it was in favour of the blacks. Richmond : 1st innings, 74, 2nd innings, 236, total, 310. Aboriginals : 1st innings, 97, 2nd innings, 82, not finished.— June 6, 1868. Gentlemen of Sussex v. Aboriginal Team. Played at Brighton; at least 5,000 spectators. The game was won by the gentlemen by nine wickets. A sum of eight guineas was collected on the ground and presented to Mullagh, to mark the appreciation of the all-round play he exhibited. Aboriginals : 1st innings, 171, 2nd innings, 89, total, 260. Gentlemen : 1st innings, 151, 2nd innings, 122.—June 9, 1868.

King Cole, one of the aboriginal cricketers, died of inflammation of the lungs.—July 30, 1868.

Mullagh distinguished himself in the Victorian Eleven against Lord Harris's team, at Melbourne, by making the highest score (36) in the 2nd innings.—March 8, 1879.

ABORIGINAL NAMES.

" The tribe of Camerra inhabit the north side of Port Jackson ; the tribe of Cadi inhabit the south side, extending from the South Head to Long Cove, at which place the district of Wanne, and the tribe of Wangal, commences, extending as far as Par-ra-mata or Rose Hill ; the tribe Wallumede inhabit the north shore, opposite Warrane or Sydney Cove, and are called Wallumatta. The space between Rose Hill and Prospect Hill is distinguished by eight different names, although the distance is only four miles."—*Hunter's Journal.*

EXAMPLES OF.

North Head (Sydney)—" Boree."
South Head (Sydney)—" Cuttai."
Middle Head (Sydney)—" Cubba Cubba."
Timbrebungie—" Big Bend." A large bend in the Macquarie, twenty miles below Dubbo.
Dubbo—" White clay or sand."
Minore—" All about."
Wollombi—" Meeting of the Waters." A village situated sixteen miles south-west from Maitland, where two streams meet.
Potts' Point (Sydney)—" Carrajeen."
Lady Macquarie's Chair (Sydney)—" Yurong."
Darling Point (Sydney)—" Yaranabe."
Manly Beach (Sydney)—" Cannae."
Cockatoo Island (Sydney)—" Warrieubah."
Goat Island (Sydney)—" Memel."
Hawkesbury River—" Deerabubbin." The aboriginals suffered at times from a disease very like small-pox, called by them " Galgala."
Botanic Gardens, Farm Cove (Sydney)—" Yoolaugh."

Milson's Point—" Kirribilli."
Blue's Point—" Warung."

Sydney	Warrane	
Parramatta	Parramatta	eels sit down.
Manaro	Manaro	the navel.

Minyago yugilla—Why weepest thou ?—is the name of a fountain springing out of the side of a mountain near the Namoi.

Manilla (River)	Muneela	round about
Culgoa (River)	Culgoa	running through
Boggabri	Bukkiber-i	place of creeks
Drill dool	Tareel dool	place of reeds
Piliga	Bilagha	head of scrub oak
Breewarina	Bureewarrina	trees (acacia pendula)
Yarra Yarra		flowing, flowing
Mooki (River)	Mook-i	flinty
Guligal	Guligal	long grass seed
Molroy or Miiroy	Murrowolaroi	having hedgehogs
Narrabri	Nurra-bur-i	forks
Botany	Zwiagal	
Bundarra	Bundarra	place of kangaroos
Balal	Balal	bare, barren
Pokataroo	Bukkitaro	river going, wide
Barwon	Ba-wun	great (river)
Gundamaine	Gundi-my-an	house on the stream
Gwydir (River)	Gu-i-da	place of red (banks)
Gunedah	Gunneda	place of white stone
North Shore (Sydney)	Walumetta	
Dromedary Mountain	Culago	
Fort Bourke	Wurtamurtah	
Lachlan (River)	Colai	
Newcastle, Mulubimba		

Names of some of the aboriginals of Sydney in the first days of the colony :—

" Benelong."
" Barangaroo"—Wife of Benelong.
" Daringha "—Ditto.
" Dilboong"—Name of native girl living in Sydney.
" Mangoran "—A chief of Sydney.
" Ballooderry "—Son of Mangoran.
" Bedia Bedia "—Chief of Parramatta.

" Yelloway "—Ditto.
" Gorne Beak "—A great fighting man.
A white man named Wilson was many years ago living with the blacks in the Port Stephens district. He was called by them " Bunboey."

ABORIGINAL, PETRIFIED. Found in a cave near Mt. Gambier, S.A., 1862. The aboriginal was shortly afterwards stolen, and no trace of it has been discovered. It was rumoured that it had been exhibited in England some years afterwards.

[Two petrified aboriginals were found on the Upper Murray or "Indi" in 1854. They were in a perfect state of preservation. One was taken to Sydney by a travelling hawker, and thence shipped to England, but the ship was lost.]

ABORIGINALS.

ANNUAL CONFERENCES WITH. Proclamation issued that an annual friendly conference be held on December 28th of each year, May 4, 1816; held at Parramatta between the Governor and the leading tribes, January 17, 1826; at same place, December 28, 1826; by Governor Darling at Parramatta, January 16, 1830.

ATTACKS BY. Very troublesome in 1796; people at farms about Parramatta plundered of provisions and clothing; settlers armed themselves, and several conflicts ensued throughout the year; many blacks were killed, and several of the Europeans were wounded; very troublesome at Lane Cove, at Bringelly on the Nepean, Bathurst Road, and at other places,

GOVERNOR DARLING AT AN ANNUAL CONFERENCE WITH NATIVE TRIBES
Rex Nan Kivell Collection

1816; large number of blacks, never before seen within the different settlements, came from the mountains, plundered the drays and farms, and mangled the bodies of their victims; annoyed settlers beyond Blue Mountains, stealing cattle for food, as they said, in exchange for their kangaroos which the settlers had shot, 1823; blacks in the neighbourhood exceedingly robust and well proportioned (*see* ABORIGINALS, REMARKABLE); a party of eighteen men travelling overland with sheep to Port Phillip attacked by 300—seven white men killed and one man wounded, 1838; fifteen shepherds and stockmen killed at Liverpool Plains, 1838; blacks having large quantities of arms in their possession, were very formidable to the settlers in the Port Phillip district, 1840; telegraph station, Barrow's Creek, attacked, February 22, 1874.

CALL OF COMMUNICATION BETWEEN. The peculiar signal-call of the natives, " Coo-ee " or " Coo-ey " with the rising inflection on the second syllable, can be heard to a much greater distance than any call made by Europeans, and its repetition from a distance at once establishes a communication between two parties. The up-country settlers have all adopted this " Coo-ey," and constantly use it.

CEREMONIES AMONGST. *The Bora.*—The name " Bora " is derived from " Bor " or " Boora," the belt of manhood, and is conferred on the neophyte of life entering that stage. This " bor " is supposed to be endowed with magical power, so that by throwing it at an enemy sickness can be ejected from the body of the thrower. It is the great national institution of the Australian Aboriginal, the rite of initiation into the duties and privileges of manhood. The sacredness of this immemorial rite, and the indispensable obligation to submit to it, are most deeply impressed on the minds of the young aboriginals. Even when they enter the service of the squatters or the settlers, and so in a great measure break off from association with their own people, they seem to be bound by an irresistible spell to submit, at the presented time, in spite of all obstacles and dissuasions, to their national rites. The " Bora " is held whenever there is a considerable number of youths of an age to be admitted to the rank of manhood. Rev. William Ridley, an authority on the subject, says :—" Old Billy Murri Bundar at Burturgate, stated that the Creator ' *Baiame* ' long ago commanded the people to keep the ' Bora,' and gave them the *Dhūrumbulūm*, or sacred wand for this purpose. He said any one of the men might demand that a ' Bora ' be held. Then they consult as to the place, and choose one of their number to be the dictator or manager of the solemnity. This dictator sends a man round to all the tribes, who are expected to join in it. This herald bears in his hand a *boomerang* and a *spear* with a *murūra* (padymelon) *skin* hanging upon it. Sometimes all the men within twenty miles are summoned, sometimes a much larger circuit is included, and Billy stated that every one summoned

must attend the " Bora," even if he have to travel a hundred miles to it. It is so done, he said, all over the country and always will be. The dictator chooses a suitable spot for the purpose, and fixes the day for the opening of the ceremony. The ground is regarded as consecrated to ' Baiame,' and his will is obeyed in carrying out the service. Notice is given three weeks at least, sometimes three months before the ceremony begins; during the interval the trees on the chosen ground are ornamented with figures of snakes and birds cut with the tomahawk. When the appointed time is come, the men leave their camps, where the women and children and youths remain. The men assemble at the selected spot, clear away all the bushes, and make a semi-circular embankment or fence ; this being done, some of the men go to the camps, pretending to make a hostile attack, on which the women run away with the children,—the young men and boys over thirteen go back with the men to the ' Bora.' Very few Europeans have been allowed to witness the ceremony, but a Mr. Honey, when a boy, was present at one held between the Barwon and Castlereagh Rivers, and has given a description of it, but the proceedings and ceremonies appear to differ widely in the different tribes, the discipline the candidates for manhood have to go through in some tribes being far more severe than in others, so much so that the young men, after undergoing the severity of the ordeal, are quite exhausted, and sometimes half-dead. Previous to undergoing the ordeal, the candidates have to be for seven or eight months under a strict rule, eating only prescribed food, and keeping themselves partially secluded from social intercourse. The day of the ceremony having been decided on and the tribes assembled, a place is cleared and prepared generally on the top of a low hill ; here the youths are kept for a week under the *surveillance* of two or three old men ; at the end of this time one of the front teeth is knocked out and the youths receive a severe flogging, during which tortures they are not expected to groan or display any signs of pain. For the next four days (in some tribes) their food is of the most revolting description that can be imagined. After the last ceremony the young men were allowed to go away. For three or four months they are not allowed to come within three hundred yards of a woman, but once in the course of the time a great smoke is made with burning boughs, and the young men are brought up to one side of it, whilst women appear at a distance on the other side. Then the young men go away for another month or so ; at the end of that time they again assemble and take part in a sham fight ; this completes the long process of initiation. From this time they are free to exercise all the privileges of manhood, amongst which are the eating of the flesh of kangaroo and emus, and the taking of wives. During the intervals between the ceremonies of the ' Bora ' the candidates are carefully instructed by the old men in the unwritten laws or traditions of their tribe and the laws of consanguinity and marriage, a breach of which latter moral law subjects the offender to the risk of death. The ceremonial of the 'Bora' is the great educational system by which this exact observance of their law is inculcated."

Circumcision. The rite of circumcision is commonly practised by the aboriginals of Australia, particularly around the Gulf of Carpentaria *(Leichhardt);—The knocking out of the front tooth* is most extensively practised by the natives of Australia. It appears to be performed on their entering into early manhood, though often when they are twelve or fourteen years of age, and consists in extracting the front tooth from the upper jaw. The patient has often to undergo the greatest agony, and eat the most vile and disgusting food for several days.

Corrobborree. [*See* CORROBBOREE.]

CONFLICTS WITH. Near Sydney, August, 1794; desperate fight at Parramatta (their leader Pemuluy wounded and captured), March, 1797; near Parramatta (between natives and military —50 natives shot), May 3, 1804; desperate fight on the Sydney Race Course (now Hyde Park) between two hostile tribes (a number of the combatants severely wounded and one killed on the spot), December 26, 1829.

FREEMASONRY AMONGST. Sturt, the explorer, relates that he met a tribe of aboriginals in Central Australia, who had an intimate knowledge of freemasonry, and gave the signs only known to the mystic brotherhood.

FUNERAL RITES. In all parts of the country the aboriginals show a great regard for their dead. Some bury them; and of those who do so, some dig the grave so deep as to place the deceased standing up; others place them sitting with the head above the surface, but covered with earth. They carefully protect their graves with boughs from the depredations of wild animals; sometimes there are as many as a hundred graves in their cemeteries. Amongst the Wailwun tribe, a chief, or person regarded with much respect, is buried in a hollow tree, the body being enclosed in a sheet of bark; in other places the body is deposited on a sheet of bark on the forks of a tree. And affection sometimes induces their relatives to carry about the bones (after the flesh is gone) for a long time; it is no uncommon thing in a mother thus to carry the bones of her child for years. Sometimes a tribe devour the heart and liver of a chief, that they may inherit the virtues and courage for which he was distinguished. The fashion of their mourning is to plaster their heads and faces with white clay, and wound themselves with tomahawks till the blood pours forth, keeping up a great wailing the while. In Northern Australia they cut off the joint of one of their fingers as an expression of grief for the death of their children.

GRANTS OF LAND TO. A piece of ground at George's Head, for the purpose of cultivation, allocated to sixteen natives with their wives and families numbering forty altogether of the Broken Bay tribe, with Boongarie as their chief, measured off and appropriated to their exclusive use, and at same time a suit of clothes given to each of them together with implements of husbandry, February 1, 1814.

LANGUAGES OF. The Rev. Canon Gunther compiled a grammar and dictionary of the Wiradhuri language, which was sent to the Imperial Government, in manuscript, in compliance with a request from Professor Max Müller for information of this kind; a work of similar character, by the late Rev. Mr. Watson, a colleague in the mission of Mr. Gunther, was also sent home; Rev. L. E. Threlkeld published, in 1834 and 1850, a grammar and a key to the language of the Lower Hunter; the Government printed and published in Sydney, in 1866, and a second edition in 1875, a work on Kamilaroi and other Australian languages, by the Rev. William Ridley, containing illustrations of twenty different dialects, and a comprehensive grammar of Kamilaroi; the Rev. Mr. Taplin has also published some works on the languages and people of South Australia; Mr. Brough Smyth, of Melbourne, and Mr. Curr, of Geelong, have been compiling works of a comprehensive character on the languages of Australia; a publication of Mr. Curr on the subject appeared some years ago.

Mr. R. Brough Smyth has just published (1879) an exhaustive work on the language and customs of the aborigines.

LAST. King Billy or William Lanne, last male Tasmanian aboriginal, died March 3, 1869; Queen Trucannimai, or Lalla Rookh, the last of the Tasmanian female aboriginals, died at Hobart Town, aged 73, May 8, 1876.

MARRIAGE LAWS OF. Many, perhaps all, tribes of Australian aboriginals have strict rules as to marriage, founded on a system of giving certain distinctive names to all children according to their parentage. The rules are numerous, but a few words may give a general idea of them. The mother's name determines that of her children. Thus all the sons of Kubbotha are Kumbo, and all the daughters are Butha. A Kumbo may have one or two other names; but every son of a woman called Kubbotha is named Kumbo. So the sons of a woman named Ippatha are all Kubbi, and her daughters are all Kubbotha. In some parts four names of men and four names of women comprehend a whole community, every one of the tribe having one of these names; in some parts there are more names, some less. The names belong to them from birth. They do not take the same names as their parents; but the mother's name fixes those of her children. The whole tribe being thus named by an inflexible rule, a law of marriage is founded upon the names. Thus Kumbo is to take his wife, or wives, from among women bearing the name of Matha; Kubbi has his choice of the Ippatha; and Ippai (brother of Ippatha), is free to take any Kubbotha (sister of Kubbi). The rule prevents a man from taking to wife a sister, half-sister, niece, or aunt, and also prevents the intermarriage of first cousins, when they are the children of two brothers or of two sisters. It is possible under this rule for a man to marry the daughter of his father's sister or the daughter of his mother's brother ; but not lawful for a man to marry the daughter of his father's brother or of his mother's sister.

MILITARY PROCEEDINGS AGAINST. As a means of checking the outrages committed by the blacks in 1816, a detachment of the 46th regiment under Captains Shaw and Wallis was sent out to make a circuit around the outposts. At a place called Aird they encountered a large body of blacks, who gave them battle, and were not vanquished until 14 of them were killed and many wounded. A large number were taken prisoners and sent to Sydney.

Martial law was proclaimed in consequence of aboriginal depredations at Bathurst, August 5, 1824.

THE CONVERSION OF THE ABORIGINES
Melbourne Punch, 1857 (With Bible and bottle — Christianity was not the only "enlightenment" brought to the natives.)

MISSIONS TO. In New South Wales the Rev. Canon Gunther (now of Mudgee) for many years carried on, under the auspices of the Church of England, a mission to the Wiradhuri-speaking tribes of Wellington Vale. The Rev. L. E. Threlkeld, of the London Missionary Society, conducted a mission at Lake Macquarie, in the Valley of the Hunter. In 1837 a band of German missionaries came out, sent by the celebrated Pastor Gössner, of Berlin, to seek the conversion of the Australian aborigines to Christianity. By the influence of the Rev. Dr. Lang, of Sydney, they were settled at Moreton Bay, and laboured there for the instruction of the blacks. One of them, Rev. J. G. Hausmann, now on the Albert River, has divided his labours during his Australian career of forty years between the aboriginals and his German fellow-countrymen. In 1853 the Rev. William Ridley carried the Gospel to the Kamilaroi-speaking tribes on the Namoi and Barwon. Mr. Daniel Matthews has recently established a mission for the aboriginals at Maloga, near Moama, on the Murray. The Rev. George F. Dillon, of the Roman Catholic Church, founded a successful mission at Burragorang, about 65 miles from Sydney. In South Australia the present Bishop of Brisbane, then Archdeacon Hale, a descendant of Sir Matthew Hale, conducted for many years a very successful mission at Poonindie, Port

Lincoln ; and Rev. Mr. Taplin did much good service in a mission in the eastern part of that colony. In Victoria there have been several missions, the most important of which is at Ramayuk, in Gippsland, conducted by the Rev. Mr. Hagenauer, and supported by the Presbyterian Church. The Wesleyan Church had a mission near Geelong. The Rev. George King, of the Church of England, conducted a mission, with good results, in Western Australia. Of these missions, those at Poonindie, Ramayuk, and Burragorang are still continued. Mr. Daniel Matthews also, is still labouring in his mission at Maloga.

NEW ZEALAND. [*See* MAORIS.]

NUMBERS OF.

Australia. Number of blacks in Australia estimated at 3,000,000.—1848.

N. S. Wales. Estimated by Governor Phillip at 1,000,000, of whom 3000 were by him supposed to be between Broken Bay and Botany Bay, June, 1788 ; estimated at 1600 between Broken Bay and Botany Bay, 1803.

South Australia. According to the census, there were 3953 aboriginals—2203 males, 1750 females.—March 26, 1876.

Tabular View, representing the Numbers of the Aboriginal Native Population scattered over various Localities of the Colony of New South Wales, in 1848.

Locality.	No.	Authority.
District of Port Phillip	5000	Robinson, C.P.A.
Grant County	200	Addis
Belfast, Port Fairy	300	Rev. J. G. Wilson
Yarra & Western Port	165	Thomas, Assist. P.A.
Upper Goulburn and	302	Parker, Do.
Lower Do.	200	Do. Do.
Country N. and W. of	350	Do. Do.
River Loddon	670	Do. Do.
Western Port District	1000	Powlett, C.C.L.
Portland Bay Do.	3000	Fyans
Murray Do.	200	Smythe
Gipps Land Do.	1000	Tyers
New South Wales	10,000	Estimate by Author
Campbelltown	17	Rev. J. Innes
Windsor	65	Bench of Magistrates
Brisbane Water	47	Do.
Gosford	50	Rev. E. Rogers
Morpeth	23	— G. A. Middleton
Newcastle	29	— C. P. N. Wilton
Wollombi & M'Donald River	73	Dunlop
Lower Hawkesbury R.	27	Rev. W. W. Simpson
Vale of Clwyd	22	— C. Stuart
Dungog	63	Bench of Magistrates
Patterson	150	Rev. W. Ross
Singleton	70	— F. Cameron
Port Macquarie	370	Gray ; Woodward
Scone	75	Bench of Magistrates
Mudgee	55	Rev. J. Gunther
Raymond Terrace	53	Bench of Magistrates
Bathurst	150	Do.
Picton	67	Do.
Berrima	40	Do.
Wollongong	93	Rev. M. D. Meares
Goulburn	25	Bench of Magistrates
Queanbeyan	60	Murray
Districts of Fish River and Lake George	150	Rev. R. Cartwright
Macleay River	429	Massie
District of Moreton Bay	4000	Wickham ; Simpson
Darling Downs	500	Rolleston

New England	550	MacDonald
Murrumbidgee	2000	Bingham C.C.L.
Manero	683	Lambie

Victoria. It is estimated that at the first colonisation of Port Phillip the Aboriginals numbered about 5,000. When Victoria became an independent colony, in 1851, the number was officially stated to be 2693. According to the report of the Central Board for the Protection of the Aboriginals, dated May 15th, 1875, the numbers then amounted to 1553. The number of either sex is not given in the Board's estimate, but taking the proportions obtaining at the census of 1871, when, however, it was found impossible to enumerate all the Aboriginals, the males should number 915 and the females 638; in January, 1878, the number was estimated at 1067. The census collectors in 1871 succeeded in falling in with 1330 Aboriginals, of whom 784 were males and 546 were females. On both occasions the returns of the Central Board for the Protection of the Aboriginals gave a higher number than those of the census. At the present time the Secretary to the Central Board estimates the total number of Aboriginals in the colony to be 1553. 557 Aboriginals, viz., 302 males and 255 females, or more than a third, are living on Aboriginal stations, which are under the control and partial support of the Government. The remainder wander about the colony at large. Every effort is made to induce them to pursue profitable employments, and the education of the young receives attention. They are trained to labour, but they are also taught reading, writing, and arithmetic, and they are, as a rule, apt scholars.

Western Australia. Number of aboriginals frequenting the settled districts of Perth, Freemantle, Swan Avon, Wellington, Sussex, and Albany estimated at 1200, 1842; estimated at 800, 1859.

OUTRAGES AGAINST.—Violation and ill-treatment of five native women by a party sent to cut rushes in one of the bays adjacent to the settlement, 1788. Twenty-eight men, women and children barbarously murdered at Mr. Henry Dangar's station, Myall Creek, June, 1838. [*See Crimes*, 1838.]

Konikoondeet (Jajowrong) and another man, name unknown, reported by the aboriginals to have been shot by two white men when exploring the country, March or April (so in official record) 1838.

About fourteen men, names unknown, shot by a party of men from Bowman's, Ebden's, and Yaldwyn' stations, in recovering a flock of Bowman's sheep, July, 1838.

Noorowurnin and another Jajowrong, shot by Bowman's assigned servants at the Maiden Hills, February, 1839.

Six men, names unknown, shot by the Mounted Police on the Campaspe, June 22, 1839.

Wikur, Keramburnin, and another Taoungurong, shot by Monro and party between the Colliban and Mount Alexander, January, 1840.

Pandarragooendeet, a Jajowrong native, shot by one of Dutton's assigned servants, who afterwards absconded, August, 1814.

Panumarramin, a Grampian native, shot by the late J. F. Francis in his sheepfold, September 1840.

Bonnokgoondeet, Jojowl, Kombonngarramin, and Per-

tunarramin, shot by J. F. Francis in the Pyrenees, December 21, 1840.

Gondu-urmin, a Kalkalgoondet native, shot by Dutton's assigned men near the Lodden, February 7, 1841.

Mokfte, (Jajowrong) shot near Mount Cole; it is said by a splitter, March, 1841.

Koenycrook, a Taoungurong, shot, it is supposed by Bennett's shepherd, who was found murdered. The black was found in a tree badly wounded, and died in Melbourne hospital, May, 1841.

Two men reported by the aboriginals to have been shot near Hall's, at the foot of the Grampians, by Hall's hutkeeper, July, 1841

Kowarramin, two other men, and a girl, reported by the aboriginals to have been shot by three white men near Kirk's, Purrumbeep, July or August (so in official record) 1841.

Bood bood yarramin, reported by the aboriginals to have been shot by Captain Bunbury's storekeeper near Mount William, August, 1841.

The bodies of three aboriginal women, and one male child, found dead, and an aboriginal wounded by a gun shot in a tea-tree scrub near the station of Messrs. Osbrey and Smith, Portland distinct (now Western Victoria), February 25, 1842.

A tribe of about sixty slaughtered in return for Frazer massacre, Dawson River, 1857.

About 170 blacks slaughtered in Medway Ranges, Queensland, by police and others, in return for Wills' massacres, Oct. and Nov., 1861.

THE HUNTED RUSHCUTTER
Artist unknown, c. 1790, British Museum

OUTRAGES BY.

Six convicts and two soldiers, cutting rushes, killed, in retaliation for the ill-treatment by them of five native women at one of the bays adjacent to the N.S.W. settlement, henceforward called Rushcutter's Bay, 1788.

The aboriginal natives during the year 1809 committed many acts of aggression, including the murdering and spearing of many of the colonists, the destruction of cattle, and other acts of violence.

Shepherd of W. Bowman's, killed by the Taoungurongs, near Mount Alexander, May or June (so in official record) 1838.

Shepherd and hut-keeper of Mr. C. Hutton's, killed near the Campaspe, May 22, 1839.

Shepherd of Messrs. Jennings and Playne's (successors to Mr. Hutton) killed near the Campaspe, June, 1840.

Hutkeeper of Mr. Wills, killed near Mount William, November 21, 1840.

Hutkeeper of Mr. Oliphant, killed near the Pyrenees by the Balkalgoondeet natives, March 19, 1841.

Shepherd of Mr. Bennett's, killed by the Taoungurongs on the Campaspe, May, 1841.

M. A. M. Alien, killed by the Mallgoondeet natives, on the Loddon, March 13, 1842.

Two men in the service of Mr. Irvine, at the Pyrenees, attacked and wounded, February, 1842.

Several head of cattle speared on Mr. Hall's run near the Grampians, March, 1842.

About thirty head of sheep scattered, and several of them stolen by the Belokepor and Utowolbulloh natives at Messrs. Birch's, 1843.

Andrew Beveridge, a young settler, murdered in Port Phillip district, Lower Murray, by a number of blacks, August 23, 1846.

Mr. Frazer, wife, children, and governess, massacred near Dawson River, 1857.

NATIVES ATTACKING SETTLERS IN QUEENSLAND

Mr. H. S. Wills, Baker, his overseer, Baker's two sons, and eleven other persons massacred at Cullinlaaringo Station, Queensland, Oct. 17, 1861.

Mr. Johnson, telegraph station-master, Daly-waters, speared by blacks, June, 1875.

Handley Regan and another white man shot by blacks on Daintree River, Queensland, December 16, 1877.

Cowardly attack on and wounding of Mr. Hartley and Capt. Sykes at the North Shore, near Cooktown, Queensland, by a large band of armed blacks, February 6, 1879.

B. Maylo, with three white men, who went with Beckett's cattle to Sulieman Creek, were found murdered by blacks, owing to the treachery of their own black boy, who had instructed the murderers to rush between the whites and the camp while the men were bathing, February 27, 1879.

Duncan Mackay, while searching for water, was supposed to have been killed by blacks, at Herbert Downs, February, 1879. [*See* ABORIGINALS, ATTACKS BY.]

PROTECTORS OF. Launcelot Edward Threlkeld, Lake Macquarie ; John and Mary Handt, Moreton Bay ; George Langhorne, Port Phillip ; William and Ann Watson, Wellington Valley— 1832. G. A. Robinson, Tasmania, 1830 to 1835.

REMARKABLE. Capture of the warlike *Ara-ba-noo* an aboriginal, 30 years of age, by Lieut. Ball and Lieut. George Johnston in Port Jackson ; was taken charge of and well treated by the Governor ; *Ara-ba-noo* soon became quite reconciled and friendly, but was seized with the small-pox, and died May 15, 1789.

Bennelong, a young native taken prisoner, and treated kindly by Governor Phillip, November 25, 1789. *Bennelong* taken with another native to England by Governor Phillip, December 11, 1792 ; returned with Governor Hunter, and quickly resumed his old habits ; claimed for himself the character of a chief, and took to the bush, September 7, 1795.

Jackey Jackey, companion of Kennedy, the explorer, received medal, 1854.

Mosquito, a noted bushranger. [*See* BUSH-RANGERS (*Van Diemen's Land*).]

Saturday, a notorious ringleader of insurrectionary blacks, New South Wales, inspired the colonists with great terror, 1823 ; 500 acres of land offered for his capture, 1824 ; was captured, but not without requiring six men to secure him, and a musket was broken on his ribs before he could be manacled.

Boongarie, a noted king, settled at George's Head, 1815 ; died, and was buried at Garden Island, November 24, 1830.

Gooseberry, Queen, wife of King Boongarie, was one of the last, if not the last, of the Port Jackson tribe.

REMARKABLE CAVES OF. Discovered by the explorer King on his fourth expedition, at Princess Charlotte Bay ; a variety of native paintings were on the walls.—1821.

SCHOOL FOR THE CHILDREN OF. Founded at Parramatta under the auspices of Governor Macquarie, December 8, 1814.

SMALL-POX AMONGST. Spread of small-pox among the Sydney blacks, hundreds died, 1788-9 ; amongst the Port Macquarie blacks ; large number died. December, 1831.

WEAPONS OF. *Boomerang*. A curious aboriginal weapon ; is of a curved form, made of a piece of hard wood, thirty to forty inches in length, two and a-half to three inches wide at the broadest part, and tapering away at each end nearly to a point ; the concave part is from one-eighth to one-fourth of an inch thick, and the convex quite sharp. A native can throw this simple instrument forty or fifty yards, horizontally skimming along the surface not more than three or four feet from the ground, when it will sud-

NATIVE WEAPONS
The Illustrated Sydney News, 1885

denly rise into the air to the height of fifty or sixty yards, describing a considerable curve, and finally fall at his feet. During the whole of this evolution, the boomerang keeps turning with great rapidity, like a piece of wood revolving on a pivot, and with a whizzing noise. It is not easy to comprehend by what law of projection the boomerang is made to take the singular direction it does. In the hands of a European it is a dangerous weapon, as it may return and strike the thrower; but the Aboriginal can inflict with it on others the most deadly wounds.

Nullah Nullah and *Waddy* are clubs of different sizes and solidity; of the latter there are several sizes.

Spear. This is about ten feet long, as thick as a man's finger, tapering to a point, sometimes jagged or barbed, and hardened in the fire; this they can throw from fifty to sixty yards with great precision, the impetus being greatly increased by the use of the *Womerawa*, or throwing stick.

Tomahawk. This is made of stone, sometimes of jasper, fastened with a hard gum between a cleft stick; one of its uses is to cut notches in trees of fifty or sixty feet high, which are too thick to be grasped in the trunk and have no lower branches.

Womerawa. This is a piece of wood from two to three feet in length, about three inches broad at one end, and going off to a point at the other, to which a sort of hook is fastened; the hook is inserted into a small hole at the extremity of the spear, and the womerawa being grasped at the broad part, acts somewhat on the principle of the sling, enabling a powerful man to send the spear above a hundred yards.

WHITE MEN WITH. *William Buckley*, " the

THE DISCOVERY OF BUCKLEY
National Library of Australia

wild white man " of the Australian Bush, was one of those implicated in the conspiracy among the soldiers of Gibraltar to assassinate the Duke of Kent. He was transported with the first fleet of convicts in "The Ocean" and "Calcutta," under Governor Collins, to settle Port Phillip in 1803 ; he escaped with several others, and Collins and his party abandoned the settlement a few days afterwards. Buckley fell in with the blacks and was received into their tribe, and lived among them for 32 years. He was found in 1835 by the first permanent white settlers in Port Phillip. He had lost his language and sunk to the level of a savage. He afterwards became useful to the white colonists as an interpreter ; he died in Hobart Town in 1856.

James Davies, son of a Scotch blacksmith, was transported to New South Wales per ship "Minstrel" in 1824, being only 16 years of age. For some offence he was sent from Sydney to Moreton Bay settlement ; shortly afterwards absconded from Capt. Logan's (of 57th Regt.), exploring party, and took to the bush. After being 14 years with the blacks, was found by Mr. Andrew Petrie, and returned to civilised life in 1842. Davis had a companion with him when he absconded, who was after a short period with the natives killed for desecrating the bones of their dead.

James Morrill, born at Maldon, Essex, England ; sailed from Sydney for China on board barque "Peruvian," Captain George Pitkelhy, of Dundee, February 28, 1846 ; on March 8th, driven by storm on Horse-shoe reef near Port Denison ; 22 souls on board, took refuge on a raft, and 7 survivors after 42 days were washed ashore near Cape Cleveland ; all these died with the exception of Morrill, who remained with the blacks, and was rescued from them in February, 1863. [*See* PAMPHLET.]

Narcisse Pierre Pellatier, son of a shoemaker of Saint Gillies, near Bordeaux ; in 1858 was cabin boy of the ship "St. Paul," of Bordeaux, during a voyage from China to Australia, where she was conveying 350 Chinese immigrants. The vessel struck on a reef in Lousida group and became a total wreck, the captain, crew and Chinese reaching an island, where the latter were deserted by the crew, the boats being insufficient to carry more than themselves, and after traversing some 600 miles they landed on the Australian shore at "First Red Rocky Point " south of Cape Direction ; here the crew abandoned Pellatier and took to the boat again, and it is said eventually reached New Caledonia. After the Chinese were deserted as above the cannibal blacks there appear to have eaten them all in the most methodical manner, slaughtering them two at a time for food when they required it ; sixteen, the sole survivors, were at last rescued by a passing vessel. The blacks of Cape Direction, however, finding the deserted and almost dying Pellatier, treated the boy with the greatest kindness, fed him and finally took him to their camp, and

with this tribe, known in their own tongue as Makadamas, he remained seventeen years until he was discovered and taken away by the crew of the "John Bell," a pearl schooner then lying at Night Island. On April 11th, 1875, when discovered, Narcisse Pellatier was stark naked like the tribe of blacks he was with ; his body was burned by the sun to a rich red colour, his skin had quite a glazed appearance, and his breast was adorned with raised lines of flesh (scarified) of the thickness of a pencil, whilst the lobe of the right ear was ornamented with a piece of wood about half an inch in diameter and four inches long. The cuts on his breast, of which he was very proud, were made with pieces of broken quartz, the lips of the cuts being raised by a series of constant pinching during the healing process. He states at first his thoughts continually reverted to his parents and his country, but as years rolled on these faded from his memory and he became thoroughly identified with the blacks, from whom at the time of his rescue it was not his wish to part, and not their wish for him to go. His life appears to have been principally passed in fishing and hunting and occasionally fighting with a neighbouring tribe. Although a mere boy when deserted he had retained his knowledge of reading and writing and counting with ease up to one hundred, and he drew some excellent sketches of the animals he had hunted. He returned to France a few months after being discovered.

John Renton, a shipwrecked sailor, who had been twenty years with the aboriginals on one of the islands north of Queensland, was rescued by the master of the "Bobtail Nag," July, 1874. Renton was killed in the South Seas by natives while acting as labour agent for Queensland Government, February, 1879.

ABORIGINES. This is a term employed to denote the original or primitive inhabitants of a country. The aborigines of Australia form a distinct race, to which the term **Papuas** or oriental negroes has been assigned ; and whether on the northern and tropical, or southern and temperate, shores of Australia, they possess the thick prominent lips, sunken eyes, high cheek-bones, and calveless legs of the African, differing, however, in the hair, which is long and coarse. The nose, though large, is not so flat as that of the Africanders ; indeed it is sometimes of a Roman form ; and the forehead is high, narrow, and at the crown formed somewhat after the manner of the roof of a house. They are of middle height, few being of lofty stature ; the women are small and well made, as indeed is generally the case with the male sex ; the hands and feet small, the shoulders finely rounded, but the abdomen frequently protuberant, and the arms long ; the features in youth are not unpleasing ; in some women the smile may be considered almost fascinating, added, as it is, to an easiness of manner and an harmonious voice. The colour of the skin and hair is in general black, but

NATIVES OF BOTANY BAY
Rex Nan Kivell Collection

some tribes have been seen of a lighter colour, approaching that of the Malay, with hair of a reddish cast. Some possess large beards, but many pluck out the hair by the root. As is the case with all savages, the head is the principal part for decoration ; some divide the hair into small parcels, each of which is matted together with gum, and formed into lengths like the thrums of a mop ; others, by means of yellow gum, fasten on the head the front teeth of a kangaroo, the jaw-bones of a fish, human teeth, feathers, pieces of wood, tails of dogs, &c. Oil of any quality is used with avidity for preserving the skin from mosquitoes, &c., and the breasts, arms, back, &c., are covered at an early age with cicatrices of every variety of form. The males of most tribes have the front tooth struck out on attaining puberty, and the women are frequently observed with a joint of the little finger cut off. When going to war, or grieving for a deceased friend, or occasionally even for ornament, white and yellow pigments are applied in streaks over the whole body, according to the taste of the decorator—such as a large white circle round each eye, waving lines down and across the thighs and legs. In general, it may be said that the whole of the aborigines of this vast island are of the same stock, though it is not a little singular that their languages differ so much that tribes within short distances of each other, unless inhabiting the bank of the same river, are quite strangers to each other, whilst almost every large community, or family as they may be termed, has its own peculiar dialect. Of their numbers it is difficult to form a correct idea ; depending, however, as they do, entirely on the chase or fishing, or on gum or bulbous roots, and subject to the effects of long droughts, the country is very thinly peopled. No houses are constructed ; an overhanging rock, or a slip of bent bark, serves for temporary shelter. In many places a log of wood, or a wide slip of bark tied at either end, and stuffed with clay, is the only mode invented for crossing a river or arm of the sea ; whilst in other parts of the country a large tree, roughly hollowed by fire, forms the canoe.

ADDRESS, EARLY.

Copy of address presented to Governor Bourke at Port Phillip, Melbourne, March 4, 1837 :—

To His Excellency Major-General Sir Richard Bourke, K.C.B., Captain-General and Governor-in-Chief of the territory of New South Wales and its Dependencies, &c., &c.

SIR,—We, the undersigned inhabitants of Port Phillip, beg to approach your Excellency, and offer you our congratulations upon your safe arrival in this portion of your Government. The pleasure we experience in thus addressing your Excellency is enhanced by the consideration that your arrival dissipates the reports which had reached us of your Excellency's resignation, and bids us hope that the colony may continue to derive advantage from the exercise of those talents which have always been exerted for, and have tended materially to advance its prosperity. We cannot sufficiently thank your Excellency for having at so early a period visited this newly settled district. It is very important that the sites of towns, and other preliminary arrangements, should be speedily and efficiently determined, and we congratulate ourselves that these will be effected under your Excellency's personal superintendence. We may, perhaps, be allowed to express our regret that so few are present to meet your Excellency on this occasion, but the absence of several from the distant position of the residences of others, have prevented many from manifesting their respect and attachment to your Excellency, and joining us in welcoming you to this interesting and important part of New South Wales.

ADELAIDE.

First arrival of cattle overland at Adelaide, April 3, 1838. First municipal election, Adelaide, South Australia, October 31, 1840; Stanley Stokes, returning officer; first aldermen—James Hurtle Fisher, A. H. Davis, Matthew Smellie, and George Stephenson. James Hurtle Fisher elected first Mayor, which office he resigned January 6, 1842. Two hundred German immigrants arrived, September 18, 1844. Foundation stone of Town Hall laid, May 4, 1864; opened, June 20, 1865; cost of erection about £25,000. Foundation stone of New Post Office, Victoria Tower, Adelaide, laid, November 1, 1867. [See SOUTH AUSTRALIA.]

ADELAIDE RIVER, falls into Clarence Straits, N.W. Australia, and so called, in honour of Adelaide, the Queen Dowager: discovered by Stokes, 1839.

AGENT, COLONIAL.

Stuart Donaldson, Esq. Agent for the Colonies January 6, 1830. [First Colonial Agency: subsequently became paid office under the title of Agent-General.]

The sum of £1400 placed on the Estimates at the disposal of Mr. Lytton Bulwer to be employed in promoting the claims of the Colonies in England, 1835.

AGENTS-GENERAL.

Hon. Arthur Blyth, appointed Agent-General for South Australia, February 16, 1877.

SUCCESSION OF.

New South Wales.—Hon. W. C. Mayne: Sir C. Cowper: Hon. William Forster.

New Zealand.—Hon. Isaac E. Featherston: Sir Julius Vogel.

Queensland.—Hon. John Douglas: Hon. R. Daintree: Hon. A. Macalister.

South Australia.—Hon. F. S. Dutton: Hon. A. Blyth.

Victoria.—Right Hon. H. C. E. Childers: Sir G. Verdon: Sir A. Michie.

[See PARLIAMENTARY AGENT.]

AGRICULTURAL SOCIETY. [See SOCIETIES.]

AGRICULTURE.

First harvest gathered in N.S.W. at Rose Hill, Parramatta, December, 1789; 1000 acres cleared and in cultivation in the Sydney and Parramatta districts, 1791; land in cultivation, 1783 acres, December 11, 1792. The year's harvest yielded 14,000 bushels of wheat, 1793; cultivation, 3361 acres of wheat, 1527 acres of maize, and 26 acres of barley, besides a

KING WILLIAM STREET, ADELAIDE
The Illustrated Sydney News, 1879

considerable quantity of garden ground, 1796. From 15,000 to 20,000 bushels of wheat, respectively, produced in the Hawkesbury district in 1798 and 1799 ; 7677 acres of land under cultivation in New South Wales, 1799 ; according to the *Agricultural Statistics*, the quantity of land under cultivation in the three principal districts —Parramatta, Hawkesbury, and Sydney—was 4392 acres of wheat and 1436 acres of maize, 1799. *Rust in wheat* first appeared in New South Wales crops, October, 1803. 12,860 acres under crop ; 48,885 acres located ; corn in the public store—15,831 bushels of wheat, 62,094 bushels of maize, besides that in possession of individuals, 1805. Agricultural Society of New South Wales founded July 5, 1822. The colony blest with an abundant harvest ; so abundant that, in one day, the price of wheat fell from 25s. to 10s. a bushel, 1824. Great failure of the crops occurred, owing to a very long drought prevailing, and the non-arrival of foreign supplies caused a scarcity to be apprehended, and the rations per head to all persons maintained by the Government were reduced, and a notification was issued requesting private families to reduce the consumption of flour, 1828. Remarkable abundance of the crops all over the colony of New South Wales, 1836. The produce of the crops of the Colonies of Victoria, New South Wales, Queensland, South Australia, Western Australia, Tasmania, and New Zealand for the years 1876-7 was as follows : — Wheat, 18,654,257 bushels ; oats, 8,091,848 bushels ; barley, 1,830,396 bushels ; maize, 5,297,318 ; other cereals (including beans and pease), 609,008 bushels ; potatoes, 318,708 tons ; hay, 630,347 tons ; and 1,868,355 gallons of wine.

ALBANY, WESTERN AUSTRALIA. The site of Albany, Western Australia, chosen 1827.

ALBERT RIVER discovered by Captain Stokes, 1839.

ALBION. Name first given to the settlement at Sydney Cove, Port Jackson, 1788.

ALEXANDRIA LAND. Added to South Australia, 1862.

ALFRED, H.R.H. PRINCE, DUKE OF EDINBURGH. Landed at Adelaide in command of H.M.S. "Galatea," October 30, 1867 ; in Melbourne, November 23, 1867 ; in Sydney, in the "Galatea," January 21, 1868 ; Brisbane, February 25, 1868 ; shot by a man named O'Farrell, at Clontarf, Sydney harbour (bullet entering at back, but not proving fatal), great indignation, O'Farrell's life being saved only by the protection of the police, March 12, 1868 ; left Sydney, April 6, 1861 ; second visit to Victoria, February 22, 1869 ; arrived in New Zealand, April 11, 1869 ; second visit to Sydney in "Galatea," September 15, 1870.

AUSTRALIA VINDEX
Sydney Punch, 1868 (After an insane attempt to assassinate H.R.H. Prince Alfred, an enraged New South Wales prepared to lynch the attacker, James O'Farrell.)

ALPACAS.

The expediency of importing them into New South Wales first suggested, 1844.

Meeting held in Sydney with a view of initiating measures to introduce alpaca sheep into the Colony, when it was proposed to raise £2000 for the purpose of importing a flock containing 400 breeding ewes, 1850.

Llamas, Alpacas, and Vicuna sheep introduced into the Colony. 280 (a mixed flock) were landed in Sydney *ex* Salvadora, from the

MR CHARLES LEDGER AND ONE OF HIS EXTRA ORDINARY FLOCK
Mitchell Library

Chilian port of Caldera, South America. The importer was Mr. Charles Ledger, who had been for a considerable time established in Peru. In obtaining these sheep he endured many hardships and privations ; he travelled through Peru, Bolivia, and the Argentine Mountains. The number of each sort landed in Sydney were : 46 male alpacas, pure bred ; 38 female ditto, pure bred ; 110 female llamas ; 27 ditto crossed in first generation, between alpaca and llama ; 11 ditto, second generation, between male alpaca and female from the first cross ; 5 ditto, third generation, from male alpaca and female from second cross ; 40 lambs of first, second, and third cross ; 4 male and 1 female vicunas. Pedro Cabreba, who had travelled with Mr. Ledger seven years, was the overseer : November 28, 1858 ; the Government became possessed of the imported flock of llama sheep (having purchased them for the sum of £15,000), and undertook measures for the management of them at a cost of £1000 per annum, April, 1859.

ANGORA GOATS. Mr. M'Cullough, of Maryborough, subscribed £600 towards the introduction of Cashmere and Angora goats, 1866.

ANNIVERSARY DAY. Anniversary of foundation of the Colony celebrated with great spirit,—public dinner given to Mr. W. C. Wentworth (then Member of the Council) at the Sydney College,—also a public dinner at the City Theatre, January 26, 1846.

ANNIVERSARY DAYS of the Foundation of the Australasian Colonies :—

New South Wales, founded ....January 26, 1788
Tasmania, separated from New South Wales
                             December 3, 1825
Western Australia, founded (1826, Lockyer) June 1, 1829
South Australia, founded ....December 28, 1836
New Zealand, founded ....January 29, 1840
Victoria, separated from New South Wales, July 1, 1851
Queensland, separated from New South Wales
                           December 10, 1859

APPOINTMENTS, Early Imperial.

Rev. Samuel Marsden, Chaplain, New South Wales, January 1, 1793.

Richard Atkins, Esq., Judge Advocate, *vice* Richard Dove, Esq., who died November 2nd, December 18, 1800.

Charles Grimes, Surveyor-General of Norfolk Island, Acting Surveyor-General of New South Wales, April 13, 1801.

Robert Fitzgerald, Esq., Inspector and Director of all the Agricultural Settlements belonging to the Crown, July 29, 1802.

Michael Rowland, appointed Superintendent of Convicts, *vice* Rowland Hassall, September 30, 1802.

Charles Throsby, Esq., Medical Officer at Castle Hill, and a Magistrate of the Territory, October 18, 1802.

Captain William Kent, R.N., Magistrate of the Territory, November 28, 1802.

Charles Grimes, Esq., Surveyor-General of New South South Wales, on the retirement of Augustus Alt, Esq., on half-pay, March 15, 1804.

Rev. William Cowper, Senior Assistant-Chaplain N.S.W., January 1, 1808.

John Macarthur, Esq., Magistrate of the Territory, February 12, 1808.

Colonel Joseph Foveaux, Colonial Secretary, 1808.

Rev. Robert Cartwright, Senior Assistant-Chaplain, New South Wales, January 5, 1809.

John Oxley, Esq., Surveyor-General, New South Wales, January 1, 1872.

John Wylde, Esq., LL.B., Judge-Advocate of the Supreme Court (arrived by the "Elizabeth"), October 5, 1816.

Rev. Richard Hill, Senior Assistant-Chaplain, New South Wales, January 1, 1818.

Major George Druitt, 48th Regiment, Chief Engineer of Roads in New South Wales, June 4, 1819.

William Balcombe, first Colonial Treasurer, arrived in New South Wales, April 5, 1824.

John Stephen, Esq., first Solicitor-General, Commissioner of the Court of Requests, August, 1824.

Rev. M. D. Meares, Senior Assistant-Chaplain, New South Wales, December 20, 1824.

Alexander Macleay, Esq., Colonial Secretary, New South Wales, June 14, 1825.

William Lithgow, Esq., Auditor of General Accounts, appointed by Secretary of State, June 14, 1825.

Henry Dumaresq, Clerk to the Executive Council, December 21, 1825.

Captain William Dumaresq to temporary charge of the Civil Engineers Department, December 24, 1825.

Captain Rossi, Police Magistrate at Sydney, *vice* D'Arcy Wentworth, resigned, 1825.

Captain William Dumaresq, Inspector of Roads and Bridges, New South Wales, January 6, 1826.

Alexander Macleay, Colonial Secretary of New South Wales and Registrar of the Records, January 7th, 1826.

John Thomas Campbell, Esq., member of the First Land Board of the Colony, February 17th, 1826.

Captain Thomas Logan, 57th Regiment, Commandant of penal settlement, Moreton Bay, March 6, 1826.

William Dumaresq, Esq., Magistrate of the Colony, March 7, 1226.

Alexander Macleay, Esq., appointed a Magistrate of the Colony, March 7, 1826.

Lachlan M'Allister, Esq., Magistrate for the County of Argyle, March 7, 1826.

William Dumaresq, Director of Public Works, May 29, 1826.

William Henry Moore, Esq., solicitor, Acting Attorney-General of New South Wales, October 13, 1826.

Rev. C. P. N. **Wilton**, Senior Assistant-Chaplain, New South Wales, October 19, 1826.

John Stephen, Esq., Judge of the Supreme

Court, November 13, 1826.

Henry Grattan Douglas, Acting Commissioner of Court of Requsts, November 3, 1826 ; appointed Clerk of Legislative Council, December 12, 1826.

John Busby, Esq., Mineral Surveyor and Civil Engineer, 1826.

John Mackaness, Esq., Sheriff of New South Wales, January 21, 1827.

Samuel Wright, Esq., Police Magistrate of Newcastle, March 9, 1827.

James Busby, Esq., Collector of Internal Revenue, and Member of Land Board, April 2, 1827.

John Thomas Campbell, Esq., Acting Collector of Customs, N.S.W., April 5, 1827.

John Dalhunty, Principal Superintendent of Police, N.S.W., May 7, 1827.

Stewart Ryrie, Auditor of Colonial Accounts, June 2, 1827.

William Lithgow, Private Secretary to the Governor, June 2, 1827.

Alexander Macduff Baxter, Attorney-General of N.S.W., August 1, 1827.

Henry Grattan Douglass, Esq., Commissioner of Courts of Requests, September 8, 1827.

Thomas de la Condamine, appointed Clerk of the Executive and Legislative Councils, September 8, 1827.

William Romaine Garrett, Surveyor, to Surveyor-General of N.S.W., September 14, 1827.

Thomas Livingstone Mitchell, Deputy Surveyor-General, N.S.W., September 14, 1827.

Ambrose Hallen, Assistant Surveyor to Government of N.S.W., September 14, 1827.

Henry S. Shadforth, appointed Magistrate of Colony, October 18, 1827.

Lieutenant-Colonel Morrisset, Principal Superintendent of the New South Wales Police, October 19, 1827.

Lieutenant Thomas de la Condamine, 51st Regiment, Private Secretary to the Governor, November 24, 1827.

William Howe, Esq., Superintendent of Police at Campbelltown, January 12, 1828.

Sydney Stephen, Solicitor-General, February 23, 1828.

Robert Humphrey Hartley, a Magistrate of the Colony, February 28, 1828.

Lieutenant George Sleeman, 39th Regiment, Resident, King George's Sound, August 11, 1828.

Captain Collet Barker, 39th Regiment, Resident, Fort Wellington, August 11, 1828.

Major H. R. Hartley, 57th Regiment, Resident of Melville Island, November 8, 1828.

Captain Robert Hunt, 57th Regiment, Commandant, Norfolk Island, November, 1828.

E. Deas Thomson, Clerk of the Executive Council, Dec. 29, 1878.

James Thomas Morrissett, Commissioner of Norfolk Island, January 31, 1829.

James Raymond, Postmaster of the Colony, April 27, 1829.

Charles Wilson, Director of Public Works, May, 1829.

Edward Hallen, Draftsman, Surveyor-General's Office, August 21, 1829.

Charles Thomas Smathman, Coroner for the City of Sydney, September 4, 1829.

Henry Colden Antill, to conduct the duties of the police in the County of Camden, October 2, 1829.

Gregory Blaxland, Esq., Magistrate of the Colony, October 26, 1829.

Captain John Douglas, Esq., Magistrate of the Colony, October 18, 1829.

Roger Therry, Esq., Commissioner of the Court of Requests for N.S.W., November 6, 1829.

Captain Wilson, Director of Public Works N.S.W., 1829.

Stuart Donaldson, Esq., Agent for the Colonies, January 6, 1830.

Roger Therry, Magistrate of the Colony, April 14, 1830.

Campbell Drummond Riddell, Colonial Treasurer, August 23, 1830.

Campbell Drummond Riddell, a Magistrate of the Colony, October 18, 1830.

Charles Cowper, Esq., Clerk to the Commissioners for managing the affairs of the Church and School Estates, April 6, 1831.

John Kinchela, Esq., Attorney-General of New South Wales, June 25, 1831.

Charles James Windeyer, Esq., Assistant Police Magistrate of Sydney, July 29, 1831.

Rev. George Innes, M.A., appointed Head Master of the King's School, Sydney, December 7, 1831.

John Nicholson, Esq., Magistrate of the Colony, February 26, 1832.

John Webb, Esq., Superintendent of Council, Norfolk Island, March 6, 1832.

Francis Allman, Esq., Police Magistrate at Wollongong, September 4, 1832.

William Westbrooke Burton, Esq., Puisne Judge of the Supreme Court of Australia, December 22, 1832.

Robert Stewart, third Police Magistrate at Sydney, November 13, 1834.

Edward Deas Thomson, Colonial Secretary, *vice* Alexander Macleay : Mr. McPherson succeeded to the office of Clerk to the Council, January, 1837.

W. Hone, Esq., Attorney-General of Tasmania, 1837.

AQUATICS.

AMATEUR RACES. Boat-race from Bradley's Head into Sydney Cove, 3½ miles (with the tide), between Captain Piper, Naval Officer, Captain Lawlie of the "Batavia," Captain Johnston of the "Guildford," and Captain Bell of the "Minerva." Won by Captain Piper. Time, 15 minutes.—May 16, 1818.

CHAMPION OF THE WORLD, THE ONLY AUSTRALIAN (1879) Edward Trickett, Sydney, New South Wales, beat J. H. Sadler, course, Putney to Mortlake, River Thames, London ; time, 23m., 24s., June 27, 1875.

Trickett, Edward, beat M. Rush for championship of the world and £400, Parramatta River, June 30, 1877.

CHAMPIONSHIP RACES.

R. Green, senior, beat Candlish (of Newcastle-on-Tyne) for £400, over the champion course, Parramatta River, June 23, 1853.

Between Dale and Gillett, won by Dale, Saltwater River, Victoria, distance 4½ miles, time 46 minutes, January, 14, 1857.

R. Green won the Scullers' Sydney Champion Cup, value 100 guineas, with 10 guineas added, Port Jackson, February, 1857.

Between Richard Green and T. M'Grath, Parramatta River, for £200 and championship, won by Green, time 26½ minutes, August 9, 1859.

Between Green and White and Punch and M'Grath, on Parramatta River; distance, 3½ miles; Punch and M'Grath won by eight boat's-lengths, in 25 minutes— May, 1861.

Between R. and H. Green and Punch and M'Grath, for £100 a-side; won by the latter crew, August, 1861.

Between W. Hickey and R. Green; won by Hickey, Parramatta River, January 20, 1866.

W. Hickey beat M. Rush for £200 and the championship, Parramatta River; time, 25 min. 30 sec., November 19, 1870.

Between Michael Rush, Edward Trickett, E. C. Laycock, W. Hickey, R. Green, and S. Newly, on the Clarence River, Grafton, for the championship of the Australian Colonies, open to all comers pulling in outriggers; prize, £200; distance, 6,262 yards, or 3½ miles and 100 yards; Rush won by 18 boat's-lengths, and two boat's-lengths separated Trickett (second) and Laycock (third); time, 19 min. 42 sec., October 7, 1874.

Between Joseph Sadler. champion of England, and Edward Trickett, of Sydney, New South Wales, for the sculling championship of the world, on the Thames; won by Trickett, June 27, 1876.

Between Edward Trickett and Michael Rush, for the sculling championship of the world, Parramatta River, New South Wales, Trickett winning easily by six boat's-lengths; distance, 4 miles; time, 23 min. 35 sec., June 30, 1877.

INTERCOLONIAL RACES.

First Intercolonial race (four-oared gigs), New South Wales beat Victoria, February 4, 1863.

Intercolonial champion gig race between Victoria and New South Wales, at Sydney; won by New South Wales, November 9, 1872.

Intercolonial champion sculling match on the Yarra, between Carter, Bell, and Orr; won by Orr, March 28, 1873.

Intercolonial gig race on the Yarra; won by Melbourne

INTERCOLONIAL GIG RACE, SYDNEY
The Australasian Sketcher, 1874

Combination crew, beating Sydney Rowing Club, Ballarat Club, Geelong and Hobart Town Clubs, March 28, 1873.

New South Wales beat Victoria, on the Parramatta River, time, 21 minutes 59 seconds, September 26, 1874.

Eight-oared race between New South Wales and Victoria, rowed on the Lower Yarra, Melbourne crew defeated ; the Sydney Rowing Club won by two lengths and a half ; time, 24½ minutes ; distance 4 miles ; March 6, 1878.

INTERCOLONIAL FOUR-OARED UNIVERSITY RACES.

Between New South Wales and Victoria, rowed at Melbourne ; won by Melbourne University, December 23, 1870. In Sydney, second contest, Melbourne won, December 21, 1871.

ORDINARY RACES.

Between Captain Piper's gig and a whaleboat belonging to the American brig "General Gates" ; course, Dawes' Battery round a boat stationed between Shark Island and Bradley's Head ; distance, 8 miles, owners steering ; Captain Piper won in 35 minutes ; July 10, 1819.

Between Captain Piper's gig and a cutter belonging to Captain Donaldson of the "Grenadine"; course, from Sydney Cove round Garden Island and back ; Captain Piper's gig won in 16 minutes ; October 9, 1821.

Between gig of the man-of-war "Rainbow," Captain Rous, and Captain Piper's gig, for £100 aside ; course, round Shark Island and back ; after a close contest, won by Captain Rous's gig by 1 minute 10 seconds ; February 24, 1827.

Thomas M'Grath (native of Sydney), beat George Mulhall over the course in Sydney Harbour ; 1855.

Deward beat M'Grath round Shark Island ; time 39 minutes 12 seconds ; February 27, 1855.

Tom M'Grath beat R. Green for £200 ; won by a boat's-length ; Port Jackson, January 21, 1856.

R. Green beat Deward (of Gravesend), for £400 ; Green won easily ; Port Jackson, April 22, 1856.

R. Green beat Thomas M'Grath for £400 ; Green won by a boat's-length ; Port Jackson, June 24, 1856.

"Challenge," owned by Mr. T. J. Dean, won the Sydney Challenge Cup, value 300 guineas, with 50 guineas added ; February 1, 1857.

R. Green won the Sculling Sydney Champion Cup, value 100 guineas, with 10 guineas added ; Port Jackson, February 1, 1857.

Henry White beat James Punch, Parramatta River, for £200 ; time, 25 minutes 15 seconds ; May 9, 1859.

James Punch beat H. White, 1 mile, Parramatta River, for £200 ; time, 5 minutes 35 seconds ; June 6, 1859.

J. Candlish beat H. Green, 3½ miles, Parramatta River, for £200 ; time, 25 minutes 7 seconds ; June 15, 1859.

M'Grath beat Deward (red buoy), in watermen's skiffs, for £100 ; February 18, 1860.

Richard Green beat Henry White for £100, Parramatta River ; time, 26 minutes 40 seconds ; December 20, 1860.

Punch and M'Grath beat Green and White for £100, Parramatta River ; time, 25 minutes ; May 25, 1861.

The Brothers Green beat Punch and M'Grath, Parramatta River, June 22, 1861.

Punch and M'Grath beat the Brothers Green for £100, Parramatta River, July 20, 1861.

R. Green beat M'Grath for £25 (heavy boats), September 7, 1861.

M'Grath, of Sydney, beat Nickel, of Williamstown, Melbourne, for £200 ; January 18, 1862.

T. M'Grath beat T. Ralph, Yarra River, Melbourne, for £200, in outriggers, 4 miles ; time 29 minutes 45 seconds ; February 21, 1863.

W. Hickey beat R. Green for £170 (watermen's boats), Parramatta River, New South Wales, June 24, 1865.

White beat Galbraith for £200 (wager boats), Parramatta River, July 29, 1865.

Hickey beat Green for £200 (watermen's boats), Parramatta River, August 20, 1865.

White beat M'Leer for £100 (wager boats), Parramatta River ; time, 31 minutes ; September 16, 1865.

Connor and Donnelly beat White and Day for £100, Parramatta River ; October 28, 1865.

W. Hickey beat H. White for £200 (wager boats), Parramatta River ; time, 24 m. 50 s., Dec. 16, 1865.

Booker and M'Leer beat Connor and Donnelly for £100, Parramatta River, April 14, 1866.

R. Green beat W. Hickey for £200 (1 mile), Parramatta River ; time, 7 minutes 21 seconds ; October 17, 1866.

R. Green beat W. Hickey for £200 (2 miles), Parramatta River ; December 15, 1866.

W. Hickey beat M. Rush, for £350 (watermen's skiffs), Parramatta River, March 26, 1870.

M. Rush beat R. Hickey, for £500 (watermen's skiffs), Parramatta River ; time, 27 m. 40 s., May 21, 1870.

M. Rush beat W. Hickey, for £100 (light skiffs), Parramatta River, December 17, 1870.

Mulhall beat Solomon for £140, round two islands ; time, 35 minutes ; January 10, 1874 ; beat Trussell Tierney for £50 (wager boats), Parramatta River ; time, 29 minutes 30 seconds ; March 14, 1874.

N. Lyons beat P. Mulhall, for £50 (outriggers), Parramatta River ; time 23 minutes 22 seconds ; July 18, 1874.

Trickett beat Pierce, for £50 (watermen's skiffs), two islands ; time, 35 minutes 40 seconds ; August 22, 1874.

W. Lyons beat J. Candlish, for £60 (outriggers), Parramatta River ; time, 24 minutes 30 seconds ; August 29, 1874.

Trickett beat Pearce, for £50 (watermen's boats) two islands ; time, 37 minutes ; September 14, 1874.

Lyons beat Mulhall, for £60 (wager skiffs), Parramatta River ; time, 22 minutes ; November 14, 1874.

E. Trickett beat E. C. Laycock, for £200 (outriggers), Parramatta River ; time, 22 minutes 55 seconds ; September 10, 1875.

E. C. Laycock beat E. Trickett for champion belt, regatta, Sydney Harbour, January 26, 1879.

[*See* SCULLING.]

REGATTAS. First regatta on the Derwent, Hobart Town, January 5, 1827. First Australian regatta took place in Port Jackson, Sydney Harbour. There were five events on the programme, April 27, 1828. Regatta in Sydney Harbour April 2, 1832. Regatta on the waters of Port Jackson, January 9, 1834. Regatta at Port Phillip, January 12, 1841.

Anniversary.—Sydney gig race, won by Sydney Rowing Club, 1873 ; won by Mercantile Rowing Club, 1876 ; won by Mercantile Rowing Club, 1877.

Woolloomooloo Bay.—December 26, 1873.

SYDNEY GARDINER CUP, *Balmain Regatta.*— Won by Sydney Rowing Club, 1870 ; won by Parramatta Rowing Club, 1871 ; won by Sydney Rowing Club, 1872 ; won by Sydney Rowing Club, 1873 ; won by Sydney Rowing Club, 1874 ; won by Sydney Rowing Club, 1875 ; won by Mercantile Rowing Club, 1876 ; won by Sydney Rowing Club, 1877.

SWIMMING EXPLOITS.—Cavill's great swimming performance on the Yarra Yarra ; 18 miles in 5 hours 58 minutes ; March 1, 1879.

ARBUTHNOT RANGE.—Gap through it discovered by Cunningham, 1827.

ARNHEIM BAY.—Explored by Flinders, 1802.

ASSIGNMENT SYSTEM.—Governor Bourke was directed to discontinue assignment of convicts, *i.e.* lending convicts out for hire to free settlers in the colony, by a despatch dated May 26, 1837 ; system ceased, 1838.

ASTRONOMY IN AUSTRALIA. Honorary medals of the Astronomical Society of London presented by the President, Sir John Herschell, to Sir Thomas Brisbane and Mr. James Dunlop, for valuable services in the cause of Astronomy in Australia, February 8, 1828.

ASYLUMS. NEW SOUTH WALES. Benevolent Asylum, Sydney, taken possession of by the Committee of the Benevolent Society, October 21, 1829. For Destitute Children (Randwick), established February 23, 1852; the following gentlemen were present at the first meeting held at Dr. Douglass's on this date : George Allen, Esq. (in the chair), Archdeacon M'Encroe, Assistant Commissary General Owen, Mr. Cowlishaw, Captain M'Lerie, Dr. Douglass, Rev. A. H. Stephen (Hon. Sec.), these gentlemen, with Mr. James Comrie, forming the first Committee. Randwick Asylum for Destitute Children first occupied, March 28, 1858. Tarban Creek Asylum, at Bedlam Point (Gladesville), Parramatta River, built by Colonial Government, at a cost of £13,000, commenced by Sir Richard Bourke, in 1835; the first patients were received from the old Asylum, Liverpool, in November, 1838; originally built to accommodate 60 patients; in 1848 it had 154, and in 1878 it had 800.

VICTORIA. There are five Benevolent Asylums, where aged and infirm persons are received as inmates, and out-door relief is also given. These institutions are situated at Ballarat, Beechworth, Bendigo, Castlemaine, and Melbourne. A small maternity hospital is attached to the Ballarat Benevolent Asylum. Benevolent Asylum at Melbourne founded 1850. [See CHARITABLE INSTITUTIONS.]

AUCKLAND, NEW ZEALAND. Founded by Captain Hobson, January 29, 1840; first Supreme Court at, February 28, 1842; first lighted with gas, April 15, 1865. [See NEW ZEALAND.]

AUSTRALIA. This great continent contains an area of 2,983,263 square miles. Its greatest breadth from north to south is 1965 statute miles, and its greatest length from east to west is about 2600 miles. It has a coast-line of 8000 miles. It is politically divided into five colonies, viz., New South Wales, capital, Sydney; South Australia, capital, Adelaide; West Australia, capital, Perth; Victoria, capital, Melbourne; Queensland, capital, Brisbane. New South Wales, the mother colony, was founded in 1788; West Australia in 1829; South Australia in 1835; Victoria in 1851; and Queensland in 1859. Victoria, however, was settled in 1835, and Queensland in 1823, but until the latter dates formed a portion of New South Wales.

NEW SOUTH WALES. Area, 323,437 square miles or 206,999,680 acres. It lies between latitude 28° 8' and 37° 0' 23", and longitude 141° and 153° 38'. Its extreme length from east to west is 900 miles, the average being 500 miles; the extreme breadth from north to south is 850 miles, the average being 500. It is bounded on the north by Queensland; on the east by the South Pacific Ocean; on the south by Victoria, from which it is separated by the Murray, and by a line drawn from the sources of that river to Cape Howe; on the west by South Australia. It has a coast line of 800 miles. [See NEW SOUTH WALES.]

QUEENSLAND. Area, 678,600 square miles, or 434,304,000 acres. It lies between latitude S. 10° 37' and 29°, and longitude E. 138° and 153° 30'. Its length from north to south is 1300 miles, its breadth 800 miles, and it has a coast line of 2550 miles. It is twelve times the size of England and Wales. It is bounded on the north by the Gulf of Carpentaria, and Torres Straits, which separate it from New Guinea; on the east by the South Pacific Ocean; on the south by New South Wales; on the west by South Australia, and by the 141st meridian of longitude, from latitude S. 29° to 26°; thence along the 138th meridian of longitude to the Gulf of Carpentaria.

SOUTH AUSTRALIA. Area, 914,730 square miles or 585,427,200 acres. It lies between latitude S. 11° 7 and 38°; and from latitude S. 26° to Cape Northumberland; it lies between longitude E. 129° and 141°; and north of latitude S. 26°, it is between longitude E. 129° and 138°, as far as the Arifura Sea and Gulf of Carpentaria. It is bounded on the west by West Australia; on the east by Victoria, New South Wales and Queensland; on the south by the Southern Ocean; and on the north by the Gulf of Carpentaria and the Indian Ocean. The coast line of the southern boundary, owing to the irregularity of the shore, is 1600 miles in length from Cape Northumberland, running north-west. NORTHERN TERRITORY of South Australia is all that tract of country north of the 26° of latitude S., and lying between longitude E., 129° and 138°, comprising about 531,250 square miles, or 340,000,000 acres.

VICTORIA. 88,198 square miles, or 56,446,720 acres. It is situated at the south-eastern corner of Australia, and lies between latitude S. 34° and 39°, and between longitude E. 141° and 150°. Its extreme length from east to west is 480 miles, and extreme breadth from north to south is 240 miles. It is bounded on the north and north-west by New South Wales, from which it is separated by the river Murray; on the west by South Australia; on the south-east by the South Pacific Ocean; and on the south by Bass's Straits, which separate it from Tasmania. It has a coast line of 600 miles.

WEST AUSTRALIA. Area, 978,298 square miles or 626,111,323 acres. It is eight times as large as the United Kingdom, and comprises all the territory between latitude S. 13° 44' and 35° 8', and lying W. of the 129th meridian of east longitude to the Indian Ocean. It has a seaboard of over 2000 miles, being 1280 miles in length from north to south, and 800 miles in breadth from east to west. It is bounded on the north and west by the Indian Ocean, on the south by the Southern Ocean, and on the east by South Australia ; but only about 600 miles from Albany, in the south, to the Murchison, in the north, by a depth of 150 miles, are occupied. [*See* WESTERN AUSTRALIA.]

TOTAL AREA of the Australian Continent, 2,983,263 square miles, or 1,909,288,923 acres.

ALLEGED EARLY DISCOVERY OF. Mr. R. H. Major, of the British Museum, alleged in 1872 that Australia was known to the French prior to 1531.

DISCOVERY OF. [*See* EXPLORERS, SEA.]

AUSTRALIA, EARLIEST MAPS OF. The earliest map of Australia (now in the British Museum), bearing the arms of the Dauphin of France, appears to have been executed in the time of Francis I., for his son the Dauphin, probable date, 1530. A map of Australia, dedicated to Henry VIII. of England, evidently a copy of the Dauphin map, executed by a Frenchman named Jean Rotz, who came to England. It bears date 1542.

[NOTE.—On the "Dauphin Map" this great country it called "Jave la Grande" ; and is distinguished from the smaller island of Java itself by the latter being called "The Lytil Java."]

AUSTRALIA FELIX. Major Mitchell gave the designation of Australia Felix to Victoria when he explored it in 1836.

AUSTRALIA NAMED. Flinders seems to have been the first who suggested for the Continent the name "Australia." He says in his work "A voyage to Terra Australis," "Had I permitted myself any innovation upon the original term (Terra Australis), it would have been to convert it into Australia, as being more agreeable to the ear and an as-

similation to the names of the other great portions of the earth." 1814.

AUSTRALIAN AGRICULTURAL CO. This Company was established August 21, 1824. The primary objects of the association were : the production of pure merino wool as an export to Great Britain ; the cultivation of the olive, vine, and such other productions as might be adapted to the soil and climate ; to encourage and assist the emigration of useful settlers and female servants, and to promote a system of useful industry. The amount of capital to be invested in the company was one million pounds sterling, divided into 10,000 shares at £10 each ; and in return for the outlay they were to receive a grant of land in the colony to the extent of a million of acres. Amongst the principal members of this company were the Attorney-General and Solicitor-General of England, 28 members of Parliament, including Mr. Brougham (afterwards Lord Brougham and Vaux), and Mr. Joseph Hume, the Governor, Deputy Governor, and eight of the directors of the Bank of England ; the Chairman and Deputy-Chairman and five Directors of the East India Company, besides many other eminent bankers and merchants of England. All the shares were speedily taken up except 500, which were reserved.

Sir Edward Parry, the Arctic Navigator, arrived with Lady Parry, from London, in the "William," to take charge of the Australian Agricultural Company's property in New South Wales, December 24, 1829.

An arrangement was effected in England with the Australian Agricultural Company, by which they gave up the monopoly of the coal mines at Newcastle.—1847.

AUSTRALIAN ALPS. The Australian Alps first seen by Hume and Hovell, November 6, 1824.

B

BALLOONING.—Many attempts have been made to ascend in balloons, resulting in nearly all cases in whole or partial failure. Mr. Thomas Gale, accompanied by Mr. John Allen, ascended in a balloon (72 feet high, 112 feet in circumference, with capacity for 32,000 feet of gas) from Victoria Park, Sydney, a height of 2½ miles, and descended in two hours' time in Delarge's Bay, Parramatta River, between Kissing Point and Tarban Creek, January 7, 1871.

BARRACKS. Hyde Park Barracks, situated at the eastern end of King-street, Sydney, were erected by Governor Macquarie, as the principal convict depôt in the colony, and were first

HYDE PARK BARRACKS

occupied June, 1819. [They are now used as an asylum for aged females, and as a Female Immigrant depôt.]

BARRIER REEF. Surveyed by Captain Blackwood, 1844.

BARRINGTON, GEORGE. A celebrated pickpocket, who was transported to Australia. He is said to have been the author of a well-known prologue delivered at the opening of the first Theatre [see THEATRES] in Sydney. He received the first warrant of emancipation ever issued, 1792 ; lived to a very old age, and died at Parramatta, N.S.W.

BARWON, KARAULA, OR DARLING RIVER, discovered Feb. 4, 1832. [The three rivers are one and the same stream under different names, being called the Karaula for some distance from its source, then assuming the title of the Barwon, and subsequently that of the Darling.—See AUSTRALIA and RIVERS.]

BALLOONING
The Illustrated Journal of Australasia

BATHURST. Governor Macquarie visited and fixed upon the site for Bathurst, so named by him in honour of Earl Bathurst, Secretary of State for the Colonies ; the road measured 140 miles from Sydney ; fifty thousand acres of good land were found to exist within ten miles of the township) May 7, 1875. Great depredations committed by blacks ; martial law proclaimed, August 15, 1824. Captain Fennell appointed commandant at Bathurst, January 5, 1825. Visited by Governor Darling, accompanied by Captain Dumaresq and Lieutenant De La Condamine, November 5, 1829. Great outbreak amongst the prison population in the district, the insurgents consisting at first of only eight persons, but shortly afterwards by intimidation and persuasion, eighty collected. In the conflict Lieutenant Brown had two men and five horses killed, but the convicts were at length subdued and ten men were convicted and hanged at Bathurst, September, 1830. Township proclaimed, 1852.

THE PLAINS OF BATHURST
Lady Georgina Sherbourne, Mitchell Library

BAUDIN, CAPTAIN (*French*) visited Encounter Bay, 1801; French claimed discovery of the whole of the South Coast of Australia, 1802; left Australia, 1803.

BAUER, MR., natural history painter, sailed with Flinders, 1801.

BAVARIA, KING OF. Instruments for Astronomical observations presented by him to Victoria, 1854.

BAXTER, JOHN, murdered by two blacks whilst with the exploring party under Eyre, 1841.

BECKER, LUDWIG, artist and naturalist, of Burke and Wills's exploring party, 1860; died near Cooper's Creek, 1861.

BEES, INTRODUCTION OF. "Captain Wallis, of the 'Isabella,' brought out a number of bee-hives on his last visit to the Colony. Mr. Parr, of George-street, has four of these thickly populated habitations, which seem not to lose any of their forces from a change of climate. A species of this industrious race was introduced into Parramatta some years ago, and lived only a short time," April, 1822; Mr. Icely, of Macquarie-place, Sydney, had one of Captain Wallis's original hives, 1823; the honey bee introduced into Tasmania by Dr. Wilson, 1834; Mr. John Hughes, of Sussex Farm, near Bathurst, the first who succeeded in bringing bees alive over the Blue Mountains, 1839; the first person who introduced bees to the Bathurst district was the late Thomas Arkell, Esq., of Charlton, Campbell's River, who received a hive from the late Nathaniel Payten, of Parramatta, and carried the bees in his gig to Charlton, 1842.

BENT, GEOFFREY HART, first Judge of the Supreme Court, N.S.W., arrived July 27, 1814.

BENTLEY MYSTERY, THE. A pianiste named Julia Bentley (formerly Miss Monk, of Exeter, England), with her husband, Thomas Charles Bentley, afterwards secretary of the Union Club, Sydney, arrived in New South Wales in January, 1860. In May, 1861, and during the seven succeeding months, a number of anonymous letters affecting the character of Mrs. Bentley were received by the leading inhabitants of Sydney. She alleged that she was insulted and violently assaulted in the streets of the city. A parliamentary inquiry was held commencing on November 14, 1862; progress report stating that no satisfactory conclusion as to the authorship of the letters had been arrived at by the committee and exonerating all those accused by the Bentleys. Sub-Inspector Harrison, of the Detective Police, gave evidence of his belief that Mrs. Bentley wrote the anonymous letters, and in support of his opinion, referred to a similar occurrence having happened to Mrs. Bentley, when a girl, some years previously, in Exeter. December 19, 1862.

BERRIMA.　　[*See* PRISONS.]

THE BERTRAND TRIAL
A & R Archives

BERTRAND CASE, THE. The murder of Mr. Henry Kinder by Louis Henry Bertrand, forms one of the most remarkable cases in the criminal jurisprudence of the Australasian Colonies, and from the revolting circumstances attending it, and the position held in society by the principal parties concerned, it is justly entitled to be considered one of the "*Causes Célèbres*" of court business. On October 2, 1865, the public of Sydney were startled by the intelligence that Mr. Henry Kinder, principal teller in the City Bank, a gentleman well-known and much esteemed, had committed suicide by shooting himself. An inquest was held on the body, when Helen Maria Kinder, the wife of the unfortunate man, gave evidence to the effect that deceased had for some days been under the influence of drink, had been very violent, and had frequently threatened to destroy himself ; that whilst in the garden she had heard the pistol fired, and on returning to the room occupied by her husband, found him lifeless. Subsequent suspicious circumstances caused the arrest of Mrs. Kinder, at Bathurst, on a charge of murder. She was remanded to Sydney, and at the same time, Louis Henry Bertrand, a well-known dentist of Sydney, and the most intimate friend of the deceased, and Jane Bertrand, his wife, were arrested on a similar charge. The hearing of the case at the Water Police Court lasted till December 9th, when all the prisoners were fully committed for trial. During the proceedings, a series of the most atrocious details ever heard in a police court came to light, and, amongst other papers produced, were the diary of the male prisoner Bertrand and a bundle of letters, written almost daily by him to Mrs. Kinder, leaving no doubt of Bertrand's intention to get rid of Kinder, with whose wife he had formed a *liaison*. Kinder had evidently been drugged day by day, till he became thoroughly demented and stupefied, and it was supposed, either that Bertrand, finding that his victim was more tenacious of life than he had expected, had fired the pistol, and had placed the weapon in Kinder's hand after death ; or, having placed the weapon in Kinder's hand whilst he was still alive, but in an almost comatose state, had bent the arm and then pulled the trigger, in either case leading to a supposition of suicide. Bertrand and Mrs. Kinder were placed on their trial at the Central Criminal Court, in March, 1866, Mrs. Bertrand having been set at liberty by the Attorney-General, as it was clearly seen that the part she had taken in the series of circumstances connected with the case had been done from fear of her husband, who had used the most terrible threats towards her, and that she had really no knowledge of the intended murder. After a long and patient trial, at which the most learned counsel were engaged on both sides, Mrs. Kinder was acquitted, and Bertrand found guilty and sentenced to death, March 21, 1866. The most strenuous efforts were, however, used by the prisoner's friends to obtain a commutation of the sentence ; every legal and technical point was made available for a fresh hearing and renewed arguments. The case was taken before the Privy Council, which upheld the conviction, Bertrand being meanwhile kept in Darlinghurst Gaol. At length, after the lapse of about two years, during which period all those skilled in medical jurisprudence were consulted and examined, the sentence was, on the ground of insanity, commuted to imprisonment for life, a sentence Bertrand is now undergoing in Parramatta Criminal Lunatic Asylum, N.S.W. Mrs. Kinder found it expedient to emigrate to New Zealand, where she was at once engaged as barmaid at an hotel, and has since re-married.

BETTING ACT (TERRY'S). The "Betting Houses Suppression Act, introduced by S. H. Terry, Esq., Member for New England, came into operation in New South Wales, April, 1876.

BILLIARDS. Mons. Pierre Carme first appeared in Sydney, April, 1826 ; John Roberts, junior, champion billiard player, first appeared in Sydney, August 14, 1876.

BIRTHS IN THE AUSTRALASIAN COLONIES FOR THE YEAR ENDING DEC. 31, 1876.

	Male.	Female.	Total.
Victoria	13,759	13,010	26,769
New South Wales .. .	11,791	11,507	23,298
Queensland	3,540	3,363	6,903
South Australia	4,134	4,090	8,224
Western Australia	474	444	918
Total	33,698	32,414	66,112
Tasmania	1,660	1,489	3,149
New Zealand	8,320	7,848	16,168
Grand Total	43,678	41,751	85,429

BIRTHS, ILLEGITIMATE, IN THE AUSTRALASIAN COLONIES.

Year.	Illegitimate Births to every 100 Children Born.			
	Victoria.	New South Wales.	Queensland.	New Zealand.
1872	2·99	4·03	2·92	..
1873	3·18	4·15	2·71	1·42
1874	3·67	4·22	2·76	1·30
1875	2·92	4·20	3·43	1·36
1876	3·64	4·08	3·21	2·23
Means ..	3·28	4·13	3·01	1·58

ILLEGITIMACY IN ENGLAND, SCOTLAND, AND IRELAND, 1871 TO 1875.

Year.	Illegitimate Births to every 100 Children Born.		
	England and Wales.	Scotland.	Ireland.
1871	5·6	9·5	2·7
1872	5·4	9·1	2·5
1873	5·2	9·0	2·4
1874	5·0	8·7	2·3
1875	4·8	8·6	2·3
Means..	5·20	8·98	2·44

Illegitimacy in England and Wales appears to be commoner than, and in Scotland more than twice as common as, it is in any of the Australasian colonies named. In Ireland, on the other hand, if the figures are reliable, it is less prevalent than in any of those colonies, except New Zealand.

BLACK THURSDAY (VICTORIA). Memorably hot day in Victoria; the thermometer was 112° in the shade, and the whole country wrapped in flames. The ashes from the fire at Macedon, 46 miles away, fell in Melbourne; many had to leave their flocks and herds and fly for their lives, February 6, 1851.

BLAXLAND, JOHN. A piece of plate was subscribed for the Hon. John Blaxland as a testimony of respect for his independence in the Legislative Council; but Mr. Blaxland dying, it was presented with a suitable address to his sons, January 9, 1846.

BLIGH, CAPTAIN WILLIAM, in the "Bounty," anchored in Adventure Bay, Van Diemen's Land, and having landed, planted some European fruit trees, 1788; mutiny of the "Bounty" April 28, 1789; arrived in New South Wales as Governor, August 14, 1806; reported and arrested by Lieutenant Minchin and soldiers, Sergeant John Sutherland, and Corporal Marlborough, by order of Major Johnston, January 26, 1808. As a condition of obtaining his freedom, entered into a written agreement with Colonel Paterson to embark and proceed direct to England in the "Porpoise," February 4, 1809; left for Tasmania, February 20, 1809; reinstated, January, 1810; left for England, May 4, 1810; arrived in England, October 25, 1810. Died in England Dec 7, 1817. [See "Bounty."]

BLONDIN, AUSTRALIAN. [See L'ESTRANGE.]

BLONDIN. First appeared in Brisbane, July 25, 1874; in a canvas enclosure (the largest in the world), first exhibition in the Domain, Sydney, August 29, 1874; first appearance in Melbourne, November 4, 1874.

MR BLONDIN IN MID AIR
The Australasian Sketcher, 1874

BLUE MOUNTAINS, CROSSING OF. Attempt made to cross the Blue Mountains by Lieutenant Dawes and a small party, December, 1789; several unsuccessful attempts made to cross them between 1789 and 1793; Captain Paterson, of the New South Wales Corps, the

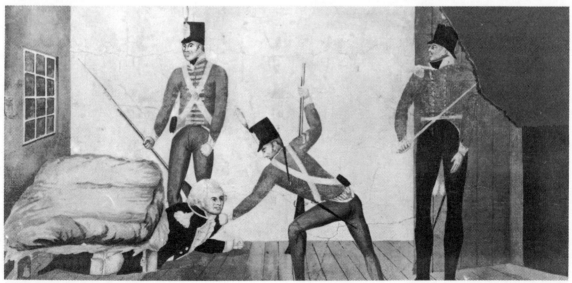

THE ARREST OF BLIGH
Mitchell Library

African traveller, began his attempt to cross them, February 18, 1793 ; Henry Hacking, quarter-master of the "Sirius," with two companions, undertook an expedition, and penetrated 20 miles further than any of his predecessors, passing over 18 or 19 ridges and gullies, and, seeing no termination to the mountainous barriers and deep descending chasms, retraced his steps, returning to the settlement after an absence of seven days, August, 1793 ; second expedition undertaken by Captain Paterson, the party being supplied with arms and provisions for six weeks, proceeded up the Hawkesbury ten miles beyond Richmond, when the rapidity of the current and trunks of trees impeded their further progress, and their boats being partially disabled, they returned, a variety of new plants being the only result of the expedition, 1793 ; Wilson, a convict (possessing some attainments), who had been for several years amongst the blacks, accompanied by a free man (a servant of the Governor), successfully crossed the Blue Mountains as far as a river, afterwards known as the Lachlan, 1799 ; Gregory Blaxland, William Charles Wentworth, and Lieutenant William Lawson crossed May, 1813 ; Mr. George William Evans made a tour over them and discovered the Macquarie River, February 12, 1814.

MILITARY GUARD AT. A military guard was stationed near the ascent of the mountains, and no one was allowed to pass without a written permission from the Government, May 7, 1815.

ROAD ACROSS. [See ROADS.]

BOAT. First boat built in the colony was called the "Rose Hill Packet," 1818.

BOGAN RIVER. Mr. Dixon visited the Bogan and followed it down 67 miles, October, 1833.

BONG BONG. [See EXPLORERS, LAND.]

BOTANIC GARDENS. Opened to the public April 30, 1838.

BOTANY BAY. A brazen tablet at Botany Bay erected in memory of Captain Cook, March 19, 1822.

"BOUNTY," H.M.S., MUTINY OF. The "Bounty," under Captain William Bligh, was an armed ship which quitted Otaheite with breadfruit trees April 7, 1789. The mutineers put the captain and eighteen men into an open boat with a small stock of provisions near one of the Friendly Islands, April 28, 1789. These reached the island of Timor after a voyage of 3,500 miles. Ten of the mutineers were tried in September, 1792 ; three were executed. John Adams and eight others of the mutineers removed from Otaheite to Pitcairn's Island, where 20 years afterwards John Adams and the descendants of his and the others were discovered. The "Bounty" was burned January 23, 1790. John Adams died March 5, 1829, aged 65.

MUTINEERS' DESCENDANTS. The descendants of John Adams and the other mutineers of the "Bounty," to the number of 198,—96 males and 102 females, removed from Pitcairn's Island to Norfolk Island, June, 1856. Returned to their original home in two parties, in 1859 and 1864 ; they now (1879) number 41 males and 49 females, the eldest of whom is Elizabeth George, 88 years of age, a daughter of one of the nine actual mutineers who took part in the events of 1789.

BOURKE, GOVERNOR SIR RICHARD *Reasons for retirement of.* Mr. Riddell, Colonial Treasurer, having been nominated by one section of the people of the colony to the office of Chairman of Quarter Sessions (*vice* Foster resigned), and contested successfully the seat against the other candidate, Mr. Roger Therry, who was the favourite of the Governor's supporters, and patronised by the Governor, Sir Richard Bourke resented Mr. Riddell's departure from official propriety by removing him from his seat at the Executive Council, 1835. On the matter being referred Home, Mr. Rid-

BAZAAR IN THE BOTANIC GARDENS
The Illustrated Sydney News, 1854

dell, Colonial Treasurer, was reinstated in the Executive Council, from which he had been suspended. In a despatch from Lord Glenelg, it was considered that suspension for a year was quite sufficient punishment for his error in allowing himself to be nominated a candidate for the office of Chairman of Quarter Sessions in 1835. The Governor, in informing the Home Government, said that he had suspended Mr. Riddell, intimating his desire of retiring in the event of its not being confirmed. In a despatch, the Secretary of State earnestly urged the Governor (Sir Richard Bourke) not to persevere in his intention of resigning; but the Governor was determined not to sit in the Executive Council with Mr. Riddell, and intimated to the Home Government his resolution to retire. The acceptance of his resignation arrived in the colony in the following September; resigned his administration December 5, and embarked on board the "Samuel Winter" for England, having administered the affairs of the colony from December 3, 1830—just seven years.

Ovation upon retirement of.

Previous to his departure, a meeting was held and a valedictory address to his Excellency was adopted, in which reference was made to the many useful reforms affected during his administration; amongst them were the severing of the connection between the Government and the Press, which had prevailed up to the time of his arrival; the many improvements in the colony, and the projecting the Circular Quay round the Cove. At this meeting it was at once determined to erect a statue to the retiring Governor, and a sum of six hundred and eighty pounds were collected in the room towards the cost of the proposed memorial. Other addresses were presented to him from the Legislative Council, the Roman Catholic and Presbyterian clergy, the Synagogue, the officers of public departments, the School of Arts, and the Freemasons' lodges. He was accompanied to the place of embarkation by a large concourse, including the Church of England Bishop, the clergy of various denominations, public officials, and persons of all grades of society.

BOWEN, LADY. Outrageous attack on Lady Bowen, wife of the Governor of Victoria, by an insane woman named Esther Gray. As Lady Bowen was entering the Athenæum, Melbourne, the woman struck her several times in the face, August 5, 1876.

Presentation of magnificent gold bracelet to Lady Bowen by the ladies of Victoria, previous to her departure, February 20, 1879.

BOWEN, LIEUTENANT, arrived in command of the "Atlantic," transport, from England, August 20, 1791.

BOWEN, TOWN OF, Queensland. Named in honour of Governor Sir George Bowen; formed, April 12, 1861.

BOWEN, PORT, Queensland. Discovered by Flinders, 1802.

BOYD, BENJAMIN. The largest squatter of his time in Australia; held 381,000 acres, for which he paid £80 license fees, 1847.

BOYNE, RIVER. Discovered November 7, 1823.

BRANDS. Registration Act of N. S. W. came into force, January 1, 1867.

BREMER, SIR GORDON. Expedition under Captain Sir Gordon Bremer, to Port Essington, in H. M. S. "Alligator" and "Britomart." A colony established, then called Victoria, October 27, 1838.

BREWERIES. The first ale made in Australia was manufactured by Mr. James Squire (a retired soldier), grandfather of James Squire Farnell, Esq., M.L.A., late Premier of New South Wales, at Kissing Point, Parramatta River, in the year 1795.

BOTTLED ALES, WINES, AND SPIRITS.

An advertisement from *The Illustrated Sydney News*, 1855

BRICKS. First bricks made in New South Wales, at Brickfield Hill, Sydney, March, 1788.

BRIDGES. First bridge commenced in Australia was Duck River Bridge, on the Sydney and Parramatta Road, N. S. Wales, 1796; Ross Bridge, Van Diemen's Land, completed, Feb. 28, 1822; foundation stone of Landsdown Bridge, Liverpool Road, N. S. Wales, laid by His Excellency the Governor, Jan. 1, 1834; opened Jan. 10, 1836; first stone bridge in N. S. Wales over Duck River opened by Governor Bourke, Jan. 26, 1836; Fitzroy Bridge, Goulburn, N. S. Wales, opened, 1855; City Bridge, Adelaide, opened 1855; Albury Bridge, over the Murray, October 3, 1861; Brisbane Bridge, foundation laid, August 22, 1864; Angaston Bridge, South Australia, opened Dec. 6, 1865; Gundagai Bridge, N.S.W., three-quarters of a mile in length, cost £45,000, over Murrumbidgee, completed, May, 1867; the Denison Bridge at Bathurst was swept away by flood, June, 1867; the Ranken Bridge was carried away soon after, thus cutting off all communication with Bathurst by means of teams — the farmers about Kelso and Peel suffered greatly

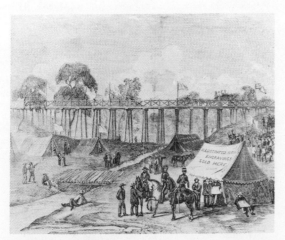

FITZROY BRIDGE, GOULBURN
The Illustrated Sydney News, 1854

in consequence, June, 1867 ; Freemantle Bridge, Western Australia, opened, Oct. 2, 1867 ; foundation stone of Prince's Bridge, Melbourne, laid, March 20, 1869 ; Victoria Bridge, Adelaide, opened 1870 ; Victoria Bridge, costing £120,000, over Brisbane River, Queensland, opened by the Marquis of Normanby, June 15, 1874 ; new bridge over the Hawkesbury, at Windsor, N. S. Wales (length, 480 ft., cost £10,280), opened by Hon. John Sutherland, Minister for Works, Aug. 20, 1874 ; bridge over the Murrumbidgee, at Hay, N. S. Wales, opened by the Hon. Henry Parkes, M.L.A., Aug. 31, 1874 ; the Moruya Bridge, N. S. Wales, opened by Mr. Henry Clarke, M.L.A., Jan. 26, 1876 ; Oxley Railway Bridge, over the Brisbane River, Queensland, opened by Governor Cairns, July 5, 1876 ; the Huon Bridge, Tasmania, opened July 13, 1876 ; Albert Bridge, over Torrens, S.A., April, 1879. [*See* RAILWAY BRIDGES.]

BRISBANE.   First settled by a detachment of soldiers, 40th Regiment, and a gang of convicts, under charge of Lieut. Miller, August, 1824. First land sale held in Brisbane, August 9, 1843 ; first Brisbane School of Arts opened, October 7, 1851 ; first public meeting in favour of separation of Moreton Bay from N. S. Wales, 1851 ; banquet given in honour of the visit of Sir Charles Fitzroy, Governor-General, April 7, 1854 ; Municipality formed, 1859 ; first daily paper published, May 13, 1861 ; foundation stone of Town Hall laid, Jan. 26, 1864 ; water works commenced, August 18, 1864 ; new School of Arts opened, July 16, 1866 ; foundation stone of Grammar School laid by H.R.H. Prince Alfred, Feb. 29, 1868 ; Chamber of Commerce established, July 1, 1868 ; Grammar School opened, Feb. 1, 1869.

BRISBANE DOWNS. [*See* MONARO PLAINS.]

BRISBANE, 1850
Rex Nan Kivell Collection

BRISBANE, COMMODORE SIR JAMES, died Dec. 19, 1826. ["The name of Sir James Brisbane will be associated with an event which forms an interesting epoch in the annals of the Colonies of Australia—the arrival of the first line of battle ship in the harbour of Port Jackson—and will be handed down with it as a record to posterity."—Extract from *Government Order*, Dec. 19, 1826.]

BRISBANE, SIR THOMAS, born in Scotland, Governor N.S.W., from 1821 to 1827; a lover of astronomy; erected observatory in Parramatta, and took active part in scientific pursuits. BANQUETS TO.

Two banquets were proposed for the purpose of inviting the Governor, previous to his retirement, one by the "Aristocracy" of the Colony, and one by the "Emancipatists," who formed the two classes of society. The former at the time were known by the names of the "Exclusionists," "Aristocrats," and "Pure Merinos." The result was, that the Governor, unwilling to attend both invitations, endeavoured to arrange between the conflicting parties, and ordered a letter to be written to the Exclusionists' Committee, expressing his wish that six individuals of the Emancipatists, whose names were given, should be invited to the banquet. Of this the committee disapproved, and in replying to the Governor's letter announced the painful necessity of declining any further preparation for the honour of his Excellency's company. The Emancipatists' party completed their arrangements, and a banquet, which was numerously attended, was given to the retiring Governor, at Nash's Hotel, Parramatta, Oct. 31, 1827.

BRISBANE, RIVER, named and explored by Oxley, Dec. 2, 1823.

BROWN, ROBERT, botanist, sailed with Flinders, 1801.

BRUNI ISLAND, Tasmania, named after Admiral Bruni D'Entrecasteaux, 1797.

BUCKLEY, WILLIAM, escaped from Collins's Port Phillip expedition, Dec. 27, 1803, and remained with the blacks 32 years. When discovered in 1835, he could scarcely remember any of his native language; his height was 6 feet 5 inches. He died in Hobart Town in 1856.

BULL-BAITING. Whitsuntide holidays celebrated at Parramatta by cock-fighting and bull-baiting. At the latter "sport" a number of useful dogs were killed or crippled, June 11 and 12, 1810.

BULLOCKS. *Largest in Australia*, property of Mr. William Edward Colston, of Barnawartha, Victoria, turned the scale at 3948lb, or 35cwt 1qr; height, 6ft 1in; length, 11ft 9in; girth, 9ft 10in; at belly, 10ft 11in; hocks, 2ft 1½in; arm, 3ft; yoke, 7ft 8in; age, 8 years, 1878.

BURDEKIN, RIVER. Discovered, March 22, 1845.

BURIAL-GROUND. The old burial-ground in George and Druitt Street was closed, and the burial ground, at what was then called the Sand-

BLACK THURSDAY
Picturesque Atlas of Australia

hills, was consecrated by the principal Chaplain, January 27, 1820. [*See* CEMETERIES.]

BURKE AND WILLS. News received in Melbourne of the death of Burke and Wills, October 10, 1861. [*See* EXPLORERS.]

BUSH FIRES. Great bush fires and intense heat throughout Victoria, causing the day to be long afterwards remembered as " Black Thursday," February 6, 1851. Disastrous bush fires throughout the South and West of N. S. Wales, in January, 1870, fires burning on each side of the line on the Southern railway, the railway porters and others beating it out with bushes, and waiting at the stations with water for the passengers to drink, and a truck on the Goulburn train catching fire near Liverpool, January 18, 1870. Disastrous bush fires (accompanied by drought) occurred throughout N. S. Wales and Queensland, December, 1874, to February, 1875.

BUSHRANGERS.

Clarke, John. Robbery under arms, at Michelago, of Levy's store, Michelago, June 1, 1866; robbery of the mail near Moruya, July 16; of W. & J. Morris's and John King's stores, at Mudmelong, July 16; of the Yass mail, July 27; of F. H. Wilson, Esq., at Manar, July 24; of the Boro mail, July 30; of Messrs. Myers and Badgery, at Jembaicumbene, August 27; of John Hoskings, at Foxlow, August 23, and again on September 10; of Guelch and Dallas, at Long Flat, September 25; of Joseph Taylor, at Little Bombay, October 20; of Messrs. Smith and Dawson, on Braidwood road, October 22; of a number of Chinamen, on the Araluen Mountains, October 28; of Ah How, at Jembaicumbene, November 20; of Chong Chang, at Major's Creek, November 20; of the Yass mail, December 7; of a Chinaman, at Mudmelong, December 31; of John Hyland, at Crown Flat, December 31; suspected of assisting to murder the four special constables, at Jindera, January 9, 1867; of Hornby and others, on the Araluen Mountains, January 15; of Henry Lamb and Chowry, Mongarlon road, January 14; of G. Myers, at Jembaicumbene, January 26; of the Yass mail, January 27; of the Goulburn mail, February 22; of Frazer's store, at Gundaroo, March 2; of F. Louise, at Bungendore, March 4; of Williams, publican, at Boro, March 7; feloniously wounded Constable Walsh and the black tracker, Sir Watkin, when being captured at Jindera, April 27; tried at Central Criminal Court, Sydney, May 29, 1867; executed at Darlinghurst, June 25, 1867.

Clarke, Thomas. Escaped from Braidwood Gaol, whilst under committal for robbery, being armed, October 3, 1865; stole a horse from C. E. Dransfield, at Jembaicumbene, October 27; stole a horse from Mulligan, at Jembaicumbene, December 1; stole a horse from John Mallon, of Mericumbene, December 13; robbery of Mr. Hoskings, at Foxlow, December 29; of Sum-

mer's store, at Jembaicumbene, January 13, 1866; of Frazer & Matthison, on Major's Creek Mountain, January 13; of the Araluen and Braidwood mail, January 15; of the Post-Office at Michelago, February 13; of John M'Elroy, at Manar, February 10; of Ed. Eaton, at Crown Flat, February 23; of Cullen and Harnett, near Cooma, March 22; of the Nerrigundah mail (Mr. John Emmett wounded), April 9; murder of Miles O'Grady, at Nerrigundah, for which he was outlawed, April 9; robbery of Morris's store at Mudmelong, February 23; of Armstrong's store, at Araluen, May 22; of Levy and others, at Michelago, June 1; of Thomas Wall, at Jindera, July 4; of the Moruya mail (mailboy's horse taken), July 16; of King and Morris's, at Mudmelong, July 16; fired at the Ballalaba police, July 17; robbery of the Yass mail, July 27; of the Queanbeyan mail, July 30; of F. H. Wilson, at Manar Station, July 24; of Hosking's, at Foxlow, August 22, and also September 10; of Myers and Badgery, at Jembaicumbene, August 27; of a Chinaman, on the Araluen Mountain, October 9; of Joseph Taylor, at Little Bombay, October 20; of R. Smith and T. Dawson, on Braidwood road, October 22; of a number of Chinese, on the Araluen Mountain, October 28; of a Chinaman, at Jembaicumbene, November 20; of a number of Chinamen, at Major's Creek, November 20; of the Yass mail, at Razorback, December 7; of a Chinaman, at Mudmelong, December 31; of attempt to rob James Hyland, at Crown Flat, December 31; suspected of murdering the four special constables at Jindera, January 9, 1867; of robbery of John Hornby, on the Araluen Mountain, January 15; of Chowry and Lamb, at Mongarlo, January 14; of James Myers, at Jembaicumbene, January 26; of the Goulburn mail, February 22; of the Yass mail, January 22; of Frazer's store, at Gundaroo, March 2; of Mr. Williams, at Boro, March 7; feloniously wounding Constable Walsh and Sir Watkin. the black tracker, when being captured at Jindera, April 27, for which they were tried at the Central Criminal Court, May 29; executed June 25, 1867.

Donohoe, John. A native of Dublin, arrived, a prisoner, in the colony by the "Ann and Amelia," 1825. Soon afterwards escaped, and took to the bush; depredations committed chiefly in the vicinity of Liverpool, Penrith, and Windsor; was joined by ten or twelve others, forming a band that carried terror through all the more populous parts of the interior during 1828 and 1829; shot dead, in a skirmish, by a soldier named Maggleton, at Raby, September 1, 1830; several of his companions afterwards caught and executed. Donohoe was 5 feet 4 inches in height, and had flaxen hair and blue eyes.

Dunn, John. One of the Gardiner gang of bushrangers, captured on the Marthaguy Creek, below Dubbo, by Constable James A. G. M'Hale, assisted by Senior-Constable Elliot and Constable Hawthorn.; Dunn shot M'Hale in the leg, and was himself wounded and afterwards tried and hanged at Darlinghurst, December 24, 1865. [*See* EXECUTIONS.]

Gardiner, Francis. Commonly known as "Frank Gardiner," *alias* Christie, *alias* Clarke ; born at Boro Creek, near Goulburn, New South Wales, in 1830, height 5 feet 8¼ inches, brown hair, sallow complexion, hazel eyes ; was first tried on the 21st and 22nd October, 1850, at the Geelong Circuit Court, Victoria, on a charge of horse-stealing, for which he received a sentence of five years' imprisonment with hard labour. On the 26th March, 1851, he escaped from Pentridge prison, Victoria, and was next convicted at the Goulburn Circuit Court, New South Wales, on 17th March, 1854, on two charges of horse-stealing, for which he received two sentences of seven years each on the roads. He obtained a ticket-of-leave for Carcoar on 31st December, 1859, but it was cancelled on 5th May, 1861, for absence from district and being suspected of cattle-stealing. For several years he kept a great part of the country in terror by his lawless deeds, aided by a gang of ruffians that he got together, the names of the principal ones being Gilbert, O'Malley, Hall, and Dunn. No less than six mail robberies under arms were committed by him, and scores of persons were bailed up and plundered. The most memorable crimes were the robbery of the gold escort from the Lachlan at Eugowra, in 1862, when the three police were overpowered by a large number of ruffians, several thousands of ounces of gold stolen ; and the shooting and wounding of Troopers Middleton and Hosie in a desperate encounter with the gang. Notwithstanding the efforts of the New South Wales Police, Gardiner escaped out of the country into the neighbouring colony of Queensland, and he set up business as a storekeeper, and successfully carried it on for two years at a place called Apis Creek, on the road from Rockhampton to the Peak Downs, where he was captured by Constables Pye, McGlone, and Wells, in February, 1864. He was brought to Sydney, and tried and convicted before Sir Alfred Stephen on the 8th July of that year for the wounding of Trooper Hosie and the robbery of Messrs. Hewett and Horsington. For these offences he received sentences amounting to 32 years' hard labour. In consequence of strong pressure being

HOW GILBERT DIED
The Illustrated Sydney News

brought to bear upon the Executive and the Governor, Gardiner was released from prison in July, 1874, on condition that he left the colony, and accordingly he went to America, where he now (1879) is. Mrs. Brown, Gardiner's paramour, was the wife of a respectable settler; having been seduced by Gardiner, she left her husband and family, breaking up a comfortable home, and lived with the outlaw until he was captured. She afterwards went to New Zealand and died a violent death by her own hands on the Thames gold-fields in 1868.

Gilbert, John, native of Canada, and the son of an old soldier, came when a boy to New South Wales with his father. He was engaged as stockman on a station near Marengo, from which place, lured by the false colouring given to bushranging in the neighbourhood, he, in 1862, joined Gardiner's gang; he was present at the sticking up of the gold escort in June of that year, and subsequently, when Gardiner had left the gang, he, in company with Ben Hall and John Dunn, made their names a terror to the country; he with his own hand shot Sergeant Parry who, deserted by his comrades, attempted to defend the Gundagai mail of November 16, 1863; on May 13, 1865, being betrayed by the farmer in whose house he and his comrade John Dunn had taken shelter for the night, he was shot in an encounter by a constable named John Bright, who, in company with Senior Constable Hales and Constable King, were brought to the spot by the informer. John Gilbert at the time of his death was about 22 or 23 years of age.

Hall, Benjamin, was for some years a small squatter in the Lachlan district, when he made the acquaintance of Francis Gardiner, then a ticket-of-leave man who was engaged in the occupation of a butcher. He was for a long time suspected by the police as being an accomplice of this man and his gang, and the close supervision under which he was kept, together with the alleged misconduct of his wife, at length drove him to desperation, and he openly joined Gardiner. On the retirement of the latter from his lawless career, Hall assumed command, and in company with Gilbert and Dunn, became the terror of the Goulburn and Lachlan Districts. At length he determined to relinquish his desperate life, and leaving Dunn and Gilbert, applied to a connection, in whose hands he had placed some money for safe keeping, for the amount. This man, under pretence of going into Forbes to obtain the money from the bank, revealed to the police Hall's hiding place, which they, under Sub-Inspector Davidson, closely surrounded at night, and as Hall arose the next morning, May 5, 1865, his body was riddled with slugs, as many as 34 wounds being counted. £1,000 reward had been offered for his capture, £500 of which his betrayer received, the other half being divided amongst the police present at his death.

Howe, Michael. Notorious bushranger in Van Diemen's Land, shot by Private W. Pugh, and captured October 21, 1818. [*See* BUSHRANGING, *Van Diemen's Land.*]

NED KELLY
The Australasian Sketcher

Kelly Gang, The. Constable Fitzpatrick, of Benalla, Victoria, whilst armed with a warrant to arrest Daniel Kelly, was overpowered at Kelly's house by the prisoner, his brother Ned, his mother, and two men, named Williamson and Skillion. The constable was maltreated and rendered insensible, but allowed to depart on solemnly promising not to report the occurrence. The three latter were subsequently imprisoned for the crime; the brothers Kelly took to the bush April 15, 1878, and thus originated the *Kelly Gang,* consisting of Edward Kelly (native of Victoria, aged 27), Daniel Kelly (native of Victoria, aged 18), Stephen Hart (native of Fish River, New South Wales, aged 20), and Joseph Byrnes (aged 21). Ned Kelly had, as far back as 1870, been arrested by the police of the Ovens District, Victoria, on suspicion of having been an accomplice of the bushranger Power. A reward of £100 was offered by the Government of Victoria for the capture of Daniel Kelly, for shooting Constable Fitzpatrick, April, 1878; their next reported act was the murder at Stringy Bark Creek, Wombat Ranges, near Mansfield,

Victoria, of Sergeant Michael Kennedy, and Constables Scanlan and Lonergan, by shooting, October 26, 1878. On October 30, the gang were outlawed, and a reward of £500 offered by the Victorian Government for the capture of each of them, dead or alive. Stuck up Faithful Creek Station, near Euroa, December 9; robbed the bank of Victoria, at Euroa, of £2,000, December 10; stuck up the Police Barracks at Jerilderie, New South Wales, and bailed up the police, Saturday evening near midnight, February 8, 1879; paraded through the township, held possession of it for two days, keeping the police in charge prisoners in the lockup, cutting the telegraph wires, and generally terrifying the inhabitants, robbing the bank of £2,000, and burning some of its valuable documents, February 10, 1879. [*See* REWARDS FOR CAPTURE OF.]

Macgregor, alias *the Wild Scotchman*, was the most notorious bushranger in Queensland; he came originally from New South Wales, and carried on for some time his depredations single-handed. As there was but little gold at that time discovered in the colony, his raids were principally on stations and travellers; was captured once, but managed to effect his escape on his way to Rockhampton Gaol; at last was, after a chase of eighty miles, captured by two magistrates, who managed to obtain fresh horses at various stations on the road whilst Macgregor had but the one; he was safely conveyed to Brisbane, where he was sentenced to twenty years' hard labour, 1863.

Melville, Captain. Born at sea. This notorious scoundrel, who gained some sympathy from a few, for his being the most daring of Victorian bushrangers, died by his own hand in the Melbourne Gaol, at the age of 35, August 12, 1859. He was undergoing his sentence of thirty-two years' hard labour when he headed the first outbreak of convicts at Williamstown, which resulted in the death of a boatman, Owen Owens, whom he was accused of having killed with a hammer, and for which he was sentenced to death at Melbourne, November 21, 1856; he was respited, but before the intelligence arrived he had strangled himself.

Morgan, Daniel, carried the palm over all bushrangers for cool audacity and blood-thirstiness. His murderous exploits at the Round Hill Station were never equalled in Australia. Five hundred pounds reward was offered by the New South Wales Government for his apprehension, January 5, 1864. In June, 1864, he shot Sergeant M'Ginnity dead, and took his horse and firearms. Verdict of the wilful murder of John M'Lean returned against him, June 23, 1864, and a reward of £1,000 was offered for his arrest by the New South Wales Government, June 27. In the following September he shot Sergeant Smith, who died a few days afterwards. Reward offered for his apprehension by Government increased to £1,500, March 8, 1865. On April 6, 1865, put in force a threat often attributed to him of making a raid upon Victorian territory—and he stuck up the station of Mr. Evans at

DANIEL MORGAN

Whitefield. Several carriers were also bailed up on the road near Wilton. On April 9 following, Morgan reached Mr. M'Pherson's house at the Peechelba Station, about twenty miles from Wangaratta. He immediately bailed up all whom he found on the station. But a servant girl ran to the house of Mr. Rutherford, a partner of Mr. M'Pherson's, situated at a distance of 400 yards. A man was despatched to Wangaratta, and the police force arrived, which, combined with Mr. Rutherford's men, made a party of about 28 men. Morgan, meanwhile, unsuspectingly was spending the night in a free and easy manner, Mrs. M'Pherson playing on the piano. In the morning, after reconnoitring in the front of the house, he prepared to start. The force had been carefully posted in ambush all round the place. After having duly breakfasted, Morgan left; Mr. M'Pherson and three others going with him to the paddock to get a mare. On his way he approached within 100 yards of the ambush of John Quinlan, a labouring man, who jumped from behind a tree and shot the bushranger through the back. He died a few hours afterwards, without confessing anything. Next day an inquest was held on the body, and the jury returned a verdict of justifiable homicide.

Power, Henry, stuck up the mail coach near Porejsukka, in the Ovens District, May 7, 1869;

stuck up the Buckland mail coach within five miles of Beechworth. The Government of Victoria offered £500 for his arrest, August 28, 1869; captured by Superintendents Nicholson and Hare and Sergeant Montford, whilst asleep in a hut on the Glenmore Ranges, at the head of the King River, Victoria; there was a revolver by his side, and a gun close to his head (he supposed that he was betrayed by Edward Kelly, who turned out bushranger in the same locality), June 5, 1870. Found guilty at the Beechworth Assizes on three charges of robbery, and sentenced to five years' imprisonment on each charge, sentences to be cumulative. He showed bravado in Court, and on being sentenced requested the Judge to "draw it mild": August 2, 1870.

Peisley John, a notorious scoundrel at whose house, in the western district, it is supposed the Gardiner gang received assistance, encouragement, and support. Peisley was tried and convicted of murder, and executed at Bathurst April 25, 1862.

Thunderbolt. [*See* WARD.]

Walmsley, one of Donohoe's gang, was captured after a slight resistance, and was condemned to death; was, however, pardoned by the Governor, in consequence of disclosures he made as to the receivers of the booty taken by this gang (it was chiefly on his evidence several convictions of receivers subsequently took place), January 5, 1831.

Ward, Frederick, alias *Captain Thunderbolt*, was a stockman on Barney Downs Station, in the New England District; was a splendid horseman, and a man of cool, determined courage. Whilst serving a sentence he escaped from Cockatoo Island. For some years he set at defiance the authorities in New England. He once stuck up a German band in the Goonoo Goonoo gap, and as they pleaded hard for their money, he promised that if he should succeed in robbing the principal winner at the Tenterfield races, for whom he was on the look-out, he would return their money, which promise he faithfully kept by sending to them, much to their astonishment, to the post office at Warwick, the £20 he had taken from them. Subsequently, when at a public house at Uralla, he was surprised by two policemen; instead of mounting his own horse he jumped on one belonging to a hawker, which turned out a bad one; a chase ensued. One constable's horse ran away with his rider; the other constable (Alexander B. Walker), a brave young fellow now sub-inspector, rode Thunderbolt down to a waterhole, when a desperate duel ensued, resulting in the death of Thunderbolt, May 25, 1870.

Webber, one of the gang commanded by Donohoe, who was shot by the police, was captured (subsequently condemned and executed), January 16, 1831.

Westwood, William John, known as *Jackey Jackey*, was not, as is from his cognomen generally supposed, an aboriginal. He was the son of a farmer in County Kent, and was transported to New South Wales in 1837, when

"THUNDERBOLT" AHORSE
A & R Archives

he was assigned to Mr. Philip King, at Gidleigh, 1840; he absconded from his employment, took to the bush, and joined a most determined scoundrel and murderer named Paddy Curran, who was hanged at Berrima in 1841; this man Curran attempting to ill-treat a married woman, Jackey Jackey defended her and threatened to take Curran's life for the base act and then left him, taking his horse, arms, and ammunition, and thenceforward he carried on his "profession" single-handed. Jackey Jackey had been arrested near Goulburn, and when being escorted from there in June, 1841, he escaped from the Bargo lock-up, taking the arms and accoutrements of one of the police. A day or two afterwards he stuck up Mr. Francis M'Arthur, and took from his carriage on the Goulburn Plains a fine horse, and he then proceeded to Gray's Inn, called the "Black Horse," some ten miles from Berrima, where he was set upon by Mr. Gray, Mrs. and Miss Gray (the latter showing extraordinary bravery), and a carpenter named Waters, and captured after being struck on the head with a shingling axe by the latter. The reward of £30 offered for his apprehension was paid to Gray, and the convict Waters received his pardon. Jackey was sentenced to imprisonment for life, and after an attempt to escape from Darlinghurst was sent to Cockatoo

Island, Parramatta River, N.S.W., from which place he, with twenty-five other desperadoes, attempted to escape by swimming to the mainland, but were followed by the police in their boat, and all captured. Jackey was then sent to Tasmania on board the brig "Governor Phillip." The prisoners were confined in the hold, nearly naked and chained to a cable, but on the way they managed to get loose and attempted a mutiny, and it was with the greatest difficulty they were landed at Hobart Town, whence they were sent to Port Arthur; there Jackey Jackey again escaped, but after

nine days' starvation was captured, one of his comrades, Frank Bailey, being shot. Twelve months afterwards he again succeeded in making his escape to the mainland, but was captured and placed in Hobart Town gaol and thence forwarded to Norfolk Island, where, on July 26, 1846, nearly all the prisoners under Jackey mutined. They murdered the overseers, and then, to the number of several hundreds, marched in military form towards Government House, under the command of Jackey. On the road, however, they were charged by the soldiers, and at last made prisoners. The principals in this

THE RIVERINA BUSHRANGERS – FINAL ENCOUNTER
The Australasian Sketcher, 1879

rising were tried, and eighteen of them, including Jackey Jackey, were executed.

Williams, Thomas, was a convict sent to Tasmania ; when his sentence expired he went to Victoria and became a bushranger ; was caught and convicted on three charges of highway robbery, for which he received sentences amounting to 30 years' imprisonment.

NEW ZEALAND.—*Garrett, Henry,* alias *Rouse,* a liberated Victorian felon, arrived in New Zealand, and at once took to the bush in the Maungatiou Ranges, sticking up twenty-three persons in one day ; was captured, and sentenced to eight years' imprisonment, 1861. [*See* CRIMES (*Henry Garrett.*)]

[*See* BUSHRANGING, VARIOUS ACTS OF.]

MEDALS FOR BRAVERY IN RESISTING AND CAPTURING.

Medals, Gold and Silver, which were ordered by Sir Charles Cowper in 1870, were in 1875 issued by the Honorable the Colonial Secretary, New South Wales, to the following recipients, in recognition of the bravery displayed by them in conflicts with bushrangers during the years 1863, 1864, and 1866. The gold medals were given to private colonists, and silver medals for distribution among the most meritorious of the constabulary. On the obverse side is the head of the Queen, with the words "The Colony of New South Wales," on the reverse the Australian Coat of Arms, below which is inscribed the name of the recipient of the medal, and a wreath of flowers and foliage of the banksia, the whole being surrounded by the words "Granted for gallant and faithful services." The gold medals were struck at the Sydney Mint.

Gold Medals were awarded to :—*Robert Lowe,* Esq., Mudgee, who shot a bushranger named Heather, near Slapdash, April 7, 1863 ; *Henry Bayliss,* P.M., who was dangerously wounded, August 21, 1863, whilst acting as a volunteer in pursuit of the bushranger Morgan, and who is supposed to have shot or caused the death of Morgan's mate ; *David Campbell,* J.P., who shot bushranger O'Meally, one of Gilbert's gang, at Goimbla, near Toogong, on the night of November 20, 1863 ; *H. M. Keightley,* P.M., Wellington, who killed the bushranger Burke, near Rockley, October 26, 1863 ; *William Macleay,* of Elizabeth Bay, who resisted and beat off Gilbert's gang from Plumb's Inn, near Goulburn, December 19, 1864 ; *J. P. Grenfell,* Crown Lands Commissioner, deceased, who was fatally wounded after a desperate encounter with bushrangers near Narramine, December 7, 1866. The town of Grenfell was named in his honour. The medal was sent to the Agent-General for presentation to Mrs. Grenfell, who now resides in the Isle of Man ; to the widow of the late *Captain M'Lerie,* to mark the services which he rendered as Inspector-General of Police from October 28, 1856, to October 6, 1874.

Silver Medals were presented to :—Constable *John Middleton,* who arrested Gardiner under circumstances of great bravery at Fogg's hut on the Fish River ; Sergeant *A. B. Walker,* who shot "Thunderbolt" near Uralla, May 25, 1870 ; Mr. *Beauvais,* innkeeper, Pine Ridge, who defended himself when attacked by an armed bushranger and murderer named Rutherford, whom he shot dead.

REWARDS OFFERED FOR APPREHENSION OF.

Large reward offered for the capture of William Underwood, the companion of Donohoe, the bushranger. Underwood was described as a native of Antrim, Ireland, a labourer, about 28 years of age, and 5 feet 8 inches in height, 1829 ; £500 was offered for the capture of Power.

The following is a list of the *highest rewards* offered for the apprehension of bushrangers :—

For the capture of	Amount.
Francis Christie, *alias* Frank Gardiner	£500
Daniel Morgan	1,000
John Gilbert	1,000
Benjamin Hall	1,000
John Dunn	1,000
— Burke	500
— O'Mealley	500
Frederick Ward	500
Thomas Clarke	1,000
John Clarke	500
Patrick Connell	250
The murderers of the special party of detectives	5,000
Edward Kelly, Daniel Kelly, Stephen Hart and Joseph Byrne (by N.S.W. and Victoria)	8,000

VICTIMS MURDERED BY.

The following list includes only those who were killed between 1862 and 1867 :—

Daniel Crotty (mailman), shot dead, near Marengo, August 16, 1862.
Peter Clarke, (drover), shot dead by Wilson.
John M'Bride (miner), shot dead by Gilbert and Lowry.
M'Ginnity (sergeant), shot dead by Morgan.
Smith (sergeant), shot by Morgan, died of his wounds.
M'Lean (station hand), shot dead by Morgan.
Parry, E. (sergeant), shot dead by Gilbert.
Chinaman (name unknown), shot dead by Morgan.
Nelson (constable), shot dead by Dunn.
Chinaman (name unknown), shot dead by Clarke's gang.
O'Grady (constable), shot dead by Clarke's gang.
Another Chinaman, shot dead by Clarke's gang.
Constable Raymond, shot dead by Crookwell and others.
Commissioner Grenfell, shot dead near Narramine.
Special constables Carroll, Phegan, M'Donnell, and Kennagh, shot dead at Jindera by Clarke's gang, January 9, 1867.
James Dornen, *alias* Bill Scott, *alias* the Long Tailor, murdered, it is believed, by Clarke's gang to prevent his giving information.
Noonang (half-caste, bush telegraph), murdered it is believed by Clarke's gang to prevent his giving information.
Total number of bushrangers shot or hanged, 23.
Total number of persons murdered by bushrangers, 20.
Total lives sacrificed, from 1862 to 1867, 44.

Of those who died of their wounds after lingering some time, or who were maimed for life, there is no return. Doubtless there were cases, also, of persons murdered by the bushrangers whose bodies were never discovered, as in the case of "German Bill," at one time mate of Morgan, who was wounded by Senior-Constable Brown, the night Mr. Bayliss was wounded, and whose sufferings there is good grounds for believing Morgan ended by shooting him through the head to prevent his giving any information to the authorities, into whose hands he must have fallen.

BUSHRANGERS RAIDING A HOUSE
Melbourne Punch, 1863

BUSHRANGERS SHOT OR HANGED, BETWEEN
1862 AND 1867 :—

Peisley, hanged.
Ross, Alexander, hanged.
Ross, Charles, hanged.
Heather, shot dead by Mr. Lowe.
Robardy, Charles, hanged.
Cummings, John, shot dead by one of his mates in an
    attempt to rescue him.
Lowry, J. F., shot dead by Sen. Sergeant Stevenson.
Burke, shot dead by Mr. Keightley.
Mr. Keightley was taken prisoner by Hall and other
    bushrangers, and £500 ransom demanded.   Mrs.
    Keightley went to Bathurst and got the money, and
    her husband was released.
O'Meally, shot dead by Mr. Campbell, at Goimbla.
Lowry, James, shot dead by Constable Ward.
Smith, shot dead at Wondilla, by Constable Saunders.
Morgan, Daniel, shot dead by a Victorian stockman,
    named Quinlan, at Peechlebar station, Victoria.
Hall, Benjamin, shot dead by Sub-Inspector Davidson,
    Constable Condell, and party and black tracker,
    near Forbes.
Gilbert, John, shot dead by Constable Bright, near
    Binalong.

Dunn, John, hanged at Darlinghurst.
Rielly, shot dead by Constable M'Glone.
Connell, Patrick, shot dead by police.
Burke (at one time belonging to Gardiner's gang),
    hanged at Melbourne.
Clarke, John, hanged at Darlinghurst.
Clarke, Thomas, hanged at Darlinghurst.
Ward, Frederick (*alias* Thunderbolt), shot dead by Con-
    stable Walker, near Uralla.

LIST OF POLICE KILLED OR WOUNDED, 1862
TO 1879,—

Detective Patrick Lyons received gunshot wound in
    right hand while escorting prisoners between Forbes
    and Young : was attacked by Davis and party ; Davis
    was arrested, April 14, 1862.
Senior constable Henry Moran shot in the groin by
    Gardiner's gang, Eugowra Creek, when escorting gold,
    June 15, 1862.
Constable Luke Cullen, while struggling with a prisoner
    pistol exploded, and was shot in leg, August 10, 1862.
Constable Thomas Rayfield, wounded with pistol ball in

side while attempting to arrest a horse-stealer named Little Jemmy, November 10, 1862.

Senior constable William Hughes fired upon from ambush, received gunshot wound in arm, June 8, 1863.

Senior constable Frederick Sutton wounded by Gilbert when attempting to rob Carcoar mail, August 6, 1863.

Senior sergeant James Stephenson received gunshot wound in the hand in an encounter with Lowry, when latter was wounded and died following day, August 29, 1863.

Senior constable Thomas Haughey received gunshot wound in the knee in an encounter with armed offenders at Toodles' shanty, Demondrille Creek, September 4, 1863.

Sergeant David M'Ginnity shot dead by Morgan near Tumberumba, June 24, 1864.

Sergeant Thomas Smyth shot while camping in his tent at night by Morgan, September 4, 1864; died, September 29, 1864.

Sergeant Edward Parry shot dead by Gilbert, November 15, 1864.

Constable Samuel Nelson shot by Dunn at Collector, January 26, 1865.

Senior constable John Ward died from a gunshot wound inflicted by a Chinaman between Mudgee and Coonabarabran, February 4, 1865.

Constable William Wiles received three gunshot wounds, two in hand and one in leg, in an encounter with Hall's gang at Byrnes', Mutbilly, February 24, 1865.

Constable John Kelly received bullet in the left breast in an attack by Hall and gang on Araluen gold-field, March 18, 1865.

Constable Robert Keane received gunshot wound in right shoulder in an encounter with bushrangers at Cunningar, March 18, 1865.

Constable Michael King received gunshot in ankle in an encounter with armed offenders at Binalong, 1865.

Senior constable J. R. Herbert accidentally shot (since died) in mistake for bushranger, April 13, 1865.

Senior constable William Lang wounded by pistol ball in the arm when attempting to arrest mail-robber Carroll, December 10, 1865.

Constable James McHale wounded when effecting the capture of the outlaw Dunn, December 24, 1865.

Constable Miles O'Grady wounded when attempting to arrest armed robbers, April 9, 1866.

Constable William Raymond shot by prisoner on escort, April 14, 1866.

Constable McCable was shot by offender Pearson at "Shearer's Inn," Bourke district, November 1, 1868.

Sergeant Andrew Sutherland shot by offender Grey, near Cowra, May 1, 1872.

Constable Michael Costigan } Shot at Bourke, September
Constable G. R. Armytage } 11, 1877.

Senior sergeant Thomas Wallings shot dead at Wonbobbie, Macquarie River, by offender Gibson, September 20, 1878.

Sergeant Michael Kennedy ⎰ Shot dead by Kelly gang
Constable Scanlan .... ⎰ at Wombat Ranges, near
Constable Lonergan ...... ⎱ Mansfield, Victoria, October 26, 1878.

Constable Power wounded in an encounter with four bushrangers near Balranald, 1879.

BUSHRANGING, VARIOUS ACTS OF.

Bushrangers committed depredations throughout the Bathurst district in the beginning of 1826; a desperate skirmish took place between the police and seven bushrangers, and one of the gang, Morris Connell, was killed on the spot by Corporal Brown, of the Mounted Police, March 16, 1826; affray between ticket-of-leave men and bushrangers at Chiplin's—one bushranger killed, and two wounded and captured, April 2, 1827; encounter near O'Brien's station between police and nine bushrangers, three bush-

rangers captured, September 3, 1828; the murder of Dr. Robert Wardell, the eminent lawyer, was committed, Sept. 7, 1834. [He was frequently associated with Mr. Wentworth in the early political contests in which the colonists were engaged. He was shot on his own land by the bushrangers, one a mere boy who turned King's evidence. The body was found next day by his servants covered over with a large bramble to keep the native dogs away, which the murderers had sufficient humanity to do. The two bushrangers, Jenkins, who fired the fatal shot, and Tattersdale, as abettor, were convicted and executed. Jenkins, whilst judgment was being pronounced, used most blasphemous curses towards the Judge, jury, and counsel, and hit his fellow prisoner who was beside him a violent blow on the ear; six constables were necessary to restrain him and to remove him from the dock. The fellow-colonists (of all classes) of Dr. Wardell testified the high respect in which he was held by crowding to his obsequies.] Consequent on the scarcity of provisions, bushranging became very prevalent in the neighbourhood of Sydney. Crime increased 50 per cent. on those of the previous year, July, August, 1839; Mr. John Kennedy Hume, a much respected colonist, shot by bushrangers at Gunning, N.S.W. The chief of the gang was executed at Goulburn for the offence, January 29, 1840. Mr. Henry O'Brien, a magistrate of Yass, headed a number of settlers in order to bring the scoundrels to justice, and in an encounter with the bushrangers, the chief of the gang was killed; another having been wounded, blew out his brains. Two were taken prisoners, and of these one hanged himself in his cell, and the other (who was instrumental in the death of Mr. Hume) was executed in Goulburn gaol, 1840; capture of the "Jew Boy's gang of bushrangers" at Doughboy Hollow, near Murrurundi, N.S.W., by Mr. Edward Denny Day and party; the gang captured consisted of Davis, Marshall, Chitty, Shea, and Buggy; two escaped, but one of these, named Glanvill, was captured the next day, December 21, 1840; capture of the first organized band of Port Phillip bushrangers on the "Plenty," through the bravery of Messrs. Snodgrass, Gourlay, Fowler, Chamberlain and Thomson, assisted by Messrs. Rider, Ewart, and Vinge. Jack Williams, the leader of the gang, was shot; Fogarty, Yankee Bill, and another were brought into Melbourne in custody, April 30, 1842.

Alexander Ross, Charles Ross, and William O'Connor, charged with robbery, firing at, and wounding Mr. Henry Stephens, found guilty at the Special Commission, Darlinghurst, and sentenced to death, February 9, 1863; a notice sent to the magistrates of all country benches, that all cases of robbery under arms and other offences of the bushranging class were, for the future, to be tried by a Special Commission, which would commence its sittings at Darlinghurst, February 2, 1863, January 20, 1863; the public-house of Mr. Cirkel was stuck up by four bushrangers,—Gardiner, Gilbert, O'Meally, and Dunn. Mr. Cirkel was shot dead by O'Meally for having, it is supposed, given information as to the movements of the gang to the police, February 15, 1863 ; Alexander Fordyce, John Bow, John M'Guire, and Henry Manns, tried by the Special Commission, Darlinghurst, February 4, 1863, for the escort robbery on June 5, 1862, but after three days' trial and one night's consideration of the case by the jury, the latter were unable to agree, and were accordingly discharged. On February 23 they were again placed on their trial, and on Thursday, 26, Fordyce, Bow, and Manns were found guilty, and sentence of death passed upon them. M'Guire was found not guilty, but was arrested upon another charge, February 26, 1863 ; Gardiner's gang captured, on the Widdin Mountains, an officer of police (sub-inspector Norton), who surrendered to them in consequence of the police he had ordered to meet him at the rendezvous having failed to obey the order, and the man Mr. Norton had with him having run away. He was kept a prisoner for some hours, when he was released unharmed, March 1, 1863 ; Clarke, one of the bushrangers present at the murder of Mr. Cirkel on February 15, was arrested by Captain Battye near Spring Creek ; he confessed to being present at the murder, and said O'Meally had fired the fatal shot, March 2, 1863 ; the two Rosses executed, March 18, 1863 ; O'Connor's sentence commuted to hard labour for life. A man named Patrick Daley was committed for trial at Forbes, charged with being one of the men who made prisoner of Sub-inspector Norton, March 24, 1863 ; petition for mercy in the case of Bow and Manns, the condemned escort robbers (Fordyce's sentence having already been commuted to hard labour for life), was signed by 13,000 persons in two days, exclusive of a large number of signatures attached to other petitions to the same purpose, March 25, 1863. Bow reprieved and sentenced to hard labour for life, Manns executed, March 26, 1863 ; bushrangers and the confessional formed the subject matter of a letter from Father M'Carthy in the *Sydney Morning Herald*, May 22, 1865 (this was in consequence of Vane, a young bushranger, giving himself up to this clergyman) ; a hawker named Charles Young robbed at Beucenya Lake, New South Wales, by William Brown, *alias* Bertram, October 15, 1869 ; the Secret Police Party, consisting of John Carroll, Eneas M'Donell, Patrick Kennagh, and John Phegan, who were sent out to capture the bushrangers (Clarke's gang) in the Braidwood district, were murdered at Jindera, January 9, 1867 ; two mates of Power savagely attacked two constables at Benalla, one of the bushrangers being captured, the other escaping, August 29, 1870 ; Sergeant Sutherland, of the New South Wales police, shot dead a few miles from Cowra by two bushrangers, May 1, 1872 ; four bushrangers, Thomas Gorman, Charles Jones, William Kay, and William Hobbs, robbed Mr. Grainger's store at Hatfield, near Balranald, New South Wales. They were under arms, and took £50, and two horses with saddles and bridles. Two shots were fired at a storeman named Day, who escaped and gave information to the police at Balranald, February 24, 1879. The bushrangers, after leaving Hatfield, stuck up a hawker named Friedman, and robbed him of £40 cash, and of some valuable jewellery and other goods, February 25, 1879. They were captured at Kilfern station and brought to Balranald by first-class constable Beresford, constable Power, and special constable Day, all of the Balranald Police, who rode 180 miles from 9 a.m. on Sunday to 7 p.m. on Monday, several shots being exchanged, and Constable Power wounded, February 19, 1879.

EUGOWRA GOLD-ESCORT ROBBERY. Policemen James Condell, Andrew Moran, and William Haviland, and mail-driver John Fagan, were stopped on the Gates Road at the Eugowra Rocks by Gardiner and seven or eight of his gang, when travelling towards Sydney with the Government Escort. The bushrangers fired a volley and then made a rush at the coach, and took the rifles of the police, the gold, amounting to 5,509 ounces, much of which belonged to the Oriental Banking Company, and bank notes to the value of £7,490 ; they also took the leaders out of the coach to serve as pack-horses but only used one ; and breaking open the boxes of gold packed them on the mail horse ; they divided the gold and notes afterwards into eight shares, five of the men taking theirs, while the other three shares (viz., Gardiner's, Charters's and Fordyce's) remained on the pack-horse which knocked up at the foot of the Widdin Mountains, and before the bushrangers could remove the gold, it fell into the hands of the police, under sergeant Saunderson who had given chase and succeeded in recovering 1239 ounces of gold ; subsequently, when Manns was arrested, 200 ounces and £135 in notes were found on him. Date of escort robbery, June 15, 1862. The names of the bushrangers engaged in this robbery were :—Frank Gardiner, *alias* Frank Christie, John Gilbert, Daniel Charters (afterwards turned informer), John Bow, Alexander Fordyce, Henry Manns, Benjamin Hall, and O'Meally.

BUSHRANGING IN VAN DIEMEN'S LAND. The welfare of Van Diemen's Land was greatly retarded in its earlier days by the number of daring and prolonged depredations committed by bushrangers. In some districts the inhabitants succoured and helped to conceal them, whilst in others the settlers assisted the authorities in trying to suppress them. Colonel Davey, in 1813, declared the whole colony under martial law, and punished with flogging persons, whether free or bound, who quitted their homes by night, and several bushrangers who were captured were speedily executed. The constables were prisoners of the Crown, and it was to their interest to detect or pretend to detect crime, this giving them a claim for quicker liberation, and consequently most atrocious perjuries were at times committed by them, implicating innocent persons, whilst it was subsequently ascertained that in many cases they received from the real culprits a share of their booty. The names of the most noted scoundrels were *Cash, Cavenagh, Brady, Mosquito,* and *Michael Howe.*

Mosquito. This bushranger was a Sydney aboriginal, transported to Van Diemen's Land for the murder of a woman. At first he was employed by the authorities as a tracker for hunting up the haunts of the bushrangers, but he afterwards effected his escape to the bush, and headed the Oyster Bay tribe of natives, over whom he appeared to exercise unbounded sway; they numbered some 200 blacks, and under the command of Mosquito committed many foul and treacherous murders upon isolated settlers and their families. He became a pest to society and a terror to the colony, and a large reward was offered for his capture; at last he was tracked to his lair at Oyster Bay by a native and two constables, and after a desperate resistance was wounded and eventually captured and conveyed to Hobart Town, where he and another native named Black Tom, and six Europeans, were executed together, February, 1825.

The love of a wild, and in a measure free life in the bush, and the wish to avoid the severity of the lash, caused many of the prisoners of the Crown to effect their escape into the bush where, collecting in gangs, they vied with one another in deeds of the most daring and sanguinary nature, till at last in 1814 Governor Macquarie, despairing of reducing their numbers by force, offered a free pardon to all who, not having been guilty of murder, would within six months of the date of his proclamation return to their duty, and this proclamation had, partly, the desired effect.

Michael Howe, who had been a seaman in the Royal Navy, and who was afterwards the owner of a small coasting craft in which he had acquired some notion of command, arrived in Van Diemen's Land in 1812, and was sent as an assigned servant to Mr. Ingle; he, however, declared he would be no man's slave, and, escaping to the bush, joined a gang commanded by a man named Whitehead. In this gang, which consisted of about twenty outlaws, were a deserter from the 73rd regiment, and two native women. Soon after Howe's joining them they attacked the settlement of New Norfolk, and there procured a good supply of arms and ammunition; thence they marched on Pittwater, committing many depredations, and sacking and burning the houses and stacks of those who had made themselves obnoxious to them; again they attacked New Norfolk, and had a fight with the settlers, in which the latter were worsted; but in the engagement Whitehead was seriously wounded. Finding that he could not recover, he appealed to Howe to finish him and to cut his head off, to prevent the reward that was offered for his capture being obtained by any of the settlers; this Howe did, and then assumed the command of the gang. It was subsequently asserted by Howe (and there is good reason to believe his statements) that some of the police presumably most active in the pursuit of him and his gang at this time were actually in communication with them, and received a share in the profits of the men's crimes. Howe at this time was accustomed to leave his gang for short periods, and retire to some mountain fastness with a native girl, to whom it was stated he was much attached; subsequently she was captured and became useful to the soldiers in discovering his favourite haunts to them. At last Howe sent, through the medium of a Yankee sailor, a proposal to the Governor to surrender. The Governor (Sorell) sent Captain Nairne to the rendezvous to meet with him and to give him an assurance of present safety and a promise of his intercession for his pardon if he would come in, which offer Howe accepted. When on the plea of ill health he was allowed to take exercise under the charge of a constable, he managed to give his guard the slip and again took to the bush. He found his gang nearly broken up, only two men remaining, Watts and Browne. Soon after his return Watts conspired with a stock-keeper named Drewe against Howe, and taking him unawares, they threw him down, disarmed him, and tied his hand behind his back. Leaving him thus lying on the ground, they ate their breakfast, and then started with him to Hobart Town, with the hope of obtaining the reward. Watts walked in front of their prisoner, and Drewe behind him. On the road Howe managed to get his hand loose unperceived by his guard, when, springing suddenly upon Watts, he seized his knife and fatally stabbed him, and then, taking his gun, shot Drewe dead on the spot. Watts managed to reach Hobart Town, but subsequently died of his wounds. A large reward was now offered for the capture or death of Howe, together with freedom and a passage home, should his captor be a convict; but for a long time he escaped all snares. But the temptation of the large reward and the free pardon, together with the passage home, was a bait that could not be long withstood, and so a transported sailor named Jack Worral conspired with one of Howe's mates, named Warburton, to effect his capture. Major Bell gave them the assistance of a soldier of the 48th regiment, named Pugh, these two secreting themselves in Warburton's hut, who was to inveigle Howe into it. This Warburton did, but Howe discovered his danger and managed to break away, the shots fired at him not taking effect. In running, however, he received a severe fall which partially stunned him, and he then turned to fight: whilst engaged with one the other crept up, and knocked him down with the butt end of his musket and with the same weapon dashed his brains out, October 21, 1818. In a kangaroo skin pouch or knapsack which he carried, was found a record of his crimes and the names of many of his accomplices, with those of the receivers of stolen property, hitherto unsuspected.

CABLE. [*See* TELEGRAPHIC.]

CAMELS purchased from India (afterwards used for party in search of Burke and Wills) at a cost of £5,500, 1858.

CAMPBELL, J. F., appointed Collector of Customs at Sydney, being the first officer who bore that title in Australia, 1827.

CAMPBELLTOWN, N. S. W., marked out and named by Governor Macquarie, December 1, 1820. First Circuit Court opened by his Honor Chief Justice Forbes: the judicial party left Liverpool for Campbelltown, and were escorted in by a guard of honour consisting of four horsemen with drawn swords, and attended by Wm. Howe (Police Magistrate) the Sergeant of Police, (Campbelltown); by the Rev. Thomas Reddall (Chaplain), and by the other Justices of the Peace. There were altogether 20 carriages, containing the leading gentlemen of the district, 40 or 50 gentlemen on horseback, and upwards of 100 persons on foot in the procession, August 3, 1839.

CANTERBURY, N.Z. Arrival of the first settlers, December 16, 1850.

CAPE, RIVER, discovered, March 18, 1845.

CAPITAL PUNISHMENT, ABOLITION OF. Punishment of death abolished in New South Wales for cattle-stealing, forgery, and stealing in a dwelling property above £5 in value, August 1, 1833.

CASHMERE GOATS. 49 Cashmere goats imported to Melbourne; of these more than half died before landing, 1863.

CASTLEREAGH, N.S.W., named, December, 1810.

CASTLEREAGH, RIVER, discovered by John Oxley, July 27, 1818. (*See* EXPLORATIONS.]

CATERPILLAR PLAGUE throughout the agricultural settlements of N.S.W.: the fields and gardens were laid waste by them at a time when the ears of wheat were full and there was no possibility of counteracting the disaster, September, 1810.

CATTLE.

ARRIVAL OF. The first horned cattle which arrived in Australia with the "first fleet," consisted of two bulls and five cows, January, 1788.

STRAYING OF. Through the negligence of a convict the whole of the horned cattle in the settlement, New South Wales, consisting of five cows and two bulls, escaped into the bush and were lost, June, 1788 [*See* COWPASTURE]: order issued against shooting any of the strayed cattle at the Cowpasture, December 18, 1795.

The first cattle, after a prohibition of five years, arrived seaward in Sydney, December 18, 1878.

NUMBER OF. On January 1, 1878, the number of horned cattle in Australia was as follows :—

New South Wales	..	..	..	2,746,385
Victoria	..	..	..	1,174,176
South Australia	..	..	..	230,679
Queensland	..	..	..	2,299,582
Tasmania	..	..	..	126,882
Western Australia	..	..	..	52,057
Total	..	..	..	6,629,761
New Zealand	..	..	..	494,917
Total in Australasian Colonies		..	..	7,124,678

CATTLE BRANDING
S. T. Gill, c. 1864

CEMETERIES.

First colonial church-yard or burial-ground was on the site of the present Town Hall, Sydney. A proposition to fence round the ground, in consequence of the pigs rooting up the earth and graves, appeared in the *Sydney Gazette*, February 5, 1804.

Burial-grounds first consecrated throughout the various towns in the Colony, 1811.

First burial-ground in Melbourne, Port Phillip, was near the Flagstaff Hill. A child named Goodman was the first buried there, 1836.

CENSUS, First (originally called "Musters") in New South Wales, 89 deaths having occurred of the 1,044 who had left England, June, 1788. General "muster" of convicts February 1, 1801 ; of free persons, July, 1801.

New South Wales gave the population at 36,598, 1828 ; first time taken in one day—population, 114,769 males, and 74,840 females, total, 189,609, March 2, 1846. [See Population.]

Punishment for Non-attendance at. Four settlers and an assistant-surgeon were charged with neglecting to attend a "General Muster," and to send in an account of their stock, as prescribed by the Lieutenant-Governor's orders. They would not recognise the new form of Government. One was fined one shilling and sentenced to six months' imprisonment. The others were sentenced to one month's imprisonment, December 11, 1808.

CHAMBER OF COMMERCE, Sydney, established. First officers : Edward Woolstoncraft, W. J. Browne, A. B. Spark, and 30 members, June 7, 1825.

CHARITABLE INSTITUTIONS. Foundation stone of new Institution for the Deaf and Dumb and Blind, on the Newtown Road, Sydney, laid by His Excellency the Governor, April 2, 1871 ; the Institution opened by Earl Belmore, March 13, 1872. Deaf and Dumb and Blind Asylum opened at Adelaide, December, 1872.

New South Wales.

There are in the colony 42 hospitals, the principal of these being the Sydney Infirmary and the St. Vincent Hospital ; 7 benevolent asylums, 3 of these being Government institutions ; 13 orphan and other schools, and 8 lunatic asylums, consisting of 7 Government institutions, and 1 private asylum at Cook's River. The number of admissions into these hospitals during 1877 was 5,228. Of these, 5,316 patients were removed or discharged during the year, and the deaths numbered 1,131. Into the whole of the charitable institutions there were 10,418 admissions. The receipts from voluntary contributions were £33,386 16s. 1d., Government contributing £117,771 13s. 10d., making a total of £151,158 9s. 11d. The disbursements during the year were £142,309 14s. 11d. In addition to the foregoing institutions, there are in Sydney a Home, a Female Refuge, a House of the Good Shepherd, a Sailors' Home, a Night Refuge and Soup Kitchen, and an Infant's Home. Into these last, during 1877, 1,453 inmates were received and supported at an expense of £3,237, derived from private benevolence : 1878.

New Zealand.

On January 1, 1877, there were 24 public hospitals throughout the colony, having 109 wards, and 942 beds. During 1876, 4,934 out-door patients and 7,478 in-door patients were relieved, 439 died, and there were under treatment on December 31, 594 patients. There are 3 benevolent asylums, with 63 wards and 128 beds ; two orphan asylums at Motueka and Lyttleton, with 16 wards and 160 beds ; eight lunatic asylums with 260 wards and 830 beds, sheltering on December 31, 785 patients ; and three reformatory and industrial schools, at Auckland, Burnham, and Caversham, in which on December 31, were 371 children of both sexes. There are also a large number of benevolent and benefit societies for the relief of the distressed and needy, 1878.

Queensland.

There are 21 public hospitals in the colony, also a benevolent asylum, and four orphan asylums. In the hospitals during the year 1876, 4,231 patients were admitted ; of these 3,234 were discharged relieved or cured, 255 removed, 380 died, and 362 were still under treatment on December 31. The number of out-door patients was 1,838. These institutions have 96 wards and 610 beds. Into the benevolent asylums the admissions were 62, and there were 123 inmates at the beginning of the year : of these 121 remained in the house on January 1, 1877 ; 371 orphans were in the four asylums on the same date. In addition to the foregoing, there are two Lock hospitals, one at Brisbane and one at Rockhampton, three lunatic reception houses and one asylum. The reception-houses have 9 wards and 30 beds ; 223 patients were under treatment during the year ; of these 110 were discharged cured, 90 were removed, 10 died, the number remaining under treatment at the end of the year being 13. The lunatic asylum at Woogaroo has 30 wards, 37 dormitories, and 389 beds. During the year 281 males and 172 females were under treatment, of whom 47 were cured and 4 were improved, and 13 died ; 382 were remaining in the asylum on December 31. The total receipts on account of the hospitals were £29,067 5s. 11d., of which £8,233 4s. 6d. were derived from private contributions ; the expenditure was recorded at £31,474 2s. 8d. The receipts for the benevolent asylum were £2,746 1s. 11d., the expenditure being the same. The receipts for the orphan asylums were £7,171 0s. 3d., nearly the whole being from the State funds ; the expenditure was £7,140 1s. 8d. : 1878.

South Australia.

Among the institutions are the hospitals throughout the colony, those at Adelaide, Kooringa, Mount Gambier, and Wallaroo being the leading ones. There are also lunatic asylums at Adelaide and Parkside, and an asylum for the destitute poor at North Terrace, Adelaide, and a Blind, Deaf, and Dumb Asylum. A Sailors' Home is in operation at Port Adelaide. During the year 1877, 2,321 patients were treated in the Adelaide hospital ; of these 1,982 were discharged, 153 died, and 185 were under treatment in the wards. In the Destitute Asylum and through its country boards during 1878, the number of destitute persons who received out-door relief was 4,819 ; the recipients of in-door relief numbered 1,437, and the expenditure for 1877 amounted to £21,355 15s. 10d. The total amount expended on these institutions for the year ending June 30, 1878, was £55,009 13s. 6d. ; of this sum £17,956 8s. 8d. went to the hospitals, £15,466 17s. 10d. to the asylums, and £21,586 7s. to the destitute poor. There are numerous other agencies of a private character, also benefit and other societies for the relief of the sick, poor, and destitute : 1878.

Tasmania.

There is a general hospital at Hobart Town, another at Launceston, and one at Campbelltown, for the care and relief of the sick and injured. At these establishments the average number of in-patients was 164 ; the total number of cases treated for both in and out-patients was 10,852. The average nett cost of each indoor patient was £66 2s. 9½d. at Hobart Town, and £40 7s. 11d. at Launceston. For the relief of the destitute poor there are five pauper establishments, and the Queen's Asylum at New Town for destitute children. In the latter institution there are generally about 127 inmates, who are supported at a cost of £19 3s. 5½d. per head. There are two hospitals for the insane, one at New Norfolk, and one at Hobart Town. The average number of inmates during 1877 was 303. There are 27 benefit or friendly societies, of which 18 are connected with the order of Odd Fellows (Manchester Unity), and 6 are Rechabite tents. The members in 1876 numbered 2,149. The total receipts were £7,118 10s., and the expenditure £6,615 19s. 1d., the capital being £16,513 5s. 4d. : 1878.

Victoria.

There are in all sixty-eight institutions for the relief of the sick, needy, orphans, refugees, and unfortunates.

These institutions have 672 wards or rooms, and 9,655 beds. They were maintained during 1876 by £235,424 from the State Funds, £31,587 from private contributions, and £31,812 from other sources The expenditure was £302,855. The average cost of each inmate was £8 19s. 2d., varying from 17s. 3d. in the Immigrant's Home to £43 13s. 9¾d. in the Blind Asylum. There are six Benevolent Asylums, with 153 wards and 1,555 beds; 45,580 persons were relieved by them There are also seven Orphan Asylums, with 68 wards and 1,552 beds. The total number of general hospitals throughout the colony is 32. For the support of the hospitals, according to a late return, the Government aid was £60,307 10s., private contributions amounting to £29,150 19s. 4d.: from other sources there was received £9,943 4s. 5d., making a total of £99,401 13s. 9d. The expenditure, including buildings and repairs, was £106,682 0s. 10d. For the support of the asylums the receipts were, Government aid £25,000, private contributions £8,327 0s. 7d., other sources £5,957 12s. 6d., total £39,284 13s. 1d., expenditure £41,200 5s. 6d. For the support of the orphan asylums the receipts were, Government grants £12,661 0s. 2d., private contributions £5,186 7s. 4d., other sources £1,897 18s. 7d., total £19,745 6s. 8d., expenditure £19,135 13s. 7d. The receipts for the lunatic asylums were, from Government £90,674 8s., other sources £4,723 4s. 6d., total £95,397 12s. 6d. The total expenditure during the year 1877, on the asylum and lunacy wards was £95,517 6s. 6d., an increase of £401 5s. 10d. on the previous year, the average weekly cost of each patient being 14s. 2¾d. The hospitals have in the aggregate 230 wards, containing 2,246,963 cubic feet of space, and 1,987 beds. During 1875, 14,477 persons were relieved, the daily average of relief being 1,536·6 persons. There are five lunatic asylums, having 72 wards and 2,642 beds. There is also a private asylum at Cremorne, near Melbourne, having 32 wards and accommodation for 40 patients. The number of registered patients on December 31, 1877, was 2,747, an increase of 112 upon the return of 1876. During 1877, 3,287 patients were under treatment, of whom 674 were admitted during the year. 258 recovered and 193 died. The number of patients on January 1, 1878, was 2,719, 1,753 males and 1,146 females. The ratio of lunatics to the entire population is 1 in every 1,510 persons; in the previous year it was 1 in 1,431 : 1878.

Western Australia.

There are eight hospitals, one lunatic asylum, two poor-houses, two native institutions, a Protestant orphanage, and a Roman Catholic orphanage, 1879.

CHESS. The history of Australian chess is necessarily brief, as it is only during the last ten or twelve years that serious attention has been devoted to this intellectual pastime. The first chess club in Sydney was established in 1860 in connection with the School of Arts. About the same time chess societies were formed in Melbourne, Adelaide, and the other capitals of Australia. As these associations increased, they became more prosperous; in course of time, talent for the game was developed in a marked degree. Match played between New South Wales and Victoria, seven players on each side, by electric telegraph, won by Victoria, 1870. Intercolonial matches have since been continued between the representatives of Victoria, New South Wales, South Australia, and Queensland. In New Zealand and Queensland chess is also liberally supported.

PROBLEMS AND PROBLEM WRITERS.—In the problem department of chess rapid strides have been made by Australian composers, many of whom have established good reputations. The tournaments initiated by the Melbourne *Leader*, Sydney *Town and Country Journal*, and *Sydney Mail, South Australian Chronicle*, and Canterbury *Times*, have created a healthy competition amongst colonial problemists, and have produced some of the most beautiful stratagems extant. The leading composers in the colonies are as follows : New South Wales—J. Willis, J. J. Glynn, E. R. James, W. Cook, G. Power. Victoria—T. D. Clarke, T. Henderson, L. Graham, E. L. Bailey, W. A. Rohner. South Australia—H. Charlick, W. J. M'Arthur, W. F. Bertram, E. J. Catlow, C. J. Shuttleworth. Tasmania—J. G. Witton. New Zealand—C. Benbow, T. F. Jacobsen, J. Snellie : 1879.

CELESTIAL HAPPINESS
Melbourne Punch, 1865 (A cartoon symbolising fears of the consequences of Chinese immigration.)

CHINESE. The first shipload of Chinese immigrants arrived in New South Wales ; they were introduced at private cost, but the introduction of this race of men was much repudiated, 1848 ; first importation of Chinese into Brisbane, May 3, 1850 ; monster meeting against the Chinese gold-diggers, at Golden Point, Lambing Flat, New South Wales, January, 1861 ; 2,000 Chinese landed at Cooktown, May 3, 1875. Great fight among Chinese at Maytown, Queensland, with fatal results, August 12, 1878.

CHISHOLM, MRS. CAROLINE, located thirty families at Illawarra, New South Wales, on land granted to them on clearing leases, the proprietor to grant them provisions for the first five months of their occupancy, 1843 ; a testimonial, valued at 200 guineas, raised by public subscription in Sydney, was presented to Mrs. Chisholm " as an expression of thanks for her active and zealous exertions on behalf of the immigrant population" during the previous seven years, April 14, 1846.

CHURCH ACT. The celebrated Church Act of 7 Wm. IV., by which religious equality was firmly and permanently established in Australia, was passed, 1836.

CIVIL ACTION. The first of any note in the colony of New South Wales was tried in 1795. [A hog, belonging to a Mr. Bolton, having been shot by some of the soldiers, an altercation took place, and some of the military assaulted Bolton with a loaded musket, as was alleged, at the instance of two officers of the corps. Damages were laid at £500, and the case occupied several days. A verdict was given for twenty shillings. An appeal was made to the Governor, who confirmed the verdict.]

CLAIMANT. *Arthur Orton*, alias *Tom De Castro*. Claimant to the Tichborne title and estates, convicted in England, perjury, in 1874, sentenced to fourteen years penal servitude. Lived formerly in Wagga Wagga, New South Wales. [*See* TICHBORNE.]

CLAN CAMPBELL. Meeting of the members of the Clan Campbell at the Chamber of Commerce, Sydney, held for the purpose of assisting in a proposed offering to the Princess Louise (on her marriage with its representative, the Marquis of Lorne), January 25, 1871.

CLARE, RIVER, discovered, March 22, 1845.

CLARENCE, RIVER. Captain Barkus, in H.M. schooner "Alligator," whilst in search of a supposed wreck, discovered a river of some magnitude south of the Tweed, supposed to be the "Clarence" or the "Richmond," of Captain Rouse, September 5, 1827. Hon. Captain Rouse, in H.M.S. "Rainbow," discovered two large rivers to the northward of Sydney, where there is a firm and safe anchorage. He proceeded a considerable distance up both rivers, and reported the country to be well wooded, the climate salubrious, and the soil apparently of the richest description. One of these rivers he named the "Clarence," the other the "Richmond." Both rivers lie between Sydney and Moreton Bay, in the usual track of vessels trading to Sydney, which makes it remarkable that they were not previously discovered. (*Sydney Gazette*, September, 1828, and August 13, 1829.) August, 1828. [*See* RICHMOND RIVER.]

CLIMATE.

CLIMATE OF THE PRINCIPAL AUSTRALIAN COLONIES.

Name of Colony.	Mean	Absolute max.	Absolute min.	Absolute range.	Mean daily range.	Mean humidity.	Average rainfall, inches.
Queensland, Brisbane....	70.0	108.0	34.5	73.5	20.9	76	51
New South Wales, Sydney	62.4	107.0	36.0	71.0	14.7	72	50
Victoria, Melbourne.....	57.5	111.2	27.0	84.2	18.8	72	26
South Australia, Adelaide	66.1	113.5	34.2	79.3	20.6	60	21
Tasmania, Hobart Town	54.4	105.0	29.0	76.0	17.9	75	23
New Zealand, Wellington	55.6	83.0	30.0	53.0	12 0	68	47

CLUB-HOUSES.

ADELAIDE (S.A.) :—*Adelaide Club ; Bushman's Club ; City Club ; Civil Service Club ; Der Deutsche Club ; Flinders Club.*

VIEW OF THE CLARENCE RIVER
The Australasian Sketcher, 1873

AUCKLAND (N.Z.):— *Auckland Club; German Club; Northern Club; Working-men's Club.*

BRISBANE (Q.):—*Brisbane Club; Queensland Club.*

WELLINGTON (N.Z.):—*Wellington Club.*

HOBART TOWN (TASMANIA): — *Tasmanian Club; Working Men's Club.*

MELBOURNE (VICTORIA):—*Athenæum Club; Cosmopolitan Club; University Club; Melbourne Club; Victoria Club; Yorick Club.*

SYDNEY (N.S.W.):—*Australian Club; Union Club; German Club; Reform Club.*

CLYDE, RIVER, (N.S.W.) Lieutenant R. Johnston, R.N., in the cutter "Schnapper," with a party, of which Mr. Hamilton Hume was one, discovered and named Clyde River (native name Bundoo); explored it for 30 miles, and learned from the natives that Captain Stewart and party, who had left Sydney a few months previously to make an examination of the coast of Twofold Bar (Lind Journal), had been wrecked, and probably murdered by the natives whilst endeavouring to make their way back overland: December, 1820.

COACH. The first hackney coach ever introduced into the colony, was owned by Mr. Hart (the stand being fixed near King's Wharf, Sydney), and commenced to ply for hire November 15, 1830.

COAL, FIRST DISCOVERY OF, at Port Stephens, May, 1796; at Mount Keira, Illawarra, February, 1797. [A vessel called the "Sydney Cove," from Bengal to Sydney, being wrecked on the coast, some of the crew made their way to Sydney, after enduring many hardships; two days before their arrival they had fallen in with a quantity of this valuable article, with some of which they had kindled a fire. A boat was dispatched to the place to ascertain the fact, and in the face of a deep cliff washed by the ocean, a stratum, in breadth six feet, and extending about nine miles to the southward, was discovered]; to the northward of Sydney, September 19, 1797. [A vessel called the "Cumberland" having been piratically seized, two boats were manned and sent in pursuit, but returned after an absence of thirteen days without discovering the fugitives, but one of the commanders, Lieutenant John Shortland, in the course of the voyage, discovered a river to which he gave the name of "Hunter," and the entrance to which he explored. Adjacent to the harbour (now called Newcastle) was found a very considerable quantity of coal of a good quality (some specimens of which were brought to Sydney) lying so near the water's edge as to be conveniently shipped]; in Van Diemen's Land, June 6, 1816; in Western Australia, September 9, 1846; seam of coal discovered at Fingal, Tasmania, February 26, 1873; discovered on the Mackenzie River, Queensland, April 10, 1878.

THE FIRST EXPORTATION OF, from N.S.W.,

MT KEIRA COAL MINE
The Illustrated Sydney News, 1855

took place by exchange with the master of the ship "Cornwallis," Captain Michael Hogan, who arrived in Sydney with convicts from Ireland: on this occasion 45 tons of coal from the Hunter River, N.S.W., were changed for a quantity of nails and iron, January, 1800 (the cargo sent to Cape of Good Hope); the first regular export of coal took place when a small brig called the "Anna Josepha," which had been built in the colony, was freighted with colonial timber and coals, and despatched to the Cape of Good Hope, both the coals and timber meeting with a ready market there, the coals being sold at £6 per ton, 1801; the monopoly of coal by the A. A. Company condemned and given up, 1847.

COCKATOO ISLAND (now BILOELA), Port Jackson, N.S.W. Prisoners removed to, and the Superintendent's department to offices in the Executive Council Chambers, Jan., 1848. [*See* PRISONS.]

COLD. The temperature at Kiandra, N.S.W., was 8° below zero, Aug. 12, 1872.

COLLINS, LIEUT.-COLONEL, continued to act as Judge-Advocate from the foundation of the Colony of New South Wales until the year 1804, when he was appointed Lieut.-Governor of Tasmania.

COLONIAL INSTITUTE, established to promote the interests of the Colonies; Lord Bury first President; held its first meeting June 26, 1868, and first annual meeting, June 29, 1869; assumed the title of "Royal Colonial Institute," March 7, 1870. The first volumes of its proceedings have been published. The formation of a National and Colonial League resolved on at a meeting held in Cannon-street, London,

January 5, 1870 ; Duke of Manchester, second President, resigned, 1878 ; H.R.H. Prince of Wales third President, 1878.

COLONIAL OFFICE. In the reign of George III, 1768, a Secretary of State for the American, or Colonial department, was appointed, in addition to the two principal Secretaries of State then existing ; but this new office was abolished in 1782 by Statute 22 Geo. III, c. 82. In 1782 the duties of the two principal Secretaries of State were divided into "Home" and "Foreign" ; the affairs of Ireland and the colonies devolving on the Home department ; those of the colonies constituting a separate branch of the Home department called "the Office for Plantations," which was at first managed by a separate Under-Secretary. At its commencement in 1793, the affairs of the War were managed by the Home department, but in 1794 a principal Secretary for War was appointed, and the business of the colonies was transferred from the Home to the War department in 1801. In 1854 a fourth principal Secretary of State was added for War, the affairs of the colonies remaining under the exclusive charge of a principal Secretary of State. In 1858 a principal Secretary of State was added for the affairs of India.

COMETS. First seen by Mr. Rumker at Parramatta, May 24, 1822 ; by Mr. Thomas Robertson at Deniliquin, January 16, 1865 ; in Melbourne, July 29, 1874.

COMMERCE. For the first time in the history of New South Wales the exports exceeded the imports, 1844.

COMMERCIAL DEPRESSION. Considerable disarrangements in commercial transactions took place in New South Wales, attributed to the scarcity of 1838 and 1839, which caused a great drain of capital from the colony for the necessaries of life ; the decline in the price of wool ; excessive consignments of goods to the colony, mostly on speculation by English merchants ; the necessity of disposing of the same, contributing to produce an undue extension of credit, and also hazardous speculation in the employment of money in investments not yielding immediate returns, June, 1841 ; a great monetary depression from the effects of overspeculation and the land mania, no less than 600 business people taking the benefit of the Insolvency Act since its coming into force—a period of 11 months, December, 1842 ; a meeting held in Sydney "to take into consideration the alarming and depressed state of the monetary affairs of the colony, and to devise measures of immediate relief," Mr. Wentworth taking a prominent part in the deliberations, 1843.

COMMISSARIAT. Deputy Commissary-General Laidley arrived to succeed William Wemyss, Esq., in charge of the Commissariat, at Sydney, May 12, 1827 ; Deputy Commissary-General Wemyss left Sydney for the Isle of France, November 10, 1828.

COMPANIES.

LIST OF PRINCIPAL AUSTRALIAN COMPANIES.

Australian Agricultural Company. Founded June 21, 1824. Capital, £500,000 ; paid-up, £430,000. Nominal price of shares, £25 ; paid-up, £21 10s.

Australian Marine Insurance Company. Established January 31, 1831.

Australian Gas Company (Sydney). Founded 1835 ; incorporated September 7, 1837.

Sydney Fire Insurance Company. Formed January 10, 1836.

Hunter River Steam Navigation Company. Incorporated September 1, 1841 ; incorporated under the style of the Australasian Steam Navigation Company, December 10, 1851.

Hunter River Steam Navigation Company. Established February 4, 1840.

Hunter River New Steam Navigation Co. December 21, 1852.

Illawarra Steam Navigation Company. Incorporated, October 7, 1858.

Australian Mining Company. Founded 1845. Capital, £400,000 ; paid-up, £128,205. Nominal price of shares, £20 ; paid-up, £7 7s. 6d.

Australian Mutual Provident Life Assurance Company. Founded 1849. Insured 45,000 policies ; amount insured, £17,000,000 ; accumulated funds, £2,500,000 ; annual income, £600,000.

Australian Mortgage, Land, and Finance Company, Limited. Founded 1863. Capital, £1,000,000 ; paid-up, £175,000. Nominal price of shares, £25 ; paid-up, £5.

Mutual Life Association of Australasia. Established 1869.

English and Australian Copper Company, Limited. Founded 1851. Capital, £210,000 ; paid-up, £175,000. Nominal price of shares, £3 ; paid-up, £2 10s.

New Zealand Loan and Mercantile Agency Company, Limited. Founded 1865. Capital, £1,000,000 ; paid-up, £85,655. Nominal price of shares, £25 ; called-up on 20,000 old shares, £2 10s. ; on 20,000 new shares, £1.

New Zealand Insurance Company. Founded 1859. Capital, £1,000,000 ; paid-up, £335,000.

New Zealand Trust and Loan Company. Founded 1862. Capital, £500,000 ; paid-up, £100,000. Nominal price of shares, £25 ; paid-up, £5.

North British Australasian Company, Limited. Registered 1857. Capital, £213,692 ; paid-up, £213,692 ; paid-up, £100.

Otago and Southland Investment Company, Limited. Founded 1864. Capital, £500,000 ; paid-up, £50,000 ; reserve fund, £10,000. Nominal price of shares, £5 ; paid-up, £1.

Peel River Land and Mineral Company, Limited. Founded 1853. Capital, £600,000 ; paid-up, £600,000. Nominal price of stock, paid-up, £100.

Port Phillip and Colonial Gold-Mining Company, Limited. Founded 1852. Capital, £200,000 ; paid-up, £97,500. Nominal price of shares, £2 ; paid-up, £1.

Scottish Australian Mining Company, Limited. Founded 1859. Capital, £150,000 all issued ; paid-up, £127,500. Nominal amount of shares, £1 ; 120,000 paid-up, £1 ; 30,000 paid-up, 5s.

Scottish Australian Investment Company, Limited. Founded 1840. Capital, £300,000 ; pref. £200,000 ; paid-up, £300,000 ; pref. £200,000.

South Australian Company. Founded 1836. Capital, £355,000 ; paid-up, £355,000. Nominal price of shares, £25 ; paid-up, £25.

Trust and Agency Company of Australasia, Limited. Founded 1861. Capital, £500,000 ; paid-up, £50,000. also £141,631 in advance of calls.

Van Diemen's Land Company. Founded 1825. Capital, £300,000, in 10,000 shares of £30 each, of which £28 10s. called up.

Victoria London Mining Company, Limited. Founded 1860. Capital, £20,000 first issue, £25,000 second issue ; paid-up, £25,000 first issue, £20,000 second issue. Nominal price of shares, both issues, £1; paid-up, £1 first issue, 16s. second issue.

Yorke Peninsula Mining Company, Limited. Founded 1864. Capital, £75,000 paid-up. Nominal amount of shares, £1; paid-up, £1.

CONFERENCES.

Statistical Conference held in Melbourne 1861; representatives N.S.W., Christopher Rolleston; Victoria, W. H. Archer; South Australia, Josiah Boothby; Queensland, F. O. Darvall; result, statistics settled on a basis comprehensive and exact.

Boundary disputes between New South Wales and Victoria in summer of 1864 settled amicably at 'a conference between the two colonies, April 19, 1865; meeting of Ministers from the Australian Colonies at Melbourne to arrange postal communication with Europe, March, 1867.

Conference on the assimilation of tariffs, a customs union, and mail contracts, held at Melbourne—members for New South Wales, C. Cowper and S. Samuel; South Australia, J. Hart, J. H. Barrow, W. Townsend; Victoria, Sir James M'Culloch, and J. G. Francis; Tasmania, J. M. Wilson, T. S. Chapman,—June 27, 1870.

Meeting of the delegates from New South Wales, Victoria, South Australia, and Tasmania, objecting to Imperial interference in their mutual fiscal arrangements, September 27, 1871.

Intercolonial Conference held in Sydney, Premiers and Colonial Secretaries of New South Wales, Victoria, South Australia, Queensland, New Zealand, Tasmania, and West Australia present, January, 1872.

Intercolonial conference at Sydney between representatives of the New South Wales, Queensland, and New Zealand Governments, September 30, 1874.

The Intercolonial Cable conference, at which New South Wales, Victoria, and South Australia were represented, agreed, subject to the approval of their respective Governments, to enter into arrangements for duplicating the present means of cable communication by the construction of a cable from Singapore to Port Darwin, February 3, 1877.

Conference held in Melbourne for duplication of cable to England, Colonel Glover present; result, agreement entered into with Eastern Telegraph Company, 1878. [See FREE SELECTORS.]

CONSTITUTION, THE AUSTRALIAN.

New South Wales. First constitutional meeting held, at which a farewell address to the Governor was adopted, in which was asserted the expediency of enlarging the freedom already given by the introduction of the principle of taxation by representation, and by the establishment of a House of Assembly, to consist of 100 members. The names of the gentlemen forming the deputation to present the address were—Messrs. D'Arcy Wentworth, W. C. Wentworth, Thomas Raine, W. J. Browne, and Daniel Cooper : October 21, 1825.

A public meeting held in Sydney, called by the Sheriff (Mr. Mackaness) in compliance with a requisition to that effect, for the purpose of memorialising the Home Government to concede to the colonists the legal and constitutional rights of complete trial by jury, and a representative Assembly, hitherto withheld on the ground of the peculiar condition of the colony. The requisition was signed by twenty-four of the most influential inhabitants, who were said to represent property to the amount of a million of money. The meeting was held at the Court-house on the Anniversary of the Foundation of the colony, and was one of the largest which had hitherto taken place. Mr. W. C. Wentworth was the proposer of the adoption of the petition to the Home Government (copies of which were intended for the King and both Houses of Parliament), Sir John Jamison seconding the proposition. A deputation, consisting of the Sheriff, Mr. Blaxland, and Mr. Wentworth, waited on the Governor to request him to forward, by the first opportunity, the petition to the King. The petition intended for the Parliament was entrusted to Mr. Blaxland (who was about returning to England) to be handed to Sir James Macintosh for the House of Commons, and to Sir Thomas Brisbane for the House of Lords, to be given by him to some friend in that House. This was the first grand effort towards the attainment of the free constitutional privileges of the colony, January 26, 1827.

Public meeting held to petition the Imperial Parliament for the extension to the colony of trial by jury and a representative Legislature. Mr. M'Quoid (the Sheriff) took the chair and gave the assemblage the highest sanction of legality. The petition for the House of Commons was entrusted to Sir James Macintosh, and to the House of Lords to the Marquis of Sligo. Mr. Stuart Donaldson was invited by letter to act as agent for the colonies, February 9, 1830.

On the accession of William IV, a meeting was held in Sydney for the purpose of sending to the King an address of congratulation, in which was embodied a hope that to "His Majesty would belong the happiness of extending to the only remaining Colony of Britain bereft of the rights of Britons, a full participation in the benefits and privileges of the British Constitution," 1831.

A public meeting was held in the Court-house, Sydney, and presided over by Sheriff M'Quoid, to petition the King and Parliament for a representative Assembly. The petition, which was carried unanimously, prayed for the granting to the colony of such an institution, to be composed of not fewer than 50 members, and claiming the right of levying and appropriating their own taxes. This petition was moved by Mr. Wentworth and seconded by Mr. Lawson. At this meeting a vote of thanks was given to H. Lytton Bulwer, — Robinson, and Joseph Hume, for their steady exertions in Parliament to promote the interests of the colony, and to Potter M'Queen and Stuart

Donaldson, for their services on various occasions : January 26, 1833. [A paid agent for the colony was first proposed at this meeting; it was agreed that the Governor should be memorialised to cause £1,000 to be appropriated for the payment of a Parliamentary agent, to be chosen every three years by the landholders and householders of the colony.]

A meeting of the Patriotic Association was held in Sydney for the purpose of discussing the form of legislature and the qualification of members and voters, which might be deemed necessary, in contemplation of the Imperial Parliament's extending to the colonists an enlarged degree of self-government. Two forms of legislation was discussed : One for two Houses, Upper and Lower ; the other proposed the junction of the two Houses into one body, to consist of 50 members, 10 to be nominated by the Government, December 8, 1835.

First published report of the Land and Emigration Commissioners was important and interesting, as it had from time to time been the subject of very considerable controversy in the colony. In September of 1841 a meeting was held in Sydney, to take into consideration the above report, and to petition the Queen for the extension to the colony of the representative form of Government, and in reference to the general question of a representative Government. The petition stated that the Legislature of the colony, as it was then constituted, had not shown itself capable or desirous of supplying the wants or representing the feelings of the colony ; it therefore prayed that Her Majesty would confer on the colony the advantages of a Government, based on popular representation. Dr. Bland occupied the chair. Other meetings, in most of the towns of New South Wales, were held, and similar petitions adopted. September, 1841.

A meeting, one of the largest in Sydney, held to petition for representative Government. After a very stormy debate it was adjourned until a future day at the Sydney College, when a petition to the Queen and Imperial Parliament was adopted, February 16, 1842. [The petition set forth : (1.) That they were free subjects, forming a population of over 10,000 persons. (2.) That their movable and immovable property was estimated at £30,000,000 ; and the property annually created by them at £2,500,000 ; that the maritime commerce of the country during the preceding ten years amounted to £22,500,000 ; that the community raised for Government purposes an annual revenue of £350,000 ; that besides the consumption of British manufacture and the employment of British shipping, the colony relieved Great Britain of the surplus population of 57,000 souls, at a cost to the colonists of £1,250,000. (3.) That, notwithstanding their numbers, wealth, the importance of their commerce, the high rate of their taxation, and the magnitude of their revenue, the community had no control over their taxation, no voice in the management of their affairs, no representation in the local Legislature, and thus

they were destitute of those free institutions which every Briton was taught to prize as the safeguard of his liberties and as the invaluable birthright of his race.]

The sum of £81,000 reserved for the control of the Council for the payment of the salaries of the Governor, the Superintendent of Port Phillip, of the Judges, the administration of justice, and the Civil and Religious establishments. An opposition was made against the Civil list, which did not cease until the Constitution was superseded by one more liberal, 1842. [The contention was, that in the United Canadas, with a population of 10,000,000 the Civil list received for the Crown was £75,000, whilst in New South Wales, with only a population of 77,000 the Civil list amounted to £81,000.]

News was received that the new Constitution Act had been passed by the Imperial Parliament July 29, 1842, and had received the Royal assent on the following day. Thus the struggles which the colonists had carried on for a responsible Government for a series of years was at last crowned with success. The Council consisted of fifty-four members, of whom thirty-six were to be elected by the people (not less than four to be returned by Port Phillip), and eighteen were to be nominated by the Crown ; of the nominated members six were to have seats by virtue of their office, viz., the Colonial Secretary, the Colonial Treasurer, the Auditor-General, the Attorney-General, the Commander of the Forces, and the Collector of Customs. These were to occupy the position of a Ministry of the House. The qualification of an elector was : a freehold of the value of £200, or the occupation of a dwelling valued at £20 per annum. The qualification of a member of the Council was £2,000, or an income of real estate of £100 per annum. The duration of the Council was limited to five years. The Act was received in Sydney Jan. 5, 1843.

A meeting was held to petition for the reduction of the franchise, 1849. [The then existing qualification was £20 per annum household, or £200 freehold, when a petition to the Queen and Parliament was adopted, praying for a reduction to £10 annual household ; or £50 freehold in Sydney, and £5 annual household and leasehold ; or £25 freehold in all other parts of the Colony. The petition received 3,255 signatures.]

"An Act for the better government of her Majesty's Colonies" received the Royal assent. Into Van Diemen's Land, South Australia, and West Australia, this Act introduced for the first time the elective principle, and on Port Phillip, now named Victoria, it conferred Colonial independence, Aug. 5, 1850.

The "Lysander" arrived in Melbourne, bringing news of the "Act for the better government of the Australian Colonies" having received the Royal assent, Nov. 11, 1850. [Demonstration lasted four days.]

The qualification of electors of the colonies of New South Wales and Victoria was reduced by the new Act to £100 freehold, or £10 household or leasehold, and a Civil list of £73,500 was established for New South Wales. By this Act power was given to Her Majesty to detach other territories of New South Wales, and to erect them into a separate colony or colonies, on the petition of the householders of the territories north of the thirtieth degree of south latitude : 1850.

On the motion of Mr. Wentworth, in the Legislative Council, a petition to the Queen and Imperial Parliament was adopted, in which was set forth the general grievances of the Colony. It consisted of a recital of a remonstrance adopted by the former Council, with this addition, that they were prepared, on the surrender to the Colonial Legislature of the entire management of all revenues, territorial as well as general, and on the establishment of a similar constitution to that of Canada, to provide for the whole cost of the internal government of the Colony, whether Civil or Military, and to provide a Civil list during Her Majesty's life, and for five years after her death : 1851.

A protest was entered on the minutes of the House of the Legislative Council against the new Constitution Act, in which the Council solemnly protested, insisted, and declared :—(1.) That the Imperial Parliament of right ought not to have any power to tax the people of the Colony, or to appropriate any money levied by the authority of the Legislative Council by virtue of Act 18 Geo. III. (2.) That the public lands, having derived their value from the colonists, were as much their property as the ordinary revenue, and should be subject only to the control of the Colonial Legislature. (3.) That the Customs and all other departments should be subject to the control of the same Legislature. (4.) That all offices of trust should be conferred on the colo-

nists, except that of Governor, who should be paid by the Crown. (5.) That plenary powers should be conferred on the Colonial Legislature, and no bills reserved for Her Majesty's pleasure, but such as affected the prerogatives of the Crown. An address was presented to the Governor on this occasion requesting his Excellency to transmit a copy to the Secretary of State, and printed copies were sent to all the rest of Her Majesty's Ministers and Privy Councillors ; copies were also sent to noblemen and gentlemen who had taken an interest in the affairs of the colony : 1851.

A select committee of the Council was obtained to prepare a Constitution for the colony, pursuant to the powers conferred on the Council by the Imperial Act. The committee consisted of W. C. Wentworth, S. A. Donaldson, E. Deas-Thomson (Colonial Secretary), J. H. Plunkett (Attorney-General), J. Macarthur, C. Cowper, J. Lamb, J. Martin, T. A. Murray, and Dr. Douglas. In September, the report was brought up and two bills were laid before the House, one to grant a Civil list to Her Majesty, and the other to confer a Constitution on New South Wales : 1852.

A despatch received from the Secretary of State for the Colonies (Sir John Pakington), stating that the control of the Customs should be subject to the direction and supervision of the local Legislature, and that the administration of the lands should be also transferred to that body, that transportation to Tasmania should be discontinued, and that it was the wish of Her Majesty's Government that the Council should establish the new Legislature on the

THE MEETING AT CIRCULAR QUAY
The Illustrated Sydney News, 1854

basis of an elective Assembly and a Legislative Council nominated by the Crown, leaving to the Council to determine the number of members of which the Chambers should severally consist. On receipt of this despatch the Council appointed a committee to prepare a Constitution of the Colony. The committee (which was by ballot) consisted of the mover (Mr. Wentworth), Messrs. E. Deas-Thomson (Colonial Secretary), J. Macarthur, J. H. Plunkett (Attorney-General), Cowper, Martin, Donaldson, Macleay, Thurlow, and Murray. The report brought up by the committee was not satisfactory to the colonists, for in the formation of the Council or Upper House they recommended the conferring of hereditary titles on the members of the House, though not to sit by right of descent, but conferring on the original patentees and their descendants (the inheritors of the titles) the power to elect a certain number of their order, to form in conjunction with the original patentees the Upper House. In consequence of this report, a meeting, condemnatory of that report, was held by the colonists at the Royal Hotel, Sydney, when the "Constitution Committee," which afterwards obtained so much celebrity, was appointed, August 3, 1853.

A general meeting of the colonists was held at the Royal Hotel, to oppose, amongst other matters, the report of the Council, recommending the creation of a Colonial nobility with hereditary privileges, and to construct an Upper House of Legislature in which the people should have no voice. Mr. John Gilchrist, a leading member of the mercantile body, occupied the chair; the principal speakers were Messrs. Darvall, Robert Johnson, Henry Parkes, Montefiore, J. W. Blyth, Deniehy, Mort, Archdeacon M'Encroe, John Brown, Piddington, and E. Flood. Amongst other resolutions adopted were the following:— (1.) That the proposed Constitution Bill was radically defective, and opposed to the interests of the colonists. (2.) That the meeting earnestly protested against any attempt in the Legislative Council to impose a Constitution on the Colony which was formed in direct opposition to the wishes of the people. (3.) That they pledged themselves by every constitutional means to resist the formation of any second Chamber, not based on popular suffrage. (4.) That the proposed alteration in the Electoral Act, instead of being increased, ought to be rectified. The resolutions were embodied in a petition for presentation to the Council: August 10, 1853.

The second reading of the Constitution Bill was moved by Mr. Wentworth. The debate occupied the House seven days. The second reading of the bill was carried by a majority of 34 to 8, and the committal of the bill was made an order of the day for December 6, 1853. [Three days after the second reading a mass meeting was held at the Circular Quay, Sydney, for the purpose of giving expression of dissent to the bill, and to petition Her Majesty to withhold her assent to it. At this meeting the Constitution Committee was made a standing body, for the purpose of taking the necessary steps to procure for the people of New South Wales a Constitution based on British liberty.] On the motion for going into committee on the bill, the clause which empowered the existing Government to sit as members of the Upper House for life was abandoned, and a clause substituted giving the first members seats for five years. The clauses providing for hereditary titles were also abandoned, August 16, 1853.

The bill passed through the third reading by a majority of 27 to 6, amidst great cheering, thus establishing two deliberate Chambers—a Legislative Council and a Legislative Assembly. The Legislative Council was to consist of not less than 21 naturalized or natural born subjects, four-fifths of whom should be persons not holding any Civil office or emolument under the Crown. The members were to hold their seats for five years; at the expiration of that time all those holding seats to be entitled to do so for life. The President to be nominated by the Crown. The Legislative Assembly was to consist of 54 members, to be elected for five years: December 21, 1853.

The qualifications of candidates and electors were:—All inhabitants of full age being naturalized or born British subjects, not convicted of crime, or if convicted, pardoned, having paid all rates and taxes, being the owners of freehold estates of the value of £100, householders, lodging occupiers, or leaseholders of three years at £10 per annum, persons receiving £100 per annum salary, boarders at £40 per annum, and holders of pasture licenses for one year. After the bill had passed the Council, a series of declaratory resolutions were moved by Mr. Wentworth, amongst which was that a copy of the bill be transmitted to the Governor-General, with a request that his Excellency would forward the same to the Secretary of State for the Colonies, as being a fit enactment to give the required validity to the bill. "Thus terminated the most important labour which had ever devolved on an Australian Legislature": 1853.

A deputation consisting of W. C. Wentworth (author of the bill) and E. Deas Thomson (Colonial Secretary, one of its warmest supporters), were sent to England to watch the progress of the Constitution Bill through the Imperial Parliament. Previous to their departure a large sum was subscribed with a view of providing a statue or a painting of Mr. Wentworth. A testimonial was also presented to Mr. Thomson by his friends and the admirers of his political conduct as Colonial Secretary for 17 years. £2,250 was collected. £1,000 was appropriated for a service of plate; the remainder was devoted to founding the "Thomson Scholarship" in the University of Sydney, and to procure a portrait of the recipient: 1854.

Wentworth left for England to take charge of the Constitution Bill during its passage through the Imperial Parliament,—Riddell appointed Colonial Secretary; Merewether, Colonial Treasurer; and Stirling, Auditor-General, 1854.

THE DEPARTURE OF W. C. WENTWORTH
The Illustrated Sydney News, 1854

A new Electoral Bill submitted to the House of Assembly and passed in November following. The number of members was increased to 72 the franchise extended to every adult male of six months' residence in any electorate, and vote by ballot made one of the provisions : May, 1858.

Victoria. The constitution of Victoria establishing separate Legislative Houses received Royal assent and proclaimed throughout the colony, November 23, 1855.

Dead-lock between Legislative Council and Assembly on introduction of Protectionist Tariff in Victoria, 1865-6.

Dismissal of 120 Civil servants in Victoria, January 8, 1878.

Crisis terminated in Victoria by the adoption of the Payment of Members Bill by the Council, and the passage of a new Appropriation Bill (not including the item for payment of members) through the Assembly, a compromise between the Council and the Assembly having been effected through the instrumentality of Mr. Lyell, M.L.A., and Mr. Munro, M.L.A., March 26, 1878. In pursuance of the agreement, Mr. Berry gave notice of motion to the Assembly for the appointment of a committee to search the records of Parliament for the Appropriation Bill laid aside by the Council 30th December, it being understood that this was the first step towards the introduction of a new Appropriation Bill without the item of payment of members. March 26, 1878.

A deputation of Victorian colonists waited on the Secretary of State for the Colonies, London, relative to the crisis, April 10, 1878.

The Government of Victoria re-appointed three additional county court judges and twelve police magistrates and a few officers (dismissed on January 8—"Black Wednesday"), April 15, 1878.

Hon. Graham Berry (Premier) and Hon. Professor Pearson (Minister for Education) appointed by the Assembly as an "Embassy" to request the British Parliament to settle the constitutional difficulty in Victoria, by the introduction of a Reform Bill, left for England in R.M.S. "Siam," December 28, 1878. [*See* PARLIAMENT.]

CONVENTION, VICTORIAN, in which Mr. Wilson Gray, Mr. (Sir) George Verdon, Mr. Walsh, and Mr. Burtt took prominent part, sat in St. Patrick's Hall, Melbourne. [Its objects were, principally, reform of the land laws and the Constitution Act.] 1865.

CONVICTS.

The "First Fleet " with 696 convicts, under the command of Governor Arthur Phillip, R.N., anchored in Port Jackson, January 26, 1788.

Freedom and grant of land in Parramatta, N.S.W., given to the first convict settler selected from the body of prisoners, 1790.

The "Gorgon " with the "second fleet," having on board 1,695 male and 68 female convicts, arrived in Sydney, September 21, 1791.

The "Lady Shore," transport, carrying 60 female convicts, and a detachment of recruits for the New South Wales Corps, was seized by the latter, and the commander and first mate murdered. She was then taken to Rio de la Plata and delivered to the Spaniards. This vessel, besides public stores, had a considerable amount of private property on board, 1798.

From January 25, 1788, to January 7, 1800, 37 transport vessels arrived in the harbour of Port Jackson, carrying 3,000 prisoners. Up to September, 1800, 12 other vessels had sailed from England and Ireland with 3,924 prisoners.

Number of convicts in New South Wales, including 1,247 on Norfolk Island, 31,186, December 31, 1836.

Assignment system ceased in New South Wales, November 2, 1838.

A meeting was held at the School of Arts, Sydney, to counteract a Report of the Parliamentary Committee on Transportation, recommending that sending convicts to the colony should cease. A petition for the continuance of transportation was adopted, but urging that the colony should not be saddled with the whole cost of the maintenance of the police and gaols, but that one half should be borne by the mother country, and that a tax for the remainder of £5 should be levied for all assigned convicts, mechanics, and others employed in towns, and £2 for all shepherds and all others employed in pastoral pursuits, February, 1839.

Transportation ceased by order of the Queen in Council, August 1, 1840.

NOTE.—Though transportation had virtually ceased at this date, it will be found on reference to p. 51 that, notwithstanding the strong and unceasing protests of the colonists, the Government of Great Britain made an attempt to revive it nearly nine years afterwards. The people of Sydney arose in indignation. Upwards of 5,000 persons assembled at the Circular Quay, and so great was the commotion and the excitement that the guard at Government House was doubled, and the guns of a ship of war were "trained" on the place of meeting. It may be here convenient to point out how small a proportion the convict population bears to that of immigration. Though 137,161 convicts arrived from Great Britain and Ireland (many for trivial offences), and it is forty years since transportation virtually ceased, on the other hand we have had over 1,250,000 free persons who emigrated from the same countries. During three years—1851, 1852, and 1853—the number of immigration to our shores amounted to 220,000.—ED.

CHAINED MEN AT WORK
From a French engraving, 1848

ATTEMPTED ESCAPES OF.

A large number of prisoners had, by means of misinterpretations of stories of the blacks, conceived the idea that there was a colony of white people about 500 miles to the south-west, and had formed a plan to escape to that place; but it being discovered, sixteen of the prisoners were brought to Sydney, and punished. In order to convince the whole of them of their error, the Governor proposed to despatch four of the strongest malcontents, with four soldiers and guides to accompany them on their journey. After an absence of ten days, three returned. One man being determined to proceed, was left with the guides, who returned after 26 days, and added to the Australian Ornithology a splendid specimen of the mœnura, or bird of paradise, for the first time procured, January, 1788.

W——— B——— with his wife and two children and seven other convicts, escaped in an open boat, March 28, 1791. [They reached Timor, and were subsequently taken prisoners by Captain Parker. B——— died at Batavia; his wife was taken to England, tried, and confined in Newgate until her sentence expired.]

Discovery by the ship "Providence," 28 guns, Captain Broughton, at Port Stephens, of four runaway convicts, who had been missing from Parramatta since September, 1790: August, 1795.

Twenty male and female convicts absconded, with the idea that they could reach China overland, November 21, 1791. [Several of them died in the bush, and the remainder were brought back in a deplorable condition.]

The Colonial vessel "Cumberland" taken by prisoners, August, 1797.

The "Venus," brig, owned by Robert Campbell & Co., seized by convicts, and taken off, 1799.

"Venus," Colonial vessel, seized at Port Dalrymple, by prisoners, June 17, 1806.

The "Harrington," brig, Captain W. Campbell, taken out of Farm Cove by prisoners, May 15, 1808. [News was received by the "Lady Barlow," on August 22, 1809, of the re-capture of the "Harrington," in the Indian seas, by the frigate "Phœnix." Shortly after she came from India she was lost on the Laconian coast, and the convicts (including the ringleader) thereby escaped, or perished.]

The "Unity," a Colonial vessel, piratically seized, and taken away by prisoners from out of the River Derwent, April 23, 1813.

The "Trial," Colonial vessel, seized by prisoners who were erecting the Lighthouse at Watson's Bay, Port Jackson, and taken away, on September 12, 1816. [She was afterwards discovered wrecked north of Port Stephens. All on board perished by famine, or were murdered by the natives. The place where the boat was found by Mr. Oxley was called Trial Bay.]

The "William Cæsar," Government boat, taken away by prisoners, and afterwards found north of Port Stephens, July 11, 1817.

INSURRECTION AT CASTLE HILL
Rex Nan Kivell Collection

The "Isabella," small craft, seized at Port Macquarie, by prisoners, and not since heard of, October, 1823.

An assigned servant of Thomas Potter McQueen, and five other prisoners of the Crown, absconded, on October 4, 1828, from his station and attempted to reach Timor or New Guinea overland. After penetrating the country for 200 or 300 miles, and enduring the most frightful sufferings, by which all his companions died, Mr. McQueen's servant returned, and gave himself up, November 26, 1828, to Peter M'Intyre, J.P., of Sigenhoe Estate.

Seizure of the Government barque "Lady Franklin," Captain Willett, by 22 convicts when on their way from Hobart Town to Norfolk Island, December 28, 1853. [The convicts overpowered the guard and retained possession of the barque for eleven days, when they loaded the ship's boats with provisions and left in them.]

INSURRECTIONS OF.

The first great insurrection of convicts commenced at Castle Hill, and extended to the Hawkesbury. This outbreak was shown to have been in agitation for a month previous. Martial law was proclaimed. The insurgents had in their possession 136 muskets, 14 pistols, and a great number of swords, bayonets fixed on poles, and pitch-forks. Ten ringleaders were taken in arms on March 4 and 5, 1804. [They were tried and condemned : three were exe-

cuted at Parramatta on the 8th, three at Castle Hill on the 9th, two at Sydney on the 10th, and two were respited.]

TABLE OF THE NUMBER TRANSPORTED TILL THE CESSATION OF TRANSPORTATION.

Year.	No.	Year.	No.	Of these, sent to Tasmania.
1788	696	1813	938	
1789	1,239	1814	1,091	
1790	—	1815	1,204	
1791	2,407	1816	1,439	
1792	368	1817	2,225	480
1793	1	1818	2,992	469
1794	94	1819	3,130	511
1795	132	1820	3,563	873
1796	206	1821	2,639	1,253
1797	380	1822	1,571	658
1798	395	1823	1,617	1,007
1799	53	1824	2,028	943
1800	593	1825	1,313	652
1801	297	1826	1,511	579
1802	673	1827	2,642	981
1803	630	1828	3,271	1,241
1804	—	1829	4,023	1,525
1805	119	1830	4,133	2,045
1806	306	1831	3,971	2,116
1807	302	1832	4,229	2,031
1808	377	1833	4,551	1,821
1809	262	1834	4,920	2,440
1810	610	1835	4,399	1,955
1811	672	1836	4,273	1,985
1812	662	1837	4,068	2,197

TOTAL NUMBER LANDED IN AUSTRALASIA, 1787 TO 1868— (Prepared by Mr. Gideon Lang.)				
Colony.	Period.	Number of Convicts Landed		
		Males.	Females	Total.
New South Wales ..	1788 to 1839	51,082	8,706	59,788
Van Diemen's Land	1803 to 1853	56,042	11,613	67,655
Western Australia ..	1853 to 1868	9,718	..	9,718
Total ..	..	116,842	20,319	137,161

REMARKABLE CIRCUMSTANCES CONNECTED WITH.

A man found guilty of stealing a pair of oars sentenced to be imprisoned one calendar month, and on the last day of his imprisonment to be publicly whipped from the Police Office to the King-street Wharf, September 23, 1829.

A conspiracy was got up among the prisoners who were being conveyed to Norfolk Island in the " Governor Phillip," to murder the crew and guard, but it was discovered and fortunately frustrated. The notorious Knatchbull, who was on board, was, it was alleged, the principal conspirator, 1832.

CONVICT SHIPS, LAST.

The "Eden" was the last convict ship but one that landed convicts in New South Wales, November 18, 1839.

The "Hashemy," 936 tons, Captain Ross, with 212 convicts, arrived in Sydney harbour June 8, 1849. [A great meeting took place to protest against transportation, June 11, 1849. Mr. Robert Campbell was chairman in the absence of Mr. Robert Lowe. Mr. Lamb moved the adoption of the "protest," which was :—

" We, the free and loyal subjects of Her Most Gracious Majesty, inhabitants of the city of Sydney and its immediate neighbourhood, in public meeting assembled, do hereby enter our most deliberate and solemn protest against the transportation of British criminals to the colony of New South Wales. Firstly,—Because it is in violation of the will of the majority of the colonists, as is clearly evidenced by their expressed opinions on this question at all times. Secondly,—Because numbers among us have emigrated on the faith of the British Government that transportation had ceased for ever. Thirdly,—Because it is incompatible with our existence as a free colony desiring self government to be made the receptacle of another country's felons. Fourthly,—Because it is in the highest degree unjust to sacrifice the great social and political interests of the colony at large to the pecuniary profit of a fraction of its inhabitants. Fifthly,—Because, being firmly and devotedly attached to the British Crown, we greatly fear that the perpetration of so stupendous an act of injustice by Her Majesty's Government, will go far towards alienating the affections of the people of this colony from the mother country. For these and many other kindred reasons—in the exercise of our duty to our country—for the love we bear our families —in the strength of our loyalty to Great Britain—and from the depth of our reverence for Almighty God—we protest against the landing of British convicts on these shores." Mr. Lowe, who had in the meantime arrived, seconded this. A deputation of six presented the petition to Governor Fitzroy for transmission to England. They asked the Governor to send the prisoners back, but he refused. A meeting was held June 18, 1849, and the first resolution prayed Her Majesty to remove Earl Grey from her counsels.]

"Tuesday, June 19, 1849.—All the convicts will be removed from the ship this morning. They have all been engaged. In addition to those previously mentioned, a large draft was sent to Parramatta on Saturday under engagement to Mr. Fitzgerald, M.L.C., and Mr. Lawson, and others. The forty-five sent to Moreton Bay were forwarded at the expense of the Government, not being under any engagement but merely sent to the district in order that the settlers there may have an opportunity of hiring them. All the rest have been taken from the ship at the expense of the employers. The only restrictions are that the men are not to be landed in Sydney and they shall not be employed in the county of Cumberland."—From Sydney newspapers.

COO–EE. [See ABORIGINALS' CALL OF COMMUNICATION.]

COOLIES.
An association was formed in Sydney to petition for persons to be permitted to introduce coolies and other Indian labourers. Permission had to be obtained from the Home Government. The Governor was averse to the introduction of this class of persons, on the ground that it would tend to deteriorate the community of the rising colony : 1842.

COPPER.

Copper ore discovered at Macquarie Harbour, Van Diemen's Land, April 20, 1827.

Copper discovered in New South Wales, January, 1829.

Burra Burra Copper mines discovered in South

A COPPER MINE, SOUTH AUSTRALIA
The Australasian Sketcher, 1875

CORROBBOREE
Nicholas-Martin Petit, c. 1804, Musée d'Histoire Naturelle, Le Havre

Australia, May 19, 1845. [Total quantity of copper raised up to 1875, 215,132 tons, valued at over £4,000,000.]

The Kapunda Copper mines, South Australia, discovered by Messrs. Dutton and Bagot, 1843; first 10 tons ore reached Adelaide and caused much excitement, January, 1844; smelting at mine, December, 1849.

Copper ore discovered West Australia, December 18, 1846.

Copper mines on Mr. Icely's land at Carcoar, New South Wales, discovered November, 1848.

John Mollard, *alias* "One-eyed Dick," discovered the Peak Downs Copper mine, Queensland, December 18, 1861.

John Manton took up three 80-acre blocks of the land discovered by Mollard, at the Peak Downs, and floated in Sydney the Peak Downs Copper Company, December, 1862. [First Peak Downs copper smelted, 1864; total expenditure to December 31, 1874, £702,040; total receipts, £268,000.]

The Wallaroo mine, Yorke's Peninsula, discovered by a shepherd on Mr. W. Hughes' run, 1860.

The Moonta mines, S.A., discovered, 1861.

[Total quantity of ore raised from Wallaroo mine to end of 1875, 290,629 tons, valued at £4,500,000.

Total quantity raised from Moonta mine, Yorke's Peninsula, to end of 1875, 255,089 tons. Amount realised on ore sold, £2,761,787. Working expenses and plant, £1,850,000. Dividends paid to shareholders, £928,000.]

Copper discovered at Bundaleer, South Australia, April 12, 1873. [*See* MINERAL STATISTICS.]

COPPER COIN. A vessel arrived from England bringing £450 worth of copper coin, the first issued in the colony, 1800.

CORNSTALKS. A term applied in New South Wales long ago to colonial-born youths.

CORONER, FIRST, appointed in N.S.W., 1825.

CORROBBOREE.

This aboriginal ceremony and festival always takes place at night, and by the light of blazing boughs. The blacks dance to beaten time accompanied by a song. The dancers paint themselves with white or red clay in such remarkably varied ways, that no two individuals are at all alike. The surrounding darkness seems necessary to the effect of the whole, all these dances being more or less dramatic; the painted figures coming forward in mystic order, from the obscurity of the background, whilst the singers and beaters of time are invisible. All produces a highly theatrical effect. Each dance seems most remarkably progressive, the movement being at first slow, and introduced by two persons, displaying the most graceful motions both of arms and legs, whilst others, one by one, drop in, until each imperceptibly wears into the true savage attitude of the corroboree jump, the legs striding to the utmost, the head turned over one shoulder, the eyes glaring and fixed with savage energy in one direction, the arms raised and inclined towards the head, the hands usually grasping waddies, boomerangs, or other warlike weapons; the jump now keeps time with each beat, and at each leap the dancer takes six inches to one side, all being in a connected line led by the first dancer. The line is doubled or trebled according to space and numbers, and this gives great effect, for when the first line jumps to the left the second jumps to the right, the third to the left again, and so on until the action acquires due intensity, when all simultaneously and suddenly stop. The excitement which this dance produces in the savage is really remarkable; however listless the individual, lying half asleep perhaps, as he usually is when not intent on game, when once set to this dance he is fired with sudden energy, every nerve being strung to such a degree that he is no longer to be recognised as the same individual, until he ceases to dance and returns to his normal condition. There can be little doubt but that the "Corrobboree" is the medium through which the delights of poetry and the drama are enjoyed, in a limited degree, even by these primitive savages.

AT MELBOURNE. A Corrobboree was held to the north of the city to which 700 natives flocked from all parts of the country; and some alarm was caused amongst the people of Melbourne at the strange and wild antics of these native warriors, who kept up their festival from sunset to dawn without intermission, June, 1844.

CORRESPONDENCE BETWEEN SIR HERCULES ROBINSON (GOVERNOR OF N.S.W.), and SIR JAMES MARTIN (CHIEF JUSTICE), on the Gardiner case, published July 21, 1875.

COTTON. First grown in the Sydney Botanic Gardens and exhibited by Mr. Charles Frazer, 1828; planted at Moreton Bay, January, 1845; first shipment from Queensland, January 29, 1854; first cotton grown in the Hunter district,

A COURSING MEETING
The Australasian Sketcher, 1873

New South Wales, 1856. [*See* MANUFACTORIES ; *also* QUEENSLAND.]

COURSING.

New South Wales.—First coursing match came off at Bathurst, N.S.W., May 8 and 9, 1876.

Victoria.—First public coursing meeting, held at Sunbury, Victoria, May 29, 30, 31, and June 2, 1873.

COURTS.

DISTRICT COURT. First District Court held in Sydney May 6, 1844.

EARLY CASES IN. The first action tried in any court in the colonies was in 1790, when a captain of one of the convict ships was sued for moneys, &c., entrusted to him for some of the convicts brought out ; a verdict was given for the plaintiffs, 1790.

LIEUTENANT-GOVERNOR'S COURT, consisting of the Deputy, Judge-Advocate, and two other persons, first opened in Van Diemen's Land, 1816.

PETTY SESSIONS. First held in Victoria, July 17, 1838.

PRACTICE established in New South Wales, May 20, 1814.

QUARTER SESSIONS. A court of civil judicature was established, to be held the first month of each quarter in the year ; and two magistrates, consisting of the Judge-Advocate and another, were constituted a Court for the recovery of small debts, 1811.

First general Quarter Sessions held in Sydney, November 1, 1824 ; at Campbelltown, New South Wales, June 3, 1828.

W. Foster, Esq., elected Chairman of Quarter Sessions for the colony, October 26, 1829.

At the Sittings of the Quarter Sessions, Sydney, the public business was delayed for three days through the Legislative Council on a constitutional point having refused to vote the Crown Prosecutor's salary. The Clerk of the Peace was ordered to act, but it was found Mr. Cheeke's commission, being under the sign manual, could not be superseded. Mr. Cheeke afterwards came forward and acted, relying on the Council re-considering their decision, January 2, 1844.

REQUESTS. The first sittings in Sydney commenced September 2, 1824.

Established in various parts of New South Wales, September 9, 1829.

Roger Therry, Esq., Commissioner of the Courts of Requests, New South Wales, arrived in Sydney, November 4, 1829.

The amended Court of Requests Act came into operation in New South Wales. By this Act the jurisdiction for the recovery of debts was extended from £5 to £30, January 1, 1844.

SUPREME COURT.

Civil and General Jurisdiction, and early Appointments.

Richard Atkins appointed Judge-Advocate, December 18, 1800.

Elias Bent, Judge-Advocate, arrived with Governor Macquarie, December 30, 1809.

A new Charter of Justice published, by which three Courts of Justice were established,—the Governor's Court, Supreme, and Lieutenant-Governor's Court. The first consisted of the Judge-Advocate and two magistrates, which took cognizance of pleas of land or subject matter of action that did not exceed £50. The second, a Judge appointed by Commission under the King's Royal Manual, with two magistrates appointed by the Governor. This was a Court of Record, and had all the powers incident thereto. The third, the Lieutenant-Governor's Court, was established in Van Diemen's Land. It consisted of the Judge-Advocate of the island, with two inhabitants nominated by the Lieutenant-Governor, its jurisdiction being the same as that of the Governor's Court : July, 1814.

Judge Barron Field arrived by the "Lord Melville," February 24, 1817.

Judge Field embarked on board the "Mermaid," Lieutenant P. P. King, commander, and sailed for Hobart Town to hold his first circuit of the Supreme Court in Van Diemen's Land, December 24, 1818.

Judge Field returned to Sydney, January 14, 1819.

First Supreme Court held at Hobart Town, January 23, 1819.

Foundation stone of Supreme Court, New South Wales, laid June 4, 1819.

Mr. George Allen, the first Colonial Attorney and Solicitor, admitted to practice, July 26, 1822.

Mr. Justice Field sailed for England from Sydney, Feb. 4, 1824.

Mr. Francis Forbes, first Chief Justice of New South Wales (appointed June, 1823) arrived March 5, 1824.

Mr. J. L. Pedder, first Chief Justice, arrived in Tasmania, March 16, 1824.

Mr. John Wylde, Judge-Advocate, appointed temporary Judge, Supreme Court, Sydney, March 24, 1824.

New Charter of Justice arrived April 5, 1824.

Supreme Court, Tasmania, established by Royal Charter, May 7, 1824, and March 4, 1831.

Mr. J. L. Pedder appointed first Chief Justice, Van Diemen's Land, May 7, 1824. (Mr. Pedder was admitted to the Bar, Middle Temple, June 16, 1820, and knighted in 1838.)

Mr. Saxe Bannister, first Attorney-General, arrived April 5, 1824.

New Charter of Justice formally promulgated (at the Georgian School-house, Castlereagh-street, Sydney) in the Colony of New South Wales, May 17, 1824.

Mr. John Mackaness, first Sheriff under His Majesty's commission, arrived, July 15, 1824.

Mr. John Stephen, first Solicitor-General and Commissioner of the Court of Requests, and Mr. William Carter, first Master in Chancery, arrived in Sydney, Aug. 1, 1824.

John Stephen appointed Assistant Judge Supreme Court, Aug. 17, 1824.

Mr. F. E. Mills, first Registrar of the Supreme Court, arrived in Sydney, Aug. 28, 1824.

Through the exertions of Chief Justice Forbes, trial by jury in the Court of Quarter Sessions of New South Wales was first instituted (at Liverpool) Oct. 14, 1824.

John Carter appointed first Master in Chancery, 1824.

Solicitors in the colony acted also as Barristers in the Supreme Court, but when Messrs. Wentworth and Wardell were admitted as barristers in the Supreme Court this year they moved for a division of the Bar, which was argued before the Court ; but the Chief Justice ruled that the existing Charter did not allow of the construction which the movers sought to enforce. The motion was resisted, on behalf of the attorneys, by Messrs. Rowe, Garling, Moore, Norton, Chambers, and Allen. The discussion on this occasion was the most severe and interesting that had ever taken place in the colony, 1824.

First Jury empannelled in the Supreme Court, to dispose of a case, the King *v.* Robert Cooper, when a verdict was returned for the defendant, Feb. 12, 1825. [The establishment of trial by jury caused considerable ill-will and contention, because the emancipists, who then formed a numerous, wealthy, and respectable class, were excluded from the jury list framed in the first instance. The emancipists, determined not to allow this exclusion to become an established usage, submitted the matter before the highest tribunal, and an order was issued for the Sheriff to show cause requiring him to insert certain names of persons in the list of jurors for the Quarter Sessions. The result was that the Chief Justice decided that the application made, as it was on affidavit, was in itself irregular, and, therefore inefficient to answer the end proposed; that when any other remedy could be obtained the high prerogative writ of *mandamus* could not be applied for, and that a more simple remedy was open to the complainants. The Solicitor-General, Mr. John Stephen, appeared for the Sheriff, Messrs. Wardell and Wentworth for the emancipists.]

Judge-Advocate Wylde embarked at Sydney for England, Feb. 12, 1825.

Mr. John Stephen, Solicitor-General, appointed Assistant Judge in the Supreme Court, August 7, 1825.

Supreme Court House, Sydney, formally opened by proclamation, July 31, 1826.

Mr. William Henry Moore appointed Acting Attorney-General *vice* Bannister, October 1826.

The King's Commission, appointing *Mr. John Stephen* one of the Judges of the Supreme Court, arrived, November 3, 1826.

Mr. James Holland, appointed Solicitor-General for New South Wales, and Commissioner of Court of Requests, December 12, 1826.

Mr. Justice Dowling, one of the Assistant Judges of the Supreme Court, New South Wales, arrived in Sydney, per ship " Hooghley," February 24, 1827.

Mr. Alexander Macduff Baxter, Attorney-General, arrived in Sydney, July 31, 1827.

Mr. William Foster arrived with appointment of Solicitor-General of New South Wales, August 21, 1827.

Sheriff Mackaness suspended, in consequence of his presiding at a general public meeting held in the early part of the year, and in his capacity of Chairman, for failing to stop language which was considered to be offensive to Church and State, December, 1827; *Lord Goderich,* Secretary for the Colonies, directed he should not be re-appointed, December 13, 1827.

Mr. M'Quoid, formerly a merchant in Java, appointed Sheriff of New South Wales, February 24, 1828.

Mr. John Sampson, Solicitor-General, arrived in Sydney, March 12, 1828.

Supreme Court buildings, King-street, Sydney, commenced in year 1820 (Court first held in one of the wings in 1862), completed August 28, 1828.

The exclusion of emancipists from the Jury list brought to a close, 1828.

Mr. William Carter appointed Sheriff, January 5, 1829.

Mr. J. E. Manning, Registrar of the Supreme Court, arrived in Sydney, May 6, 1829.

Mr. Henry Moore appointed Crown Solicitor of New South Wales, August 1, 1829.

Division of the Bar Supreme Court, New South Wales, made by order of the Judges, the legal gentlemen being given the option of choosing which branch of the profession they would adopt, September 5, 1829.

First Act of Council establishing trial by jury in civil cases passed, October 19, 1829.

Mr. John Kinchela, LL.D., Attorney-General for the colony, arrived, June 24, 1831.

Mr. Edward M'Dowall appointed Solicitor-General of New South Wales, December 16, 1831.

Mr. John Stephen (aged 64), one of the Puisne Judges of the Supreme Court of New South Wales, was allowed, by a Treasury minute, to retire on a pension of £500 per annum, March 27, 1832.

Mr. John Hubert Plunkett, Solicitor-General, arrived in New South Wales in the ship "Southwark," June 14, 1832.

Judge Burton (from the Cape of Good Hope) arrived with the appointment of Judge of the Supreme Court, Sydney, 1832.

Mr. Justice Stephen formally retired from the Bench through ill health, an address being presented to him by the members of the Bar, March 16, 1833.

Mr. Justice Dowling proceeded to Norfolk Island with a special commission for trial of prisoners at that settlement charged with capital offences, September 5, 1833.

The qualification of emancipists to sit as jurymen finally decided by the formal opinion of the Judges (Chief Justice Forbes, and Justices Dowling and Burton), under the statute of 6th George IV, according to which Act, persons perfectly free, within the limits of the colony, whether by absolute or conditional pardon, were entitled to all the privileges of freedom, 1833.

Announcement made by the Judges that the rule of the Court promulgated three years before, relative to the division of the profession had been confirmed by the King and would be accordingly acted upon, November 1, 1834.

Judge Burton visited Norfolk Island and tried one hundred and thirty capital charges, 1834.

Mr. Justice Burton announced from the Bench his determination to prevent all but properly qualified parties from practising as solicitors or conveyancers, October 5, 1835.

Mr. Justice Dowling was appointed Acting Chief Justice, and *Mr. J. Kinchela* second Puisne Judge, April 14, 1836.

Chief Justice Forbes retired from the Bench, a public meeting being held, and an address voted and presented to His Honor, July, 1837.

Mr. J. Walpole Willis arrived with appointment as second Puisne Judge, November 3, 1837.

First Court in Port Phillip held in a small brick building at the corner of King and Bourke streets, His Honor J. W. Willis being the first Judge, 1841.

Mr. Justice (now *Sir*) *Alfred Stephen* arrived in Sydney from Hobart Town with the appointment of second Puisne Judge, May 7, 1839.

Sir Charles Cooper first Supreme Court Judge, South Australia, 1839 to 1849.

The Judges decided that the English bankrupt laws were not applicable to the Colony of New South Wales, November 26, 1839.

New insolvency laws came into operation, February 2, 1842.

First Supreme Court New Zealand opened February 28, 1842.

A. W. Young arrived in New South Wales with the appointment of High Sheriff, October 8, 1842.

Judge Willis removed from the Colonial Bench, November 12, 1842; he was Resident Judge at Port Phillip. [The Superintendent of that place officially reported that the Judge did not possess the confidence of the public. The complaint specifically urged against him was want of dignity, and petulance unbecoming a Judge. Judge Jeffcott was appointed his successor.]

Mr. Samuel F. Milford, the first Master-in-Equity in the Supreme Court, New South Wales, arrived in the colony, January 1, 1843.

Mr. G. P. F. Gregory, Prothonotary, Supreme Court, New South Wales, arrived, August 13, 1843.

Mr. (afterwards *Sir) J. Nodes Dickinson* arrived in New South Wales to fill the second Puisne Judgeship, vacant by the removal of Mr. Justice Burton to the Judicial Bench of Madras, October 13, 1844.

Sir James Dowling, Chief Justice, died, having been Judge in the colony from August 6, 1827, and Chief Justice from April, 1836, to September 27, 1844.

Mr. Justice Stephen appointed to succeed Sir James Dowling as Chief Justice, 1844.

Mr. Roger Therry appointed Resident Judge of Port Phillip, *vice* his Honor Mr. Justice Jeffcott, January 18, 1845. [Mr. Alfred Cheeke succeeded to the Commissionership of the Court of Requests, his office of Crown Prosecutor being given to Mr. Thomas Callaghan, January 18, 1845.]

Mr. W. A'Beckett appointed Resident Judge of Port Phillip, succeeding Mr. Roger Therry, who was gazetted as being appointed by Her Majesty a Puisne Judge of the Supreme Court of New South Wales, February 3, 1846.

New Charter of Justice issued to New Zealand, by the Queen December 23, 1846.

INTERIOR OF THE POLICE COURT
The Illustrated Sydney News, 1854

Sir Charles Cooper first Chief Justice S. Australia, 1849.
Thomas Horne appointed Acting Puisne Judge, Tasmania, 1850.
Sir William A'Beckett, Chief Justice of Victoria, 1851.
Sir Redmond Barry, Puisne Judge, Victoria, 1851.
Benjamin Boothby, Puisne Judge, South Australia, February, 1853.
Mr. Justice Williams appointed Supreme Court Judge, Victoria, 1854.
Hon. Robert Molesworth, Puisne Judge, Victoria, June 17, 1856.
Sir Valentine Fleming, Knt. (who was admitted barrister of Gray's Inn, November 21, 1848, and for many years Attorney-General of Tasmania), appointed Chief Justice of Tasmania, 1856.
First Supreme Court, Brisbane, April 5, 1857.
Alfred J. P. Lutwyche appointed Supreme Court Judge, Moreton Bay district, October 21, 1859.
Edward Castres Gwynne, Primary Judge in Equity, South Australia, February, 1859.
Mr. Edward Wise appointed Puisne Judge, New South Wales, February 15, 1860.
Sir R. D. Hanson appointed Chief Justice of South Australia, 1861.
Sir Archibald Caul Burt, Chief Justice, Western Australia, 1861.
Sir James Cockle, first Chief Justice of Queensland, 1862.
F. D. Fenton, Chief Judge of Native Lands Court, New Zealand, 1864.
Alfred Cheeke, Puisne Judge of Supreme Court, Sydney, June, 1865.
George Hibbert Deffell, Master-in-Equity, N. S. Wales, 1857; Commissioner in Insolvency, 1865.
Peter Faucett, Puisne Judge, Supreme Court, New South Wales, October 6, 1865.
Arthur Todd Holroyd, Master-in-Equity, New South Wales, 1866.
William Lambert Dobson appointed Puisne Judge, Tasmania, February 5, 1870.
Sir Francis Smith appointed Chief Justice of Tasmania (admitted to the Bar, Middle Temple, May 27, 1842), February 5, 1870.
T. H. Fellows, Puisne Judge, Victoria, 1872.
Sir James Martin appointed Chief Justice, New South Wales (*vice* Sir Alfred Stephen, retired), Nov., 10, 1873.
Charles Lilley, Puisne Judge, Queensland, July, 1874.
Sir William Montagu Manning, Q.C., sworn in as Judge of the Supreme Court, New South Wales (*vice* Cheeke, deceased), May 4, 1876.
James Penn Boucaut, Puisne Judge, S.A., Sept., 1878.
New Law Courts at Brisbane opened, March 10, 1879.

Criminal Jurisdiction.

The Criminal Court was convened for the first time in the settlement of New South Wales, when a person was sentenced to receive 150 lashes and another to be confined on Pinchgut Island for a week on bread and water (this fact giving the name to the island), February 11, 1788.

Criminal Court convened in New South Wales; six convicts received sentence of death for robbery of stores; one was sentenced to be executed the same day, one was pardoned, and the four others were reprieved, February 26, 1788.
A criminal libel case took place. Dr. W. Bland was convicted of libelling the Governor by the composition and publishing of various letters and verses contained in a manuscript book, dropped on the Parramatta Road, and thus brought to light. He was sentenced to be imprisoned for twelve months, to pay a fine of £50, and to find two sureties for two years, himself in £200 and two sureties in £100 each. September 24, 1818.
The first sittings of the Supreme Court, in its criminal jurisdiction, established by the new charter, held by Sir Francis Forbes, Chief Justice, June 10, 1824.
The first official return of trials before the Court of Criminal Jurisdiction, from the year 1810 to 1824 inclusive, published 1825. [Up to 1822 crime increased; after that time the scale turned and crime rapidly decreased; during the first six years 95 persons paid the extreme penalty of the law, 16 of which were for murder.]
First Circuit Court at Maitland (Wallis Plains) opened by Mr. Justice Dowling, August 17, 1829.
First criminal session held in Melbourne, April 12, 1841.
The Criminal Court was removed from the present Supreme Court to the court-house, Darlinghurst, 1842.

COWPASTURE. Lost Cattle discovered here, 1797.

COWPASTURE ON THE NEPEAN RIVER
Joseph Lycett, an engraving from *Views in Australia, 1824-5*

CRICKET INCIDENTS AND CURIOSITIES.

A Long Score.—The largest number of runs ever put together in a one-day match in Sydney was obtained in a contest between elevens from the Commercial and Australian Joint Stock Banks, on the Association Ground. The Commercial Bank players went to the wickets first, and remained in nearly all day, scoring, with 16 sundries, exactly 500 runs. Cape contributed 139, Moses 136, Cooper 92, and Docker 77. The Joint Stock Bank team scored only 65 runs, of which Blaxland made 38. Mr. Blaxland went in first, and his was the last wicket down.
Another Long Score.—The above was eclipsed in April, on the same ground, in a one-day's match between King's School, Parramatta, and Oaklands; the former scoring 532 in their only innings. W. S. Brown 114, J. Hillas 120, E. Pell 105, and C. Wade 95, were the chief contributors.
Seven Wickets in Two Overs.—In the match played between the Australian Eleven and eighteen of Elland and district, an English paper says:—"After thirty-five minutes' play 8 wickets had fallen for 10. Soon after this Mr. Boyle did the 'hat trick,' taking 3 wickets in 3 balls. In his next over he did even a greater performance, taking 4 wickets in 4 balls. Thus in 8 balls he obtained 7 wickets." This feat (as it deserved to be)

PRACTISING FOR THE ALL ENGLAND MATCH
The Australasian Sketcher, 1873

was "received with great cheering." No wonder the Elland eighteen all retired for 29 runs.

Big Hits.—A player in Hyde Park once hit a ball over the houses in Elizabeth-street into Castlereagh-street. Mr. G. H. Gordon hit a ball in the Domain to the fountain opposite the garden gates ; 8 runs were scored for it. Messrs. T. Docker, G. Morgan, and G. H. Gordon have each sent the ball outside the Albert Ground. Mr. Docker's was a front hit from the northern wicket, the others were leg hits. Mr. T. Docker made 5 fourers off an over of 6 balls bowled by G. Abbott on the Albert Ground, but the wickets were nearer the fence than usual. Nat. Thompson hit a ball in the Domain which struck the Infirmary wall and bounced back across the road.

Mr. G. H. Gordon threw a ball 122 yards on the Albert Ground, which is the best known in New South Wales. The nearest approach was by F. Spofforth, who has thrown a ball 120 yards.

A century in a single innings has only been reached twice in the Intercolonial matches. R. W. Wardill scored 110 first innings at Melbourne in 1867, and Lieutenant Gordon 121 second innings at Melbourne in 1870. In the memorable match between Eleven Australians and Lillywhite's Eleven, C. Bannerman scored 165 not out, retiring hurt.

The largest score ever recorded took place in a match played on Moore Park in the season 1874-5 between the Ulster and Macquarie Clubs. The former club went in first, and retained possession of the creases for four consecutive Saturdays, scoring (including 100 sundries) 1,238 for 9 wickets. The Macquarie thought it was time to abandon the game. Many doubt this match ever having been played, but on reliable authority we are assured of its being a fact.

In a match for the Warehousemen's Challenge Cup, between Myers and Solomon and Prince, Ogg and Co., played at Redfern in January, 1877, Mr. Henry Cooke, for the former named side, bowled 7 wickets for 10 runs, threw one out, and caught the other two, thereby putting out all the opposing side himself.

In the Intercolonial match played at Melbourne, December, 1877, Evans and Coates each bowled 104 balls, 12 maidens, for 35 runs. The former obtained 3, the latter 6 wickets.

Frisquette or Ladies' Cricket, an Australian winter game, invented by Mr. F. J. Ironside, of Sydney, and first played there July, 1878.

CRIMEAN WAR. Meeting held in Sydney for co-operating with Great Britain in providing for the relief of the widows and orphans of those who fell in the war. February, 1855. [As the result of this meeting the Patriotic Fund was established ; in a few days the sum of £8,000 was subscribed, of which £1,000 was given by Sir Daniel Cooper, who also promised £500 annually during the continuance of the war.]

CRIMES AND CRIMINALS, REMARKABLE.

Murder of John M'Intyre, by an aboriginal, 1789.
Marion Du Fresne was murdered in New Zealand, June 14, 1799.

Murder·in Sydney of Samuel Clode, a missionary of Tahiti, by a soldier, his wife, and a free man, July, 1799.

A great fraud was practised by clerks (prisoners) who had access to the records of the names and periods of transportation of prisoners. The sentences of 200 prisoners were found to be altered to make them appear less ; from £10 to £12 was given by each prisoner for the alteration, 1801.

Joseph Luker, a constable, was inhumanely murdered whilst on duty, August 26, 1803.

Rev. Dr. Halloran, tutor to the Earl of Chesterfield, was transported for forging a frank to a letter (postage 10d.), September 9, 1818.

Murder perpetrated by a man named Barry, at Birch Grove, on the defenceless persons of Mr. and Mrs. Bradley, an aged couple, August 15, 1822.

At the Criminal Sessions 34 prisoners were sentenced to death, principally for bushranging, October, 1822.

An atrocious murder committed within three miles of Kissing Point, on a poor woman named Martin, whilst her husband was at church, the murderer never having been discovered, June, 1823.

£5,000 stolen from the Government Treasury, Hobart Town, 1824.

Captain Piper, "the Naval Officer" (as the Collector of Customs was then called), was found to be a defaulter to the amount of £13,575, 1827.

Singular robbery of the Bank of Australia, George-street, Sydney, by excavating from a house across the street. £750 in British silver, 2,030 dollars, and a large number of notes (£14,500), and bills stolen, September 15, 1828.

Captain Logan, whilst surveying, murdered by the Moreton Bay blacks November, 1830.

Sarah M'Gregor and *Mary Maloney* tried and convicted of the murder of their master, Captain Waldron, at Illawarra (to whom they were assigned), February 22, 1834. [They were respited until the pleasure of His Majesty was known, when their sentences were committed to three years' imprisonment.]

The body of *James Hamilton*, murdered by strangulation and his bowels ripped open, found by two lads named Lovett and Anderson, on their way home from the races, near Mount Renny. Kilmartin was executed for this crime, May 11, 1834.

Dr. Wardell was murdered in his own grounds at Petersham, by John Jenkins and Thomas Tattersdale. A man named Emanuel Brace turned informer. September 7, 1834.

William Fineas Bowles, convicted of the murder of his wife in open day, in Bathurst-street, Sydney, with a knife, February 13, 1835 ; executed February 16, 1835.

John Dow, alias *Lutterell*, alias *Lord Viscount Lascelles*, tried and convicted of forgery, and transported for life, May 5, 1835. [In this assumed title he travelled over the Colony for several months on Her Majesty's commission, to make enquiry into the state of the prison population.]

Samuel Onions, extensive ironmonger in Sydney, convicted of perjury : sentenced to seven years' transportation, August 10, 1837.

Eight men were tried, charged with the murder of aboriginals at a station called Myall Creek, belonging to Henry Dangar, Esq. The number killed was 28 men, women and children, under circumstances of most cruel heartlessness. The victims were shot and burnt indiscriminately, no regard being paid to age or sex. The accused were assigned servants as stockmen and labourers to various settlers. The occasion of this uncalled-for slaughter of these aborigines was for spearing cattle, but there were grounds for supposing that those murdered were not given to violence and plunder, being under the protection of Mr. Dangar and his servants. At the first trial the men were not convicted. On the second occasion, November 27, 1838, Mr. Chief Justice Dowling presided, Mr. Plunkett (Attorney-General) and Mr. Roger Therry appeared for the prosecution, Mr. A'Beckett, Mr. Foster and Mr. Windeyer appeared for the defence. Seven of the prisoners were convicted and were executed December, 18, 1838.

Harrington, the notorious swindler, taken from the "Roslyn Castle" in Sydney Harbour as she was proceeding to sea, bound for England, January 26, 1839.

A surgeon in Sydney sentenced to pay a fine of £50 for illegal dissection, September 16, 1839.

John Thomas Wilson purchased the brig "Venus," and put on board her a full cargo of merchandise which he had purchased from a number of merchants and tradesmen, and left the colony in her, his debts being £30,000, October 18, 1839. [He left the bulk of his property behind, which he had previously assigned over to Mr. A. Polack ; the deed being found faulty, Polack agreed to pay the creditors 75 per cent. of their respective claims.]

Defalcations of *Murray*, Registrar of the Supreme Court, discovered, 1842.

Street robberies prevalent in Sydney. Mr. Noble murdered in his own house by three ruffians, who were afterwards arrested for the crime, 1843.

Mrs. Jamieson, a widow, barbarously assaulted with a tomahawk by one John Fitz, otherwise Knatchbull, January 6, 1844. [She died in a few days afterwards. Knatchbull was subsequently tried for the murder, and defended by Mr. Robert Lowe, when the defence set up (for the first time in the colony) was *self-delusion*. He was, however, found guilty, and executed 13th January following.]

Mrs. Hoadley, murdered in her house in King-street, Sydney, May 19, 1845.

John Tawell, born in 1784, in Aledby, county of Norfolk, in 1798, entered the service of a widow who kept a general store, and who belonged to the Society of Friends, of which society he afterwards became a member. In 1804 he went to London, and entered the service of Mr. Janson, a large linendraper. He married a housemaid in the employ of his master, and then left. He was engaged by a Mr. Marsden, wholesale druggist and chemist, to travel for the establishment, and evinced so much activity and business tact, that for seven years he was trusted and highly prized by his employer. At length it was found that he had committed extensive forgeries on the Uxbridge Bank for which, if he had been tried, he would have lost his life ; nevertheless, the bank officials, being members of the Society of Friends, were disinclined to be instrumental in taking life, so proceeded against him on the charge of having a forged note in his possession, for which he was transported to Sydney in 1814. Here he was employed as an assistant in the Convict Hospital. For his assiduity, intelligence, and carefulness he soon obtained a ticket-of-leave from Governor Macquarie, who very shortly afterwards gave him his emancipation ticket. Tawell then commenced as a chemist in Hunter-street, Sydney, and also traded in various kinds of produce. He rapidly grew rich, embarked in the shipping trade and in oil speculations, and was successful in all his ventures. He built a chapel for the Society of Friends in Macquarie-street, Sydney, and emptied 600 gallons of rum in Sydney Harbour in order to encourage temperance. His wife, hearing of his altered condition, came out in 1824. After an absence of 16 years he returned with a large fortune to England, 1831 ; made one or two trips to Australia on business speculations, which brought him in a large sum. His wife, during her last illness, was attended by a nurse named Sarah Hart, with whom Tawell formed an illicit intercourse, and kept her in seclusion at various places. He married again, in 1841, a widow named Mrs. Cutforth. Fearing that his connexion with Sarah Hart would be found out, he planned and perpetrated her murder, for which he was placed on his trial March 12, 1845. In his confessions he stated that he had previously attempted to kill her with morphia put in some porter, and that on this last and fatal occasion he had used prussic acid. He was executed March 21, 1845. Throughout his whole life he always appeared to be religious and charitable : to one school he gave £30 per annum. He took apparently great interest in all matters belonging to the religious society of which he was so unworthy a member.

The Nelson Gold Robbery, in Hobson's Bay, Melbourne, April 2, 1852. [The ship which had arrived the previous day in Hobson's Bay from Geelong with treasure, was boarded by a daring gang of robbers and plundered of gold to the value of £24,000. (There were only three sailors and three passengers on board.) The gold was bought by a Melbourne storekeeper (who met the robbers on the beach) at thirty shillings an ounce. He then sailed for England and was never prosecuted. Four men—John Jones, James Morgan, James Duncan, and John Roberts were indicted for the offence and found guilty. One was afterwards released, his arrest being found to be a case of mistaken identity. April 2, 1852.

Robbery of the M'Ivor (now Heathcote, Victoria) Gold Escort, July 20, 1853.

Dr. Alexander Cuthill, an old-established and much-esteemed medical practitioner of Sydney, shot by an insane person named James Gray, while returning in his gig to town from Cook's River, April 27, 1854. [Dr. Cuthill left a legacy of over £10,000 to the Destitute Children's Asylum, Sydney, the bulk of which has since been expended in erection of the Asylum at Randwick. He died from the effects of the wound May 1. Gray was tried, condemned to death, and his sentence afterwards commuted to 15 years' imprisonment.]

Murder of *James Scobie,* near Eureka Hotel, Ballarat, Victoria, October 7, 1854. [The hotel-keeper, Bentley, suspected, arrested, and acquitted; indignation amongst the diggers in consequence.]

Francis Brannagan arrived in Tasmania in 1842, under a sentence of 14 years, Went over to Melbourne in 1854, and in November, 1854, was committed for highway robbery by the Maryborough bench, and whilst *en route* for Castlemaine for trial, broke out of the Tarrangower lockup, together with another prisoner, Brannagan escaping, December 7, 1854. [£100 reward was offered for his capture, which was accomplished by the police near Ballarat; he was sentenced to 15 years, the first three in irons.]

Captain Melville was undergoing a sentence of 32 years' hard labour when he headed the first outbreak of the prisoners at Williamstown, which resulted in the death of Owen Owens, a boatman, whom he killed with a hammer. Sentenced to death at Melbourne, November 21, 1856, but was commuted. Strangled himself in the gaol, August 12, 1859.

Richard Rowley assaulted Kilmartin, an overseer at Pentridge, while under cumulative sentences amounting to 32 years, July 26, 1859.

Eugowra Escort robbed, June 15, 1862.

George Williams tried at special sessions, Darlinghurst, for robbery under arms on October 14, 1862, of John George Pile; pleaded guilty, and sentenced to 12 years' hard labour, the first year in irons, February 9, 1863.

George Williams and *Frank Britten,* for robbery under arms November 5, 1862, of the Bathurst mail, in company with another man, when Arundel Everett was robbed of £6, and Owen Malone of £990, the property of the Bank of New South Wales, found guilty at the special commission, Darlinghurst, and each sentenced to 15 years' hard labour, the first year in irons, February 9, 1863.

Charles, alias *James Mackay,* for the robbery under arms of two carriers at Mount Victoria; sentenced at the special sessions, Darlinghurst, to hard labour for 15 years, first year in irons, February 9, 1863.

John Healey, for robbery under arms near Goulburn, sentenced at the special commission at Darlinghurst, to 15 years' hard labour on the roads, the first year in irons, February 9, 1863.

Charles Foley and *John Brownlow,* tried at the special commission at Darlinghurst, for having, on December 18, 1862, robbed at the Laggan, O'Brien, a publican, of £75; found guilty and sentenced, Foley to 12 years' hard labour on the roads, the first year in irons; Brownlow to 7 years' hard labour, February 9, 1863.

An attempt was made about 10 o'clock on Tuesday night, February 24, 1863, to rob the Western escort. The coach was attacked between Big and Little Hartley, by a party of some five or six armed men, who fired upon it, some logs having been thrown by them previously across the road so as to block it. One shot slightly wounded Sergeant M'Lure, and one of the horses was shot dead; the gold, however, was not interfered with, and after an interval of half-an-hour, the escort proceeded on its way.

Wilson, a noted Melbourne street-walker in female attire, sentenced to death, December 1, 1863. [Sentence commuted to hard labour for life on the roads of the colony.]

John Woods, alias Young, was transported for 15 years for a serious offence from England; also sentenced afterwards to seven years on the roads at Norfolk Island, and arrested by J. Dowling, Esq., while attempting to rob the English, Scottish, and Australian Chartered Bank, Fitzroy, June 12, 1864.

William Carver, alias Foster, alias Thornley, convicted at home, and sentenced to seven years' transportation to Van Diemen's Land. Eight years for horse-stealing at Castlemaine, Victoria; and two years for bestiality at Ballarat. Arrested for shooting at Percy de Jersey Grut, Esq., with intent to murder him and rob the English, Scottish, and Australian Chartered Bank, Fitzroy, Melbourne. This man was arrested June 15, 1864, by Detectives Williams and Berliner, who also afterwards captured his companions, Jeremiah Phillips and James Anderson.

Henry L. Bertrand and *Jane Bertrand,* his wife, charged at the Water Police Court with the wilful murder of Henry Kinder, principal teller at the City Bank, Sydney, N. S. W., on the 2nd December previously, at Kinder's residence, St. Leonards, North Shore; and Maria Helen Kinder, charged as an accessory to the murder, November 29, 1865. All three prisoners committed for trial, December 9, 1865. Henry Louis Bertrand found guilty of the murder of Henry Kinder (Jane Bertrand and Maria Helen Kinder having been liberated by order of the Attorney-General, being acquitted), sentenced to death March 21, 1866. Appeal of Louis Henry Bertrand to Privy Council sustained, and prisoner reprieved from death, but ordered to be imprisoned for life on the ground of insanity, September 9, 1868. [*See* BERTRAND CASE, THE.]

Desperate conflict between four police and eleven prisoners at Bargo Brush, N.S.W.; Constable Raymond shot dead by a prisoner named James Crookwell, April 15, 1866.

Series of murders committed by Thomas Kelly *alias* Noon, Richard Burgess *alias* Hill, and Phillip Levy, who with John Joseph Sullivan, were known as the New Zealand murderers. The latter turned Queen's evidence, he proved how they planned the murder of Mathieu, Kempthorn, Dudley (storekeeper), and De Pontius (a miner), who, on June 12, 1866, left Deep Creek for Nelson, and were murdered the following day whilst crossing the Maungatapu Mountain. Three of the party were shot by the murderers, and the fourth was strangled with Sullivan's scarf. They also murdered poor "Old Jamie" in a manner even more horrible than that of the above four men, and took from him £3. Besides Mr. G. Dobson, surveyor, whom they strangled, and left at the foot of a tree in a sitting position (as if he had died from exhaustion), but whom they afterwards buried, these fiends are supposed to have committed more than thirty murders in New Zealand alone. They carried with them a bottle containing strychnine, having resolved that if any party they encountered were too strong for them, they would make friends, and whilst drinking with them administer the poison, and then rob them. Burgess stated that he began his criminal career at the age of eight. He had been a lawyer's clerk, and was the chief of the band. June 13, 1866.

Murder of four constables at Jindera Mountains, January 9, 1867.

Andrew Anderson and Thomas Campbell tried before Mr. Justice Cheeke, and found guilty for conspiring to blow up a portion of the outer wall at Darlinghurst, February 13, 1867.

William Henry Scott, tried at the Central Criminal Court, before Mr. Justice Cheeke, for the murder of his wife Annie, and sentenced to death, February 22, 1867. [Scott after murdering his wife cut up the body and placed it in a box, and with the assistance of a boy carried it from his house in Sussex-street. The body was subsequently found by a lad named James Kirkpatrick, at the back of Barker's mills.]

Fifteen prisoners sentenced at Bathurst Assizes, 1867, on their way to Sydney, made a desperate attempt to escape, two got away—(one, Rutherford afterwards captured), Constable Holmes being shot dead, April 23, 1867.

T. J. Griffin, Police Magistrate at Clermont, Queensland, tried at the Police Court, Rockhampton, and committed for trial, November 21, 1867.

Henry Garrett *alias* Rouse, robbed the Bank of Victoria at Ballarat in 1855 and was sentenced to ten years imprisonment ; in 1861 was granted a ticket-of-leave ; he then went to New Zealand, commenced bushranging and stuck up 23 persons in one day on the Maungatien Ranges, was captured and sentenced to eight years imprisonment ; after serving six years was again liberated and sent over to Melbourne, where he was brought before the magistrates under the Influx of Criminals Act ; he complained bitterly of not being allowed to settle anywhere and threatened to commit a murder, in order that his life might be ended for him. 1851—1867.

The remains of two German hawkers, named Pohlman, were found in the ashes of a fire on the Yanko Creek, about 8 miles from Narranderra.   April 1, 1868.

A ticket-of-leave man named William Munday or Collins committed five brutal murders at Conroy's Gap, sixteen miles from Yass. He got up in the night and killed with an axe a shepherd, who was sleeping alongside of him. Smith, a man who was sleeping in a room on the opposite side of the hut, hearing the noise, got up, but Munday quickly killed him with a shears. Conroy and Mrs. Conroy also hearing the struggle ran into the murderer's room, when he killed them both with the sheepshears.   Next morning a shepherd named White, who slept in a detached hut, came over to Conroy's house ; he was met by Munday, who first disabled him with the shears and then struck him down with the axe. [Munday said he intended murdering Conroy's son, but fortunately he was absent on that fatal night. The reason assigned by Munday for the murders, was that he was badly treated whilst in Conroy's employ and that he could only obtain £1 for six months service as a shepherd.   He was tried at Goulburn for murder found guilty and sentenced to death.] April 8, 1868.

Rev. W. Hill murdered at Pentridge Gaol, Victoria, by a prisoner named Ritson, May 13, 1869.

Scott *alias* Captain Moonlight, tried at Ballarat for the Egerton (Victoria) bank robbery in 1870, found guilty of the offence, sentenced to ten years' imprisonment, 1872.

Triple murder committed at Forest Reefs, in the Orange district, by a man named Martin. His wife and his wife's father and mother killed.   January 3, 1871.

Martha Elizabeth Rumph,-wife of a shepherd near Bombala, cut the throats of several of her children, two of whose heads were nearly severed from their bodies by a knife, and then attempted to kill herself.   She was tried at the Criminal Court, Sydney, February 16 following, and acquitted on the ground of her being insane at the time of the murders. January 11, 1871.

A threatening letter sent to the Governor of N.S.W., stated in the Assembly to have been the work of a boy of thirteen years.   June 1, 1871.

A man named Savage found murdered in a hut on his own property, about three miles from Parramatta, and on the Kissing Point Road, near Sydney, June 27, 1871.

William Hartley, *alias* George Cox, sentenced to death at the Bathurst Assizes for the Wren's Nest murder.   October 28, 1871.

Mail coach stuck up near Merriwa by two armed men. November, 1871.

Arrival of the " Jessie Kelly," schooner, from Noumea, bringing intelligence of the massacre of Bishop Patteson, of the Melanesian Mission, and the Rev. Mr. Atkin.   November 4, 1871.

Keropa tried at Napier, New Zealand, for the murder of Rev. Mr. Volkner ; found guilty and sentenced to death, December 21, 1871.

James Stewart, murdered with a knife, at Camden Park, New South Wales, by Robert Boyd, who committed suicide same day. January 5, 1872.

G. R. Nicholls and Alfred Lyster, tried before Mr. Justice Hargrave, for the murder on Parramatta River, New South Wales, of William Percy Walker, March 13, 1872 ; they were convicted and sentenced to death, May 22, 1872.

" Carl " murders and kidnapping investigation commenced, Water Police Court, Sydney, July 27, 1872.

Captain Joseph Armstrong and the mate of the " Carl," convicted on the (Queen's) evidence of Dr. James Patrick Murray, of kidnapping Polynesians, were sentenced to death, but the sentence was afterwards commuted ; five of the crew were also tried, and received two years' imprisonment, for assault on the high seas.   November 19, 1872.

Release of Mount and Morris (of the " Carl " kidnapping expedition), who had been sentenced at the Melbourne Criminal Sessions some time before to fifteen years' imprisonment ; grounds of release being that it was not shown that they were detained for their crimes in some place appointed by the Secretary of State.   September 18, 1873.

THE CARL CASE — DISCHARGE OF MOUNT AND MORRIS
The Australasian Sketcher, 1873

Extensive forgeries of bank notes discovered in Parramatta Gaol, October 1, 1873.

H. J. O'Ferrell, a clerk in the Lands Office, Melbourne, absconded; £14,000 deficient in his accounts, November, 1873; was arrested in Singapore in 1874, brought back to Melbourne, tried, convicted, and sentenced to fourteen years' imprisonment. 1874.

A girl named Mary Buchan foully murdered at Mount Gambier by a married man named William Page *alias* Walker, who was executed for the crime. July 11, 1875.

Case of attempt to bribe a member of the New South Wales Parliament. A sentence of three years' imprisonment with hard labour was passed, which however was quashed on appeal to the full Court, August 17, 1875.

Richard W. Sawers, teller, Bank Victoria, arrested Melbourne, embezzling £1,400, October, 27, 1875.

Attempt was made to upset the up-train from Ballarat and Geelong to Melbourne by placing three iron rails and a sleeper across the line; the train cut through the rails. December 9, 1875. [£200 reward was offered for the conviction of the perpetrator.]

Commercial Bank at Cannonbar, New South Wales, broken into, and the manager bailed up at night and robbed of £1500. January 13, 1876. [The robbers were subsequently captured, and a large amount of the money recovered.]

Bank of N.S.W. Brisbane, robbed of £1,300 by a clerk, December 5, 1877.

[*See* EXECUTIONS.]

CRIME IN AUSTRALIAN COLONIES, 1876.

Name of Colony.	Number of Offences for which persons were—			
	Apprehended or Summoned.	Summarily Convicted or held to Bail.	Committed for trial.	Convicted after Commitment.
New South Wales	45,105	30,404	1,391	822
New Zealand	22,141	16,100	414	249
Queensland	10,180	6,126	285	132
South Australia	9,375	7,929	239	124
Tasmania	9,207	7,208	96	51
Victoria	42,297	27,505	680	384
Western Australia	7,509	5,847	95	47
Total	145,814	101,119	3,200	1,809

PROPORTION OF ARRESTS, COMMITMENTS, AND CONVICTIONS IN AUSTRALIAN COLONIES TO POPULATION, ETC., 1876.

Name of Colony.	Proportion per 1,000 of—		Proportion per 1,000 of—		Proportion per Cent. of—	
	Apprehensions and Summons Cases to Population.	Summary Convictions to Population.	Commitments for Trial to Population.	Convictions after Commitment to Population.	Summary Convictions to Apprehensions and Summons Cases	Convictions after Commitments to Commitments.
New South Wales	72·96	49·18	22·50	13·30	67·40	59·10
New Zealand	57·14	41·55	10·68	6·43	72·72	60·14
Queensland	55·27	33·26	15·47	7.17	60·18	46·32
South Australia	42·99	36·36	10.96	5·69	84·58	51·88
Tasmania	88·04	68·93	9·18	4·88	78·29	53·12
Victoria	50·92	33·11	8·19	4·62	65·03	56·47
Western Australia	277·95	216·43	35·17	17·40	77·87	49·47
Total	61·52	42·66	13·50	7·63	69·35	56·53

A box, the property of the Oriental Bank, containing £5,000 extracted from the mail room of the "Avoca," during the passage from Sydney to Melbourne, Aug. 4, 1877. Twelve months afterwards the carpenter of the vessel,

Martin Wieberg was captured and confessed to the robbery, implicating Ellison, the first officer. Wieberg escaped from the Victorian police when pretending to lead them where the hidden treasure was, Oct. 28, 1878. Ellison was arrested in England, but acquitted. Nov., 1878.

A messenger at the Sydney Observatory, arrested on suspicion of having attempted to destroy Mr. Russell, the Government Astronomer, by an infernal machine, September 8, 1877.

Mr. and Mrs. Askell murdered at Booral, Raymond Terrace, New South Wales, February 1, 1878.

Senior Sergeant Wallings shot whilst after bushranger, September 20, 1878. [His murderer, Gibson, was shot by Sub-inspector Duffy and party, on the Queensland border, Oct. 6, 1878.]

CULTIVATION.

The following table gives the number of acres under crop in the Australasian Colonies on January 1, 1878 :— [*See* "AGRICULTURE."]

	Acres.
New South Wales	546,556
Queensland	99,891
Tasmania	131,013
South Australia	1,828,115
Victoria	1,420,502
Western Australia	50,591
Total	4,076,668
New Zealand	641,833
Total for Australasian Colonies	4,718,501

CUMBERLAND DISEASE. A distemper known as the Cumberland Disease made great ravages amongst the cattle of the colony of New South Wales. It was confined to the county of Cumberland, but attacked herds that were brought from other parts 1851.

CURIOSITIES : FACTS AND SCRAPS.

Destruction of Rum. John Tawell, a member of the Society of Friends, to show his devotion to the cause of temperance, ordered upwards of six hundred gallons of rum to be emptied into Port Jackson March 9, 1836.

An Extraordinary Sentence. The following took place in Sydney, September 23, 1829 :— the prisoner was tried before Mr. Justice Dowling and found guilty of stealing a pair of oars; sentence, to be imprisoned one calendar month, and on the last day of his imprisonment to be publicly whipped from the police office to the King-street wharf.

Remarkable case of a series of wrecks suffered by the same people. The "Mermaid," Colonial Government cutter, left Sydney for Raffles Bay, but on entering Torres Straits she got on shore, and was lost. All on board were saved upon a rock. In three days afterwards the "Swiftsure," Captain Johnson, which sailed from Tasmania, hove in sight, and took on board the captain and crew of the "Mermaid," but in three days she also got on shore, and was wrecked. Two days afterwards the "Governor Ready," also from Hobart Town, Tasmania (April 2), passing within sight, took the shipwrecked people belonging to the "Mermaid" and "Swiftsure" on board; but was itself wrecked on May 18, but all the people saved by taking refuge in the long boats. The ship "Comet," also from Tasmania, soon after took the whole of the collected crews of the lost ships "Mermaid," "Swiftsure," and "Governor Ready" on board, but was herself wrecked, but all hands saved. At last the ship "Jupiter," from Tasmania, came in sight, and taking all on board, steered for Port Raffles, at the entrance to which harbour she got on shore, and received so much damage that she may be said to have been wrecked. 1829.

Mungo Park's offer to Explore Australia. In the New South Wales official correspondence, there is a letter to John King, Esq., of the Treasury, dated May 15, 1798, from Sir Joseph Banks, communicating Park's offer, as follows: —"It is impossible to conceive that such a body of land, as large as all Europe, does not produce vast rivers, capable of being navigated into the heart of the interior, or, if properly investigated, that such a country, situate in a most fruitful climate, should not produce some native raw material of importance to a manufacturing country as England is. Mr. Mungo Park— lately returned from a journey in Africa, where he penetrated further into the inland than any European before has done by several hundred miles, offers himself as a volunteer to be employed in exploring the interior of New Holland by its rivers or otherwise, as may in the event be found most expedient. His moral character is unblemished, his temper mild, and his patience inexhaustible, as he has proved during his African expedition; he is sufficiently versed in astronomy to make and to calculate observations to determine both latitude and longitude: he knows geography enough to construct map of the counties he may visit, draws a little, has a complete knowledge of botany and zoology, and has been educated in the medical line. He is very moderate in his terms; he will be content with ten shillings a day and his rations, and happy if his pay is settled at twelve shillings. The amount of his outfit for instruments, arms, presents, &c., will not, I think, exceed £100. He will want a decked vessel of about thirty tons under the command of a lieutenant, with orders to follow his advice in all matters of exploring. Such a vessel may easily be built in the country, if one already there, which is found to have very bad qualities as a sea-boat, cannot be made sufficiently trustworthy; and Lieutenant Flinders, a countryman of mine, a man of activity and information, who is already there, will, I am sure, be happy if he is entrusted with the command, and will enter into the spirit of his orders, and agree perfectly with Park. The crew of such a vessel need not, in my opinion, consist of more than ten men—four for boat-keepers, and six to proceed in the country with one or both the commanders, as may happen when inland journeys are to be attempted. If either or both these projects are carried into execution I will readily undertake to draw up instructions for all parties, and to correspond with them during the execution of their plans,

under the superintendence of your office, such hopes have I of material discoveries being made and such zeal do I really feel for the prosperity of a colony in the founding of which I bore a considerable share."—*Abridged from "Laballiere's Early History of Victoria."*

CURRENCY.

The following proclamation was issued by Governor King:—

PROCLAMATION.

November 19, 1800.

Whereas, representations of the want of small money experienced here, has induced His Majesty to take into gracious consideration the immediate relief from this great inconvenience to all classes of his subjects in this colony, a quantity of copper coin has been received in His Majesty's armed vessel "Porpoise," and will be circulated by being paid for grain and animal food supplied His Majesty's stores.

These are therefore to give notice, that a copper coin weighing one English ounce, and stamped with the profile of His Majesty on the one side, and of Britannia on the other, will be issued as above, at the rate of two-pence for each copper, and that the same shall pass current in the colony, and is to circulate at the aforesaid rate of two-pence.

And that no one may plead ignorance of the rate or legality of this or any other of the coins circulating in this colony, of which it does not appear that any regular proclamation has ever collectively been issued, I have judged it most expedient herewith to publish the following tables of all the specie legally circulating in this colony with the rates affixed to each, at which they shall be considered, and be a legal tender in all payments or transactions in this colony:—

TABLE OF SPECIE.

A guinea	..	..	..	£1	2	0
A johanna	..	..	..	4	0	0
An half ditto	..	..	..	2	0	0
A ducat	..	..	..	0	9	6
A gold mohur	..	..	..	1	17	6
A pagoda	..	..	..	0	8	0
A Spanish dollar	..	..	..	0	5	0
A rupee	..	..	..	0	2	6
A Dutch guelder	..	..	..	0	2	0
An English shilling	..	..	..	0	1	1
A copper coin of one ounce	..	..	..	0	0	2

GOD SAVE THE KING.

When a sufficient quantity of copper coin is received in the colony, of which notice will be given, no private notes or cards will be allowed to circulate. This supply of copper having been sent to relieve the inconvenience of persons requiring to make small payments; no persons are to collect the same, for the purpose of making large payments; nor shall it be deemed a legal tender to offer the same in payment for any sum exceeding five pounds.

And it is hereby declared that the exportation or importation of any sum in copper exceeding £5 shall be punished by fine of treble the value, and forfeiture of the sum exported or imported.   November 19, 1800.

First issue of copper coin took place December, 1800. The coins and their standard value circulating in the colony at this time were:—A guinea, which was current for £1 2s.; a Johannes, £4; a half Johannes, £2; a ducat, 9s. 6d.: a gold mohur, £1 17s. 6d.; a pagoda, 8s.; a Spanish dollar, 5s.: a rupee, 2s. 6d.; a Dutch guelder, 2s.; an English shilling, 1s. 1d.; a copper coin (penny) of one ounce, 2d; a copper coin, half ounce, 1d.; a copper coin, quarter ounce, ½d. In consequence of the scarcity of copper coin in circulation, orders were given by the Governor that no sum of this coin exceeding £5 should be deemed a legal tender, and that no larger sum than £5 should be exported in copper, under a severe penalty. 1801.

THE HOLEY DOLLAR

H. M. S. "Samarang" arrived from India, with treasure dollars for Government, February 3, 1812.

The constant draining of sterling money for the payment of supplies, which the colony was necessitated to procure from England and other countries, occasioned a great scarcity of money. The Governor sanctioned the issue by individuals of five shilling promissory notes, payable on demand in copper coin. It was named "Currency" money. This was the commencement of that system of money orders, which afterwards played so conspicuous a part of the monetary history of the colony of New South Wales. 1812.

The expediency of persons being allowed to issue the five shilling promissory notes, or "Currency" money as it was called, only benefited the colony for a short time ; in consequence of shilling money becoming shorter every day, and many persons issuing these notes being unable to meet them, and others who were not responsible for payment of the amount of orders, they became depreciated as low as fifteen shillings in the pound. An order was subsequently given which more effectually remedied the evil, which was the issue of what was known as the holey dollar, which was by cutting a circular piece out of the centre of the Spanish dollar, and giving the piece cut out the value of fifteen pence, whilst the rim or ring represented five shillings, at once increased the amount of sterling money in the colony, and increased the quantity of current coin. The circular piece cut out of the dollar was called a "dump," and its value represented fifteen pence ; thus every dollar realised 6s. 3d. July 1, 1813.

"The Holey Dollar," and the piece taken out—"the dump"—officially countenanced, 1821.

First Act of Parliament passed in Australia. Its object was to make promissory notes and bills of exchange payable in Spanish dollars available as if such notes had been drawn payable in sterling money of the realm, September 28, 1824.

The system of currency or dollar system abolished by Act of Council, February 12, 1826.

Gazette notice appeared, officially prohibiting the further use of the holey dollar and the dump, a large amount of British coin having been received, and put in circulation, August 15, 1829.

Public meeting held in Sydney respecting the currency of dollars, dumps, and rupees, determining only to deal in sterling pieces. Resolutions were passed that dollars and rupees be retained in circulation at the following rates: Dollars, 4s. 2d., and rupees, 1s. 9d., November 23, 1829.

Counter meeting held which resolved that the dollar be retained at 5s. currency, November 30, 1829.

Money in circulation very scarce, as much as seventy-five per cent. being given for loans, 1834.

Withdrawal by proclamation of old British copper coins from circulation in the colonies, on August 21, 1876.

A notice to the effect that old copper would be exchanged at the Sydney Branch of the Royal Mint for bronze coin, up to March 31, 1877, published March 24, 1876.

CURRENCY LADS AND CURRENCY LASSES.
A term formerly applied to the native born population of New South Wales to distinguish them from the immigrant portion of the inhabitants, who were designated as "sterling."

CURTIS ISLAND.
Discovery of Curtis Island, (after Timothy and William Curtis, Esqs.) and Macauley Island (after G. M. Macauley, Esq.) by Captain Lever, in the "Lady Penrhyn," June 1, 1788.

CUSTOMS.

Despatches sent to the Governor to cause a register of all ships entering the harbour and clearing out to be instituted, 1799. [This was the first step taken towards the establishment of Custom House duties, and port regulations.] The first imposition of import duties commenced in Australia, 1800. [The immediate object of this impost was to raise a fund for the purpose of finishing a gaol in Sydney; the work had been carried on at first by voluntary assessment, levied on the inhabitants of Sydney and the settlers generally, but this was found inadequate for that purpose.] *Francis Rossi*, appointed Comptroller of Customs, May 7, 1827. *J. F. Campbell* appointed first Collector of Customs in New South Wales, being the first officer who bore that title, 1827.

CUSTOMS DUTIES. Meetings held in Sydney and different parts of the colony, and petitions adopted praying the Home Government for admission of wheat, maize, and flour into the English ports on the same terms on which the Canadian grain was allowed, 1845; the duty on spirits reduced one-half, in order to put a stop to illicit distillation, 1845; a resolution passed in the Legislative Assembly, New South Wales, to abolish the duty on tea and sugar, on the motion of Mr. Parkes, was carried by a majority of one, 29 voting for it and 28 against it, September 3, 1859. [A motion was afterwards moved for rescinding the resolution, which was carried by a majority of 40 to 21. The revenue derived from this source was £150,000 per annum.] abolition of *ad valorem* duties New South Wales, January 1, 1874.

CUSTOMS FRACAS in Melbourne between the authorities and the soft-goods firm of Stevenson and Sons, Flinders Lane, April 15, 1876.

TARIFF. The Border Customs tariff treaty between New South Wales and Victoria passed 1867; a despatch from Lord Kimberly received, objecting to the complex tariff between the Australian Colonies, July 13, 1871.

THE CUSTOMS HOUSE
Sydney Punch, 1864 (A satirical comment on border customs.)

D

DARLING, RALPH.

Governor of New South Wales, arrived in 1821; party feeling was very high against the Governor in 1829. The Governor was assailed by the Opposition, and an impeachment was got up and sent home for his alleged mis-government. The friends of the Governor, consisting of "landed proprietors and merchants," presented an address to him, in which they stated that they were convinced that every act of his administration emanated from the purest motives. This address was presented by Messrs. A. Berry, R. Jones, W. B. Browne, G. Bunn, Icely, and A. B. Spark, and bore the signature of 120 persons. The Governor was openly insulted whilst in conversation with the Colonial Secretary after Divine Service on the Sabbath. The assailant came up to the Governor and exclaimed "You are a —— scoundrel." He was immediately seized. A carving knife and two pistols were found on him. The alleged cause of this assault was disappointment in regard to an application for a grant of land, to which the applicant imagined he had a right, but could produce no proofs in support of his claim, and it was rejected, December 20, 1829. [See SUDDS AND THOMPSON.]

Proceedings touching the impeachment of Governor Darling brought forward in the House of Commons, 1830. [The impeachment was supported by Mr. Stewart, Mr. Joseph Hume, and Mr. Daniel O'Connell, and was opposed by Sir George Murray, who then held the office of Secretary for the Colonies. The discussion brought no other result than to show that the affairs of the colony had raised an interest in the highest quarters, and the proceedings were brought to a termination.]

DARLING DOWNS, discovered and named by Allan Cunningham, June 5, 1827.

DARLING, RIVER, discovered by Captain Sturt. [Known at its rise as the Karaula, or Calewatta, changing afterwards to the Barwon, and subsequently to the Darling.] February 4, 1829. [See RIVERS.]

DAWSON, RIVER, discovered November 11, 1844. [See RIVERS.]

DECEASED WIFE'S SISTER, MARRIAGE WITH. Colonial Acts of Parliament have been passed to declare valid the marriage of a man with his deceased wife's sister. Assented to in South Australia, June, 1871; in Victoria, November, 1873; and in New South Wales, July 21, 1875. [It has also become law in Queensland.]

DEFENCES. The Home Government proposed to send out military labour to execute the necessary works for the defence of Port Jackson, provided the colony paid the men, but the Council refused the offer until the local Legislature was invested with the entire control of the colonial revenue, territorial as well as general: ultimately carried by the casting vote of the Speaker, Dec., 1851; meeting held in Sydney in consequence of the intelligence of the news of the war between Russia and Turkey, when upwards of two thousand persons were present, and an address to the Queen was adopted, in which it stated unalterable devotion and loyalty to Her Majesty, and to assist to the utmost of their ability to maintain the honour of the British flag and the safety of this portion of Her Majesty's dominions. Two resolutions were adopted, one to call in the combined action of all the available strength of the colony, the other that the citizens were prepared to support the Executive Government in all the needful measures for the protection of the colony against foreign invasion, 1854; to enable the colonies to take effectual measures for their defence against attacks by sea the "Colonial Naval Defence Act" was passed in 1865; Colonial Branch Army Act passed, 1866; "Cerberus," monitor, for the defence of Port Phillip,

DEFENCES AT PORT PHILLIP HEADS
The Australasian Sketcher, 1878

arrived in Hobson's Bay, April 7, 1871; trial of harbour defences, Sydney, nearly three thousand men mustered, March 25, 1871; a sum of £30,000 voted by the Legislative Assembly of New South Wales for works of fortification and defence, June 12, 1871; telegram received that Sir W. F. D. Jervois and Colonel Scratchley had been selected by the British Government to report upon the capabilities for defence of the Australian colonies, February 22, 1877; Sir William Jervois arrived in Sydney to report on the Australian defences, April, 1877; Sir W. Jervois and Lieutenant-Colonel Scratchley arrived in Melbourne, June 11, 1877; Sir H. Parkes submitted resolutions to the New South Wales Assembly substantially embodying the scheme of defences advised by Sir W. Jervois in his report, June 14, 1877; Sir William Jervois' report on the defences of Port Phillip Bay, Victoria, published, July 24, 1877; scheme of Sir W. Jervois for defence of Adelaide submitted to Parliament, December 12, 1877.

DIAMONDS. E. H. Hargraves reported discovery of diamonds and other precious stones in New South Wales, July 2, 1851; several diamonds found at Oberon, New South Wales, October 3, 1872; three hundred and seventy-five diamonds received in Sydney from Bingera, New South Wales, March 8, 1873.

DISTILLATION. Private distillation extensively practised, 1796; distillation first permitted, December 30, 1821. One person was fined £500 for illicit distillation in Sydney. The fine was paid, July 21, 1843. A conviction against another, for illicit distillation, caused some excitement; the offender appealed to the Supreme Court, Sydney, against the conviction of the Parramatta Bench of Magistrates, when the conviction was set aside, through some oversight in the Crown law offices, in the issue of Commissions of Peace, for certain parties to act as magistrates in the city of Sydney and the county of Cumberland, whereby all the magistrates in the colony except those who had been mentioned in the new commission, had been acting for fourteen months without authority. The result was, that, three days after the circumstance was known, a new Commission of the Peace was issued, and the Legislative Council was immediately summoned, when a bill of Indemnity was passed for what had been magisterially transacted during that time; 1844. Seizure of illicit stills at a wholesale grocery establishment in George-street, Sydney, September 12, 1870; [the stills, plant, and materials confiscated, and the defendants were punished by being fined in heavy penalties]; seizure of illicit stills in a house, near Victoria Bridge, Ipswich Road, Queensland, March 1 and 2, 1879; seizure of

DRY DOCK AT WATERVIEW BAY
The Illustrated Sydney News, 1854

illicit stills in a vinegar manufactory in Fortitude Valley, Queensland, March 3, 1879.

[*See* SMUGGLING.]

DOCKS.

Dry dock at Waterview Bay, Port Jackson, better known as Mort's Dock. Length 365 feet, width 70 feet, depth 19 feet, finished, 1856.

Fitzroy Dock, Cockatoo Island, length 356 feet; width 83 feet, depth 21½ feet; foundation stone laid, June 5, 1854; first vessel entered, December 1, 1857.

Alfred Dock, Williamstown, Victoria, completed, September 6, 1873; [the Albert Graving Dock at Williamstown is the property of the Government, and is by far the largest dry dock at present in the southern hemisphere. It is constructed of the basalt or bluestone of the neighbourhood, and is 450 feet in length on the floor, and 465 feet over all. It is 97 feet between the copings, and 80 feet wide at the entrance; and it has a depth of water, over the sill, at ordinary tides of 24 feet 6 inches at low water, and of 26 feet 6 inches at high water. The cost of the dock proper has been about £223,000, and the pumping machinery and caisson, both of which were made in the colony, cost about £20,000 in addition]; first ship entered the Alfred Dock, March 2, 1874.

Graving dock, Brisbane, commenced, (contracted to be finished in three years) January 28, 1876; [dimensions: 300 feet long; width, inside dock on top, 75 feet, at bottom, 40 feet; depth of water on sill at low water, 12 feet 2 inches; at high water, 22 feet; cost of dock, £62,796].

DRAMA, THE.

First theatrical performance in Australia. Play of Farquhar's comedy "The Recruiting-officer," performed by some prisoners to celebrate the King's birthday, at Sydney, N.S.W., June 4, 1789.

The first theatre erected in Sydney (at a cost of £100) was opened January 16, 1796. The performance was Dr. Young's tragedy "The Revenge," and "The Hotel" as an after-piece. The manager's name was Sparrow, and the actors were Messrs. Green, Hawkes, Hughes, Chapman, and Mrs. Davis. George Barrington, the notorious pickpocket, is the accredited author of the celebrated Prologue, which was read on the rising of the curtain, as follows:—

PROLOGUE.

From distant climes, o'er wide-spread seas we come,
Though not with much *éclat*, or beat of drum;
True patriots, all, for be it understood,
We left our country for our country's good:
No private views disgrac'd our generous zeal,
What urg'd our travels, was our country's weal;
And none will doubt, but that our emigration,
Has proved most useful to the British nation.
But you inquire, what could our breasts inflame,
With this new passion for theatric fame;

What, in the practice of our former days,
Could shape our talents to exhibit plays?
Your patience, sirs, some observations made,
You'll grant us equal to the scenic trade.
He who to midnight ladders is no stranger,
You'll own will make an admirable Ranger.
To seek Macheath we have not far to roam,
And sure in Filch I shall be quite at home.
Unrivalled there, none will dispute my claim,
To high pre-eminence and exalted fame.
As oft on Gadshill we have ta'en our stand,
When 'twas so dark you could not see your hand,
Some true-bred Falstaff, we may hope to start,
Who, when well-bolstered, well will play his part.
The scene to vary, we shall try in time
To treat you with a little Pantomime.
Here light and easy Columbines are found,
And well-tried Harlequins with us abound;
From durance vile our precious selves to keep,
We often had recourse to th' flying leap;
To a black face have sometimes ow'd escape,
And Hounslow Heath has proved the worth of crape.
But how, you ask, can we e'er hope to soar
Above these scenes, and rise to tragic lore?
Too oft, alas! we've forced th' unwilling tear,
And petrified the heart with real fear.
Macbeth a harvest of applause will reap,
For some of us, I fear, have murdered sleep;
His lady too, with grace will sleep and talk,
Our females have been used at night to walk.
Sometimes, indeed, so various is our art,
An actor may improve and mend his part;
"Give me a horse," bawls Richard, like a drone,
We'll find a man would help himself to one.
Grant us your favour, put us to the test,
To gain your smiles we'll do our very best;
And without dread of future Turnkey Lockits,
Thus, in an honest way, still pick your pockets.

[The price of a seat in the gallery—the most commodious and fashionable part of the house—was fixed at a shilling's worth of spirits, flour, meat, or other articles of general use. After the theatre had been opened a short time it became very popular, and every device was practised by the worst class of convicts to obtain the means of admission. One fellow killed a fine greyhound belonging to an officer, and after skinning it succeeded in palming its joints off for kangaroo flesh, at the rate of 9d. per pound. Crime increased to such a marked extent, that the Governor issued an order for levelling the place with the ground. 1798.]

Sir Richard Bourke granted a license to Mr. Barnett Levy for dramatic performances. Mr. Levy was at that time owner of the Royal Hotel, and he fitted up the saloon of that establishment as a theatre. He caused a theatre to be built, which was termed the "Theatre Royal," in 1833. The first manager was Mr. Meredith, who was succeeded by Mr. Simmons.

Victoria Theatre, Sydney, opened March 17, 1838.

Queen's Theatre Royal, in Queen-street, Melbourne, opened May 1, 1845.

Mr. George Coppin's first appearance, Queen's Theatre, Melbourne, June 21, 1845.

George Coppin built Olympic Theatre, Melbourne, 1854.

Julia Mathews, youthful Australian actress, appeared at the Victoria Theatre, Sydney, January 2, 1855.

George Coppin appeared at the Victoria

SCENE FROM OTHELLO
The Illustrated Sydney News, 1854

Theatre, Sydney, January 8, 1855.

Joseph Rayner and Mrs. Charles Poole appeared at Victoria Theatre, Sydney, April 16, 1855.

G. V. Brooke, Fanny Cathcart (Mrs. Robert Heir, now Mrs. Geo. Darrell), Robert Heir, and Richard Young appeared at Victoria Theatre, Sydney, May 15, 1855.

Lola Montez appeared at Victoria Theatre, Sydney, August 23, 1855.

Charles Young, Mrs. Charles Young (now Mrs. Herman Vezin), and J. P. Hydes appeared at Prince of Wales Theatre, Sydney, November 6, 1855.

G. V. Brooke appeared at Queen's Theatre, Melbourne, as Othello, February 26, 1856.

Mr. and Mrs. James Stark appeared at Victoria Theatre, Sydney, April 18, 1856.

William Hoskins appeared at the Victoria Theatre, Sydney, July 7, 1856.

Julia Harland (Mrs. W. Hoskins) appeared at Victoria Theatre, Sydney, July 8, 1856.

Marie Duret appeared at Victoria Theatre, Sydney, July 14, 1856.

John Dunn appeared at Victoria Theatre, Sydney, July 21, 1856.

Adelaide and Joey (Mrs. Constable) Gougenheim appeared at Lyceum Theatre, Sydney, October 6, 1856.

M'Kean Buchanan appeared at Victoria Theatre, Sydney, October 6, 1856.

Charles Burford appeared at Victoria Theatre, Sydney, October 30, 1856.

First appearance of Mary Provost at the Victoria Theatre, Sydney, March 14, 1859.

First appearance of John Drew, the Irish Comedian, at Victoria, Sydney, June 8, 1859.

Sir William Don arrived in Melbourne 1860.

Prince of Wales Theatre, Sydney, destroyed by fire, October 3, 1860; rebuilt, 1863.

Barry Sullivan appeared as "Hamlet" at Theatre Royal, Melbourne, 1863.

Mr. J. J. Bartlett's first appearance in Melbourne, July, 1863.

Charles Kean, accompanied by Mrs. Kean, arrived in Victoria from England, September 25, 1863.

Mr. and Mrs. Charles Kean made first appearance at the Haymarket Theatre, Melbourne, in "The Gamester," October 10, 1863.

Joseph Jefferson appeared as "Rip Van Winkle" at the Princess Theatre, Melbourne, 1863.

Madame Celeste appeared in the "Woman in Red" at the Haymarket Theatre, Melbourne, 1866.

Anderson appeared as "Hamlet" at the Haymarket Theatre, Melbourne, 1867.

Walter Montgomery, the celebrated actor, made his first appearance in Australia at the Theatre Royal, Melbourne, July 20, 1867; last appearance in Sydney, May 25, 1869; departed for England, June 3, 1869.

Mr. Charles Mathews, the accomplished comedian and actor, reappeared at the Prince of Wales Opera House, Sydney, January 14, 1871.

Last appearance of Mr. and Mrs. Charles Mathews in Australia. Farewell address read at the Prince of Wales Opera House by Mr. Bartlett, January 28, 1871.

Mr. Howe, the tragedian, appeared at the Prince of Wales Opera House as "Rip Van Winkle," February 9, 1871.

Madame Agatha States (with Signor Orlandini, Signor Susini, and Signor Cecci) Opera Company—conductor, Signor Giorza—first appeared at Masonic Hall, Sydney, January 3, 1872.

Prince of Wales Opera House, Sydney, destroyed by fire, January 6, 1872.

Theatre Royal, Melbourne, opened November, 1872.

Mr. and Mrs. F. M. Bates' first appearance in Australia, at Melbourne, August 4, 1873.

Hattie Shepparde (Mrs. Hy. Hallam), the well-known actress, died in Melbourne, aged 26, September 21, 1874.

J. C. Lambert, well-known on Australian stage, died in England April 30, 1875.

Lady Don, an actress very popular in Australia, widow of Sir Wm. Don, Bart., died in London, September 24, 1875.

Adelaide Ristori, celebrated tragedienne, appeared at the Victoria Theatre, Sydney, July 26, 1875.

Theatre Royal (formerly Prince of Wales Theatre), Sydney, opened December 11, 1875.

News received from California of the death of Miss Julia Mathews, a favourite actress on the Australian stage, June 20, 1876.

Mrs. Alfred Phillips, for many years a popular actress in Melbourne, died August 12, 1876.

Majeroni (Italian tragedian, Ristori Company) appeared for the first time in English at the Theatre Royal, Sydney, April 17, 1876.

Wm. Creswick appeared in "Hamlet" at the Victoria Theatre, Sydney, February 16, 1878.

Mrs. Scott-Siddons opened a farewell season at the Queen's Theatre, Sydney, March 23, 1878.

DROUGHT. A long drought prevailed and great heat experienced, the thermometer standing at 80° at 4 o'clock in the afternoon and frequently at midnight at 70°, 1823; three years' drought occurred in the colony of New South Wales, 1825-6-7; one of the most severe droughts ever known in New South Wales, with great scarcity of water in Sydney and suburbs, only two months' supply being left in the Botany dams, and water being sold at a very high rate in Parramatta-street and other localities for people in the suburbs, occurred March, April, 1876; [the water was cut off nearly all day in the city, and in the suburbs turned on only for an hour or two in the evening; a water famine was daily expected, when rain came and relieved apprehension].

DUELLING.

The following are the only particulars of a duel between Lieutenant-Colonel Paterson and Captain Macarthur, New South Wales Corps. "Governor's Order, Sydney, September 14, 1801. The Governor deeply laments that circumstances should have operated so forcibly on the mind of Lieutenant-Colonel Paterson, commanding officer of the New South Wales Corps, as to exact private satisfaction for the injury it appeared to him that his honour had received from Captain Macarthur, of the same corps, whereby the King's service and the welfare of the colony may experience a great loss. In consequence of the

result of the encounter, and the surgeons having declared that the Lieutenant-Colonel's life is by no means out of danger, Captains Macarthur, Piper, and M'Kellar are to be put under a close arrest until the surgeons pronounce him in a state of convalesence, or that the officer's life being out of danger." "Governor's Order, September 21.—Although the surgeons have this day reported that Lieutenant-Colonel Paterson is not yet out of danger from the wound he received on the 14th instant, yet, as the eight days limited for a military arrest expire this day, Captains Macarthur, Piper, and M'Kellar, principal and seconds in the unfortunate encounter, in which Lieut.-Colonel Paterson was wounded, are to be released from arrest, into which they were ordered by the general orders of the 14th instant, and notwithstanding the impropriety of admitting persons to bail situated as these officers are, yet the same reasons that operated with the Governor in committing them to a military arrest, rather than to the public gaol, induces him to admit of their giving bail, and proper security for their appearance before a court of criminal judicature. These officers, as well as Lieutenant-Colonel Paterson, are to give security, and to enter into recognisances for keeping the peace towards each other as long as they are in this territory and its dependencies." It appears by an order dated September 23, that Lieutenant-Colonel Paterson and Captains Piper and M'Kellar entered into sureties to keep the peace, but Captain Macarthur would not, and therefore declined to free himself from arrest. It was therefore ordered by the Governor "that Captain John Macarthur do prepare himself to embark for England in the arrest he has thought proper to place himself under." The affair was afterwards settled amicably. [Colonel Paterson was subsequently acting Governor of New South Wales, during the time that Bligh was under arrest, and Captain Macarthur was then acting Colonial Secretary.]

Mr. Saxe Bannister, the Attorney General of New South Wales, and Dr. Wardell fought a duel of a harmless character, October 21, 1826.

Mr. Henry MacDermott, an alderman and afterwards Mayor of Sydney, challenged Robert Lowe, M.P., to a duel. Mr. Lowe declined the combat, and had Mr. MacDermott and his seconder, Captain Moore and Dr. M'Farlane, bound over to keep the peace, 1844.

Duel between Mr. Stuart Alexander Donaldson, a member of the Legislative Council of New South Wales, and Sir Thomas Mitchell, Surveyor General of the colony of New South Wales, in consequence of the latter characterising the statement of Mr. Donaldson to his constituents of Durham county, relative to the expenses of the Surveyor General's department, as "false;" three shots were exchanged—one shot whizzed close to the ear of Sir Thomas, and Mr. Donaldson's hat was penetrated by a bullet from his adversary's pistol; the seconds here interfered, and the combatants left the ground, but without a reconciliation, September 27, 1851.

EARTHQUAKES.

The first earthquake recorded in Australia is thus described by Governor Phillip :—" Slight shock of earthquake in the newly formed settlement of Sydney Cove. It did not last more than two or three seconds. It was felt by most people in camp, and by the Governor himself, who heard at the same time a noise to the south, and which he took at first to be the reports of guns fired at a great distance. The earth teemed with a sulphurous odour for some time after," June 22, 1788.

Earthquake felt in Sydney Jan. 17, 1800.

Shock of earthquake felt at Sydney, Jan. 17, 1801.

Earthquake in Sydney, Feb. 7, 1801.

Shock of earthquake felt at Parramatta, Prospect, and the Hawkesbury, May 7, 1804.

Earthquake strongly felt at Richmond, New South Wales, Sept. 24, 1806.

Earthquake at Launceston, Nov. 28, 1823.

Smart shock of earthquake felt at Melbourne and neighbourhood, " being the third similar visitation which had been experienced since the formation of the settlement," Aug. 21, 1841.

Earthquake experienced in New South Wales, and felt at Windsor, Newcastle, Port Stephens, Macleay River, and Patrick's Plains, Oct. 28, 184

Earthquake at Wellington, New Zealand, Oct. 16 and 17, 1848.

Earthquake at Melbourne, Sep. 17, 1852.

Earthquake at Christchurch, New Zealand, Jan. 23, 1855.

Earthquake in Melbourne, Jan. 10, 1867.

Earthquake in New Zealand, Oct. 19, 1868.

Shock of earthquake felt at Bombala, N.S.W., 1869.

Smart shock of earthquake at Braidwood, N. S. W., Jan. 3, 1871.

Shock of earthquake felt at Goulburn, Yass, Albury, and Wagga Wagga, as well as other townships of New South Wales, June 8 and 12, 1871.

Severe shock of earthquake at Braidwood, N. S. W., June 2, 1872.

Earthquake in Sydney and throughout New South Wales, Oct. 18, 1872.

Shock of earthquake at Queanbeyan, N.S.W., Nov. 18, 1872.

Shock of earthquake felt at Buman, South Australia, Jan. 25, 1873.

Sharp shocks of earthquake experienced at Maryborough, Avoca, and other districts in Victoria.

Earthquake at Wellington, March 13, 1875.

Shock of earthquake felt at Bega and Eden, N. S. W., July 11, 1875.

Earthquake at Warwick, Queensland, Nov. 24, 1875.

Earthquake at Port Darwin, Dec. 7, 1876.

Smart shock of earthquake felt at Castlemaine and the surrounding districts, Victoria, Jan. 21, 1877.

Shock of earthquake felt at Melbourne, June 25, 1877.

EDUCATION is provided in all the Australian colonies and New Zealand largely at the expense of the Government. The system of education is by the aid of universities, colleges, grammar schools, and public and private schools. By the " Public Schools Acts" of Queensland, Victoria, South Australia, Western Australia, and Tasmania, education is compulsory, and in these and all the colonies it is secular and free, though denominational tenets are taught outside specified school hours.

New South Wales is indebted for her Public Schools Act passed in 1867, to Sir Henry Parkes.

Mr. (now Judge) Lilley introduced, for the first time, free education into Australia (Queensland) in 1870.

EMANCIPISTS. A first general meeting of emancipated colonists was held to petition His Majesty George IV. for a redress of their grievances. The grievances complained of were that they had acquired and had become possessed of property in the colony, and that from the commencement of the colony until April, 1820, it had been resolved that persons arriving in the colony under sentence of transportation and afterwards obtaining their pardon, might acquire and possess landed and other property, and enjoy all the civil rights of free citizens, but by a determination of the Court of King's Bench, and acted upon by the civil courts of the colony, that conditional and absolute pardons granted by governors in the colony were of no effect to the parties holding them in restoring them to any legal enjoyment of any civil right, until their names should be inserted in some general pardon under the Great Seal of England; they had in consequence been exposed to infinite prejudice and danger, that this state of the law affected a very considerable part of the property possessed by the emigrant colonists, and that this had been derived through and from the emancipists : January 23, 1821.

EMIGRATION. Great number of persons emigrated from New South Wales to Valparaiso, 1843.

RICH EMANCIPIST, THE LEGENDARY SAMUEL TERRY
The Penny Satirist, London, 1838

EPIDEMICS.

Severe epidemical catarrh prevailed throughout the colony; many people, whites and blacks, died after a few days suffering, August, 1820.

Whooping cough first made its appearance in the colony, being introduced by the ship "Morley," and many persons, old and young, were swept off, amongst whom was the son of Governor Darling, March, 1828.

The ship "America," Captain M'Donald, arrived from London with 169 male prisoners. In consequence of measles appearing on board, and a soldier and seven prisoners dying, the vessel was put in quarantine, August 18, 1829.

The ship "Minerva," with 285 immigrants, arrived in Port Jackson, having typhus fever on board. She went into quarantine, January 23, 1838. [The passengers were finally relieved on April 16th following. 18 males and 15 females died.]

The influenza very prevalent in the colony, it being estimated that no less than 10,000 persons were afflicted, many of whom died, 1838.

Scarlatina made its first appearance in Sydney and prevailed to a considerable extent, a large number of children died, 1841.

Asiatic cholera appeared in Melbourne, 1841.

Measles prevalent in Victoria, November, 1874.

[*See* SMALL-POX.]

BRING OUT YOUR DEAD; OR, WHAT IT MAY COME TO
Melbourne Punch, 1869

EUREKA STOCKADE, taken by storm on the morning of Sunday, December 2, 1854. [It occupied about an acre, and was situated in Ballarat East, Victoria, between the present Eureka, Stawell, Rodier, and George streets.]

[*See* Riots.]

EXECUTIONS.

The First Execution in Australia was that of a youth aged 17, named James Barrett, executed for robbery in New South Wales, March 6, 1788.

EXTRAORDINARY FAILURE OF.

Joseph Samuels, who, on September 12, 1803, was tried and convicted at the Criminal Sessions for the robbery of a desk containing money, the property of Mary Breeze, at Sydney, was thrice suspended, September 20, 1803. [The cord first separated in the middle, and the criminal fell prostrate; on the second attempt the rope unrove at the fastening, and he again came to the ground; and the third time being launched off, the rope again snapped short. The Provost-Marshal Mr. Smith, (a man universally respected) compassionating his protracted suffering, proceeded to Government House, and represented all those extraordinary circumstances to the Governor, who was pleased to reprieve Samuels.]

PLACES OF. The gallows in Sydney were removed in 1804 to the corner of Park and Castlereagh streets, where the Barley Mow publichouse now stands; afterwards erected near the site of Barker's Mills, in Sussex-street; again on the east corner of the Protestant burial ground, near Strawberry Hill; then on the sand hills to the back of the new Military Barracks; and in the year 1820 to the old Gaol, in Lower George-street; and finally to the gate of the new Gaol at Darlinghurst. The first execution at the Darlinghurst Gaol took place, October 29, 1841.

LIST OF.

New South Wales.

Styles, for murder of Thomas Roberts, executed at Sydney, July 5, 1815.

Nineteen prisoners (out of twenty-six capitally convicted at the Criminal Sessions) executed at Sydney, August, 1821.

Black Tommy, aboriginal native of Bathurst district, for murder, executed at Sydney, December 31, 1827.

John Holmes, for setting fire to a barn belonging to James Bem, executed at Sydney, August 21, 1829.

A young desperado, named Tierney, 17 years of age, executed at Sydney, 1830. [When on the scaffold, he threw the executioner with himself to the ground; the former, being much bruised by the fall, could scarcely be persuaded to proceed with his duty.]

A soldier of the 39th Regiment, named Brennan, under sentence by a Court-Martial, shot, at Dawes' Battery, Sydney, April 6, 1832.

Hitchcock, Poole, Riley, Perry, Jones, and Ryan, six assigned servants of Major Mudie, for being concerned in an insurrection at "Castle Forbes" station, executed at Sydney, December 12, 1834. [The men did not attempt to deny their offence, but persisted in the statement that they had been goaded on to their crime by the tyranny and ill-treatment which they had been subject to on the station. A Commission was appointed to inquire into the circumstances, the result being a condemnation of the mode in which the assigned servants were dealt with at "Castle Forbes," and Major Mudie was struck out of the Commission of the Peace.]

Kilmartin, for murder, executed at Sydney, May 11, 1834.

John Jenkins, for murder of Dr. Wardell, executed at Sydney, November 10, 1834.

Thomas Tattersdale, for murder of Dr. Wardell, executed at Sydney, November 10, 1834.

Wm. Morris, for murder, executed at Sydney, November 26, 1839.

Joseph Saunders, for murder and robbery, executed at Sydney, November 26, 1839.

Peter Scullion, for murder and robbery, executed at Sydney, November 26, 1839.

George Carey, for having stolen property in possession, executed at Sydney, November 26, 1839.

George Gorman, for murder, executed at Sydney, November 26, 1839.

Alexander Telford, for murder and having firearms, &c., executed at Sydney, November 29, 1839.

James Davis, for murder and having firearms, &c., executed at Sydney, November 29, 1839.

Llewellyn Powell, for murder, executed at Sydney, November 29, 1839.

James Lynch, for murder, executed at Sydney, November 29, 1839.

Charles Clipp, for murder, executed at Sydney, November 29, 1839.

Archibald Taylor, for felony, executed at Sydney, November 29, 1839.

John Hunt, for murder, executed at Sydney, March 10, 1840.

A CARICATURE OF CONVICT PUNISHMENT
A Muster Master by An Old Van Diemean, Mitchell Library

Thomas Whitton, for murder and arson, executed at Sydney, March 19, 1840.

Enoch Bradley, for murder, executed at Sydney, December 11, 1840.

Thomas Legg, for rape, executed at Sydney, December 11, 1840.

William Newman, for murder, executed at Sydney, December 8, 1840.

James Martin, for murder, executed at Sydney, December 8, 1840.

James Mason, for being an accessory to murder, executed at Sydney, December 8, 1840.

Michael Hinnigan, for murder, executed at Sydney, December 11, 1840.

Ed. Davis, Robt. Chitty, Jas. Everett, John Shea, John Marshall, Jas. Bryant, and Richd. Glanville were part of what were termed the Jew Boy's Gang (Davis being the Jew Boy), who for nearly twelve months had kept the residents of the Hunter River district in terror by numerous daring outrages and murders. They were executed in Sydney, March 16, 1841.

Michael Bradley, for murder, executed at Newcastle, N.S.W., April 5, 1841.

Patrick Curran, a notorious bushranger, for the murder of an overseer, executed at Berrima, October 21, 1841.

George Stroud and Robert Hudson, for murder, executed at Berrima, October 29, 1841.

Patrick Clearham, executed at Berrima, April 22, 1842.

John Lynch, or Dunleary, for the murder of Landregan; he confessed to having committed seven other murders; executed at Berrima, April 22, 1842.

Martin Beech, for murder, executed at Berrima, October 22, 1842.

Lucretia Dunkley, for murder, executed at Berrima, October 22, 1842.

Thomas Horner, for murder, executed at Newcastle, November 10, 1842.

George Wilson, shooting with intent, executed at Newcastle, 1843.

George Forrester, for murder, executed at Newcastle, 1843.

Melville (aboriginal), for murder, executed at Newcastle, 1843.

Harry (aboriginal), for murder, executed at Newcastle, 1843.

Therramitahie (aboriginal), for murder, executed at Port Macquarie, 1843.

Benjamin Harris, for murder, executed at Port Macquarie, 1844.

Mary Thornton, for murder, executed at Port Macquarie, 1844.

Joseph Vale, for murder, executed at Port Macquarie, 1844.

Benjamin Stanley, for murder, executed at Port Macquarie, 1844.

John Knatchbull, for murder of Mrs. Jameson, executed at Sydney, February 13, 1844.

Henry Atkins, for murder, executed at Berrima, October 8, 1844.

John Viddall, for murder, executed at Sydney, February 7, 1845.

John Ahern, for murder, executed at Sydney, August 12, 1845.

James Fitzpatrick, for murder, executed at Newcastle, 1845.

William Shea, for murder, executed at Newcastle, 1846.

Patrick Ryan, for murder, executed at Newcastle, 1848.

Charles Henry Mackie, for rape, executed at Bathurst, November 10, 1848.

William Fyfe, for murder, executed at Sydney, July 4, 1848.

Robert Walsh, for murder, executed at Bathurst, October 26, 1849.

George Waters Ward, for murder, executed at Newcastle, 1849.

William Hayes, for murder, executed at Newcastle, 1850.

James Whelan, for murder, executed at Sydney, November 5, 1850.

Mago (aboriginal), for murder, executed at Sydney, November 5, 1850.

Michael Collihanee (*alias* Mickey-bad-English) for rape, executed at Newcastle, 1851.

Thomas Wilmore, for murder, executed at Bathurst, April 14, 1852.

Thomas F. Green, for murder, executed at Sydney, September 21, 1852.

Timothy Sullivan, for murder, executed at Bathurst, September 30, 1852.

Newina (Chinese), for murder, executed at Bathurst, September 30, 1852.

Patrick Macnamara, for murder, executed at Newcastle, November 3, 1852.

Patrick M'Carthy, for murder, executed at Bathurst, April 11, 1853.

Paddy (aboriginal), for rape, executed at Bathurst, April 11, 1853.

Daniel Thomas Gardner, for murder, executed at Maitland, February 23, 1854.

James M'Laughlin, for murder, executed at Bathurst, April 25, 1854.

Billy Palmer, for murder, executed at Bathurst, April 25, 1854.

James Tabbott, for murder, executed at Goulburn, May 30, 1854.

Christopher Walsh, for murder, executed at Maitland, August 28, 1854.

Samuel Wilcox, for murder, executed at Sydney, July 5, 1855.

Mary A. Brownlow, for murder, executed at Goulburn, October 11, 1855.

Addison Mitchell, for murder, executed at Bathurst, May 7, 1857.

Henry Curran, for rape, executed at Bathurst, May 7, 1857.

Patrick Walsh, for murder, executed Goulburn, November 4, 1857.

James Moyes, for murder, executed at Sydney, September 7, 1858.

John Arrow, for murder, executed at Bathurst, May 11, 1859.

William Martin *alias* Thomas Ryan, robbery with firearms, and rape, executed at Bathurst, May 11, 1859.

John Scabby Harry, for rape, executed at Goulburn, May 18, 1859.

John Norris, for rape, executed at Sydney, July 22, 1859.

Robert Davis, for murder, executed at Bathurst, November 3, 1859.

Frederick Clarke, for murder, executed at Goulburn, May 8, 1860.

Ellen Monks, for murder, executed at Goulburn, May 8, 1860.

William Goodson, for murder, executed at Sydney, May 16, 1860.

John Jones, for murder, executed at Maitland, November 15, 1860.

Harry (aboriginal), for murder, executed at Maitland, September 16, 1861.

William Johnstone, for rape, executed at Goulburn, December 3, 1861.

John Peisley, for murder, executed at Bathurst, April 25, 1862.

Jackey Bull (aboriginal), for murder, executed at Bathurst, April 25, 1862.

John Smith *alias* Regan, for stealing gold and stabbing, executed at Goulburn, May 5, 1862.

Henry Kane, for murder, executed at Goulburn, May 5, 1862.

Benjamin Allerton, for robbery with arms, executed at Goulburn May 5, 1862.

Jackey (aboriginal), for rape, executed at Bathurst, October 23, 1862.

Alexander Ross, for robbery and wounding, executed at Sydney, March 18, 1863.

Charles Ross, for robbery and wounding, executed at Sydney, March 18, 1863.

William Marcus, for robbery and wounding, executed at Sydney, March 26, 1863.

Charles Robaay, for murder, executed at Goulburn, May 13, 1863.

Mahommet Cassen, for murder, executed at Goulburn, May 23, 1863.

Henry Wilson, for murder, executed at Maitland, August 3, 1863.

Thomas M'Cann, for wounding with intent, executed at Sydney, February 1, 1864.

James Stewart, for murder, executed at Bathurst, November 22, 1864.

George Gibson *alias* Paddy Tom, for mail robbery and murder, executed at Bathurst, May 20, 1865.

Ah Lun, for murder, executed at Bathurst, November 21, 1865.

Sam Poo, for murder, executed at Bathurst, December 19, 1865.

John Dunn, for murder, executed at Sydney, March 19, 1866.

Michael Green, for murder, executed at Sydney, June 11, 1866.

Charles Crookwell, for murder, executed at Sydney, July 2, 1866.

Spider (aboriginal), for rape, executed at Bathurst, November 26, 1866.

Michael Maher *alias* Murray, for murder, executed at Bathurst, December 3, 1866.

Henry Sues, for murder, executed at Goulburn, December 10, 1866.

William H. Scott, for murder, executed at Sydney, March 18, 1867.

William Peters, for assault with intent, executed at Bathurst, June 19, 1867.

John Clarke, for wounding with intent, executed at Sydney, June 25, 1867.

Thomas Clarke, for wounding with intent, executed at Sydney, June 25, 1867.

O'Farrell, H. J., for shooting H.R.H. Prince Alfred, at the Sailor's Home Picnic, March 12, 1868, at Clontarf, Middle Harbour, Sydney, New South Wales, was executed at Sydney, April 21, 1868. [O'Farrell shot His Royal Highness in the back, and with a second shot, before he could be seized, wounded Mr. Thorne in the foot. His trial took place before Mr. Justice

Cheeke, on the 30th and 31st of the same month, when sentence of death was passed upon him. He was executed at Darlinghurst Gaol on April 21, 1868.]

Robert Barnes, for murder, executed at Bathurst, May 26, 1868.

John M'Kervett, for murder, executed at Bathurst, May 26, 1868.

William Munday *alias* Collins, for murder (Conroy Gap), executed at Goulburn, June 2, 1868.

Ah Sun, for murder, executed at Bathurst, November 24, 1868.

Robert Campbell *alias* Palmer, for murder (Pohlman Brothers), executed at Wagga Wagga, October 5, 1870.

Chong Gow, for murder, executed at Deniliquin, June 6, 1871.

Michael M'Mahon, for murder, executed at Maitland, October 21, 1871.

Thomas Kelly, for felonious assault, executed at Sydney, January 2, 1872.

John Conn *alias* Coins, for murder, executed at Bathurst, June 4, 1872.

William M'Crow, for murder, executed at Sydney, April 8, 1872.

Thomas Scource, for murder, executed at Sydney, April 8, 1872.

George Robert Nicholls, for murder at Parramatta River, executed at Sydney, June 18, 1872.

Alfred Lyster, *alias* Froude, for murder at Parramatta River, executed at Sydney, June 18, 1872.

William Krauss, for murder of Captain Longmuir, executed at Sydney, July 1, 1873.

Henry V. Jarvis, for murder, executed at Sydney, December 23, 1873.

John Hawthorne, for attempt to murder, executed at Goulburn, May 19, 1874.

John Glover, for murder, executed at Goulburn, May 19, 1874.

Gottleb Eichborn, for rape, executed at Armidale, June 23, 1874.

John M'Grath, for murder, executed at Sydney, September 14, 1875.

George Rope, for murder, executed at Mudgee, December 7, 1875.

George Pitt, for murder, executed at Mudgee, June 21, 1876.

Michael Connolly, for murder, executed at Mudgee, June 28, 1876.

Daniel Boon, for shooting with intent (Alexander M'Mahon), executed at Wagga Wagga, April 5, 1876.

Ah Chong, for murder, executed at Sydney, April 18, 1876.

Thomas Newman, convicted of murder, executed at Dubbo, April 5, 1877.

Peter Murdick *alias* Peter Higgins, convicted of murder of Henry Flood, executed at Wagga Wagga, October 4, 1877.

Queensland.

Thomas John Griffin, Gold Commissioner, for the murder of troopers John Francis Power and Patrick William Cahill, executed at Rockhampton, June 1, 1868. [Griffin robbed the gold escort in charge of these troopers after murdering them on the Mackenzie River.]

Palmer and Williams, for the murder of Halligan a storekeeper, executed at Rockhampton, November 24, 1869.

Archibald, executed at Rockhampton, for murder of Halligan, December 22, 1869.

William Brown *alias* Bertram, for wounding Mr. Baker, and for robbery under arms, executed at Toowoomba Gaol, April 29, 1870. [He was a native of Germany, and came to South Australia at 12 years of age; was a reputed horse-stealer in New South Wales.]

Cunningham executed at Brisbane Gaol, January 14, 1878.

Victoria.

George Melville, George Wilson, and William Atkins, for the M'Ivor escort robbery, executed, 1852.

James Condon, John Dixon, Alfred H. Jackson, convicted November 19, 1855, of highway robbery with violence, on Mr. Rutherford, near Ballarat. Took £1500 from him. Kept Geelong and Ballarat road in terror for a time; executed at Melbourne, November 24, 1855.

Chong Sing Hang Tzan, for murder of Sophia Lewis, whilst in a state of intoxication. Robbed her of a large amount of money and jewels, 1856; executed at Melbourne, September 2, 1857.

John Mason. Killed his mate with an axe near Ballan; was found burning the body (which he had previously cut to pieces), near his hut. Executed November 6, 1857.

William Jones, Edward Brown. Robbery with violence. Executed at Melbourne, March 1, 1858.

George Robinson. Murdered his wife by throwing her down a hole at Castlemaine. Executed at Melbourne, March 16, 1858.

Edward Cardanna, *alias* John Nelson. Murder of John Armstrong, at Long Gully, executed at Melbourne, March 10, 1858.

Owen M'Queeny. For murder of Elizabeth Lowe, near Geelong, executed at Melbourne, October 20, 1858. [At the execution of this criminal a woman applied for permission to have her hands "streaked over" with the hands of the dead man.]

Samuel Gibbs, George Thompson. Murder of Mr. Anderson at Ballarat, executed at Melbourne, November 6, 1858.

Edward Hitchcock. Murdered his wife at Strathlodden, executed at Castlemaine, November 23, 1858.

Christian Von See. Murder of his mate, countryman and benefactor Leoman, a puddler at the Terricks, Bendigo, executed at Melbourne November 29, 1875.

Thomas Ryan. For murder of L. Hartweg, a gardener at Indigo, executed April 11, 1859. [Ryan shot him to obtain £14, the produce of his day's sale of vegetables; was originally sent out as a convict on board the "Calcutta," in 1803. Afterwards returned to England from which he sailed as an emigrant.]

George Chamberlain, for murder of Mr. Cornelius Green, at Omeo, and William Armstrong, shooting with intent to murder Joseph Green, executed July 12, 1859. [The first criminal shot, and the latter tomahawked the dying man.]

William Siddons. For rape, at Pleasant Creek, on a child eight years old, attended with circumstances of peculiar atrocity, executed November 7, 1876.

Henry Brown. For murder of his mate, executed November 21, 1876. This (coloured) man, was formerly a slave in Maryland, whence he escaped to Canada. He murdered his mate in a fit of passion while both were at work in a drive.

George Waines. For murder of Mr. and Mrs. Hunt, of Casterton, executed July 16, 1860. [A well-to-do farmer, possessed of £1,400, in order to save some £50 he owed his victims, murdered them and then buried their bodies, and eight months afterwards disinterred them and burnt Mrs. Hunt's body to cinders. The male body he put in a sack and threw it into a pond. He confessed to a detective who had been put into a cell with him, and who persuaded the murderer he was a fellow prisoner.]

Edward Fenton. For murder, executed August 20, 1860.

John M'Donald. For murder of his wife at Ironbark Gully, Bendigo, whilst in *delirium tremens*. Knew nothing of his crime till told by his little girl; executed September 3, 1860.

William Smith. Drowned his wife in a waterhole, near Beechworth, executed April 22, 1861. [The night before his execution he attempted to cut his own throat with a small piece of razor, which he managed to conceal in the lining of his shoe.]

Henry Cooley. For murder of his wife, executed at Melbourne, July 11, 1861. [Made a confession to another prisoner.]

Nathaniel Horatio Ruby. Killed his mate by striking him with a piece of quartz, executed at Melbourne, August 5, 1861.

Martin Rice. Murder, executed at Melbourne, September 20, 1861.

Thomas Sanders. For rape on a servant in the family of Mr. Cropley, a farmer in Keilor Plains; an atrocious case. His accomplice Johnson's sentence commuted to hard labour for life. Sanders was an old "flogger" at Norfolk Island; executed at Melbourne, October 31, 1861.

Samuel Pollet. For rape on a child of his own, aged 11, executed at Melbourne, December 29, 1862. [He was previously worth £4,000.]

Thomas M'Gee. Murder of a miner named Brown at Sandhurst, executed at Melbourne, February 19, 1863.

James Murphy. Murder of Constable O'Boyle at Warrnambool, executed at Geelong, November 6, 1863. [The executioner sent from Melbourne to Geelong was an old mate of the criminal, and was so much affected that he had difficulty to perform his duty.]

David Gedge, Julian Cross, Elizabeth Scott. At the instigation of the woman the two men murdered her husband Robert Scott, a refreshment tent-keeper near Mansfield, whilst lying in bed with *delirium tremens* ; executed at Beechworth, November 11, 1863. This being the *first* and *only* execution of a female in Victoria fears of a disturbance were entertained, leading to the execution of the three taking place half-an-hour before the time publicly announced.]

James Barratt *alias* Birmingham. Hacked Mrs. Elizabeth Beckinsale to pieces with a tomahawk in her own house at Woodstock, for the sake of £6, a silver watch and a pair of boots, executed at Melbourne, December 1, 1863.

Alexander Davis. Murder of George Sims at Smythesdale, executed at Melbourne, February 29, 1864.

Samuel Woods, William Cower. Robbery in company and shooting with intent to murder, executed at Melbourne, August 3, 1864.

Christopher Harrison. Murder of his partner Marsh, executed at Melbourne, August 3, 1864. [They were contractors ; Marsh delayed certain payments ; Harrison thought his good name lost, and shot his partner at the back of the Public Works office. Great exertions were made to obtain a respite on the ground of " emotional madness."]

John Stacey *alias* Michael Stacey. Murder of a child named Macdonell, executed at Melbourne, September 5, 1865. [The boy was son of a woman who lived with Stacey, and the brute in revenge for having been beaten by another man took the boy out of a bed where he was sleeping with four of Stacey's own children and threw him down the water closet.]

Joseph Brown. For murder of Emanuel Jacobs, at the Whittington Tavern, Bourke-street, executed at Melbourne, May 1, 1865.

Pierre Dotsellaere. For murder in Latrobe-street, of Catherine Sarah Jacobs, his paramour, who was about to be married to another man, executed at Melbourne, July 6, 1865.

David Young. For murder of a young married woman, named Graham, at Daylesford, her husband being away on his night-shift, executed at Castlemaine, August 21, 1865. [On the scaffold Young denied his guilt, but subsequently abundant evidence was given that he had been the perpetrator of many crimes besides that for which he suffered.]

Thomas Mendid *alias* Yankee Tom. For murder of James Sweeney, executed at Geelong, October 28, 1865. [Before capture he fired four shots at the police, but without effect.]

Patrick Sheehan. For murder, executed at Melbourne, November 6, 1865.

Poy Long. For murder, executed at Melbourne, March 10, 1866.

James Jones. For murder, executed at Melbourne, March 19, 1866.

Robert Burke *alias* M'Clusky. Notorious N. S. W. bushranger. Passing through Victoria back to his old haunts at Diamond Creek, he got some refreshment at house of Mr. Hurst ; at some fancied insult of the son, H. F. Hurst, he deliberately shot him ; executed at Melbourne, November 29, 1866.

Denis Murphy. Murder, executed at Melbourne, April 17, 1867.

John Kelly. For unnatural offence, executed at Melbourne, May 4, 1867.

— Duffers. For rape on his own daughter, executed at Castlemaine, May 22, 1867.

William Henry Terry. Murder of his mate Peter Reddick at the Coliban, executed at Castlemaine, July 31, 1867.

Joseph Ballan and George Searle. Murder of Mr. Alick Burke, manager of the Bank of Australasia, Smythesdale, executed at Ballarat, August 7, 1867. [They left the dead body in a sitting position in the buggy.]

Joseph Whelan and Bernard Cunningham. Murder, executed March 31, 1868.

John Hogan. Murder of Martin Rooney at Bullock Creek, executed at Castlemaine, August 14, 1868. [He killed Rooney in his own tent with a hammer, and stole some £200.]

Michael Flannigan. Murder of Sergeant Hull, at Hamilton ; executed at Melbourne, March 31, 1869. [Dressed for death in his old mounted police uniform.]

James Ritson. For murder of the Rev. Mr Hill, at Pentridge, executed at Melbourne, August 3, 1869. [Had been sentenced to death for shooting at a Market Inspector named Kinsella ; the sentence was commuted to imprisonment for life. Mr. Hill went to see him in the usual course of his prison duties.]

James Smith. Murder of his wife, executed at Beechworth, November 11, 1869.

Ah Pew. Violation and murder of Elizabeth Annie Hurst, a child aged 9 years, at Glenluce, executed at Melbourne, March 23, 1869.

Patrick Smith. Murder of his wife at Hotham, executed at Melbourne, August 4, 1870.

Andrew Vair. Murder of Amos Gheale, executed at Ararat, August 15, 1870.

James Cusick. Barbarous murder of his wife at Gooley's Creek, executed at Melbourne, August 30, 1870.

James Seery. Murder of his mate Auguste Topfar, at Grant, executed at Melbourne, November 14, 1870.

James Quinn. Murder of Ah Cow ; died protesting innocence ; executed at Beechworth, Nov. 10, 1871.

Patrick Geary. Murder of Thomas Brookhouse, in February, 1854, at Colac ; his wife was acquitted ; circumstantial evidence and confession ; when sentenced to death said, " Amen ! this is the last of poor Patrick"; executed at Melbourne, December 4, 1871.

Edward Freny. Murder of Charles Manks in the Treasury Gardens in March, 1872 ; executed at Melbourne, May 14, 1872. [A singular case, in which other crimes were involved.]

James Wilkie. Murder of Henry Pensom, at Daylesford, executed at Castlemaine, May 20, 1872.

Samuel Wright. A convict, attempted murder of Hogan, executed at Castlemaine, March 11, 1873.

Thomas Brady, James Smith. Murder of Mr. Watt of Woragee, executed at Beechworth, May 12, 1873.

Pierie Borhuu. Murder of Mrs. Smith of Kangaroo Flat, Sandhurst, who kept a public house where he spent most of his gains ; executed at Castlemaine, May 20, 1873.

Oscar Wallace (Negro). Rape at Mount Beckwith, executed at Ballarat, August 11, 1873. [A hardened ruffian who danced a jig the night before his execution.]

Ah Cat (Chinese). Murder, executed at Castlemaine, August 9, 1875.

Ah Gaa (Chinese). Murder of his mate at Vaughan, near Maryborough ; executed at Melbourne, August 30, 1875.

Henry Howard. Murder of Elizabeth Wright, of Frankston, executed at Melbourne, October 4, 1875.

John Weechurch, real name John Taylor. Murderous assault on Warder Moran with the iron handle of a tub sharpened at both ends, whilst undergoing a sentence at Pentridge ; executed at Melbourne, December 6, 1875. [On the scaffold he said he had been a professional thief for years, and had never known a thief die worth a shilling. He had been " in trouble" since 1850. This man was a deep scoundrel.]

Basilio Bondietto. Murder at Sandy Creek of Carls Comisto his mate on September 4, 1876 ; executed at Melbourne, December 6, 1876. [Circumstantial evidence ; Sir George Stephen formally protested against his execution, and a public meeting was held in the Town Hall two days before and a petition presented to the Governor, but the Cabinet stood firm.]

John Duffus. Rape on his own children ; executed at Castlemaine, May 22, 1876.

James Ashe. Rape and assault on Mrs. Reece, of Burrumbeet ; executed at Melbourne, August 21, 1876. [Had no knowledge of a Creator or any religion ; had lived the life of an ignorant herd-boy. Died penitent.]

William Hastings. Murder of his wife near Frankston ; executed at Melbourne, March 1, 1877.

NUMBER OF IN N.S.W., from 1825 to 1877 (inclusive.)
1825, 9 ; 1826, 21 ; 1827, 29 ; 1828, no return ; 1829, 52 ; 1830, 50 ; 1831, 32 ; 1832, 82 ; 1833, 31 ; 1834, 44 ; 1835, 40 ; 1836, 26 ; 1837, 12 ; 1838, 19 ; 1839, 22 ; 1840, 8 ; 1841, 15 ; 1842, 24 ; 1843, 9 ; 1844, 8 ; 1845, 3 ; 1846, 1 ; 1847, 8 ; 1848, 9 ; 1849, 4 ; 1850, 4 ; 1851, 2 ; 1852,

5 ; 1853, 2 ; 1854, 6 ; 1855, 5 ; 1856, nil ; 1857, 4 ; 1858,
1 ; 1859, 7 ; 1860, 5 ; 1861, 2 ; 1862, 6 ; 1863, 6 ; 1864,
2 ; 1865, 3 ; 1866, 6 ; 1867, 4 ; 1868, 5 ; 1869, nil ;
1870, nil ; 1871, 3 ; 1872, 3 ; 1873, 4 ; 1874, 3 ; 1875,
2 ; 1876, 4 ; 1877, 2.   Total, 554.

N.B.—Port Phillip separated from New South Wales in
1851 ; Queensland, in 1859.   [*See* CRIMES.]

EXHIBITIONS.

Opening of **New South Wales** exhibits for the
Paris Exhibition, at Sydney. by Sir Charles
Fitzroy, 1854 ; **first Victorian Exhibition, opened
December 17, 1854** ; first Queensland Exhibition opened, October 29, 1861 ; second Victorian
Exhibition, opened October 1, 1861 ; New Zealand Exhibition opened at Dunedin, January 12,
1865 ; third Victorian Exhibition, opened October
24, 1866 ; opening of Intercolonial Exhibition at
Sydney, New South Wales, August, 1870 ;
opening of Intercolonial Exhibition, Melbourne,
1872 ; New South Wales Intercolonial Exhibition opened by Sir Hercules Robinson, April
3, 1873 ; opening at Melbourne of Victorian
contingent for Philadelphia Exhibition, September 2, 1875 (78,000 feet of space occupied
with 4,892 exhibits) ; New South Wales Intercolonial Exhibition opened in Sydney, April
6, 1875 ; opening of first Intercolonial Exhibition in Queensland (15,000 persons present on
first day), August 20, 1876 ; foundation stone
of building in Domain, for first Australian International Exhibition to be held in Sydney, 1879,
laid by Lady Robinson, February 13, 1879.
Foundation stone of Melbourne International
Exhibition, 1880, laid by Governor Bowen
February 19, 1879.

Number of visitors who paid for admission
at the Agricultural Society's Exhibitions in
Sydney :—1869, 37,380 ; 1870, 184,375 ; 1871,
31,100 ; 1872, 64,700 ; 1873, 66,020 ; 1874,
68,640 ; 1875, 93,700 ; 1876, 70,486 ; 1877,
131,186.

EXILE, PRESENTATION TO.   Testimonial
amounting to nearly £900 presented to William
Smith O'Brien in Victoria, July 22, 1854.

EXILES, POLITICAL.   Henry Fulton, clergy-
man of the Church of England ; William
Harold, clergyman of the Church of Rome ;
Joseph Holt, one of the leaders of an army of
Irishmen who had risen in 1797-8 against British
rule in Ireland, exiled 1799.

EXMOUTH, MOUNT, New South Wales, discovered by Oxley, 1818.

EXPEDITIONS.

Bruni D'Entrecasteaux, a French Rear-
Admiral, with two ships of war, the "La
Recherché" and "L'Esperance," anchored in
Recherché Bay, Van Diemen's Land, April 20,
1792.

Two Spanish ships on a voyage of discovery
and science, the "Descovierta" and "Atrevida"
arrived in the colony ; they had been three
years absent, visiting all the Spanish provinces
in South America.   Each ship (in addition to
other officers) had on board a botanist and

OPENING CEREMONY OF THE PARIS EXHIBITION, 1854
The Australian Picture Pleasure Book

RECEPTION OF THE SPANISH AT BOTANY BAY, 1793
Juan Ravenet, Spanish Government Archives

a limner. They erected an Observatory in the vicinity of Sydney Cove. Before leaving, the chief of the expedition, Malaspina, presented to Major Grose a copy of the astronomical observations which had been made at the Observatory, by which it appeared that the longitude from that place deduced from 42 sets of distances from the sun and moon was 151 degrees 18 minutes 18 seconds east of Greenwich, and the latitude 33 degrees 51 minutes 28 seconds south, March 13, 1793 ; French discovery ships " La Naturaliste," Captain Hamelin, and " La Geographe," Captain Baudin, visited Sydney, M. Peron, naturalist to the expedition. They reported the discovery of that part of the Australian coast westward of Captain Grant's discovery, May, 1802. [*See* NAPOLEON'S LAND ; *also,* **EXPLORERS, SEA.**]

Mr. William Macleay and *Captain Onslow,* R.N., M.P., sailed in the " Chevert " (Captain Edwards), on a scientific exploring expedition to New Guinea, May 18, 1875.

EXPLORERS, LAND.

Governor Phillip, being settled at Sydney, attempted, in March, an exploration towards the Blue Mountains. He named the Carmarthen, the Lansdowne, and the Richmond Hills, and went overland to Botany, 1788 ; subsequently, the Hawkesbury, in July, 1789.

Captain John Hunter, being sent from Sydney, in October, to the Cape in the " Sirius " for supplies, conjectures the existence of Bass Strait, 1786.

In August, *Lieutenant Dawes, Captain Trench,* and *Captain Paterson* attempted exploration of the Blue Mountains, 1793 ; followed by similar attempts by *Hacking,* quartermaster of the " Sirius," *Dr. Bass,* of the " Reliance " (1794-6), *Mr. Barveillier* (in 1802), and *Mr. Cayley* (1804).

Lieutenant Bowen visited Jervis Bay, 1796.

Charles Grimes, Assistant-Surveyor-General, surveyed Port Stephens, 1796.

Captain Hamilton lost in the " Sydney Cove," in Bass Strait, on passage from India to Sydney ;

some of the crew landed near Cape Howe, and made their way overland to Sydney ; the first white foot in Victoria. 1797.

Gregory Blaxland, Lieutenant William Lawson, of the 102nd Regiment, and *William Charles Wentworth* started from Back Creek, May 11, in an attempt to cross the Blue Mountains ; they succeeded, after much toil and hardship, in finding a spur from the Dividing Range which led them into a valley down the slopes of Mount York into country which improved at each mile ; having successfully accomplished their mission, and being short of supplies, they returned to Sydney, and arrived June 6, 1813.

Mr. George W. Evans, Deputy-Surveyor-General, was sent by Governor Macquarie to follow up the above discoveries ; on November 20, he reached their furthest point ; on 30th, crossed the Dividing Range between the eastern and western waters, and named and crossed the Fish River, which fell into the Macquarie [native, " Wambool "] (discovered, December 7, 1813). Evans returned to Emu Plains, having penetrated 100 miles due west of the Nepean, January 18, 1814.

[These two expeditions created great excitement. A road was commenced and completed to Bathurst in January, 1815. On opening it Governor Macquarie bestowed various names ; amongst others, Cayley's Repulse, King's Table Land, Prince Regent's Glen, Pitt's Amphitheatre, Cox's Pass, The Vale of Clwydd (now the site of Hartley), Clarence Range, Mount Evans, Sidmouth Valley, Campbell's River, Mitchell's Plains, O'Connell and Macquarie Plains, &c.]

Mr. Evans, with a small party, again sent out with one month's provisions, to explore Queen Charlotte's Valley, found Limestone Creek, and two days afterwards came on the Lachlan. The course of the Macquarie and Lachlan flowing into the interior and diverging at each mile became the problem to be solved, 1814.

Hamilton Hume, and his brother, *John Kennedy Hume.* The Government expedition of Evans awakened the enterprise of two native born

AN EXPLORING PARTY
A lithograph from Allan Cunningham's *An Account of the State of Agriculture and Grazing in New South Wales,* 1826

youths of this name, who in 1814, made their way through the mountains, and discovered the country around Berrima and Bong Bong. A few years after, H. Hume, in company with Mr. Meehan, a surveyor, opened up the Goulburn Plains and the country adjacent.

Mr. John Oxley, the Surveyor-General of New South Wales, took charge of a party equipped for the purpose of tracing the Lachlan. The expedition left Sydney, April 6, arriving at Bathurst on the 14th. The party consisted of Mr. Evans, Deputy Surveyor-General; Mr. Allan Cunningham, the King's Botanist; Charles Frazer, Colonial Botanist; Wm. Parr, mineralogist; and eight men; five months provisions, and two boats. August 29th, they returned to Bathurst, having explored the Macquarie to the marshes and traced the Lachlan for 500 miles. Returning, they took an oblique course, and crossed some splendid country, several fine rapid streams running north-east, which they named the Elizabeth River, Mary River, Molle Rivulet, and Bell's River. Twice he was on the point of discovering the Murrumbidgee. For 50 miles not a pebble was seen. He came to the conclusion that the interior of the country was a marsh, and uninhabitable, 1817.

Oxley's Second Journey. Party consisted of Mr. Evans, Dr. Harris, surgeon of the 102nd Regiment, Mr. Nazer, botanist, and 12 men. In June they reached a depôt which had been formed at Wellington Valley. The boats were laden and dropped slowly down the Macquarie, while the horses followed along the banks. July 3, reached Mount Harris. July 27 discovered the Castlereagh River. August 8, ascended Mount Exmouth, Arbuthnot's Range, Liverpool Plains (after Lord Liverpool). September 2, discovered and named, in honour of Sir Robert Peel, the Peel River (native Namoi), and soon afterwards discovered and named the Goulburn Valley and Cockburn River, flowing into the Peel. The Apsley River was next named, followed by the Hastings, the Forbes, the Ellenborough, and the King Rivers. November 5, Oxley reached Newcastle, having traversed the whole of the country between Mount Harris and Port Macquarie. They carried a stranded boat on their shoulders for 90 miles, from one inlet to another, in their progress to Port Stephens, 1818.

The result of this remarkable journey was the necessity of finding a track to Liverpool Plains, whilst to the puzzle of mysteriously flowing rivers was now added the theory of an inland sea.

Captain Stewart, being sent from Sydney by Governor Macquarie, with a small party in a boat to search for a supposed passage from Lake Bathurst to the sea, lost his boat at Twofold Bay, and was cut off by the natives in the endeavour to reach Sydney by land, 1820.

Lieutenant R. Johnson, R.N., in the cutter "Snapper," sent in search of Stewart, discovered the Clyde River, up which he sailed for 30 miles, 1820.

A small Government station formed at Port Macquarie, at the mouth of the Hastings, 1822.

Oxley, accompanied by Lieutenant Stirling, and Mr. John Uniacke, left Port Jackson October 23, 1823, in the "Mermaid," to ascertain the best site for a penal settlement north of Sydney. They examined Port Curtis November 6, 1823; discovered the Boyne River November 10, 1823; reached Moreton Bay November 29, 1823. At Moreton Bay met with a white man named Pamphlet, who gave him information which led to the discovery, December 2, of the Brisbane River, on which is now planted the capital of Queensland. Lieutenant Miller formed a settlement there, August, 1824.

Allan Cunningham, sent out to explore from the Cudgegong River as far as Liverpool Plains, left Bathurst with five men and five horses. Examined the Cudgegong and Goulburn. June 2, discovered Pandora's Pass, opening out a fair and practicable road to Liverpool Plains. 27th returned to Bathurst by the Cudgegong, 1823.

Major Ovens and *Captain Currie* discovered June 1, the Murrumbidgee, and explored the country about Lake George, and thence Monaro Plains, which he called Brisbane Downs, after Governor Brisbane, 1823.

Hamilton Hume and *Captain W. H. Hovell*. A private expedition towards Western Port. Party consisted of six prisoners, named Claude Bossawa, Henry Angell, James Fitzpatrick, Thomas Boyd, Samuel Bollard, and Ben Smith, three horses, two carts drawn by four bullocks. Left Appin, October 2, 1824, and on 13th arrived at Hume's Station, at Lake George. Started again October 17 towards Yass, named Mount Lookout, and forded the Gundorroo branch of the Murrumbidgee, swam that river with great difficulty; successively named M'Dougall's Plains, the Midway River, Battery Mount. On the 16th November, they reached a river named "the Hume," after the father of Mr. Hume. It is now called throughout its length the Murray. A monument, erected by the inhabitants "in honour of Hamilton Hume," gives the date as November 17. Crossed the river on the 20th. On the 27th they crossed the eighth river met with, and named it the Ovens, after Major Ovens, private secretary to Governor Brisbane. Next named Mount Buffalo, Oxley's Creek, Mount Bellevue, and Berry's Plains. On December 3, they reached a river, to which the name of Hovell was given. It had been previously seen higher up by Dawson, and named the Goulburn. At the crossing place, two hills received the names of Mounts Throsby and Meehan. On December 7, they discovered King Parrot Creek, and the country from Muddy Creek to Mount Disappointment "Bannister's Forest," after the Attorney-General. Mount Piper and Sandy Creek follow. The Julian Range, Bland's Mount, Mount Hodometer, Relief and Broughton Creeks, and 20 miles further on the Arndell, after Dr. Arndell, the father of Mrs. Hovell. On December 16, they camped on the beach at Bird Rock Point, near the site of Geelong, and Kennedy's Creek was named. Mount Woolstonecraff is identified with Vila Minarter or Station Peak, which they

ALLAN CUNNINGHAM
Picturesque Atlas of Australia

ascended. Other remarkable hills were named Mount M'Intosh, after the Barrack Master, Mount Campbell (after Mr. Campbell, of Harrington Park), and Mount Berry, after Mr. Alexander Berry, and finally the Julian Range. On the 19th December, they recrossed the Arndell and Broughton, Bland's Plains, and the Julian Range, at a point called Hume's Pass. This lies between Mount Disappointment and Mount Wentworth, named after the leading colonist of that name. Mount Wentworth is the Mount Macedon of the maps, and the Mount Ginburrh of the blacks ; it should be called Mount Hume. Christmas Day was spent on the Hovell, and on the last day of 1824 they recrossed the Ovens. January 18, 1825, the party arrived at Hume's Station, at Lake George. This was a remarkable exploration. Unhappily differences existed between the leaders. Labilliere's History [1878] gives the full details, which are contradictory. Each leader received a grant of 1200 acres, 1824.

Captain Wright, of the Buffs, sent down from Sydney with a detachment to occupy Western Port, owing to some reports that the French intended to form a settlement in Australia. Captain Hovell accompanied this expedition. They sailed in H.M.S. "Fly," Captain Wetherall, and the colonial brigs "Amity" and "Dragon," October, 9, 1826. Major Lockyer, with another detachment in the same ships, continued the voyage, and for the same reason established a settlement at Albany, Western Australia, which was abandoned in 1830, when the settlement was merged in the Swan River Colony. Each party consisted of two officers, eighteen soldiers, and twenty prisoners.

Mr. Wishart, the master of a small cutter, driven into a bay, which received the name of Port Fairy from the vessel, 1827.

Mr. William Sutton, master of a sailing vessel, visited Portland Bay, and built a house at Whaler's Point in 1829. In 1831 he occupied it for some time while sealing, and in 1832 he formed a whaling station there, erected building, and grew vegetables. He died at his farm, Narrawong, near Portland, July 20, 1878—1828-9.

Allan Cunningham, with a party of six men and eleven horses, started from the Upper Hunter 30th April, and crossed Oxley's track till he fell in with a branch of the Peel River, at an elevation of 1,900 feet. Discovered the Darling Downs and the streams which are tributary to the Condamine. His furthest point was 75 miles west of Brisbane. The discovery of the Downs and the Dumaresq, the Gwydir and the Barwan, or Upper Darling Rivers, were the features of this important exploration, 1827.

Cunningham traced the Brisbane to its sources, 1829.

Captain Charles Sturt 39 Regt., first expedition, accompanied by Hamilton Hume, Staff-Surgeon M'Leod, two soldiers and eight prisoners, left Sydney November 10, 1828 ; February 4, 1829, discovered the Darling, which they traced down to lat. 29°37 and long. 145° 33' ; reached New Year's Creek, or the Bogan, and traced it up for 50 or 60 miles ; followed the Castlereagh for 100 miles. 7th April reached Mount Harris, and thence hastened home.

Sturt's second expedition started Nov. 3, 1829, accompanied by Mr. George M'Leay, son of the Colonial Secretary, Mr. Frazer, botanist, Harris, Hopkinson, Robert Harris, Clayton, Mullholland and Macnamara. In January, 1830, embarked on the Murrumbidgee, and followed it down to the junction with the Murray ; 14th January discovered the junction with the Darling ; discovered the Rufus and Lindesay Rivers, and on 3rd February entered Lake Alexandrina. On the 23rd they reached the sea at Encounter Bay. Sturt re-entered the river, and after a month of almost incredible hardship, regained the Murrumbidgee, and Sydney on 25th May. This 2,000 miles pull in a boat was a very remarkable exploration. Sturt died at Cheltenham, England, June 16, 1869.

Captain (Sir James) Stirling, in H.M.S. "Success," surveyed the coast of Western Australia, 1829, a settlement formed at Perth this year, when Captain Freemantle in the "Challenger" took possession. Before the end of that year twenty-five ships from England had landed 850 emigrants and a vast quantity of stock. In 1830 over 1100 more settlers arrived.

Captain Bannister, first explorer of overland route from Swan River to King George's Sound, 1829.

THE SWAN RIVER 50 MILES UP
Captain Stirling's bivouac, March 1827, Mitchell Library

Mr. Hay explored the back country; discovered the Denmark River, and returned to Parry's Inlet, 1829.

Mr. Dale made a journey from the Canning or Upper Swan followed up the Avon to York and Beverley, 1830.

Captain Stirling and *Lieutenant Roe,* then Surveyor-General of Western Australia, made several explorations of a limited character to the eastward from Perth, 1831.

Moore
Bunbury } Exploration in the neighbourhood
Wilson   } of the Swan; the Moore River
Collier } named by the first, 1831.
Hillman

Captain Collett Barker, of the 39th Regiment, who had been at Port Raffles on the N. Coast, and Mr. Kent were sent from Sydney, in April 1831, to search for some communication between Lake Alexandrina and St. Vincent's Gulf, following up the conjectures which arose from Sturt's wonderful boat voyage. Ascended Mount Lofty and saw the plains on which now stand Adelaide, Norwood, and Kensington. Barker was killed by the natives on the beach at the Murray entrance, and Kent returned in the ship to Sydney, 1831.

Major (Sir Thomas) Mitchell, Surveyor-General of New South Wales, with a strong party of fifteen men, and Messrs. White and Finch, two volunteers, with seventeen horses, carts, and canvas-boats. Some information of a river named Kindur (Gwydir) by the blacks was brought in by an escaped prisoner named Clarke, who had lived with the tribes about Liverpool Plains. Acting Governor Sir Patrick Lindesay gave Mitchell leave to search in this quarter. They started November 24, 1831; on December 29 they reached the Peel, then the limit of exploration in this direction, and on December 22 the Namoi. Here the canvas boats were launched, and a man sent back with the news, but was never afterwards heard of. On January 9, 1832, they made the Gwydir, and Cunningham followed it for twelve days, and reached the head-quarters of the Darling, called by the natives Kavuala (Macintyre). On February 4, they reached the Darling. Finch had been sent back from the Peel to the Hunter; his party were killed by the blacks. On July 11, when 100 miles from junction of Murray and Darling, they started on their return and reached Sydney in safety. Places named in their expedition and their signification :—Pic of Tangùlda, December 15, 1831, (native); River Namoi, December 22; Emerguendi Hill, December 23; Bullabalakit Hill, Mount Frazer (after the botanist), January 4, 1832; the Karaula, February 6; Maule's Creek

MAJOR THOMAS MITCHELL
Picturesque Atlas of Australia

(Colonel Landerdale Maule), February 24; Mount Forbes (Captain Forbes, 39th Regiment), February 24; Mount Lindesay (Sir Patrick Lindesay), February 24; Mount Warrogo (native), February 27; Mount Idive (native), Mullaba Plains, Mount Albueva, Mount Conrada (native), 1831-2.

Captain Forbes, who had been sent after bushrangers on the Namoi, also tried to find the Kindur but without effect.

Mr. Dixon, in October, 1833, traced the ranges between the Lachlan and the Macquarie, by crossing the Bogan, which he followed for 67 miles.

Mr. Edward Henty visited Portland, in July 1834, in the "Thistle," Captain Liddell. He returned November 19, with stock, whaling gear and boats, and formed, with his brother Francis, who arrived a month later, the First Permanent Settlement in Port Phillip. Mr. Henty's career in Victoria is historical; he died at Melbourne, August 14, 1878. Captain Liddell died at Queenscliff, February, 1878, and by the desire of the English Government a notice of "the upright and honourable founder of the Colony of Victoria" was published in the Victorian "Government Gazette," January 17, 1879.

John Batman, as agent for an association formed in Tasmania, crossed Bass Strait from George Town in the "Rebecca," 30 tons, on May 12, 1835, and entered Port Phillip Heads 29th. Ascended Station Peak, and traversed the country around Geelong. On 2nd June anchored at mouth of the Yarra, next day ascended that river, which he named after himself. He re-

turned to Tasmania, leaving a party behind him. He returned to Port Phillip with his family in April, 1836, and became a permanent settler, and died in May, 1839. The disputes between him and Fawkner as to priority of discovery are well known. The truth is that both sailed by the charts of Port Phillip published by Flinders in 1814.

John Pascoe Fawkner, who had been a boy on board the "Ocean" in the attempted settlement at Port Phillip in October 1803, having prospered as a Tasmanian colonist, this year fitted out the "Enterprise," in which his associates, William and Samuel Jackson, J. Lancy, R. H. Marr, and George Evans, on the 27th July, 1835, left Hobart Town to cross the Straits in search of country at Port Phillip. They entered Western Port August 8th, and on the 16th passed through Port Phillip Heads. On the 29th they carried the vessel up the Yarra, and tied her to the tea-tree growing on the banks of the river where the Queen's Wharf now stands. The career of Mr. Fawkner is historical. He died September 4th, 1869.

Mitchell's journey to the Darling, and through Australia Felix. A party of 25 men, with drays, horses and two boats, March 9, 1835, started and explored down the Lachlan. Tried to strike across for the Darling. Reached the Murrumbidgee, the Murray Scrubs, and the Darling junction. Explored up the Murray in June, and passed without knowing the junction of the Edward.* On June 20 they reached the junction of the Loddon, and traced it for three days. Arrived at Swan Hill, 21st June. Discovered and named River Yarrayne, Boga Lakes, Moonlight Creek, Mount Hope, Pyramid Hill, Mount Burrabungale July 4, Tarray Creek 18th, Dyanbooro Creek, Weelbang Creek (native names), Mount Freeth after Major Freeth of the Royal Engineers, Avoca River 10th, and Avon, July 11, Small Owen Creek, Doseasa's Creek, Richardson River, after the botanist of the exhibition; Lake Lonsdale, after Captain Lonsdale of the 4th Regiment, first police magistrate of Melbourne; the Grampians, 16th July, the highest point of which was named Mount William, after the King; Mount Zero,

* Names given in this portion of the Expedition :
County of Cook, 1st April.
Pass of Mount Victoria (opened 1832).
Farmer's Creek.
Mount Juson, 11th April, after Mr. Cunningham's mother.
Mount Laidley, after the Commissary.
Cookopie Lagoon ⎫
Coogoonderoy Creek ⎪
Turangeno Plain ⎬ Native.
Boors Hill ⎪
Tandogo Creek ⎭
Berry Ridge, 17th April.
Burrqudine ⎫ 2nd May, native names of places on the
Curdenda ⎬ Bogan, where Cunningham the botanist
Cudduldurg ⎭ was killed by them.
Mount Hopeless, 15th May (5-day search on his tracks).
Fort Bourke, 27th.
M'Culloch's Range, 24th June (Dr. M'Culloch).
Mount Lyre, 26th (Sir Charles Lyre).
Mount Danberry (Dr. Danberry).
Mount Murchison (Sir Roderick Murchison).
Affray with natives, 11th July.
Greenough Range, 26th (G. B. Greenough, geologist).
Mount Macpherson, 29th (after the Revenue Collector, Sydney).

82 EXPLORERS, LAND

on 17th, the northern peak of the range; the river Wimmera, 18th; Mitre Rock and Lake; Boga Lakes; Mackenzie River, 21st, after Captain Mackenzie; River Norton, after James Norton, of Sydney; the Victoria Ranges, 22nd, after Princess Victoria, now Her Majesty the Queen; Mount Arapiles, originally Mount Howick, because it was ascended on the anniversary of the Battle of Salamanca, called by the French Arapiles; Greenhill Lake; Bed Lake, 25th; Salt Lake; White Lake; Sorauvin Creek, a village in the Pyrenees; the Glenelg River, 31st, after the Secretary for the Colonies; Nangeela Valley (native); the Pigeon Ponds, 3rd August, (from a bronzewing pigeon); Chetwynd River 6th August, (after W. Stapylton, the 2nd in command); Mud Hill; Wando Vale 10th, (native, Temiantgand geen); River Wannon 11th; the Rifle Range (after the 95th, now the Rifle Brigade); River Stoke 14th, (after a brother officer who fell at Badajos); Fort O'Hare 18th, (after Major O'Hare of the 95th, who led forlorn hope at Badajoz); Isle of Bags 20th; Discovery Bay 20th; River Crawford 22nd, (after General Crawford of the Light Division); Mount Eckersley 28th; Mount Napier (after Sir George Napier, who commanded advance at Ciudad Rodrigo); River Fitzroy (after Lord Fitzroy Somerset—Lord Raglan); Mount Kincaid 30th, (an old friend in Peninsula); River Surry (at request of Mr. Harty); Mount Abrupt 31st; Mount Clay (Sir William Clay, G.P.); River Shaw 4th September, (after an old comrade); Lake Linlithgow; Mount Rouse; Mount Eccles; Mount Gavooch; Mount Shadwell; Mount Clarke (from Major Shadwell Clarke); the Pyrenees 10th September; Mount Hotspur (proximity to Lady Julia Percy, 3rd); Pange Creek 11th; Mount Pierrepoint 12th; Mount Bainbrigge (General Sir Phillip Bainbrigge); Lake Nivelle 13th; Mount Sturgeon (Colonel Sturgeon, of the Staff Corps); Dundee Range (Sir Robert Dundee, K.C.B.); The Serra Range; Lake Repose 13th, (here Stapylton remained behind to rest the cattle whilst Mitchell with a large party pushed on homewards; Mount Stavely 10th, (General Sir William Stavely); The Hopkins (after Sir John Paul Hopkins); The Cockajemmy Lakes 20th, (native); Mount Nicholson (from Dr., now Sir Charles Nicholson, Bart.); Mount Cole 23rd, (after General Sir G. Lowry Cole); The Mammaloid Hills 26th; Mount Greenock; Mount Beckwith (Colonel Sir Sydney Beckwith, Rifle Brigade); Mount Byng 28th, (after Earl of Stafford); Mount Alexander (a new name for Mount Byng); River Barnaud 30th September, (after General Sir A. F. Barnaud); Mount Macedon (Mitchell saw Port Phillip from summit and the tents of Batman and Fawkner); Mount Blackwood; River Campaspe 5th October, (native); Mount Campbell 6th, (General Sir Arch. Campbell, Bart.); Deegay Ponds (native); Violet Ponds 10th October, (from flowers); Swampy River 13th: Mount Barnaud (see River); Mount Darwin; Fuller's Range (after "a successful and public-

spirited colonist of New South Wales"); Mount Dingee 16th, (native); Mount Aberdeen; Mount Buller; Mount Ochtertyre 17th. Reached Sydney November 3, 1835.
[This highly successful exploration, commonly called "the Major's line," resulted in the cumbersome name of *Australia Felix* being given to the country passed through. It has since been replaced by that of VICTORIA, to the opening up of which district Mitchell's expedition gave an immense impetus.]

Captain Hobson of H.M.S. "Rattlesnake," afterwards the first Governor of New Zealand, on a visit to Port Phillip, surveyed and named Hobson's Bay, 1836.

Captain Sir John Hindmarsh, in H.M.S. "Buffalo," 28th December, founded Adelaide, 1836.

Mr. George Hamilton, with a party of seven prisoners of the Crown, made his way overland in May from Sydney to Melbourne. The names of these first overlanders, among whom may be named Gardiner, Bonney, Hawdon and Faithful, are preserved in Mr. H. F. Gurner's Chronicle of Port Phillip, 1837.

Messrs. Gellibrand and *Hesse*, while exploring the Cape Otway country, were murdered by the natives, 1837.

Settlement formed in May, 1839, by the New Zealand Company at Port Nicholson (Wellington). Auckland founded by Hobson the same year, which was the capital till 1865. In January, 1848, the islands, which had hitherto been a dependency of New South Wales, were formed into an independent colony,—Sir George Grey the Governor at Auckland, and E. J. Eyre, Lieutenant-Governor at Wellington, 1839-40.

Angus M'Millan started from Corrowong May 28 1839, with Matthew Cameron, one stockman, and a blackfellow, to seek country to the south. From the top of Mount M'Leod (Haystack) he had a view of Corner inlet. On a second expedition on 20th December he reached the Glengarry January 23, 1840, and again starting February 9, 1841; on the 14th of that month tasted the sea water at Port Albert. He called the country "Caledonia Australia," a name which has given place to Gippsland. M'Millan named January 16, the Nicholson River; 17th, the Mitchell; 21st, the Avon; 22nd, Lake Victoria, Macarthur's Plains and the Macalister River. Lake Victoria is the Lake King of Strzlecki. He died May, 1865.

Count Paul E. von Strzlecki, a distinguished Polish exile, who had travelled some 700 miles on foot over Australian ground in his scientific travels, in **January 1840** joined at Sydney Mr. James Macarthur and Mr. James Riley in search of country towards Western Port, 15th February ascended and named Mount Kosciusko,—6510 feet high. On 7th March they called at M'William's Camp on Dowman's River. They suffered great hardships before reaching Western Port. Names given :—the Thomson River (after Sir Deas T.); the King (after Admiral P. P. K.); the Riley, Macarthur,

Perry, Dunlop, and Barney, and the Latrobe after the Superintendent of Port Phillip ; the Maconachie after Captain M., formerly Superintendent at Norfolk Island, 1840.

Captain George Grey of the 83rd, with Lieutenant Lushington and a party of 12 men, landed in December at Hanover Bay, Northwest Coast. Sent vessel to Timor for ponies. These sickened and died, and Grey made his way back to Hanover Bay, and was picked up by Captain Wickham, who was surveying the coast in the "Beagle," 1837.

Grey's Second Journey. His party of 13 landed in February from a whaler in Shark's Bay,—3 whale boats and provisions for six months. They suffered great privations before they reached Perth. Discovered the Arrowsmith, the Karie, the Chapman, the Greenough, the Gascoyne, and the Hutt Rivers, 1839.

John Orr, Dr. Stewart, and Messrs. Rankin, Kersop, W. A. Brodribb, Kinghorne, M'Leod, and James Macfarlane, in the barque "Singapore" to explore Gippsland. 13th February they arrived at Corner Inlet. The Albert and Tarra and Kersop Rivers, Mount Wellington and Mount Singapore named by them. 1841.

Dr. Edward Barker, Albert Brodribb, (brother of W. A. B.) and *Edward Hobson,* with two blackfellows, were the first to travel on foot, June, 1841, from Melbourne into Gippsland, and thence to Port Albert and back to Melbourne. They suffered great hardships, being

EYRE AND WYLIE
Picturesque Atlas of Australia

for days without any food. Their supplies, carried on their backs, were soon exhausted, and they lived on what animal food the blacks could procure for them. 1841. [The present road into Gippsland follows their tracks.]

Edward John Eyre, with a single black boy, made his astonishing journey round the Great Australian Bight to Albany, W. A., 1840. In June, 1840, with a party consisting of Mr. Scott, John Baxter, three men, and three natives, he started from Adelaide with the intention of planting the Union Jack in the centre of the Continent. He was beaten back, and abandoning the hope of going north, found a passage between the head of Spencer's Gulf and Lake Torrens, now known by his name. Scott went back in the open boat from Port Lincoln to Adelaide for supplies, to be sent to Fowler's Bay Governor Gawler sent to dissuade Eyre from his rash intent, but without avail. On March 7, 1841, Eyre and Baxter, with three black boys, pushed into the desert, 135 miles, five days without water, till they reached the coast. When 600 miles from King George's Sound, they had but three weeks' provisions left. Baxter was murdered by two of the black boys ; and alone with the other, Wylie, Eyre pursued his journey. They were succoured at Rossiter Bay by a French whaler, and eventually reached Albany.

The *Messrs. Russell* made some explorations of the Darling Downs, the Condamine, and the country around Wide Bay, 1841-42.

Captain Frome, Surveyor-General of South Australia, made some explorations of the Lake Torrens country, 1842-43.

J. A. Horrocks, a South Australian explorer of much promise, in an attempt to examine the head of Spencer's Gulf, was killed by the explosion of his gun, 1846.

Ludwig Leichhardt. An expedition to connect the surveys of Wickham and Stokes and the settlement of Port Essington, which had been abandoned in 1823, and a second time established in 1831, with a view to a market in India for Australian horses. Party of nine persons (two natives), all volunteers. Their names were Calvert, Roper, Murphy, Hodgson, Gilbert (naturalist), and Phillips. Sixteen oxen and seventeen horses. On October 1, 1844, they were on the Condamine. Discovered and named the Dawson, Gilbert's Ranges, Lynd's Range, Expedition Range, Mounts Nicholson and Aldis, the Boyd River, the Christmas Ranges, Comet Creek, Albinia Downs, the Mackenzie, Mount Stewart, Peak Range, Coxen's Range, and the Isaacs River, the Suttor. Thus far they had proceeded under the influence of the sea-breezes. On March 9, 1845, they reached a fine lake in the channel of that river. Discovered Mount M'Connell, the Burdekin, the Clarke, and the Perry. At the end of April they were in latitude 18° 59', hoping that the Burdekin would lead them to the Gulf. Separation Creek and the Mitchell, May 20. On June 25 they had passed the head of the Gulf. On the 28th, an onslaught was made on the party by the natives. Gilbert

LEICHHARDT'S CAMP ON THE NIGHT OF GILBERT'S
DEATH
National Library of Australia

was killed, and Roper and Calvert dangerously
wounded. The Gilbert was next seen and
named, and on the 6th August a river Leichhardt,
thought to be the Albert of Stokes. Gregory
subsequently called it the Leichhardt. They
were now in country like "the Plains of Promise;"
Breame's Brook, and the Nicholson, Turner and
Wentworth Creeks, the Tasman, Seven Emu,
Cycas, Robinson, and Macarthur Rivers were
crossed and named in succession. October 13,
Limnen Bight River, the Wickham, the Roper,
the head of which—a bubbling spring—they
reached on the 28th. Onthe 22nd November,
they were on the South Alligator River, and on
the 3rd December, on the eastern river of that
name. Mounts Beddome and Roe on the 15th
December ; and on the 17th, after a journey of
3000 miles, extending over fifteen months
"ragged and famished, with no stores but a few
steaks and dried strips of their last bullocks, and
no animals but the horses they rode, they reached
Port Essington." The return to Sydney was made
by sea. The country they passed through is now
all occupied by stock. Port Essington was, however, abandoned. The explorers were received
with enthusiasm, and rewarded by the State, and
£1,400 subscribed as a present: 1844-45.

Sturt's Expedition to the Central Desert—
1844-5.

[The party consisted of Mr. Poole, assistant surveyor ; Mr. J. H. Burton, surgeon ;
and Mr. J. M'Douall Stuart, draughtsman (who
afterwards crossed Australia), and twelve men.

They had a boat, 4 drays, 200 sheep, 30 bul-
locks, and eighteen months' stores. In Sep-
tember, 1844, they left the junction of the
Murray and Darling. Discovered and named
Laidley's Ponds [native, Williorara], Cawn-
dilla, Stanley, or Barrier Ranges. Saw there
Mr. Serle, of Frome, and Eyre, and the
Byell and Babbage, of Mitchell ; Hood's Creek,
Mount Arrowsmith, Browne's Creek, Grey and
Stokes Ranges, &c. For six months they were
confined, by the want of water, to one spot.
The heat was intense. "The tubes of the
thermometer burst, the bullocks pawed the
ground to get a cooler footing, the men's shoes
were scorched as if by fire ; their finger-nails
were brittle as glass ; the lead dropped from
the pencil and the ink dried on the pen as
Sturt wrote up his daily journal ; the drays
almost fell to pieces, the screws loosened in
their boxes ; the horn handles of the instruments and their combs split, and the wool on
the sheep and their own hair ceased to grow."
They clung to the shelter of their tents. Poole
died, and was buried near where Burke and
Wills now lie. They were glad to eat some
bacon fat and suet which the dogs had buried.
To sit their horses was an agony. The water
was as blue as indigo, and as salt as brine.
Sturt's furthest north, after repeated efforts,
was 25° 58', long. 139° 26'. The Barcoo
(Cooper's Creek) was just struck in lat. 27° 44',
long. 40° 22', and his turning point was in lat.
27° 56', long. 142° E. A dark purple sea of

NOTHING IN SIGHT
Sturt's expedition to the Central Desert, *Picturesque Atlas of Australia*

stony desert. The expedition reached Adelaide at the end of 1845.]

Mr. Commissioner Mitchell, a son of Sir Thomas Mitchell, explored in the direction of the junction of the Macquarie and Castlereagh. Discovered the Narran and Bokhara, both tributaries of the Darling. In 28° 25′ he came on the junction of two very large rivers, named the Balonne and Culgoa, 1845.

Augustus C. Gregory, C. F. Gregory, and Frank T. Gregory, three young surveyors, with a modest equipment of four horses and seven weeks' provisions, started in August from the outlying districts of Australia, and penetrated through a large tract of salt swamp country, to the mouth of the Arrowsmith, discovered by Grey. Found coal. 1000 miles of exploration in 47 days, 1846.

Lieutenant Helpman was sent in a small schooner to Champion Bay to look for this coal. He travelled with a cart up the Greenough, and following the track of the Gregorys', reached the coal deposit. His companion, Frank Gregory, with a small party, made a flying survey of the country adjacent, December, 1846.

J. S. Roe, Surveyor-General of Western Australia (*See* KING), who had been concerned with nearly every effort at exploration in Western Australia, started in September, 1848, from York, with a party of six persons, 11 horses, and four months' provisions. Reached the Palinup—the last water crossed by Eyre—in October, Bremer Range and Fitzgerald Peaks. Retreated to Mount Ridley, and after great exertion reached the Russell Range. Returned to Esperance Bay. Coal found on the Phillips. An exploration of 1800 miles, 1848.

Augustus C. Gregory, with a party of six men, started in September from 80 miles west of Perth, northward, to explore the Gascoyne. Grassy plains between the Moore and the Arrowsmith. Pene-

trated 350 miles north of Perth, and found a galena lode on the Murchison, 1848.

Governor Fitzgerald, in December, went to examine this mineral deposit, and named the Geraldine. He was speared by the blacks, and narrowly escaped with life.

Sir Thomas Mitchell, to Tropical Australia, 1845. [An expedition fitted out at the expense of the Home Government, E. B. Kennedy second in command, W. Stevenson, naturalist, and 76 men, 8 drays, 80 bullocks, 2 boats, 17 horses, 3 light carts, 250 sheep, and provisions for a year, in search of a port for the shipment of horses to India. Left Parramatta 17th November, and Buree 15th December, 1845; reached the junction of Barwon and Macquarie 28th February, 1848, Carawy Ponds, Narran River 7th March, the Balonne 1st April, Cawan, Culgoo, St. George's Bridge (depôt), 23rd April, Turanimga Lagoon 30th, Cogoon River, Mount Toolumba 3rd May, Mount First View, Mounts Minute, Insiting, and Red Cap, Mount Abundance 7th May, the Fitzroy Downs and Grafton Range (the Governor and the Duke of G.), 8th May, Frosty Creek (thermometer at 19 degrees in tent), Mounts Bindango, Bindyego, and Lake Tagande 11th, the Amby, the Maranoa 17th, Mount Mevivale 21st, River Head Range, head of the Maranoa 24th, Mount Lonsdale 27th, Mount Kennedy (depôt camp), 4th June :—here Mitchell started in advance) ; Possession Creek 10th, Mount Owen (after Professor O.), Mount Cliff, Mount Ogilby, Mount Faraday, Hope's Table Land, Buckland's Table Land, Mount Aquarius 21st, Mount F. P. Kennedy (28th), Mount Salvator 5th July, Salvator Rosa valley, River Salvator, the Claude 14th, Stephenson's Pass 17th, (after Dr. S.), Tower Almond, Glen Turret, and Mount Kitsyth (from early association), Mount Mudge (Col. M.) 19th, Mount Beaufort (in honour of Sir Francis B., Hydrographer to the Admiralty), the River Belyando (native), 21st, Mount Narrien (Professor N.) 27th. The ex. party returned 12th August, with the intention of exploring to N.W. The River Nogoa discovered 29th, Balmy Creek 30th, Mantuan Downs and Plains 2nd September, Mount Pluto 10th, Mount Hutton (Professor H.), Mount Playfair (Professor P.), the Nive and Nivette Rivers (commemoration of Wellington's battles) 13th, the River Victoria (the Barcoo, "the future highway to the Indian Ocean"), 15th, Yuranigh Ponds 25th, Mount Gray 28th, Gowen Range, Mount Kœnig (Professor K.), Mount Northampton (after the Marquis, President of the Royal Society), 1st October, Mount Inniskillen (after the Earl of I.), River Warrego (native), 11th, Mount Sowerby, (Professor S.) 20th. On the 6th October Mitchell returned to his depôt camp at the Pyramids, and on the 19th Kennedy's depôt. Kennedy being sent S., found the Mooni River. This expedition returned to Sydney in January, 1847. "Modern times present no achievements of a similar character which can bear comparison with these journeys in Australia." Sir Thomas Mitchell died 5th October, 1855.

Mr. Kennedy, with a party of 8 men (mounted) and leading spare horses, 2 light carts, and 8 months' provisions, started in March to determine whether the Barcoo (Victoria) of Mitchell's last expedition and Sturt's Cooper's Creek were the same. On August 13, having travelled up the Warrego, he reached Mitchell's furthest point on the Barcoo, discovered the Thomson (named after Sir E. Deas-T.), and having run the Victoria to a dry channel in a desert instead of a highway to a shipping port on the north coast, as was expected, turned back in latitude 26° 13' and longitude 142° 20', and reached Sydney early in 1848.

Leichhardt's last expedition with the intention of crossing the continent from Mitchell's, Victoria River, to Swan River. The party consisted of H. Classen, his brother-in-law, Mr. Bunce, naturalist, and six men. They had 100 sheep, 270 goats, 40 bullocks, 15 horses, and 13 mules. They started in December, 1847, from their former station on Harley's Creek. In January, 1848, they lost most of their horses and cattle near the Condamine. They followed their old track to the head of the Dawson, and came on the Mackenzie, where they were all laid up with fever and ague. The news of Mitchell's discoveries of the Fitzroy Downs and Grafton Range having reached Leichhardt, who, impeded by his flocks of goats and sheep, had been wandering for many months over the Fitzroy Downs, he organised another expedition, and on the 9th August, 1847, accompanied by Mr. F. N. Isaacs, Mr. Bunce, Mr. Perry, and a blackfellow, started from the Darling Downs, and reached the Cogoon, 54 miles west of the Horsetrack River, 1847-8.

Mr. Kennedy's expedition towards Cape York. The party consisted of Mr. W. Carron, botanist, Mr. T. Wall, naturalist, nine men, and a native called Jacky Jacky, 28 horses, and 100 sheep. They were landed from the "Tam-o-Shanter," at Rockingham Bay, May 30. H. M. S. "Rambler" was to meet them at Cape York. At Weymouth Bay Kennedy left eight of his party behind, and pushed on with the others and the natives. When a few miles distant from Cape York they were attacked by the blacks, and all but Jacky Jacky murdered. He succeeded in carrying the distressing news to the "Ariel," which vessel was waiting at Port Albany, 23rd December, 1848. The party left at Weymouth Bay were reduced by the constant attacks of the natives and starvation to only two survivors, Mr. Carron and Mr. Goddard, when they were rescued, 1848.

Messrs. Oakden and Hulkes. Exploration of Lake Torrens country, whilst searching for sheep runs at the head of Spencer's Gulf, South Australia. 1851.

Mr. Hovenden Hely and a party of six with 12 months' provisions, started in January from the Darling Downs towards Peak Downs in search of Leichhardt. Misled by various reports received from the blacks, he found some old sheep

THE DEATH OF KENNEDY
Picturesque Atlas of Australia

bones, &c., left by Mitchell at one of his camps on the Maranoa. He gave up the attempt at the Nivelle of Mitchell, and returned to the Balonne in July, 1852. [The details of the various expeditions sent forth on the search for Leichhardt are far beyond the limits of this work.]

William A. Randall, in his steamer the "Maryanne," first navigated the Murray by steam as far as Maiden's Punt, Echuca, 1853.

Captain Francis Cadell opened up the Murray to steam navigation as far as Swan Hill, 1853.

R. Austin, Assistant Surveyor-General, despatched by the Government of Western Australia, with eight men and a native, 27 horses, and stores for 120 days. They went to search for gold, and the direction to be towards the Gascoyne. Left Northam July 10. Cowcowing, Mount Kenneth, Recruit Flats, Mount Magnet, the Sandford, Mount Luke, Mount Murchison and River, Mount Welcome. Furthest point 26° 15', longitude 115° 16'. Reached Shark's Bay and the vessel waiting for them, 1854. [Mr. Austin received much credit for his perseverance and courage, but the fruits of this expedition were very meagre.]

Augustus C. Gregory. Expedition up the Victoria (of Stokes), and in search of Leichhardt, under the auspices of the Royal Geographical Society of London. Party of 11, among whom were his brother, H. Gregory, Dr. (now Baron von) Mueller, then botanist, and W. Wilson, geologist. The "Tom Tough" and "Monarch" landed them on the "Plains of Promise" of Stokes, 24th September, 1855. The leader, Dr. Mueller, and seven men proceeded to explore the upper part of the Victoria. Wilson formed the camp. In six days Gregory made Macadam Range, and eight days after the Fitzmaurice. The early part of November was spent in emptying the "Tom Tough," which had been damaged in the ascent of the river. On 3rd January, 1856, Gregory started from his depôt with eight men (including Dr. Mueller, Mr. Elsey, surgeon, and Mr. H. Gregory, 30 pack and six saddle horses), and reached the head of the Victoria in 18° 12', longitude 130° 39'. A further journey of 300 miles brought them to Sturt's Creek, the waters of which became salt, ending in Termination Lake. Gregory pushed back to his depôt on the Victoria, and from thence made his way across Arnheim's Land to the Roper of Leichhardt, and followed that traveller's line all the way to the eastern settlements. This expedition cost a large sum of money, 1855.

Benjamin Herschell Babbage, geologist of S. A., sent to examine this country north and east of Adelaide and in search of gold, collected specimens of stones, but found no indication of the precious metal, 1856.

In a second expedition the same year, accompanied by Mr. Bonney and three miners, they made a further search to the north of Adelaide by way of Mount Remarkable and beyond the head of Spencer's Gulf to Mount Arden and Mount Seale. In October Babbage discovered a fine stream of water (and small lakes) which he called after the Governor, " Macdonald Creek " and the long reach of water, Blanch Water.

G. W. Goyder, Deputy Surveyor-General, South Australia, an expedition to examine the country about Blanch Water, and to make a trigonometric survey of it. Gave a glowing report of magnificent pastoral country, named the Freeling and Werter water. Came upon the Lake Torrens and found the water fresh. The Government were besieged by applications for pastoral licenses in consequence of Mr. Goyder's report, 1857.

Colonel Freeling, R.E., Surveyor General of South Australia, was sent to test Goyder's reports. His report decidedly unfavourable ; all the marked features of the country seen by Goyder were the result of mirage, the whole country round the lake even of the most desolate description, 1857.

A. C. Gregory, in search of Leichhardt. This expedition was sent out by the New South Wales Government, the party consisting of his brother C. F. Gregory and seven experienced bushmen and 40 horses each carrying 150 lb. of provisions. They started from Sydney 12th June, 1858. They reached the Barcoo (Victoria of Mitchell) in April, and found the fine stream seen by the explorer a dry watercourse and the country a desert. In lat. 24° 25′ long. 145° S., they found a tree marked L and some stumps of others which had been felled with an axe. In May they reached the Thomson and followed it till it ran out in plains of baked clay. This river in 1862 was seen by Landsborough and described as one of the most charming in Australia. Gregory pushed down Cooper and Strzlecki Creek and arrived at Adelaide 31st July, after a seven months exploration which left the fate of Leichhardt as much in doubt as ever, 1858.

Frank T. Gregory. An expedition to examine the country between the Gascoyne and Mount Murchison, Western Australia. The party consisted of J. S. Roe, W. Moore, C. Navin, A. Chainer and a native. They started 16th April, 1858, from the Geraldine mine. Dis-

covered and named Mount Nairn, Lockyer Range, Lyons River, the Alma, Mount Augustus, Mount Gould, and Mount Hall. A million acres of good land were found, and they returned to Adelaide 10th July, 1861.

B. Herschell Babbage, third expedition. The party consisted of W. G. Harris, surveyor and second in command ; T. Warriner, assistant ; Mr. Herrigolt, botanist ; J. Jones, H. Cornell, S. Thompson, G. Mason, teamsters ; H. Lewin, cook and wheelwright ; and J. Stranger, shepherd. They left Adelaide in February, intending to proceed to the N. W. Babbage discovered the remains of Coulthard, who was lost in March, 1853, near Steep's station, Mount Remarkable ; examined the whole eastern shore of Lake Gairdner, Lake Finnis, Lake Blyth, Lake Macfarlane ; the eastern and western shores of the Island Lagoon or " Great Salt Lake," and Red Lake, Lake Heart, Lake Hanson, Lake Young Husband, Lake Reynolds, &c. Some of these had been previously discovered by Messrs. Macfarlane, Seymour, and Smith when searching for country. Major E. Warburton (with Charles Gregory as second in command) sent out to recall and supersede Babbage, reached him on the western shore of Lake Gregory in November, 1858. In searching for Babbage, Warburton found Mount Hamilton and some fine springs, Pasley's Ponds, Beresford Hills, Strangway's Springs, Douglas Creek and Davenport Range, Coward Springs, Gregory Creek, the Hermit Range and Finnis Springs. Major Warburton and the Hon. S. Davenport, in May, 1858, made an exploration N. and N. W. of Adelaide to Lake Gairdner. Mr. Davenport advanced and reported on the western shore of the Lake for 60 miles beyond Hacks furthest point, 1858.

Stephen Hack with *Mr. Miller* in command of a party of five men with 12 horses, a dray and six months provisions, an expedition from Streaky Bay to examine to the north and east. He did not penetrate far, but discovered a considerable extent of available country, 1857.

Messrs. Murdoch Campbell, of Mount Remarkable, Chas. Swinden, of the Gilbert, D. Thompson, Tariara, and Edwin Stock (for part of the way) crossed the head of Spencer's Gulf. Bedack Yanaherry, Bonney's Bluff, the Elizabeth Run, Pernatty, Swinden's Country and excellent pastoral country 50 miles further, 1857.

Messrs. Miller and *C. W. Dutton* (of Hack's Expedition) in the same year exploration at the back of Fowler's and Denial Bays. Discovered a good deal of available country, 1857.

Samuel Parry, Government Surveyor, S.A., made a journey into the country lying within the sweep of Lake Torrens, Lake Gregory, and Blanch Water ; from Mount Searle to Illusion Plains, and Agapena. He reported much good country, 1857.

Sir Richard Graves M'Donnell, Governor of South Australia, made an exploration to Mount Searle and the Strangways and Loddon Springs. The following year, in February, His Excellency, who had taken very great interest in the prospect, accompanied Captain Cadell in the steamer "Albury" 600 miles up the Darling above the Murray junction to Mount Murchison, 1858.

George Elphinstone Dalrymple with a party of five started on an exploration in the districts of Burdekin, Suttor and Belayando, between the parallels of 19° and 20° S. They greatly extended the knowledge of the country which Leichhardt, Mitchell, Kennedy, and Gregory had given us, 1859.

William R. Randall navigated in the steamer "Gemini" (constructed for the purpose) the Darling, starting February 2, from the Murray junction. Reached Fort Bourke on the 20th and Gunneewarra, on the Barwan, on the 23rd. He reached his highest point at Nonah or the Blacks Fishing Ground, now Brewarrina, 2400 miles by its windings from the sea and 1800 miles reckoning from the Murray Junction, 1859.

THE BURKE AND WILLS EXPEDITION
The first day's march, La Trobe Collection, State Library of Victoria

STUART REACHES THE GEOGRAPHIC CENTRE OF AUSTRALIA
National Library of Australia

John M'Douall Stuart, who had been of Sturt's party to the Central Desert in 1844-5, was in 1860 engaged in looking for suitable pastoral runs for his employers, Messrs. Chambers, and Finke, and had seen much of the interior. A reward of £2000 had been offered by the South Australian Government to the man who should cross from sea to sea. In March, 1860, he started from Chambers Creek with 13 horses and a party consisting of three, Keswick, Head and Massey. Discovered and named the Neale River, the Finke River, and Chamber's Pillar,

the M'Donnell Range. On 22nd April he stood in the *centre of the Continent* when the Union Jack was unfurled and the place called Central Mount Stuart. His next effort was to reach the source of the Victoria River, and they attained within 300 miles but he had to turn back at Mount Turnbull. The Barker Range was named after the Governor of Victoria, and the Hanson Range after the Chief Justice of Adelaide. They reached the settled districts September 2, 1860, more dead than alive, when Stuart was received with enthusiasm.

Robert O'Hara Burke and *William John Wills*. In September, 1858, Mr. Ambrose Kyte, of Melbourne, initiated a subscription for a Victorian expedition by a gift of £1000. Mr. Burke, an officer of police, was selected to lead it, and with him were joined Mr. Landels, who had brought from India the camels intended for the exploration; Mr. Wills, surveyor and astronomer; Hermann Beckler, botanist; Ludwig Becker, artist; and ten assistants, of whom it is only necessary to mention Charles Gray and John King. They left Melbourne August 20, 1860. Thirteen months after, one survivor returned, broken down by hardship, having left three of his comrades, with whom he had *crossed the continent*, dead in the desert. In that time the continent was crossed by various searching expeditions four times, and more knowledge of the interior obtained than in the previous 30 years. Landels and Beckler left the party. A station superintendent named Wright was engaged by Burke; Becker died before they found the camp at Cooper's Creek. From this depôt on the 16th December, accompanied by Wills, King and Gray, the leader dashed into the unknown interior with, it appears, but one idea—to cross the continent at all hazards. The pitiful tale is too long to tell here. They reached the estuary of the Flinders River (which Burke mistook however, for the Albert) on February 4, 1861, and then hurried back; on the way Gray died. In the last stage of exhaustion they again arrived at the depôt on the 21st April to find that Brahe, the officer

THE FINDING OF JOHN KING LIVING AMONG THE ABORIGINES
Mitchell Library

left in charge, had that very day departed south. The rest of this unhappy business belongs to history. The following names appear on the file map showing the tracks of all the Australian explorers, compiled by Mr. Skene, the Surveyor-General of Victoria, from the imperfect records left by Burke and Wills of their line of work : De Little's Ranges, Mount Standish, Mount Meorlin, Mount Bruce, Bindon's Creek, Mount Aplin, Mount Murray, Mount Barry, Mount Forbes, Mount Birnie, Mount Collis, Mount M'Gowan, Mount Ligar, Cloncurry Copper Mine, Mount Nicholson, Mount O'Shanassy, Mount Morrah, and the Cloncurry River, along which they travelled till they reached the Flinders, 1860.

BURKE AND WILLS RELIEF EXPEDITION. *Alfred W. Howitt* : The anxiety of the Exploration Committee of the Royal Society regarding Burke and Wills, led to a relief party being sent to Cooper's Creek, of which Mr. Howitt, an admirable bushman, was the leader. Near Swan Hill he met Brahe returning with the intelligence that Burke had not returned to the depôt. Howitt was reinforced and sent forward. This party consisted of E. J. Welch, surveyor, and S. Wheeler, Brake, Atkins and two others. He crossed the Darling near Wilcannia, and directing his course towards the Stokes Ranges (reached and named by Sturt in 1845) passed M'Adam Range, Torowoto, Canulta, Poria, Wilkie's Creek, Mount Shillinglaw, M'Leay's Plains, and finally the depôt at Fort Wills on Cooper's Creek, September 8. On the 16th the party found King the survivor ; two days after they buried the remains of Wills, and on the 21st those of Burke. Carrier pigeons brought from Menindie were despatched with intelligence but never reached home. The relief party with King returned to Melbourne 28th November, 1861.

Alfred Howitt. It having been determined the remains of Burke and Wills should be brought to Melbourne, Mr. Howitt was again sent to Cooper's Creek, (the Barcoo). This party con-

sisted of E. J. Welsh, Dr. J. P. Murray, Western Phillips, A. Aitken, Henry Burrell, H. D. Galbraith Williams, Short, and four others. They left Melbourne 9th December, 1861, reached Port Wills 18th February, 1862, after making several excursions in various directions and discovering Bateman's, Barrell's, Phillips, O'Donnell's Williams Creeks, Lake Short, Howitt finally left Cooper's Creek in October 1862, for Adelaide. The remains of Burke and Wills arrived in Adelaide, December 11, and in Melbourne, December 28, 1862. The public funeral took place January 21, 1863. A monolith weighing 34 tons was placed over the grave, and a bronze statue of the gallant Burke and his illustrious comrade Wills, the work of Charles Summers, was erected at the cost of £4000, in the principal street of Melbourne. An annuity of £180 per annum was granted by Government to John King, and other grants made to Dr. Wills, the father of the

explorer, and to Mrs. Dogherty, Burke's foster-mother. King died of phthisic, January 15, 1872. A Royal Commission sat and reported on the whole subject of the Burke and Wills Expedition. It consisted of General Sir Thomas Pratt, Sir Francis Murphy, Mr. Matthew Hervey, Mr. J. F. Sullivan, and Mr. E. P. S. Sturt, the brother of the great explorer. The total cost of the Burke and Wills Expedition was more than £57,000.

J. M' D. Stuart. Third expedition *crossed the continent.* In Stuart's first expedition the

JOHN McDOUALL STUART
Picturesque Atlas of Australia

natives had driven him back when two thirds of the way across. In the second he reached the centre but was stopped by waterless scrubs to the east of Newcastle water, when in latitude 17°. In the present journey he accomplished the great exploit. This party consisted of William Keckwick second in command, F. W. Thring third officer, W. P. Auldass, Stephen King, John Billiat, James Frew, Herth Nash, John M'Gorrerey and J. W. Waterhouse, naturalist. Leaving the settled districts of South Australia in January 1862, in April he reached the northern part of his former expedition. The names bestowed on Stuart's line of route, along which now runs (nearly) the Electric Telegraph from sea to sea, were The New, or Upper Wales, The Hamilton, Bagot's Range, The Stevenson, The Lindsay, The Coglin, The Coyder, The Fricke, The Thigh, Owen's Springs, Mount Hay, Mount Harris, The Woodforde, The Stirling, The Taylor, Mount Morphett, Sullenlands Creek, Younghusband's Range, The Bonney, Gilbert's Creek, Tennant's Creek, Bishop's Creek, Hayward's Creek, Allack Creek, Morphett's Creek, Tompkinson's Creek, The Burke, The Hunter, The Gleeson, The Hawker, The Ferguson, The Lawson, Acion Sturt's plains towards the Ashburton Range. Reached his old camp at north end of Newcastle water, April 8; thence with a small party he endeavoured to reach the Victoria. Excursions in several directions from Howell's Ponds, Frew's and King's waterholes—named in token of approbation of two other party; Nash's Spring, Auld's Ponds, M'Gorrerey's ponds, Daly waters, (in honour of the Governor of South Australia, May 23). From this point he struck for the sources of the Wickham, Purdie's Ponds, The Strangeways), after the Commissioner of Crown Lands, South Australia), June 14, Mount Mueller, (after Baron Von Mueller, the distinguished botanist). On the 22nd June they were in the country discovered by Gregory in 1856; on the 27th they were in the magnificent country on the Roper River, a branch of which Stuart named after his friend and patron, James Chambers, of Adelaide; another large branch was named the Waterhouse, after the naturalist of the expedition, and a high tent hill Mount Shillinglaw, after a friend who had sent him the Admiralty charts of the coast he was striving to reach. From the top of Mount Helpman he saw Mounts Levi and Watts, and the Chambers Range. The Fanny and Katherine were named in honour of two daughters of Mr. Chambers. Mount Stow and the Keckwick Springs. On July 11 the party reached the Adelaide River, a branch of which was named after Miss Mary Chambers and William Creek from a son. Billiat's Springs, Pricilla's and Ellen Creeks, The Daly Range, Mount Daly and Mount Goyder (after the Surveyor General), Anna's Creek, Thring's Creek. On the 24th July Stuart stood on the beach of Van Diemen's Gulf and looked on the waters of the Indian Ocean, in which, according to a promise he had given Governor M'Donnell, he dipped his feet and washed his hands, then the Union-Jack was hoisted and left flying. From Newcastle water to the sea beach, the main body of the horses had been only one night without water. If this country is settled, says Stuart, it will be one of the finest colonies under the Crown, suitable for the growth of any and every thing. The party got back to Adelaide in December. The South Australian Government bestowed a reward of £2000 on the leader, and the Royal Geographical Society sent him their medal. His sufferings however, on his various journeys had been very great, and he sank and died in 1869.

H. and F. William and J. Neilson, from Mount Rankin, on the Darling, towards Cooper's Creek, looking for country. Left 22nd June. Route: Talywalka Creek, Mulyoh Spring, Paaroo Creek, Boree Creek. Turned back when 35 miles from Cooper's Creek, at a creek thought to be identical with the Nive of Mitchell, 1861.

William Landsborough. This relief party was sent from Brisbane in the "Firefly" transport with horses, &c., to the Albert River, where Captain Norman, of Her Majesty's ship "Victoria," had fixed his depôt for the various searching expeditions. The party consisted of H. M. Campbell, G. Bourne, W. Allison, W. Gleeson, Charley, Jemmy, Fisherman, and Jackey, aboriginals. Of these, Mr. Campbell, Allison, Fisherman, and Jemmy accompanied Mr. Landsborough on a preliminary search to the S.W.; on his second journey, or across the continent, his companions were Bourne, Gleeson, and three of the blacks. The "Firefly" was wrecked in Torres Straits, but by great exertion Captain Norman towed her round to the

Albert, and landed 25 horses. The party started first November 16 in the direction of Central Mount Stuart, and made some 200 miles, and then returned to the depôt, where news of Burke's tracks had been brought by Walker from Rockhampton. Landsborough on this trip gave the following names :—The Gregory River ; Mount Macadam and Creek (after the secretary of the Agricultural Society) ; Heales Ranges (after the Premier of Victoria) ; Hull Ranges, Mount Moore, Stawell Creek (after the Chief Justice of Victoria) ; Mount Kay (after Captain Kay, R.N.) ; Smith Range ; Prior Range ; The O'Shanassy River (after Sir John O'Shanassy) ; Verdon Creek (after Sir George Verdon); Haines Creek (after a former Chief Secretary of Victoria) ; Balfour Creek ; Murphy Creek (after Sir Francis Murphy, Speaker) ; Wilson Creek ; Campbell's Tower ; Haughton Creek ; Dodwell Creek ; Fullerton Creek ; Dixon Creek ; Abbot Creek ; Barkly Tableland (in honour of his Excellency Sir Henry Barkly, Governor of Victoria) ; Pratt Creek (after General Sir Thomas Pratt) ; Burrows Creek ; Elliot Creek (after an officer of the "Victoria") ; Pring Creek ; Clifton Creek ; Darvall Creek(after B. Darvall, Esq., of Sydney) ; Wilkie Creek ; Allison Creek ; Turner Creek ; Manning Plain ; Mary Lake ; Lake Nances ; The Herbert River ; Chester Creek. On the return journey from this point, January 4, 1862, Harris Creek ; Thornton River ; Seymour River ; Beame's Brook ; Barkley River. Arrived at the depôt on the Albert January 19, 1862. On the 10th of February, Landsborough again started south on that brilliant expedition which has placed him in the front rank of explorers. Their first camp was at Fort Bowen (named in honour of the then Governor of Queensland, and now of Mauritius), following up the Flinders, Mount Brown, Mount Little, O'Connell Creek, Branston Range, Sloane Creek, Walker Range, and Table Mountain, Jardine Creek, Coxen Creek, Tower Hill, Landsborough Creek and River, which, lower down, is The Thompson, Cornish Creek. The Plains to the east were those discovered by Mitchell between the Alice and the Barcoo. Here Landsborough was near some old camp of his own ; Aramac Creek, Mackenzie and Herbert Ranges, Stark, Salton and Isabella Creeks, Porteous Creek, Bowen Downs, Bourne Creek, Mount Pring, Dunsmore Creek, Mount Johnstone. On the 19th April they reached the Barcoo River, and on the 21st May they reached Mr. William's station, on the Warrego, whence they travelled to the Darling and Menindie, and in June arrived in Melbourne. A remarkable incident of the expedition was that Landsborough brought across with him a foal dropped on the Flinders, at Carpentaria, 1861-2.

RELIEF PARTY. *Frederick Walker*, from Rockhampton (Port Curtis), with a party of the Queensland native police, of which corps Walker had been an officer. Mr. Walker started August 25, 1861, traversing known country till he reached the Barcoo. There he found some supposed tracks of Leichhardt. On 7th October he started from the Barcoo in a N.N.E. direction, crossed the Alice on the 13th. Subsequently discovered and named the Coreenda River, Mount McAlister, Mount Horsfeldt, Mounts Casfort and Pollux, the Buckley River (the Flinders), Mount Norman, Mounts Mayne and Ward, Jingle Creek, the Stawell River. Near this they had an encounter with the blacks, in which 12 of their assailants were killed. The Norman River (formerly the Bynor). In lat. 18° 7', they came on well-defined tracks of four camels and one horse (Burke's), and, pushing forward, Walker reached the depôt formed by Norman on the Albert on the 7th December. Starting again on the 21st, he endeavoured to follow Burke's tracks south, in which he showed his excellent bush knowledge, but failed. On the 25th December they reached the Norman, and on the 1st February, 1862, the Jardine, whence crossing the Great Cordillera of the east coast, and so by the Burdekin, until they reached Port Denison, on 5th June, 1861-2.

John M'Kinlay's party consisted of Mr. Middleton (Mr. Hodgkinson till February 24) second in command, Davis, Palmer, Wylde, Kirby, Poole, Maitland, and three blacks, with camels, bullocks, sheep, and a cart. Started from Adelaide on August 16, 1861, Blanchewater September 24, and arrived at Lake Pando October 6, where they heard reports from the Lake Torrens blacks of white men travelling with camels. On October 20 they reached Lake Kadhi-baerri (Lake Massacre) and found tracks of camels and horses and a white man's grave. They picked up a canteen, an exploded Eley's cartridge, and a piece of the *Nautical Almanac*, horse-hair, &c. The body was that

JOHN McKINLAY
Picturesque Atlas of Australia

of a European enveloped in a flannel jacket with short sleeves. This was Gray's grave. Here M'Kinlay had a brush with the natives. Having, as he thought, found traces of the destruction of Burke's party, M'Kinlay sent the news back to Adelaide, and establishing a depôt in lat. 27° 41' long. 139° 30', he waited the return of Hodgkinson, who brought from Adelaide the news of the rescue of King by Hewitt. In an excursion to the eastward he visited the graves of Burke and Wills. Starting from his depot, he got into a country of lakes—Lake Buchanan, Lake M'Kinlay, Lake Jeannie, Lake Hodgkinson, Lake Goyder, Browne's Creek, Mount M'Donnell (after the Governor), and Lake Lady Blance, Lake Sir Richard—where they camped from the 6th to the 18th January, 1862. These latter were covered with wild fowl, and the country was very good. Hayward Creek (after the owner of Aroona, in S. A.), Lake Strangways, Alfred Creek, Ellar's Creek, Mount Wylde, Caddry-yerra. On February 14 they found the remains of Burke's horse and saddle. Near this M'Kinlay left his cart and sundry things. Several of his party were very ill and the heat was intense. Some of the bullocks were killed by it, but the sheep throve wonderfully. At the beginning of March the rain fell, and the country became flooded and difficult to travel. March 9, at Escape Creek, Will's Range, Elliott's Knob, Browne's Creek (after J. H. Brown, of Booboorowie's, S.A.); Ellar's Tier, and Warren's Tier of Table Tops (after G. Warren, of Gawler), The Downs of Plenty, Scott Ranges (after John Scott, of Adelaide), Emu Downs, Carbine Creek, Davenport Creek (after George Davenport, of Melbourne), Brown's Creek (after Charles Brown, of Bourke-street, Melbourne); The Hamilton Range (after the Inspector of Police, Adelaide); Hunter, Mary, and Moses Islands, Jeannie Lagoon, Euro Hill, Kell's Creek, Mueller's Creek and Mount (after Baron von Mueller, now called the Diamantina, after Lady Bowen); The Robinson River (after J. Robinson, of Hume River); The Mansergh River; The Fletcher River (after G. B. Fletcher, of Tapis, Darling River); The Cadell River (after Captain Cadell, "the enterprising and indefatigable navigator of the Murray and Darling"); The Middleton Creek, Savillis Creek, M'Kinlay's Range, The Hamilton River. The Warburton (after the Commissioner of Police); Crozier Range (after J. Crozier, of Murray River); William's Range, Kirby's Ranges (where a man of that name was lost with sheep for three days, to the great distress of the leader and himself); Black-eyes Creek (after a noted bullock); Marchant Creek (after William Marchant, of Mananarie); The Williams (after Edward Williams, Esq., North Adelaide); The Elder (after Sir Thomas Elder); Poole's Creek (after R. T. Poole, of Willaston); Mounts Elephant, Macpherson, and Margaret; The Jeannie and William Creeks (the latter being the Cloncurry of Burke); Davis Creek. On May 5, 1862, the party were on Gregory's track, 20 miles east of

where he crossed the Leichhardt, which river they struck next day. At Rowdy Creek Camp, on May 17, he killed one of his remaining bullocks, which only gave them 70 lb. weight of meat without a particle of fat. They were now surrounded by salt water creeks and the river and within four or five miles of the coast. On May 21, they commenced their return journey towards Port Denison. Passed Fisher Creek (after C. B. Fisher, of Adelaide); Boord's Creek (after Samuel Boord, of Adelaide); got on Landsborough's tracks. On June 7, struck the Flinders (Norman or Bynoe); Gregory's Ranges, Mount Wildash (after W. Wildash, of Queensland); Hawker's Bluff (after Hon. G. C. Hawker); Morphett's Peak (after John Morphett, of Adelaide). So through very rough country, in which the horses knocked up, provisions failing, flavouring their soup with the pickled green-hide reserved for the camels' boots, slowly towards the station on the Burdekin, passing Ross Creek, Cole Creek, Beveridge Creek, Clark's Creek, till July 11, when they reached the Campbell and Bowen Rivers, Gibson Creek and Brown and Kirsock Rivers. On the 20th they reached the M'Keachie Creek (named after Alexander M'Keachie, of Delagate, Monaro, N.S.W.); and two days after the Burdekin. Only two pack horses and one camel left Forster's Peak and River (after A. W. Forster, of the Murray; M'Leod's Bluff (after James M'Leod, of the Darling); and the Fletcher Range (after G. B. Fletcher, of Ta-pio, Darling); Mount Buchanan (after Alexander Buchanan, of Anlaby, S.A.); the Scott River (after E. B. Scott, of Moorna, on the Murray); and Mount Middleton ("after our right hand man"); Mounts Frederick and Philip (after the brothers Fletcher, of Melbourne); Mount Poole (after R. T. Poole, of Adelaide); Mount Bertram (after Alexander Bertram, of Sandhurst); Mount Haverfield (after Robert Haverfield, of Echuca); Mount Grierson (after R. Grierson, of Melbourne); Mount Roberts (after G. Roberts, of the Murray). On July 30 they killed and boiled down their last camel. On August 2, with only the horses they rode and one pack horse, they struck Hawey and Somers's out-station on the Bowen. Finally, the party reached Port Denison and Melbourne, where a great ovation was given to him and his party, together with Landsborough and King, at the Exhibition Building, 1861-2.

Captain W. H. Norman, H.M.C.S. "Victoria." This expedition was intended as a support and deport on the Albert River for the explorations of Landsborough, M'Kinlay, and Walker. Commander Norman had a general supervision of the whole, a duty which he performed admirably. The officers of the "Victoria" were—G. A. Woods, 1st Lieutenant; C. C. Gascoyne, 2nd Lieutenant; R. Griffiths, Chief Engineer; G. Elliot, Paymaster; S. Paterson, Surgeon; — Frost, gunner (killed by a gun-shot accident). The "Victoria" sailed from Melbourne August 21, 1861. Succoured

Landsborough's party (26) ; found the depôt on the Albert September 12 ; searched and surveyed the neighbouring coast ; left the river February 16, and reached Melbourne February 31, 1862 ;—1861-2.

C. E. Dempster and *A. Dempster*, with their companions, B. Clarkson, C. Harper, and a native, made an exploration from the settled districts of W. A., as far as Mount Kennedy. Discovered an extensive chain of lakes, and heard from the blacks of three white men who had perished. These were surmised to be of Leichhardt's party. Another party, composed of C. and W. and A. Dempster, and Maxwell and Larnock, made an expedition to the S. E., setting out from Northam, thence to Port Malcolm, and thence northward to the interior, which was found barren country, 1861-3.

Frank T. Gregory. Expedition to De Witt's Land. Party : J. Turner, assistant, E. Brockman, W. S. Hall, J. M'Court, A. James, J. Harding, M. Brown, and P. Walcott. They left Freemantle in the " Dolphin " April 23, and landed at Nickol Bay. Discovered and named the Maitland River, the Fortescue River, Hammersley Range, Chichester Downs, Harding River, Samson and Bruce Hills, Sherlock River. Reached the sea between Pickard and Depuch islands, and thence to their camp at Nickol Bay. On July 30 they again set out ; discovered and named the Yule River, the Strelley River, the Shaw River, the De Grey River, the Oakover, and the Ashburton, (named after Lord A., the President of the Geographical Society). Pearl oyster beds were found by the crew of the "Dolphin" on the coast of Nickol Bay. The party got on board that vessel October 21, and returned to Freemantle, 1861.

Dalrymple's second Journey. Traced an opening from the Valley of Lagoons to Rockingham Bay, Queensland, 1862.

Thomas M'Farlane, of Western Australia, started from Streaky Bay in August, and made extraordinary efforts to penetrate the country around the great Australian Bight, 1863.

Messrs. *H. M. Le Froy*, superintendent of convicts, and *Robinson*, with a party of four men equipped by Government, in May, penetrated eastward from York to long. 122° 40′ to the lake which bears the leader's name ; three months in the field. Much valuable pastoral and agricultural land was found, 1863.

C. C. Hunt and *Ridley*. Explorations in the cutter "Mystery," in April, May, and June, along the coast, and a land journey from Tien Tsin harbour to the De Grey River, 1863.

An immense extent of country on all the rivers flowing into the Gulf of Carpentaria taken up, 1864-6.

J. G. Macdonald, made a successful journey from the head water of the Lynd River to the Albert in August, established the first store there, and chartered the first vessel from Sydney, 1864.

Settlement founded in June, 1864, at Adam Bay, Alexander Land, B. T. Finnis, first Government Resident—abandoned ; and, in 1869, Port

Darwin selected by Mr. G. W. Goyder, Surveyor-General, who founded Palmerston. The same year in June, a settlement was founded at Port Albany, Queensland, by Capt. Carneigie, in H. M. S. "Salamander."

C. C. Hunt, W. Australia, with a family of four and two natives and twenty-three horses. Exploration east of York. Found a fine tract of land 350 miles east of that town. Absent 22 weeks, 1864.

Messrs. Jardine, Cape York County, a private exploration from Leichhardt's track on the Mitchell in 1845, in a northern direction along the west shore of the Gulf ; discovered and named Holroyd Creek, Kendal Creek, Kinloch Creek, Archur River, Coran River, Batavia River, Jardine River, and Somerset Town at Cape York, 1864-5.

Duncan M'Intyre, in looking for country on the Flinders, heard a report of supposed traces of Leichhardt. A Ladies' Committee was formed in Melbourne, and £4000 raised to send M'Intyre in search. Party consisted of leader's brother, five others and an Afghan in charge of the camels, lent by the Victorian Government. The notorious Dr. J. P. Murray (of the "Carl" case), was surgeon. His misconduct was the principal cause of this expedition proving a shameful failure. The traces were no doubt those of Landsborough and M'Kinlay. M'Intyre subsequently got across to the Gulf and died there. 1865.

Delisser and *Hardwicke*, started from Clona, the out-station of Fowler's Bay, across the Nullabor Plain to the edge of the great Victorian desert, in latitude 30°, 1865.

John Forrest, West Australia. The native tribes on the border of the settled districts having reported supposed massacre of white men, another Leichhardt search party was equipped and sent from Perth. Forrest penetrated 250 miles to the east of former expedition, named Lake Barlee, Mount Alfred, Mount Alexander, Mount Malcolm, Mount Leonora, Mount Floro, Mount Margaret, and Mount Weld, 1869-70.

John Forrest's second journey. On his return Forrest was equipped for a journey to Adelaide, the Government being desirous of learning something of the country through which the telegraph wire was to pass. He started with his brother Alexander and five others, on the 30th March, and travelled nearly over Eyre's tracks. On 2nd July they arrived at Eucla, and in August reached Adelaide, where they received a cordial welcome. The party were never 30 miles inland, and had a little vessel coasting the route, 1869-70.

Ernest Giles. Between the years 1872–1876 Mr. Giles made five expeditions west of the Telegraph line. The first party, equipped at the expense of Baron von Mueller and himself, consisted of Mr. Carmichael and A. Robinson, with 15 horses. They started from the Telegraph Line in August, 1872, reached "Chambers's Pillar," and departing thence travelled 40 miles through Glen Edith to

Gill's Range, a fine pastoral country. Lake Amadeus (named after the King of Spain) prevented Giles reaching Mount Olga. After being three months in the field, and exploring 250 miles of new country, Giles returned. Places named on this expedition : Chandler's Range, M'Minn Creek, Phillip Creek, the Glen of Palms, Ellery's Creek (after the Government Astronomer, Victoria), Todd Glen (after Mr. Todd, C.M.G., the Postmaster-General, South Australia), Krichauff Range (after the Hon. F. K., of Adelaide), Rudall Creek (Dr. R., of Melbourne), Gosse's Range (after a brother explorer), Carmichael Creek, Haast's Bluff (after Dr. Von H., Government Geologist, N. Zealand), Mount Musgrave (after the Gov. of S.A.), the Leibig Mountains (after Baron Von L.), Gardiner's Range, Mount Peculiar, Ehrenberg Range (Professor E., of Berlin), The Tarn of Auber, Vale of Tempe, M'Nicol's Range, Worril's Pass, Johnny's Creek (after J. M'Culloch, of Gottlieb-Wells), King's Creek, Carmichael's Crag, Penny's Creek (after Mr. P., of Yorke's Peninsula), Stokes Creek (after F. S., of Coonatto), Bagott's Creek (after J. B., of the Peake), Trickett's Creek, Gill's Range (after his brother-in-law, G. D. G., of Melbourne), Mount Levi (after P. L., of Adelaide), Petermann's Creek (after the celebrated geographer of Gotha), Middleloni Pass (after A. D. M., of Mena-Marty), Rogers Pass (after Murray R., of the Darling), Mounts Reginald and Alfred (after sons of Major Campbell), Seymour Range (after Robt. S., a brother explorer), Mount Prim (after E. P., of the Darling), Mount

Omerod, Peddle's Ponds (after J. G. A. P., of the Darling), Bacon's Range (after Harley B., of the Telegraph Line), Briscoe's Ponds (after H. H. B., of the Darling), Mount Sonder (after Dr. W. O. S., of Hamburg), Mount Zeil (after Count Z.), Mount Heuglin (after Baron von H.) Giles and his party returned to the Telegraph line at the Finke and Hugh Junction, on 21st November, 1872. His second expedition consisted of W. H. Tietkans, A. Gibson, and J. Andrews, with 24 horses. The funds were mostly found by Victorian subscriptions. They left the Telegraph line at the junction of the Stevenson and Alberga Creeks, on Aug. 4, 1873. On this expedition Giles penetrated 700 miles, discovered four distinct ranges, seven mountains, and extensive pastoral country, since occupied. They were nearly 12 months in the field, 1873. Places named : Anthony's Range (after the Governor, Musgrave), the Krichauff Range, Mount Sir Henry and Ayers Range (Sir H. Ayers, K.C.M.G.), Mount Barrow (the Hon. J. B.), Mount Reynolds (the Hon. T. R.), Mount Cavenagh (the Hon. W. C.), Everard Range (the Hon. W. E.), Tietkens Creek (after the second in command), Mount Ferdinand (Baron von Mueller), Mount Winter (Jas. W., of Rushworth), Mount Officer (S. H. O., of Victoria), Currie Creek (J. C., of St. Kilda), Levinger Creek (B. L., of Melbourne), Winter Creek (after S. P. W., of Newindale), Mount Davenport (after Hon. S. D., of Adelaide), Moffat's Creek (after R. M., of Ravenswood), Glen Watson (J. B. W., of Sandhurst), Bowen Range (Gov. of Victoria), Fraser's

JOHN FORREST ARRIVES AT THE GREAT AUSTRALIAN BIGHT, 1870
National Library of Australia

GILES AT QUEEN VICTORIA SPRING, 1875
National Library of Australia

Wells (W. F., of Wagga). On the 4th September they cut the dry track of Gosse's Government Expedition, which altered the plans and course of Giles. Christy Bagott's Creek, Wilson Lake (Sir S. W., of Horsham), Hector's Pass (nephew of do.), Stevenson's Creek (Geo. S., of Melb.), Hogarth's Wells (Hon. T. H., of Smithfield), Glen Osborne (S. O., of Elsternwick), Mount Scott (A. S., of Jolimont), Sladen Water (Sir C. S., C.M.G., of Victoria), Glen Cumming (Hon. J. C., of Melbourne), Mount Russel (Hon. Phillip R., of Melbourne), Glen Gerald, Glen Fielder, Mount Barlee (after Colonial Sec., W.A.), Mount Buttfield, Rawlinson Range (Sir. H. R., President R.G.S., London), Carnarvon Range (after the Secretary of State), Mount Sargood (Hon. F. S., of Melbourne), Docker Creek, Livingstone Pass, Mount Skene (Hon. W. S., of Victoria), M'Bain Springs (James M'B., of Toorak) Hull Creek, Curdie's Range, Blood's Range, Chirnside Creek, Shaw Creek, Glen Robertson (G. R., of Casterton), Alfred and Marie Range (the Duke and Duchess of Edinburgh), Gibson's Desert (where one of the party met with his death), Mount Forrest (after J. F., the explorer).—1875. Giles was again fitted out, this time by Sir Thomas Elder, the well known patron of exploration, who supplied him with 19 camels and provision for 18 months. They started from Youldah 27th July, 1875. The party consisted of Mr. Tietkens, Mr. Young, A. Ross, P. Nicholls, Saleh (an Afghan), and a black boy. This re-markable journey carried them through desert after desert for some 1500 miles. One stretch of 325 miles from water to water occupied 17 days in the travelling, and the little band were saved by a spring in the Great Victoria Desert, 600 miles from the W. Aust. settlement, which they reached 4th November, 1875. Departing from Perth 13th January, 1876, Giles pushed north and struck the Ashburton, thence passing thorugh 150 miles of desert towards the Rawlinson Range. On August 23, they reached the Peak Telegraph station, and subsequently Adelaide.

The great overland telegraph running over the tracks of J. M'D. Stuart from Adelaide to Port Darwin, was on 22nd October placed in connection with the cable laid by the British-Australian Company between Java and that place. The distance from Port Darwin to Adelaide is 1,973 miles. The cost of the overland telegraph line was £370,000. The first message through from England came to Messrs. M'Ewan

and Co., of Melbourne. The cable end arrived at Port Darwin in October, and the shore end was laid on 7th November. The ships employed were the "Edinburgh," 2800 tons, the "Hibernia," 3100 tons, and the "Investigator," 600 tons. Captain Halpin was in command. 1872.

Colonel Peter Egerton Warburton, from Central Australia to the West Coast; equipped by Sir Thomas Elder and Captain Hughes, of Adelaide; started from Alice Springs, April 15. Party : R. Warburton (son of the leader), J. W. Lewis, D. White, two Afghans, and a black boy; with 17 camels and six months' provisions. They traversed the continent from the M'Donnell

COLONEL WARBURTON TOASTS THE QUEEN, MAY 24, 1873
National Library of Australia

Ranges to the coast north of Nickol Bay, passing over 800 or 900 miles of ground never before trodden by a white man. When they reached the Oakover the party were utterly exhausted, with only a few pounds of dried camel flesh left. They were rescued by Messrs. Grant, Harper, and Anderson, of the De Grey River, the furthest outlying station-holders, who sent the party down 150 miles to Roebourne (Tsien Tsin). 1873.

John Forrest. The great Western Desert crossed, 1874. [Party consisted of Alexander Forrest, five whites, two aboriginals, and 21 horses. The party left Champion Bay on April 1, and the outlying stations on the 18th. On May 4 they reached Mount Hale on the Murchison, and beautifully grassed country. From the head of a branch in lat. 25° 50′, long. 119°, they proceeded to the watershed of the river. Passing over undulating spinifex desert, they slowly attained long. 127°; thence to the Barrow Ranges and Giles's tracks, the Cavenagh Ranges

(Giles), Mount Cooper (Gosse), Tomkinson Ranges, Lungdey's Gully, Musgrave Ranges, and on to the Alberga, which they traced down, and reached the Peake telegraph station, Sept. 30. The horses knocking up, they had to walk turn about nearly 2000 miles. The Tomkinson, Mann, and Musgrave Ranges were beautifully grassed. For 600 miles in one portion of the journey they travelled through nothing but a spinefex desert.]

William C. Gosse. South Australia Government Expedition, 1874. [An expedition almost simultaneous with that of Colonel Warburton; accompanied by three white men (Mr. E. Berry, the leader's brother, and another), three Afghans and a black boy, with a cart and horses. Started from Alice Springs; explored 60,000 square miles of territory of which previously nothing had been known to the west, across the West Australian boundary. We discovered and named Ayer's Rock, a remarkable high mass of granite, 1100 feet higher than the surrounding country, and in extent two miles east and west, rising abruptly from the plain. It contains caves with many remarkable drawings. The expedition penetrated 600 miles west of the telegraph line, over country which no other white man had seen. The furthest point west reached was 26° 21′ S., 126° 59′ E.]

J. W. Lewis and *W. Beresford.* The leader had proved himself an excellent explorer when a member of Warburton's party. They were sent out by the Government of South Australia, to survey the country about Lake Eyre, and did good service in correcting the maps of previous explorations in that direction by Warburton. The camels were lent by Sir Thomas Elder. A block of country 200 miles across from Lake Hope to Eyre Creek in Queensland, and about 250 miles broad, stretching from the telegraph line to Sturt's Stony Desert, was examined, 1875.

Gilbert M'Minn and *A. W. Sergison.* South Australian Government, 1876. [A party sent to ascertain the course of the Katherine River, which they followed down into fine country. They then made for Mount Hayward, the head of the navigation of the Daly, and traversed 113 miles of splendid country. Returning, they made for the head of the Adelaide, and descended it till it opened into large plains. From thence they rode to Southport, where they arrived November 3. The following year (1877) Mr. Sergison and Mr. Roderick Travers formed a party, and explored the country about the Daly and Fitzmaurice Rivers. They found 5,000,000 acres of the finest pastoral land on Roe Downs.]

Ross and *Harvey,* South Australia. From Mount Crisse, on the Stevenson, through Charlotte Waters to the Todd River. Followed up the Waite River, which was the limit of exploration in this direction, 1877.

EXPLORERS, SEA

[Australia was practically discovered by Lieut. James Cook in 1770. In a work of this compendious character, therefore, the following brief reference to the earlier navigators of Australasian seas must suffice.]

The learned researches of Mr. R. H. Major, of the British Museum, on the subject are well known. He awards the priority of discovery to Guillaume Le Testu, a Provençal pilot, born at Grasse. A map indicating Australia, bearing the date of 1542 and his name, is now in the Depôt de la Guerre at Paris. The claims of De Gonnville, of Honfleur, 1503; Magalharn, the First Circumnavigator, 1520; the Portuguese, in 1540; and the Spaniard Manoel Godinho de Eredia, 1601, are doubtful.

The voyage of Don Jorge de Menezes, from Malacca to the Moluccas, in 1526; of Alvarez Mendana, in 1595, to the Marquesas; of Alvarez de Saavedra, in 1526, and Ruy Lopez de Villalobos, in 1543, and James le Maive and William Schouten, in 1616, to the coast of New Guinea, (Papua), may all be said to have been in search of the Great South Land.

The Dutch yacht "Duyfhen," (the Dove) from Bantam, commander unknown, sailed along the east coast of Carpentaria as far as Cape Keerweer (Turn again), 1605.

Pedro Fernandez de Yuisos and *Luis Vaes de Torres.* Discovery of Straits known by name of the latter, 1606.

Theodoric Hertoge or *Hatichs,* commonly called Dirk Hartog, in the "Endraght," whence the coast is now known, to Shark's Bay, Western Australia, left a record on a tin plate, 1616. [*See* Vlemingh.]

JANZOON'S DRYFKEN
Picturesque Atlas of Australia

Captain Zeachern, discoverer of Arnhem's Land (doubtful), 1618.

John Van Edels, on the west coast, named after him, 1619.

The "Landt Van de Leeuwin," or "Land of Lions," the south-west cape of Australia, named from the vessel, 1622.

Jan Carstens, from Amboyna, in the "Peera" and "Arnhem," north-west coast, 1623.

Pieter Nuytz, in the "Gulde Zeepard," "outward bound from Fatherland for the space of 1,000 miles," western and southern coasts, 1627.

Willem de Witt (of the "Vianen"), north-west coast; named after him, 1628.

Francis Pelsart, in the "Batavia" frigate lost on Houtman's Abrolhos, 1629.

Pieter Carpenter, with a squadron, discovered the Gulf of Carpentaria, 1628.

Gerrit Tomaz Pool, in the "Amsterdam" and "Wezel," from Banda; coasts of New Guinea and Arnhem's Land, 1636.

TASMAN'S CARPENTER LANDING
Picturesque Atlas of Australia

Abel Jansen Tasman. The "Happy Voyage" in the "Heemskirk" and "Zeehaan," the latter commanded by Gerritt Jansan, sailed from Batavia August 14, 1642; discovered Van Diemen's Land November 24; anchored in Fredrick Hendrik's Bay (now Prince of Wales Bay), on December 1, and took possession for Holland. Sailing hence, on December 9, Tasman discovered New Zealand, 1642.

Tasman, in a second voyage, surveyed in the "Limmen," the "Reemeaw," and the "Brak," several thousand miles of the north and north-

west coasts (Carpentaria), 1644. [No journal exists, but his chart was published and his track "depicted" in 1648, on the floor of the Stadthouse at Amsterdam. Tasman born at Hoovu, in New Holland, about 1600. Subsequent career to date of death unknown.]

NEW HOLLAND, the name by which Australia henceforth known.

The "Vergulde Draeck," from Batavia, lost on the Abrolhos, 1656.

William Dampier, in the "Bachelor's Delight," and "Cygnet," on a voyage round the world (which lasted eight years), along with his buccaneer comrades, made the north-west coast at Roebuck Bay on January 4, 1688; left the coast February 12th. Dampier born in Somersetshire, in 1652. Date of death unknown.

WILLIAM DAMPIER
Picturesque Atlas of Australia

Willem de Vlemingh, in the "Geelvink," "Nyptang," and "Wezel" sailed from Holland in search of the Dutch ship "Ridderschap," thought to have been lost on the Abrolhos. Sighted land near Swan River 25th December; landed on main 5th January; named place from the black swans now first seen; sailed north and found the record left by Hertoge; added another record on a tin plate; both found by Baudin in 1803; Grey, in 1838, could find neither, 1695.

William Dampier, in the "Roebuck," sailed from England to explore the north-west coast of New Holland 14th January; anchored in Shark's

Bay 6th July; coasting till 30th without finding a landing-place; visited the archipelago that bears his name; left the coast in September, 1699. [Dampier was, with Woodes Rodgers, again in these seas, 1710.]

Three Dutch ships from Timor explored north-west coast, then called Van Diemen's Land, 1705.

Commodore Roggewein, fitted out from Holland, discovered "the Thousand Islands." 1721.

The "Zeewyck" lost on the Abrolhos; the crew escaped to Batavia in a boat built from the wreck, 1727. [Stokes found a gun and some other relics on an island 1839.]

Captain Carterat at Santa Cruz, New Britain, and New Zealand. 1767.

M. de Bougainville, the Louisiade archipelago, 1768.

Captain de Surville in the "St. Jean Baptiste," 32 guns, from Pondicherry, cast anchor in Doubtless Bay, New Zealand, 16th December, at the very time Cook in his first voyage was quitting that place. They saw nothing of each other. 1769. [De Surville made some discoveries in the "Argacides" on his voyage to Callao. He was drowned going ashore there.]

Capt. James Cook. The Australian Continent, for all practical purposes, first discovered by Lieut. Cook when engaged on his first voyage round the world. His ship, the "Endeavour," 370 tons, sailed from Plymouth, August 26, 1768, came on to the Australian coast, April 19, 1770, at a point now within the colony of Victoria, in latitude 38° S., longitude 24° 7' E., now identified with Cape Conran. Land first seen by Lieutenant Zachary Hicks, after whom it was named. Sailing north, Cook passed and named Ram Head, Cape Howe, Mount Dromedary, Port Upright, Bateman's Bay, The Pigeon House, Cape St. George, Long Nose and Red Points. April 28, reached, named, and anchored in Botany Bay; here on May 1 was buried a seaman named Forby Sutherland, *the first white man buried in Australia.* May 6, passed an opening which he named "Port Jackson," after Sir George Jackson, one of the Admiralty Secretaries. Ranged along the coast, naming Broken Bay, Cape Three Points, Cape Hawke, Smoky Cape, Cape Byron, Mount Warning, Point Danger, Point Look-out, Moreton Bay, The Glass Houses, Double-Island Point, Indian Head, Sandy Cape, Break-Sea Spit, Hervey's Bay, Cape Capricorn, Cape Manifold, Keppel Bay and Islands, Cape Townshend, Thirsty Sound, Cape Palmerston, The Bay of Inlets, Cape Conway, Repulse Bay, Whitsunday Passage, Cumberland Islands, Cape Gloucester, Holborne Isle, Edgecumbe Bay, Cape Upstart, Cleveland Bay, Magnetical Isle, Halifax Bay, Cape Sandwich, Rockingham Bay, Dunk Isle, Frankland's Isles, Cape Grafton, Green Island, and Trinity Bay. June 10, near Cape Tribulation, the "Endeavour" struck on a coral reef, but with great exertion was got off on the 12th, and on the 17th got to an anchor in Endeavour River. Here they repaired the

vessel, and saw the first kangaroo. August 4, sailed again. Named Cape Bedford, Cape Flattery, Lizard Island, Eagle Island, Direction Island, Providential Channel, Cape Weymouth, Forbes Islands, Bolt Head, Cape Grenville, Temple Bay, Sir Charles Hardy's Isles, and Cockburn Isles. August 21, Cook reached Cape York, the northern promontory of the continent, and at Possession Island hoisted the British colours, and claimed the whole of the coast he had traced for King George III, under the name of NEW SOUTH WALES. Thence he proceeded on his scientific voyage to the North Pacific. In this voyage Cook tested the chronometer made by Kendall upon Harrison's description, and Cook's favourable report procured to Harrison the additional £10,000 voted by Parliament. The "Endeavour" returned to England, July 13, 1771. In his third voyage he was killed by the natives of Owhyhee, February 14, 1779. [A magnificent statue, the work of Woolner, has been erected to the great navigator in Hyde Park, Sydney, at a cost of £4,000. The foundation-stone was laid by H.R.H. the Duke of Edinburgh, on March 27, 1869. The statue was unveiled February 25, 1879, by His Excellency Sir Hercules Robinson, Governor of New South Wales. Cook was born at Marton, in Yorkshire, on October 27, 1728. The names of his officers and colleagues in the famous voyage of the "Endeavour" were— First lieutenant, Zachary Hicks; second do., John Gore; master, Robert Molineaux; mate, Charles Clerke; boatswain, John Gathray;

THE ENDEAVOUR IN ROUGH SEAS
British Museum

gunner, Stephen Forward; carpenter, John Slatterley; surgeon, Wm. B. Munkhouse; clerk, Richard Orton. The scientific staff consisted of Mr. (afterwards Sir) Joseph Banks, then President of the Royal Society : Charles Green, assistant to the Astronomer-Royal at Greenwich; Dr. Solander, Swedish botanist, one of the librarians of the British Museum; and Messrs. Buchanan and Parkinson, draughtsmen for natural history and landscape. The following changes took place during the course of the voyage :—

Nov. 6, Wm. Perry, surgeon, in the room of W. B. Monkhouse, died November 5, 1770, at Batavia.

Feb. 5, Saml. Evans, boatswain, in the room of John Gathray, died February 4, 1771.

Feb. 13, George Nowell, carpenter, in the room of John Slatterley, died February 12, 1771.

April 16, Richard Pickersgill, master, in the room of Robert Molineux, died April 15, 1771.

May 25, John Gore, second lieutenant, in the room of Zachariah Hicks, died May 25, 1771.

May 26, Charles Clerke, third lieutenant, in the room of John Gore, appointed second lieutenant.

} At sea.

1770.]

M. De St. Alouarn, anchored near Cape Leeuwin, 1772.

Captain Marion du Fresne, in the "Mascarin and Castres" (Captain Crozet), from Nance, the first visitor to Tasmania since Tasman ; spent six days in Fredrick Hendrik Bay, March 4; thence to New Zealand, where he and 26 others were massacred by the Maories. "They treated us," says Crozet, "with every kind of friendship for 33 days, with the intention of eating us on the 34th." The Maori version, given by Dr. Thomson, is, "We treated Marion's party with every kindness for 30 days, and on the 31st they put two of our chiefs in irons and burned our sacred places :" 1772.

Cook's second voyage in the "Resolution" and "Adventure" (Captain Furneaux, who had been second lieutenant with Wallis) left Plymouth July 15, 1772; searched for southern continent ; visited Dusky Bay (New Zealand), Resolution Island, Doubtful Island, Tongataboo, Oytstack, South Seo, Easter Island, Marquesu, Society Islands, New Hebrides; discovered New Caledonia; discovered Norfolk Island; corrected his former position of New Zealand, Tierra del Fuego, Georgia, Fernando, Novembe, Azores; arrived in England, July 30, 1775. He lost but one man from sickness in a voyage of 3 years and 18 days, and in a navigation that extended through all climates from 52° N. to 71° S. On this voyage he had four chronometers. The officers were Messrs. Wales and Bayley, astronomers; John Reinhold Forster, and his son, and Dr. Sparreman (a Swede), naturalists; an artist, and a draughtsman.

Captain Tobias Furneaux, the "Adventure." [Separated from Cook, who had gone south towards the Pole.] On coasts of Tasmania. Gave it as his opinion that Tasmania and New South Wales were joined, with a deep bay intervening, which opinion, when he met Cook, was deemed sufficient to prevent a further examination by Cook himself.

Cook's third voyage in the "Resolution" and "Discovery" (Captain Clerke). Sailed from Ply-

THE DEATH OF COOK
Mary Evans Picture Library

mouth July 12, 1776. [Touched Mt. Kergusten's Land, Tasmania, and New Zealand ; discovered Wangee Island and Wateeo, Friendly Islands, Tahiti, Bolabola ; discovered Christina's Island, Sandwich Island and Albion Woolka Sound ; Coast to Oonalashka and thence to northward ; Coast north ; discovered Owhyhee (Hawaii), where he was killed (Bay of Karakokooa), February 14, 1779. There were killed at the same time Corporal Thomas of the marines, Theophilus Hinks, John Allan and Thomas Habchatt, a lieutenant, a sergeant and other seamen were wounded. Captain Clerke to Kamstchatka in search of N.W. Passage died. Captains Gore and King brought the ship home, October 4, 1780. Mr. Anderson, who had been sergeant of the "Resolution," was the naturalist.]

Captain Forrest of the East India Company's Service, in a vessel of 10 tons, on the coasts of New Guinea, 1776.

Don Francis Anthony Maurelle, do. 1781.

Governor Phillip arrived at Botany Bay with the "First Fleet" Jan. 3. The British flag hoisted at Sydney Cove, Jan. 26, 1788. [*See* "FIRST FLEET."]

Jean François Galup de la Perouse in the "Boussole" and "Astrolabe" (M. de Langle) French discovery ships. Sailed from Brest August 1, 1784. Touched at Madeira, Teneriffe. Savages. Martin Vas. Trinidad. Searched for Ascension Island. St. Catherine Island. Searched for Island Grande. R. Gallego. Patagonia. Le Maire Shaiti. Cape Horn. Searched for Drake's Island. Mocha. Conception. Easter Island. La Mesa, &c. doubtful. Sandwich Islands. Mount St. Elias. Port des Français and Coast to Monterey. Isle Neckar. Marianas Bashee Islands. Macao. Manilla. Japan Corea. Avatska Bay. Navigation Islands. Friendly Islands. Tongataboo. Norfolk Island. Pylstaart. Entered Botany Bay as Governor Phillip with the "First Fleet" was departing to remove the British settlement to Sydney Cove, January 24, 1788. The naturalist of the "Astrolabe," Father Le Receveur, died at Botany, February 17, 1778. La Perouse left Botany March 10, 1788, and was lost at Manicolo, New Hebrides. His fate unknown till Captain Dillon, of the "Research," in 1827 discovered the traces for which he was created Chevalier by the French Government.

Lieutenant Shortland with three ships from Sydney bound to England passed through Bougainville's Straits, 1788.

J. H. Cox in the brig "Mercury" South Coast of Tasmania, now known by his name and Oyster Bay, 1789.

Don Alexandro Malaspina in the "Descobierta" and "Atrevida" (Don Jose di Bustamente) Spanish discovery ships, left Calais January, 1789. Examined Coast of South America. Found Cape Horn. Juan Fernandez ; thence the coast to the supposed Strait of Juan de Fuca. Acapulco. Philippines. Macoa. Arrived at Sydney, March 21, 1793, sailed April 12. Friendly Islands. Returned to Cadiz, September, 1794. [Malassima was imprisoned on his return and most of his observations were lost.]

Captain George Vancouver in the "Discovery" and "Chatham" (Broughton), explored 110° of the S.W. Coast. Discovered King George's Sound. Broughton discovered Chatham Islands, 1791.

Captain William Bligh (afterwards Governor of New South Wales) in his memorable voyage in the "Bounty's" launch, passed Cape York in his voyage to Copang, 1791.

Captain Edward Edwards of H.M.S. "Pandora" in search of mutineers of the "Bounty," Discovered the Murray Islands. Lost on the reefs; reached Timor in his boats, 1791.

John M'Cluar, Lieutenant in the Bombay Marine in surveying the Coast of New Guinea, sailed along Arnheim's Land to Cape Van Diemen, 1791.

Admiral Bruni D'Entrecasteaux in the "Recherché" and "L'Espérance" (Huon de Kermadec) left Brest September 28, 1791, to seek La Perouse. Voyage to Moluccas. New Caledonia. Hammond Island. Tesoriere Island. Isle Banca. New Hanover. Admiralty Island. New Guinea. Timor. Java. Nuytz Land. Esperance Bay. South Coast of Australia. Anchored in Slovni Bay, called the Derwent "La Riviere du Nord" (*See* HAYES). Tasmania, April 12. New Zealand. Tongataboo. Erronan. Discovered Isles Beaupré. Solomon Islands. Dampier's Strait. Wagion. Cajali, Sourabaya. D'Entrecasteaux, de Kermadec, and D'Auribeau having died the journals were published by the late Admiral Rossel. Labillardiere was the naturalist of the expedition, 1792.

Captain William Bligh and *Nathan Portlock* in the "Provident" and "Assistant." Transport of bread-fruit from Pacific Islands to West Indies. Exploration of Torres Straits. Planted fruit and vegetables in Tasmania, 1792.

William Bampton and *Matthew B. Alt* in the ships "Hormuzeer" and "Chesterfield" near Norfolk Island through Torres Strait, 1793.

John Hayes, Captain in Bombay Marine in the "Duke" and "Duchess" visited Tasmania and gave names to the Derwent, &c., which have replaced the names of the first discoverer, D'Entrecasteaux, 1794.

Matthew Flinders and *George Bass,* with a boy, in a boat 8 feet long, called "Tom Thumb," in October, 1795, traced the George River 20 miles further than previously known ; in March following, in same boat, reached Port Hacking. Returned April 2, 1796.

Captain Wilson in the "Duff" missionary vessel. Line Islands, 1797.

Bass, in a whale boat, with six hands, left Sydney 3 December ; on 19th, discovered Twofold Bay, and next day rounded the Howe, and in the evening landed near Ram Head. Could not identify the "Point Hicks" of Cook. January 3, 1798, found some convicts who had escaped from Sydney, on an island near Promontory. On 4th reached, and until 18th, explored Western Port. On return, rounded Promontory 26th. On 24 February, this remarkable exploration of 600 miles of coast line ended by arrival in Sydney, 1798.

Flinders, in the "Francis," to the wreck of the

MATTHEW FLINDERS AND GEORGE BASS IN THE "TOM THUMB"

Picturesque Atlas of Australia

"Sydney Cove" in the Straits, February 1, 1798.

Flinders and *Bass*, in the "Norfolk," a little sloop of 25 tons, built at Norfolk Island, sailed from Sydney 7 October. Circumnavigated Tasmania. Discovered the Tamar River. Returned to Sydney January 11, 1799. Bass Strait named by Governor Hunter after this voyage, 1799.

Flinders, in the "Norfolk," sent by Governor Hunter to explore the coast northward, sailed 8 July; on 15th cleared Point Danger, and entered Moreton and Glasshouse Bays. Conflict with the natives at Point Skirmish. Ascended Pumice Stone River. Went on to Hervey Bay, 1799. [The inlet he entered, Shoal Bay, was afterwards found to be the mouth of the Clarence.]

James Grant, Lieutenant in the "Lady Nelson," 60 tons, tender to the "Investigator," left Portsmouth 17 March, arrived on Australian coast 3 December. The first vessel to pass through Bass Strait. Named Cape Northumberland, Cape Banks, Schanks and Gambier Mounts, Cape Bridgewater, Cape Nelson, Cape Solicitor (Sir William Grant's Cape), Lawrence Islands, Lady Julien Peircy Islands, Cape Albany Ottway, Cape Patten, Portland Bay, Cape Danger, Wight Land, Foveruax King's Bay, Cape Liptrap, South Cape (Promontory), King George's Sound (between Liptrap and Promontory), Sir Roger Curtis Island, Rodondo, The Devil's Tower and Moncur Island, The Hole in the Wall, The Glenine Island. Here Grant's discoveries joined those of Flinders. The "Lady Nelson," called "His Majesty's Tinder-box," arrived in Sydney 16 December. The second ship through Bass Strait was the "Harbinger," Captain Black, from the Cape of Good Hope, January 11, 1801, who sighted and named King Island; the S. part of which was sighted by Captain Reid in 1798. The third ship through was the "Margaret," Captain Byers, from England, 7 February, 1801.

Christopher Dixson, in the ship "Ellegood," most probably a whaler, visited King George's Sound. A sheet of copper bearing these names and the date August 27, 1800, was found by Flinders, when he came on that part of the coast in November, 1801.

James Grant, again in "Lady Nelson," to explore Bass Strait, sailed from Sydney, 8 March, accompanied by Mr. Murray, 1st mate Francis Barreillier (*See* EXPLORERS, LAND), Mr. Cayley, botanist, and Mr. Boven, 2nd mate. Named Cape Paterson; entered Western Port, 21 March. Named Churchill and Margaret Islands (Elizabeth); verified Bass's explorations. Left Western Port 29 April; returned to Sydney 14 May, 1801.

John Murray, Lieutenant, succeeded Grant in "Lady Nelson." Further exploration of the Straits, and discovery of Port Phillip. Left Sydney 23 November, Mr. Bowen 1st mate. Obervsations at Kent's Group and the Promontory Islands. Entered Western Port 6 December, and explored till January 5, 1802, when they were able to get out. On the neighbouring coast until the 31st, when the "Lady Nelson" had again to take shelter in Western Port, and there remain till 15 February. From Western Port, on the 1st February, Murray despatched Bowen with five men, in the launch, to examine the entrance of Port Phillip, which they had seen in their cruize. Bowen got in, and the vessel was carried round on February 15 and anchored off what is now the quarantine ground. Murray remained in the Bay (which he called after the Governor, Port King) a month, and returned to Sydney March 24, 1802.

Captain Matthew Flinders, in the "Investigator," 334 tons, accompanied by R. M. Fowler, (afterwards Admiral) 1st Lieutenant; S. W. Flinders, 2nd Lieutenant; John Crossley, astronomer; Dr. R. Brown, botanist; William Westall, A.R.A., artist; Ferdinand Bauer, natural history painter; John Thistle, master; John Atkin, 2nd master; Hugh Bell and Robert Purdie, surgeons; midshipmen, John Franklin (subsequently the great Arctic explorer), Thomas Evans, William Taylor, Thomas Bell, Nathaniel Bell, Kennet Sinclair, Sherrard P. Laird, and James Wolsey: boatswain, Charles Douglas; gunner, R. Colpits; carpenter, R. Mart; Clerk, John Olive. Total, 88 persons. Sailed for the exploration of the coasts of Australia, from Spithead. July 11, 1801. Sighted Cape Leeuwin December 6. After examining King George's Sound, coasted the Great Bight to Fowler's Bay, the known limits of former exploration, February 16. Named Coffin Bay. Entered Port Lincoln 26th. Next examined Spencer's Gulf on both sides. Entered Investigator Strait, north coast Kangaroo Island, Gulf of St. Vincent, discovered and searched. Sailed through Backstairs Passage April 7. Next day met with Commodore Nicholas Baudin, in the "Géographe," place now called Encounter Bay, lat. 35° 40′ S., 138° 58′ E. Baudin had separated from his 2nd captain in the "Naturaliste" (Hamelin), in a gale after examining Tasmania. Stated he had explored the S. coast from Western Port to the place of meeting.

NICHOLAS BAUDIN
Picturesque Atlas of Australia

Baudin and *Hamelin*. Baudin's explorations extend only over 50 leagues of the coast line. He had passed Port Phillip without noticing the entrance. The wrong subsequently attempted to be done by the French navigators, respecting the discoveries of Flinders, is a matter of history. Parting from Baudin, Flinders pursued his voyage to Sydney. On April 27th, Flinders entered Port Phillip, surveyed the entrance channels, and the coast line of the bay on both shores as high up as Geelong Bay and the opposite shores, landing both at Arthur's Flat, and walking to the top of Station Peak. whence he saw Western Port and at the head of

Port Phillip Bay. On May 9 he arrived at Sydney, and found the "Naturaliste" there. On the 20th her consort the "Géographe" arrived.

Flinders refitted and sailed from Sydney July 22, 1803. He discovered Port Curtis and Port Bowen; spent 105 days in exploring the Gulf of Carpentaria and Arnheim Bay, and proceeding thence to Timor, *circumnavigated Australia for the first time*, and returned to Sydney June 9, 1803. Here the "Investigator" was condemned as unseaworthy. Desirous of getting to England to show what he had done, and obtain another vessel, Flinders took passage with his officers and crew in the "Porpoise," which vessel was homeward bound through Torres Strait. They sailed August 10, 1803, and seven days after were cast away on the Barrier Reef. Flinders made his way back to Sydney, 700 miles, in an open boat, and pursuaded Governor King to let him have a sloop of 30 tons (the "Cumberland"). In this crazy vessel he proceeded home, and putting in to the Mauritius, was there made prisoner by General De Caen, the Governor, and cruelly detained for six years and a-half. Meantime the account of the voyage of Baudin was published in France, in which the whole of the S. coast of Australia, from the Promontory to the Leeuwin, was claimed as the discovery of the French expedition, a claim which was dispelled the day that Flinders' account of his voyage appeared, which was the day of his death, July 19, 1814. He was born in 1774. His grand-daughter enjoys a pension from the two Colonies of New South Wales and Victoria of £200 a year, since 1856. He gave Australia its name, and she has had no more illustrious or more modest explorer.

Charles Grimes, Surveyor-General of N.S.W. in the "Cumberland," in charge of Lieut. Robbins, sent down in Nov. 1802, by Governor King to "walk round" Port Phillip. His assistants were James Meehan and James Flemming. Having sought for Baudin at King's Island, and warned him from attempting a settlement on any station ground, Grimes passed into Port Phillip and thoroughly fulfilled his orders. He was the first to discover the Yarra, (upon which Melbourne now stands). January 30, 1803. [His long-missing chart and journal were found by Mr. T. J. Shillinglaw, F.R.G.S., 1878, and have been published by the Government of Victoria.]

Captain Nicholas Baudin in the "Géographe," and Hamelin in the "Naturaliste," 1802.

Expedition of *Lieut.-Governor Daniel Collins* to form a penal settlement at Port Phillip, left England April 27, on board H.M.S. "Calcutta," 50 tons, Capt. Daniel Woodriff, and the transport "Ocean," John Mertho, master, arrived at Port Phillip, October 9, 1803. Landed the settlement at a place now called "The Sister," near Sorrento. [A very partial exploration of the bay was made by Collins, who seems to have been prejudiced against the place, and on January 30, 1804, a portion of the settlement again embarked on board the "Ocean" and proceeded to Tasmania, where, on February 15, Hobart Town was

LOUIS DE FREYCINET AT SHARK BAY
National Library of Australia

founded. The rest of the detachment followed, and on June 25, 1804, were all killed at Hobart Town. The records of this attempted settlement have recently been published by the Victorian Government.]

Lieut. Bowen had previously been sent from Sydney, in the "Lady Nelson" with a small party of fifteen persons to Tasmania, and had camped at Risdon, near Hobart Town, June 11, 1803.

Lieut.-Colonel Paterson, of the N.S.W. corps, sent from Sydney by Governor King to examine Port Dalrymple with a view to a settlement being formed there, June, 1804.

Lieut. Charles Robbins and *John Oxley* sent by Governor King in the cutter "Integrity" to examine Western Port, 1804-5. This expedition put an end to the idea of a settlement on the South Coast.

L. de Freycinet, in "L'Uranie," sailed from London, September 15, 1817. [Saw Edels Land, Shark's Bay, Simao Island, Coepang, Moluccas, Waigion, Umata, Sandwich Island, Rose Island, Pylstaart, Sydney, Campbell Island, Tierra-del-Fuego. February 15, 1820, touched at the Falklands. Proceeded in "La Physicienne" to Monto Video, Rio, Azores, Cherbourg.]

Captain Philip G. King (born at Norfolk Island, son of Governor King). First voyage, accompanied by Messrs. Roe* and Beddome, (mates,) and Mr. Allan Cunningham, botanist, sailed in the cutter "Mermaid" of 84 tons, from Sydney, December 22, taking a "west-about" route round the Leeuwin; Dampier's N.W. Cape February 10, 1813. In this barren and desolate land met with ant-hills eight feet high; the sea swarmed with turtles, snakes, sharks, and dolphins; the copper-coloured air filled with venomous insects. Anchored in Nicol Bay, March 4, little dreaming of the rich

* Called the "Father of Modern Explorers."

plains in the back country—Goulburn group, Port Singleton, and Van Diemen Gulf. Explored the Alligator, traced it for 40 miles, refitted at Timor, and returned to Sydney, July 28, 1818. Employed in survey of Macquarie Harbour in Tasmania, Port Macquarie, and the Hastings which had just been discovered by Oxley, 1817.

Captain Sutherland on a sealing voyage visited Port Lincoln, and remained for seven months on Kangaroo Island, 1819.

King. Second voyage in "Mermaid." In May, 1819 sailed from Sydney, and passing through Torres Straits took up the survey at the point left off by Flinders—Wessells Heads. Examined coast from Clarence Straits to Cambridge Gulf, overrunning the work of the French Commodore Baudin; returned to Sydney January 12, 1820.

King. Third voyage, accompanied by Allan Cunningham, resumed the survey in June on the "Red Coast." Had to leave off at Prince Regent's River, near present Camden Harbour Settlement. Returned to Sydney in September, 1820.

King's Fourth voyage. Messrs. Roe and Cunningham accompanying in the "Bathurst," 1821. [Some remarkable caverns at Princess Charlotte Bay. Sailed 50 miles up the Prince Regent River. Refitted at Mauritius. Returned and surveyed Swan River and the coast northward to the Buccaneer Archipelago, which had been partially examined by Baudin. Returned to Sydney April, 1822. This was King's last voyage in our waters. He was subsequently engaged in the survey of the "Beagle" in South America, and he died a Rear-Admiral in 1855. A settlement at Port Cockburn was made in 1824 by Sir Gordon Bremer as a result of King's exploration. This was abandoned in 1826, and which another settlement formed at Raffles Bay, also had to be abandoned in 1829.]

Captain Duperry in "La Coquille." Voyage amongst the Line Islands, 1822-4.

Captain Bougainville in the "Thetis." Left Brest March 2, 1824. Malacca, Singapore, &c., explored to south of Tasmania. Refitted at Port Jackson, sailed 21st September, and crossed the Pacific to Valparaiso without seeing land, 1824.

D. H. Kolff, Lieutenant in the Dutch brig "Dourga." Exploration of the islands about New Guinea and the Arafura Sea, 1825. [Corrected by Lieutenant Modera in 1828 in corvette "Triton."]

Captain (Chevalier) *Dillon* in the "Research" [De La Perouse] on the South Coast about Port Lincoln and Encounter Bay. 1826.

Captain Gould visited the South Coast about Port Lincoln, 1827-8.

Captain Dumont D'Urville in the "Astrolabe" sailed from Toulon in April. Touched at Bass Straits, North part of New Zealand, and Pacific Islands, 1826.

Captain James Stirling, H.M.S. "Success," Survey of coast from King George's Sound to Swan River, 1828.

Captain R. Fitzroy in the "Beagle." Visited New Zealand, Port Jackson, Hobart Town, King George's Sound, 1829.

Captain La Place sailed from Toulon 30th December. Visited East Indies, Hobart Town, New Zealand, 1829.

Survey of the coasts of Australia by the "Beagle" and "Fly," 1837-1841. [The "Beagle" left England June, 1837. Her officers were T. C. Wickham, Commander, retired through ill health March, 1841; J. B. Emery, Lieutenant, retired in 1841; Henry Eden, Lieutenant, retired in 1841; John Lort Stokes, Lieutenant, succeeded Wickham 1841, and continued survey till 1843; Charles Darwin, F.R.S., Naturalist. The ship reached Swan River November 15, 1837; 1838, discovered the Fitzroy River; 1839, left Sydney for Port Essington, 22nd May; arrived there January. Discovered and named Adam Bay (after Admiral Sir Charles A.) 1840. Discovery of the Adelaide River at Clarence Straits by L. R. Fitzmaurice, Mate. Discovered Port Darwin, Victoria River, Fitzmaurice River. Found memorials of the wreck of the "Zerouk" (*which see*).

Again left Sydney to examine Gulf of Carpentaria, 1842. Discovered the Flinders River, which they ascended 20 miles. Discovered the Albert River (the Maatsuycker of Tasman); explored it for 50 miles. At Treachery Bay, Captain Stokes was speared and nearly lost his life. 1842-1845. Captain Blackwood in the "Fly" continued the survey, and made a minute survey of the Great Barrier Reef and of the South Coast of New Guinea.

EXPLOSIONS.

Two and a half tons of gunpowder on a dray belonging to a carrier named Gamble, exploded on the Bathurst Road, near Penrith, New South Wales, November 16, 1865. [Gamble and his six horses were killed on the spot, and his dray smashed to atoms.]

A terrible nitro-glycerine explosion in Bridge-street, Sydney, March 4, 1866. [100lbs. of the material ignited. Two large stores (Molison and Black, and Thompson's) completely shattered.]

Explosion at the Kaitangata Coal mine, Otago, New Zealand, 35 lives lost, February 1, 1879.

THE "PLAINS OF PROMISE" DISCOVERED BY STOKES
National Library of Australia

F

FAIR. First fair in New South Wales settlement took place at Parramatta, and drew together a large concourse of visitors, March 11, 1813.

FAMINE.

In consequence of a destructive flood on the Hawkesbury, which rose 8ft. higher than on any previous occasion, £36,000 worth of property was destroyed, and several lives were lost. It commenced in the last week of February, and its greatest height was on March 22. This reduced the colony to a state of famine—wheat rose to 70s. and 80s. a bushel, the 2lb. loaf from 4s. 6d. to 5s., and vegetables were not procurable at any price, March, 1806; in consequence of a great drought, the necessaries of life became scarce and accordingly dear. The 2lb. loaf was raised to 2s. 6d. Vessels were sent to Valparaiso and China for grain provisions. A public subscription was raised, from which funds, flour, &c., was purchased, and distributed gratuitously to the sufferers, July and August, 1839.

NEW SOUTH WALES CONTRIBUTION IN AID OF THE FAMINE IN GREAT BRITAIN. A large and influential meeting, at which the Mayor presided, was held in Sydney to take measures for collecting subscriptions to relieve the famine then prevailing in Ireland and Scotland, in consequence of the failure of the crops in those countries. Similar meetings were held in various parts of the colony, and large sums were subscribed for that benevolent purpose, August, 1846.

CRIMEAN WAR FUND, LANCASHIRE COTTON AND FAMINE FUND, INDIAN MUTINY FUND. A sum of £92,000 was collected in New South Wales for these objects.

FUND FOR THE RELIEF OF, IN INDIA. Indian Famine Relief meeting held in Melbourne. A sum of £2,000 subscribed by Mr. W. J. Clark, October 1, 1877; the total Victorian contributions amounted to £28,790, January 25, 1878; South Australian contribution amounted to £11,450, New South Wales £16,000, Queensland £2,500, Tasmania £3,875, New Zealand £2,500. Total, £65,110. February 19, 1878.

FUND FOR THE RELIEF OF, IN CHINA. Sydney contribution amounted to £3,970 14s. 10d., Victoria £4,200. November 20, 1878.

FANCY DRESS BALLS. The first of these popular gatherings, at which 700 persons were present, was given by the Mayor of Sydney, (Alderman Wilshire) at the Victoria Theatre, August 21, 1844; held at the Prince of Wales Theatre, Sydney, 1858; held at the Exchange, Sydney, in aid of School of Industry, 1855; given by the Mayor of Melbourne, 1866; again in Melbourne 1870; held in honour of Prince Alfred at a building erected in Hyde Park, Sydney, 1868; given by the Mayor of Sydney (Alderman C. J. Roberts), 1,600 guests present, March 19, 1879. Return ball at Exhibition Building, Sydney, May 7, 1879.

THE MAYOR'S FANCY DRESS BALL
The Australasian Sketcher, 1874

FASTDAY, AND DAY OF HUMILIATION IN NEW SOUTH WALES, on account of the drought, November 2, 1838; for the success of the British arms in the Crimea, and the restoration of peace, August 18, 1854; for rain, November 2, 1858; for rain, November 2, 1876; for breaking up of drought, March 1, 1878.

FEDERATION. A Select Committee of the Legislative Council reported on the subject of Australian Federation 1857. [They recommended a meeting of delegates from the Legislatures of the four Colonies of New South Wales, Victoria, South Australia, and Tasmania, with the view to devising a plan for a General Assembly for all the Colonies, (Mr. E. Deas-Thomson, who was the chief mover in this important question, was Chairman of the Committee,)] ; Sir

Hercules Robinson delivered an able speech at Albury in favour of Australian Federation, October 31, 1876.

FENIANS, ESCAPE OF. A number of Irish political prisoners escaped from Freemantle, Western Australia, by the American whaler "Catalpa," April 17, 1875.

FIRES.

Auckland (N.Z.). Very extensive conflagration occurred in this city, 1871 ; Post Office, Custom House, and five stores, destroyed, November 19, 1872 ; 63 houses in Queen-street, destroyed, September 7, 1873 ; 15 shops burnt in Queen-street, May 5, 1874.

Ballarat (V.). Row of houses in Plank Road, destroyed (two children burnt to death), July 9, 1857 ; Adelphi hotel and other buildings burnt, February 23, 1859 ; Town Hall (Ballarat, West), burnt, September 24, 1859 ; disastrous conflagration in Bridge-street, much property destroyed, December 4, 1859 ; most disastrous fire commenced at the Montezuma Theatre, January 10, 1861 ; Star Hotel, Main Road, June 1, 1861 ; large fire, Main Road, April 27, 1862 ; United States Hotel, Main Road, April 11, 1866.

Brisbane (Q.). Great fire, April 10, 1864 ; second great fire, December 1, 1864 ; third great fire, April 11, 1865 ; total destruction of Mr. Pettigrew's extensive steam saw-mills (estimated loss, £25,000), October 18, 1874.

Cooktown (Q.) Destructive fire, August 11, 1875 ; second large conflagration (estimated damages, £8000), October 14, 1875.

Dunedin (N.Z.) Extensive fire, August 31, 1874.

Gawler (S.A.) Dawson's flour mills destroyed, January 14, 1877.

Geelong (V.). Bell's grocery store, April 13, 1860 ; Rosemary Branch Hotel, July 12, 1860 ; Spedding's general store, July 31, 1860 ; Haworth's tannery, August 26, 1860 ; house unoccupied, next Roebuck Hotel, January 23, 1860 ; house unoccupied, next Bush Inn, March 13, 1861 ; Holding's Victoria Hotel, October 9, 1861; Fyff's-buildings, March 9, 1862 ; Fowle, chemist's December 21,1862 ; Jacobs, clothier's, August 18, 1863 ; Brearley Brothers' tannery, February 1, 1864 ; Passelaigne's wine shop, March 24, 1864 ; Shepherd's, next Olive Branch Hotel, September 6, 1866 ; Smith and Aitchison, painters, &c., October 31, 1866 ; Burrow's, January 27, 1867 ; Cathcart's, December 7, 1867 ; M'Lean's, December 9, 1867 ; Collins's tannery, April 4, 1868 ; Ibbotson's, May 6, 1868 ; Espinasse's, May 8, 1868 ; Beamond's, fruiterer, April 13, 1869 ; Fuller's, May 16, 1869 ; Hourigan and Dunn, July 15, 1869 ; Turner, Bartlett, Pearson, Goode, and M'Callum, October 9, 1869 ; ship "Lightning," October 30, 1869 ; Sturn's, November 13, 1869 ; Gant, Coade, and Crawcour, November 23, 1869 ; Carpenter's coach factory, December 18, 1869 ; Burn's, December 20, 1869 ; Hardie, Ritchie, and Floyd, February 2, 1870 ; Nicholson's, fruiterer, June 20, 1870 ; Davies, cabinetmaker, October 16, 1870 ; Clanchy, Queen's Head Hotel, October 16, 1870 ; M'Lauchlan, M'Ewen, and Montgomery, November 5, 1870 ; L. Webster's, November 7, 1870 ; Welsh's haystack, December 6, 1870 ; Ascherberg's bone mills, January 20, 1871 ; Hughes, framemaker, February 18, 1871 ; Tinney's general store, April 24, 1871 ; stabling, Convent, June 25, 1872 ; Messrs. Hawksford, Allen, Jermyns, Rowsell, Synnott, and Haslaw's, September 5, 1872 ; Victoria woollen cloth factory, August 15, 1873 ; M'Inerney's Junction Hotel, September 17, 1873 ; Messrs. M'Lauchlan, Jenyns, and D'Helin's, October 30, 1873 ; stables, Union Bank, December 9, 1873 ; Wesleyan School, January 16, 1874 ; *Advertiser* Office, April 10, 1874 ; Messrs. Gates and Dimmelow, April 22, 1874 ; Volum's brewery, June 24, 1874 ; Sach and Heady, grocers', &c., July 4, 1874 ; Reid's flour mill, August 15, 1874 ; Tannock's, confectioner, September 9, 1874 ; Langhorne's, November 6, 1874 ; Cotton's store, June 19, 1875 ; Tonkin's store, September 30, 1875 ; Groll and Thorne, saddlers', November 25, 1874 ; Glennister and Symons's, December 22, 1875 ; Palmer's store, January 4, 1876 ; Victorian woollen factory, January 30, 1876 ; Hennessy's, February 16, 1876 ; Fowler's, February 26, 1876 ;

Lockwood's Rosemary Hotel, March 8, 1876 ; Kettle's, March 28, 1876 ; Lawson's, July 25, 1876 ; Lamble's, September 10, 1876 ; S. V. Bucklard, September 6, 1876 ; Messrs. Hughes, Cantlow, and Penrose's, January 2, 1877 ; Graham's, February 8, 1877 ; Reidey's, February 26, 1877 ; Tannock's, May 27, 1877 ; Graham's Supreme Court Hotel, June 19, 1877 ; Fanning's, October 6, 1877 ; Pride's, October 23, 1877 ; Messrs. Malcolm and Flannagan, October 27, 1877 ; Rice's, November 9, 1877 ; Welsh's Royal Mail Hotel, December 26, 1877 ; Victorian woollen factory, February 21, 1878 ; Leven's, March 3, 1878 ; Donahy's rope works, April 23, 1878 ; Bannister's, October 29, 1878 ; Railway gate-keeper's house, December 1, 1878 ; Grant's, December 27, 1878 ; Sinclair's boat-shed, January 5, 1879 ; Fleming's, January 10, 1879 ; Mulligan and Perry's, January 13, 1879 ; Thear, Bartlett, and Bowen's, January 23, 1879 ; Howarth and Rickett's, January 24, 1879 ; Allen's, February 3, 1879 ; Robinson and Cullen's sale yards, February 4, 1879 ; Matthews and Bennett, February 4, 1879.

Gerringong (N.S.W.). The township nearly destroyed by fire, July 1, 1872.

Inglewood (V.) Destructive fire, December 24, 1876.

Invercargill (N.Z.) Thirteen houses burnt, October 11, 1871 ; disastrous conflagration, March 23, 1875.

Lyttleton (N.Z.) Great fire, October 24, 1870.

Maitland (N.S.W.) Great fire, March 14, 1865.

Maryborough (N.S.W.) Extensive fire (estimated damage, £20,000), January 3, 1876.

Melbourne (V.). Extensive fire at Palmer and Balls, general stores, Collins-street West May 29, 1855.

Fire in Queensbury-street, Carlton, 22 houses destroyed, July 23, 1855.

Easy and Co's., auction mart and store, in Collins-street West, June 14, 1857.

An advertisement from *The Illustrated Sydney News*, 1855

James M'Ewan and Co., wholesale ironmongers' store, Little Collins-street, February 8, 1858.

Greenwood, Lee, and Smith's timber yards, Elizabeth-street, February 18, 1858.

Carmichael and Forbes's naphtha and asphalt works, Australian Wharf, November 16, 1858.

Mason and Firth's printing office, Sutherland's steam mills, and Stephen's ironmongery stores, Flinders-lane, March 1, 1859.

Union Hotel, Bourke-street, and several places of business, December 1, 1861.

Dove and Oswald, ship chandlers' store, Flinders-street, January 23, 1862.

A large fire, Beach-street, Sandridge, Garton's Hotel, and large number of places of business (estimated loss, £60,000), November 13, 1862.

Beauchamp and Rocke's, auction rooms, Collins-street East, February 19, 1866.

Olympic Theatre, Lonsdale-street East, October 29, 1866.

Large fire in High-street, St. Kilda, 14 places of business, January 1, 1867.

The Oriental rice mills, Flinders-street, July 10, 1867.

Halstead and Kerr's timber yards, Elizabeth-street North, and several business places, April 15, 1868.

Trenson and Hill's flock mills, and several houses in Lygon-street, Carlton, August 5, 1869.

Large fire. Mill's timber yard and Solomon's store, Flinder's-street West, destroyed, January 6, 1869.

Varieties Hotel, Bourke-street, July 5, 1870.

Haymarket Theatre, Bourke-street, September 22, 1871.

Timber yard and saw mills in Victoria-street, Hotham, March 9, 1872.

Theatre Royal, Bourke-street, March 20, 1872.

Victorian Rope Works, Sandridge Road, Emerald Hill, March 21, 1872.

Connell, Watson, and Hogarth, wholesale grocery store, Flinders-lane, March 3, 1872.

Ramsden's paper mills partly destroyed, January 28, 1873.

Detmold's, wholesale stationer and bookbinders' store, Collins-street East, partially, April 21, 1874.

Extensive fire at Emerald Hill, January 19, 1875.

Extensive fire at the Victoria Sugar Company's Works, Sandridge, June 8, 1875.

Luke and Co., wholesale grocery and tea merchants, King-street, destroyed by fire, and J. G. Francis' store, June 21, 1875.

Falk and Co.'s store, Little Collins-street, May 19, 1876.

Hanssens and Co's. spice and coffee mills, Flinders-street, May 25, 1876.

Extensive fire and destruction of Flinder's Bonded store, Flinders-street, May 25, 1876.

Sanders and Lazarus', fancy goods store, Elizabeth-street, partially, May 25, 1876.

Cunning and Co's. chemical works, Yarraville, destroyed, September 9, 1876.

Matlock (*V.*). Township burnt, December, 16, 1873.

Nelson (*N.Z.*). Destructive fire, March 20, 1875.

Newcastle (*N.S.W.*). Fire in Hunter-street, March 30, 1873 ; fire in the co-operative colliery, January 6, 1876 ; destructive fire in town, March 27, 1879.

Horsham (*V.*). Disastrous fire ; several properties destroyed (loss £6,000), January 12, 1876.

Rockhampton (*Q*). Large fire in East-street, August 6, 1872.

Roma (*Q*). Large fire, January 15, 1871.

Sydney (*N.S.W.*). The Royal Hotel and Theatre Royal destroyed by fire, March 18, 1840.

John Debenham's, 309 Pitt-street (caused through fire-works), May 24, 1852.

Alexander Waddell's, George-street South, June 8, 1852.

Hyland and Co.'s, Lower George-street, July 5, 1852.

Joseph Fogg's, Underwood's-buildings, Lower George-street, October 20, 1852.

Scott, Dickson, and Co.'s sugar works, Bathurst-street, October 31, 1852.

Tooth and Co.'s brewery (engines working five days), January 16, 1853.

Robey and Co.'s distillery, February 17, 1853.

Robey and Co.'s sugar works, Parramatta-street, October 5, 1853.

Macdonald's brushmakers, George-street (upper portion of premises destroyed), October 11, 1853.

Thomas Holt's stores, George-street South, July 5, 1854.

Youngman's, druggists, Pitt-street, February 28, 1854.

W. Wallis, back premises and workshop, Elizabeth-street, March 11, 1854.

Stewart and Co., George-street West, store with contents totally destroyed, May 5, 1854.

Rich, Langley, and Butchardt, premises totally destroyed, December 30, 1854.

Linker and Scott, ship chandlers', Lower George-street, March 16, 1855.

Furlong and Kennedy's flour mills, Dixon-street, totally, January 18, 1856.

Dudgeon's stores, Hunt's-buildings, George-street south, grocer, several houses destroyed, June 28, 1856.

Cummings H., poulterer, two houses destroyed, October 18, 1856.

Foss, Son, and Co., Pitt-street, druggists, upper portion of stores destroyed, January 20, 1857.

Boylson's store, Ashfield, June 12, 1857.

J. H. Goodlet, saw mills, partially destroyed, June 25, 1857.

Daniel's bowling saloon and Wright and Johnson's, September 15, 1857.

Williams, cooper's, New Pitt-street, December 23, 1857.

M'Guiggan's brewery, Bathurst-street (machinery destroyed), January 11, 1858.

Berkleman and Bate's, millers, Lower George-street totally destroyed, April 19, 1858.

Phillip M'Carroll's, butchers, Botany Road, totally destroyed, February 14, 1859.

W. Ellis, grocer's, George-street, totally destroyed (loss £15,000), April 21, 1859.

St. Andrew's Cathedral (temporary) slightly burnt, caused by boys lighting a fire outside the building, September 2, 1858.

John Carey's ironmongery premises, opposite present City Bank, Pitt-street, totally destroyed, August 17, 1859.

J. Goldstein's shop, lower George-street, totally destroyed February 5, 1860.

Dean and Co., auctioneers', O'Connell-street ; fire by explosion of gun cotton, March 1, 1860.

Prince of Wales Theatre (three lives lost), October 3, 1860.

A. Cooper, wine and spirit stores, Sussex-street south ; upper portion of stores destroyed, December 8, 1860.

Michael Boylson's flour mills, several buildings, totally destroyed, January 24, 1861.

G. Lind, tobacconist's, King-street, April 21, 1861.

Curran, furniture dealer's workshops, &c, Pitt-street, totally destroyed, June 20, 1861.

Buchanan, Skinner and Co's. ice-house, totally burnt, May 24, 1862.

R. Johnson, fire at Gunnedah ; store and workmen's dwelling destroyed, June 5, 1862.

J. and E. Row, chemists, stores, Bank Court, totally destroyed, August 3, 1862.

Foster, confectioner's, buildings, George-street, totally destroyed, August 29, 1862.

St. Mary's Cathedral totally destroyed, June 29, 1865.

John Frazer and Co's., York-street, totally destroyed, July 20, 1865.

Thomas Walsh, grocer's, three shops totally destroyed, December 14, 1865.

John Hill and Co., furniture dealers', King-street, totally destroyed ; steam engines first used, December 21, 1865.

Joseph Wearne's Anchor Flour Mills, Barker-street, totally destroyed, January 16, 1866.

Mollison and Black, merchants, great explosion nitro-glycerine, Bridge-street, March 4, 1866.

James Hurley's (grocer), Glebe road, and six wooden cottages, totally destroyed, August 2, 1866.

Victoria Theatre, fire under stage, ignited by an incendiary, October 20, 1866.

Portion of roof of St. Vincent's Hospital, Victoria-street, November 18, 1866.

R. Neivike and others in King-street and George-street, several premises destroyed, December 21, 1866.

R. Forster, hairdresser's, and three others, destroyed, February 5, 1867.

A. A. Lackerstein, pickle merchant, 394 George-street, known as "Sands' fire," April 18, 1867.

Michael Goldstein, draper's, shop and contents, Pitt-street, destroyed, September 23, 1867.

J. B. Holdsworth, ironmonger's back stores, George-street, totally destroyed, March 1, 1868.

St. Mary's temporary cathedral, weatherboard building, totally destroyed, January 5, 1869.

The temporary Town Hall, Wynyard-square, some records were destroyed, December 30, 1869.

Blackwall wool stores, Circular Quay, large quantity of wool and flax, both stores and contents destroyed, February 9, 1870.

Fire in Hunter-street, the roof of Nos. 16, 18, 20, 22, 24, and 26 destroyed, September 20, 1870.

D. F. Metcalf's back premises and contents, Pitt-street, destroyed, C. Newton Brothers narrowly escaped, November 2, 1870.

A. S. N. Co.'s works, Pyrmont, large quantity of patterns destroyed, November 22, 1870.

J. Pemell and Co.'s flour mills, Parramatta-street, totally destroyed, sugar works narrowly escaped, only saved by the stream of water thrown by steam-engine. December 11, 1870.

Wm. Foy, ironmonger's, front building Hunter-street, totally destroyed, several stores narrowly escaped, December 18, 1870.

Prince of Wales Opera House, King and Castlereagh streets, Sydney, totally destroyed with four houses in King-street, crushed by the falling of walls, two persons injured in King-street, seven houses partially destroyed, three houses Castlereagh-street partially destroyed, flour mill destroyed, three lives lost by the southern wall falling, January 6, 1872.

Barker and Co.'s tweed factory, Sussex-street, building gutted, May 17, 1872.

Mrs. J. Ellis's and three other houses destroyed, five buildings altogether damaged, January 29, 1873.

Seamer & Robertson's saw-mills, Woolloomooloo, totally destroyed, three cottages also injured, April 19, 1873.

The roofs of six cottages (called the "Rookery"), John street, Pyrmont, June 21, 1874.

J. Booth and Co.'s saw mills, Balmain, totally destroyed, December 14, 1874.

Back premises of Lane, Chester, and Co., ship chandlers, Lower George-street, totally destroyed, August 3, 1875.

Destructive fire, Kent-street north, four houses totally destroyed, no water available, September 21, 1875.

Castlemaine brewery, Darling Harbour, malt-house destroyed, September 24, 1875.

Town and Country Journal and Evening News offices, (damages, £6,000), December 13, 1875.

Mort and Nichol's meat preserving works, Darling Harbour, great damage done, December 26, 1875.

Saywell's tobacco factory, Clarence-street, October 5, 1876.

J. G. Hanks and Co., grocers', George-street, totally destroyed, April 23, 1877.

Ten offices, Albert-street, Circular Quay, with contents destroyed, February 26, 1878.

Eglinton Lodge, Glebe Point, totally destroyed, including valuable library of over five hundred volumes, belonging to Mr. H. N. Montagu, May 3, 1878.

Timaru (N.Z.). Disastrous fire, May 13, 1872.

Wellington (N.Z.). Large fire, March 20, 1875.

FLAGSTAFF, First, was set up at the South Head, Sydney, by which the intelligence of the approach of any vessel could be immediately communicated to those in Sydney, 1790.

"FLEET, First." The "Sirius," frigate, Captain Hunter, ; "Supply," armed tender, Lieutenant H. E. Ball ; "Golden Grove," "Fishburn," "Barrowdale," storeships ; "Lady Penryhn," "Friendship," "Charlotte," "Prince of Wales," "Alexander," "Scarborough," transports, commissioned, 1787.

FLOGGING. [*See* CONVICTS.]

FLOODS

Hawkesbury River. A most destructive overflowing of the River Hawkesbury took place in March, 1806 ; 6,000 bushels of corn were destroyed, one hundred persons, men, women, and children, who had taken refuge on the roof of their houses and "on rafts of straw floating on the deluge," were saved by the exertions of one Mr. Arundell, a resident, and Mr. Biggers. The value of property destroyed amounted to £35,000 ; by this flood the colony was almost reduced to a famine,—wheat rose to £4 a bushel, and the 2-lb. loaf to 5s : September 24, 1806.

A tremendous fall of rain was experienced in Sydney, March 30, 1834. [During five hours some of the streets had the appearance of swollen rivers, and to such an extent did the waters accumulate, that youths were seen swimming about in the carriage ways. The foundations of many houses were injured, and the main guard-house in Lower George-street gave way, the roof falling in with a crash. It was estimated that £10,000 would not cover the loss occasioned by the torrents of water which saturated dwellings and ploughed up streets during the short period of a few hours.]

Gundagai. First Gundagai flood, February, 1844. The Valley of the Murrumbidgee was converted into an inland sea ; the town of Gundagai was swept away, only seven buildings remaining out of 78, and 89 persons perished out of a population of 250. The waters commenced rising on Thursday night, and did not begin to fall until Saturday morning : June 26, 1852.

A great flood took place in almost all parts of the colony, the country adjacent to the Shoalhaven and Araluen Rivers, in the south, suffering most from this visitation. The prospects of the agriculturists and the diggers were alike blasted by the overwhelming waters. Many lives were lost, and in some instances whole families were drowned. Entire houses were overwhelmed, and cattle, crops, fences, agricultural implements, the wreck of households and farms were carried to the sea, strewing the sea coast for a distance of miles ; one proprietor near Goulburn lost 2,000 sheep. At Braidwood, another proprietor lost to the extent of £5,000 ; the railway works lost to a great extent, embankments being washed from under the rails, culverts burst, and bridges destroyed by the combined force of the rushing waters and masses of floating timber : February, 1860.

Bathurst. Town of Kelso partly submerged, December 16, 1872.

Inverell. Heavy floods, December 21, 1872.

Cooma. Heavy floods, June 1, 1873 ; March, 1879.

Clarence River district. Devastating floods and loss of life. The damage done at Grafton alone estimated at £50,000, July 22, 1876.

Date and Height in feet above mean tidal level.

June 20, 1857, very small flood.

	ft.	in.		ft.	in.
			April 29-30, 1860	36	8
July 29, 1857	32	1	July 26, 1860	34	3
August 22, 1857	37	1	Nov 19, 1860	35	4
Feb. 12, 1860	26	9	April 30, 1861	26	8

From May, 1861, to June, 1864, several freshes and small floods occurred, but none of any consequence.

	ft.	in.		ft.	in.
June 13, 1864	47	4	Nov. 21, 1870	25	8
July 16, 1864	35	6	April 30, 1871	31	3
June 15, 1866	26	0	May 2, 1871	36	4
July 12, 1866	26	9	Feb. 26-27, 1873	41	10
April 30, 1867	25	8	June 17-18, 1873	27	4
June 23, 1867	62	7	Feb. 23, 1874	26	7
Feb. 19, 1868	29	2	June 7, 1875	38	2
May 9, 1869	36	9	May 2-3, 1877	29	7
March 31, 1870	27	6	July 16-17, 1877	26	0
April 28, 1870	44	4	Feb. 9-10, 1878	25	9
May 13-14, 1870	34	9			

In 1870, at Palmer's Farm of 100 acres, 50 acres were washed away and the confluence of the Hawkesbury and the Grose entirely changed.

Since the Richmond Bridge was built in 1862-3, the river has so encroached on the south side as to necessitate the bridge being lengthened 60 feet.

The highest flood in the memory of any of the white inhabitants occurred in June 1867.

Tumut and Riverina districts.—After the great drought in 1839 very favourable seasons took place up to 1843. In 1844 occurred the first heavy flood in the Tumut and Murrumbidgee Rivers, in September. From 1845 to 1850 the seasons were favourable, the river occasionally flooded, but not to any serious extent The winter of 1849 was dry, and nothing but light showers fell till May, 1851, being the severest drought remembered, and most serious in its consequences. This drought was confined to the western slopes, and was so severe that large quantities of stock perished from thirst. The winter of 1852 was the wettest known, and then occurred the great flood at Gundagai (which see) on June 26, 1852. The next severe drought was in 1868, most felt in the Lachlan and Murrumbidgee Rivers. The principal floods in the Murrumbidgee River since have been—

		Gundagai.		W. Wagga.	
		ft.	in.	ft.	in.
1863, when the river rose		38	10 ..	35	9
1867	,, ,, ,,	28	9 ..	30	7
1867 (second flood)	,,	26	4 ..	27	10
April 27, 1870	,, ,, ,,	38	0 ..	35	0
May 14, 1870	,, ,, ,,	32	0 ..	32	6
May 24, 1870	,, ,, ,,	28	6 ..	28	0
June 4, 1870	,, ,, ,,	28	6 ..	28	0
October 30, 1870	,, ,, ,,	30	4 ..	31	0

Hunter River.

Year.	Feet above high water mark.	
1820	....	37 0
1826	....	29 0
1832	....	29 0
1840	....	26 0 very sudden rise, and several people drowned.
1857	....	26 0 June.
,,	....	27 0 July.
,,	....	29 0 August.
1861	....	21 0 April.
,,	....	25 0 July.
,,	....	25 6 August.
1864	....	28 0 February.
,,	....	24 0 June 4.
,,	....	26 0 June 11.
,,	....	25 0 July 15.
,,	....	24 9 August 9.
1867	....	30 0 June.
1873	....	July 27, flood, no note of height.
1874	....	January, high flood, 33 ft. 9 in.
1875	....	March 2, high flood.
,,	....	June, high flood.

FLOODS IN OTHER AUSTRALIAN COLONIES :—
Greatest flood ever known in Port Phillip (now Victoria), 1844.
Great floods in Ipswich, December 17, 1845.
Great floods at Hobart Town, Tasmania, February 27, 1854.
Great flood at Ballarat, April 24, 1860.
Heavy floods in Queensland, 1863.
Heavy floods in Queensland, 1869.
Great floods in Victoria, September 9, 1870.
Great floods in West Australia, October, 1870.
Great floods in New Zealand, September, 1871.
Great floods in Tasmania, June 11, 1872.
Great flood of the Condamine River, Queensland, January 14, 1873.
Disastrous floods (2) at Normanton, Queensland, February 14, 1873.
Heavy floods in Queensland, February and March, 1875.
Heavy flood of Fitzroy River, Queensland, April 25, 1875.
Destructive floods in South Australia, May 10, 1875.
Heavy flood of the Campaspe, Victoria, June 9, 1875.
Disastrous floods at Sandhurst, February 20, 1878.
Serious flood in Melbourne—the heaviest since 1863. Several chains of the Yan Yean aqueduct swept away, March 16, 1878.

FLYING-FOXES.
Plague of flying-foxes (then called bats) visited Rose Hill, N.S.W., Feb., 1791. [From the numbers which fell into the brook at Rose Hill, the water was tainted for several days, and it is supposed that more than 20,000 of them were seen within the space of one mile. Many of these were of great size. Governor Phillip saw one which measured four feet between the tip of each wing.]

FOOTBALL.
The Sydney *Monitor* reported for the first time that the soldiers in the Sydney barracks amused themselves with a game called Football, July 25, 1829.

FOOTBALL
The Australasian Sketcher, 1874

FORT BOURKE.
Sir Thomas Mitchell reached the Darling, and whilst there erected a stockade, which was named Fort Bourke, May, 1835. [This place is now an important flourishing town.]

FORTS.
A half-moon battery completed at the east end of Sydney Cove, May, 1798. [On it were mounted some guns of a tender which accompanied the original expedition.]
Two other batteries, one commanding a position on the west side of the town, and another on Garden Island, completed 1799.
The foundation-stone of Fort Phillip (on the site of the present Observatory), Sydney, laid, Sept. 4, 1804.

FOSSIL.
Important discovery of fossil remains in Gowrie Creek, Queensland, Aug. 5, 1873.

FRAUD.
John Thomas Wilson absconded from the colony in the brig "Venus," which vessel he had bought a short time previously, and put on board her a full cargo purchased from Sydney merchants and tradesmen, Oct. 19, 1839. [His debts amounted to upwards of £30,000. Giving his horse to a porter to take care of, he left the Commercial Wharf by the "Sophia Jane" steamer, proposing only to go down the harbour; boarded the brig outside the Heads. The great bulk of the property left behind him was claimed by A. Polack, who paid the creditors 75 per cent. of their claims.]
[*See* SWINDLERS.]

FREE SELECTORS.
FIRST CONFERENCE IN SYDNEY HELD IN 1877. Delegates from various districts of New South Wales (Mr. Barbour, M.P., Chairman, and Mr. J. Boulding of Yass, Vice-Chairman) assembled in conference at Sydney, and published their Manifesto, Oct. 12, 1878.

G

GALENA. Lode found in West Australia, 1846.

GAOL, DARLINGHURST, was first used, June, 1841. [*See* PRISONS.]

GAS.

Gaslight Company formed in Sydney, April 13, 1836; Sydney first lit with gas, May 24, 1841; Hobart Town lit with gas, March 12, 1857; Melbourne first lit with gas, August 10, 1857; Adelaide first lit with gas, June 22, 1863; Brisbane first lit with gas, 1865; Newcastle lit with gas, October 29, 1867; Parramatta Gas Company incorporated, August 13, 1872;

Warrnambool, Victoria, first lit with gas, August 29, 1874; Rockhampton, Queensland, first lit with gas, December 17, 1874; the Three Melbourne Gas Companies decided to amalgamate and form the Metropolitan Gas Company, August 13, 1877.

GEELONG, reached by Hume and Hovell, 1824; laid out by Governor Bourke, March 1837; railway to township commenced, September, 1852; telegraph line opened, December, 1854; railway opened 1857.

GEELONG BAY, explored by Grimes, 1803; traversed by Batman, 1835.

GENOA, DUKE OF, visited Melbourne, April 28, 1873.

GEOLOGY.

Wonderful geological discovery of curious balls of granite, &c., made by a geologist in the Raymond Terrace district (County Gloucester, New South Wales); some specimens were sent to the British Museum and Royal Geographical Society, London, 1847.

Samuel Stutchbury appointed to make a geological and mineralogical survey of New South Wales, to ascertain the mineral resources of the colony, January 10, 1851.

Dr. Bruhn, of Melbourne, started on a tour of mineralogical research to Mount Macedon district, Victoria; he proved the existence of silver, copper, antimony, sulphur, and iron, February, 1851.

Mr. A. R. C. Selwyn arrived and commenced

YARRA ST, GEELONG
The Illustrated Sydney News, 1854

the geological survey of the colony of Victoria, 1853.

GEORGE'S RIVER, N.S.W. Lieut. Flinders and Mr. Bass, in a boat called the "Tom Thumb," 8 feet long, explored George's River 20 miles further than Governor Hunter's survey, 1795.

GERMAN FESTIVAL. Great German Peace Festival held in South Australia, October 13, 1871.

GIPPSLAND, discovered by Alexander M'Millan, January 1, 1870.

GLADSTONE, QUEENSLAND, proclaimed a municipality, February 21, 1863.

GOLD, DISCOVERY OF.

Discovery of a gold mine in the settlement reported by a convict, August 20, 1788. [The report was afterwards proved to be a *canard*.]

Some convicts who were employed cutting a road to Bathurst are said to have found gold in a considerable quantity, and were only compelled to keep silence on the point by menaces and flogging, 1814.

Assistant Surveyor James M'Brian discovered gold on the Fish River, about 15 miles east of Bathurst, New South Wales, February 15, 1823. [The following extract from his Field Book is preserved in the Surveyor-General's Office, Sydney:—"At 8 chains 50 links to river and marked gum-tree, found numerous particles of gold in the sand and in the hills convenient to the river."]

A convict flogged in Sydney on suspicion of having stolen gold, which he stated he had discovered in the bush, 1825.

Count Strzlecki discovered gold associated with pyrites at the Vale of Clwydd, in the Blue Mountains, New South Wales, April, 1839. [At the request of the Government, who feared an outbreak amongst the convicts, the discovery was kept scrupulously secret.]

Rev. W. B. Clarke, M.A., F.R.G.S., found gold in the Macquarie valleys, and near Vale of Clwydd, New South Wales, April, 1841.

Rev. W. B. Clarke reported that the first gold he had ever seen in Australia he procured from granite, October 29, 1841.

Rev. W. B. Clarke was the first explorer who proclaimed, on true scientific grounds, the probable auriferous veins of Australia. He found gold and exhibited it to several members of the Legislature of New South Wales, April 9, 1844.

Mr. Alexander Tolmein, sent by Governor Grey to Kangaroo Island to capture a gang of bushrangers, reported that he had when about 20 miles S.S.W. from Melbourne seen a quartz reef with yellow metal in it, which he was afterwards convinced was gold, 1844.

Sir Roderick Murchison pointed out the singularity of the Blue Mountain Chain of Australia (the Cordilleras) to that of the Ural, and predicted the presence of gold, 1844.

Gold specimens found on the spurs of the Pyrenees Mountains, Victoria; exhibited in the shop window of Mr. Robe, jeweller, Melbourne, January, 1848.

Rev. W. B. Clarke wrote in a letter to *The Maitland Mercury*:—"It is well known a gold mine is certain ruin to the first workers; and in the long run, gold washing will be found more suitable for slaves than British freemen," January 25, 1849.

Gold discovered at the Pyrenees, Port Phillip, by a shepherd, January 31, 1849.

Thomas Chapman discovered gold at Daisy Hill, Victoria, and sold to Mrs. Brentani, Collins-street, Melbourne, a nugget which weighed 16 ounces. Afraid of the Melbourne authorities, the discoverer "bolted" to Sydney in the "Sea-Horse," January, 1849.

Announcement that gold had been discovered in California, February, 1849. [By June of the same year nearly 300 persons had left New South Wales for that place. In a short time the emigration to the auriferous region resulted in a great depreciation of property in the colony; many availing themselves of the crisis to become purchasers, afterward realised fortunes to a great extent.]

Mr. Latrobe, the Superintendent of Port Phillip, sent Captain Dana in command of 16 mounted native police to prevent digging for gold at Daisy Hill, Victoria, 1849.

William Clarke, junior (afterwards gold-broker, Elizabeth-street, Melbourne) with William Vicary, found auriferous quartz at Smythesdale, Victoria, 1849.

Mr. Austin brought to Sydney a nugget of gold worth £35, which he had found in the Bathurst district, January, 1581.

Gold discovered in New South Wales at Summerhill Creek, by Mr. Edward Hammond Hargraves, Feb. 12, 1851. [There were indications of the existence of gold in considerable quantities at this Creek. Some nuggets and dust having been exhibited in Sydney, a rush to that locality immediately took place. The ordinary means of conveyance being so inadequate, the fares of the coaches were at once doubled. Provisions rose to a very high price,—flour to £30 a ton. A license of 30s. a month was imposed on all persons seeking for gold.]

DIGGERS ON ROUTE TO THE DIGGINGS
S. T. Gill, 1854

Gold discovered by Edward Hammond Hargraves, at Lewis Ponds Creek, New South Wales, February 12, 1851.

Dr. Bruhn traced gold in quartz, whilst travelling to explore the mineral resources of Victoria, April, 1851.

Nugget of gold weighing 13 ounces found at Summer Hill Creek, N.S.W., the earliest nugget found in New South Wales after the gold discovery there by Hargraves, May 13, 1851.

The first proclamation issued in Sydney by Sir Charles Augustus Fitzroy, Governor-General of Australia, declaring gold to be the property of the Crown, was on May 22, 1851. [On the following day another Governmental order was issued, comprising six clauses and containing also the form of license, to the following purport:—Clause 1 prohibited digging after June 1, 1851, without a license. Clause 2 enacted that "for the present and pending further proof of the extent of the goldfield," the license fee to be fixed at thirty shillings per month. Clause 3 provided that no person should be eligible to dig for gold unless he could produce a certificate of discharge, or prove to the satisfaction of the Commissioner that he was not a person improperly absent from hired service. Clause 5 stated that rules adjusting extent and position of land to be covered by each license, and for the prevention of confusion, should be the subject of early regulation. Clause 6, " with reference to lands alienated by the Crown, in fee simple, the Commissioner will not be authorised for the present to issue licenses under these regulations to any person but the proprietors, or persons authorised by them in writing to apply for the same."]

Dr. Bruhn started for the Pyrenees from Melbourne on a mineralogical research. The *Argus* of the day said : " Where gold undoubtedly is, he (Dr. Bruhn) is pretty sure to find it :" March, 1851.

Gold said to have been discovered at the Pyrenees, Port Phillip, by a person named Chapman, June 6, 1851.

Gold found on a creek north of the Pyrenees, Victoria, afterwards called Navarre by William Richfould, shepherd to J. Wood Beilby, who informed the Government, June 7, 1851.

Despatch to Earl Grey from Sir Charles Fitzroy, Governor of New South Wales, June 11, 1851. [The despatch stated that two years previously a Mr. Smith who was attached to some ironworks near Berrima, had announced to the Government the discovery of gold in New South Wales, had shown a lump of quartz to the Colonial Secretary, and had offered on certain terms to reveal the locality.]

Gold discovered at the Turon, June 19, 1851.

The following is a short statement of the order in which the Select Committee appointed by the Legislative Council to consider claims for rewards for gold discoveries in Victoria, placed the various claimants in their report dated March 10, 1854 :—

The Hon. W. Campbell discovered gold in March 1850, at Clunes ; concealed the fact at the time from the apprehension that its announcement might prove injurious to the squatter on whose run the discovery was made ; but mentioned it in a letter to a friend on June 10th, and afterwards on July 5, 1851, which friend, at Mr. Campbell's request, reported the matter to the gold-discovery-committee July 8th. Mr. L. J. Michel, and six others, discovered gold in the Yarra Ranges, at Anderson's Creek, which they communicated to the gold-discovery committee July 5th. Mr. James Esmond, a California digger, and three others, obtained gold on the quartz rocks of the Pyrenees, and made the discovery public July 5th, Dr. George Bruhn, a German physician, found indications of gold in quartz " two miles from Parker's station," in April, 1851, and forwarded specimens to the gold-committee June 30th. Mr. Thomas Hiscock found gold at Buninyong August 8th, and communicated the fact to the editor of the *Geelong Advertiser* on the 10th of the same month. This discovery led to that of the Ballarat gold-fields. Mr. C. T. Peters, a hut-keeper at Barker's Creek, and three others, found gold at Specimen Gully July 20th ; worked secretly to September 1st, then published the account. This led to the discovery of the numerous gold-fields about Mount Alexander.

Gold discovered at Clunes, Victoria, by James William Esmond. July 1, 1851.

Large nuggets of gold found by an aboriginal at Meroo or Louisa Creek, Turon, on a station belonging to Dr. Kerr, five miles from Bathurst and 29 miles from Mudgee. July 16, 1851. [When discovered it was in three pieces, though generally supposed to belong to one mass. One piece weighed 70 lbs. and the others 60 lbs. each.]

Discovery of gold at Ballarat by Richard Turner, Thomas Dunn, James Merrick, George Wilson, and Charles Gerrard, August 24, 1851. [Another party, consisting of Connor, Woodward, Brown, Jeanes, Smith, and Thornton were on the field at the same time, and Woodward said that the discovery of gold at Ballarat was first made by Brown on the Monday morning, August 25, 1851.]

Gold found at Buninyong by Hiscock, August, 1851.

Bendigo gold-field discovered, December 8, 1851.

Araluen gold diggings, N.S.W., discovered by A. Waddell, and Hicken, 1851.

Gold found at Anderson Creek, Victoria, 1851.

Abercrombie gold diggings, N.S.W. discovered, 1851.

Meroo gold-field, New South Wales, discovered, 1851.

Large nugget of gold, called " the Brennan," weighing 364 ounces 11 dwts., found at Meroo or Louisa

Creek, twenty-four yards from the spot where the three large pieces had previously been discovered, 1851. [It was sold in Sydney for £1,156.]

Two tons of gold were exported to England from the colony of New South Wales in one vessel in the month of January, 1852.

Two nuggets found at Louisa Creek, one, called the " King of the Watercourse Nuggets," weighing 157 ounces, and the other 71 ounces, 1852.

First Bendigo escort despatched with 20,937 ounces gold, July 25, 1852.

Mr. Charles Ring, a settler, first discovered gold in New Zealand, on Cape Cobulle, forty miles east of Auckland, in the vicinity of Coromandel Harbour, October, 1852.

The " Nil Desperandum," nugget, weighing 540 ounces, found, November 29, 1857.

Gold found at Fingal, Tasmania, in 1857. [The Government gave £2,000 for a further search, but without success.]

Nugget, weighing 53 ounces, found at Louisa Creek, New South Wales, 1857.

" Blanche Barkly," nugget, found, August 23, 1857.

"The Welcome " found at Bakery Hill, Ballarat, Victoria (valued at £8,376), June 9, 1858.

A party of four at Burrandong, near Orange, New South Wales, at a depth of 35 feet found a nugget of gold, the standard weight of which was 1,127 ounces 6 dwts. and was valued at £4,389 8s. 10d. at the Sydney Mint, November 1, 1858.

Gold discovered at Snowy River, New South Wales, January 27, 1860.

Two large nuggets, one weighing 160 ounces, and the other weighing 93 ounces 18 dwts., found at Kiandra, New South Wales, March, 1860.

Lambing Flat gold-diggings discovered on Mr. James White's Station, Burrangong, by his nephew Denis Regan, and the cook named Alexander, June, 1860.

Large nugget, weighing 400 ounces, found at Kiandra, Snowy River, New South Wales, October, 1860.

Large and nearly solid nugget, weighing 140 ounces, found on the Tooloom diggings, New South Wales, 1860.

Burrangong, Lambing Flat, further prospected and discovered to be a payable gold-field, January 1861. [A great rush took place, when samples of gold were exhibited in Sydney.]

Two nuggets were found at New Chum Hill, Kiandra, one weighing 42 ounces, the other 200 ounces, July, 1861.

A nugget, weighing 64 ounces 7 dwt., found by two boys at Gundagai, New South Wales, July, 1861.

Gold found at Tuapeka, New Zealand, by Mr. Gabriel Reed, 1861.

Gould found traces of gold in Tasmania, at the Gordon, the Franklin, and the King River, 1861.

A nugget of 20 ounces of gold found in Red Jacket Gully, Whipstick, Victoria, March, 1863.

Calliope gold-field, Queensland, proclaimed, May 26, 1863.

The Great Britain Co., Gibraltar Hill, Majorca, Victoria (eight shareholders), raised in a week six tons of quartz, yielding 34 ounces 18 dwts., or over 5·8 ounces to the ton, April, 1864.

A goldfield and copper-mine discovered on the river Cloncurry, 1865.

Gympie (Queensland) gold-field discovered by a man named Nash, 1867.

The " Welcome Stranger," nugget, found at Moliagul, eight miles from Dunolly, Victoria, the gross weight was 210lbs., and it yielded 2,302 ounces 18 dwts. 5 grs. of smelted gold, February 5, 1869.

Gold discovered at Waterhouse, Tasmania, March 19, 1869.

A specimen, weighing 350lbs., two-thirds being estimated to be pure gold, was found near Braidwood, November, 1869.

A large nugget found at Berlin, Victoria, weighing 1,121 ounces, May 31, 1870.

A large nugget found at Berlin, Victoria, weighing 896 ounces, September, 1870.

Discovery of a rich gold reef at New Walcha, New South Wales, November 9, 1870.

A cake of gold from John Krohmann's claim at Hill End, Tambaroora, New South Wales, weighing 5,612 ounces and valued at £20,000, the result of one crushing of 16 tons of quartz, exhibited at the Sydney Intercolonial Exhibition, May 1, 1872.

TO EMIGRANTS.

The following GUTTA PERCHA ARTICLES will be found of great value to Emigrants, especially such as are proceeding to the

GOLD DIGGINGS.

GUTTA PERCHA LINING FOR BOXES.

BUCKETS.	LIFE-BUOYS.	WASHING BOWLS.
DRINKING-MUGS.	FLASKS.	SYPHONS.

GUTTA PERCHA TUBING.

SUCTIONS FOR PUMPS.	CARBOYS FOR GUNPOWDER.
JUGS.	MINERS' CAPS.

SOLES FOR BOOTS AND SHOES.

TO KEEP THE FEET DRY is of the utmost importance to the Emigrant. This may be secured by the use of Gutta Percha Soles, which are perfectly Waterproof, cheaper and more durable than Leather. They can be put on with ease by any one. This cannot be too extensively known amongst Australian Emigrants, as it is now difficult to find a Shoemaker in that country.

Gold-washing Vessels of every variety of shape may be had to order.

Directions to Emigrants for lining Boxes with Gutta Percha Sheet (so as to preserve the contents from injury by Sea-water), also for putting on Soles of Boots and Shoes, &c., may be had GRATIS on application to any of the Gutta Percha Company's Dealers.

The Gutta Percha Company, Patentees, 18, Wharf-road, City-road, London.

Advertisement from *The English Emigrant in Australia*, 1852

Another monster nugget found at Berlin, Victoria; valued at £1,953, May 14, 1872.

The second largest result obtained from one crushing in Australia, was at Beyer's and Holtermann's claim, Hill End, Tambaroora, New South Wales. The weight of the mass was 630lbs., its height 4ft. 9in., its width 2ft. 2in., and it was valued at £12,000, June 23, 1872.

Auriferous reef found at Yam Creek, one hundred miles from Port Darwin, August 16, 1872.

Discovery of a nugget at Smythesdale, near Ballarat, weighing 13lbs., February, 1873.

Extensive gold diggings found at Palmer River, Queensland, 1873.

At Beyers and Holtermann's mine, Hill End, New South Wales, 102cwt. of gold was in 10 tons of stuff. From the same mine a slab of vein-stuff and gold weighing 6½ cwt. was exhibited which was estimated to contain 2 cwt. of gold.—Feb. 1, 1873.

Gold found at Tumbling Waters, Northern Territory.—March 22, 1873.

The mint returns for gold from 415 tons of vein-stuff from Messrs. Beyers and Holtermann's mine at Hill End, N.S.W., were 16,280 ozs., the value being £63,235.—1873.

Krohmann's Company, Hill End, N.S.W., raised 436 tons 9 cwt. of stuff, for which the mine returns were 24,479 ozs. 9 dwts. of gold, valued at £93,616 11s. 9d.—1873.

A nugget weighing 30 ozs., found at Copperfield, Queensland, Oct. 27, 1878.

Opening of Mr. Iceley's private gold-field at Manduramah, near Carcoar, N.S.W., Jan. 26, 1878.

The Hodgkinson, Northern Queensland, officially reported as discovered by J. V. Mulligan, M'Leod, Warner, Abelson, Kennedy, and Crosley, Feb. 10, 1876.

A Chinaman, at Jericho, near Berlin, Dunolly district, Victoria, found a nugget of gold weighing 400 oz., June 23, 1873.

A nugget weighing 250 ozs., found near Buninyong, Victoria, July 11, 1878.

GYMPIE GOLD-FIELDS, RUSH TO.

Rush to the Gympie gold-field, Queensland, July, 1868.

LICENSES TO SEARCH FOR. The following is a copy of the first license to search for gold in Australia, and was issued on Queen's Birthday anniversary :—

No. 1.   GOLD LICENSE.   May 24, 1851.

The bearer, *Richard Roe*, having paid to me the sum of one pound ten shillings, on account of the Territorial Revenue, I hereby authorise him to dig, search for, and remove gold from any such Crown lands within the country of Bathurst, as I shall assign to him for that purpose, during the month of May, 1851.

This license must be produced whenever demanded by me, or other persons acting under the authority of Government.   (Signed)   J. R. HARDY, J.P., Commissioner.

First license issued in Victoria, Sep. 21, 1851.

The number of gold licenses issued in N.S.W. was 12,186, of which 2,094 was issued at the Ophir; 8,637 at the Turon; 1,009 at the Meroo and Louisa Creek; 41 at the Abercrombie; and 405 at Araluen, up to Oct. 31, 1851.

Delegates from Victorian miners, asking for reduction of gold miner's license, waited on Governor Hotham, who reduced the charge from 40s. per month to 40s. per quarter, 1854.

The monthly gold license fee was repealed in Victoria, and a small export duty imposed instead, 1855.

NUGGETS FOUND IN NEW SOUTH WALES.

The annexed statement is from Mr. Liversidge's pamphlet on Minerals of New South Wales :—
Examples of New South Wales Nuggets.

No. 1. Found in July, 1851, by a native boy, amongst a heap of quartz, at Meroo Creek or Louisa Creek, Turon River, fifty-three miles from Bathurst, and twenty-nine miles from Mudgee, New South Wales. It was in three pieces when discovered, though generally considered as one mass. The aboriginal who discovered these blocks " observed a speck of glittering substance upon the surface of a block of the quartz, upon which he applied his tomahawk, and broke off a portion." One

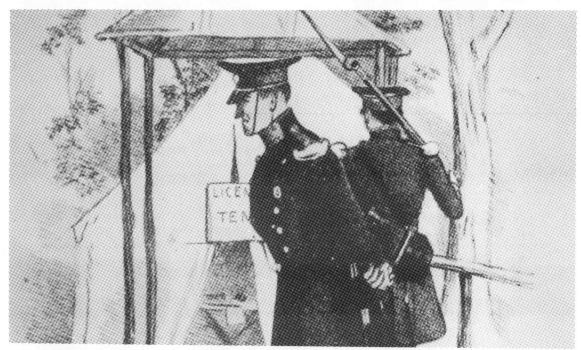

A LICENSING TENT AND "JOES"
S. T. Gill, c. 1852, Government Printer, Melbourne

of the pieces weighed 70lb. avoir., and gave 60lb. troy of gold ; the gross weight of the other two about 60lb. each. These three pieces, weighing 1¾cwt., contained 160lb. troy of gold, and about 1cwt of quartz. In the same year another nugget, weight 30lb. 6oz., was discovered in clay, 24 yards from the large pieces ; and in the following year, also near to No. 4, there were found two nuggets, weighing 157oz. and 71oz. Gross weight (troy), 106lb. 1272oz.

No. 2. A model of what is said to be the first large nugget found in New South Wales, is to be seen in the Australian Museum, Sydney. Found in Ophir Creek.

No. 3. A nugget weighing 26oz. was found at Bingera in 1852.

No. 4. Found by a party of four, on 1st November, 1858, at Burrandong, near Orange, New South Wales, at a depth of 35ft ; when pounded with a hammer it yielded 120lb. of gold, for which £5,000 were offered. Melted at the Sydney Mint, when it weighed 1286oz. 8dwt.; after melting, 1182oz. 7dwt.; loss 8 per cent.; fineness, 87·4 per cent.; the standard weight of gold being 1127oz. 6dwt. Value, £4,385 8s. 10d The gold was mixed with quartz and sulphide of iron (mundic). Assay, 87·40 per cent. gold, equal to 20 car. 3¾ car. grs. Gross weight (troy) 107lb. 2oz. 8dwt. ; 1,286oz. 8dwt.

No. 5. Found at Kiandra, Snowy River, New South Wales, October, 1860. Gross weight (troy) 33lb. 4oz. ; 400oz.

No. 6. "The Brenan Nugget." Found in Meroo Creek, Turon River, New South Wales, embedded in clay ; measured 21in. in circumference. It was found 24yds. from No. 1. Sold in Sydney, 1851, for £1156. Gross weight (troy), 30lb. 6oz. ; 364oz. 11dwt.

No. 7 Found at New Chum Hill, Kiandra, New South Wales, July, 1861. Gross weight (troy), 16lb. 8oz. ; 200oz.

No. 8. Found at Kiandra, Snowy River, New South Wales, March, 1860. Gross weight (troy), 13lb 4oz ; 160oz.

No. 9. Found in 1852, at Meroo Creek, Turon River, New South Wales, close to No. 1. This was called "The King of the Waterworn Nuggets." Gross weight (troy), 13lb. 1oz. ; 157oz.

No. 10. Found in 1860, at the Tooloom diggings, New South Wales ; nearly solid gold. Gross weight (troy), 11lb. 8oz. ; 140 oz.

No. 11. Found at Kiandra, Snowy River, New South Wales, March 1860. Gross weight (troy),7lb. 9oz. 18dwt; 93oz. 18dwt.

No. 12. Found in 1852, at Louisa Creek, New South Wales ; a solid lump of gold. Gross weight (troy), 6lb. 10oz. ; 82oz.

No. 13. Found by two boys, in July, 1861, at Gundagai (new diggings), New South Wales. Gross weight (troy), 5lb 4oz. 7dwt. ; 64oz. 7dwt.

No. 14. Found in 1857, at Louisa Creek, New South Wales ; gold and crystalised quartz. Gross weight (troy), 4lb. 2oz. ; 50oz.

No. 15. Found at New Chum Hill, Kiandra, New South Wales, in July, 1861. Gross weight (troy), 3lb. 6oz. ; 42oz.

No. 16. Found at Summer Hill Creek, New South Wales. The earliest nugget found in New South Wales, after the gold discovery there by Hargraves, May 13, 1851. Gross weight (troy), 1lb. 1oz. ; 13oz.

No. 17. A nugget weighing 22oz. 18dwt. 12gr. was found on "M'Guiggan's Lead," about nine miles from Parkes. The metal was of dark colour, and free from gangue, 1876.

No. 18. A nugget weighing 19oz. 12dwt. was found early in 1876 at the "Wapping Butcher" mine, near Parkes.

NUGGETS FOUND IN VICTORIA.

			When found.	Weight. lb. oz. dt.
Black Hill ..		..	14 Oct., 1851 ..	7 6 0
Canadian Gully	..	..	20 Jan., 1853 ..	93 1 11
,,	,,	..	22 Jan., 1853 ..	84 3 15
,,	,,	..	31 Jan., 1853 ..	134 11 0
,,	,,	..	Feb., 1853 ..	30 8 0
,,	,,	..	Feb., 1853 ..	30 11 2
,,	,,	..	Feb., 1853 ..	11 11 15
Eureka	..	..	7 Feb., 1854 ..	52 1 0
Dalton's Flat, Canadian, "Lady Hotham"		..	8 Sep., 1854 ..	98 1 17

SUCCESSFUL DIGGERS ON THE WAY FROM BENDIGO
S. T. Gill, 1854

Bakery Hill	..	..	6 Mar., 1855 ..	47 7 0
,, ,,			Mar., 1855 ..	40 0 0
"Union Jack," Buninyong ..			28 Feb., 1857 ..	23 5 0
Black Hill Lead, "Nil Desperandum"			29 Nov., 1857 ..	45 0 0
Bakery Hill, "Welcome"	..		9 June, 1858 ..	184 9 16
Koh-i-Noor Claim ..		..	27 July, 1860 ..	69 6 0
"Sir Dominic Daly"	..	..	Feb , 1862 ..	26 0 0
Moliagul, "Welcome Stranger" ..	..	..	9 Feb., 1869 ..	190 0 0
Webbville, Buninyong		..	1 Aug., 1869 ..	12 0 0

PORT CURTIS, RUSH FOR.—Announcement made of the discovery of gold at Port Curtis, at a place called Canoona, on the banks of the Fitzroy River, in 1858. In October 10,000 persons had congregated in that district ; the rush was however a failure, and resulted in great misery and want, and in November there were only 4,000 or 5,000 persons left, but it has been the means of forming a prosperous settlement in that port. Port Curtis is situated on the verge of the tropic of Capricorn on the eastern part of Australia. It was discovered by Flinders in 1802, and named after Admiral Sir Roger Curtis, who then commanded at the Cape of Good Hope. The harbour is nearly as large as Port Jackson.]

REWARDS FOR DISCOVERY OF. The Parliament of New South Wales voted £10,000 to Mr. Hargraves as a reward for the discovery of gold in the colony, and £1,000 as a gratuity to the Rev. W. B. Clarke as a mark of appreciation for his geological reports, addressed by him to the Government, 1853. [£5,000 was afterwards paid to him.]

The Prospecting Board, Victoria, made the following awards in 1860 :—

J. Mitchell and others, Wahgunyah ..	..£1,000	0 0
E. W. Gladman, Baw Baw ..	.. 250	0 0
R. Ellison and others, Londonderry ..	.. 250	0 0
J. Parker and others, Hines. &c. ..	.. 750	0 0
J. Dunleary and others, Redbank ..	.. 300	0 0
J. and J. Thomas, Mountain Creek ..	.. 750	0 0
J. Middlemiss and another, Redbank, &c.	.. 300	0 0
W. M'Crea, Hawthorn, Icy and Pleasant Creeks ..	 950	0 0

The Government of Victoria paid the following amounts to discoverers of gold in 1861 :—

Mr. Hargraves ..	1855..	..£2,381 0 0

Rev. W. B. Clarke	..	1855..	£476	4	0	}	1,000	0	0
Further reward	..	1861..	523	16	0	}			
Mr. Michael & others	1855..		576	4	0	}	1,000	0	0
Further reward	..	1861..	523	16	0	}			
Mr. Bruhn	..	1855..	238	0	0	}	500	0	0
Further reward	..	1861..	262	0	0	}			
Mr. Hiscock	..	1855..	476	4	0	}			
Further reward	..	1861..	523	16	0	}	1,000	0	0
Mr. Esmond	..	1855..	476	4	0	}			
Further rewards Clunes	..	1861..	523	16	0	..	1,000	0	0
J. Mechosk, Tarrangower and Kingower		1857..	476	4	0	}	1,000	0	0
Further reward	..	1860..	523	16	0	}			
Mr. Campbell	..	..	..	..	..	..	476	4	0

Awards made by the Board appointed in Victoria to consider aplications for rewards for the discovery of new gold-fields :—

J. Donnelly and others, Donnelly's Creek	..	£650	0	0
J. M. Connell and others, Walsh's Creek	..	200	0	0
C. Donovan, Donovan's Creek	.. ..	200	0	0

The Select Committee of the Legislative Assembly of Victoria, appointed March 4, 1863, to inquire into claims of prospectors and discoverers of new gold-fields made the following awards :—

J. Pollard and others, Ararat	..	..	£1100	0	0
A. Thompson and others, Inglewood	..		800	0	0
J. Law and others, Navarre	..	..	600	0	0
W. Gooley, Gooley's Creek, Upper Goulburn			100	0	0
E. Hill, Mount Blackwood	..	..	300	0	0
W. Pierce and another, Alma	..	..	300	0	0
J. Geraghty and others, Emerald, Nicholson, and Britannia	..	.. ...	500	0	0
J. O'Hanigan, Emerald	..	..	100	0	0
T. Potter and others, New Inglewood	..		300	0	0
A. Franktovich, Redcastle	..	..	100	0	0
D. Torquoy and others, Campbell's, near Ararat	.	..	.. ..	400	0

GOLD REWARDS under the Regulations of the Gold-fields Reward Fund of the Colony of Victoria. A Board specially appointed, recommended awards as follows (January 22, 1864) :—

MOUNT ALEXANDER—£1,000—equally divided between John Worley, C. T. Peters, George Robinson, and Robert Keen.

INDIGO—£500—J. H. Conness.

AVOCA—£400—equally divided between Daniel Burn, George Bell, senior, George Bell, junior, and John Cox.

CRESWICK—£800—to be divided as follows: J. P. Main, £150; John Hogben, £100; the remaining £550 to be divided equally between Robert Ormand, James Williams, Patrick Brannigan, William Lyons, William Giles, Charles Tandy, Lawrence Lawrenson, William Leary, Alfred———, John———.

REEDY CREEK—£100—J. Jones.

DAYLESFORD—£800—to be divided thus: John Egan, £600 ; and Thomas Connell, £200.

McIVOR—£400—William Bulling.

KORONG—£400—to be equally divided between H. T. Cullen, —Adams, R. Higgs, and T. W. White.

FIERY CREEK—£400—to be equally divided between Matthew M. Johnston, William Jewell, Edward Windus, and John Thomas.

ELYSIAN FLAT—£350—to be equally divided between P. G. Emmett, Eugene Ross, Alexander Lovell, Robert Jamieson, Christopher Smith, and W. T. Glover.

WARDY YALLOAK—£600—to be divided thus: Herbert Swindells, £100 ; and the remaining £500 to be equally divided between H. V. Smith, T. Kemp, and J. Hardy.

B. B. AND JORDAN—£200—to be equally divided between William Quinn, Owen Whittle, Gilbert Jones, and P. Sandford.

EASY GOLD
Melbourne Punch, 1854 (A satirical comment on dreams of easily won gold.)

UPPER GOULBURN—£200—Terence T. Gaffney.
    Total, £6,150.

160 applications sent to the Board appointed by the Victorian Parliament, claiming rewards for the discovery of new gold-fields.—January 22, 1864.

Amounts paid by Government of Victoria:—

1855	..	£4,523 16 0	1860	..	£2,623 16 0
1856	..	Nil.	1861	..	3,857 4 0
1857	..	£ 476 4 0	1862	..	833 6 8
1858	..	Nil.	1863	..	2,300 0 0
1859	..	Nil.	1864	..	6,150 0 0

These sums do not include £476 4s. paid to Mr. Campbell, and £950 to Mr. W. M'Crae, paid before 1864. The total rewards paid for the decade ending 1864 amounted to £22,190 10s. 8d.

Mr. E. H. Hargraves granted a pension of £250 per annum for life from N.S.W. Government for gold discovery, from January 1, 1877.

RIGHT OF THE CROWN TO GOLD, found on private property, confirmed by the Privy Council, February 8, 1877.

RIOTS IN CONNECTION WITH. Riots at Ballarat were caused by the way in which the gold licenses were collected, and by other matters which the Government appeared to ignore. The diggers erected a stockade, called the Eureka, which, after some fighting, was captured by the military. 1854.

Riots at Lambing Flat in consequence of the influx of Chinese, June 1, 1861.

TOTAL QUANTITY OF GOLD, obtained in Australia and New Zealand from date of first discovery :—

Colony.	Quantity.	Value.
	oz.	£
1 New South Wales	8,436,114	31,413,940
2 New Zealand	8,359,552	32,599,281
3 Queensland	1,889,458	6,940,417
4 South Australia ..	—	600,000
5 Tasmania in 1876 (gold exported)	10,278	41,861
6 Victoria	46,444,188	185,776,753
Grand Total	65,139,590	£257,372,252

(*For later return see* MINERAL STATISTICS.)

VICTORIAN DISCOVERER OF. James William Esmond, the discoverer of gold in Victoria, had, like Hargraves, been at the Californian goldfields, and felt convinced of the auriferous nature of the Australian soil. He left Port Phillip for California in June, 1849, observed the similarities in soil and general features between Clunes and California, and decided to return to explore his Australian home for gold. Circumstances made Esmond and Hargraves fellow-passengers on their return from California to Sydney. Esmond found gold at Clunes, Tuesday, July 1, 1851; and published his discovery at Geelong, July 6, following. [Several other parties were said to have discovered gold in Victoria before this, particularly Wm. Richfould, at Amherst, in 1848, and Chapman, at the Pyrenees, on June 6, 1851.]

GOLD ESCORT. First gold escort from the Etheridge, Queensland, started, April 13, 1872.

GOLD-FIELDS REGULATION ACT, VICTORIA, came into operation, January, 1853. [The license fee was thirty shillings per month, and gave summary jurisdiction to commissioners and justices of the peace; a double fee was imposed on foreigners. A public meeting of miners was held to protest against the provisions of the Act, on account of the largeness of the fees and of giving summary jurisdiction to commissioners and justices.]

"GOLDFINDER," EARLY. M'Gregor, a shepherd in the Wellington district, N.S.W.—better known by the *soubriquet* of "Goldfinder"—used to create temporary excitement on his periodical trips through Bathurst on his way to sell gold in Sydney. He never revealed the secret of the place of discovery. [This was several years before the discovery of gold in Australia was published.]

GOLD MINE, THE DEEPEST IN AUSTRALIA. The Magdala Goldmining Company's mine, at Stawell, Victoria, is 2,032ft. below the surface, and 1,200ft. below the level of the sea, 1879.

GOLD REGISTER, FIRST, issued in New South Wales, March 30, 1857.

GOLD REVENUE THE, placed at the disposal of Colonial Legislatures by a despatch received from the Colonial Ministers, September, 1852.

GOLD ROBBERIES. The "Nelson,' gold-ship, which was lying in Hobson's Bay with £24,000 of gold in bullion, was boarded by a gang of thieves who carried off the treasure, which has never been recovered; there were at the time three sailors and three passengers in the ship, April 2, 1852.

WEIBERG ROBBERY. The "Avoca" gold robbery. 5,000 sovereigns, the property of the Oriental Bank, stolen from on board the P. & O. steamer on the passage from Sydney to Melbourne by a ship's carpenter, Martin Weiberg, who also accused the first officer of being concerned in it, August, 1877.

[*See* BUSHRANGERS and CRIMES, *M'Ivor* and *Eugowra Escort Robberies.*]

GOLD.

GOLD.—PALMER RIVER.—The quantity of gold which has been obtained from the Palmer River since its discovery by James V. Mulligan and party, in June, 1873, has been very large. Between June and December 1873, all the gold that was obtained on the Palmer—and there were during that period from 4 to 5,000 miners on the field, all doing well—was brought to Charters Towers and Townsville, and that goldfield and port were of course, accredited with the gold, and it was not till the establishment of a Custom House at the then newly discovered port of Cooktown, in December, 1873, that any of the gold from the Palmer was brought to the latter port.

The following is an official statement of gold exports at Cooktown :—

Year.	Ozs.	Value.
1874	121,481	£485,924
1875	162,864	651,456
1876	169,972	679,888
1877	154,979	619,916
1878	108,214	432,856
Total	717,510	£2,870,040

Gold exported from Cleveland Bay from opening of the port until the end of the year 1878—

Year.	Quantity.			Value.		
	ozs.	dwt.	gr.	£	s.	d.
1866	98	0	0	343	0	0
1867	1,693	9	0	5,927	1	6
1868	20,550	2	0	71,925	7	0
1869	30,870	17	0	108,047	19	6
1870	52,000	9	0	182,001	11	6
1871	95,118	6	0	332,914	1	0
1872	111,749	7	0	391,122	14	6
1873	90,925	5	0	349,094	0	0
1874	108,849	0	0	385,780	0	0
1875	108,872	0	0	385,109	0	0
1876	90,428	0	0	318,626	0	0
1877	102,865	0	0	365,504	0	0
1878	81,379	4	22	276,422	0	0
	895,398	19	22	3,172,814	15	0

GOLDEN HORSESHOES. Mr. Cameron, a storekeeper at the Woolshed, New El Dorado (the first member of the Victorian Legislative Assembly returned for the Ovens), rode into Beechworth, Victoria, on a horse called Castor, (belonging to Mr. Brown, of Wagga, who was in Beechworth at the time), shod with golden shoes. The weight of each shoe was 7oz. 4dwt. The shoes were on the horse three days, 1856.

GOULBURN River, discovered by Hume and Hovell, and so named by them in honour of the Colonial Secretary of New South Wales, December 3, 1824.

GOVERNORS.

Colonel Arthur, Governor of Tasmania, belonged to the York Chasseurs ; appointed Superintendent of Honduras, 1814 ; arrived in Tasmania, 1824.

Lieutenant-Colonel Barney appointed Lieutenant Governor of Northern Australia, the only Governor of that intended colony, arrived in the "William Hyde," September 15, 1846. He left shortly afterwards in the "Columbia" with a party, in search of a proper site for the settlement of Northern Australia, and returned on November 28 following, having discovered a splendid harbour at Port Curtis, 1846.

LIST OF, AND EVENTS IN CONNECTION WITH
THEIR GOVERNMENTS.

New South Wales—

Captain A. Phillip, R.N., from January 26, 1788, to December 10, 1792.

Captain F. Grose (Lieutenant-Governor), from December 11, 1792, to December 12, 1794.

Captain Paterson, New South Wales Corps (Lieutenant-Governor), from December 13, 1794, to September 1, 1795.

Captain Hunter, R.N., from September 7, 1795, to September 27, 1800.

Captain P. G. King, R.N., from September 28, 1800, to August 12, 1806.

Captain W. Bligh, R.N., from August 13, 1806, to January 26, 1808.

During Governor Bligh's suspension the Government was successively administered by—
Lieutenant-Colonel G. Johnstone, Lieutenant- Colonel Foveaux, and Colonel William Paterson, all of the New South Wales Corps, afterwards 102nd Regiment, from January 26, 1808, to December 28, 1809.

Major-General L. Macquarie, from January 1, 1810, to December 1, 1821.

Major-General Sir T. Brisbane, K.C.B., from December 1, 1821, to December 1, 1825.

Colonel Stewart, 3rd Regiment of Buffs (Acting Governor), from December 6, 1825, to December 18, 1825.

Lieutenant-General R. Darling, from December 19, 1825, to October 21, 1831.

Colonel Lindsay, C.B. (Acting Governor), from October 22, 1831, to December 2, 1831.

Major-General Sir R. Bourke, K.C.B., from December 3, 1831, to December 5, 1837.

Lieutenant-Colonel K. Snodgrass (Lieutenant-Governor), from December 6, 1837, to February 23, 1838.

Sir George Gipps, from February 24, 1838, to July 11, 1846.

Sir Maurice O'Connell, from July 12, 1846, to August 2, 1846.

Sir Charles A. Fitzroy, Governor General, from August 3, 1846, to January 17, 1855.

Sir William Thomas Denison, K C.B., Governor General, from January 20, 1855, to January 22, 1861.

[Colonel Henry Keane Bloomfield, John Hubert Plunkett, Esq., and Charles Cowper, Esq., Administrators during absence of Sir W. Denison at Norfolk Island, from September 17 to October 27, 1857.]

Colonel John Maxwell Perceval, Sir William Westbrooke Burton, Kt., and Charles Cowper, Esq., Administrators during absence of Sir W. Denison at Norfolk Island, from June 16 to July 8, 1859.]

Lieutenant-Colonel John F. Kempt (Administrator), from January 23, 1861, to March 21, 1861.

Right Honorable Sir John Young, Bart., K.C.B., G.C.M.G.,

Privy Councillor, afterwards Lord Lisgar (Administrator,) March 22, 1861, to May 15, 1861, Governor-in-Chief, May 16, 1861, to December 24, 1867.

Sir Trevor Chute, K.C.B. (Administrator) from December 25, 1867, to January 7, 1868.

Somerset Richard Lowry Corry, Earl of Belmore, January 8, 1868, to February 22, 1872.

Sir Alfred Stephen, Kt., C.B., K.C.M.G., (Chief Justice), from February 23 to June 2, 1872.

Sir Hercules G. R. Robinson, G.C.M.G., June 3 to March 19, 1879.

Sir Alfred Stephen, C.B., K.C.M.G., Lieutenant-Governor (Acting-Governor), from March 20, 1879.

Right-Honourable Viscount Loftus (Privy Councillor), 1879.

New Zealand—

Captain William Hobson, R.N. Proclamation of British Sovereignty by Captain Hobson in January, 1840, New Zealand a dependency of the Colony of New South Wales until 3rd May, 1841, at which date it was proclaimed a separate colony. From January, 1840, to May, 1841, Captain Hobson was Lieutenant-Governor of New Zealand under Sir George Gipps, Governor of New South Wales, and from May, 1841, Governor of New Zealand, the seat of Government being at Auckland, where he died in September, 1842. From the time of Governor Hobson's death in September, 1842, until the arrival of Governor Fitzroy in December, 1843, the Government was carried on by the Colonial Secretary, Lieutenant Shortland, from January, 1840, to September 10, 1842.

Lieutenant Shortland (Administrator), from September 10, 1842, to December 26, 1843.

Captain Robert Fitzroy, R.N., from December 26, 1843, to November 17, 1845.

Captain Grey (became Sir George Grey, K.C.B., in 1848). Held the commission as Lieutenant-Governor of the colony until January 1, 1848, when he was sworn in as Governor-in-Chief over the islands of New Zealand, and as Governor of the Province of New Ulster and Governor of the Province of New Munster. After the passing of "The New Zealand Constitution Act," Sir George Grey was, on September 13, 1852, appointed Governor of the colony, the duties of which he assumed on March 7, 1853. In August, 1847, Mr. E. J. Eyre was appointed Lieutenant-Governor of New Munster : he was sworn in January 28, 1848. On January 3, 1848, Major-General George Dean Pitt was appointed Lieutenant-Governor of New Ulster : he was sworn in February 14, 1848 ; died January 8, 1851 ; and was succeeded as Lieutenant-Governor by Lieutenant-Colonel Wynyard, appointed April 14, 1851 ; sworn in April 26, 1851. The duties of the Lieutenant-Governor ceased on the assumption by Sir George Grey of his office of Governor, March 7, 1853 : from November 18, 1845, to December 31, 1853.

Lieutenant-Colonel Robert Henry Wynyard, C.B. (Administrator), from January 3, 1854, to September 6, 1855.

Colonel Thomas Gore Browne, C.B., from September 6, 1855, to October 2, 1861.

Sir George Grey, K.C.B., Administrator from October 3, 1861 ; Governor, from Dec. 4, 1861, to Feb. 5, 1868.

Sir George Ferguson Bowen, G.C.M.G., from February 5, 1868, to March 19, 1873.

Sir George Alfred Arney, Chief Justice (Administrator), from March 21, 1873, to June 14, 1873.

The Right Hon. Sir James Fergusson, Baronet, Privy Councillor, from June 14, 1873, to December 3, 1874.

The Right Hon. the Marquis of Normanby, Privy Councillor, (Administrator) from December 3, 1874 ; Governor from January 9, 1875, to March, 1879.

Sir Hercules Robinson, G.C.M.G., from March 24, 1879, still in office.

Queensland—

Sir George Ferguson Bowen, G.C.M G., December 10, 1859, to January 4, 1868.

Colonel Maurice Charles O'Connell, President of the Legislative Council (Administrator), January 4, 1868, to August 14, 1868.

Colonel Samuel Wensley Blackall, August 14, 1868, to January 2, 1871.

Colonel Sir Maurice Charles O'Connell, Kt. (Administrator), January 2, 1871, to August 12, 1871.

Most Honorable George Augustus Constantine, Marquis of Normanby (Privy Councillor), August 12, 1871, to November 12, 1874.

Colonel Sir Maurice Charles O'Connell, Kt. (Administrator), November 12, 1874, to January 23, 1875.

William Wellington Cairns, C.M.G., January 23, 1875, to March 14, 1877.

Colonel Sir Maurice Charles O'Connell (Administrator), March 14, 1877, to April 10, 1877.

Sir Arthur Edward Kennedy, C.B., K.C.M.G. (Administrator), April 10, 1877, to July 20, 1877.

Sir Arthur Edward Kennedy, C.B., K.C.M.G., Governor, July 20, 1877 ; still in office.

South Australia—

Captain John Hindmarsh, R.N., K.H., from December 28, 1836, to July 16, 1838.

George Milner Stephen, Esq. (Officer Adm. Govt.), from July 16, 1838, to October 12, 1838.

Lieut. Col. George Gawler, K.H., from October 12, 1838, to May 15, 1841.

George Grey, Esq., from May 15, 1841, to Oct. 25, 1845.

Lieut.-Col. Fred. Holt Robe, from October 25, 1845, to August 2, 1848.

Sir H. Ed. Fox Young, Kt., from August 2, 1848, to December 20, 1854.

Boyle Travers Finniss, Esq. (Officer Adm. Govt.), from December 20, 1854, to June 8, 1855.

Sir Richard Graves MacDonnell, C.B., Kt., from June 8, 1855, to March 4, 1862.

Sir Dominick Daly, Kt., from March 4, 1862, to February 19, 1868.

Lieut.-Col. Francis Gilbert Hamley (Officer Adm. Govt.), from February 20, 1868, to February 15, 1869.

Right Hon. Sir James Fergusson, Baronet, from February 16, 1869, to April 18, 1873.

Hon Sir Richard Davies Hanson, Kt., Chief Justice (Officer Adm. Govt.), from December 7, 1872, to June 8, 1873.

Sir Anthony Musgrave, K.C.M.G., from June 9, 1873, to January 29, 1877.

Hon. Samuel James Way, Chief Justice (Officer Adm. Govt.), from January 29, 1877, to March 24, 1877.

Sir William Wellington Cairns, K.C.M.G., from March 24, 1877, to May 17, 1877.

Hon. Samuel James Way, Chief Justice (Officer Adm. Govt.), from May 17, 1877, to October 2, 1877.

Sir William Francis Drummond Jervois, K.C.M.G., C.B., R.E., sworn in October 2, 1877.

Hon. Samuel James Way, Chief Justice (Officer Adm. Govt.), from February 14, 1878, to August 15, 1878.

Sir William Francis Drummond Jervois, K.C.M.G., C.B., R.E., from August 15, 1878 ; still in office.

Tasmania—

Colonel David Collins (Lieutenant-Governor), from February 19, 1804, to March 24, 1810.

Lieutenant Edward Lord and Captain Murray, 73rd Regiment (Commandants), from March 24, 1810, to February, 1812.

Lieutenant-Colonel Geiles, 73rd Regiment (Commandant), from February, 1812, to February 4, 1813.

Colonel Davey (Lieutenant-Governor), from February 4, 1813, to April 9, 1817.

Colonel Sorell (Lieutenant-Governor), from April 9, 1817, to May 14, 1824.

Colonel Arthur (Lieutenant-Governor), from May 14, 1823, to December 3, 1825.

Lieutenant-General R. Darling (Governor-in-Chief) from December 3, 1825, to December 6, 1825.

Colonel Arthur (Lieutenant-Governor), from December 6, 1825, to October 30, 183.

Lieutenant-Colonel Snodgrass (Acting Lieutenant-Governor), from October 31, 1836, to January 5, 1837.

Sir John Franklin, K.H. (Lieutenant-Governor), from January 6, 1837, to August 21, 1843.

Sir J. C. Eardley-Wilmot, Bart. (Lieutenant-Governor), from August 21, 1843, to October 13, 1846.

C. J. Latrobe, Esq. (Administrator of the Government), from October 13, 1846, to January 25, 1847.

Sir W. T. Denison, Kt. (Lieutenant-Governor), from January 26, 1847, to January 8, 1855.

Sir H. E. F. Young, C.B., Kt. (Governor-in-Chief), from January 8, 1855, to December 10, 1861.

Colonel T. Gore Browne, C.B. (Administrator), from December 11, 1861, to June 16, 1862 ; (Governor-in-Chief), from June 16, 1862, to December 30, 1868.

Lieutenant-Colonel W. C. Trevor, C.B. (Administrator), from December 30, 1868, to January 15, 1869.

C. Du Cane, Esq. (Governor and Commander-in-Chief) from January 15, 1869, to November 28, 1874.

Sir Valentine Fleming, Kt. (Administrator), from March 26, 1874, to June, 1874.

Sir Francis Smith, Kt. (Administrator), from November 30, 1874, to January 13, 1875.

F. A. Weld, Esq., C.M.G. (Governor and Commander-in-Chief), from January 13, 1875 ; still in office.

Victoria—

Charles Joseph La Trobe (Superintendent of the district of Port Phillip), from September 30, 1839, to July 1851, and (Lieutenant-Governor), from July 15, 1851, to May 5, 1854.

John Vesey Fitzgerald Foster (Administrator), from May 8, 1854, to June 22, 1854.

Sir Charles Hotham, K.C.B. (Lieutenant-Governor), from June 22, 1854, to December 31, 1855.

Major-General Edward Macarthur (Officer administering the Government) from January 1, 1856, to December 26, 1856.

Sir Henry Barkly, K.C.B. (Captain-General and Governor-in-Chief of the colony of Victoria, and Vice-Admiral of the same), from December 26, 1856, to September 10, 1863.

Sir Charles Henry Darling, K.C.B. (Governor and Commander-in-Chief), from September 11, 1863, to May 7, 1866.

Brigadier-General George Jackson Carey, C.B. (Officer administering the Government), from May 7, 1866, to August 15, 1866.

The Right Hon. John Henry Thomas Manners Sutton, Viscount Canterbury, K.C.B. (Governor and Commander-in-Chief), from August 15, 1866, to March 2, 1873.

Sir William Foster Stawell (Officer administering the Government), from March 3, 1873, to March 19, 1873.

Sir George Ferguson Bowen, G.C.M.G. (Administrator, from March 31), 1873, to July 29, 1873 ; (Governor and Commander-in-Chief), from July 30, 1873, to December 31, 1874.

Sir Redmond Barry (Administrator of the Government), from January 3, 1875, to January 10, 1875.

Sir William Foster Stawell (Administrator), from January 11, 1875, to January 14, 1876.

Sir George Ferguson Bowen, G.C.M.G. (Governor and Commander-in-Chief), from January 14, 1876, to February 22, 1879.

The Most Noble the Marquis of Normanby (Governor and Commander-in-Chief), from March 1, 1879 ; still in office.

Western Australia—

Captain James Stirling (Lieutenant-Governor), from June 1, 1829, to September 30, 1832.

Captain Irwin, (Acting Lieutenant-Governor), from September, 1832, to September, 1833.

Captain Daniell, (Acting Lieutenant-Governor), from September, 1833, till May 11, 1834.

Captain Beete, (Acting Lieutenant-Governor), from May 11, to May 24, 1834.

Sir James (formerly Captain) Stirling, (Governor), from August, 1834, to December, 1838.

John Hutt, Esq. (Governor), from January 2, 1839, to December, 1845.

Lieutenant-Colonel Clarke, (Governor), from February, 1846, to February, 1847.

Lieutenant-Colonel (formerly Captain) Irwin, (Governor), from February, 1847, to July, 1848.

Captain Charles Fitzgerald, (Governor), from August, 1848, to June, 1855.

Arthur Edward Kennedy, Esq., (Governor), from June, 1855, to February 17, 1862.

Lieutenant-Colonel John Bruce, (Acting Governor), from February 17 to February 27, 1862.

John Stephen Hampton, Esq. (Governor), from February 27, 1862, to November, 1868.

Lieutenant-Colonel John Bruce, (Acting Governor), from November, 1868, to September, 30, 1869.

Frederick Aloysius Weld, Esq. (Governor), from September 30, 1869, to November, 1874.

Sir William Cleaver Francis Robinson, K.C.M.G., (Governor), from November 14, 1874, to August 28,

1877. Lieutenant-Colonel E. D. Harvest, (Acting Governor), from August 28, 1877, to November, 1877.
Sir Harry St. George Ord, C.B., K.C.M.G., (Governor), from November, 1877; still in office.

SALARIES OF. The salaries of Governors Hotham and Barkly (Victoria) were £15,000 per annum.
The present salaries of Governors are :—
New South Wales, £7,000.
New Zealand, £5,000, and allowance, £2,500.
Queensland, £5,000.
South Australia, £5,000.
Tasmania, £3,500.
Victoria, £10,000.
Western Australia, 2,500.

GOVERNMENT HOUSE, FIRST. The first stone of a building to be used as a temporary Government House was laid May 15, 1788. [A piece of copper recording that Governor Phillip, with his party, landed January 24, 1781, placed beneath it. The site of the first Government House was in Pitt-street, Sydney, where are now situated Vickery's buildings. The remains were pulled down in 1868.]

GOVERNMENT ORDERS. In the early days of the Colony of New South Wales some extraordinary "Government Orders" were issued, which throw some light on the manners, customs, and evil propensities of the criminal class. The following are selected as examples :—

Selling of Rations.—"Although repeated orders have been given to prevent the convicts from selling or exchanging their provisions issued from the Public Stores for money, spirits, or tobacco, that practice is still continued, and as those who sell their own provisions must support themselves by stealing from others, it is the duty of every individual to put a stop to a practice which distresses the honest and industrious, whose gardens are robbed, and provisions stolen by those who sell their rations, no provisions are ever to be purchased or received from a convict on any consideration whatever, and the Commissary is directed to give 30 ℔. of flour as a reward for discovering any person who may in future be guilty of a breach of this order. BY ORDER OF THE GOVERNOR. February 11, 1790."

Boat Building.—"No boat is to be built by any individual in this settlement whose length from stem to stern exceeds fourteen feet (*sic !*), without having first obtained permission from Head Quarters.—April 9, 1791." [This was to prevent convicts escaping by sea.]

Against Imprisonment for Debt.—"It having been represented to the Governor that many people who are concerned in petty dealings with every description of inhabitants in this colony consider themselves at liberty to imprison the persons of their debtors when unable to discharge their demands, by which means the public interest is materially injured and the Crown deprived of the service of such debtors : Notice is hereby given, and the Governor expects it to be seriously attended to, that the public labouring servants of the Crown are not to be detained from their duty by imprisoning their persons in this way, the property they possess being considered as belonging to Government; and if any such dealers shall be desirous at any time of accommodating the labouring servants of the Crown with credit, it must be wholly and absolutely upon the strength of their good faith in the integrity of such people, and not under a notice that they can arrest and imprison by forms of law; and it is from henceforth to be generally understood that Government will by no means dispense with the labour of its servants for the partial accommodation of any private dealings whatever.—October 4, 1798."

Spirit Smuggling.—"All spirituous liquors and other strong drinks that are attempted to be smuggled from any ship arriving here will on condemnation be the exclusive property of the person or persons making the seizure.—Nov. 28, 1800."

Reprieve in consequence of Rain, and Caution to Evildoers.—"The regiment to be under arms on Monday next, 19th instant, at half past nine in the morning, to attend the execution of John Boatswain, private soldier

GOVERNMENT HOUSE, SYDNEY, c. 1790
George Raper, British Museum

in the New South Wales Corps, sentenced to die by a general court martial, for desertion.—April 14, 1801."

* * * * * * *

"Raining in torrents. The execution of the prisoner as directed by the orders of the 14th instant, on account of the inclemency of the weather, is deferred until further orders."

* * * * * * *

"Still raining in torrents. Execution further deferred. April 20, 1801."

* * * * * * *

"Favourable circumstances having been reported, the Governor of the settlement is pleased to extend a reprieve, and grant a free pardon to the prisoner John Boatswain, sentenced to death for the unsoldierlike crime of desertion ; but the Governor trusts that the example of the awful position in which the wretched man was placed will deter others from following his example.—April 25, 1801."

"Rum" Reward for Apprehension of Absconding Prisoners.—"Whereas William Knight and James Warwick have by regular form been outlawed, and are supposed to associate and commit violent acts of depredations in conjunction with the natives, on the public, the Governor is pleased to offer a reward of thirty gallons of spirits to any person who shall lodge the bodies of the said William Knight and James Warwick in jail, or deliver them to the nearest magistrate in command.—May 11, 1801."

Nomenclature.—"His Excellency the Governor is pleased to direct that in all spiritual, judicial, and parochial proceedings, deeds, instruments, and registers, the districts of Sydney, Petersham, Bullanaming, Concord, and Liberty Plains be comprised within a parish to be henceforth named St. Phillip, in honour of the first Governor of this territory. And the districts of Parramatta, Bankstown, Prospect Hill, Toongabbie, Seven Hills, Castle Hill, Eastern Farms, Field of Mars, Northern Boundary Ponds, and Kissing Point be comprised within a parish to be henceforward named St. John, in honour of the late Governor Captain John Hunter. And that the churches now building at Sydney and Parramatta be respectively named Saint Phillip and St. John.—July 23, 1802."

Caution against Runaways.—Government issued notice, pointing out the falsity and wickedness of the report generally believed in by the convicts, that a settlement of white people existed on the other side of the mountains, and cautioning them, by the dreadful fate of the runaways, against following their example, Oct. 20, 1802.

Strayed Cattle.—Proclamation issued against persons crossing the Nepean to the Cowpastures (whither the strayed cattle had resorted), without a permit signed by the Governor. "If any persons not authorised shall presume to kill any of the said black cattle, male or female, they will be punished to the utmost extent of the law.—July 6, 1803."

Boatmen's Fares.—Government order issued fixing the fare to be charged by boatmen for a passenger from Sydney to Parramatta, or *vice versâ,* at one shilling, and stringent regulations issued for the better conduct of the boatmen towards passengers, July 6, 1803.

Caution against Cutting Timber.—In consequence of heavy floods on the Hawkesbury, the Governor issued an order cautioning settlers against cutting down trees or cultivating the banks of the river, whereby many acres of ground had been removed, houses, stock, &c., washed away, and river blocked with trees ; a penalty of £50 imposed for each tree cut down after this notice, Oct. 4, 1803.

Importation of New Zealand Skulls.—In consequence of the traffic in human skulls with the New Zealand natives, a Government order was issued prohibiting the importation, April 19, 1831. [*See* TRAFFIC IN HUMAN MAORI HEADS.]

Cutting Timber, &c., on Garden Island.—"It being deemed expedient that the island situated in the harbour of Port Jackson, and near to Farm Cove, called Garden Island, should be comprised in and considered in future as forming a part of the Government Domain : Notice is hereby given that all the growth and produce of said island, whether timber or grass, is to be appropriated in future to the exclusive use of his Excellency's establishment, and all persons are cautioned not to cut grass or timber there, as any person detected so in doing after this public notice will be prosecuted and severely punished. Persons detected or convicted of having set fire to any wood or grass in Garden Island will be most severely punished for such wanton mischief. (Signed) LACHLAN MACQUARIE. September 7, 1811."

GOVETT'S LEAP. W. R. Govett, Surveyor, N.S.W., discovered the remarkable falls which now bear his name, 1832.

GOVETT'S LEAP FALLS, BLUE MOUNTAINS
Gibbs, Shallard, & Co.'s *Illustrated Guide to Sydney,* 1882

GRANT, CAPTAIN. Left England in the "Lady Nelson," March 18, 1800 ; arrived in Sydney, December 16, 1800. [*See* PORT PHILLIP.]

GRAPE-VINES. The first grape vine was planted on land in Parramatta, November 15, 1791. [*See* VINES.]

GRASSHOPPERS, devastated large areas of country in South Australia, and in Riverina, New South Wales, November 27, 1872.

GUNPOWDER, first manufactured by Mr. Robert Cooper, of Sydney, October 6, 1829.

H

HANDBALL MATCHES. Series of Inter-colonial handball matches between Victoria and New South Wales resulted in a victory for the former, March 24, 1877.

HARBOUR TRUST COMMISSION, VICTORIA. Sir John Coode accepted the offer of the Harbour Trust Commission to report on direct communication between Melbourne and Hobson's Bay, Victoria, December 8, 1877. Sir John Coode forwarded report to Victoria Government in which he recommended improving the Yarra Yarra River instead of constructing a canal from Sandridge to Melbourne, March, 1879.

HARGRAVES, EDWARD HAMMOND, found gold at Lewis Ponds Creek, near Bathurst, February 12, 1851 ; awarded a grant of £15,000 by Sydney and Melbourne Legislatures in 1855.

EDWARD HAMMOND HARGRAVES
Picturesque Atlas of Australia

HASTINGS, RIVER, surveyed by Oxley, 1818.

HAWKESBURY, RIVER (*native name* VENRUB-BIM), discovered by Governor Phillip and named by him in honour of the head of the Council of Trade and Plantations, June 6, 1789.

AN EXPLORING PARTY AT BEROWRA WATERS
Mitchell Library

HAWKESBURY, SETTLEMENT OF THE. The first settlers on the Hawkesbury established themselves on that river, in January, 1794. [The blacks at first refrained from troubling their outpost, but it was only for a short time, for, the next year, the Government schooner was sent to the Hawkesbury with a military guard, to prevent acts of violence which frequently occurred between the Europeans and the blacks.]

VISIT OF THE GOVERNOR TO. Governor Hunter visited the Hawkesbury, and having seen the settlers at the chief settlement there (now Windsor) and settled disputes between them, he proceeded to Richmond, where bearings were taken to cut a road to Parramatta, 1796.

HAYES, SIR HENRY BROWNE, who had served the office of Sheriff of the City of Cork, was tried in 1801 for the abduction of a wealthy Quaker lady, and was sentenced to suffer death ; this sentence was, however, commuted to imprisonment for life. His case at the time excited much attention, in consequence of the position in life of the parties implicated. Some time elapsed after the commission of the offence before Sir Henry was captured and brought to justice. A large reward having at length been offered for his apprehension, he walked into the shop of a hairdresser at Cork, named Coghlan, and after some conversation said that as it was his intention to surrender himself Coghlan might as well reap the benefit of the reward by giving him up. Whilst in the colony he resided at Vaucluse, a beautiful spot near the entrance to Sydney harbour, for many years afterwards the residence of Mr. W. C. Wentworth. He received a pardon and left the colony for Ireland in 1812. There is a singular story current respecting him, which is implicitly believed by the more ignorant part of the old colonists, to the effect that, finding his place at Vaucluse much infested with snakes, and firmly believing that these reptiles could not exist on Irish turf, he sent home for several casks of that article, which he scattered over the place. His faith in his native land and its patron saint was amply rewarded, for, from that time to this, says the story, a snake has never been seen at Vaucluse.

HAYES, CAPTAIN, the notorious pirate and kidnapper, captured in the South Seas, July 13 1872.

HEALEY, REV. WILLIAM.

Sergeant Timothy Foley and Mounted Constable Wm. Townsend, of the N. S. W. police, shot Rev. Wm. Healey, a Roman Catholic priest, in mistake for a bushranger, at Deepwater, on the Murrumbidgee River, August 6, 1876.

Foley and Townsend tried at Yass and acquitted of the manslaughter of Father Healey, April 4, 1877.

HEAT.

Great heat in Sydney (thermometer 102° in the shade), December 27, 1790.

Great heat experienced, settlement visited by myriads of flying foxes, birds dropped dead from the trees, January, 1791.

Great heat in the settlement. The country around Rose Hill and Parramatta on fire for many miles, February 12, 1791.

The thermometer stood at 90° in the shade and 146° in the sun at Parramatta, December 18, 1813.

Lieutenant Lowe, at the floods on the Namoi, was perched on the trunk of an uprooted tree ; the rains had ceased, the thermometer was at 100°, a glaring sun and a coppery sky were above him ; he looked in vain for help ; but no prospect of escape animated him, and the hot sun began its dreadful work. His skins blistered, dried, became parched and hard like the bark of a tree and life began to ebb. At length assistance arrived ; it came too late, he was indeed just alive, but died almost immediately. He was literally scorched to death." His remains were buried on Tibbereena Station, belonging to the late W. C. Wentworth, January, 1840.

In New South Wales.

(1)	1791 January 10, in Sydney	..	105 in the shade
(1)	1791 ,, 11 ,,	..	105 ,,
(2)	1798 December, on the Hawkesbury	107	,,
(3)	1826 November 29, in Sydney	104	,,
(4)	1832 March 18 ,,	130 in the sun
(5)	1833 February, in Bathurst	..	105 ,,
(6)	1833 ,, ,,	...	107 ,,
(6)	1833 ,, ,,	..	107½ ,,
(7)	1835 January 31, in Sydney	..	109 in the shade
(8)	1837 February 23 ,,	..	132 in the sun
(9)	1839 January 29, in Yass	..	120 ,,
(10)	1845 January 21, Central Australia	131 in the shade
(10)	1845 November 11 ,,	127 ,,
(11)	1847 ,, 1, on the Paterson	127 in the sun
(11)	1848 January 1 ,,	128 ,,
(11)	1848 ,, 1 ,,	108 in the shade
(11)	1848 ,, 3 ,,	109 ,,
	At 10·30 p.m. it was ..	92 ,,
(11)	1863 January 5, in Sydney	.. 106·9 ,,
(11)	1866 ,, 8, in Lochinvar	.. 108 ,,
	At 9·30 p.m. it was ..	95
(11)	1867 January 2, in Lochinvar	.. 107 ,,
(11)	1867 November 16 ,,	.. 104 ,,
(11)	1867 December 25 ,,	.. 106 ,,
(12)	1870 January 3, at Sydney	.. 105·2 ,,
(12)	1871 December 22 ,,	.. 103·8 ,,
(12)	1878 November 21 ,,	.. 102·5 ,,
(12)	1878 ,, 21 ,,	.. *131 in the sun

*Glass burst, and the temperature must have been over 131 to do this.

AUTHORITIES.—1 and 2, Colonel Collins ; 3, 4, 5, 6, 7, and 8, Sydney *Gazette* ; 9, Sydney *Monitor* ; 10, Sturt's Central Australia ; 11, Rev. A. Glennie's iournal ; 12, H. C. Russell, Government Astronomer.

The following extracts will convey some idea of the awful effects of the heat on some of the hot days :—

On February 10 and 11, 1791, on which days the temperature at Sydney stood in the shade at 105°, the heat was so excessive at Parramatta, made worse by the bush fires, that immense numbers of the large fox-bats were seen to drop from the trees into the water, and many dropped dead on the wing. At Sydney about the harbour in many places the ground was found covered with small birds, some dead, others gasping for water. At Parramatta, an officer of the relief guard left the boat to find a drink of water, and had to walk several miles in a dry watercourse before he found it, many birds dropping dead at his feet. The wind was north-west, and burned up everything before it. Persons whose business obliged them to go out declared that it was impossible to turn the face for five minutes to the wind.

The Sydney *Gazette* of February 8, 1822, says :—The other day a professional gentleman was induced to dig for some moist soil to preserve a few choice plants, and he found the ground at 20 feet down as much heated as it was within a few inches of the surface.

From the same paper, November 29, 1826 :—The heat and hot wind of Saturday last excelled all that we ever experienced in the colony. On board the " Volage," man-of-war, in the shade, the thermometer was 106°, and on the shore it was, in some parts of the town, 100°, and in others 104°. To traverse the streets was truly dreadful, the dust rose in thick columns, and the N.W. wind, from which quarter our hot winds invariably proceed, was assisted in its heat by the surrounding country being all on fire, so that those who were compelled to travel felt themselves encircled with lambent flames. Sydney was more like the mouth of Vesuvius than anything else. Sunday, however, brought a change of wind, since when the weather has been somewhat more endurable.

Again, in March, 1829 :—We are all burnt up ; it is frightful to go into the garden. Not a drop of water but what we send for from Botany Swamps. Fourpence per gallon was paid for water in Sydney during 1829.

Sydney *Gazette*, Tuesday, Feb. 21, 1832, says :—Saturday was one of the hottest days ever remembered. The recent rains having saturated the earth, the atmosphere was impregnated by an aqueous vapour not unlike steam issuing from a boiler, while the sun poured down all the fury of his heat. It was dreadful. Man and beast groaned beneath the oppression, and numbers of working oxen dropped down dead on the public roads. In the evening we were, " as usual," relieved by a stiff southerly gale, wafting health and vigour on its blessed wings. On Sunday night we were visited • by a tremendous storm of thunder, lightning, rain and hail. The lightning was magnificent beyond description, spreading over the whole canopy of heaven, and assuming a thousand various forms. The storm broke heaviest over Parramatta, where the artillery of the skies roared and cracked in deafening peals, making the very houses totter.

Saturday, March 18, 1832, was insufferably warm. At 1 p.m., the thermometer was 130° in the sun. The cattle suffered much. Working bullocks dropped dead.

Captain Sturt's account of a hot day experienced in Central Australia on November 11, 1845, is as follows :—"The wind which had been blowing all the morning hot from the N.E. increased to a gale, and I shall never forget its withering effects. I sought shelter behind a large gum tree, but the blasts of heat were so terrific that I wondered the very grass did not take fire; everything both animate and inanimate gave way before it; the horses stood with their backs to the wind and their noses to the ground, the birds were mute, and the leaves of the trees fell like a shower around us. At noon I took out my thermometer graduated to 127° and put it in the fork of a tree, and an hour afterwards when I went to examine it the tube was full of mercury, and the bulb burst; about sunset the wind shifted to W., and a thundercloud passed over us, but only a few drops of rain fell."

On the Lower Macquarie River, on January 11, 1878, at half-past 2 o'clock p.m., the thermometer registered 117° in the shade. On the same date at half-past 5 p.m., 110° in the shade. On January 18 the glass rose to 119° in the shade. On the same date at 10 p.m. it was 98°.

In Queensland.—Four sudden deaths caused by the great heat occurred at Rockhampton, Queensland, February 21, 1878.

In Victoria.—The following is a table of the hottest days in Melbourne; the years 1861 and 1864 are omitted, as the thermometer did not reach 100° in those years :—

Year	Date	°	Year	Date	°
1858—	Jan. 5	101·6	1868—	Mar. 20	100·0
"	27	106·8		Nov. 28	101·3
"	28	107·8		Dec. 11	101·0
"	31	101·0		" 24	110·0
	Nov. 22	103·2	1869—	Feb. 19	100·8
1859—	Feb. 6	104·0		Dec. 15	100·0
	3	100·3		" 20	108·4
	Dec. 4	103·0		" 21	101·3
	" 20	100·1	1870—	Jan. 12	104·1
1860—	Jan. 21	108·8		" 23	107·0
	" 22	111·0		" 24	107·1
1862—	Jan. 13	105·0		Feb. 3	102·8
	" 14	111·2		" 15	109·0
	Dec. 31	107·2		" 21	102·0
1863—	Jan. 8	104·6	1871—	Dec. 4	101·0
	Feb. 1	103·9		" 21	100·2
	" 2	104·0		" 22	106·0
1865—	Feb. 27	103·4		" 30	102·8
	Dec. 27	101·8	1872—	Jan. 9	101·0
1866—	Jan. 15	103·0		" 10	102·0
	" 16	108·2		" 16	103·3
	Feb. 7	100·9		" 21	100·8
	" 8	102·5	1873—	Jan. 20	101·0
	" 11	102·0		Feb. 16	102·4
1867—	Jan. 12	108·4		Dec. 8	101·2
	" 22	101·0		" 9	100·6
	" 25	103·0		" 15	100·1
	Dec. 19	104·6	1874—	Feb. 14	101·0
1868—	Jan. 25	100·3		" 17	102·7
	Mar. 1	104·6		" 28	102·2
	" 6	100·7			

Hottest day ever experienced in Melbourne. Thermometer 110·4° in the shade. Jan. 20, 1875.

Five days' intense heat in Victoria. At Melbourne, in the shade, the thermometer rose to 110 degrees; in the sun 146·0°, being the greatest heat recorded in Melbourne. Jan. 22, 1875. [*See* METEOROLOGY.]

HEROES.

Presentation at Sydney, by Sir John Young, of the Victoria Cross to *Samuel Mitchell* of the Marines, for valour in the New Zealand war, September 24, 1864.

Presentation at Sydney, by Earl Belmore, of the Royal Humane Society's medal to *Samuel Bennett Bailey,* for courageous conduct on the occasion of the wreck of the " Walter Hood," near Ulladulla, New South Wales. [*William Harrison,* of the Richmond River, had a similar medal sent to him for courageous conduct in saving life on the same occasion]: January 26, 1872.

Cecil Herbert M'Meikan, aged eleven years, a native of Victoria, presented by Governor Bowen with the Royal Humane Society's silver medal, for bravery in rescuing two boys who were drowning in the Saltwater River, Victoria, January 1, 1875.

James Henry Brownhill, nine years of age, presented by Sir George F. Bowen, Governor of Victoria, with the Royal Humane Society's silver medal, for saving the lives of three children who were in danger of drowning, whilst bathing in the Loddon River, Victoria, in January, 1874, January 1, 1875.

John McDonald, Inspector of Queensland Police, saved the lives of thirteen persons wrecked in the "Queen of the Colonies." Queensland Government awarded him £100 for his bravery, 1860.

John P. Sheehan, saved the lives of thirty-three persons on the occasion of the Gundagai floods. June, 1852. [New South Wales Government presented him with a silver jug in recognition of his humanity and bravery on the occasion.]

John Bennett, a native of Sydney, N.S.W., for saving the lives of seventeen persons on various occasions, presented with 1,000 sovereigns by Hon. Lady Robinson (on behalf of the colonists), on board the s.s. " Whampoa," Sydney, November 9, 1876.

HOBART TOWN. [*See* TASMANIA.]

HOBSON, CAPTAIN, first Governor of New Zealand, installed February 4, 1840.

Surveyed Hobson's Bay 1836. He was afterwards Governor of New Zealand. He founded Auckland (which was the capital of that colony until 1865). 1839.

HOBSON'S BAY, VICTORIA. Captain Hobson anchored in Hobson's Bay, Victoria, September 29, 1816.

Batman anchored in Hobson's Bay May 29, 1835.

The Bay was called after Captain Hobson, of H.M.S. " Rattlesnake," 1836.

HOPS. The first plantation of hops gathered at Kissing Point, on the Parramatta River, Feb., 1812. [It was formed a few years previously by Mr. Squire, and contained five acres, which yielded fifteen hundredweight of hops of good quality. This gentleman brewed the first ale in the colony, and was the grandfather of James Squire Farnell, late Premier of New South Wales.]

HORSES.

One stallion, three mares, and three colts arrived in Australia with the first fleet, January, 1788.

SHIPPING HORSES AT SANDRIDGE
The Australasian Sketcher, 1875

The number of Horses in the colonies on January 1, 1878, was as follows :—

New South Wales	328,150
New Zealand	99,859
Queensland	140,174
South Australia	110,684
Tasmania	22,195
Victoria	203,150
Western Australia	30,691
Total	934,903

First export of horses to India, 1830.

Three vessels laden with horses left Port Jackson for Calcutta, April, 1844, [From this date commenced the regular export to India of this description of stock.]

ENDURANCE OF. A gentleman named Mossman, of Sydney, undertook for a wager to ride his horse from Sydney to Maitland, a distance of 140 miles, over rough country, in 24 hours. The journey was performed in 20 hours, but the horse died immediately afterwards, 1853. [*See* RACES.]

LOSS OF. Nine valuable racehorses worth £20,000 lost from " City of Melbourne " in a gale on her passage from Melbourne to Sydney. Sep. 11, 1876.

ROBBERY OF. Remains of Mr. J. T. Tindale's valuable imported horse, " Duke of Athol " (stolen a few weeks previously) found at the foot of a cliff near Merriwa, July, 1875. [Large rewards had been offered for recovery of the horse.]

HOSPITALS.

When the portable hospital, brought from London, was put up in Sydney, nearly 500 patients were placed under medical treatment, of whom a great many died, 1809.

The first stone of the General Hospital in Macquarie-street, Sydney, laid by Governor Macquarie, Oct. 23, 1811. [This building, afterwards known as the Infirmary, was pulled down in 1879, and the materials ordered to be destroyed. The parties who contracted for its erection had a monopoly of the spirit trade of the colony whilst the work was in progress. This circumstance led to the building being known to the early colonists as the "Rum" Hospital.]

Hospital founded in Melbourne, 1846.

Miss Osborne with five trained nurses arrived in Sydney from England, March, 1868.

Foundation stone of Prince Alfred Hospital laid by Sir Henry Ayres at Adelaide, South Australia, June, 1870.

The Alfred Hospital, Melbourne, opened by the Duke of Edinburgh, 1870.

Foundation stone of Prince Alfred Memorial Hospital, Sydney, laid by his Excellency Sir

Hercules Robinson, April 24, 1876.

HOVENDEN, MAJOR FREDERICK. Major Hovenden's remains were found in Bungaribee Brush. The words "Frederick Hovenden, died of hunger," cut with a penknife on the peak of a travelling cap, left no doubt of the immediate cause of death, 1845.

HUME (or GOOLWA), RIVER, discovered and named by Hamilton Hume, November 16, 1824. [The Hume, formerly known as the Indi, on its upper portion beyond Wallerawang, is the boundary between New Sonth Wales and Victoria. The name of the "Murray," was subsequently given to its western portion, which was discovered by Sturt.]
[See RIVERS.]

HUNTER, JOHN. [See NEW SOUTH WALES.]

HUNTER RIVER, named after Governor Hunter (native name Coquon), discovered by Lieut. John Shortland, September 19, 1797; Governor Bourke visited the Hunter River district, 1833.

HUNTING.

The first (recorded) hunt with the hounds in Australia took place October 8, 1812. [A kangaroo was hunted at the Nepean, towards Cowpasture Plains, and killed after an exciting run of two hours.] A hunt after a deer near Sydney, the hounds threw off near Ultimo House, the seat of Mr. Harris, June 27, 1820; Captain Hunter's pack of hounds hunted weekly in the vicinity of the Dog Trap road, April 1836.

Hunt Club formed at Parramatta, "to improve the breed of horses, and to rid the country of native dogs and of bushrangers," May 27, 1833.

HURLING MATCH, proposed, between the natives of four counties of Ireland, to come off on Hyde Park, Sydney; but it being rumoured that an intention to break the public peace existed, the Vicar-General, Dr. Gregory, on the assembling of the parties about to engage in the match, prevailed on them by an address and considerable exertion, at once to separate, July 13, 1846.

THE FIRST SYDNEY GENERAL HOSPITAL
Mitchell Library

I

ILLAWARRA.

DISCOVERY OF, by Bass and Flinders, who left Sydney in the "Tom Thumb," the first place noted being Hat Hill, Mount Keira, March 25, 1796.

SETTLEMENT OF. Captain Bishop formed a settlement at Illawarra, N.S.W., 1827.

IMMIGRANT. "The first free immigrant, and indeed the first person of any class in society, who obtained a grant of land in the colony of New South Wales was a German, of the name of Philip Schaeffer. He had been sent out in the "First Fleet" as an agricultural superintendent, chiefly with a view to attempt the cultivation of tobacco, on account of Government; as the province of Virginia, from which that article had previously been obtained, had then ceased to be a British colony, and as the soil and climate of New South Wales were supposed likely to prove not unfavourable for its cultivation, Schoeffer's grant was the largest of all those I have enumerated, comprising an extent of one hundred and forty acres. Unfortunately, however, he had contracted habits of intemperance, and accordingly contrived to get rid of it. He afterwards obtained a grant of fifty acres, in what now constitutes an exceedingly valuable locality in the town of Sydney, but was induced to surrender it to the Colonial Government for public purposes about the year 1807, receiving as a compensation twenty gallons of rum, which was then worth £3 a gallon, and a grant of similar extent at Pitt Water, one of the inlets of Broken Bay. There had been a female convict in the "First Fleet"—a native of the Isle of Skye in Scotland—of the name of Margaret M'Kinnon, who had been transported for the crime of arson, having set fire to her neighbour's house in a fit of jealousy. Schoeffer married this woman, and settled on his farm at Pitt Water, where he lived many years; but old age, poverty, and intemperance induced him at length to sell it piecemeal, and he died at last in the Benevolent Asylum, or Colonial Poor House. I have introduced this episode chiefly to point out the sort of accidents on which the acquisition of wealth in a new country not unfrequently depends; for if Schoeffer had only retained his fifty-acre farm in Sydney for about thirty years longer, he could have sold it for at least £100,000, which, at the usual rate of interest in the colony, at that period, would have yielded him a permanent income of £10,000 a year."— DR. LANG'S HISTORY OF NEW SOUTH WALES.

IMMIGRANTS.

The "Bellona" arrived in Sydney with immigrants. These immigrants were granted farms of from 80 to 100 acres, a few miles from Sydney, and from the fact that the new settlers were originally free, the site of the farms received the name of "Liberty Plains," January 16, 1792.

The first body of free settlers introduced at the public expense on the recommendation of the Colonial Governor, 1796.

Arrival of four free settlers with their families, May, 1798.

First Government free immigrants arrived at Hobart Town, September 18, 1816.

Michael Henderson (of the Hunter) long afterwards a resident of Roslyn Castle, Raymond Terrace, and Wm. Howe (of Glenlee), the first settlers who paid their own passages to New South Wales, arrived, 1818.

Free immigration to New South Wales commenced during Governor Brisbane's time, 1822.

To encourage the officers in the navy to emigrate to the colony, grants of land were proportioned in extent to the capital of the settler, and the conditions were that the settler or his family were to reside in the colony for seven years; a proclamation to this effect issued, July 3, 1828.

First female immigrant ship arrived; the immigrants consisted of fifty young women from an orphan school in the City of Cork, June, 1831.

The "Stirling Castle," with fifty-nine Scotch mechanics and other artisans in the building trade with their families, engaged in Great Britain by Dr. Lang, arrived, October 15, 1831. [The vessel was placed in quarantine in consequence of typhoid fever making its appearance on board.]

The first appropriation for immigration purposes made by the Legislative Council placing the sum of £10,000 on the Estimates, the Imperial Government having expressed their intention to contribute for the same purpose double the sum voted by the colony. The reduced sum of £3,600 was eventually voted, 1832.

[The "Immigrants' Friends' Society," was formed for the regulation of immigrants landing in the colony; the objects being for the benefit of the immigrants, to assist in procuring comfortable settlements on their arrival, and to aid such families as might require pecuniary assistance, 1832].

2,685 free persons arrived, of whom 1,432 came without the assistance of Government, the rest being assisted immigrants, 1833.

Number of immigrants who arrived in New South Wales from 1829-1835 :—

564 in 1829
309 in 1830
457 in 1831
2,006 in 1832
2,685 in 1833
1,564 in 1834
1,428 in 1835.

Fourteen agricultural families, numbering 56 persons, from the county of Dorset, left England in "The Brothers," Captain Towns, for Sydney, November 20, 1836.

H.M.S. "Buffalo" landed immigrants at Kangaroo Island, South Australia, December, 1836.

A public meeting was held in Sydney to petition the Governor on the subject of immigration and the discontinuance of transportation. The petitioners prayed "That a more effective course might be pursued with a view to purchasing the largest possible portion of British labour with the produce of land sales," so as to avoid the necessity of importing Indian labour, May, 1838.

The bounty system of immigration was found to work badly, 1839. [The provisions were so sparingly supplied and so deficient in quality in the ships chartered under that system, that women were frequently led to barter their virtue for the necessaries of the table.]

Mr. James Macarthur returned to the colony, bringing with him from Germany six vinedressers and their families, to be employed in the vineyard at Camden, 1839.

The second selection of immigrants arrived at Port Phillip from Sydney in the "John Barry," April 29, 1839.

An Immigration Committee appointed by the Council of New South Wales for the purpose of devising the best means to promote immigration. After due deliberation, they reported thereon ; amongst many recommendations to accumulate funds for the purpose of supporting immigration, it was proposed that a loan of one or two millions should be raised in England for the purpose of carrying on immigration on a large scale ; but this did not meet with the approbation of the public. A meeting was held in Sydney to protest against it, on the grounds that if the scheme were carried out it would amount to the creation of a national debt. A petition to the Secretary of State was adopted in which the memorialists stated that the demand for the Crown lands was the true standard by which the supply of immigrants should be regulated. 1841.

The Governor of New South Wales received a despatch from the Secretary of State in respect of bounties on immigration, which to some extent conveyed a vote of censure on the Governor for having given orders for bounty payable in two years for a sum of £979,562 and directed that for the future bounty orders should not be issued exceeding the net amount of the land revenue clearly applicable for the next succeeding year. The nature of these bounty orders was an engagement on the part of the New South Wales Government to pay out of the Colonial Land Fund, on the arrival in Sydney of approved immigrants, certain sums of money per head to those through whose instrumentality they had been brought out. 1842.

A report made by the Immigration Agent, Mr. Merewether, of the number of immigrants who arrived in 1841. [It appeared that 4,563 English, 1,616 Scotch, and 13,440 were Irish. This caused much discussion on the preponderance of Irish immigration, but was defended by the Governor in his place in the Council.]

The number of immigrants who arrived in the Colony during the four years previous to December 31, 1841, was 49,684.

First German immigrants arrived in Adelaide, South Australia, September 18, 1844.

The number of immigrants arrived in the colony of New South Wales during ten years ending 1846 was 55,063, at a cost of £992,729, being £18 3s. 1d. per head.

The first immigrant ships, the "Philip Lang" and the "John Wickliffe," for Otago, New Zealand, left Greenock, the leader of the colonists being Captain William Cargill, of the 74th Regiment, November, 1847.

The "Artemesia," first Government immigrant ship, arrived at Brisbane, Dec. 13, 1848.

About a thousand Germans were introduced into Port Phillip, and soon settled down to useful pursuits, February 11, 1849.

The "Culloden" arrived in Melbourne with a large number of distressed needlewomen, July, 1850.

The sum of £108,000 appropriated by the Parliament of New South Wales for the purpose of immigration, 1853.

Mr. (now Sir) Henry Parkes and Mr. W. B.

IMMIGRANTS ON BOARD SHIP
Illustrated London News, 1844

Dalley sent to England as N.S. Wales emigration lecturers, May, 1861.

IMMIGRATION TO THE SEVERAL AUSTRALASIAN COLONIES FROM 1838 TO 1875.

Year.	New South Wales.	New Zealand.	Queensland.	South Australia.	Tasmania.	Victoria.	Western Australia.	Total.
1838	10,189	—	—	3,143	571	3	115	14,021
1839	8,455	—	—	4,856	328	1,161	268	15,786
1840	7,648	1,458	—	2,748	299	3,473	224	15,850
1841	17,492	3,901	—	175	806	9,804	357	32,625
1842	1,450	3,064	—	145	2,448	864	563	8,534
1843	2,439	343	—	45	24	627	—	3,578
1844	1,179	68	—	47	1	934	—	2,229
1845	73	14	—	300	20	423	—	830
1846	36	6	—	2,224	—	81	—	2,347
1847	726	316	—	3,512	8	387	—	4,949
1848	7,622	751	—	7,852	218	7,399	62	23,904
1849	8,403	1,825	—	10,855	535	10,562	11	32,191
1850	3,661	2,005	—	5,013	270	4,682	316	16,037
1851	4,508	2,677	—	7,048	800	6,212	287	21,532
1852	12,736	1,718	—	7,552	1,417	63,719	739	87,881
1853	10,673	1,420	—	6,883	991	40,469	965	61,408
1854	14,647	1,050	—	11,457	4,312	51,291	480	83,237
1855	14,050	2,301	—	11,333	3,457	21,072	96	52,309
1856	9,810	4,004	—	4,512	1,815	24,314	129	44,584
1857	10,379	3,807	—	3,646	2,113	40,921	382	61,241
1858	7,214	5,872	—	3,982	306	21,666	255	39,295
1859	5,439	8,558	—	1,556	931	14,030	499	31,013
1860	3,671	5,242	393	1,245	483	12,979	379	24,302
1861	1,626	4,555	2,480	422	258	14,256	141	23,738
1862	4,100	11,440	8,575	1,365	387	15,353	623	41,843
1863	6,379	13,919	10,339	1,898	38	20,261	220	53,054
1864	4,689	11,970	7,183	2,842	50	13,909	299	40,942
1865	2,623	7,037	12,551	5,145	40	9,713	174	37,283
1866	1,648	4,298	6,054	3,392	7	8,531	167	24,097
1867	1,318	3,984	454	624	25	7,898	163	14,466
1868	1,318	3,703	685	351	18	6,566	168	12,809
1869	796	2,636	2,318	161	315	8,649	26	14,901
1870	1,043	3,332	2,593	311	27	9,103	56	17,065
1871	966	2,948	1,315	381	11	6,570	36	12,227
1872	1,102	6,616	2,380	281	196	5,269	32	15,876
1873	941	11,651	5,689	1,544	713	5,680	30	26,428
1874	1,579	36,704	8,352	1,958	13	5,233	99	53,958
1875	2,157	18,763	5,482	2,819	2	5,673	629	35,525
Total 38 years	194,785	124,556	76,783	122,713	24,353	479,877	8,990	1,102,897

INSOLVENCIES IN AUSTRALIA, for the year ending December 31, 1877 :—

	No.	Liabilities.	Assets.	Deficiency.
New South Wales ..	588	508,352	210,851	297,531
†New Zealand ..	326	324,178	284,161	60,006
Queensland ..	132	190,534	112,720	77,814
*South Australia ..	176	158,766	81,879	76,887.
Tasmania ..	33	24,228	13,373	11,885
Victoria ..	715	£462,650	£272,727	£189,931
‡Western Australia ..				

* Besides 82 private arrangements under the Insolvent Act.
† This return is for the year ended December 31, 1876.
‡ No returns published.

The Judges decided that the English Bankrupt Laws were not applicable in the Colony of New South Wales, November 26, 1839 ; four Official Assignees appointed in the Insolvency Court, New South Wales, February 7, 1844. [They were appointed to abolish the system of trusteeship, as many of these trustees had escaped from the colony, or made away with the assets of estates which had been placed under their charge.]

IPSWICH, QUEENSLAND. First sale of Crown Lands held, October 11, 1843 ; the first steamer between Brisbane and Ipswich started, June 29, 1846 ; first Supreme Court Sittings held at Ipswich, February 6, 1860 ; Ipswich gazetted a municipality, March 3, 1860 ; Ipswich Grammar School opened, September 25, 1863.

IRON.

Iron smelting commenced in New South Wales, at the Fitzroy Iron Works, near Berrima, in 1847.

Derwent Iron Works, Tasmania, first smelted iron, July 5, 1875.

The Lithgow Valley Iron Works, New South Wales, were commenced in 1875.

THE LANDING PLACE, IPSWICH
Conrad Martens, Mitchell Library

J   K

JAMIESON, Sir John, awarded the gold medal of the London Society for the Encouragement of Art and Manufacture, for a method of extirpating stumps of trees, 1829.

JOHNSTON, Major, proceeded to England with Mr. John Macarthur, to attend the court-martial regarding the conduct of the former *re* Bligh's arrest and deposition, March, 1809. Court-martial, consisting of fifteen officers—six lieutenant-generals, two major-generals, five colonels, and two lieutenant-colonels—was held over Captain Johnston for the arrest of Bligh, the trial commencing May 7, 1811. The result of this trial was that Lieutenant-Colonel Johnston (he having been promoted shortly before the trial to that rank) was found guilty of an act of mutiny in the arrest of Bligh, and was sentenced to be cashiered, July 2, 1811. [Lieut.-Colonel Johnston shortly afterwards returned to the colony, which he had served long and faithfully, where he spent the remainder of his days. He died May 5, 1826.]

JOHNSTON, Rev. Richard, first colonial chaplain, arrived 1788. He received 10 shillings per day as chaplain. He first planted the orange in N.S.W., and on leaving sold his farm of 600 acres and 150 sheep to Mr. Cox. He returned to Europe, January 17, 1802 ; died 1814.

JUBILEE. A grand Jubilee was held in New South Wales on the fiftieth anniversary of the foundation of the colony, January 26, 1838.

KANGAROOS. The dimensions of one caught near Goulburn were—From tip to tip, 9ft.; tail, 4ft.; head, 11½in.; tail weighed 18½lb. Another one was caught which measured 10ft. 6in. from tip to tip. In June, 1875, Mr. Licensed-surveyor James Evans killed a very large kangaroo near Cootamundra; the measurement from tip to tip being 11ft. 7in., and its weight 207lb.—the tail alone weighing 22½lb.

8,000 kangaroos killed in a battle at Trunkey Station, N.S.W., August 11, 1877.

KIAMA. Opening of the Robertson Basin at Kiama (cost £75,000), September 20, 1876.

KING'S BIRTHDAY. The Royal Standard hoisted for the first time (at Dawes Battery) in the territory of New South Wales, Australia, on the anniversary of His Majesty's birthday ; a free pardon given, in consequence, to a large number of persons, June 4, 1803.

KING'S SCHOOL. [*See* Parramatta ; *also*, Schools.]

KING, William Francis, known under the *soubriquet* of "The Flying Pieman." William Francis King, born in London in March, 1807, was the eldest son of Francis King, Esq., at one time Paymaster of Accounts in the Treasury at Whitehall. His father intended him for the Church, but it soon appeared that his innate love of field sports and boisterous recreations was not befitting the sacred office, and he entered into partnership with Smith and Simpson, stock and sharebrokers in London. He did not remain long connected with this firm ; fancying that this business was getting into difficulties, he sold his share, and obtained a situation as clerk in the Treasury Office in the Tower of London. But his restless disposition soon took him from this work ; and he left England for New South Wales in 1839, with the expectation, from the high recommendations he brought with him, of obtaining a Government situation. In this hope he was, however, disappointed ; and he took the situation of schoolmaster and clerk at Sutton Forest, near Bong Bong, an appointment given to him by Archdeacon Broughton, afterwards Bishop of the diocese. From this he went as tutor to the children of Mr. William Kern, with whom he remained for several years. Here again his unsettled temperament prevailed over every feeling; and he left Mr. Kern with the intention of returning to England. Many unforeseen difficulties, however, presented themselves, and he was induced to hire as a barman to a Mr. H. Doran who then kept the "Hope and Anchor," at the corner of King and Pitt streets, afterwards the "Rainbow Tavern." This kind of life did not suit King, and he commenced a series of pedestrian feats in which he took great delight, and so far from considering on such occasions that he was executing a task he always enjoyed it as a pastime. Some of the exploits of this extraordinary individual were as follows :— A pedestrian feat of walking 1,634 miles in 5 weeks and 4 days, out of which period he only had nine days fair weather; but it did not appear that the poor pieman reaped any advantage beyond his self-gratification at having acquitted himself so well. He then walked to Mr. Kern's estate near Campbelltown and back, a distance of 62 miles in 12½ hours; from the obelisk in Macquarie Place, Sydney, to the 16-mile stone at Parramatta and back again in 6 hours; beat the coach from Windsor to Sydney, arriving 7 minutes before it; walked from Sydney to Parramatta and back twice a day for 6 consecutive days; on one occasion undertook to carry a dog, weighing upwards of 70lb., from Campbelltown to Sydney between the hours of half-past 12 at night and 20 minutes to 9 the next morning, which feat he accomplished 20 minutes within the given time; was backed to carry a live goat weighing 92lb., with 12lb. dead weight besides, from the old "Talbot Inn" on Brickfield-Hill, Sydney, to Mr. Nash's at Parramatta, in 7 hours, which task he performed having 12 minutes to spare; walked from the Parramatta church to the church at Windsor, a distance of 43½ miles, for 3 consecutive days—the first day he occupied 8 hours in going to and fro, the second 7½ hours, and the third 7 hours 25 minutes. There were numerous other feats performed by this remarkable man, which, with his occupation earned for him his cognomen of "The Flying Pieman." No doubt his natural bent for such undertakings, and his readiness on all occasions to be backed for them made him the dupe of many, whilst his peculiar and vivacious manner rendered him the butt of almost all. King died at the Liverpool Asylum, N.S.W., August 12, 1874.

A KANGAROO DRIVE
The Australasian Sketcher, 1874

LABOUR, SCARCITY OF.

A great scarcity of labour existed for gathering the harvest, which was one of the most abundant that had ever been, the want of sufficient labour being severely felt. At the Hawkesbury alone the settlers required 400 labourers to reap the harvest, but the Government could only supply 112; in consequence, several immigration schemes were suggested and proposed, 1830.

A great scarcity of labour prevailed throughout New South Wales, Jan., Feb., 1847.

LACHLAN, RIVER, discovered by Evans, 1815; visited by Governor Bourke, 1832.

LAKES.

The largest lake in Victoria is called Corangamite; its area is about 48,640 acres. Lake Hindmarsh, area 35,840 acres; Lake King, area 13,440 acres; Lake Albacutya, 13,000 acres; Lake Tyrrell, 45,440 acres; Lake Victoria, 38,700 acres; 'Lake Wellington, 46,080 acres, and Lake Reeve, 9,000 acres are all in Victoria.

Lake George, New South Wales, discovered, 1817. [It is 25 miles in length and 8 in breadth.]

Lake Bathurst, New South Wales, 8 square miles in area, discovered 1817.

Lake Macquarie, New South Wales, 20 miles long by 3 miles broad.

The largest lakes in Tasmania are the Great Lake, covering an area of 28,000 acres; Lake Sorrell, 17,000 acres; Lake St. Clair, 10,000 acres; and Arthur's Lake and Lake Echo, occupying 8,000 to 12,000 acres. These lakes form the head waters of the principal streams flowing south, west, and north.

In South Australia, Lake Torrens is a vast inland salt lake, 90 miles north of Spencer Gulf; Lake Eyre is also salt, and lies about 40 miles east of the Denison Range; Lake Gardiner is an immense salt lake to the north of the Gawler Ranges, at an elevation of 366 feet above the ocean level. Lakes Gregory, Blanche and Blanchwater lie to the north-east of Lake Eyre. There are also several curious volcanic lakes, notably the Blue Lake, lying in the extinct crater of Mount Gambier, in the south-eastern district. Lakes Alexandrina (60 miles long by 40 in breadth) and Albert, into and through which the Murray flows, are extensive sheets of water, navigable for steamers of light draught. The Coorong is an arm of the sea, and at parts from half a mile to two miles in width, separated from it by a narrow strip of sand-hills, and running parallel with the coast line for about a hundred miles.

The largest lake in New Zealand is Lake Taupo, situated in the province of Auckland, which has a diameter of 20 miles, and an area of about 200 square miles.

LAND.

The quantity of land in New South Wales which had been granted up to the time of the departure of Governor Hunter in 1800 was as follows :—47,678 acres, viz., 3,389 by Governor Phillip, 10,671 by Lieutenant-Governor Grose, 4,965 by Lieutenant-Governor Patterson, and 28,650 by Governor Hunter.

Land Board, to which applications for land were to be made, first appointed in New South Wales, January 10, 1826. [The names of the Board were :—Wm. Stewart, Lieutenant-Governor ; Wm. Lithgow, Auditor of Accounts ; Captain Wm. Dumaresq, Civil Engineer.]

Letters patent erecting a Corporation for the management of the Church and School Lands in the Colony of New South Wales, issued March 9, 1826.

Grant of land, two square miles, to each Australian-born lady on her marriage in New South Wales, January, 1, 1829.

Major Mitchell assumed the office of Surveyor-General, New South Wales, May, 1829.

S. A. Perry, Deputy Surveyor-General, arrived August 3, 1829.

Definite regulations determined upon by the Home Government with regard to the disposal of Crown lands in New South Wales. Prior to this date Crown lands were given away. The system of grants was abolished and no land to be alienated but by public auction. The whole territory was divided into counties, hundreds, and parishes, each parish to comprise an area of about 25 miles. The lowest price for land was fixed at 5s. per acre. These and other regulations appertaining to Crown lands were proclaimed in the colony, August, 1, 1831.

The adjustment of titles to land in Tasmania, granted by the various Governors, was a vexed question during the whole of Governor Arthur's administration. Many of the limits of the grants had been defined by a curious expedient said to have been practised in Ireland. A string was tied to a dog's tail and when the dog stopped running that was taken to be a mile ! Thousands of acres had been so measured off, and endless confusion resulted from the claims made in 1824, which the *Caveat Board* rectified in 1831.

The New South Wales Commissioners for the determining of land grants held their first meeting, April 11, 1834.

The quantity of land alienated in the colony of New South Wales according to return prepared by the Surveyor-General was 3,518,300 acres, exclusive of town allotments, June 30, 1834.

Letters patent passed the Great Seal erecting into counties certain portions of land in the Colony of New South Wales, and fixing boundaries for the same. Seventeen counties were named—Camden, St. Vincent, Northumberland, Durham, Hunter, Cook, Westmoreland, Argyle, Murray, King, Georgiana, Bathurst, Roxburgh, Phillip, Brisbane, Bligh, and Wellington—November 26, 1835.

First sale of Crown Lands in Adelaide, South Australia, March 27, 1837.

The first land sale in Melbourne took place, the average price being £35 per lot of half an acre, June 1, 1837.

A case of conspiracy for preventing Crown lands from being disposed of at a higher rate than the upset price, was tried at the Supreme Court, Sydney, when John T. Hughes, G. Porter, P. M'Intyre, and J. Eales, were convicted and sentenced to pay £100 each, 1837.

The minimum price of land in the Colony of New South Wales was increased from 5s. per acre to 12s., January 7, 1839.

Squatting Act of New South Wales passed, March 22, 1839.

Commissioners were appointed to revise claims put forward by some individuals, to large tracts of land purchased in New Zealand. A Bill was introduced during the Session of 1840 for the purpose, when Mr. W. C. Wentworth and Mr. Busby, who had been acting as consul at New Zealand, and some others who had purchased land from several New Zealand chiefs, resisted the inquiry. These persons had purchased land to the number of ten millions of acres in the Middle Island, and two hundred thousand on the Northern Island, for which they paid £200 each, and stipulated to allow £100 per annum to each of the chiefs for their lifetime, who had ceded their territory. The claimants were permitted to be heard at the Bar of the Legislative Council against the bill, both personally and by counsel in defence of their claims and in opposition to the bill. Messrs. Wentworth and Busby were heard personally, the others were heard through their counsel, Mr. W. A'Beckett (afterwards Chief Justice of Victoria) and Mr. Darvall. The principles on which the bill was framed and advocated were :—First, that the savages possessed no other right in the country they inhabited than that of mere occupation, until they became civilised to put it to some proper use, that of cultivation, consequently they were incapable of giving legal title of land to any other person ; second, that if a country inhabited by men of this description were afterwards taken possession of by any civilized colonising power, the right of pre-emption existed only in that power ; third, that British subjects, either as individuals or as bodies, possessed no right to form colonies without the consent of the Crown ; and that in the event of their doing so, they became liable to be ousted by the Crown from their possessions.

The Bill was passed and after the Act became law, a number of the claimants, comprising subjects of Great Britain, France, and the United States, resident in New Zealand, protested against the enforcement of the Act, and appealed to their respective Governments against the right of the Governor and Council of New South Wales to enact and enforce such a measure. The Commission, however, was appointed assuming the title of a Court of Claims, which resulted in deciding, in most instances, that the land to which the claimants were entitled was a mere fraction of the quantity said to be purchased, and some claims were disallowed altogether. The occasion of this bill being brought into the Council was that in the course of the year 1839 it was announced to the colony that a Treasury minute had been made, sanctioning an advance from the revenue of New South Wales for the expense of the Government of New Zealand as a dependency of New South Wales, with a Lieutenant-Governor ; the funds so advanced to be repaid out of the revenue received from the territories ceded from time to time by the aboriginal proprietors in accordance with the ordinances of the Governor and Council of the older colony for that purpose enacted.

The price of Crown lands in the Port Phillip district was fixed at £1 per acre, the sale to be effected without competition. In the other two districts into which the colony was divided, viz., the Northern or Moreton Bay district, and the middle or New South Wales district, a minimum price of twelve shillings per acre was established, but the auction system was retained, 1840.

The first land sale of town allotments in Auckland, New Zealand, took place April 19, 1841.

The new Imperial Act regulating the disposal of waste lands, received in New South Wales, 1842. [By this measure the auction system was universally brought into operation ; the lands were divided into town, suburban, and county lots, and the minimum price of county land was fixed at £1 per acre, all over the colony.]

Proclamation for regulation of pastoral leases issued. Great meeting of squatters in Sydney. The Pastoral Association of New South Wales was formed, April, 1843.

First sale of Crown lands held at Brisbane, August 9, 1843.

First sale of town land at Ipswich, Queensland, October 11, 1843.

A Pastoral Association formed in 1844. [The first business transacted was to petition the Queen and both Houses of Parliament against the new squatting regulations, and to pray that the management of the Crown lands should be transferred from the Executive to the Governor and Legislative Council.]

A proclamation was issued altering the terms on which licenses for Crown lands were granted. This caused a great contest between the holders of pastoral licenses and the Executive Government ; numerous public meetings were held throughout the colony, and much subsequent discussion ensued in the Legislative Council.

A LAND SALE
The Australian Picture Pleasure Book

In consequence of this alteration a society was formed called the " Pastoral Association of New South Wales," April, 1844.

The total number of occupants of Crown lands beyond the settled districts of N.S.W. was 1,865, in 1848.

First land sales at Ipswich, Drayton, and Warwick, Queensland, July 31, 1850.

First land sale in Moreton Bay district, 1850.

First land sale at Geelong, November, 1852.

A land bill was introduced into Parliament by the Cowper Administration. A call of the House took place. The bill was read a second time by a majority of 36 to 8 ; but in committee a motion for its further consideration to be

THE WOES OF FREE SELECTORS
Sydney Punch, 1865

deferred to that day six months, was negatived only by the casting vote of the chairman. The Ministry withdrew the bill, and announced that they would recommend a dissolution of Parliament and appeal to the country, 1857.

Land order system of Queensland—"That each emigrant from the mother-country paying his own passage out, or having it paid for him, is entitled to a bonus in land, at the minimum price at least equivalent to the cost of his passage out"—became law, 1860.

Mr. (now Sir) John Robertson's famous New South Wales Land Act (introducing "Free Selection before Survey") passed October 18, 1861; came into operation January 1, 1862.

Duffy Land Act, Victoria, passed June 18, 1862.

First land sale at Rockhampton Bay, Queensland, March 22, 1865.

Land Laws of Queensland passed, 1868.

Victorian Land Act of 1869 came into operation, February 1, 1870.

Land Laws of Western Australia proclaimed, 1870.

Land Laws of South Australia passed, 1870.

Land Laws of Tasmania passed 1870; amended 1871 and 1872.

The Amended Land Act of New South Wales assented to, August 10, 1875.

Yanko Reserve, New South Wales, thrown open for selection October 18, 1876.

Crown Lands Alienated in Australasia up to January 1, 1877.

Name of Colony.	Area in Statute Acres.	Acres Granted and Sold.			Amount realised on Land Sales.						Extent Unalienated at end of 1876.
					Total.			Average per Acre.			
		Prior to 1876.	During 1876.	Total.	Prior to 1876.	During 1876.	Total.	Prior to 1876.	During 1876.	Total.	
					£	£	£	£ s. d.	£ s. d.	£ s. d.	Acres.
New South Wales..	199,000,000	19,249,658	4,051,908	23,301,566	15,800,144	4,089,507	19,889.651	0 16 5	1 0 2¼	0 17 0⅜	175,698,434
New Zealand	67,136,000	13,116,405	528,561	13,644,966	7,347,395	846,831	8,194,226	0 11 2½	1 12 0½	0 12 0	53,491,034
Queensland........	428,492,800	1,745,102	315,219	2,060,321	1,932,620	170,000	2,102,620	1 2 1¾	0 10 9½	1 0 5	426,432,479
South Australia....	585,427,200	6,398,823	714,421	7,113,244	8,588,212	1,013,161	9,601,373§	1 6 10	1 8 4¼	1 7 0	578,333,956
Tasmania..........	16,777,600	4,024,808	27,007	4,051,815	1,640,396	36,490	1,676,886	0 8 1¾	1 7 0¼	0 8 3¼	12,725,785
Victoria	56,446,720	10,351,195	476,584	10,827,779	17,416,200	584,913	‖18,001,113	1 13 7¾	1 4 6½	1 13 3	45,618,941
Western Australia..	640,000,000	1,908,083	30,073	1,933,156	*a*	8,461	8,461	*a*	0 5 7½	0 5 7½	638,066,844
Total ..	1,993,280,320	56,789,074	6,143,773	62,932,847	52,724,967	6,749,363	59,474,330	0 19 8	1 1 2	0 17 8	1,930,367,473

* The figures for Victoria do not include land of which the purchase was not completed, which at the end of 1876 amounted to 6,463,148 acres. The figures for New South Wales and South Australia do include such land, but the area has not been given. Portion of this land in the last-named colonies might revert to the Crown in consequence of non-fulfilment of conditions, &c.

† To compute the amount in these columns the money realised has been divided by the sum of the acres granted and sold. The amounts therefore express the average price realised for all the land parted with, including not only that for which money was paid, but that which was granted without payment.

‡ In Victoria the land in process of alienation is included under this head. See note (*)

‖ Including an amount of £6,884,362, which represents the estimated balances due at the end of 1876 on land in process of alienation.

§ Including balances of payments due for lands sold on credit, which amounted at the end of 1876 to £2,957,929.

Note.—Where *a* occurs the information has not been furnished, or is incomplete.

LANDS-OFFICE. Foundation stone of the new Lands Office, Sydney, New South Wales, laid by Hon. Thomas Garrett, M.L.A., Secretary for Lands, October 14, 1876.

LAND-TAX.

Hon. R. Le Poer Trench (Attorney-General), Sir Bryan O'Loghlen, and Mr. Archibald Fisken gazetted Commissioners of Land Tax, Victoria, October 6, 1877.

Sir George Bowen assented to the Victorian Land Tax Bill, Oct. 11, 1877.

LA PEROUSE. (Of the French Exploring Expedition "Boussole" and "Astrolabe" sighted Botany Bay January 22, 1788; landed January 24, 1788; departed March 11, 1788.) M. De Clonard, captain of the "Astrolabe," brought to Governor Phillip La Perouse's despatches for the French Government, the last ever forwarded by that navigator, February 16, 1788.

Relics of this navigator found on an island called Tucopid, South Pacific Ocean, by Captain Dillon, 1827. [These relics are preserved in the Museum at Paris.]

"LARRIKIN," a name given to young vagabonds in Australia. The term was first applied in a Melbourne Police Court by an Irish police officer (Dalton), who, in reply to the Magistrates, said the youths before the Court were "larrikin," meaning larking.

LAUNCESTON. [*See* Tasmania.]

LAWSON, Lieutenant William, with Wentworth and Blaxland crossed the Blue Mountains, May, 1813; was appointed to the command of the military forces stationed in the country to the westward of the Blue Mountains; he was also placed at the head of the Civil department at Bathurst, and through all that country which had received the name of the County of Westmoreland, July 31, 1819.

LEAD found in South Australia, 1843. [*See* Minerals.]

LEGAL.

The separation of the two branches of the legal profession in New South Wales took place, 1829. [*See* Court, Supreme.]

LEGISLATIVE ASSEMBLY. [*See* PARLIA-
MENT *and* CONSTITUTION.]

LEGISLATIVE COUNCIL. [*See* PARLIAMENT.]

LEICHHARDT, MADAME. The Legislative
Council of New South Wales voted a pension of
£100 per annum to Madame Leichhardt, the
mother of the explorer, 1853.

LEICHHARDT, SEARCH FOR.

The sum of £2,000 voted by the Legislative
Council of New South Wales, to fit out an
expedition for the search of Dr. Leichhardt, 1851.

An exploring expedition, under Mr. Hovenden Hely, was undertaken to search for Dr.
Leichhardt, January 1, 1852. The party consisted of seven white men and three blacks,
was provided with sixteen horses and fifteen
mules, and supplied with provisions for nine
months. But very little information of the fate
of the explorer was obtained.

The Australian Cordillera crossed by Leichhardt Search Party, under A. C. Gregory,
August 11, 1855. [*See* EXPLORERS.]

L'ESTRANGE, the Australian Blondin, crossed
Sydney (Middle) Harbour on a tight rope
stretched from cliff to cliff. The length of the
rope was 1,420 feet, and its height above the
water 341 feet, March 29, 1877.

LIBELS.

Andrew Bent fined £500 and imprisoned for
publication of letters written by Mr. Robert
Lathrop Murray against Governor Arthur, in
the *Hobart Town Gazette*, July 25, 1825.

A criminal prosecution was instituted against
Dr. Wardell, the proprietor and editor of the
Australian newspaper, for libel on the Governor,
in which, it was alleged, an attempt was made
to bring the King's representative into hatred
and contempt. The jury not agreeing, the
defendant was discharged, on the understanding
that there should be no further prosecution.
December 22, 1827.

Robert Howe, proprietor of the *Sydney
Gazette*, found guilty of libelling Dr. H. G.
Douglas. He was ordered to enter into recogni-
zances to appear when called upon for judgment,
December 24, 1828.

Hayes, editor of *The Australian*, convicted of
libelling Governor Darling *re* Sudds and
Thompson's case, was sentenced to a fine of £100,
with six months' imprisonment, April 14, 1829.

E. S. Hall, editor of *The Monitor*, convicted
of libelling Governor Darling *re* Sudds and
Thompson's case, was sentenced to twelve
months' imprisonment, September 15, 1829.

R. Mansfield, editor of *The Sydney Gazette*,
criminally prosecuted for libel, for publishing
an article favourable to the Governor, and
against petitions for his impeachment. Verdict
against Mansfield, who was fined £10. 1829.

E. S. Hall was, on December 21st, found guilty
of libelling Governor Darling; on December 23rd
of libelling James Laidley, Deputy Commissary

General; on December 23rd of libelling F. A.
Healy, Superintendent of Convicts; and on
December 24th of libelling Alex. Macleay,
Colonial Secretary, 1829.

Stevens and Stokes, proprietors of the *Sydney
Morning Herald*, obtained a verdict against F.
Stephen and J. R. Nichols, of *The Australian*,
March 25, 1834.

Cavenagh, editor of *The Sydney Gazette*, obtained a verdict against W. C. Wentworth, with
£225 damages, July 1, 1837.

James Mitchell obtained £100 damages
against Dr. Thompson, for the publication of
certain letters in the Sydney newspapers, March
23, 1838.

The editor of the *Satirist*, an obscene publication in Sydney, sentenced to two years' imprisonment; the printer and publisher were
also each sentenced to twelve months imprisonment, 1843.

Messrs. Hawkesley and Williamson, charged
with libelling Captain Fitzroy, A.D.C. to the
Governor, by publishing an article in their
paper—*The People's Advocate*—to the effect that
plaintiff was assaulted at Parramatta by Mr.
Beit for cheating at cards. Defendants were
committed for trial, found guilty, and sentenced
to six weeks' imprisonment in Darlinghurst Gaol,
and a fine of £25 each, February 25, 1845.

The *Sydney Morning Herald* having commented
on the unseaworthiness of a vessel named the
"Caroline," belonging to Isaac Simmons, that
person prosecuted Messrs. Kemp and Fairfax.
Verdict for the defendants. August 29, 1845.

The Argus published a libel against William
Frazer, member for Creswick, April 4, 1862.

Philpots and wife *v.* Bishop of Newcastle, for
using defamatory expressions in a letter to the
Rev. J. R. Thackeray, of West Maitland.
Verdict for the plaintiffs; damages, 40s. April,
1874.

Mr. E. Langton, M.L.A., Victoria, obtained
a verdict of £1,000 damages (subsequently
reduced to £750) for a libel published against
him by *The Age* newspaper, March 3, 1877.

In Frazer *v.* Syme (Melbourne *Age*), the jury
awarded £250 damages to the plaintiff, June 22,
1878.

LIBRARIES.

Sydney Parliamentary Library is the most
valuable of the kind in Australia. On
August 8, 1843, a select committee of the
Legislative Council was appointed "to make
necessary arrangements for the fitting up
and opening the library of the Council."
The committee reported "that they regret
to find that the books at present belonging
to the library of the Council are comparatively
few in number, and do not comprise those books
which may be considered indispensable as books
of reference or of general utility." The last report of the library committee of the Council in
1855—previous to the establishment of Responsible Government—states :—"The new Legislature will, therefore, have at its command a

library raised from 337 volumes—which were found on its shelves at the time of its formation in 1844—to 6,999 volumes of standard works in the various departments of literary and science." Since 1855 to the end of 1878 large additions have been made, including many scarce and valuable works, and the number of volumes in round numbers is between 25,000 and 30,000.

AUSTRALIAN SUBSCRIPTION, THE, established March 7, 1826.

FREE. Australian Free Library, in Terry's buildings; originated through the efforts of Thomas De La Condamine, Private Secretary to Governor Ralph Darling. It was first known as the Australian Subscription Library. Alex. Macleay, first President, October 1, 1827.

The foundation stone of the Australian Library, Sydney, was laid by Alexander Macleay, Esq., February 14, 1843; opened January, 1846.

The Public Library, Melbourne, costing £110,000, and now containing 80,000 volumes, was founded July 3, 1853. [Library opened February 11, 1856.]

The Melbourne University Library, costing £7,406, and containing 9,168 volumes, was founded 1854.

The library of the Supreme Court, Victoria, cost £8,722, and now containing 10,454 volumes, was founded 1854.

Free Public Library, Sydney (previously the Australian Subscription Library), opened by Earl Belmore, September 30, 1869. Mr. R. C. Walker appointed first librarian of Sydney Free Library, November 10, 1869.

Branch of Free Library opened as a Lending Library, July 1, 1877.

Free Public Library, Sydney, New South Wales, opened on Sundays, April 21, 1878.

LIST OF THE PRINCIPAL LIBRARIES IN AUSTRALIA.

	vols.
Sydney Free Library, opened 1869	37,000
,, Lending Branch, July 1, 1877	5,981
,, School of Arts, established March 22, 1833	19,000
,, Parliamentary Library, opened 1844 ..	30,000
Melbourne Public Library, 1854	80,000*
,, Parliamentary Library, 1856 ..	27,000
,, Supreme Court Library	13,000
,, Athenæum, 1840	11,760
,, University, 1854	9,168
Adelaide, South Australian Institute, 1863 ..	25,000
,, Law Library	2,000
Brisbane School of Arts	7,500
,, Parliamentary Library	12,000
Ipswich	3,000
Rockhampton	4,500
Ballarat Mechanics' Institute	11,500
,, Free Library	10,000
Sandhurst Mechanics' Institute	6,000
Hobart Town Public Library	7,800
Launceston Mechanics' Institute	7,000
Geelong Mechanics' Institute	12,000
Beechworth Athenæum	3,700
Castlemaine Mechanics' Institute	4,781
Goulburn Mechanics' Institute	3,000
Bathurst School of Arts	5,254
Mudgee Mechanics' Institute	4,000
Newcastle School of Arts	2,500

And 14,000 pamphlets.

MELBOURNE LIBRARY
The Illustrated Journal of Australasia

LICENSES. The sale of intoxicating liquors by persons unauthorised to sell them having increased to a degree threatening the welfare of the settlement, the Governor ordered licenses to be issued for that privilege; ten were granted, 1796. [These licenses extended over twelve months, the person being bound by sureties not to infringe the conditions imposed by the authorities.]

LIGHTHOUSES.

Foundation stone of Sydney lighthouse and "Macquarie Tower" laid by Governor Macquarie, July 18, 1813. [Its height is 76 feet, or 353 feet above sea level.]

The Superintendent of Port Phillip selected Cape Otway as a site for a lighthouse, April 21, 1846.

C. J. Tyers, C.C.L., sent to select a site for a lighthouse at Cape Howe, April 23, 1846.

Gabo Island selected as a place for a lighthouse by Mr. C. J. Tyers, 1846.

Lighthouses erected at Cape Borda and Northumberland, 1857.

LIST OF PRINCIPAL LIGHTS ON THE COAST OF AUSTRALASIA (1879).

NEW SOUTH WALES.

Eden.—Twofold Bay, 1 light, fixed, seen nine miles. Red Harbour Light on Point Lookout.

Ulladulla Harbour Light.—On Pier, fixed, green, visible from seven to nine miles.

Shoalhaven. — Position light, visible eight miles.

Jervis Bay.—Near Cape St. George, 1 light, revolving, seen fifteen to twenty miles.

Wollongong.—On coast Illawarra, 1 light, red, fixed, visible ten miles. On east side of Pier Head.

Macquarie. — On South Head, entrance to Port Jackson, 1 light, revolving, seen twenty-five miles. Shows a bright flash every minute and a-half.

Hornby.—On Inner South Head, 1 light, fixed, seen fifteen miles. Tower, painted in vertical stripes of red and white.

Sow and Pigs Lightship.—On N.W. edge of Sow and Pigs Shoal, 2 lights, fixed, seen fifteen miles.

Fort Denison.—On Fort Denison, 1 light, fixed, seen five miles. Harbour light to guide vessels up Sydney harbour.

Broken Bay Lights.—Two fixed, E.S.E. and W.N.W. from each other, seen three miles off.

Newcastle.—On Nobby Island, 1 light, fixed, seen seventeen miles.

Newcastle Leading Lights.—For entering, red and bright.

Newcastle Leading Lights.—For the North Harbour, red and bright.

Port Stephens.—On Port Stephens, 1 light, revolving, seen sixteen miles. Shows alternately red and white flash.

Nelson Head.—One light, fixed, bright to seaward, visible eight to ten miles.

Sugar Loaf Point.—Revolving, bright, flashing every half minute, and visible twenty-two miles. Green light of fourth order shown also from the same tower.

Manning River.—Bright fixed light shown from Pilot Station, seen from ten to twelve miles.

Seal Rocks.—Revolving bright light.

Clarence River.—Bright fixed light shown from Pilot Station, visible from a distance of six or eight miles.

Richmond River.—Two bright fixed lights exhibited from Pilot Station, visible six or eight miles. W.N.W. and E.S.E., 550 feet apart.

Cape Fingal.—Pilot Station, Tweed River, 1 light, bright, fixed, visible to seaward from six to eight miles.

New Zealand.

Cape Foulwind.—Revolving white light flashing every half minute, visible 19½ miles.

Tiri Tiri (Hauraki Gulf).—Fixed white light, visible 23½ miles.

Manukau Heads.—Fixed white light, visible 26½ miles.

Sandspit (Firth of Thames).—Fixed red and white light.

Bean Rocks (Auckland Harbour).—Fixed red, white, and green light.

Napier Bluff (Napier).—Fixed white light, visible 18 miles.

Pencarrow (Port Nicholson).—Fixed white light, visible 30 miles.

Soames Island (Wellington Harbour).—Fixed red, white, and green light.

The Brothers, Cook's Straits.—Second order flashing white light, visible 22 miles (in place of the Mana Island light).

Farewell Spit.—Revolving light, white with red arc over spit-end, visible 17 miles.

Nelson.—Fixed white light, visible 12½ miles.

Cape Campbell.—Revolving light, white, visible 19 miles.

Port Lyttelton (entrance).—Fixed white light, 29 miles.

Port Chalmers.—Fixed red light, visible 20 miles.

Nugget Point.—Fixed white light, visible 23 miles.

Dog Island (Foveaux Straits).—Light revolving every half minute, visible 18 miles.

Centre Island (southern extremity, Foveaux Strait).—First order fixed red and white light, visible 22½ miles.

Portland Island (Hawkes Bay).—Revolving white light, visible 24 miles.

Timaru.—Fifth order fixed white light, visible 14½ miles, in place of the red light.

Manawatu River (entrance of).—White light, visible 11 miles.

Wanganui North Heads.—White light, visible 12 miles.

Port Ahwiriri (Napier).—Harbour light is exhibited, visible 9 miles.

Buller River Head (Port of Westport).—Harbour light, visible 10 miles.

Queensland.

Cape Moreton.—On N.E. part of Moreton Island, 1 light, revolving at intervals of one minute. Tower white.

Middle Channel, Moreton Bay, two leading lights are established to guide vessels over the West Banks.

Comboyuro Point Light.—Used in connection with the leading lights for taking the Middle Channel.

Cowan Cowan Point Light.—Fixed, bright light, eight feet above high water mark.

Brisbane Bar.—Lightship, fixed, also leading lights for crossing the bar.

Sandy Cape Light.—Dioptric, first order, obtaining its greatest brilliancy every two minutes, visible twenty-six miles.

Burnett River (Mouth of).—Fixed, white.

Cape Capricorn.—Revolving, 310 feet high. Intervals between periods of greatest brilliancy one minute.

Bustard Head.—Fixed, and flashing.

Gatcombe Head (Port Curtis).—1 fixed light, fifty feet high.

Oyster Rock.—One bright apparent light, visible S.W. by W. ½ W. to N.W. by W. about fourteen miles.

Lady Elliott's Island.—One bright, revolving light, flashes every thirty seconds, visible twelve miles.

Woody Island.—Leading lights.

Maryborough.—Leading lights, colour red and bright.

Keppel Bay. — Lightship, 1 bright light,

THE NEW LIGHTHOUSE, PORT ADELAIDE
The Australasian Sketcher, 1874

S.S.W. ½ W., off the elbow buoy.

Floating Light.—Upper flats, Fitzroy River, red.

Flattop Island.—Signal station, temporary light, visible ten miles.

Port Denison.—One white fixed light, on North Head, eighty-six feet above the level of the sea.

Cape Bowling Green.—Revolving every minute, visible fifteen miles.

SOUTH AUSTRALIA.

Cape Borda.—On Cape Borda, Kangaroo Island, 1 light revolving, bright; seen thirty miles; red phase of same light fifteen miles. Exhibits a bright and red flash alternately every half minute.

Tipara Reef (Spencer's Gulf).—Lighthouse exhibiting a bright revolving light, having eclipses every thirty seconds.

Troubridge.—On Troubridge Island, St. Vincent's Gulf, 1 light revolving every half minute.

Cape Jervis.—One bright fixed light.

Hulk off Glenelg.—Two bright vertical.

Glenelg Jetty, Holdfast Bay, Gulf of St. Vincent.—1 light, fixed, red.

Port Adelaide Pilot Station, Semaphore Jetty.—One green fixed light points out landing place; visible four miles.

Port Adelaide.—Lighthouse on south side of outer bar; white, flash, shown every thirty seconds.

Sturt.—On Cape Wellington, Kangaroo Island, 1 light, revolving; seen twenty-four miles; exhibits a flash every one and a-half minute.

Macdonnell.—On Cape Northumberland 1 light, revolving, shows alternately every minute; white, red, green; visible from seaward; white light 18 miles, red 15 miles, green 8 miles.

Cape Jaffa.—1 light, revolving every thirty seconds.

TASMANIA.

D'Entrecasteaux.—On Bruni Island, 1 light, revolving, seen twenty-four miles. Shows a bright flash every fifty seconds. Tower, white.

Iron Pot.—On Cape Direction, 1 light, fixed, seen eight miles. Guide to the River Derwent. Tower, red.

Port Dalrymple.—On Low Head, entrance to River Tamar, 1 light, revolving, seen eight miles. Shows a bright flash once every minute. Tower, upper part red, lower white.

Swan Island.—In Banks's Straits, 1 light, revolving, seen twenty miles.

Goose Island.—On Goose Island, Bass's Straits, 1 light, fixed, seen twenty years.

Kent's Group.—On Deal Island, Bass's Straits, 1 light, revolving, seen thirty-six miles.

THE IRON POT LIGHTHOUSE
The Illustrated Sydney News, 1855

VICTORIA.

Portland Bay.—On Battery Hill, red and white dioptric. Tower, white.

Port Fairy.—Light fixed and flashing. Exhibits a red flash every three minutes. Tower, red. Jetty, 1 light, green.

Warrnambool.—Two lights, upper one fixed, white; lower light fixed, red.

King's Island.—On Cape Wickham, 1 light, fixed, white. Tower, white.

Cape Otway.—One light, revolving, white, showing a bright flash of four seconds duration every minute. Tower, white.

Queenscliff (High Light). — On Shortland's Bluff, fixed red and white light. Tower, white. The upper and lower lights in one, lead in mid-channel.

Queenscliff (Low Light).—On Shortland's Bluff, fixed red and white light. Tower, white. The upper and lower lights in one, lead in mid-channel.

Queenscliff Jetty.— One light, fixed, green, seen four miles.

Swan Spit Light.—On Swan Spit, fixed, red and white light, fixed on piles.

Lonsdale Point Light.—On Lonsdale Point; fixed, red and green.

South Channel, Melbourne.—Eastern Light, immediately under Arthur's Seat, fixed dioptric, eighty feet above sea-level, visible about fourteen miles in clear weather, and shows red between S. by W. ½ W., and S.E. ¼ E., and white between S.E. ¼ E., and E. by N. ½ N.

South Channel.—Pile Light is fixed twenty-seven feet above sea-level, visible in clear weather about ten miles; it shows red from W. ½ S. round northerly to N.E. ¼ N., and white between N.E. ¼ N. and S.S.E. Between the bearings of S.S.E. to W. ½ S., this light is obscured.

West Channel Light Ship.—On north end of West Channel, two lights, fixed, white, seen ten miles. Visible all round the compass; gong sounded in thick or foggy weather.

Geelong Ship Channel Lightship.—On entrance to Corio Bay, 1 light, fixed, bright, seen nine miles. Visible all round the compass; gong sounded in thick or foggy weather.

Geelong Harbour.—A red light from lantern, placed on first red dolphin inshore of the light-ship.

Gellibrand's Point Lightship.—Off Gellibrand's Point, 1 white light, revolving, seen ten miles. Visible all round the compass; gong sounded in thick or foggy weather; exhibits bright flash once every thirty seconds.

Port Arlington.—Fixed red light.

Schnapper Point.—Fixed white light.

Cape Schanck.—On Cape Schanck, 1 light, white, fixed, and flashing; shows a bright flash of ten seconds duration every two minutes. Tower, white.

Western Point.—Hastings Jetty, bright light, seen five miles off.

Promontory.—On Wilson's Promontory, 1 light fixed, seen twenty-four miles. Tower, white.

Port Albert.—On Latrobe Island, 1 light, revolving, seen ten miles; shows a bright flash every three minutes. Tower, white.

Flinders.—On Gabo Island, 1 light, fixed, white, seen eighteen miles.

WESTERN AUSTRALIA.

Champion Bay.—Leading lights are fixed red lights, elevated 65 and 41 feet respectively above the level of the sea, and should be visible in clear weather, through an arc of 75 degrees, from a distance of 8 or 9 miles. The towers painted white, with keeper's dwelling attached, are 202 yards apart, and bear from each other E. by N. ⅛ N., and W. by S. ⅛ S. The upper tower, 26 feet high, is square; the lower tower, 37 feet high, is octagonal. The illuminating apparatus of the lower light is of the fourth order.

NOTE.—These lights in line (bearing E. by N. ⅛ N.) lead between the shoals that extend northward of Moore Point and the shoal ground southward of Four-fathom Bank.

Position of lower light latitude 28 degrees 44 min. 35 sec. S., longitude 114 deg. 37 min. 25 sec. E.

Rottenest.— On Rottenest Island, Western Australia, 1 light revolving; seen twenty-five miles; flashes once a minute for 8 seconds, and is obscured for 52 seconds.

Freemantle.— On Freemantle, entrance to Swan River, 1 light fixed, seen fifteen miles; intended only as a guide to Gages Road.

Bunbury.—(Lisschenault Inlet) 1 fixed, bright; 117 feet high; visible fifteen miles in clear weather.

Breaksea.—On Breaksea Island, King George's Sound, 1 light, fixed; seen twenty-seven miles.

Princess Royal Harbour.—On Point King, King George's Sound, north point of entrance to the harbour, 1 light fixed; seen ten miles.

LIVERPOOL, N.S.W.

Called the district of George's River, named by Governor Macquarie, December 10, 1810.

Courts of Quarter Sessions appointed to be holden twice a year at this township (closed June 3, 1828), October 26, 1826.

"LOCH ARD," SURVIVORS OF.

Sir George Bowen, on behalf of the Government of Victoria, presented, at the Town Hall, Melbourne, Thomas Pearce, midshipman of the ship "Loch Ard," with a gold watch and chain, in recognition of his gallantry in saving Miss Carmichael's life (on June 1) at the time of the wreck of the "Loch Ard." June 19, 1878.

The gold medal of the Victorian Humane Society presented at Melbourne to Thomas Pearce, midshipman, for rescuing Miss Carmichael from the wreck of the "Loch Ard." June 20, 1878.

Presentation of a large sum of money at the Exhibition Building, Alfred Park, Sydney, N.S.W., to Thomas Pearce, midshipman of the "Loch Ard," for saving the life of Miss Carmichael, at the wreck of that vessel. July 27, 1878.

[*See* WRECKS.]

LODDON (YARRAYNE, *or* CAMPASPE), RIVER. named Yarrayne, by Sir T. L. Mitchell, 1835.

LODGING-HOUSE, MODEL, erected in King-street, Melbourne, June 20, 1873.

LOGAN, CAPTAIN, Commandant of Moreton Bay settlement, discovered a magnificent river 50 miles to the southward of that settlement: the name Darling River given to it, October, 1826; Captain Logan murdered, November 16, 1830.

LONSDALE, CAPTAIN WILLIAM, formerly of 4th Regt., Resident Magistrate of Victoria, arrived September, 1836; nominated by Governor Latrobe as Colonial Secretary, July, 1850.

LORD HOWE ISLAND. Lieutenant Henry Lidgbird Ball, on his passage to Norfolk Island, in the "Supply," discovered and named Lord Howe Island, February 17, 1788. [On his return Lieutenant Ball stopped at, and surveyed the island.]

LOWE, RIGHT HON. ROBERT, M.P. (England), barrister-at-law, arrived in Sydney, 1842.

LUNATIC ASYLUMS.
Tarban Creek (Gladesville) Lunatic Asylum, at Bedlam Point, on the Parramatta River, New South Wales, built by the Colonial Government at an expense of £13,000, to accommodate sixty patients, December 14, 1835. First patient received from the old Asylum, at Liverpool, in 1838. In 1848 there were one hundred and fifty-four inmates, and there were about eight hundred patients in 1877.

Yarra Bend, Melbourne, opened for reception of lunatics, October, 1848.

LUNATICS IN AUSTRALIA, FOR YEAR ENDING DECEMBER 31, 1877.

	Population.	Lunatics.
New South Wales ..	662,212	1,749
New Zealand........	417,662	865
Queensland	203,084	432
South Australia	236,864	478
Tasmania	107,104	349
Victoria	860,787	2,688
Western Australia ..	27,838	....*
Total........	2,515,551	6,561

* No records published of the number.

VIEW OF LIVERPOOL
Joseph Lycett, an engraving from *Views in Australia, 1824-5*

M

MACARTHUR, JOHN. Trial of Mr. John Macarthur, of Sydney, for contempt of law, January 25, 1808. [The Court was composed of six officers — Captain Anthony Fern Kemp, Lieutenant J. Brabyn, Lieutenant W. Moore, Lieutenant T. Laycock, Lieutenant W. Minchin, and Lieutenant W. Lawson—the Judge-Advocate (Atkins) presiding.]

MACARTHUR, RIVER, discovered, September 21, 1845.

MACKENZIE, RIVER, discovered by Leichhardt, 1844.

MACQUARIE, LACHLAN, GOVERNOR-IN-CHIEF, New South Wales, Lieutenant-Colonel of 73rd Regiment, arrived in Sydney in the "Hindostan," frigate, 50 guns, from England, December 28, 1809, entered on his government, January 1, 1810. [His first measure was to take cognizance of the events which resulted in the suppression of his predecessor, by issuing a proclamation, in which he stated His Majesty's deep regret and displeasure on account of the late tumultuous and mutinous conduct of certain persons towards his (the Governor's) predecessor, William Bligh, and commanded him, before opening the Royal Commission, to reinstate that officer in his position of Captain-General and Governor-in-Chief of the colony, who was, at the expiration of twenty-four hours after being so reinstated, formally to receive Governor Macquarie as his successor. The absence of Governor Bligh from the colony prevented this order from being carried into execution. A proclamation was issued to the effect that all persons appointed to offices during the deposition of Bligh were ordered to be displaced, and all grants of land made null and void. In a week afterwards another proclamation was made, indemnifying the magistrates, gaolers, and constables from prosecutions for acts done by them, they not being otherwise illegal than having been performed by virtue of powers granted by persons not authorised by law to grant them. When Governor Macquarie arrived, Governor Bligh was in Tasmania, and a vessel was sent with despatches to him. He returned to Sydney, and was received with honours due to the rank of Commodore.]

Governor Macquarie made his first tour of the colony, being absent from Sydney about a month. He visited the Hawkesbury and George's River, inspecting the farms and establishing and naming the following towns:— Windsor (called Green Hills), Richmond, Wilberforce, Pitt Town, and Castlereagh and Liverpool on George's River. The result of the Governor's tour was that measures were adopted for the advancement of agriculture and pastoral pursuits, and for the distribution amongst the settlers of breeding cattle on reasonable terms, premiums being offered for the cultivation of certain products, He started on November 6, and returned to Sydney, December 23, 1810.

Governor and Mrs. Macquarie embarked for Van Diemen's Land (calling at Jervis Bay), in the schooner "Nelson"; arrived at Hobart Town, November 23, 1811; visited Newcastle January 3rd, and returned to Sydney, January 11, 1812.

Bathurst visited by Governor Macquarie, who fixed upon the site for a town, which he named in honour of Earl Bathurst, Secretary of State for the Colonies, April 25, 1815.

Governor Macquarie's second visit to Van Diemen's Land, April 4, 1821.

Governor, Mrs., and Master Macquarie sailed for England in the "Surrey," Captain Raine, February 12, 1822.

MACQUARIE, RIVER, (native name, *Wambone*), N.S.W., discovered by Mr. G. W. Evans, December 7, 1813; explored by Oxley, 1818.

MAGISTRACY. A new Commission of the Peace was issued, when thirty-two of the old magistrates were left out, causing much dissatisfaction; and the Governor's enemies were unremitting in their attacks on his administration, and a petition to Parliament was got up by the faction opposed to the Governor, but a counter-petition, signed by 5,000 "free inhabitants of the colony," was sent to England. The petition was prepared by Mr. Wentworth, and it stated that the petitioners "feel it their bounden duty to record their entire and cordial approval of the wise, disinterested, liberal, just, paternal, and constitutional policy which has marked his administration": 1836.

MAGISTRATES. A Commission issued appointing 120 magistrates for the colony of New South Wales, January 1, 1830.

MAITLAND. A settlement was formed at Maitland by eleven well behaved convicts who were allotted land to cultivate. A few others were located at the Paterson, eight or nine miles off. 1818.

MAIZE, FIRST SALE OF. The Government

purchased from the settlers 1,200 bushels of maize, being the first ever sold in New South Wales, September, 1793.

MANHOOD SUFFRAGE, introduced into Victoria. The first Parliament under its provisions elected, October 13, 1859.

MANUFACTURES. First attempt in the Colony to produce a textile fabric, made, April, 1799; three hundred yards of blanketing were woven from wool, the produce of previous years, and one hundred and seventy yards of linen were manufactured from Colonial flax, 1801; tweed first manufactured in New South Wales, 1843; Fulton and Langlands established the first iron foundry in Melbourne, 1852.

MANUFACTORIES.

NEW SOUTH WALES.

In 1877 163 flour mills, of 2,623 h. p., driving 382 pairs of stones, were in work; 151 were steam, of 2,529 h. p., 8 water, of 80 h. p., 1 windmill, of 10 h. p., and 3 were worked by horse power, employing in all 623 hands. The total number of works and manufactories of all kinds was 11,911, of which 9,233 were connected with or dependent upon agriculture, 415 were for working on the raw material, the production of the pastoral interest, 265 were for the manufacture of feed of which the raw material was not the produce of agriculture, 688 were connected with the building interests, 155 were machine factories, brass, lead and iron works; the remainder were of a miscellaneous character. Among them being 4 chemical works, 11 gas works, 2 organ builders, 6 rope walks, 10 railway carriage works, 13 account-book factories, 104

boot factories, 42 clothing factories, 140 coach and waggon works, 1 glass silvering establishment, 4 ice works, 2 kerosene work, 2 paper mills, 106 ship and boat yards, 22 smelting works, and 11 steam joinery works. The total number of workpeople employed was 23,807—20,590 males and 3,217 females. There are 8 woollen factories employing 207 hands, the out-turn being 271,452 yards of cloth and tweeds; 33 soap and candle factories, employing 156 hands, the produce for the year being 92,958¼ cwt. of soap, and 36,909 cwt. of candles; 20 tobacco factories (not all at work, with 532 hands, who manufactured 19,180½ cwt. of tobacco; 29 steam power and 34 cattle power sugar mills (12 of them not being worked), the sugar manufactured being 150,744 cwt., and 78,823 gallons and 1,667 tons of molasses, from 1,999,560 cwt. of cane; and 2 sugar refineries turning out 259,653 cwt. of refined sugar. During the year 150,737 gallons of rum were distilled from 26,531 cwt. of molasses. 1878.

NEW ZEALAND.—There are 80 flour mills, driven by 1,289½ horse power, with 191 pairs of stones; 82 breweries, employing 432 hands, and 191 horses, the beer brewed amounting to 4,247,402 gallons; 110 flax mills, having 187 machines, driven by an aggregate of 963 horse power, principally water, 4,255½ tons of flax being manufactured in 1873—this industry is now in a languishing condition owing to the low price of flax in the English market. In addition to this there are 657 manufactories, works, &c., employing 7,999 male hands and 195 female hands, and machinery of the aggregate of 4,203 horse power. The principal of these factories are 6 agricultural implement, 1 basket, 4 biscuit,

THE OLD MILL, PARRAMATTA
The Illustrated Sydney News, 1854

10 boiling down and meat preserving, 84 potteries, 12 candle and soap works, 19 coachbuilding, 2 distilleries, 71 fellmongeries and tanneries, 6 furniture, 2 glue, 22 iron and brass foundries, 4 cooperage, 17 rope, cordage, and mat, 162 saw-mills, sash and door, 20 ship and boat building, 1 varnish, 2 woollen cloth. Railway trucks are now made in the colony, both at Government and private works.

QUEENSLAND.—There are in the colony 5 steam mills for grinding and dressing corn, 70 sugar mills, 37 steam saw mills, 3 cotton gins, 15 soap works, 4 meat preserving establishments, 12 distilleries, 4 tobacco manufactories, 2 steam biscuit manufactories, 1 salt works, 20 agricultural implement manufactories, 4 boiling-down establishments, 6 fellmongeries, 5 breweries, 42 cordial manufactories, 8 lime kilns, 5 potteries, 21 iron and tin works, 10 foundries, 33 coach factories, 8 cooperages, 34 printing establishments, 10 ship and boatbuilding yards, 3 smelting works, and numerous other works for the manufacture of articles of general requirement.

SOUTH AUSTRALIA.—Among the leading manufactories are 43 for agricultural implements, 3 for soap and candles, 20 for coach and carriage building, 6 for jam, 8 for boat building, 1 for meat preserving, 4 for ship building, 5 for marble polishing, 1 tweed factory, 13 clothing factories, 24 boot and shoe factories, 3 flax mills, 3 rope walks, 2 brush manufactories, 10 biscuit bakeries, 4 confectionery manufactories, 9 dried fruits, and 3 olive oil factories. Among works may be enumerated 25 breweries, 135 distilleries, 27 foundries, 8 gas works, 7 potteries, 31 saw mills 34 tanneries, 102 wine presses, 30 soda water manufactories, and 1 ice works. Flour mills are very numerous, there being, in 1876, 101, containing 320 pairs of stones, driven by steam machinery, of the aggregate horse-power of 1,978. During 1876, 727,272 gallons of wine were manufactured, and 37,299 gallons exported. Sericulture is attracting considerable attention, and the silk produced has been pronounced by Marseilles merchants to be equal to any ever wound by them. 1878.

TASMANIA.—The climate of Tasmania is especially adapted to malting and brewing, and also to the growth of hops. The Tasmanian brewed ale is that which is chiefly drunk in the colony, and an export trade is carried on with New South Wales and Victoria. There are 19 breweries, 29 tanneries, 5 soap and 6 candle manufactories, 10 jam-boiling establishments, 54 saw-mills, 41 agricultural implement works, 6 brass foundries, 12 coachbuilding factories, 76 fellmongeries, 2 iron smelting works, 32 steam flour mills, 40 water mills, 3 potteries, 3 tin smelting works, and there is also now one manufactory of cloths, tweeds, blankets, &c., from Tasmanian wool, which have been stimulated by the offer of a bonus of £1,000 by Parliament. The firm offered its first production of tweeds, flannels, &c., for sale by auction in August, 1874. Wool is the principal product,

next to which in importance are tin and jam, 1878.

VICTORIA.—The number of manufactories, large and small, according to the returns made up to March 31, 1878, is 1,763, employing in the aggregate 27,618 hands and 957 engines, principally steam of 8,636 h. p., the machinery and plant being of the value of £2,157,052, the land, £1,145,414, and the buildings £1,795,133—a total of £5,097,599. Among the industries are manufactories, foundries, &c. : 10 account books, 2 organ building, 8 pianoforte, 40 agricultural implement, 8 cutlery, 45 engine machine, 127 coach and waggon, 39 saddle and harness, 17 ship and boat, 4 graving and floating docks, 1 patent slip, 15 bedding, 36 cabinet making, 6 looking-glass, 20 chemical, dye, and essential oil works, 1 fuse, 8 ink and blacking, 1 match, 3 blasting powder, 142 clothing and boot and shoe, 1 jute, 2 oilskin, 15 rope and twine, 16 meat preserving, 10 biscuit, 8 confectionery, 8 jam, 3 maizena, starch, &c., 104 aerated waters, 11 coffee and spice, 4 sauce and pickle, 2 sugar, 13 tobacco and snuff, 6 brush, 3 curled hair, 3 flock, 1 glue, 2 fancy leather, 38 soap, candle, and tallow, 4 tar distilling (asphalte), 116 tanneries and fellmongeries, 5 distilleries, 13 malthouses, 2 sugar refineries, 4 whip, 8 basket, 11 blind, 1 broom, 17 cooperage, 3 earth closet, 2 fancy box, 150 moulding, framing, and saw, 2 paint and varnish, 1 paper, 5 paper bag, 16 gas, 5 glass, 2 stone-sawing and polishing, 3 ice, 4 antimony smelting, 1 bell, 6 electro-plate, 2 fire-proof safe, 88 iron, brass, and copper, 61 iron and tin works, and 8 wire working. During 1877, 145 patents were applied for, and 168 articles, of which 65 are described under the head of " Literary, Dramatic, and Musical productions," were copyrighted. Meat-preserving is also conducted on an extensive scale, and large quantities are exported to Great Britain. A mauufactory for the utilizing and making of the skins of the various indigenous birds and animals of the colony bas been established, also a silk company, which has for its object the cultivation of silk and grain. Very large paper mills have recently been opened near Geelong. The mills for grinding and dressing grain number 150, of which 141 are driven by steam and 9 by water, there being 487 pairs of stones, operated in all by 2,871 h. p.; estimated value of machinery and plant is £225,500. The woollen mills are eight in number, employing 8 steam-engines of 530 horse-power. The cloth, tweed, and flannel produced during the year ending March 31, 1878, was 957,265 yards, and 2,984 blankets, and 2,496 shawls from 1,511,514lbs. of wool. The value of the machinery and plant is £130,871. The tanneries numbered 116, employing 37 machines worked by steam, 32 by horse-power, and 47 by manual labour, the total amount of horse-power being 384, 3,101 pits, and having tanned during the year 3,309,162 hides and skins, the leather produced being valued at £646,968; the value of plant and machinery was £81,040. There were also in operation at the same date 224 brick yards and potteries, employing 272 machines for tempering and crushing clay, and for making bricks or pottery 18 engines of 101 h. p.; 69,250,400 bricks were made during the year, of the value of £145,766, and pottery to the value of £27,322, the machinery and plant valued at £56,326. There are 109 breweries in Victoria; the beer brewed during 1877-78 being 15,141,835 gals., the value of the machinery and plant employed being £163,216, and the number of hands employed being 939, of horses 647, and of drays and waggons 367. The materials used during the year were 11,157,151 lbs. of sugar, 1,071,261 bushels of malt, and 1,220,528 lbs. of hops. There are 140 stone quarries at work employing 7 steam-engines of 58 h. p, The stone operated on during the year was 212,644 cubic yards of bluestone, 1,202 of flagging, 7,173 of sandstone, 900 of granite. The approximate value of stone raised was £48,015, the value of machinery and plant £13,130. 1877-8.

WESTERN AUSTRALIA.—The manufacturers in the colony are few. They consist of—one soap factory, five water and twenty-three steam flour-mills, two water and eight steam saw-mills, and thirteen mills worked by horse-power, also four tanneries, one smelting works, three breweries, two iron foundries, two coach factories, and a bone-crushing mill. A salt factory is being worked at Rottnest Island by the Government. A European superintendent conducts the works, which are supplied with labour from the native penal establishment situated on the island. Two very successful breweries are also at work in Perth. 1878.

MAORIES.

The aboriginal natives of New Zealand, supposed to be of Malayan origin, and to have peopled these islands about the fifteenth century. There are in New Zealand about 60 Native Schools under the auspices of the Government, in which about 1,500 children are instructed; the girls are also taught domestic duties.

The number of Maories was estimated at 2,000,000 in 1835.

The Maori population consisted of 18 tribes, and the number 45,470—24,363 males, 20,335 females, and 772 persons whose sex were not indicated in the returns, January 1, 1876.

MASSACRES BY. The Maories of New Zealand attacked the settlers of Mallewherowhero District, committing dreadful atrocities amongst them. They massacred about thirty Europeans, including women and children who could not get away. They also butchered Major Briggs, Captain Wilson, Lieutenant Walsh, Messrs. Dodd, Poppard, Nairn, McCulloch, Coddle, and Hedbury who were in one party, besides twenty of the friendly natives, some of whom were dreadfully mutilated, November 1868. [See NEW ZEALAND.]

SYDNEY MARKETS ON SATURDAY NIGHT
The Australian Picture Pleasure Book

MARKETS.

The usual prices given at Sydney for grain and live stock:— Wheat 10s. per bushel; maize 7s. Live stock: The value of a Cape ewe was £6 to £8 8s.; a she goat £8 8s.; a full grown hog, £3 10s.; an English cow was sold for £80. 1794.

First Public Market established in the Colony, at the southern end of George-street, Sydney, October 20, 1810.

A fair and market established at Parramatta, New South Wales, December, 1810.

MARRIAGE. First in Port Phillip took place April 30, 1837.

ENDOWMENT ON. The practice of bestowing two square miles of the public lands on each native-born young lady on the occasion of her

HEAVILY TATTOOED, THE SON OF A MAORI CHIEF
A & R Archives

ROBINSON AND FINLAY, THE MARRIAGE CEREMONY
The Australasian Sketcher, 1878

marriage, established in the Settlement of New South Wales, January, 1829.

MARRIAGE BILL. Marriage with Deceased Wife's Sister Bill of South Australia received the Royal assent and became law, June 1871.

DISTINGUISHED. Mrs. Putland, daughter of Governor Bligh, married in Sydney to Lieutenant Sir Maurice O'Connell, 73rd Regt., May 3, 1810.

Hon. (now Sir) Edward Deas-Thomson married in Sydney to Anna Maria, second daughter of Governor Sir Richard Bourke, 1833.

Sir Henry Barkly, Governor of Victoria, married, at Melbourne, to the only daughter of Major-General Sir Thomas Simpson Pratt, 1860.

Mr. Charles Bright married in Melbourne, to Anna Maria Georgina Manners Sutton, daughter of Viscount Canterbury, 1868.

Sir James Ferguson, Governor of New Zealand, married to Olive, youngest daughter of John Henry Richman, Esq., of South Australia, 1873.

Earl Donoughmore married at Hobart Town to a Tasmanian lady, Miss Isabelle Stephens, daughter of Colonel Stephens, May 19, 1874.

Captain Stirling, R.N., A.D.C. to the Queen, married to Helen Cecilia, daughter of Sir E. Deas-Thomson, and grand-daughter of Sir Richard Bourke, July 15, 1874.

Norah Augusta, daughter of His Excellency Sir Hercules Robinson, the Governor of New South Wales, married to Mr. A. K. Finlay, August 7, 1878.

Lord Henry Phipps, third son of Marquis of Normanby to Norma Leith Hay, second daughter of Mr. James Leith Hay at Ipswich, Queensland, November 21, 1878.

MARTIAL LAW. Great convict insurrection at Castle Hill, martial law proclaimed March 5; repealed March 9, 1804; martial law proclaimed in consequence of attacks by blacks at Bàthurst. 500 acres of land offered for the capture of "Saturday," the aboriginal ringleader, August 5, 1824; martial law proclaimed at Taranaki, New Zealand, February 23, 1860.

MARYBOROUGH, QUEENSLAND, established February 2, 1851; first Circuit Court, held April 2, 1860; proclaimed a municipality March 23, 1861.

MASSACRES.

Report reached Port Hunter, Duke of York Group, that a few days previously a number of Wesleyan mission agents at New Britain had been killed and eaten by the natives. An expedition of friendly natives, under the Rev. G. Brown, the originator and head of the missions, some ten days later attacked and killed a number of the men concerned in the murder, and burnt several villages, April 8, 1878.

Crew of the schooner Marian Renny was massacred at the Solomon Islands, only one escaped, January, 1868.

M'KEAN, HON. JAMES. Member of the Legislative Assembly of Victoria, expelled from the House, for alleging in a Police Court that the Members were drunk most of their time, were a disgrace to their country, and not competent to deal with public affairs, July 27, 1876.

MEETINGS. First public meeting ever held in New South Wales, its object being to raise funds to build a gaol, June 17, 1799; first public meeting held in the Court House, Sydney, to petition the King and Parliament for the privileges inherent in every British community—Taxation by representation, or a House of Assembly, May 29, 1835.

MELBOURNE, VICTORIA.

First settled, August, 1835.
Melbourne named, March, 1837.
Post-office opened, August 12, 1841.
Savings' Bank established, September 1, 1841.
First Coroner (Dr. Wilmot) appointed, February 2, 1841.
Foundation-stone of Presbyterian Church, Melbourne, laid January 22, 1842.
Melbourne incorporated [See MUNICIPAL] July 20, 1842.
Mr. Condell elected first Mayor, December 9, 1842.
Boundaries of Melbourne proclaimed, March 13, 1843.
Melbourne Hospital founded, January, 1846.
The *Argus* first issued, June 2, 1846.
Melbourne Hospital opened, July 15, 1847.
Melbourne formed into a separate bishopric, 1847.

Great flood in Melbourne, November 28, 1849.
Public meeting held for the purpose of establishing gas works, August 28, 1850.
Prince's Bridge across the Yarra Yarra opened with great ceremony, November 12, 1850.
First sod turned for the Yarra Yarra embankment, Melbourne Water Supply, December 20, 1853.
The *Age* established October 17, 1854.
Public Library erected, July 3, 1855.
Yan Yean Waterworks opened by Major-General Macarthur, January 1, 1858.
Memorial-stone of Melbourne Town Hall laid by H. R. H. Prince Alfred, November 29, 1867.
Town Hall, Melbourne, opened August 9, 1870.
Clock presented to the Town Hall by W. V. Condell, son of the first Mayor, 1873.
First shade-trees planted in Collins-street by the Mayor, Mr. James Gatehouse, May 24, 1875.
Victoria Arcade, Bourke-street, opened, Nov. 25, 1876.
First election of Harbour Trust Commissioners under the Melbourne Harbour Trust Act of 1876, March 30, 1877.
Foundation-stone of the Eastern Market laid by Councillor Pigdon, Mayor of Melbourne, May 9, 1878. [See PORT PHILLIP.]

MELVILLE ISLAND. Melville Island Settlement, at the mouth of Van Diemen's Gulf, founded by Captain Bremer, in H.M.S. "Tamar," November 1, 1824. [It consisted of 126 people, who erected a stockade at Fort Dundas in

MELBOURNE IN 1875
The Australasian Sketcher, 1875

Apsly's Strait, but abandoned it, March 31, 1829.]

MERCHANDISE. Ten ships freighted with Colonial produce left Sydney for England, 1821.

MERCURY BAY. The Transit of Mercury observed by the astronomer, Mr. Green, at a place named in consequence Mercury Bay, November 9, 1869.

METEOROLOGY.

Awful storm of wind and rain at Norfolk Island ; large pines 180 to 200 feet in height and 20 to 30 feet in circumference blown to the ground, February 26, 1795.

An extraordinary phenomenon observed in the New South Wales settlement. An appearance presented itself in the north-west about dusk in the evening which had the resemblance of a ray of forked lightning. It remained the whole time stationary, lasting five minutes, 1793.

Heavy hailstorm or fall of ice on the Hawkesbury. The produce of four farms completely destroyed ; some of the frozen flakes found on the second day 8 inches in length, December, 1795.

Severe hailstorm. Many of the stones (6 inches in circumference) killing the poultry and knocking down lambs, May 14, 1798.

Two seamen killed by lightning on board the "Atlantic" in Sydney Cove, 1806.

Heavy hailstorm—did much damage to crops at the Hawkesbury, September 24, 1806.

Severe hailstorm 10 miles from Sydney. Some of the stones literally flakes of ice and 8 inches circumference. January 18, 1812.

A hailstorm visited Sydney, one of the severest ever experienced in the colony. It set in about 2 p.m., and in *less than 12 minutes* it demolished nearly the whole of the glass windows in the town and destroyed the gardens. 1814.

Terrific hailstorm in New South Wales, February 17, 1823.

A great storm passed over the district of Prospect and the Pennant Hills. It was accompanied by thunder, lightning, and hail ; and so great was the fall of the mass that it was 10 feet in some parts of the low grounds. Four days afterwards a piece of ice was found still 12 inches in circumference. 1824.

The most violent storm of wind and hail ever known in New South Wales, January 11, 1829.

Heavy fall of snow in Sydney, lasting half an hour, between 8 and 9 a.m., June 28, 1836.

A great comet first seen in New South Wales, March 4, 1843.

House unroofed in Melbourne during a tornado from the north, February 11, 1846.

Tremendous dust storm and hot wind at Melbourne, March 1, 1853.

Great comet, tail of 30 degrees, seen at Melbourne, March 3, 1853.

Great comet seen in Melbourne, April 3, 1853.

Terrific hailstorm at Brisbane, October 20, 1859.

Large comet seen in Victoria, May 16, 1861.

Greatest heat ever reached in Sydney, according to H. C. Russell, Government Astronomer, the glass showing 106·9 deg., was on January 5, 1863.

Great storm in New South Wales, July 12, 1866.

Terrific gale—three pilot boats upset and eight lives lost outside Sydney Heads, July 29, 1867.

The greatest heat experienced in Adelaide, in the shade, was 113·5, in January, 1867. The greatest heat in Adelaide, in the sun, was 164·0, in January, 1870.

Great cyclone at Townsville, Queensland, February 21, 1870.

Great storm at Sydney, attended with loss of life, November 6, 1870.

Great storm in Tasmania, July 23, 1871.

Large meteorite discovered by Mr. Thomas Robertson on the Barratta run, near Deniliquin ; weight, 2cwt., April 9, 1871. Described by Archibald Liversidge, Esq., before Royal Society, Sydney, May 22, 1871.

Great gale at Auckland, New Zealand, May 30, 1874.

Heavy gale in Sydney from the eastward, with rain, May 2, 1875.

Remarkable waterspout observed near Inverell (inland town of N S.W.), May 6, 1875.

Heavy storms on the coast of New South Wales, June 28, 1875.

Destructive hailstorm in Tasmania, January 28, 1876.

Fearful tornado at Bowen, Queensland, February 16, 1876.

Heaviest gales on record on the Australian coast. On Sunday night (10th) the wind obtained the remarkable velocity of 135 miles per hour, September 10, 1876. [The "Dandenong" was lost in this gale.]

The s.s. "City of Melbourne" on passage to Melbourne was caught in this gale off Jervis Bay, and racehorses to the value of £20,000 were lost.

A terrible hurricane occurred at the Lacipede Islands, February 18, 1877.

Severe hurricane devastated the Grenfell district in New South Wales, November 27, 1877.

Greatest heat ever registered in New South Wales, Brewarrina (according to Mr. Colin C. Fraser, of Milroy), the glass showing 127 deg. (in the sun) and 124 deg. (in the shade), was on January 18, 1878.

Extraordinary fall of rain in Sydney, nearly 8 inches in 24 hours. Heavy rains very general throughout Riverina. February 6, 1878.

Extraordinary meteor of unusual size seen about 3 p.m. in New South Wales and Victoria, June 8, 1878.

Extraordinary shower of sulphur at Warrnambool, Victoria, September 16, 1878.

The average rainfall in Adelaide, South Australia, for 36 years was 21·155 inches. Greatest rainfall in 1851, when 30·663 inches fell ; least rainfall was in 1865, when 14·750 inches fell. The average rainfall in Palmerston, Northern territory, for six years was 63·252 inches.

I.—THE GREATEST RAINFALL IN ONE DAY.

New South Wales, at South Head, October 15, 1844 .. .. 20·41 inches.
Sydney Observatory, February 25, 1873.. 8·90 „
Victoria—The results published do not contain the daily amounts.
South Australia—Not published.
Queensland—Not published.

II.—GREATEST RAINFALL RECORDED IN ONE YEAR.

New South Wales	..	..	1860	..	82·81 inches.
Queensland	..	..	1870	..	79·06 „
South Australia	..	..	1875	..	31·45 „
Victoria	..	..	1849	..	44·25 „

III.—LEAST RAINFALL RECORDED IN ONE YEAR.

New South Wales	..	..	1849	..	21·49 inches.
Queensland	..	..	1865	..	24·11 „
South Australia	..	..	1869	..	13·85 „
Victoria	..	..	1865	..	15·94 „

LIST OF COMETS OBSERVED IN NEW SOUTH WALES.

Encke's Comet	..	..	1822
Comet IV. ..	..	..	1822
„ I. ..	..	..	1824
„ I. ..	..	..	1825
„ IV. ..	..	..	1825
Comet of ..	..	..	1833
Comet of ..	..	..	1834
Comet I. ..	..	..	1843
„ II. ..	..	..	1853
„ III. ..	..	..	1853
„ VI. ..	..	..	1858
„ III. ..	..	..	1860
„ II. ..	..	..	1861
Encke's Comet	..	..	1862
Comet III. ..	..	..	1862
Comet II. ..	..	..	1864
„ I. ..	..	..	1865
Encke's Comet	..	..	1865
Comet III. ..	..	..	1874
Encke's Comet	..	..	1875
Encke's Comet	..	..	1878
Brorsen's Comet	..	..	1879

A few of the above list have been also observed in Victoria.

THE DELIGHTFUL CLIMATE OF AUSTRALIA.

I.
An eminent Melbourne Merchant (resident in the Toorak Road), resolves to walk into Town this delightful morning.

II.
Before he reaches the St. Kilda road, he is unfortunately overtaken by a slight dust storm.

III.
Bountiful Nature, however, soon relieves him with a change of weather.

IV.
The Eminent Melbourne Merchant reaches his Counting House,

THE DELIGHTFUL CLIMATE OF AUSTRALIA
Melbourne Punch, 1865

MILITARY.

The "Surprise," "Neptune," and "Scarborough" (transport), arrived with New South Wales corps, afterwards 102nd Regiment or "condemned regiment," June, 1790.

Lieutenant-Governor Francis Grose arrived in the "Pitt," with the remainder of the New South Wales Corps, December 10, 1792.

Dawes' Battery, at Sydney (N.S.W.), erected by Lieutenant Dawes, March, 1798.

Lieutenant-Colonel Patterson returned to take command of the New South Wales Corps, 1799.

New South Wales Corps reduced to a peace footing. 1803.

The New South Wales Corps, or 102nd Regiment, embarked for England in the "Hindostan," April 17, 1810.

First detachment 73rd Regiment embarked for Ceylon on board the "Earl Spencer," January 26, 1814.

The "Windham" arrived with the Head Quarters of the 46th Regiment, commanded by Lieutenant-Colonel Malle, February 7, 1814.

The Head Quarters of the 73rd Regiment, with Lieutenant and Lady O'Connell, embarked for Ceylon on board the "General Hewitt," March 26, 1814.

Third division of the 73rd Regiment embarked for Ceylon with Lieutenant-Colonel Gelb, April 2, 1814.

Military Barracks, Lower George-street, Sydney, completed, May, 1815.

The Head Quarters of the 43rd Regiment arrived with the "Matilda" to relieve the 46th under the command of Lieutenant-Colonel Erskine, August 9, 1816.

Captain James Wallace, of the 46th Regiment, stationed at Newcastle (N.S.W.), 1871.

Major George Druitt, 48th Regt., appointed chief commander of the Military Engineering, 1819.

Head Quarters of the 3rd Buffs arrived in the "Commodore Hayes," August 29, 1823.

The Royal Veteran Company, the name under which were embodied as a local corps those officers and soldiers of the old 102nd Regiment or new corps who chose to remain in the colony after that regiment was recalled for the part it had taken in the arrest of Governor Bligh, was disbanded, and informed that they would be conveyed home at Government expense. September 24, 1823. [Only four availed themselves of the offer of the Government; the rest remained n the colony, and received grants of land.]

The 48th Regiment embarked for Madras, March 5, 1824.

Colonel Thornton and Captain Coghill, with Head Quarters of 40th Regiment, arrived in the "Mayles," October 27, 1824.

Head Quarters of the 3rd Regiment of Buffs, under Colonel Stewart, embarked at Sydney for England, November 28, 1827.

Captain Wright, of H.M. 39th Regiment, tried for the alleged murder of a prisoner named Clinch, at Norfolk Island, acquitted, October 9, 1829.

Recruiting for the army first commenced in New South Wales, April 1, 1839.

A despatch received in New South Wales from the Secretary of State, to the effect that the charge of. the future providing and maintaining a military force in the colony must be undertaken by the colonists, otherwise the military would be withdrawn. 1850.

A company of the 40th Regt. was mounted and equipped as light cavalry for bush service, and was employed in the escort of treasure from the various gold-fields, May, 1853.

British Military Forces withdrawn from Australia: from Victoria, 1870; from New South Wales, August, 1870.

Vote of £20,000, passed in the Assembly, on the motion of the Colonial Secretary, for two companies of artillery and two companies of infantry, May 25, 1871.

GRAND REVIEW OF TROOPS
The Illustrated Sydney News, 1855

MINERALS, LIST OF, FOUND IN AUSTRALIA :—

Actinolite
Adamantine Spar
Adularia
Agalmatolite
Agate
Albite
Alum
Amethyst
Amianthus
Amphibole
Analcime
Anatase
Andalusite
Anglesite
Anhydrous Silicates
Anthracite
Antimonite
Antimony, Native
Antimony Oxide
Antimonial Copper Ore
Antimony Sulphide
Apatite
Argentite, Silver Sulphide
Arragonite
Arsenic, Native
Arsenical Pyrites
Asbromstus
Asteria
Atacamite
Augite
Azurite
Barklyite
Barytes
Bellmetal Ore
Beryl
Bismuth, Native
Bismuthite
Bitumen, Elastic
Blende
Bog-butter
Bog Iron Ore, Limonite
Bornite
Brick Clay
Brookite
Brown Coal, Lignite
Cacholong
Cairngorum
Calcite
Cornelian
Cassiterite
Cerussite
Cervantite
Chabasite
Chalcedony
Chalcopyrites
Chalcotrichite
Chalybite
Chert
Chiastolite
Chlorite
Chromite, Chrome Iron
Chrysoberyl
Chrysocolla
Chrysolite
Cinnabar
Clays
Coal, Common
   ,,   Brown, Lignite
   ,,   Cannel
   ,,   Anthracite
Cobalt, Oxide
Condurrite
Copper, Native
Copper Black Oxide, Tenorite
   ,,   Red Oxide,

Cuprite
   ,,   Chloride, Atacamite
   ,,   Blue Carbonate, Chessylite
   ,,   Green Carbonate, Malachite
   ,,   Grey Sulphide, Copper Glance
   ,,   Pyrites
   ,,   Purple, Bornite
Copper-nickel
Corundum
Cuprite
Cyanite, Kyanite
Cymophane
Delessite
Diallage
Diamond
Disthene
Domeykite
Earthy Minerals
Eisenkiesel
Elaterite
Emerald
Emery
Epidote
Epsomite
Fahlerz
Felspar, Common
   ,,   Glassy
Figure-stone
Fire-clay
Flos-ferri
Fluor-spar
Galena
Garnet
Gems
Girasol
Gmelinite
Gold
Göetheite
Graphite
Green Earth
Gypsum
Hæmatite
Halloysite
Hauyne
Heavy-spar
Herschelite
Hornblende
Hyacinth
Hyalite
Hydrous Silicates
Hypersthene
Ice-spar
Ilmenite
Iridium
Iron, Native
   ,,   Brown Hematite
   ,,   Carbonate
   ,,   Chromate
   ,,   Limonite
   ,,   Pharmacosiderite
   ,,   Phosphate
   ,,   Magnetic pyrites, Pyrrhotine
   ,,   Pyrites
   ,,   Scorodite
   ,,   Spathic
   ,,   Specular
   ,,   Sulphide
   ,,   Titaniferous
Iron-ores
   ,,   Brown
   ,,   Magnetic
Iserine
Jamesonite

Jargoon
Jasper
   ,,   Ribbon
Jet
Kampylite
Kaolin
Kerosene Shale
Kupfernickel
Kupfermanganerz
Kyanite
Laumonite
Lead, Native
   ,,   Arseniate
   ,,   Carbonate
   ,,   Molybdate
   ,,   Oxide, Red Lead
   ,,   Phosphate
   ,,   Sulphate
   ,,   Sulphide, Glance
Lignite
Lime, Carbonate
   ,,   Phosphate
   ,,   Sulphate
Lydianstone
Magnesia, Carbonate
   ,,   Sulphate
Magnesite
Magnetite
Magnetic Pyrites
Malachite
Manganese
Marble
Marcassite
Marmolite
Meerschaum
Melaconite Tenorite
Menaccanite
Mercury, Native
Mercury, Sulphide Cinnabar
Mesotype
Mica
Mineral Wax
Mimetite
Minium
Mispickle
Molybdenite
Moonstone
Muller's Glass, Hyalite
Muscovite
Natron
Nepheline
Nickel, Arsenides
Nigrine
Olivenite
Olivine
Oolitic Limestone
Opal
Orthoclase
Osmo-iridium
Ozokerite
Pectolite
Peridot
Pharmakosiderite
Phosphacalcite
Picrolite
Plakodine
Platinum
Pleonaste
Plumbago
Porcelain Clay, Kaolin
Prehnite
Pyrites, Iron
   ,,   Marcassite
   ,,   Magnetic
Pyromorphite
Pyroxene
Pyrrhotine
Quartz
Quicksilver

Redruthite
Resinite
Rock-crystal
Ruby, Oriental
   ,,   Spinelle
Rutile
Sahlite
Salt, Common
Saponite
Sapphire
Scheelite
Schorl
Scolezite, Skolezite
Scorodite
Selenite
Serpentine
Siderite
Silica
Silicified Wood
Silver, Native

   ,,   Antimonial
   ,,   Sulphide
Smaragdite
Soapstone
Soda, Carbonate
Sodium, Chloride
Specular Iron Ore
Sphærosiderite
Shene
Spinelle
Spodumene
Staurolite
Steatite
Stilbite
Strontianite
Sulphur
Talc
Tellurium, Native
Tenorite
Tetrahedrite

Tin-ore
Titanium
Topaz
Torbanite
Tourmaline
Travertine, Freshwater Limestone
Tremolite
Tungsten
Wad
Wavellite
Websterite
Williamsite
Wolfram
Wood Opal
Wulfenite
Zeolites
Zinc-blende
Zircon

MINERAL STATISTICS OF AUSTRALASIA.

GOLD.

New South Wales, to December 31, 1878 : 8,846,990 ozs.

Victoria, to Dec. 31, 1878 : 48,012,670 ozs.

Queensland, to December 31, 1878 : 2,993,482 ozs.

South Australia, to December 31, 1877 : 7,508 ozs.

Tasmania, to December 31, 1878 : 66,510 ozs.

New Zealand, to December 31, 1877 : 8,648,966 ozs.

COAL.

New South Wales, to December 31, 1877 : 17,481,197 tons, and 137,299 tons shale.

Queensland, to December 31, 1877 : 484,115 tons.

SILVER.

New South Wales, to December 31, 1878 : 494,942 ozs.

Victoria, to December 31 : 1878, 127,539 ozs.

Queensland, to December 31, 1877 : 279 ozs.

New Zealand, to December 31, 1877 : 317,936 ozs.

South Australia, to December 31, 1877 : 4 tons ore.

TIN.

New South Wales, to December 31, 1878 : 29,874 tons ingots ; 12,080 tons ore.

Victoria, to December 31, 1877 : 4,196 tons 10 cwt. ore.

Queensland, to December 31, 1877 : 17,042 tons.

Tasmania, to December 31, 1878 : 16,656 tons.

South Australia, to December 31, 1877 : 7 tons 13 cwt.

COPPER.

New South Wales, to December 31, 1878 : 25,060 tons ingots ; 22,713 tons ore.

Victoria, to December 31, 1877 : 2,641 tons ore.

Queensland, to December 31, 1877 : 82,955 tons.

South Australia, to December 31, 1877— value £18,000,000 : 121,504 tons metal ; 419,572 tons ore ; 2,215 tons regulus.

IRON.

New South Wales, to December 31, 1878: about 9,466 tons.

Victoria, to December 31, 1871 : value £2,111.

South Australia, to December 31, 1877 : 444 tons.

MINES.

Hon. J. B. Humffray, first Commissioner for Mines in Victoria, 1860.

Department of Mines established in Victoria, 1870.

Mining Department, Sydney, N.S.W., established by Act of Parliament ; Hon. James S. Farnell, first Minister ; Mr. Harrie Wood, from School of Mines, Ballarat, Victoria, specially chosen first Under-Secretary. 1874.

DEEPEST MINES. The deepest mines in Australia are some gold mines in Victoria. The depth of the Magdala shaft is 2,032 feet; the Newington and Pleasant Creek is 1,940 feet, and the Prince Patrick 1,530 feet.

In New South Wales the deepest mine in which payable gold has been obtained is at Adelong. Government offered £1,000 for payable gold at 800 feet, and the reward was obtained by the "Great Victoria Mining Co., Adelong." obtained gold at a depth of 816 feet, 1877.

MINT, ROYAL.

The establishment of a Mint, or branch of the Royal Mint, in Australia, first considered in the Legislative Council, 1851.

The formal sanction of Her Majesty's Government for the establishment of a branch of the Royal Mint at Sydney, received, July, 1853. [The stipulation was, that the dies from which the colonial coins were to be struck were to be provided by the Master of the Mint in London. Precise directions were given as to the fineness and weight of the coins, which were in those respects to correspond with the coin of the realm ; colonial coins were from time to time to be transmitted to England, to be assayed and tested by the Master of the Royal Mint, and the principal officers were to be appointed by the Crown. Captain (now Colonel) Edward Wolstenholme Ward, of the Royal Engineers, was appointed first Deputy-Master of the branch of the Royal Mint in the colony, at a salary of £1,000 per annum, May 13, 1855.]

Victorian Mint, Melbourne, opened, June 12, 1872. Colonel Ward first Deputy Master.

First issue of 40,000 sovereigns from the Melbourne Mint, July 8, 1872.

Total quantity of gold dust or bullion received at Sydney branch from its opening to December, 1878, inclusive, 11,591,320,465oz.; its total value being £44,488,539 19s. 3d. Total value of gold dust or bullion issued during the same period, £44,490,307 4s. 1d.

Total quantity of gold dust or bullion received at Melbourne branch from its opening to December 31, 1877, was 2,159,166·71oz.; its total value being, £8,590,158 16s. 10d. The total value of

gold dust or bullion issued during the same period was £8,560,568 5s. 7d.

MISSIONARIES.

Arrival of the "Nautilus" with the "Duff" missionaries from Tahiti, April 14, 1798.

Wesleyan Missionary Society established in Hokianga, New Zealand. 1822.

Rev. D. Tyerman and G. Bennett, Esq., deputation from London Missionary Society, visited Australia, August 20, 1824.

The German mission projected by Dr. Lang to Christianize the blacks at Moreton Bay, and to afford security to ships wrecked on the adjacent coast. Two clergymen and 18 lay missionaries formed the mission, the chief missionary being Schmidt, arrived from Berlin. 1838.

The Rev. Joseph Holbert Smales, for many years a town missionary in Hobart Town, died, December 30, 1870. [Sixty-seven years previously, in 1803, Mr. Smales, then a midshipman on the sloop-of-war "Porpoise," performed divine service to the first assembly of Tasmanian Christians, on her deck, when she was lying off Flagstaff Battery, Hobart Town, long before there was a place of worship built on the banks of the Derwent.]

MORETON BAY, 1835
Rex Nan Kivell Collection

MOA, THE, an enormous bird which inhabited New Zealand up to seventeenth or eighteenth century, ranging from size of a goose to 12 or 14 feet in height; though now extinct remains have been found to form almost perfect skeletons.

MONARO PLAINS. Captain Currie and Brigadier-Major Ovens discovered Monaro Plains, and called them Brisbane Downs. June 3, 1823.

MONEY. [See CURRENCY.]

MORETON BAY.

Captain Cook entered a Bay which he named Moreton Bay in honor of the Earl of Moreton, who was president of the Royal Society, May 17, 1770.

Captain Flinders, whilst exploring the northern territory entered Moreton Bay, 1800.

Mr. Oxley, Surveyor-General of New South Wales, was sent on an expedition to Moreton Bay to search for a spot to form a penal settlement.   He was accompanied by Lieutenant Stirling and Mr. Uniacke, October 23, 1823.

The expedition under Oxley, after having visited Port Curtis and surveyed the Boyne River, returned and anchored (in the " Mermaid ") in Moreton Bay, November 28, 1823.

Mr. Oxley and party, of the " Mermaid," rescued two men, named Pamphlet and Finnegan, from the blacks ; Pamphlet told Oxley of the existence of a fine river flowing into the Bay, November 30, 1823.

Mr. Oxley explored the river falling into the Bay, which he named the Brisbane, in honor of Sir Thomas Brisbane, Governor of New South Wales, December 2, 1823.

Mr. Oxley sent in a report of his explorations, in which he recommended Moreton Bay as a place for establishing a penal settlement, February, 1824.

Lieutenant Miller, of the 40th Regiment, appointed first Commandant of the Moreton Bay settlement, September 12, 1824.

A settlement was formed at a place called Redcliffe Point, under direction of Mr. Oxley, but it was soon found unsuitable, and was removed to the present site of Brisbane (aboriginal name Meganchan), September 12, 1824.

Sir Thomas Brisbane was the first Governor who visited Moreton Bay ; and Brisbane, the town, was called after him, November 10, 1825.

Moreton Bay appointed a place to which offenders convicted in New South Wales, and being under sentence of transportation, should be sent, August 15, 1826.

Visit of Governor Darling to Moreton Bay, 1827.

Allan Cunningham made an overland journey from Sydney, 1827.

Rev. John Vincent, C.E., appointed Chaplain of the Moreton Bay settlement by Governor Darling, September 18, 1828.

During the sixteen years of the "convict period" there were 8 commandants.   The following table gives the duration of their command :—

Captain Miller	1824		
Captain Bishop	1824	to	1825
Captain Logan	1825	to	1830
Captain Clunie	1830	to	1835
Captain Fyans	1835	to	1837
Major Cotton	1837	to	1839
Lieutenant Gravett	May, 1839 to July, 1839		
Lieutenant Gorman	1839	to	1840

Captain Logan, third commandant, was represented as being remarkably unpopular, and charged with being excessively tyrannical : "old hands" say that the lash was ever resounding in the camp during his sway.   He was murdered by the blacks (supposed at the instigation of the convicts), while on a botanical expedition in the neighbourhood of the Limestones (Ipswich), November 16, 1830. [His remains were brought to Sydney, and interred with military honours, at Garden Island, in the same tomb as those of Judge Bent, a friend of his early youth.]

The first squatters on the Darling Downs were Patrick Leslie, James Leith Hay, and Arthur Hodgson, about 1830.

The convict hospital (now Police barracks) erected, 1827.

The Chaplains residence (now Colonial Secretary's office) erected. 1828.

The Prisoners' barracks (now Supreme Court) erected, 1828.

The Military barracks (now Treasury) erected, 1828.

The Windmill (now Observatory) erected, 1829.

Female factory (now Central Police Court) erected, 1830.

The Superintendent of Convicts' quarters (now Railway Engineers' office) erected, 1829.

The Surgeon's quarters (now occupied by Inspector of Police) erected, 1831.

Military hospital (now Public Works office) erected, 1832.

First steamer, "James Watt," anchored in Moreton Bay, August, 1837.

A young convict who had escaped fourteen years previously, was found with the natives on the Mary River ; he had almost forgotten his own language, 1837.   [He was found by an expedition party, among whom were Andrew Petrie, Hon. Mr. Wriothesley, H. Stuart Russell, and Mr. Jallath ; another convict was also found by the same party, who had been twice with the blacks, once seven years and this time eighteen months.]

Andrew Petrie appointed Foreman of Works, Royal Engineer department, 1837.

The convict settlement broken up, May 21, 1839.

First free settlers arrived in Brisbane, 1840. [Their names were John Williams, Thos. Dowse, G. Edmondstone, G. S. Le Breton, David Bow, John Richardson, Wm. Holman Berry, R. Little, P. Phelan, and M. Moriarty.]

First drays brought over Cuningham's Gap to Brisbane, October 19, 1840.

Sir George Gipps visited Moreton Bay settlement, March, 1842.

Moreton Bay proclaimed open to settlement, May 4, 1842.

First sale of Moreton Bay land held in Sydney, December 7, 1842.

The Governor visited Moreton Bay to make arrangements for the sale of lands and to mark out the chief reserves, 1842.

First land sale took place in Brisbane, August 9, 1843.

Moreton Bay proclaimed a warehousing port, July 20, 1846.

First Government emigrant ship the "Artimesia" arrived, December 13, 1848.

The "Fortitude," emigrant ship, sent out under Dr. Lang's auspices, arrived Jan. 21, 1849.

First exile ship, "Mount Stuart Elphinstone," reached Moreton Bay, October 31, 1849.

First bank opened in Moreton Bay, November 14, 1850.

First Circuit Court in Moreton Bay District held, 1851.

The first direct shipment of wool to England was made February, 1851.

Government Resident first appointed at Moreton Bay, January 1, 1853.

CLEMENT HODGKINSON ON AN EXPEDITION TO MORE-
TON BAY, 1843
Rex Nan Kivell Collection

Governor Sir Charles Fitzroy visited Moreton
Bay, March 20, 1854.

Separation granted from N.S.W., December
10, 1859.

MORRILL, OR MURRELL, JAMES, who was
wrecked in 1846 on a voyage from Sydney to
China in the barque "Peruvian" on Cape Cleveland, N.E. Coast of Australia, and who had lived
with the blacks for 17 years, made himself known
to some stockmen in the North of Queensland,
on January 25, 1863. Born near Maldon,
England, in 1824; died at Port Denison, Queensland, October 30, 1865.

MOUNTAINS.

The highest mountain in Australia is Mount
Kosciusko, in the Australian Alps ; its altitude
is 6,510 feet. The Bogong Range, Gipps Land,
Victoria, is 6,508 feet.

New South Wales.—The principal ranges of
mountains are the Interior Ranges, the Great
Dividing Chain, and the Coast Ranges. The
former lie near the western boundary of the
colony, and form the western watershed of the
Darling River ; the chief of them are the Grey
Range, and the Stanley or Barrier Range. The
loftiest elevation in the Grey Range is Mount
Arrowsmith, 2,000 feet high ; and in Stanley
Range, Mount Lyell, about the same height.
The Great Dividing Chain extends throughout
the whole length of the eastern and south-eastern
coasts of Australia, and forms the main watershed of the country. It consists of seven main
branches, viz. : (1) the New England Range
(highest point Ben Lomond, 5,000 feet ; (2)
the Liverpool Range (highest point Oxley's
Peak, 4,500 feet) ; (3) the Blue Mountain
Range (highest point, Mount Beemarang,
4,100 feet) ; (4) the Cullarin Range (highest
point, Mundoonen, 3,000 feet) ; (5) the
Gourock Range (highest point, Jindulian,
4,300 feet) ; (6) the Monaro Range (highest
point, head of Kybean River, 4,010 feet) ;
and (7) the Muniong Range (highest point, Mount
Kosciusko, 6,510 feet). This last is about 700 feet
below the line of perpetual snow. All this series is
connected with the Cordillera dividing the

eastern and western watersheds. The Coast
Ranges lie on the east side of the Great Dividing Chain, and parallel to it for a very considerable distance. They generally form the
edge of the elevated table-land, upon which lies
the Great Dividing Chain. The loftiest peaks
of these are Mount Seaview, 6,000 feet, Mount
Coolungubbera, 3,712 feet, and Mount Buda-
wang, 3,800 feet high. The most remarkable
of the isolated mountains and groups are Mount
Doubleduke, Whoman, Elanie, Yarrahappini,
Kibbora, The Three Brothers, Mount Talawah,
Dromedary, Mumbulla, and lastly, Imlay, or
Baloon—2,900 feet high.

New Zealand.—The mountains of New
Zealand are more lofty than those in Australia.
In the province of Wellington is an active
volcano called Tongariro, 6,500 feet, the peak
of Ruaperhui rises to an elevation of 9,100 feet
above the sea-level. Mount Egmont is about
8,300 feet high ; it rises in an almost perfect
cone from a base of 30 miles in diameter, and
its summit, which is an extinct crater, is
covered with perpetual snow. In the Southern
Island, Mount Cook, in the province of Canterbury, is the loftiest peak, being 13,000 feet high.
Mount Arthur, near Nelson, is about 8,000 feet
high. Amongst the peaks in Otago province is
Mount Earnslaw, at the head of Lake Wakatipu,
9,000 feet, and Mount Tutoko, near Martin's
Bay, 8,000 feet.

Queensland.—The highest peak on the Coast
Range is Mount Dalrymple, 4,250 feet. The
Bellenden Kerr Range is in the north ; its
highest point is 5,400 feet.

South Australia.—The highest points of the
Main or Flinders Range are Mount Lofty, 2,334
feet above the sea-level — overshadowing
Adelaide ; Mount Barker 2,331 feet, Mount
Horrocks 1,984 feet, the Razorback 2,992 feet,
Mount Bryan 3,012 feet, and Black Rock Hill
2,750 feet. The highest elevation of the Gawler
Range, in Port Lincoln Peninsula, is about
2,000 feet.

Tasmania.—The highest mountain in Tasmania is 5,069 feet in height. Among the peaks
are Row Tor 3,895 feet, Mount Barrow 4,644
feet, Mount Victoria 3,964 feet, Ben Nevis 3,910
feet, Ben Lomond 5,010 feet, Mount Nicholas
2,812 feet, Brown Mountain 2,598 feet, Table
Mountain 3,596 feet, Miller's Bluff 3,977 feet,
Dry's Bluff 4,257 feet, Quamby Bluff, Ironstone
Mountain, 4,736 feet, Cradle Mountain 5,069
feet (the highest in the colony), the Du Cane
Range, Mount Olympus, Mount Humboldt,
Mount Hugel, Mount William 4,360 feet, and
Mount Hobhouse 4,031 feet, Mount Roland,
4,047 feet, Black Bluff 4,381 feet, Valentine's
Peak 3,637 feet, the Elden Range 4,789 feet,
the Frenchman's Cap 4,756 feet, Wyld's Crag
4,399 feet, Mount Field 4,721 feet, Mount
Anne, the Arthur Range, 3,668 feet, Mount
Picton 4,340 feet, Mount Wellington 4,166 feet,
Adamson's Peak 4,017 feet, and Mount La
Perouse 3,800 feet.

Victoria.—The highest peaks of the mountain
system of Victoria are the following :—Bogong

6,508 feet, Feathertop 6,303 feet, Hotham 6,100 feet, Cobboras 6,025 feet, Cope 6,015 feet, Buller 5,911 feet, Gibbo 5,764 feet, Wills 5,758 feet, Howitt 5,715 feet, Buffalo 5,645 feet, Twins 5,575 feet, Wellington 5,363 feet, Tamboritha 5,381 feet, Cobbler 5,342 feet, Kent 5,129 feet, Forest Hill 5,000 feet.

Western Australia.—The highest mountain in the colony is Mount William, of the Darling Range. It is situated in the Murray district, about 60 miles inland, and has an altitude of 3,000 feet above the sea-level. The Blackwood, the Victoria, and the Roe Ranges rise to the height of 1,500 to 2,000 feet above the sea-level.

MUNICIPAL.

The Corporation question agitated at Sydney, 1832.

A Bill for incorporating the City of Sydney, introduced in the Council of New South Wales; but the agitation with respect to the qualification clauses produced so much discussion that the Bill was withdrawn. 1840.

First municipality, Adelaide, established August 19, 1840.

First municipal elections, Adelaide, October 31, 1840.

A Bill was passed, after several amendments, to incorporate the towns of Sydney and Melbourne. On the Bill, at first, being brought in, it met with much opposition, and several meetings were held to petition against the same, on the grounds that the Legislative Council, being composed of nominees of the Crown, had no right to establish corporate bodies with powers of taxation, such power belonging only to the representatives of the people; that they ought to have assigned to them, as well as all town taxes and assessments, all public lands within the precincts of the town, not vested in the ordnance department, including Hyde Park and Sydney Common, and also certain fees, tolls, and other such sources of revenue. The qualifications of voters and candidates were:—A person entitled to vote must have occupied a house or warehouse, twelve months previous to enrolment, of the annual value of £25. The qualification for alderman, councillor, auditor, or assessor was real estate of £100, or property valued at the annual value of £50. The city was divided into six wards, each of which was to elect four councilmen, and these again were to elect an alderman for each ward amongst their own body, or choose one of the citizens at large; the Mayor to be elected by the aldermen and councilmen. July 20, 1842.

The first municipal election took place in Sydney, when four councillors for each of the respective wards were elected, and on the 9th of the same month six aldermen, and the Mayor (John Hosking) were elected in the marketshed by the councillors. The first aldermen elected were:—Bourke Ward, Mr. John Hosking (elected first Mayor); Gipps Ward, Mr. Robert Owen; Brisbane Ward, Mr. George Allen; Phillip Ward, Mr. J. R. Wilshire; Macquarie Ward, Mr. Thomas Broughton; Cook

Ward, Mr. Francis Mitchell. November 1, 1842.

First Civic Election, Melbourne, December 1, 1842.

Henry Condell, the first Mayor of Melbourne, was elected by a majority of 34 over Edward Curr. 1842.

Sir George Gipps, in a despatch dated November 27, 1842, stated that he had decided that the Mayor of Sydney should be styled "Right Worshipful," and that the Mayor of Melbourne should be "Worshipful." This was approved of by Lord Stanley, in a despatch of July 3, 1843.

A select Committee of the Legislative Council was appointed to inquire into the working of the Corporation of Sydney. Amongst other matters the report stated, that "the committee was perfectly satisfied, from the evidence they had taken, that the body had entirely lost the confidence of the citizens, and was regarded as an impediment to the improvement of the city." The committee recommended that the Act of Council incorporating the City of Sydney should be repealed, and that an Act should be passed, appointing three commissioners, in whom should be vested all the powers then exercised by the corporation, and an Act to that effect was afterwards passed. 1849.

First Municipal Election in Tasmania, January 1, 1853.

An Act was passed, abolishing the Municipal Corporation, Sydney, substituting in its stead three paid commissioners to carry out the works necessary for draining the city and supplying it with water. 1853.

Commissioners, who superseded the Sydney City Council, commenced their duties, January, 1854.

Municipality of Emerald Hill, Victoria, was the first to avail itself of Captain Clarke's law of Local Self-Government. 1855.

William Carter, first Mayor of Hobart Town, 1857.

An Act passed for the re-establishment of a Municipal Council in Sydney, 1857.

Brisbane incorporated, September 7, 1859.

Sydney Municipal Council unable to meet its liabilities. Half the employes discharged. The Government advanced £10,000, January 7, 1875.

Estate of the Sydney Corporation sequestrated by order of the Chief Commissioner of Insolvency, November 24, 1876.

Sydney Municipal Council unable to meet its liabilities. Half of the employés discharged; the Government advanced £10,000. 1879.

MURRAY, River. Upper part, the **Hume**, discovered by Hamilton Hume, November 16, 1824; lower part, named after Sir **George** Murray, Secretary of the Colonies, discovered by Captain Sturt, 1829; Captain Sturt **sailed** down the Murray in 1833; first navigated **by** W. R. Randall in his steamer the "Mary Anne," July, 1853; first navigated by Cadell as far as Albury in the steamer "Albany." August 27, 1853. [*See* Rivers.]

MURRUMBIDGEE, RIVER, discovered by Captain Currie and Brigadier-General Ovens (who went on an expedition to examine the country south of Lake George), June 1, 1823; Hume and Hovell reached the Murrumbidgee, October 19, 1824; Hume and Hovell crossed the Murrumbidgee, October 22, 1824; the Murrumbidgee first traversed by a steamer, as far as the town of Gundagai, 1858. [*See* RIVERS.]

MUSEUMS.

The Australian Museum, Sydney, originated by a number of gentlemen interested in the promotion of science in Australia. Founded, 1836. [The first president was Alexander Macleay, then Colonial Secretary.]

National Museum, Melbourne, opened in present building, May 1, 1864.

South Australian Museum opened, 1855.

Queensland Museum, Brisbane opened, 1870.

Canterbury, New Zealand, 1858.

The Industrial and Technological Museum of Victoria opened, September 7, 1870.

The Legislative Assembly of New South Wales decided on opening the Museum and Free Library on Sundays, March 26, 1878.

MUSIC, OPERA, AND MISCELLANEOUS ENTERTAINMENTS.

Vincent Wallace left Sydney Feb. 14, 1838.

Isaac Nathan, the great pianist and composer, arrived in Melbourne February 5, 1841. [He gave some concerts prior to his departure for Sydney.]

Catherine Hayes first appeared at the Victoria Theatre, Sydney, September 25, 1854; received a public testimonial at the Victoria Theatre, Sydney, October 17, 1854; left Sydney October 18, 1854.

Miska Hauser appeared at the Victoria Theatre, Sydney, November 11, 1854.

Ali Ben-Sou-Alle appeared at the Victoria Theatre, December 21, 1854.

The wizard, Jacobs, appeared at the Victoria Theatre, March 12, 1855.

The Bacchus Minstrels (first negro troupe) appeared at the Victoria Theatre, Sydney, October 29, 1855.

N. C. Bochsa (celebrated harpist), appeared at the Prince of Wales Theatre, Sydney, December 22, 1855.

Anna Bishop appeared at the Prince of Wales Theatre, December 22, 1855.

Tonic-Sol-fa, introduced to Sydney by Mr. J. C. Fisher. (2000 teachers have been trained; and in 1876, 32,460 public school children in New South Wales were being instructed in the method.) 1855.

Catherine Hayes gave concerts in Sydney and Melbourne. Two concerts given for the charities of the two cities produced an amount of £1,000. 1856.

Linley Norman appeared at the Prince of Wales Theatre, Sydney, July 8, 1856.

Walter Sherwin appeared at the Prince of Wales Theatre, Sydney, July 8, 1856.

Mme. Clarisse Cailly appeared at the Royal

THE SYDNEY MUSEUM
Gibbs, Shallard, & Co.'s *Illustrated Guide to Sydney*, 1882

THE LEICHHARDT CONCERT
The Illustrated Sydney News, 1854

Hotel, Sydney, August 15, 1856.

Farquharson appeared at the Prince of Wales Opera House, Sydney, July 8, 1856.

Herr Strebinger, first appearance at Victoria Theatre, Sydney, January 29, 1859.

First appearance of Carandini Opera Company at the Prince of Wales Theatre, Sydney, Mme. Marie Carandini, Mme. Sara Flower, Miss Emma Howson, Messrs. W. Sherwin, John Gregg, Frank Howson, and others ; Conductor, Mr. L. H. Lavenu. June, 1859.

Emma Stanley, in her entertainment of Seven Ages, at the Victoria Theatre, Sydney, July 4, 1859.

Madame Jaffa, pianist, first appearance at Exchange, Sydney, September 19, 1859.

Grand (Sydney) University Festival, to inaugurate the opening of the new hall, lasting six days ; concerts on two of the days both morning and evening. Commenced, July 19, 1859.

H. Squires, Lucy Escott, and Armes Beaumont appeared in Sydney, 1863.

Madame Simonsen, vocalist, Herr Martin Simonsen, violinist, gave first concerts in Australia in Melbourne, August 25, 1865, and at the Exchange, Sydney, December, 1865.

Signor Cesare Cutolo, an eminent musician, killed on board the "Alexandra" by a spar falling on him. 1867. [The untimely fate of Signor Cutolo was deeply lamented in Sydney, Melbourne, Adelaide, and other places in the colonies, where he was well known and highly esteemed for his talent as a musician, and his rare

personal qualities causing him to be a welcome guest wherever he visited. Born in 1826, he early imbibed the idea of freedom for his country. After passing through the Conservatoire of Music at Naples, where he obtained the highest diplomas from the various professors (amongst whom were some of the greatest composers of the day), he joined the Garibaldians, being appointed on the staff of the Italian liberator, and serving in most of his campaigns, becoming the personal friend of his two sons, Ricciotti and Menotti Garibaldi. In 1860 he arrived in Sydney, New South Wales, where he settled as a professor of music, and married the widow of Mr. Heath, a chemist of that city, both of whom were well known for their love and support of music, being themselves talented amateurs. Amongst his other pupils was the son of the Governor General, Sir William Denison. A concert, given by Signor Cutolo in aid of the Randwick Asylum for Destitute Children, realised a large sum for the institution. Signor Cutolo subsequently accepted a very influential invitation to settle in Victoria, and it was during his return passage to that colony, after a visit to his friends in Sydney, that the terrible accident happened to him which resulted in his death. Signor Cutolo was reclining on the poop of the "Alexandra," Signora Cutolo by his side reading to him, when the spanker-boom, which had been only carelessly fastened, came down with a run, striking the unfortunate gentleman on the neck. He lingered a few hours, dying just as the vessel entered Port Phillip Heads. An action was brought by his widow against the A.S.N. Company; it was settled by arbitration, the Company paying £1,500 and costs. A beautiful tombstone, in the form of an obelisk, was erected in Melbourne to his memory by his widow and friends.]

Charles Edward Horsley, eminent composer and musician, gave his first concert in Sydney, July, 1866.

Maud Fitz-Stubbs, juvenile amateur pianist, first appeared in public at six years of age, at C. E. Horsley's concert, Academy of Music, December 21, 1867.

Signora Barratti, opera singer, first appeared in Melbourne, February 5, 1868.

Robert Heller and Miss Haidee Heller, prestidigitateurs and pianists, performed in Sydney, January, 1871.

Robert Heller gave a largely attended farewell entertainment at the School of Arts previous to his departure from the colony, January 21, 1871.

Arabella Goddard, pianist, appeared at the Masonic Hall, Sydney, June 12, 1873.

Ilma de Murska, vocalist, appeared at Masonic Hall, Sydney, November 2, 1875.

Marriage at Sydney, by Dr. Fullerton, of Ilma de Murska, the "Hungarian nightingale," to Alfred Anderson, R.A.M., December 29, 1875.

Mr. Alfred Anderson, celebrated Australian pianist died in Melbourne, aged 28 years, March 22, 1876.

Marriage at Otago, N.Z., of Ilma (de Murska) Maria Thea Anderson (widow of Alfred Anderson) to John Thomas Hill, K.S.R.A.M., May 15, 1876.

Davenport Brothers, spiritualists and conjurors, first appeared in Australia, at Melbourne, September 2, 1876.

Victorian Academy of Music (Bijou Theatre) opened, November 6, 1876.

Ernest Hutchinson, the Australian Mozart, 7½ years of age, gave an exhibition of extraordinary musical ability at the Athenæum, Melbourne, March 22, 1877.

Eliza Wallace Bushelle, died, August, 1878. [She was the daughter of Mr. Wallace, for many years bandmaster to the 29th Regiment, and sister of the late Mr. Vincent Wallace, the composer. At ten years of age she was able to play difficult airs on the violin, and possessed remarkable vocal ability. About the year 1843 she appeared at Sydney, at public concerts, in company with her brother and Mr. John Bushelle, the latter of whom she subsequently married. At the early age of 21 she became a widow, and returning to Europe with her brother, was engaged by Mendelssohn to sing in the "Elijah" at Vienna. After fulfilling a series of engagements in Europe and America, she again came to Australia, about the year 1864, and settled in Sydney as a teacher of music, in which capacity she was remarkably successful.]

The first of the Elmblad concerts given in the Town Hall, Melbourne, June 8, 1878. [Mrs. Elmblad was a Miss Menzies, of Melbourne.]

The first of the Elmblad concerts in Sydney commenced, July 15, 1878.

Madame Carlotta Tasca, English pianist, first appeared in Melbourne, July, 1878.

Madame Olga Duboin, Russian pianist, first appeared in Melbourne, August, 1878.

Grand musical recitals at the University in honour of Beethoven, December 16, 1878. [*See* DRAMA.]

MUSTARD. First Mustard Factory, South Australia, established, May 28, 1873.

MUSTER. Muster was the term originally employed in place of census. It was usual to have periodically a general muster of the inhabitants of the settlement of N.S.W. [*See* CENSUS.]

MUTINIES.

A vessel bound to Norfolk Island with provisions was piratically seized when within one day's sail of the port. Mr. Harwood, the master, and crew where compelled to navigate the ship under the direction of one Watson, the leader of the mutiny; but arriving in the Bay of Islands, New Zealand, they were captured by two whalers who were anchored in that port, and were carried back by Mr. Drake in his vessel to Sydney. 1827.

The "Admiral Benbow" seized and plundered by pirates in lat. 13° N., long. 26° 40′ W., April 11, 1829.

Mutiny and murder on board the "Indefatigable" (formerly the "Calder," Captain Dillon), July 22, 1829. [The "Indefatigable," Captain Joseph Hunter, with F. W. Lofgren, chief officer, which left Conception June 11, 1829, with a cargo of wheat for Sydney, was seized by the Chilian crew in lat. 17° 13′ S., and long. 127° 51′ W. The captain was murdered, and five of the crew were turned adrift in an open boat, but managed to reach Resolution Island on August 7, and Otaheite on August 18. From the latter place the "Tiger" brought them to Sydney. Lofgren was compelled to navigate the "Indefatigable," and brought it to the Island of Guam, where he gave information which led to the imprisonment of the mutineers. They were brought from Antigua to Manila by the influence of Captain Rous, of H.M.S. "Rainbow," and six of them were tried and executed. The "Indefatigable" was condemned as a prize to the Spanish Government.]

Mutiny on board the ship "Eleanor," in Sydney harbour; two of the prisoners were shot and several others wounded by the guard, August 1, 1831. [*See* NORFOLK ISLAND.]

N

NAMOI (OR PEEL) RIVER. Discovered by Sir Thomas Mitchell, Dec. 22, 1831. [It had previously been described by one George Clarke.]

NAPOLEON'S LAND. M. M. Baudin and Hamelin in command of the French ships "Le Géographe" and "Le Naturaliste," commenced their survey of the coast of New Holland from Wilson's Promontory to Cape Leuwin, and called it Napoleon's Land, (M. Peron was naturalist to the expedition), 1801. Concluded the survey March 8, 1802.

NATIONAL GALLERY, VICTORIA, opened May 24, 1875.

NATURALIZATION. Aliens in Victoria not entitled to vote at Parliamentary elections until after a period of three years after naturalization. 1859.

NEPEAN POINT, so called by Lieutenant James Grant in honour of Sir Evan Nepean, Secretary to the Admiralty, 1802.

NEPEAN RIVER, New South Wales, discovered by Governor Phillip, July 6, 1788.

NEW CALEDONIA.

New Caledonia is an island in the South Pacific Ocean, about 200 miles in length and 30 miles in breadth, lying between 20° and 22° 30' S. lat., and 164° and 167° E. long. It was discovered by Captain Cook, September 4, 1774. It lies about 720 miles E.N.E. of the coast of Queensland, and Noumea, the capital, is distant from Sydney 1,050 miles. The island is of volcanic origin, and a range of mountains run down its length, in some parts attaining an elevation of 8,000 feet; it is surrounded by coral reefs and sandbanks, and possesses secure harbours,—Port Belade on its N.E. and Port St. Vincent on the S.W. coasts. The soil is very fruitful, producing cocoanuts, bananas, and bread-fruit. Sugar-cane also grows when cultivated, and vines grow wild. The inhabitants

BALARDE, THE FRENCH SETTLEMENT AT NEW CALEDONIA
The Illustrated Sydney News, 1854

resemble the Papuan race, and were for a long time considered docile and well disposed.

The island was seized by the French Government, September 20, 1853, and colonized. The principal interests in this island are British. The French Government, in December, 1864, redressed the outrages committed on the British missionaries at a station established in 1854. Its population is estimated at 60,000 souls. It has been used by the French Government as a penal settlement, both for déportés and transportés. The European population is about 16,000, 3,000 of whom are civilians, the remainder military, convicts, and exiles.

Rochefort and five other Communists escaped from New Caledonia, reaching Newcastle, New South Wales, March 27, 1874. Rochefort left Sydney by Californian mail, April 11, 1874.

Eleven Europeans massacred and fourteen wounded by New Caledonia natives, October 12, 1867.

In June, 1878, the aboriginals in the Bouloupari district rose and slaughtered a man named Chene and his family at Dezarnauld's station. To this man's abuse of the power entrusted to him, and general cruelty towards the natives may be attributed the rebellion. After the murder of Chene and family the gendarmes from La Fou proceeded to arrest the murderers, whereat the natives rose *en masse* and massacred General Gally Passe Bosc and gendarmes, and at Goinde, Dogny, and Bouloupari, killing all the whites with whom they came in contact (June 24, 25, 1878) to the number of 128. The total strength of the rebels was estimated at about 1,000 men under a chief named Atai, a man of great intelligence and strong physique. He was ably seconded in his command by a chief named

Baptiste. For some time the rebels held their ground against the troops and volunteers sent to quell the rising, but other tribes of blacks having been enlisted on the side of the Government, and the chiefs Atai and Baptiste being slain, the rebellious tribes were by degrees driven back from their strongholds ; and from a despatch, dated Bourail, January 6, 1879, it appears that a severe blow has been given to them at Cape Goulvain in an engagement in which an immense number of the insurgents fell, whilst the French loss was two killed (one an officer) and four wounded. A large quantity of arms and ammunition were also captured from the natives. Since this fight parties of the Kanakas are daily tendering their submission.

Heads of rebel chiefs Atai and Baptiste exhibited in New Caledonia, September 3, 1878.

Thirteen Europeans massacred on river Poya by natives, November, 1878.

Nine persons massacred at Kone, November 20, 1878.

Agreement with Mr. Higginson, an English colonist, signed by the French Government, granting him the services of 300 convicts for a period of 20 years, at the charge of one penny per day per man, the Government agreeing to feed and clothe them during that time. 1879.

5,000,000 francs voted by the French Government for the construction of a cable from Moreton Bay to New Caledonia, January, 1879.

NEWCASTLE.

New South Wales (Native name, *Mulubinba*). Settlement formed, April, 1804.

Christ Church founded by Captain James Wallis of 46th Regiment, 1817.

Christ Church opened, 1821.

Newcastle appointed a place for holding Quarter Sessions, June 19, 1826.

Newcastle formed into a separate bishopric, 1847.

Newcastle lighted with gas, October 29, 1867.

A VIEW OF NEWCASTLE
The Illustrated Sydney News, 1855

A GROUP OF NEW GUINEA NATIVES
The Australasian Sketcher, 1875

NEW GUINEA.

This large island lies immediately south of the Equator and north of Australia, between the Asiatic Sea on the west and the Pacific Ocean on the east. The general direction of the island is W.N.W. and E.S.E. The northern part is situated in 0° 19′ S. lat., the west point in nearly the same latitude and in 131° 12′ E. long., and the south-east point (Cape Moresby) in 10° 34′ S. lat. and in 151° 2′ E. long. New Guinea is about 1500 miles in length from north-west to south-east, with a varying breadth of from 200 to 400 miles, and an area of 250,000 square miles. The climate of New Guinea is far more humid than the opposite continent of Australia, owing no doubt to the equatorial stream of vapours and the height of its mountain range, which average more than double that of the Australian Alps. Mount Owen Stanley (so called after the commander of H.M.S. "Rattlesnake") is 13,205 feet, Mount Suckling 11,226 feet, Mount Obree 10,246 feet, Mount Yule, 10,046 feet, and many others of nearly equal altitude, whilst Mount Kosciusko, the highest mountain in Australia, is but 6,510 feet. The country, as far as is known, is covered with dense and varied forests and vast alluvial plains, intersected by noble rivers. The natives, who appear to be far superior to the Australian aboriginals, live in well-built and cleanly-kept villages, and cultivate, with more or less success, rice, maize, yams, cocoa-nuts, sugar-cane, bananas, and other tropical productions ; their patches of cultivation are well dug, kept properly weeded, and are neatly fenced. The natives appear to be of a mixed race, there being a great variety of feature (the Malay, the Jewish, and the Papuan) as well as of colour, whilst some of the explorers brought home by H.M.S. "Basilisk" in 1874, stated that they had seen a tribe with the features of white men, but, of course, dark in colour. The animals are few and mostly marsupial, there being two species of kangaroo which climb trees. The birds are remarkable for the brilliancy of their plumage. Amongst them are varieties of the birds of Paradise, and some remarkable species of fly-catcher and innumerable flocks of parrots.

Don Jorge de Menenis, a Portuguese navigator, appears to have been the first European who visited New Guinea; he remained a month and called it Papua. 1526.

Alvarez de Saavedra, another Portuguese, landed in New Guinea, and forming the idea that it abounded in gold, called it Isla del Dra. 1528.

Yuigo Ortiz de Retz, a Spanish mariner, sailed 250 miles along the northern coast, and named it Neuva Guinea. 1545.

Luis Vaez de Torres sighted New Guinea and sailed for 300 miles along its coast, doubled the south-east point, and landed in several places. 1606.

Schouten visited New Guinea and discovered several volcanoes, 1616.

Dampier visited New Guinea, and on landing met with considerable resistance from the natives, 1699.

Bougainville touched on the coast and called the place where he landed, "Louisade." 1768.

Captain Cook sailed along the coast, but was prevented landing on account of the hostility of the natives, 1770.

Forrest anchored in the Bay of Dory, on the northern extremity of New Guinea, 1775.

D'Entrecasteaux passed along northern coast and through Dampier's Straits, 1792.

Bampton visited New Guinea, 1793.

Captain Bristow visited the northern shores of the smaller islands which were discovered by D'Entrecasteaux, 1806.

Captain Staboomee, of the Dutch ship "Triton," made the earliest attempt to form a European settlement in New Guinea; he took possession in the name of the Dutch Government of all the territory from 141° E. long. westward to the sea, but the unhealthiness of the climate caused the subsequent abandonment of the settlement. 1828.

Another Dutch ship surveyed what was then called the River Doorga, but discovered it was a channel dividing Frederick Henry Island from the south-west mainland. 1835.

Captain D'Urville attempted a flying survey of the southern shore in the "Astrolabe," 1840.

Captain Blackwood in H.M.S. "Fly," surveyed 140 miles of the south-east coast of New Guinea within the great bight, 1845.

Lieutenant Yule, H.M. schooner "Bramble," laid down coast line from termination of Blackwood's survey, along south-east coast of bight 1846.

Captain Owen Stanley in H.M.S. "Rattlesnake," accompanied by the "Bramble" (Lieut Yule), surveyed the south-east peninsular of New Guinea and Bougainville's Louisade, and decided that the latter was a separate island. June, 1848.

An attempt was made in Sydney to form a company for the colonization of New Guinea. A number of subscribers joined with a large amount of capital, but finding the express sanction of the Imperial Government was required, the organization was broken up. 1864.

A party (chiefly gold miners, and including Mr. Percy Tanner, the well-known young caricature artist) attempted to reach New Guinea in the brig "Maria," for the purpose of exploring and searching for gold. They left Sydney January 25, 1872. The vessel was wrecked on the coast of Australia, and some of the survivors were rescued by H.M.S. "Basilisk," Captain Moresby, March 12, 1872. The survivors arrived in Sydney, March 28, 1872.

"Basilisk," Captain Moresby's expedition, left Cape York January 24, 1873; reached Bramble Bay February 8; anchored Redscar Bay February 13; discovered and named Port Moresby and Fairfax Harbour (named in honour of Captain Moresby's father, Admiral Sir Fairfax Moresby) February 20; anchored and remained here February 21; blacksmith of "Basilisk" reported he found gold in quartz a few miles inland, February 25; "Basilisk" returned to Cape York March 1. Second trip: "Basilisk" left Cape York March 20, 1873; reached Yam Bay April 14; discovered and named, in honour of the second Lieutenant, Hayter Island, April 24; Captain Moresby unfurled the British flag on Hayter Island and formally read proclamation taking possession of it and New Guinea in the name of Queen Victoria and by right of discovery April 24, 1873; discovered and named Sir Thomas Dyke Ackland's Bay and Discovery Harbour April 26, 1873.

A minute from the Colonial Secretary, Hon. H. Parkes, was sent to Governor Robinson, advising an effort to be made towards the colonization of New Guinea under British auspices, but no definite answer was received from the Home Government. 1874.

Large meeting held in Sydney in favour of annexing New Guinea, May 11, 1875.

Brig "Chevert" was fitted out by Mr. Macleay, and started from Sydney to explore south-east of New Guinea. The expedition, however, resulted in no discoveries being made, but after an absence of several months it brought back an immense collection of specimens of great interest to naturalists. May 18, 1875.

Andrew Goldie, a botanical collector to a London firm, landed in New Guinea, and commenced explorations along coast in his small vessel, the "Explorer," from Yule Island to the most northerly point of New Guinea, April, 1876.

Mr. M'Farlane visited Kerepenu on the east side of Hood Bay, in the missionary steamer "Ellangowan," May, 1876.

Signor D'Alberti (with party) penetrated upwards of 400 miles up the Fly River, September, 1876.

Expedition under Lieutenant Powell, R.N., left Sydney, and is at present (1879) engaged on a scientific exploring expedition on the north-east of New Guinea. June 1, 1877.

Mr. Goldie, in one of his journeys inland, discovered a large river, which has been named the "Goldie," and also found unmistakable traces of gold. October, 1877.

Mr. Goldie discovered two large and safe harbours, suitable for vessels of the largest size: one he named Millport, and the other Glasgow Harbour. 1878.

The news of Mr. Goldie having discovered gold in New Guinea caused some excitement in New South Wales, and a party of gold-miners started in the "Colonist" to prospect for it, but their search was not attended with much success, although traces of the precious metal were found in some of the streams. Fever caused the party to break up, and the members of it returned as best they could to Australia. Some, however, having become acclimatized, remained, and are carrying on their prospecting. 1878.

Murder of Mr. Ingram, Queensland Government Agent, and party, 1878.

Six native teachers died through New Guinea natives poisoning the water with the Upas tree, January, 1879.

Baron Maclay and Chevalier Bruno started from Sydney on an expedition to New Guinea, March 27, 1879.

Mr. Goldie, who appears up to the present time to have made the most explorations into New Guinea, describes the interior as far as he has penetrated, as a splendid grazing country, covered with many grasses, identical with those of Australia, and well watered with numerous small rivers, and dotted with stunted eucalyptus; here and there are native villages, surrounded by plantations of cocoa-nuts and banana. The natives Mr. Goldie met appeared to be accustomed to fire-arms, but did not appear to consider them of any use except to kill birds with. All the natives are physically powerful, and were in general obliging and civil, but none could be induced to cross the line into the country of another tribe. The Flora of New Guinea he describes as splendid in the extreme, but the Fauna does not present a corresponding variety, except in the class of birds ; snakes are not at all numerous, whilst the peculiar pig indigenous to the country abounds in many places. The butterflies, too, are most gorgeous, and some are of an enormous size. The coast he describes as very unhealthy. The great obstacle to the settlement of the country appears to be the hostility of some few tribes of the natives and the deadliness of the climate, except in the elevated land in the interior. 1879.

DISCOVERIES IN, BY H.M.S. "BASILISK."

The "Basilisk" Captain Moresby, made two trips to the New Guinea coast. The first extended from Cape York to 100 miles east of Redscar Head, and resulted in the discovery of Port Moresby, a magnificent harbour 40 miles east of Redscar Head on the south coast. On inspecting the place whither the ill-fated "Maria" was bound, three channels were discovered, and named Fortegne Straits, Rocky Pass, and China Straits. During the second trip it was discovered that Heath Point consisted of three large islands, which were named respectively Moresby, Mounlyan, and Hayter Islands, their altitude ranging from 800 to 1,600 feet. Possession of these islands by right of discovery was taken in the usual way. A quantity of quartz in which gold is visible, was brought home from the southern side of Fairfax Bay. 1873.

NEW HEBRIDES. Benjamin Boyd imported labour in the shape of natives of the New Hebrides to N.S.W., but the experiment proved a failure. 1847.

NEW SOUTH WALES CORPS. [See MILITARY.]

NEW SOUTH WALES, EARLY SETTLEMENT OF.

Thomas Townshend Viscount Sydney, principal Secretary of State for the Colonies in the administration of Pitt, adopting Captain Cook's suggestion, recommended the establishment of a colony in New South Wales. 1785.

Orders-in-Council for establishing a settlement in New South Wales, December 6, 1785.

H.M.S. "Sirius," 540 tons, 20 guns, 160 men, lying at Deptford, commissioned, and the command given to Arthur Phillip, Esq., for the projected expedition to found an English settlement in New South Wales, October 25, 1786.

H.M.S. "Supply," armed tender brig, 8 guns, 55 men, put in commission, under the command of Lieutenant Henry Ligbird Ball, for the same service, October 25, 1786.

John Hunter appointed second Captain of the "Sirius," with the rank of Post-Captain, December 15, 1786.

The first fleet began to rendezvous at the Mother Bank, Isle of Wight, as follows :— "Sirius," H.M. frigate, Captain John Hunter ; "Supply," H.M. armed tender, Lieutenant Henry Lidgbird Ball ; "Golden Grove," store-

ship ; "Fishburn," storeship ; "Borrowdale," storeship ; "Scarborough," transport, carrying 1 captain, 33 marines, 208 male convicts ; "Lady Penrhyn," transport, carrying 1 captain, 2 lieutentants, 3 privates, and 102 female convicts ; "Friendship," transport, carrying 1 captain, 44 marines and privates, 77 male and 20 female convicts ; "Charlotte," transport, carrying 1 captain, 43 men, 88 male and 20 female convicts ; "Prince of Wales," transport, carrying 2 lieutenants, 30 marines, and 50 female convicts ; "Alexander," transport, carrying 2 lieutenants, 35 marines, and 213 male convicts. March 16, 1787.

Captain Arthur Phillip hoisted his flag on board the "Sirius" as Commodore of the Squadron, and weighed anchor at daybreak, setting sail for New South Wales, May 13, 1787.

Total number of persons who embarked in the first fleet, on Sunday, May 13, 1787 :—

Civil officers	10
Marines, including officers	212
Wives (28) and children (17) of above	45
Other free persons	81
Male convicts	504
Female convicts	192
	1,044

SYDNEY COVE 1819 — WESTERN VIEW
Mitchell Library

The "Supply," having on board Governor Phillip and Lieutenant Gidley King, sighted the coast of New South Wales, January 3, 1788.

The "Supply" anchored in Botany Bay, January 18, 1788.

The "Alexander," "Scarborough," and "Friendship" cast anchor in Botany Bay, January 19, 1788.

The "Sirius," with the remainder of the convoy, the "Golden Grove," "Fishburn," "Borrowdale," "Lady Penrhyn," "Charlotte," and "Prince of Wales," arrived in Botany Bay, January 20, 1788.

Total number of persons landed, 1030. January 20, 1788.

Governor Phillip, accompanied by Captain Hunter and several other officers, set out in boats for a bay north of Botany Bay mentioned by Captain Cook and called Broken Bay. They entered a place on the way marked "Port Jackson," and selected a cove "about half-a-mile in length and a quarter-of-a-mile across the entrance," situated six miles inside this harbour, as the place for the new settlement. In honor of Lord Sydney the Governor named it Sydney Cove. January 22, 1788.

In passing a point of land in the harbour of Port Jackson, the Governor named it Manly Cove, in consequence of the confidence and manly behaviour of the natives there. January 23, 1788.

Governor Phillip, having sufficiently explored Port Jackson and found it in all respects highly calculated to support such a settlement as he was appointed to establish, returned to Botany Bay, January 24, 1788.

Governor Phillip quitted Botany Bay in the "Supply," and, together with the whole of the first fleet, sailed into Port Jackson, January 25, 1788.

The British flag displayed on shore in the harbour of Port Jackson, and around the flagstaff the Governor and principal officers assembled and drank the King's health and success to the new colony. January 26, 1788.

The colony of New South Wales formally taken possession of in the name of the King of England by Governor Arthur Phillip. British colours hoisted on Dawes Battery. Jan. 26, 1788.

On a space previously cleared, the whole colony was assembled; the military drawn up under arms; the convicts stationed apart; and around the Governor those who were appointed to hold the principal offices in the new British settlement. The Royal Commission establishing a regular form of Government on the coast of New South Wales was read by Mr. David Collins, the Judge Advocate. February 7, 1788. [By this instrument Arthur Phillip was constituted Captain-General and Governor-in-Chief over the territory called New South Wales (thus named by Captain Cook), including all the islands adjacent thereto. The office of Lieutenant-Governor was conferred on Major Ross, of the Marines. The Act of Parliament establishing the Courts of Judicature was also read; and, lastly, the patents under the Great Seal.]

OFFICERS OF THE NEW COLONY. Arthur Phillip, Captain, Governor, and Commander-in-Chief of New South Wales; Robert Ross (Major), Lieutenant-Governor; Richard Johnson, Chaplain; John Long, Adjutant; Andrew Millar, Commissary; David Collins, Judge-Advocate; James Furzen, Quarter-master; John White, Surgeon; Thomas Arndell, Assistant-Surgeon; William Balmain, Assistant Surgeon; John Hunter, Captain of the "Sirius;" Phillip Gidley King, Second Lieutenant of the "Sirius;" H. L. Ball (Lieutenant), in command of the "Supply;" John Shortland (Lieutenant), agent for transports; officers in charge of garrison of 200 marines—Captain Campbell, Captain Shea, Captain Meredith, Captain Tench, Lieutenant Johnson, Lieutenant Collins, Lieutenant Kellow, Lieutenant Morrison, Lieutenant Clarke, Lieutenant Faddy, Lieutenant Cresswell, Lieu-

tenant Poulden, Lieutenant Sharp, Lieutenant Davey, Lieutenant Timmins. May 13, 1788.

Three of the transports—the "Scarborough," "Lady Penrhyn," and "Charlotte"—which brought the first convicts to Australia, left for China to load tea for the East India Company. The "Supply" also sailed for Lord Howe Island. May 6, 1788.

Four other ships under Lieutenant Shortland, first fleet, sailed for England—the "Alexander," "Friendship," "Prince of Wales," and "Borrowdale." The "Sirius," "Fishburn," and "Golden Grove" remained. July 14, 1788.

The "Sirius," Captain Hunter, sent to the Cape of Good Hope for supplies. Great want of food in the Colony of New South Wales for seven months. September 30, 1788.

Names of officers on duty in the Settlement of New South Wales, October 1, 1788 :—Major-Commandant, Robert Ross; Captains—James Campbell and John Shea; Captain-Lieutenant—James Meredith and Watkin Tench; First Lieutenants—George Johnstone, John Cresswell, Robert Kellow, John Poulden, John Johnstone, James M. Shairp, Thomas Davey, and Thomas Timmins; Second Lieutenants—Ralph Clarke, William Dawes, and William Faddy; Adjutant, Second Lieutenant John Long; Quarter-master, First Lieutenant James Furzen; Judge-Advocate, David Collins; with 160 privates.

Return of the "Sirius," with four months' provisions. Great rejoicing in the colony. May 9, 1789.

Excursion of Governor Phillip, with Captain Hunter and party, to examine Broken Bay and the Hawkesbury. Returned after a few days' excursion. June 6, 1789.

Again started, June 30, 1789. The Windsor and Richmond bottoms examined. The Kurrajong Mountain and the Nepean Grose River seen. Returned to the Settlement overland, July 13, 1789.

The "Supply" sent to Batavia, under the command of Lieutenant Ball, for provisions. April 17, 1790.

The store ship "Justinian," from England, arrived with a timely supply of provisions for the colonists, June 20, 1790.

The "Gorgon," 44 guns, convoying what is termed the "Second Fleet," arrived in Sydney, with 1,695 male and 68 female convicts; 198 died on the passage. September 21, 1791.

Arrival of the "Atlantic" from Calcutta with a much-required cargo of rice and other provisions, June 20, 1792.

The Settlement placed on full rations after many months' privation, July, 1792.

Parliamentary enquiry into the state of the colony held in England, 1812.

NORTHERN BOUNDARY OF. An Act was passed which provided the limit of New South Wales to the north, in case other Colonies should be formed in that part of Australia. No territory lying to the south of the 26th degree of latitude was to be detached from New South Wales. 1843.

POPULATION OF. On January 1, 1879, the population of New South Wales was estimated by the Registrar General to be 693,743.

NEWSPAPERS.

The first newspaper published in Australia was *The Sydney Gazette and New South Wales Advertiser*, printed by George Howe, Saturday, March 5, 1803. *The Sydney Gazette* issued every Sunday from April 2, 1803 ; *Sydney Gazette* ceased December 23, 1843.

The Derwent Star (first newspaper in Van Diemen's Land), editor, G. P. Harris ; printer, George Clark ; first published January 8, 1810.

The Van Diemen's Land Gazette and General Advertiser (G. Clark, printer), established May 21, 1813.

The Hobart Town Gazette (Andrew Bent), established June 1, 1816. [In 1824 the title of the paper was changed to *The Gazette and Van Diemen's Land Advertiser ;* it ceased August 19, 1825.]

The Australian (editors, William Charles Wentworth and Dr. R. Wardell), established in Sydney October 14, 1824.

The Tasmanian, first newspaper in Launceston, established January 5, 1825.

The Monitor, established in Sydney, 1826.

The Gleaner, Sydney, established 1827.

The Cornwall Press, V.D.L., established April, 1829.

The Launceston Advertiser, V.D.L., established February 9, 1829.

The Sydney Morning Herald first issued as a weekly newspaper April 18, 1831, title *Sydney Herald ;* published bi-weekly May, 1832, on Mondays and Thursdays ; published tri-weekly in July, 1838, on Mondays, Wednesdays, and Saturdays ; published as a daily paper from Thursday, October 1, 1840 ; assumed its present title, August 1, 1842.

The Government Gazette, N.S.W., established March 7, 1832.

The Colonist, Sydney, N.S.W., established 1835.

Port Phillip Advertiser, established January 1, 1836.

The South Australian Register (first printed in London under the title of the *South Australian Gazette* and *Colonial Register*, June 18, 1836), Adelaide, established June 4, 1837.

Bent's News, Sydney, N.S.W., established 1837.

Port Phillip Patriot, established March 5, 1838.

Melbourne Herald, established 1840.

Perth Inquirer, West Australia, established August 16, 1840.

New Zealand Herald and Auckland Gazette, established July 10, 1841.

The Weekly Register, Sydney (Duncan's, ceased in 1846), established 1843.

The Shipping Gazette, Sydney (ceased in 1860), established 1843.

The Atlas, Sydney, established 1844.

The Moreton Bay Courier, established June 24, 1844.

Bell's Life in Sydney (ceased 1872), established 1845.

The (Melbourne) Argus, first issued June 2, 1846.

Heads of the People (ceased 1849), established Sydney, 1847.

The People's Advocate, first issued December 13, 1848.

The Empire, first published in Sydney Dec., 1850 ; temporarily stopped Aug. 28, 1858 ; revived May 26, 1859 ; ceased Feb. 9, 1874.

The Freeman's Journal, Sydney, established 1850.

The Illustrated Sydney News, established 1853.

The Age, Melbourne, established October 17, 1854.

Punch, Melbourne, established 1855.

Punch, Sydney, established 1856.

The Leader (Melbourne), established January 5, 1856.

Darling Downs Gazette, June, 1858.

South Australian Advertiser first issued July 12, 1858.

Queensland Times, Ipswich, July, 1859.

Sydney Mail, established July 7, 1860.

First daily paper published in Brisbane, May 12, 1861.

Rockhampton Bulletin, established July, 1861.

Toowoomba Chronicle, July, 1861.

Northern Argus, Rockhampton, established 1863.

The Australasian, Melbourne, established October 1, 1864.

The Queenslander, Brisbane, established February, 1866.

The Evening News, Sydney, established July 29, 1867.

Bell's Life in Victoria, last issue, January 11, 1868.

The Australian Town and Country Journal, Sydney, established January 8, 1870.

Ipswich Observer, June 1, 1870.

The Telegraph, Brisbane, established October 1, 1872.

The Capricornian, Rockhampton, established January 2, 1875.

The Echo, Sydney, established May 1, 1875.

The Week, Brisbane, established July 1, 1876.

Queensland Punch established October 1, 1878.

Australian (Brisbane) established 1878.

INTERFERENCE WITH THE LIBERTY OF.

An Act passed by Governor Darling and Council " for preventing the mischiefs arising from the printing and publishing newspapers and papers of a like nature by persons not known, and for regulating the printing and publication of such papers in other respects, and also for restraining the abuses arising frem the publication of blasphemous and seditious libels." April 25, 1827. [Banishment for a second offence was one of the punishments.]

An Act passed by Governor Darling and Council imposing a duty upon all newspapers and all papers of a like nature printed to be dispersed to the public. May 3, 1827.

[This was suspended on May 31, 1827, and never enforced.]

Governor Darling's newspaper gagging Act repealed so far as related to banishment of newspaper proprietors for second offence, January 29, 1830.

[*See* Press, Liberty of the.]

NEW ZEALAND.

The colony of New Zealand consists of three principal islands, called respectively the North, the Middle, and the South, or Stewart's Island. There are several small islets (mostly uninhabited) dependent on the colony ; the chief of these are the Chatham Isles and the Auckland Isles. The entire group lays between 34° and 48° S. lat. and 166° and 179° E. long. The principal islands extend in length, 1,100 miles ; but their breadth is extremely variable, ranging from 46 miles to 250 miles ; the average being about 140 miles.

	Sq. miles.	Acres.
The total area of New Zealand is about	100,000 or	64,000,000
Ditto of North Island	44,000 or	28,000,000
Ditto of Middle Island	55,000 or	36,000,000
Ditto of Stewart's Island	1,000 or	640,000

[By this it will be seen the area is somewhat less than that of Great Britain and Ireland.]

The estimated population of New Zealand is, at the latest date, exclusive of Maories.. 417,622
The estimated number of Maories, including half-castes, was, on June 1, 1874 45,570

All of whom dwell on the North Island, except 1,932, who are scattered over the other islands.

Captain Abel Jansen Tasman, the Dutch navigator, discovered New Zealand, December 9, 1642. [He traversed the Eastern Coast from lat. 34° 43″, and entered the strait now called Cook's Straits, but being attacked by the natives, soon after he landed in a place called Massacre Bay. Tasman took possession of New Zealand in the name of Holland.]

Captain Cook, in the " Endeavour," discovered New Zealand, October 7, 1769. [A boy, named Nicholas Young, on board the " Endeavour," first sighted New Zealand. The " Endeavour " first anchored at Poverty Bay.]

Doubtless Bay named, November 9, 1769.

Possession taken of New Zealand by Captain Cook in the name of the King of Great Britain, November 15, 1769.

De Surville, French navigator in the " St. Jean Baptiste," visited Doubtless Bay, and visited Mongonia, N.Z., December, 1769.

Captain Cook left Cape Farewell, New Zealand, March 31, 1770.

Marion Du Fresne, with Crozer, second in command, anchored his two ships, the " Mascarin " and the " Marquis de Castres " in the Bay of Islands, N.Z., May 11, 1772.

Captain Cook arrived at Dusky Bay, N.Z., in the " Resolution," March 26, 1773.

Captain Cook again returned to New Zealand ; anchored in Ship's Cove, Queen Charlotte's Sand, October 18, 1774.

Captain Furneaux, in the " Adventurer," anchored in Ship's Cove, N.Z., April 6, 1773.

Captain Cook, after visiting the South Seas, again returned to New Zealand, October 21, 1773.

The Islands were included in the Royal Commission as a part of the British dominions in virtue of sovereignty established by Captain Cook, 1787.

A vessel was sent to cruise about New Zealand with the avowed purpose of kidnapping one of the aborigines to teach the inhabitants of Norfolk Island the method of dressing flax. Two men were enticed on board off the Bay of Islands and taken to Norfolk Island ; unfortunately, one was a priest and the other a chief, and they would not admit that they knew anything about such work ; they were sent back by the Governor, Captain King, after six months' detention. 1793.

First visit of Maories to Sydney, November 22, 1803.

George Bruce, an English sailor, married the daughter of a Maori chief (Te Pahi) and settled at the Bay of Islands, 1804.

Tippahee, a New Zealand chief, with several others, mostly of rank, arrived and remained some months in the Colony of New South Wales, November 22, 1805, and were the first Maories who visited New South Wales. They returned to New Zealand in the " Lady Nelson," February 25, 1806.

The Gospel first preached in New Zealand, December 25, 1807.

Massacre of the crew and passengers of the " Boyd," numbering 70 souls, at the Bay of Islands. With the exception of one woman, two children, and a cabin boy, all were murdered and eaten, in revenge for the cruelty exercised by the captain towards a chieftain's son. 1809.

A Yorkshire blacksmith, who afterwards became a chaplain, named Samuel Marsden, proposed sending missionaries to New Zealand ; and, in consequence, 25 persons left England for the conversion of the New Zealanders, but subsequently were delayed in Sydney through the news of the massacre of the " Boyd." 1810.

The Rev. Mr. Marsden, accompanied by Messrs. Kendall, Hall, and King, their wives, and several mechanics, with some sheep and cattle, embarked for New Zealand, from New South Wales, in a brig manned by convicts, and were well received by the natives of the Bay of Islands, from whom they purchased 200 acres of land (for 12 axes) on which to form a mission station. November, 1814.

Kidnapping and outrages carried on by Europeans on the New Zealanders. It was attempted to be suppressed by the New South Wales Government appointing Mr. Thomas Kendall and three chiefs (Ruatara, Hongi, and Koro Koro) magistrates for the Bay of Islands territory. 1814.

The right of Great Britain to New Zealand recognised at the peace, 1814.

The first vessel built in New Zealand, by European whalers, was launched at Dusky Bay, Cod-fish Island ; it was 150 tons burthen. 1814.

Massacre by Maories of several of the crews of the ships " Brothers " and " Trial " in Mercury Bay, August 20, 1815.

First vessel in the Waitemata, August 21, 1820.

Mr. William Fairburn, a missionary, purchased 400 acres of land for £10 worth of merchandise, 1821.

Baron de Thierry bought, through Mr. Kendall, of the Mission Society, 40,000 acres of land on the Hokianga River for 36 axes, 1822.

A company was formed in London for the purpose of colonizing New Zealand, in 1825.

A vessel was fitted out by it, and with 60 settlers on board arrived in New Zealand, 1826.

A Sydney vessel with 80 convicts on board, having overpowered their guard, anchored in the Bay of Islands ; an old trader named Duke, with the assistance of the Maories, fought and conquered them, and took them back to Sydney, where nine were hanged. 1827.

Proclamation issued by Governor Darling against the traffic in human heads, carried on by some traders with New Zealand, 1830.

Benjamin Turner opened first grog-shop in New Zealand, 1830.

The " Beagle," with Mr. Charles Darwin on board, visits New Zealand, 1831.

Mr. James Busby was appointed first British Resident, subordinate to the New South Wales Government, to watch over the interests of New Zealand, March 6, 1832.

Barque " Harriet " wrecked at Taranaki ; twelve sailors were slain, and Mr. and Mrs. Guard, two children and 10 sailors were made prisoners. 1834.

Captain Lambert, of H.M.S. " Alligator," presented the native chiefs of New Zealand with a National Flag by order of Sir Richard Bourke, 1834.

17,000 acres of land, or 27 square miles of country, were purchased by missionaries up to this year. 1835.

Baron de Thierry claimed to have purchased for 36 axes all territory north of Auckland, and stated to the British Resident (Mr. Busby) his intention of establishing there in his own person an independent sovereignty; he accordingly issued a proclamation worded, "Charles de Thierry, Sovereign-Chief of New Zealand and King of Muhuheva, &c., &c.," 1835.

Baron de Thierry issued a second and more moderate address to the white inhabitants, dated from Sydney, 1837.

Baron de Thierry landed in his dominions with 93 street loafers from Sydney, unfurled a silken banner, ordered his subjects to back out of his presence, and offered to create the captain of the ship which conveyed him to his kingdom an admiral; funds running short, however, his subjects deserted him, and he subsequently lived in Auckland in an humble way, cleaning flax fibre. 1838.

20,000 acres of land were claimed as having been purchased by white men up to 1839.

New Zealand despatched expedition under command of Colonel William Wakefield to purchase land and form settlement in New Zealand, May 12, 1831.

Captain William Hobson was despatched from England in the "Druid," frigate, Captain Lord Churchill, as Lieutenant-Governor, to take possession of all the islands of New Zealand, in the name of Queen Victoria. The colony was to be a dependency of New South Wales. August, 1839.

"William Byron," March 31, 1841.

First Supreme Court opened, February 28, 1842.

The Waira Massacres occurred, June, 1843. Waira is an extensive valley about 70 miles from the township of Nelson; it was being surveyed by the New Zealand Company's surveyors, when the chief Te Kauparaha forbad the work and destroyed the surveyors' hut, their rods, flags, &c., &c. June, 1843.

A warrant was issued against Kanparaha and Rangihaeata for the destruction of the surveyors' hut and property; and Mr. Thompson, Police Magistrate, accompanied by Captain Wakefield, R N., Captain England, J.P., Mr. Richardson, Crown Prosecutor, Mr. Howard, Company's storekeeper, Mr. Cotterell, surveyor, and several others, and an interpreter, four constables and 12 special constables, the whole amounting to 90 persons, proceeded to put the warrant in force. June 16, 1843. These chieftains resisted the execution of the warrant, when a shameful panic seized the police, who fled disgracefully, and in the utmost disorder, leaving the officers and English gentlemen at the mercy of the Maories, who numbered about 40; they surrendered, but were all massacred, to the number of 17 souls. June 17, 1843.

Captain (afterwards Admiral) Fitzroy appointed Governor, December, 1843.

Government House at Russell, N.Z., burnt May 6, 1844.

Honi Heki, a Maori chieftain, and formerly an assistant in the missionary station, having collected a

THE BAY OF ISLANDS, NEW ZEALAND
Conrad Martens

Wellington founded by the New Zealand Company, January 22, 1840.

Captain Hobson landed, January 29, 1840.

The treaty of Waitangi signed, by which the chiefs ceded a large amount of land, and the town of Auckland established, February 5, 1840.

Mr. C. Wentworth's claim to 10,000,000 acres of land in New Zealand, in the southern island, which he had purchased from Maories, disallowed. [See LAND.] 1840.

New Plymouth founded by the New Zealand Company, 1840.

"Aurora," first emigrant ship to Wellington, anchored in Port Nicholson, January 22, 1841.

New Zealand made an independent Colony of Great Britain; proclamation issued May 3, 1841.

Foundation-stone of Metropolitan Church, St. Paul's, Auckland, laid by Governor Hobson, July 28, 1841.

Captain Arthur Wakefield was sent in command of expedition (by New Zealand Company) to form a settlement to be called Nelson; his three vessels, the "Whitby," the "Will Watch," and the brig "Arrow" left London, April, 1841.

First batch of emigrants for Taranaki arrived in

couple of hundred Maories, cut down the English flagstaff at Kororareka, and held possession of the settlement for two days, bullying the men and brutally assaulting the women, and actually held a prayer meeting with arms in their hands. July, 1844. [He afterwards (March 11, 1845), at the head of about 500 followers, surprised, sacked, and burned the same town, and drove the English soldiers and settlers to take refuge on board the vessels in the harbour.]

The English made an unsuccessful attempt to take Heki's pah, May 8, 1845.

The English troops, under Colonel Despard, attempted to take Honi Heki's new pah by escalade, and in 10 minutes were beaten back, one-third of them being killed. June 30, 1845.

Sir George Grey appointed Governor; arrived November 14, 1845.

Kowatti, a powerful chief, commenced a system of plunder on the settlers of Kowrorapi (Bay of Islands); hostilities commenced between the Europeans and natives in that part, and Kowatti being joined by other chiefs, among whom was Heki. A general war in that part of the island ensued, when a number of Europeans were killed. Kowroriki was abandoned by the settlers; some of the sufferers came to New South Wales, and a meeting was held in Sydney, when a resolution was adopted to the effect that a large number of troops ought to be immediately sent to New Zealand with two steamers, one to Cook's Straits, and the other to the Thames. A deputation waited on the Governor, but he refused the deputation other than as individuals capable of giving information relative to New Zealand. He declined to receive the resolution, which he deemed dictatorial in its nature, and to listen to which would be to forego that authority and responsibility with which the Executive alone was invested. This war, which was the first commencement of hostilities between Europeans and the natives, was long and harassing, which the Imperial Government was afterwards necessitated to carry on. 1845.

Boulcott's farm, in the Hutt Valley, garrisoned by an officer and 50 men of the 58th Regiment, was surprised, and six killed and four wounded. May 16, 1846.

Te Kauparaha's stockade surrounded by Major Last, 99th Regiment, Captain Stanley, of the "Calliope," and party, numbering about 830, and the chief was captured and taken on board the "Calliope," July 23, 1846.

Rangihaeata's forces were finally defeated and dispersed by friendly Maories under Wiremu Kingi, August 13, 1846.

The Gilfillan family, residing about five miles from Wanganui, were attacked by six Maories, the mother, two sons, and one daughter slain, and others wounded, April 18, 1847. Friendly natives pursued and captured five out of the six assassins; they were tried by Court-martial and found guilty of murder and robbery (one of the miscreants openly boasted that they had cut off and devoured part of the mother), four were condemned to death, and one (a youth) sentenced to transportation for life. April 24, 1847. The four murderers were executed Monday, April 26, 1847.

General Pitt arrived in Auckland, 1847.

The New Zealand Loan Act passed July 23, 1847.

The Province of Otago was formed by a Scotch company, 1848.

Canterbury created a Province, 1848.

A charter, founded upon an Act passed in 1846, creating powers municipal, legislative, and administrative, not having been up to this time acted upon, Legislative Council was opened by the Governor, December 20, 1848.

Dr. Monro drove the first sheep from Nelson to Wairu, 1849.

New Zealand company relinquished charter, 1850.

Canterbury founded in connection with the Church of England, 1850.

New constitution granted, 1852.

Cattle driven from Otago to Canterbury, 1853.

Under new Constitution the first elections took place, 1853.

First Provincial Council of Otago met, December 30, 1853.

Colonel Wynyard appointed Acting-Governor, January, 1854.

Colonel Sir James Gore Brown, G.C.B., K.G.M.G., appointed Governor, October, 1855.

An earthquake, but little damage done, Jan. 23, 1855.

Constitution modified, 1857.

Hawkes Bay separated from Wellington, and created a province of itself, 1858.

The 58th Regiment left New Zealand November 28, 1858.

Insurrection of the Maories, under a chief named Wirremu Kingi (the same chief who, in August, 1846, as an ally of the English, beat Rangihaeata), arising out of disputes regarding the sale of land, March, 1860.

Indecisive actions between the militia, volunteers, and Maories, March 14 to 28, 1860.

The Waireka colours presented to Governor Browne, April 3, 1860.

The 40th Regiment arrived at Taranaki, April 24, 1860.

War at Taranaki, British repulsed with loss, June 30, 1860.

Troops sent from Australia to New Zealand under General Pratt; they landed August 3, 1860.

Indecisive actions September 10 and 19, and October 9 and 12, 1860.

General Pratt defeats Maories at Mahoetahi and destroys

their fortified places, November 6, 1860.

New Zealand colonists in England justify conduct of the Governor, November 22, 1860.

The Maories defeated, December 2, 1860.

Marlborough separated from Nelson, and created a province by itself, 1860.

Gold discovered in Otago, 1861.

The Maories defeated January 23 and February 24 and March 16 and 18, 1861.

The war ends; surrender of the natives, March 19, 1861.

Sir George Grey reappointed Governor, June, 1861.

A native sovereignty proclaimed; 5,000 British soldiers in the island. July, 1861.

Cyclone in Auckland April 8, 1862.

The Abertland settlers left London May 29, 1862.

New Zealand telegraph opened July 2, 1862.

Loyalty of the natives increasing, May, 1862.

Dunstan diggings (Otago) discovered by Hartley and Reilly, 1862.

The Maori chiefs sent poetical address of condolence to the Queen on death of Prince Consort, received November, 1862.

Natives attacked a military escort and killed eight prisoners, May 4, 1863.

Waikato tribe driven from a fort July 17, 1863.

The Auckland militia were called out July 19, 1863.

War spreads, natives construct rifle pits, August, 1863.

Proposed confiscation of Waikato land, September, 1863.

General Cameron defeated Maories at Rangariri, November 20, 1863.

The Lyttelton and Christchurch railway opened December 1, 1863.

Continued success of General Cameron; capitulation of the Maori King, December 9, 1863.

British attack on the Gate Pah, repulsed with loss of officers and men, April 29, 1864.

Loan of £1,000,000 to New Zealand guaranteed by Parliament, July, 1864.

Several tribes submit, August, 1864.

Maori prisoners escape and form the nucleus of a new insurrection, September, 1864

Wellington chosen the seat of Government, October 3, 1864.

Sir George Grey issues proposals of peace, October 25, 1864.

The Aborigines Protection Society send religious, moral, and political advice to the Maories, November, 1864.

Change of Ministry; seat of Government shifted from Auckland to Wellington, November 24, 1864.

The Wanganur campaign began, January, 1865.

Outbreak of the Pai Mariri or the Hau Hau heresy, a compound of Judaism and Paganism. The Rev. C. S. Volkner murdered. And many outrages committed. March 2. Proclamation of Sir George Grey against it; it is checked by the agency of a friendly Maori chief named We-tako, April, 1865.

Auckland first lighted with gas, April 15, 1865.

William Thompson, an eminent chief, surrenders on behalf of the Maori King, May 25, 1865.

The Hau Haus beaten in several conflicts, August; the Governor proclaims peace, September 2; British troops about to leave, September 15, 1865.

The Maories treacherously murder the envoys of peace; resignation of the Weld Ministry; one formed by Mr. Stafford. October, 1865.

Bishopric of Dunedin, Otago, founded, 1865.

The Rev. Mr. Volkner murdered at Opotiki, March 3, 1865.

General Chute subdued the Hau Haus, January, 1866.

Murderers of Mr. Volkner executed, May 17, 1866.

Governor announces cessation of war, July 3, 1866.

The Maungatapu murders—John Kempthorne, Felix Matthieu, James Dudley, storekeepers, and James Pontius, a miner, were waylaid and murdered on the road between the Wakamarina and Nelson, by four scoundrels, Richard Burgess, Phil Levy, a Jew, Thomas Kelly, and Joseph Thomas Sullivan, who were afterwards arrested, and Sullivan having been allowed to turn Queen's evidence before Levy (who was anxious to do so), the other three were hanged. These murders took place June 13, 1866.

A threatened attack on the town of Napier by Maories, about 100 strong, who were beaten off and nearly all slain, October, 1866.

WELLINGTON, NEW ZEALAND
The Australasian Sketcher, 1875

Wm. Thompson surrendered to General Carey, May 27, 1867.

Death of William Thompson, the Maori chief, December 28, 1866.

Thames gold-field proclaimed, August 1, 1867.

Last Panama mail arrived in Wellington, February 24, 1868.

First Maori elected, M.H.R., April 16, 1866.

Act relating to Government of New Zealand passed in British Parliament, 1868.

Te Kooti, a convict, and about 150 Maori convicts, escape from Chatham Island to the main land, July 4; they repulse the troops sent against them September 7; and massacre the whites at Poverty Bay, Nov. 10, 1868.

Te Kooti and rebels defeated by Colonel Whitmore; 130 Maories killed, Jan. 5, 1869.

Taurangaika Pah taken, Feb. 3, 1869.

Massacre of settlers at Taranaki, Feb. 12, 1869.

Change of Ministry; proposal to pay the British troops declined by the home Government, September, 1869.

Te Kooti, thrice defeated by the colonists and friendly natives, a fugitive, October, 1869.

Despatch from Earl Granville insisting upon the withdrawal of British troops (18th Regt.) causes much dissatisfaction, Oct. 7, 1869.

Friendly interview between Mr. M'Lean and the Maori King's minister, Nov. 8, 1869.

Departure of last British troops, Jan. 22, 1870.

Te Kooti, refusing to surrender, narrowly escapes, Feb. 5, 1870.

Troops left Auckland, March 20, 1870.

Auckland constituted a borough, May 5, 1871.

Te Kooti's party attacked and dispersed, July 31, 1870.

The Duke of Edinburgh, in the "Galatea," arrived at Wellington, Aug. 27, 1870.

Loan of £4,000,000 proposed, Aug., 1870.

Political union of the Islands effected, August, 1870.

Right Rev. Octavius Hadfield, consecrated Bishop of Wellington, October 18, 1870. [He had previously been Archdeacon of Kapiti, and Commissary to Dr. Abraham, the first Bishop of Wellington. Dr. Hadfield was con-

secrated without the Royal mandate.]

Murder of Mr. Todd, surveyor, by Maories, Dec. 28, 1873.

Dunedin University opened, July, 1871.

Te Kooti, reported as living by plunder, acting as a fanatical potentate, November, 1871.

Kereopa hanged at Napier, Jan. 5, 1872.

Friendly meeting of Mr. M'Lean with Wirremu, Kingi, and other chiefs, who submit to the British Government, March, 1872.

Auckland Post Office burned, Nov. 19, 1872.

Auckland Steamship Company formed, May 2, 1873.

Auckland market opened, June 19, 1873.

Onehunga railway opened, Dec. 20, 1873.

First sod Wakaito railway extension, Jan. 10, 1874.

Opening of the Hutt railway, Jan. 21, 1874.

Destructive hurricane at Auckland, Feb. 8, 1874.

Mikado, the first San Francisco steamer, left Auckland, Feb. 15, 1874.

The Maori King submits to the British Government, February, 1875.

Foundation-stone of the Auckland waterworks laid, March 27, 1875.

Bill to abolish provinces in New Zealand passed by the Legislature of that colony, Sept. 29, 1875.

Abolition of Provinces Bill passed, Oct. 15, 1875.

Kaipara railway opened, Oct. 29, 1875.

Dr. Haast, at Christchurch Philosophical Institute, gave an account of a remarkable ancient rock-painting in the Weka Pass Range, representing animals of foreign countries, and weapons and dresses of semi-civilized people, April 6, 1877.

Remarkable tidal disturbances, East Coast, May 11, 1877.

Fire at Auckland Lunatic Asylum, Sept. 20, 1877.

Sir George Grey meets Maori King, Feb. 2, 1878.

Katikati settlers (second lot) left Belfast, May 30, 1878.

Sir George Grey offered Maori King £500 a year, May 9, 1878.

Sir George Grey met Rewi at Waitara, June 27, 1878.

"Lady Jocelyn" arrived with Katikati Immigrants, August 17, 1878.

Wellington steam tramway opened, August 23, 1878.

Railway opened, Dunedin to Christchurch, Sept. 5, 1878.

Great explosion in the Kaitangata coal mine, 35 persons killed, Feb. 1, 1879.

Great Maori meeting at Waikato. 3,000 present; had interview with Sir George Grey and Hon. J. Sheehan, May 9, 1879.

CONSTITUTION OF.

A constitutional form of Government was established in New Zealand by the Imperial Statute 15 and 16 Vic., cap. 72, passed in 1852. By that Act the Colony was divided into six provinces, since increased to nine—viz., Auckland, Taranaki, Wellington, Nelson, Canterbury, Otago, Hawke's Bay, Westland, and Marlborough—each governed by a Superintendent and Provincial Council, elected by the inhabitants according to a franchise which practically amounts to household suffrage.

By an Act of the General Assembly, 39 Vic. No. 21, passed in 1875, the provincial system of Government was abolished; the powers previously exercised by superintendents and provincial officers are henceforth to be exercised by the Governor or by local boards. The Act provided that the abolition of the provinces should not have any operation until the day after the conclusion of the then next Session of the Assembly. Before the next Session there was a general election, and the first Session of the new Parliament ended on the 31st of October, 1876. Nothing was done during the Session to repeal the Abolition Act, and the provinces, therefore, ceased to exist the day after the Session concluded. The provincial system being abolished provision was made for the division of the country into counties, and the necessary machinery for their self-government was provided.

A Central Legislature, called the General Assembly, was established by the Imperial Statute of 1852, and consists of the Governor, a Legislative Council, and of a House of Representatives. The Governor is assisted by an Executive Council, composed of the Responsible Ministers of the Colony for the time being, according to the usual practice of Parliamentary Government. The Legislative Councillors are appointed by the Governor, and hold their seats for life. The Members of the House of Representatives are chosen by Electors possessing the same qualifications as those who vote for the Provincial Councillors. Every Elector is qualified to become also a Member. The House of Representatives now consists of 88, including four Maori members, elected by the natives.

The control of native affairs, and the entire responsibility of dealing with questions of native Government, was transferred in 1863 from the Imperial to the Colonial Government. In 1864 the seat of the general Government was removed from Auckland to Wellington, on account of the central position of the latter city.

EXPLORATIONS.

Mr. Charles Darwin, the naturalist, visited New Zealand in the " Beagle," with Captain Fitzroy, 1835.

Messrs. Bidwell and Dyson looked down into the crater of Tongariri ; Lieutenant-Governor Eyre, ascended in the Middle Island, Kai Kora Mountain, from Wairu Valley, March 2, 1839.

Dr. Dieffenbach, naturalist to the N. Z. Company, who arrived in the ship " Troy," from England, ascended Mount Egmont, August, 1839.

Dr. Dieffenbach and Captain William Cornwallis Symonds explored from Manukau to Central Lake, Taupu, December 3, 1840.

Captain Wm. Cornwallis Symonds, Deputy Surveyor-General of New Zealand (who accompanied Dieffenbach, and who himself made various explorations, especially to the sources of the Wanganui and Manematu Rivers), was drowned in the Bay of Manukau, November, 1841.

Mr. Thomas Brunner made a journey across the Middle Island, New Zealand, 1846.

James Dana, of the American Exploring Expedition, visited the Bay of Islands, N. Z., and scientifically examined the surrounding country, 1849.

Dr. Monro drove the first flock of sheep from Nelson to Wairu, 1849.

Mr. Hamilton and Mr. Spencer, of the surveying vessel " Acheron," examined the Mataura and Jacob Rivers, and explored the intermediate country to Otago, 1849.

Captain Mitchell and Mr. Dashwood discovered a track from Nelson to Canterbury, 1850.

Captain Lort Stokes examined and chartered the seaboard from Otago to Preservation Harbour, 1850.

The insularity of the South Island discovered by Stewart, a sealer and whaler who died at Poverty Bay, 1851.

Mr. G. H. Braun and Mr. George Duppa rode from Nelson to Canterbury by Mr. Weld's track, who first explored it by the Wairu Gorge and Lake Tennyson, 1856.

Captains Stokes and Drury, of the Royal Navy, and D'Arville, of the French marine, made a complete outline survey of the coast of New Zealand ; and Captain Richards, R.N., and Mr. Evans, R.N., also gave an excellent description of the N. Z. coast. 1856.

Mr. Dobson, Provincial Engineer, discovered a route over the mountains to the west coast of the Middle Island, 1857.

Mr. Leonard Harper and party started on an expedition to the western coast, Middle Island, from Wartoki Valley, which they reached in 23 days, November 4, 1857.

Mr. J. Turnbull Thomson, Chief Surveyor of Otago, with his companions, Drummond and Lindsay, explored in successive trips the southern extremity of Otago—over 1,500 miles of country. 1857.

Mr. Rochfort's (Government surveyor) excursion from the north of the Buller, on the West Coast. [One of his hands—F. Millington—discovered gold. On November 8 he pursued the coast downwards, crossing the Okari, the Waitakeri, and the Waitohi ; on the latter found seams of coal.] 1858.

Mr. John Rochfort's excursion from Port Cooper, up the Hurunui to the Taramaku, across Lake Brunner, and down the Arnold River to the Grey, on the West Coast, took place in 1858.

QUEEN STREET WHARF, AUCKLAND
Picturesque Atlas of Australia

Mr J. T. Thomson gave the first sketch of the province of Otago, 1858.

Dr. Ferdinand Hochstetter, accompanied by Dr. Julius Haast (who both arrived in the Austrian frigate "Novara," in December, 1858), made a geological, scientific, and general survey of New Zealand coast and interior, and published the result of researches in 1863, in two volumes. 1859.

Dr. Julius Haast, Government Geologist of Canterbury, accompanied by Mr. James Burnett, surveyor, three other Europeans, and two Maories, started from Nelson and made an exploration of the mountainous regions and the rivers of the Middle Island of New Zealand, January 8, 1860.

Dr. Julius Haast, Government Geologist, explored the mountains of Canterbury and up the river Rangitata, and its tributaries, the Havelock and Clyde. In attempting to cross a river he lost his companion, Dr. Sinclair, 1861.

Dr. J. Haast explored the sources of the Rowai, among the mountains of that name. Above the plains of Christchurch he discovered several beds of iron ore, and found his way to Lake Takapu and Lake Pukaki, the great Tasman glacier, and the Moorhouse Range, 1862.

Dr. Hector left Port Chalmers to examine the numerous inlets and sounds on the west coast of Otago. He discovered the Kaduka river, Kakapo Lake. 1863.

Dr. Haast penetrated into the mountains of Otago, 1863.

STATISTICS OF (FOR 1877).

Population :—234,803 males, and 182,819 females; total, 417,622; births, 16,856; deaths, 4,685; marriages, 3,111; Crown Lands sold, 777,862 acres; Crown Lands amount realised, £1,316,597; free grants, 40,314 acres, land under cultivation, 2,940,711 acres; horses, 99,859; cattle, 494,917; sheep, 11,704,853; pigs, 123,921; letters received and despatched, 13,054,870; newspapers received and despatched, 8,066,311; postal revenue, £143,600; shipping belonging to the Colony, 535 vessels, of which the registered tonnage was 42,479 tons; gold raised, 371,685 ozs., value £1,496,080; wool exported, 64,481,324 lbs., valued at £3,658,938; flax (phormium), 1,053 tons, valued at £18,826; gum (Kauri), 3,632 tons, valued at £118,348; total exports the produce of New Zealand, £6,078,484; total imports £6,973,418; revenue, £3,916,023; telegraphs :—miles open, 3,307; number of messages, 1,182,955; cash value, £85,589; railways :—Miles open, 1,052; under construction, 251; Savings Banks :—Number of depositors, 35,709; amount at credit, £964,430; convictions, 250.

NOBBY, LIEUTENANT, of the N. S. W. Corps, Court Martial on. Proceedings leading to no result, and Lieut. Nobby ordered to return to duty at Parramatta. February 8, 1803.

NORFOLK ISLAND.

A party under the command of Philip Gidley King (Second Lieutenant of the "Stirling") sent out in the "Supply" (Lieut. Ball) to form a settlement at Norfolk Island. The party consisted of Lieut. King (with the title of Superintendent and Commandant of the Settlement of Norfolk Island), 1 subaltern officer (James Cunningham), a surgeon (Dr. T. Jamieson), Assistant-surgeon John Altree, Roger Morley, Mr. William Westbrooke, Mr. Sawyer, John Batcheldor, and Charles Heritage, with nine men and six women convicts, 24 in all. February 14, 1788.

Anson Bay named by Lieut. King in honour of the Parliamentary representative of Lichfield, England, March 5, 1788.

Norfolk Island taken possession of by Lieut. King and party, who celebrated the occasion by hoisting the British colours and drinking the healths of His Majesty the King, the Queen, the Princess of Wales, and success to the settlement, March 6, 1788.

First harvest (wheat) reaped in Norfolk Island, December 24, 1789.

Lieut.-Governor Ross relieved Lieut.-Governor King in the command, whilst the latter proceeded to England to report to His Majesty's Ministers on the new settlement at Norfolk Island, March 24, 1790.

Inhabitants of Norfolk Island, 498, of whom 191 men and 100 women were convicts. March 24, 1790.

Lieut.-Governor King resumed command at Norfolk Island, having returned to New South Wales by the "Gorgon," December, 1791.

The wheat harvest of Norfolk Island amounted to 1,000 bushels, December, 1791.

The state of affairs at Norfolk Island was such that the settlers were enjoying the greatest prosperity; 2,000 bushels of wheat and 50 tons of potatoes were produced. The population of the island was 1,008 persons. 1793.

Major Foveaux appointed Lieutenant-Governor of Norfolk Island. June 29, 1800.

Mr. D. Wentworth, surgeon, appointed to proceed to Norfolk Island, July 6, 1802.

Mr. D'Arcy Wentworth ordered to duty at Norfolk Island, February 8, 1803.

Lieut. James Bowen, of H.M.S. "Glatton," appointed to take charge and command, as Deputy Lieutenant-Governor of Norfolk Island, during the absence of Lieutenant-Governor Foveaux, March 19, 1803.

Lieutenant-Governor Foveaux arrived from Norfolk Island, leaving the command of the settlement to Captain Wilson, September 29, 1803.

The abandonment of the settlement of Norfolk Island took place in 1805. [The order for the abandonment had been issued in 1803. The settlers on that island were mostly emancipists, and had farms of from 33 to 40 acres. These settlers were conveyed either to Van Diemen's Land or New South Wales at the public expense, and had grants of land given to them, double the amount of their former possessions, with cattle on loan, and rationed at the public stores as new settlers. The majority of the settlers from Norfolk Island went to Van Diemen's Land, and there founded a settlement, naming the place where they located New Norfolk and Norfolk Plains after the name of the island they had been compelled to leave.]

Extraordinary high tide at Norfolk Island, May 8, 1805.

Norfolk Island appointed a place to which offenders convicted in New South Wales, and being under sentence of transportation, should be sent, August 15, 1826.

Harwood's brig seized and taken away by convicts whilst on passage from Sydney, 1827.

Serious outbreak amongst the prisoners at Norfolk Island; fifty escaped to Phillip Island, seven miles distant, where after three had been killed, the rest were captured, or after a time surrendered. September, 1827.

Captain J. Wakefield, 39th Regiment, resigned his position as Commandant of Norfolk

Island, June 29, 1839. [He was succeeded by Lieut.-Colonel Morissett, late Superintendent of Police, Sydney.]

The "Governor Phillip," a vessel employed by Government to carry supplies to and from Norfolk Island, was piratically seized by the prisoners of that island. The boat's crew, numbering 12 men, all prisoners, who were employed between the island and the vessel, by a preconcerted plan, disarmed the sentry on board, compelled such of the crew who were on deck to jump overboard, and secured the captain, mate, and soldiers below deck. The captain and mate, by breaking through a partition, got in communication with the soldiers, and commenced an attack by firing through the crevices, which took effect, when they rushed on deck, and after a brief struggle with the pirates, recaptured the vessel. The soldiers lost one man, and five others were wounded; of the convicts, five were killed and two wounded. The others were tried, and four were convicted and executed. 1842.

The Governor visited Norfolk Island on a tour of inspection, with instructions from the Secretary of State, February 28, 1843.

Norfolk Island declared no longer a dependency of New South Wales, April 2, 1844.

Government of Norfolk Island passed from New South Wales to Tasmania, October 1, 1844.

Major Childs, Governor of Norfolk Island, replaced Maconochie, 1845.

The Pitcairn Islanders, numbering 194 souls, established themselves at Norfolk Island. They were allotted land for cultivation, and supplies for a limited period; they were also supplied with seeds and implements of husbandry. A magistrate and chaplain were appointed. The instructions from the Secretary of State were that the islanders should be as little interfered with as possible, and that their existing social system was to be maintained. The Governor of New South Wales visited Norfolk Island on the establishment of that place by the Pitcairners. 1857.

Lord Belmore visited Norfolk Island in H.M.S. "Virago," returning to Sydney October 16, 1870.

NORTH AUSTRALIA. Colonel Barney arrived at Sydney from England *en route* to form the colony of North Australia, September 8, 1846.

NORFOLK ISLAND, THE CONVICT SYSTEM
Mitchell Library

OBELISK.

The Obelisk, Macquarie Place, Sydney, erected by Governor Macquarie as a starting point from which distances on the roads of the colony might be calculated. 1818.

The Obelisk, Hyde Park, opposite Bathurst-street, Sydney, erected during the mayoralty of George Thornton, Esq., for the dispersion of sewage effluvia, 1857.

THE OBELISK
The Illustrated Sydney News, 1854

OBSERVATORIES.

A sketch of Sydney Cove, Port Jackson, includes a view of the first Observatory, July, 1878. [It is thus described at page 126 of "Phillip's Voyage to New South Wales" :—"On that point that forms the west side of the Cove, and on an elevated spot, a small Observatory has been raised under the direction of Lieutenant Dawes, who was charged by the Board of Longitude with the care of observing the expected comet. The longitude of this observatory is ascertained to be 159 deg. 19 min. 30 sec. east from Greenwich, and the latitude 32 deg. 52 min. 30 sec. south."]

Observatory built at Parramatta, under the inspection of Sir T. Brisbane, 1822.

Charles Luis Rumker appointed Government Astronomer at Parramatta, N. S. W., December 27, 1827.

James Dunlop appointed Superintendent of the Observatory at Parramatta, November 11, 1831.

Parramatta Observatory closed, 1847.

An Observatory was erected at Williamstown, Victoria, 1853. [A temporary one had been erected on Flagstaff Hill, Melbourne, in 1858, which was afterwards removed to the building specially built for observatory purposes on the south side of the Yarra Yarra. According to the latest computation, the position of these Observatories is as follows :—

	Latitude S.	Longitude E.
	° ′ ″	° ′ ″
Williamstown Observatory..	37 52 7	144 54 42
Flagstaff Observatory	37 48 45	144 58 15
Melbourne Observatory	37 49 53	144 58 42

ASTRONOMERS : Australia—

Henry C. Russell, New South Wales.

John Tebbutt (amateur), Windsor, N.S.W.

R. L. J. Ellery, Victoria.

Charles Todd, C.M., South Australia.

J. M'Donnell, Queensland.

Mr. H. C. Russell, Government Astronomer, New South Wales, announced that the longitude of the Sydney Observatory was 10 h. 4 m. 50–8 s. earlier than that of London, May 6, 1878.

OCEAN STEAM SERVICE. Intelligence received that a company had been formed in England to carry out steam communication between England and the Colonies, and that the Government encouraged the project. 1847.

O'CONNELL, LADY, the heroic daughter of Governor Bligh,—who was married first to Lieutenant Putland of H.M.S. "Porpoise" (who died in Sydney, January, 1808), and secondly, in January, 1810, to Lieutenant, afterwards Sir Maurice, O'Connell,—died in England, 1864.

O'CONNELL, LIEUTENANT.

Arrived with large detachment of 73rd Regiment, in H.M.S. "Dromedary" and H.M.S. "Hindostan," December 28, 1809.

Lieutenant O'Connell married to Mrs. Putland (the faithful and heroic daughter of Governor

Bligh, who confronted the soldiers when they came to arrest her father), May 3, 1810.

Headquarters of the 73rd Regiment, with Lieutenant and Lady O'Connell, sailed for Ceylon, April 6, 1814.

ODDFELLOWS' SOCIETY, first established in the Colony of New South Wales, February 24, 1836. Foundation stone new hall, Elizabeth-street, Sydney, laid by Hon. John Sutherland November 19, 1870; hall opened May 24, 1871.

OPALS. Opal mine discovered in Queensland, near the head of the Bulla Creek, south of the Barcoo. 1870.

ORANGE, CULTIVATION OF THE, introduced into New South Wales by Rev. Richard Johnson at Kissing Point, from seeds obtained at Rio Janeiro, May, 1718.

OTAGO, founded by the arrival of the "Philip Lang" and "John Wickliff," engaged ships of Free Church Association of Scotland, March 23, 1848.

OVENS RIVER, discovered by Hume and Hovell, and named in honour of Major Ovens, November 24, 1824.

OXLEY [See EXPLORERS.]

AMATEUR ASTRONOMERS
The Australasian Sketcher, 1874

P

PALMER, John P., of Ballarat, took out writs against members of the Legislative Council, Victoria, claiming £252,000 penalties for illegally sitting and voting in that chamber. November 29, 1877.

PAMPHLET, Thomas, with Thomas Thompson, Parsons, and Finnegan, left Sydney in a small coasting craft, March 21, 1823, to procure a

THE FINDING OF PAMPHLET
Picturesque Atlas of Australia

cargo of cedar at Illawarra. A storm arose, and they were driven out to sea; on the sixteenth day, Thompson, who became raving mad for the want of water, died, and on the twenty-fourth day they reached land. They imagined they were to the south of Sydney Harbour, but they had been driven to the north, and after touching land they travelled on in a northerly direction as far as Moreton Bay. Pamphlet and Finnegan remained with the Moreton Bay blacks five months, until they were discovered by Lieutenant Oxley in the "Mermaid." Pamphlet then informed Oxley of the existence of the Brisbane River. November 29, 1823.

PANDORA, Captain Edwards, which had been sent out to search for the mutineers of the "Bounty," succeeded in capturing fourteen—that is all but nine. Two had died. Returning with them to England the "Pandora" was wrecked on the Australian coast on August 29, 1791. Thirty-one of the ship's crew and four of the mutineers of the "Bounty" were drowned. Eighty-nine of the "Pandora's" crew and ten prisoners were saved.

PARLIAMENT.

The first Legislative Council, New South Wales, opened August 11, 1824. [Names of first members: Wm. Stewart, Lieutenant-Governor; Francis Forbes, Chief Justice; Frederick Goulburn, Colonial Secretary; John Oxley, Surveyor-General; James Bowman, Principal Colonial Surgeon; John Macarthur, of Camden.]

THE FIRST ACT OF PARLIAMENT PASSED IN AUSTRALIA was an Act to make promissory notes and bills of exchange payable in Spanish dollars available as if such notes and bills had been drawn payable in sterling money of the realm. September 28, 1824.

The first Executive Council of Tasmania nominated, the population amounting at the time to 12,000. 1825.

New Executive Council appointed, N. S. W., consisting of Frederick Goulburn, Colonial Secretary; Francis Forbes, Chief Justice; Saxe Bannister, Attorney-General; John Stephen, Solicitor-General and Commissioner Court of Requests; John Mackaness, Sheriff; John Carter, Master in Equity; D'Arcy Wentworth, Police Magistrate of Sydney. December 20, 1825.

Archdeacon Scott, Alexander Macleay, Robert Campbell (sen.), and Charles Throsby, appointed to the new Legislative Council by Governor Darling, 1825.

List of Members of the Legislative Council of New South Wales, appointed March, 1828 :—

Francis Forbes, Chief Justice.
The Officer next in command to the Commander of the Forces in New South Wales.
The Venerable Thomas Hobbes Scott, Archdeacon.
Alexander Macleay, Esq., Colonial Secretary.
John Macarthur, Esq.
Robert Campbell (senior), Esq.
Charles Throsby.

Royal Charter received, appointing New Executive and Legislative Council. Executive :— The Venerable Archdeacon Scott, the Colonial Secretary, and Colonel Lindesay (34th Regt.), who with the following formed also the Legislative Council :—

Francis Forbes, Chief Justice.
Alex. Macduff Baxter, Attorney-General.
Michael Culley Cotton, Collector of Customs.
William Lithgow, Auditor-General.
John Macarthur.
Robert Campbell.
Alexander Berry.
Richard Jones.
John Blaxland.
Captain Phillip Parker King.
Edward Charles Close.
Governor Darling, as President.

Captain King being absent from the colony, John Thomas Campbell was appointed temporarily to fill his place. July 13, 1829.

The New Council commenced its Legislative labours, August 21, 1829. [In this session a bill for instituting Courts of Jurisdiction, to be called Courts of Requests, in different parts of the Colony, was passed ; a bill for the slaughtering of cattle, and a Jury bill, were also passed. In this last-mentioned bill the much-debated and momentous question of qualification was dealt with.]

Archdeacon Broughton sworn in as a member of the Legislative Council, September 22, 1829.

John George Gibbes, Collector of Customs, nominated member of the Legislative Council, November 19, 1834.

Mr. John Blaxland objected to certain items of expenditure, and, in his place in the Council at this time, entered " protests." Among the items protested against were the salary of the Colonial Secretary, which was £2,000 per annum, the reduction of which he proposed to £1,500 ; the salary of the resident at New Zealand, £500 per annum ; the salary of the Archdeacon, £2,000 (to be reduced to £1,000). These " protests " were entered in the minutes of the Council, and copies transmitted to the Secretary of State. 1834.

Important measures were passed in the Legislative Council, 1834. [They were :—Fixing the rate of interest recoverable in the Courts of the colony at eight per cent. ; an Act to remove all doubts as to the legality of marriages by Roman Catholic and Presbyterian ministers ; all lands that had been granted by the Crown to the Church and School Corporation having reverted to His Majesty, the income of such lands to be appropriated in discharging the expenses of the Orphan Schools, and to the general education of the youth of the colony.]

Measures adopted at the sittings of the Legislative Council :—Reduction of the rate of postage on letters, and the postage on colonial newspapers abolished ; a Court of criminal jurisdiction at Norfolk Island instituted as occasion might require ; a sum of £55,040 voted for the maintenance of the police and gaol establishments, and for a certain portion of the colonial marine. (Before this time the expenses of these establishments were paid by the Imperial Government.) It was announced to the House that this maintenance of the police and gaol establishments by the colony was by command of His Majesty's Government, and that His Majesty was graciously pleased to place at the disposal of the Council the surplus of the land revenue and other casual revenues of the Crown, beyond the sums appropriated for the assistance of emigrants. This was one of the initiatory steps towards the establishment of the self-supporting system which the colony had so long desired. This vote was not passed, however, without opposition. It was only carried by a majority

of one, there being seven to six ; six official members and one non-official member formed the majority. 1835.

The Legislative Council first thrown open to the public to hear the debates June 6, 1838. [Up to this time the reporters of the Press, as well as the public at large, had been excluded. From this period, which was the first Council assembled in Sir George Gipps' administration, the proceedings of the House, including the speeches of the members, were published in the newspapers.]

First session of the Legislative Council of New Zealand opened, May 24, 1841.

First Executive Council in New Zealand, consisted, in addition to Governor Hobson, of Willoughby Shortland, Colonial Secretary, Francis Fisher, Attorney-General, and George Cooper, Colonial Treasurer and Collector of Customs, *ex officio* members. 1841.

The first election of members for the City of Sydney took place. Five candidates nominated, June 13, for seats in the Parliament, when Messrs. Wentworth and Bland were returned by a very large majority. At this election a very disgraceful riot took place. One man lost his life, and much valuable property was destroyed. Messrs. O'Connell, Cooper, and Hustler were the unsuccessful candidates. June 15, 1843.

The first representative Legislature of New South Wales assembled, the ceremonial inauguration being conducted by E. Deas-Thomson, Esq., Colonial Secretary, when the election of Speaker took place. The election was contested by Mr. Macleay and Mr. Hamilton, a Crown nominee, when Mr. Macleay had a majority of 17 to 13, and assumed the weight of a new and onerous office in his 77th year. August 1, 1843. [During the session several measures were passed—the appointment of a committee moved by Mr. Terence A. Murray, to inquire into the provisions of Lord Stanley's Land Act, as far as they applied to New South Wales ; an Act to protect the interest of debtors, who, owing to the depression of the times, were in insolvent circumstances and unable to meet their claims ; and an Act to give a preferable lien on wool from season to season, and to make mortgages of sheep, cattle, and horses valid without delivery to mortgagee. This Act in a great measure alleviated the pressure of these times.].

Robert Lowe retired from Parliament of New South Wales, August 28, 1844.

A Select Committee of the Legislative Council was appointed, to take into consideration the best means of providing for the safety of life and property, having reference to the increase of outrages committed in Sydney. 1844.

Governor Gipps informed Lord Stanley of the first Parliamentary election in Australia, July 18, 1843. The following is the list of members :—

Sydney	{ Wentworth W. C. { Bland William
Parramatta	Macarthur H. H.
Cumberland Burghs	Bowman William
Northumberland Burghs	Wentworth D'Arcy

Cumberland County .... { Lawson William
                            { Cowper Charles
Northumberland County.... Foster William
Argyle County............. Bradley William
St. Vincent and Auckland .. Coghill John
Murray, King, and Georgiana Murray Terence A.
Roxburgh, Phillip, and Wel- } Suttor William H.
  lington. .... }
Bathurst .... Lord Francis
Brisbane, Bligh, and Hunter Dumaresq William
Durham.................... Windeyer Richard
Gloucester, Macquarie, and } Macleay Alexander
  Stanley Counties .... }
Cook and Westmoreland .... Panton John
Camden................... Therry Roger
Melbourne Town........... { Condell Henry (Mayor of
                           {   Melbourne).
                          / Ebden Charles Hobson
                          | Walker Thomas
Port Phillip ....< Nicholson Charles
                          | Thomson Alexander
                          \ Lang John Dunmore

The official nominees to the Legislative Council
were :—

The Lieutenant command-   The Auditor-General
  ing Her Majesty's Troops The Collector of Customs
The Colonial Secretary   The Colonial Engineer
        The Colonial Treasurer

Non-official.

Jones Richard   Berry Alexander
Blaxland John   Icely Thomas
Hamilton Edward   Elwin Hastings

The "Patriotic Six" (Tasmania), who protested against transportation of convicts to that
colony, resigned, October 3, 1845.

Responsible Government was for the first time
discussed in New South Wales, 1845.

Sir Charles Nicholson appointed Speaker of
the Legislative Council, N. S. Wales, vice
Macleay resigned, May, 1846.

A contest between the Executive and the
Legislature arose. The Governor having submitted to the Legislative Council a bill to renew
the Border Police Act, after two nights it was
rejected by a large majority, and an address to
the Governor was carried by 19 to 10 (the
majority being all representatives, and the
minority consisting exclusively of nominees).
The address voted was nominally a vote of censure on the Government Policy in reference to
its views on the Crown lands question. To the
address the Governor answered briefly : "He
was happy to say that this address was one
which required no reply, and he did not intend
to give any." This brought the contest to a
crisis. In consequence of the Governor being
on the eve of his departure to England, the
Council resolved not to transact any more business, passing not even the Estimates, until the
new Governor arrived, and on the motion of
Mr. Wentworth the Council adjourned on June
12 until July 21. In adjourning for a month,
the Council was prepared to carry on a great
part of their business through Committees
which they had appointed. But the Council,
by this adjournment, did not gain their point,
for the Governor on the following day issued a
proclamation proroguing the House until August
25 following, by which means he at once prevented the sittings of the Committees, and

thereby inconveniently prolonged their labours,
thus completely outwitting his opponents. June
12, 1846.

Orders in Council issued by Imperial Government, March 9, 1847.

Earl Grey was nominated and elected in Melbourne, as a representative in the New South
Wales Parliament. This was done to prevent
the non-electionists from having a representative, July, 1848.

First Legislative Council held at Auckland,
New Zealand, November 16, 1848.

The candidates nominated for election to the
Parliament of New South Wales for Port Phillip
district were Lauchlan M'Kinnon, Jas. William-
son, Jas. Dickson, J. F. Palmer, Ed. Curr,
Wm. Macarthur, Duke of Wellington, Viscount
Palmerston, Lord Brougham, Lord John Russell,
and Sir Robert Peel ; the first five were elected,
December, 1848.

The Imperial Parliament notified its intention
of giving representative Government to Tasmania and South Australia, by adding to the
existing Legislature elected members. 1848.

The new Legislative Council assembled—Sir
Charles Nicholson re-elected Speaker. The
Governor formally read opening speech, and
announced that Her Majesty had deemed it
expedient to revoke the Charter establishing
the new Colony of North Australia and had re-
annexed it to N. S. Wales, and that H. M.
Government had authorised a contract to be
entered into with the Indian and Australian
Steam Packet Company for conveyance of mails
between England and Australia by way of
Singapore and Torres' Straits. May 15, 1849.

Earl Grey elected to represent Melbourne in
the N. S. W. Parliament by a large majority
over Mr. J. F. V. Foster. 1848.

Indignation meeting, against Earl Grey, on the
transportation question, held in Sydney, 1849.

Last Legislative Assembly of N. S. Wales
and Port Phillip terminated May 2, 1851. The
Superintendent of Port Phillip, the Members
of the Council, and the Melbourne delegates to
the Anti-Transportation League left Sydney for
the new Colony, May 5, 1851.

First Executive Council of Victoria, July 16,
1851.

J. F. Palmer elected first Speaker, Victorian
Parliament, December, 1851.

The question of a Representative House of
Assembly was agitated in New South Wales in
1827; debated in the House of Commons and
lost, 1832; agitated again 1833 by Wentworth
and others. First Legislative Assembly in
N. S. Wales opened by Governor Fitzroy,
October 16, 1851.

The first Tasmanian Legislative Council
elected October 24, 1851.

The first Act of Parliament in Victoria
passed December 18, 1852.

First Melbourne Election Committee decide
F. J. Sargood M.L.C. for Melbourne instead of
H. Langlands, October 18, 1853.

Responsible Government granted in New
South Wales, 1856.

OPENING OF THE LEGISLATIVE COUNCIL
The Illustrated Sydney News, 1854

First Parliament opened under responsible Government in New South Wales, May 22, 1856.

List of the Members and the Constituencies they represented in the First Parliament under Responsible Government in New South Wales. (First Dissolution, December 19, 1857.)

Name of Member.	Constituency.
Arnold, William Munnings ..	Durham and the Paterson
Barker, Thomas	Gloucester and Macquarie
Bowman, William	Cumberland Boroughs
Buckley, Henry	Stanley (County)
Byrnes, James	Cumberland (S. Riding)
Campbell, John	Sydney Hamlets
Campbell, Robert	Sydney (City)
Cooper, Daniel	Sydney Hamlets
Cowper, Charles	Sydney (City)
Cox, George Henry	Wellington (County)
Dalley, William Bede	Sydney (City)
Deniehy, Daniel Henry	Argyle
Dickson, James	Northumberland Boroughs
Donaldson, Stuart Alexander	Cumberland (S. Riding)
Egan, Daniel	Monaro
Faucett, Peter	King and Georgiana
Flood, Edward	North-eastern Boroughs
Forster, William	Murray
Garland, James	Lachlan and Lower Darling
Gordon, Samuel Deane	Durham
Hargrave, Richard	New England and Macleay
Hay, John	Murrumbidgee
Hely, Hovenden	Northumberland and Hunter
Holroyd, Arthur Todd	Western Boroughs
Holt, Thomas	Stanley Boroughs
Irving, Clark	Clarence and Darling Downs
Jamison, Robert Thomas	Cook and Westmoreland
Jones, Richard	Durham
Lang, Gideon Scott	Liverpool Plains and Gwydir
Lee, William	Roxburgh
Leslie, Patrick	Moreton, Wide Bay, Burnett, and Maranoa
Lord, George William	Wellington and Bligh
Macarthur, James	Western Division of Camden
Macleay, George	Murrumbidgee
Macleay, William, junr.	Lachlan and Lower Darling
Marks, John	Eastern Division of Camden
Martin, James	Cook and Westmoreland
Murray, Terence Aubrey	Southern Boroughs
Oakes, George	Parramatta
Osborne, Henry	Eastern Division of Camden
Oxley, John Norton	Western Division of Camden
Parker, Henry Watson	Parramatta
Piddington, William Richman	Northumberland and Hunter
Pye, James	Cumberland (N. Riding)
Richardson, John	Stanley Boroughs
Robertson, John	Phillip, Brisbane, and Bligh
Rusden, Francis Townsend	Liverpool Plains and Gwydir
Rusden, Thomas George	New England and Macleay
Scott, Alexander Walker	Northumberland and Hunter
Smith, Thomas Whistler	Cumberland (N. Riding)
Suttor, William Henry	Bathurst (Country)
Thompson, James	St. Vincent
Weekes, Elias Carpenter	Northumberland Boroughs
Wilshire, James Robert	Sydney (City)

A collision took place between the Assembly and the Council of New South Wales arising out of the Indemnity Bill. After the passing of the then Appropriation Act, and before the expenditure for which the Indemnity Bill was asked, votes of credit were granted to the Government by the Assembly. The Council held that their sanction was required also, to give effect to the Vote of Credit, as well as to the Appropriation Act, and when the Bill of Indemnity was transmitted to them for their concurrence, they did not demur to give the required indemnity, but included all the appropriations which had been made since the preceding Session. The Government and their supporters rejected the amendments of the Council, as it was deemed they had converted the Bill into a money measure contrary to their privilege. The Assembly declined to proceed further with the Bill. 1856.

First free Parliament in Victoria opened by Major-General Macarthur, acting Lieutenant-Governor, November 25, 1856.

Sir James F. Palmer, first President Legislative Council, Victoria, 1856.

The first Tasmanian Parliament met December 2, 1856.

A new department created called the Department of Public Works, and Mr. Geoffrey Eagar was appointed to the office, with a seat in the Upper House, New South Wales, 1859.

First Victorian Parliament under Manhood Suffrage elected, October 13, 1859.

First elections for Queensland Parliament, April 27, 1860.

First Queensland Parliament under Responsible Government met, the first Ministry being as follows :—Robert G. W. Herbert, Colonial Secretary ; Ratcliffe Pring, Attorney-General ; R. R. Mackenzie, Colonial Treasurer ; St. G. R. Gore, Secretary for Lands and Works ; and Sir Maurice O'Connell, J. J. Galloway, W. Hobbs, and John Bramston without portfolios ; May 29, 1860.

MEMBERS OF FIRST LEGISLATIVE COUNCIL IN QUEENSLAND.

Balfour John	M'Dougall John Frederic
Bigge Francis Edward	Massie Robert George
Compigne Alfred William	Nicholson Sir Charles
Fullerton George	O'Connell Maurice Charles
Galloway John James	Yaldwin William Henry
	Laidley James

MEMBERS OF FIRST LEGISLATIVE ASSEMBLY IN QUEENSLAND.

Brisbane	{ Raff George Jordan Henry Blakeney W. C.
East Downs	Pring R.
West Downs	{ Taylor J. Moffatt De Lacy T.
South Brisbane	Richards Henry
Fortitude Valley	Lilley Charles

Drayton and Toowoomba....	Watts John
Warwick	Gore R. St. George
East Moreton	{ Edmonston George { Buckley Henry
Northern Downs...........	Coxen Charles
West Moreton	{ Thorn George { Broughton A. D. { Nelson Dr.
Maranoa	Ferrett J.
The Burnett...............	{ Mackenzie R. R. { Haly C .R.
Leichhardt	{ Herbert R. C. W. { Royds C. J. { Forbes F. A.
Ipswich	{ O'Sullivan P. { Macalister A.
Wide Bay	Eliott G.
Port Curtis	Fitzsimmons —

THE PAYMENT OF POLITICIANS
Touchstone, Melbourne, 1870

First Tasmanian Parliament dissolved, May 5, 1861.

Weston Ministry resigned, Chapman Ministry formed, August 2, 1861.

A member of the Legislative Assembly of Victoria expelled for personating voters at the Mornington election, 1861.

A member expelled from the Victorian Parliament "for being the agent of a corrupt Association for bribing Members of Parliament," 1869.

A Member expelled from the Victorian Legislative Assembly "for receiving money from a corrupt association for bribing Members of Parliament" in order to pass measures for their benefit. Was re-elected in same year 1869.

Longest Parliamentary sitting on record in Australia. New South Wales Parliament sat continuously for 37½ hours, January 28-29, 1873.

Commencement of the "stone-walling" struggle by the Opposition in Legislative Assembly of Victoria, January 12, 1876.

A Member expelled from the Victorian Parliament for referring to the Members (during the hearing of a Police Court case) in terms of derision, 1876.

A disturbance threatened in Parliament-yard, Victoria, owing to the excited state of feeling in consequence of the refusal of the majority of the Assembly to agree to a dissolution demanded by the Opposition, February 8, 1876.

"The Iron Hand" or "Gagging Motion" introduced by Sir James M'Culloch. Motion in the Victorian Legislative Assembly, for the adoption of a new standing order to authorise the stoppage of further discussion, by any Member moving, during a debate, "that the motion be now put" was carried on a division by 41 votes against 20, February 10, 1876.

A Member's seat declared vacant in consequence of malpractices imputed to him (Victoria), November 2, 1877.

A Member found guilty of bribery. The seat was awarded to Mr. Ince (Victoria), Dec. 4, 1877.

Sir John Robertson resigned his seat (for Mudgee) in the Legislative Assembly of New South Wales, December 13, 1878.

Seat of Edward Coombes, C.M.G., declared vacant by reason of his acceptance of an office of emolument under the Crown (Executive Commissioner for New South Wales at the Paris Exhibition), 1879.

Committee of Elections and Qualifications of New South Wales Parliament declared, on the petition of J. Wilton and others, Mr. Rouse not to be elected for Mudgee, and that Mr. David Buchanan was elected for the vacant seat, March 18, 1873. [Mr. Rouse had been declared by the Returning-Officer duly elected, by a majority of one, he (the Returning Officer) and two minors having voted during the election.]

Death (in his rooms at the Houses of Parliament) of Sir Maurice O'Connell, President of the Queensland Legislative Council, March 22, 1879.

CONTEMPT OF.

A Bill was passed in the New South Wales Legislative Council, declaratory of privileges to protect its members against being called to account for words used in debate in the House. Mr. Lowe, in a speech, having had occasion to refer to Mr. Henry Macdermott, accompanied his remarks by language derogatory to Mr. Macdermott; the latter challenged the former to a duel, which led to the famous "Privilege Question." The Speaker was ordered to request the Crown Law Offices to file a Bill of criminal information against Macdermott and his seconds, in consequence of which a large meeting was held in Sydney, and a resolution adopted that the proceedings of the Legislative Council, in initiating on behalf of Mr. Lowe at the public cost a prosecution against Macdermott and his seconds, were unconstitutional, oppressive, and unjust; a petition to the Governor to the effect that he would not place on the Estimates any sum to defray the expenses of the prosecution, was presented. The prosecution was proceeded with, being brought before the Supreme Court on many occasions, but it finally broke down through informality. 1844.

In the *Argus* newspaper, Melbourne, an article appeared, in which a Goldfields Member was called "a ruffian who had been pitchforked into Parliament." For this offence Mr. George Dill, the publisher of that paper, was arrested and charged at the Bar of the House with a breach of privilege and contempt. He was committed to the custody of the Sergeant-at-arms, and on May 24 was discharged on payment of fees. April 4, 1862.

The Melbourne *Argus* published a leading article, in which Sir James M'Culloch was accused of making a speech "bristling with falsehoods," March 19, 1866.

[Hugh George, publisher of the *Argus*, summoned to the Bar of the House for contempt, March 20, 1866 ; applied to be heard in defence, but refused by 39 to 21 votes, March 21, 1866 ; imprisoned in the Parliament house on the same day ; the Legislative Assembly agreed to liberate Hugh George on payment of fees, March 28; 1866 ; Hugh George declined to pay the fees, March 29, 1866 ; Parliament prorogued, at noon, April 11, 1866; Hugh George liberated at 5 p.m., April 11, 1866.]

PARLIAMENTARY AGENT.

Appointment of Parliamentary Agent in England for the Colony of New South Wales conferred on the Hon. Francis Scott, M.P. for Roxburgh, to represent the interest of the Colony in the House of Commons at a salary of £500 a year. 1844. Act passed appointing him agent for N.S.W. for three years, Oct. 30, 1846 ; re-appointed for one year ending August 3, 1849.

Edward W. T. Hamilton appointed agent for the Colony of N.S.W., resident in London, January 20, 1863.

PARRAMATTA.

Settlement of then Government farm, called Rose Hill, at the head of the navigation of the harbour, fifteen miles distant from Sydney, February 16, 1788.

Rose Hill, becoming a regular town, had its name changed to Parramatta, June 14, 1791.

John Macarthur appointed to the command of the settlement at Parramatta, January, 1793.

St. John's, C.E., Parramatta, completed, September 29, 1796.

School opened by Mr. Tull. 1797. [The School was conducted by Mr. Tull until 1877.]

First "Independent" service in New South Wales held here, by Mr. James Cover. 1798.

Instructions issued by Governor King to the Rev. Samuel Marsden upon delegating to him the general superintendence of the Police Convict Settlement and Government Affairs at Parramatta, September 28, 1800.

St. John's Church, Parramatta, opened, April, 1803.

First R. C. Service held at Parramatta by Rev. James Dixon, May 24, 1803.

Boatmen's fares to Parramatta arranged, July 6, 1833. [*See* GOVERNMENT ORDERS.]

The foundation stone of the Church of England parsonage, Parramatta, laid by the daughter of Rev. Samuel Marsden, May 5, 1816.

First Wesleyan Chapel opened in Macquarie-street, Sydney, April 21, 1821.

Observatory built by Mr. Dunlop, Astronomer, 1822.

Parramatta Show. First prize for best thoroughbred colt awarded to Sir John Jamieson's horse, "Bennelong" which afterwards won many races on the turf of the colony, October 4, 1827.

School of Industry opened, July 1, 1829.

An Act was passed by the Legislative Council of New South Wales to compel married men to withdraw their wives from the female factory at Parramatta or to maintain them after the expiration of their service, September 14, 1829.

Daring robbery of St. John's Parsonage (Rev. S. Marsden). A quantity of valuable property, and the communion plate of St. John's Church carried off. November 26, 1879.

Annual conference with the aboriginals in the Market Place, by Governor Darling, January, 1830.

Foundation of King's School by the Home

PARRAMATTA
The Australasian Sketcher, 1880

Government; Rev. Robert Forrest first Head Master, May, 1831. [Rev. W. B. Clarke, Simpson, Troughton, Walker, H. Hobart, Thos. Druitt, H. Armitage, and G. F. Macarthur were the successive Head Masters since. The present building was completed about the year 1836. The King's School was closed from 1866 to 1869, and then re-opened by the present Head Master.]

Lady Elizabeth Jane Bourke, wife of Sir Richard Bourke, K.C.B., Governor of New South Wales, died at Parramatta, aged 56. She was buried in the Church of England cemetery, Parramatta, May 7, 1832.

King's School (present building) Parramatta, opened, November 8, 1856.

Abbott, gaoler, was shot in the gaol, and three prisoners made their escape, December, 1842.

Observatory closed, 1847.

Lady Mary Fitzroy killed December, 1847.

PARRY, Sir Edward.

Celebrated Polar navigator, arrived in Sydney December 23, 1829.

Sir William Edward Parry, Arctic explorer, and for some years commissioner of the Australian Agricultural Company, died 1855.

PARDONS.
Lieutenant King arrived in the "Gorgon" with his Majesty's authority to grant absolute or conditional pardon to a number of convicts. September 21, 1791.

PATERSON River;
settlement on, formed, 1818.

PATERSON, Colonel,
succeeded Lieutenant-Governor Foveaux. Colonel Paterson, as superior military officer at the time of Bligh's suspension, was entitled to the office of Lieutenant-Governor, and remarked in the proclamation announcing his assumption that "Successive causes had until that period protracted his receiving the trust that devolved on him for the time being." January 9, 1809.

Colonel Paterson and lady embarked for England, April 17, 1810.

PEDESTRIANISM, &c.
Old Racecourse (Hyde Park) Sydney—Dicky Dowling to carry 14st. and run 50 yards, whilst another ran backwards and forwards same distance; Dowling won. October, 1810.

Hyde Park—100 yards to be run by Lieutenant Raymond, while Captain Glenholm rode the same distance; the Lieutenant won. July 24, 1811.

Parramatta Racecourse—Mr. T. Nicholls and Mr. J. Lawson, 200 yards. The first trial resulted in a dead heat; Mr. Nicholls won the run off. September 26, 1829.

Hyde Park—A 200 yards backwards race took place between two amateurs, which was won by 3 yards in one minute. August 13, 1830.

Parramatta Road—A man leaped over three horses, January 15, 1832.

Great foot race at Campbelltown between Merritt and Warby, two celebrated runners; both claimed the victory. May 22, 1833.

Parramatta Road—Welch and Farrell, 100 yards. The winner had a wooden leg and received 10 yards start. May 5, 1834.

Parramatta Road—A gentleman, for a stake of £10 and a dinner, undertook to run a mile in 5min. 30sec.; he won by 3sec. March 31, 1835.

Parramatta Road—T. Wall and C. Hearne ran a 100 yards backwards race for £20; Hearne won; time, 15sec. May 4, 1835.

Hunt undertook to walk from Macquarie Place to Parramatta, against time—3 hours; time taken, 2h. 51min. October 13, 1840.

Elizabeth-street—W. Sparkes and W. Burcher, 200 yards, £20; Burcher won by 5 yards. January 27, 1842.

Parramatta Road—The famous Flying Pieman (King) undertook to walk from Macquarie Place to Ireland's public-house, carrying 6st., in 3 h. 20 min. He carried a boy, making up the weight with shot, and won with 9 min. to spare. October 28, 1842.

St. Aubin's—Abraham Nicholls, of Scone, picked up 100 stones, yard apart, dropping each into a basket (about 5¼ miles). Time, 1 h. 42 min. December 26, 1844.

Petersham—One mile, between N. Dillon and a native boy, latter receiving 20 yards start, and won easy. January 24, 1845.

Windsor—Mad Arthur and Kurragong Sawyer to roll from Freeman's Australian Hotel to Blanchard's Signpost; the sawyer won in 9 min. The same distance was done immediately afterwards in 5 min. by Black Bobby. It was very muddy. September 13, 1845.

Woolpack, Petersham—A wager was laid that a man would go one mile without touching the ground, and would not be drawn or ride; it was accomplished on a bicycle. December 8, 1845.

Windsor—Thompson and an aboriginal (Neddy), £20, 100 yards; Thompson won by a foot. December 9, 1845.

Cook's River Road—Nap Dillon and Smith (the Flying Tailor), 100 yards, £10 a-side; Dillon won by 14 yards. March 8, 1847.

Hyde Park—H. Manuel and J. Farnell, 150 yards, £20; Manuel won by 5 yards. April 8, 1847.

Maitland—On a Friday the Flying Pieman was backed to pick up 100 cobs of corn, yard apart, in 55 min.: won by 2 min. On the Saturday he walked 5 miles for a wager—no time given; and on the Monday, at 3 o'clock, he commenced to walk 192 miles in 48 hours, the conditions being not to stop for a minute; three men to watch him—one to keep tally, second to keep a fire going, and the other asleep. At the end of the first 24 hours he had accomplished 102 miles. He failed in the attempt. August 27, 1847.

Maitland Racecourse—King, the Flying Pieman, successfully accomplished the feat of walking 192 miles in 48 hours; time, 46 h. 30 min. September 28, 1847.

Maitland—King successfully accomplished the great feat of walking 1000 quarter miles in 1000 quarter hours, at the back of the Fitzroy Hotel, November 8, 1847.

Maitland, "Fitzroy Hotel"—Flying Pieman to perform the following in 1 h. 30 sec., which he won by 45 sec. Started at 3·29 p.m.:—Ran a mile, 3·36-30; walked a mile, 3·47-45; wheeled a wheelbarrow ½ mile, 3·57-2; 2½ minutes rest; drew a gig with a lady in it ½ mile, 4·13-15; at 4·15 he commenced to walk backwards ½ mile, 4·24-47; rest, 2¾ min.; picked up 50 stones, 4·43-30; now had 15½ min. to perform 50 leaps, 4·58-15. December 26, 1847.

Dungog—Flying Pieman wheeled a barrow one mile, took 50 flying leaps, picked up 50 stones yard apart, ran backward ½ mile; after this he carried a live goat weighing 80lbs., 1½ mile in 12 min. January 8, 1848.

Dungog—Flying Pieman, 500 half miles in 500 half hours, accompanied by his dog Faithful, which was knocked up. February 28, 1848.

Singleton—Flying Pieman walked backwards ½ mile, 6 min.; ran a mile, 7½ min.; wheeled a barrow 1 mile, 15 min.; 50 leaps, 2 ft. 6 in., 10 ft. apart, 6 min. 25 sec.; 50 stones, yard apart, 14 min.; walked a mile, 11 min.; wheeled a cart ½ mile, 20 min.; won by 8½ min. The whole was to be done in 90 min. He stopped 1 min. 45 sec. April 28, 1848.

Singleton—Flying Pieman to do 60 miles in 12 hours—completed 50 miles in 11 hours 40 minutes; he walked several yards over the measured mile. May 4, 1848.

Flying Pieman beat the coach from Brisbane to Ipswich by one hour, carrying a carriage pole 100 lbs. weight. October, 1848.

THE FLYING PIEMAN
The Illustrated Sydney News, 1855

Parramatta—Ben Watsford and Tom New, 150 yards; Watsford, 2 yards. December 11, 1848.

Hyde Park— Paddy Sinclair and Hoppy Meharty, 100 yards; Meharty by 6 yards. After the above the latter ran a match with "Little Billy the Tailor," which he won. January 3, 1849.

Hyde Park—M. Morrissey and E. Byrnes, 100 yards; won by the latter by 6 inches. July 16, 1849.

Maitland—Mr. Hughes, of Patrick's Plains, to run 10 miles in 1 h. 20 min.; lost by 1½ minute. It was raining. November, 1849.

Waterloo Flats—M. Comerford and Nat Dillon ¼ mile; Comerford won by 50 yards. July 1, 1850.

Hyde Park—Richards and Hutchinson, latter 3 yards start; Richards fell down. August 5, 1850.

Newtown—W. Sparkes and Hanslow, 200 yards; Hanslow easy. January 3, 1853.

Cook's River—Adelaide stag and W. Sparkes, ¼ mile; stag won easy. January 17, 1843.

Neich's, Burwood—Adelaide stag and Mr. Watsford, 100 yards; Watsford by 3 yards. January 20, 1853.

Neich's, Burwood—Two hours after the above, Adelaide stag and T. Farnell, 150 yards; Farnell, 5 yards. January 20, 1853.

Newtown—Adelaide stag and Hatfield, 200 yards, £100; stag won. March 21, 1853.

Cook's River—Eather and Hatfield, 150 yards, £50; Eather easy. March 28, 1853.

Cook's River—Adelaide stag and Farnell, of Parramatta, 200 yards, £200; Farnell, 2 yards. April 18, 1853.

Cook's River—Eather and Farnell, 150 yards, £200; Eather by less than a foot. April 25, 1853.

Cook's River—Alcorn, of Maitland, and Eather, of Windsor, 100 yards, £200; Alcorn, 2 yards. May 31, 1853.

Cook's River—Alcorn and Farnell, 100 yards, £200; Farnell, 2 yards. June 20, 1853.

Cook's River—Alcorn and Farnell, 100 yards, £100; Farnell, 1½ yard. June 21, 1853.

Farmer's Inn, Parramatta Road—W. Grigsby, walking, running, and wheeling a barrow a mile, and picking up 50 stones, yard apart; time, 47 minutes. Perry,

of Parramatta, ran a mile against time. July 21, 1853.

Maitland—G. Rutherford, of Parramatta, and T. Wise, of West Maitland, 100 yards; Rutherford easy. November 7, 1853.

Essendon—Mr. Manuel, of Victoria, and T. Farnell, of N.S.W., 100 yards, £600; Farnell won by 3 yards. November, 1853.

St. Mary's—Pictori stag and Charles Roberts, 100 yards, £20; stag won. January 2, 1854.

Hyde Park—Dr. Watsford and Thompson, the former laying £100 to latter's £50; Dr. won easy. January 16, 1854.

Parramatta—Rutter and Perry, 50 yards, £100; Rutter, half yard. January 18, 1854.

Wilberforce—Oxley and Bushell, 100 yards, £20; Oxley by one foot. May, 1854.

Goulburn—John Hill and Patrick Byrne, 100 yards, £50; Byrne by 5 inches. In a return match next day Hill was the winner. April, 1854.

Hyde Park—Rutherford and The Stranger, 100 yards, £50; Rutherford, 4 yards: time, 10 seconds. July 3, 1854.

South Head Road—The elder of the Thomas Brothers, undertakers, to walk from Spink's public-house to the Lighthouse and back in 3 hours; time, 2 h. 43 min. The junior brother walked it the next evening in 2 h. 33 min. This was beaten the next week by 9 min. Distance, about 13 miles. July, 1854.

Hyde Park—Great foot hurdle race, 150 yards, four 3 ft. 6 in. hurdles; won by Lindsay, of Windsor. July 31, 1854.

Parramatta—Rutherford and Schofield, 150 yards; won by the former. Welsh and Rutter, 75 yards; was won by Welsh. August 14, 1854.

South Head—Welsh and the Stag, six score yards; Welsh, 1 yard. August 19, 1854.

Hyde Park—Welsh and Eather, 100 yards, £50; Welsh easy. August 28, 1854.

Hyde Park—Farnell and a Penrith boy, Farnell to carry 33 lbs.; the boy just won. September 18, 1854.

Surry Hills Boundary Stone—Welsh and Farnell, £500 and championship, 100 yards; Welsh won easy. October 9, 1854.

Hyde Park—Devonport and Farnell, 125 yards, £500; Devonport by a breast. Three quarters of an hour after, Farnell ran Rutherford, 150 yards; Farnell won. October 23, 1854.

Homebush—Devonport and Farnell, 125 yards, £100, championship; Devonport by a yard. November 27, 1854.

Museum, Geelong—Williams backed to perform the following 8 feats in 30 min.:—1. To run 100 yards against the best man in the town. 2. To pick up 30 eggs, yard apart, with his mouth, without touching the eggs or his knees the ground. 3. To throw 20 56lb. weights over his head. 4. To run 100 yards backwards. 5. To hop 100 yards. 6. To throw a 10lb. hammer 80 feet. 7. To throw a 2lb. quoit 140 feet. 8. To roll a coach wheel ½ mile. Time, 25 min. 30 sec. December, 1854.

Windsor Racecourse—Judd and Dalton, 150 yards, £100 a-side; Dalton, 3 yards. January 15, 1855.

Parramatta Road—Dalton and Devonport, 150 yards, £100, and championship; Dalton was never headed. January 31, 1855.

Perth, Tasmania—J. Gibson, of Tasmania, and Mr. Best, of Victoria, championship of Tasmania and £200; Mr. Best won. March, 1855.

Windsor—Devonport and Dalton, 150 yards; Devonport, 3 yards; time, 17 sec. April 2, 1855.

South Head—Mr. Baker, an amateur, 8½ miles in 1 hour; lost by 43 sec. March 3, 1855.

Flying Pieman to pick up 50 stones, yard apart, in 17 minutes; he won by 15 sec. April, 1855.

Homebush—Devonport and Dalton, championship and £200, 150 yards; Devonport, easy, 17 sec. April 25, 1855.

Hyde Park—Messrs. Jones and Holman, to walk from St. James' Church round the Park; Holman won. Shortly after a Billy Humphries undertook to walk from Market-street round in 20 min.; his time was 17½ min. June 4, 1855.

Windsor—Dalton and Beasley, 50 yards; Dalton easy. June 18, 1855.

Homebush—Devonport and a darkey, 300 yards over hurdles. The pistol went off accidentally; the darkey

ran over the ground. July 9, 1855.
Wilberforce—Bushell and a darkey, 300 yards, £200; darkey, 4 yards. July 16, 1855.
Canterbury—Mr. Baker against a horse, 50 yards; Mr. Baker was beaten. August 20, 1855.
Yass—D. Douglass and J. Quigley, 150 yards; Quigley easy. September 3, 1855.
Bendigo Camp enclosure—Devonport and Hayes, £400, 200 yards; Devonport, by a breast; time, 20 sec. May, 1856.
Kissing Point—Dalton and Farnell, 100 yards, £100; Dalton, by 18 inches. March 17, 1857.
Ryde—Farnell and Rutter (the latter 3 yards start), 100 yards, £100; Rutter, smallest possible win. April 13, 1857.
Randwick Road—Chamberlain and Murphy, 150 yards, £50; Chamberlain easy. April 13, 1857.
Melbourne Cricket Ground—450 yards Steeplechase, championship of St. Kilda and Brighton, between H. Ryder and J. Were; Ryder, 10 yards. June, 1857.
Brisbane Road, Launceston—G. M'Kertchy and Thos. Prosser, 150 yards, £20; Prosser, 2 yards; 17 sec. July 23, 1857.
Liverpool—Martineer and Hall, 136 yards, £100; Martineer 2 yards. March 29, 1858.
Domain, Sydney—Mr. C. R. Robinson and Mr. Alexander Black, 100 yards, £200; both these gentlemen were verging on 60 years of age. Robinson won easy. September 3, 1858.
Victoria Theatre, Ballarat—Allen M'Kean commenced the feat of 1000 miles in 1000 hours; finished on November 27, at 10 o'clock, with the greatest gameness, doing the last mile in 22½ minutes, and successfully completing the 1000 miles. September 19, 1858.
Armidale—J. Scholes and J. Jones, 3 miles, £20. Jones fell down, and Scholes finished alone in a walk. Time 33 minutes. September, 1858.
Wowingragong course—John Robinson and William Ragen, championship of the Lachlan and £300, 100 yards; Robinson by 2 yards. September 15, 1858.
Barwon Park—Martineer and White, 100 yards, £200; Martineer, 5 yards. February 14, 1859.
Lyceum Theatre, Sydney—Allen M'Kean commenced 1000 miles in 1000 hours, at 31 min. 21 sec. past 12; on the 12th March he had 270 miles finished, when there was no further news. February 28, 1859.
Government Paddock, Melbourne—Hammond and Mills, £200, 200 yards; Hammond after a hard race. July 11, 1859.
Lower Araluen—J. P. Sweeny and W. Frost, 100 yards, £200; ended in dispute. August, 1859.
Tasmania—W. Guest and Allen M'Kean, the latter to give one minute start in 5 miles walk; Guest easy. Time 50 min. 37 sec. September, 1859.
Camp Reserve, Bendigo—Tom Moran and Joe Whitley, 200 yards, £300; Moran, 1 yard. March, 1860.
Randwick—J. R. Clarke, of George street, Sydney, walked round the Randwick course (1¼ mile) in 14 min. 10 sec.; Mr. Goyder wagered £5 that he would do the same feat. He accomplished it in 13 min. 26 sec. He had no training. July 28, 1860.
Punt Road, Richmond (V.)—Harry Sallars, of the P. R. to receive 250 yards start from G. Moore, in a 4 mile walk; Sallars gave up. October 30, 1860.
M. C. C. Ground—Charles Harrison, of Richmond, and Mr. Mount, of Ballarat, a match at 100 and 140 yards over hurdles, for the championship of Victoria; won by Mr. Harrison. June, 1860.
Mudgee—W. Freeman and J. Webster, of Mudgee, £100; Freeman won easily. August, 1861.
Bathurst—W. Freeman, of Bathurst, and John Webster, of Mudgee, 100 yards, £200; Webster, 3 yards. October, 1861.
Copenhagen Grounds, Ballarat—Alexander Mount and Harrison, three distances, viz.: 100 and 140 yards flat, and 880 yards over 16 hurdles; Mr. Mount won the 100 yards; time, 10½ sec.; Mr. Harrison the 140 easy in 14 sec., and Mr. Mount the 880. December, 1861.
Penrith—Webster of Mudgee, and Single of Penrith, 100 yards, £400; Single, 2 yards. Time 11 sec. March 10, 1862.
Bourke-street—Rankin and J. Earp, 130 yards, £30; Earp 5 yards. October 6, 1862.
Copenhagen Grounds, Ballarat—Mr. Harrison and Mr. Mount for the amateur championship, 100 yards, 140 yards, and 660 yards over 12 hurdles; Mr. Harrison won the 100 yards by a yard in 10½ sec., and the 140 yards by 4 yards, in 13½ sec. The 660 hurdle race was a dead heat—Mr. Mount running over the ground. December 2, 1862.
Lake Macquarie Road—Jones and Earp, 150 yards, £40; Earp 3 yards. December 6, 1862.
Wangaratta—T. Cusack of Wangaratta, and T. Holmes of Geelong, best two out of three at 150 and 300, and to decide at 200 yards; £400; Cusack won the 150 in 15½ sec., by a yard and a half, and the 300 by 8 yards in 32½ sec. December 22, 1862.
A. A. Company's Paddock, Newcastle—E. Jones of Newcastle, and J. Honeysett of Mudgee, 100 yards, £100. Jones, 2 yards. January 8, 1863.
Elsternwick Road—G. Moore and G. Shaw; 7 mile walk, £100; Moore won by 1 min. 53 sec. Time 1 h. 3 min. and 2 sec. September 14, 1863.
Double Bay—J. Earp and W. Malone, 120 yards, £40; Malone, 3 yards. Time, 11½ sec. June 10, 1864.
Opening day of the Albert Cricket Ground, Redfern, October 29, 1864.
Randwick—E. Jones and W. Malone, 155 yards, £200; Malone, 3 yards. Time 18 sec. March 11, 1865.
Randwick—Braithwaite and Lennon, 120 yards, £50; Braithwaite easy. December 14, 1865.
Double Bay—Braithwaite and Kelly, 200 yards, £50; Braithwaite, 2 yards. February 9, 1866.
Liverpool—Braithwaite and Newtown, 125 yards, £165; Braithwaite, 3 yards. April 4, 1866.
Red House, Northcote (V).—George Moore, of Melbourne, and William Payne of Ballarat, 7 miles championship and £100; G. Moore easy. A mistake was made in the distance; they walked 7 miles 1346 yards. Time 1 h. 2 min. 7½ sec. July 21, 1866.
Red House, Northcote—Mat Higgins, 10 miles in 59 min. 35 sec. September 22, 1866.
Albert Ground—Hincks and Leahart, 1½ mile walk £100; Hincks easy. Time 12 min. 50 sec. October 6, 1866.
Albert Ground—Strettles and Grisdale, 4 miles, £50; Strettles by 229 yards. Time 37 min. 50 sec. October 20, 1866.
Dunedin (N. Z.)—Wain of Dunedin, and Brown of Green Island, for championship of Otago and £100; 1 mile. Brown easy. October 19, 1866.
Albert Ground, Sydney—Mat Higgins, 5¼ miles in half an hour; it was raining heavily; Higgins was beaten by 1 min. 40 sec. December 1, 1866.
Albert Ground—Hincks and Hamilton, 3 mile walk, £800 and championship; Hamilton by 55 sec. Time 24 min. 48 sec. February 8, 1867.
Albert Ground—Mat Higgins and S. Manning to pick up 50 apples yard apart; Higgins won by 2, or 120 yards. Time 9 min. 58 sec. March 23, 1867.
Albert Ground—Young Austin to run 10 miles in the hour. Time taken, 66 min. 15 sec. July 6, 1867.
Albert Ground—First 5 mile handicap, won by Mat Higgins. Time, 29 min. 28 sec. July 13, 1867.
Albert Ground—Match against time, 19 miles in 2 hours by Mat Higgins; he failed. Time 15 miles, 1 h. 36 min. 50 sec. August 10, 1867.
Albert Ground—Hamilton and Hincks, walk 1 mile, £30; Hincks came in first but was disqualified. Time 6 min. 30 sec. August 17, 1867.
West Maitland—F. Mitchell and R. Bogg, 100 yards, £60; Mitchell, 2 yards. August 31, 1867.
Albert Ground—Mat Higgins and M. Ryan, ¼ mile, £50; Higgins 10 yards. Time, 53¼ sec. September 21, 1867.
Red House, Northcote—Mat Higgins and Cusack, 450 yards, Higgins easy. Time, 57 sec. February 28, 1868.
Wangaratta—Higgins and Cusack, three distances, viz.: 150, 200, and 300 yards. Higgins won the 200 in 23¼ sec., and 300 in 36 sec. June 15, 1868.
Red House, Northcote—J. G. Harris, of Victoria, v. Simon Hanrahan, of Sydney, 200 yards, £200; Harris 7 yards. Time, 22 or 23 sec. August 1, 1868.
Red House, Northcote—J. G. Harris, (V.) v. W. Braithwaite (N.S.W.), 150 yards, £400; Harris, 11 yards. Time, 15½ sec. August 8, 1868.
Mowbray Course (T.)—J. G. Harris (V.) v. R. Collins (T.) 150 yards, £400; Harris, 5 yards. Time, 15¾ sec. September 28, 1868.
Albert Ground—First Sydney Athletic Cup won by Yeomans, December 26, 1868.

Albert Ground—W. Baker v. W. Hamilton, 7-mile walk, £110; Baker, 50 yds. Time, 1 h. 41 sec. November 9, 1869.
Albert Ground—W. Hamilton v. W. Baker, 7 miles—£175. Baker gave up. Time, 56 min. 50 sec. December 17, 1869.
Melbourne—English pedestrians arrived at Melbourne: Bird, Hewitt, and Topley. December 16, 1869.
Croxton Park—J. G. Harris v. Bolton, latter 5 yds. start—150 yards—£200. Harris easily. Time, 15 sec. December 17, 1869.
M. C. C. Ground—J. G. Harris and Frank Hewitt, 100, 200, 300, 440.—Hewitt won the 100 by 1 foot in 10¼ sec., the 440 finished alone in 51½ sec. The 300 was a dead heat in 33¾ sec. Harris won the 150 by 4 yds. in 15¼ sec., and the 200 by 3 yds. in 20½ sec. March 5-7, 1870.
Albert Ground—First appearance of English pedestrians in New South Wales, April 18, 1870:
Albert Ground—G. Topley v. W. Baker, 7 miles, £200. Baker, 300 yds. start. Topley won. Time, 57 min. 10 sec. May 7, 1870.
Friendly Societies Ground—F. Hewitt v. J. G. Harris—300 yards, £200. Hewitt, 5 yards. Time, 30½ sec. June 23, 1870.
Albert Ground—Mat. Higgins v. A. Pyke—150, 300, and 440 yards, £100. Higgins won the 150 yards by a yard in 15¼ sec., and the 300 by 2 yards, in 32½ sec. September 17, 1870.
Albert Ground—Hewitt v. Harris, 150 and 200 yards. Hewitt won the 150 by ½ yard in 15½ sec., and Harris the 200 by a breast in 24½ sec. October 5, 1870.
Albert Ground—W. Lyall and W. Baker, walk 2 miles, championship. Baker gave up. October 22, 1870.
Albert Ground—H. Teddick and J. Wheeler, 1 mile, £100. Wheeler easily. Time, 4 min. 58 sec. November 9, 1870.
Christchurch, New Zealand—F. Hewitt, ½ mile, to beat a certain time. Time taken, 1 min. 53¼ sec. (Fastest half mile on record.) September 17, 1871.
Eastern Oval, Ballarat—G. Cronk v. W. Sansom, ½ mile, championship and £100. Sansom, 2 feet. Time, 2 min. 2-10 sec. February 2, 1874.
West Maitland—R. F. Watson v. F. Brown, 200 yards, £200. Watson, 6 yards. April 4, 1874.
Hamilton—R. F. Watson v. G. Cronk, ¼ mile, £200. Watson won in 50¼ sec. July 11, 1874.
Parkes—J. Applitt v. G. Thompson, 100 yards, £100. Applitt easily. April 11, 1870.
Albert Ground—L. Pyke v. Henderson, 1 mile, £100. Pyke, 7 yards. Time, 5 min. July 25, 1870.
Launceston—Bird, 10½ miles in 56 min. August 29, 1870.
Parkes—Applitt v. Baxter, 250 yards, £400. Applitt by 8 yards. Time, 29 sec. December, 1874.
Narrandera—R. Williams v. T. Green, 100 yards, £100. Williams, 8 yards. January 1, 1875.
Albert Ground—First Sheffield Handicap, prize £40; won by H. Thompson, W. H. Morgan, second, and R. Hill, third. January 26, 1875.
West Maitland—R. F. Watson v. J. M. Watson, 200 yds., £500. R. F. Watson, 4 yards. Time, 19 8-10th sec. May 22, 1875.
Dunedin—W. Edwards to walk 70 yards—Burke to run 100, £80. Dead heat. June 12, 1875.
Auckland—Collins v. Delaney, 100, 150, and 300 yards. Delaney won the first two. June 12, 1875.
R. F. Watson v. F. Hewitt, 200 yards, £400. R. F. Watson, 1 yard—20 1-10th sec. May 6, 1876.
Parkes—R. F. Watson v. J. Applitt, 200 yards, £400. Applitt easy. Time,. 19¼ or 20¼ sec. November 4, 1876.
South Melbourne Ground—Hewitt v. F. S. Davis, 100 yards, £200. Hewitt easy. November 8, 1876.
West Maitland—R. F. Watson v. F. S. Davis, 150 yards, £200. Won by Watson by 9 inches. Time, 14 6-10th sec. January 13, 1877.
Richmond—C. Carver v. J. Griffiths, 150 yards, £200. Carver won in 15 sec. August 15, 1877.
Longest hop, step, and jump in Australia done at Mortlake (Victoria) by a half-caste named Frank Clarke—distance covered 42 feet 7¼ inches. December 26, 1877.
West Maitland—R. F. Watson v. C. Carver, 200 yards, £400. Watson easily. May 18, 1878.
West Maitland—R. F. Watson v. J. Applitt, 200 yards, £400. Watson won by 6 yards. Time, 20 sec. 1878.
W. Edwards to walk 110 miles in 24 hours, at Guild Hall, Sydney, walked 102 miles in the specified time. October 5, 1878. [He performed the feat in Bathurst same year.]

Charles Langton Lockton, the champion amateur jumper and hurdle-racer of England, is a Tasmanian by birth. His father was many years ago the Anglican minister at Windermere, East Tamar, and Charles was born there on 2nd July, 1856, but was taken to England early and educated at the Merchant Taylors' school. In 1869 he first entered the pedestrian arena, and for the next two years confined his successes to his school sports, not appearing in public competitions till April, 1872. During the past seven years up to 1879 however his success has been wonderful, and his performances in high jump, wide jump, hurdles, and handicaps, have been simply unparalleled in the history of athletics. Contesting at nearly all classes of sports, he contested 17 high jumps, winning 14 and being second thrice. In long jumping he has won 27, twice second, and once unplaced, out of 30 events, and he has won all the spring high jumps he contended for. In handicaps he has won 26 trial heats, second four times, and unplaced three, while in the final heat he has competed 34 races, winning 12, six times second, six times third, and ten times unplaced. Twice he has put the weight, winning once and being third another time, and was victorious in the only tug of war he contested. In level races, country trial, and final heats he has competed 67 times, winning 60, being second four times, twice third, and once unplaced. Altogether he has contested in 187 competitions, winning no less than 144, being second 19 times, third 9 times, and unplaced 15 times.

W. Edwards, a native of London, aged 28, 5 feet 7½ inches high, undertook to walk 180 miles within 48 hours at the Guild Hall, Sydney. He completed the distance half-an-hour within time, May 17, 1879.

PEERAGE, COLONIAL.

Attempted Creation of. A committee, consisting of Messrs. Charles Cowper, T. A. Murray, George Macleay, E. Deas-Thomson, J. H. Plunkett, Dr. Douglas, W. Thurlow, James Macarthur, James Martin, and W. C. Wentworth, appointed on the motion of W. C. Wentworth, held its first meeting, Sydney, May 27, 1853. Fifteen meetings were called. Half the members did not attend meetings. The Bill was reported July 28, 1853. [It was almost universally condemned by the people, and a large public meeting was called to oppose it. In the advertisement convening the meeting were the following paragraphs:—"A committee of the Legislative Council has framed a new Constitution for the colony, by which it is proposed (1.) To create a colonial nobility with hereditary privileges. (2.) To construct an Upper House of Legislature in which the people will have no voice. (3.) To add eighteen new seats to the Lower House, only one of which is to be allotted to Sydney while the other seventeen are to be distributed among the country and squatting districts. (4.) To squander the public revenue by pensioning off the officers of the Government on their full salaries! thus implanting in our institutions a principle of jobbery and corruption. (5.) To fix irrevocably on the people this oligarchy in the name of free institutions, so that no future Legislature can reform it even by an absolute majority. The Legislative Council has the hardihood to propose passing this unconstitutional and anti-British measure with only a few days notice, and before it can possibly be considered by the colonists at large." The meeting was addressed by Mr. (now Sir) Henry Parkes and other Liberals, and the result of the agitation was that the most objectionable clause, to create an hereditary colonial peerage was struck out.]

PELLETIER. Rescue by the crew of the schooner "John Bell" from the blacks at Rocky Point, Cape Direction, Northern Queensland, of Narcisse Pelletier, who had been wrecked 17 years previously, April 11, 1875. [Pelletier had been a cabin-boy on the ship "St. Paul," of Bordeaux, which in 1858 was wrecked on the Louisaida Group, whilst carrying 350 Chinese to Australia. The captain and crew escaped; all the Chinese except 16 were eaten by the blacks.] [See "ABORIGINALS, WHITES AMONGST."]

PHILLIP, GOVERNOR ARTHUR, was, through a misunderstanding, speared by a blackfellow at Manly Beach, September 20, 1790. Died at Bath, England, whither he had retired on a pension of £500 a year, with the rank of a Vice-Admiral in the Royal Navy, 1814.

PICTURE GALLERIES, NATIONAL.

Queen's Room, Melbourne, opened May 24, 1859.

In the Public Library Buildings, Melbourne, opened May 24, 1875.

Academy of Art Sydney, founded May 24, 1871; opened in present premises May 1, 1875.

Opening of seventh annual exhibition of Academy of Fine Arts, Melbourne, March 17, 1877.

"PIEMAN, THE FLYING." [See KING, WILLIAM FRANCIS.]

PIGEON MATCHES.

Pigeon match at Parramatta, October 8, 1831.
At Maitland, October 8, 1833.
Mr. Gumbleton won pigeon shooting wager. He undertook to kill 30 pigeons out of 50, with an ounce of shot to each charge, at 25 yards rise, the backer of the birds finding them and laying 15 to 10. Mr. Gumbleton won by scoring 30 birds for 32 shots. January 28, 1871.

PIGS.

74 Pigs, viz., 49 hogs and 25 sows, came out in the "first fleet," January, 1788.

NUMBER OF PIGS IN AUSTRALIA, DEC. 31, 1877.

New South Wales	191,677

FINE ART EXHIBITION
The Illustrated Sydney News, 1854

New Zealand	123,921
Queensland	52,371
South Australia	104,527
Tasmania	55,652
Victoria	183,391
Western Australia	18,942
Total	730,481

PILLARS, REV. JAMES, Unitarian clergyman, killed by falling off the cliffs at Sydney Heads, July 31, 1875.

PINCHGUT (native name MATTEWAE), an island situated in the harbour of Port Jackson, near Sydney. It was named Rock Island by Governor Phillip, but called Pinchgut by some of the "first fleet," who had, for bad conduct, been sent there and placed on short allowance of food.

PIPER, CAPTAIN, DEFALCATIONS OF. 1827. [See CRIMES.]

PIRACY.

The "Cyprus," convict ship, seized by Captain Swallow and 31 other prisoners, in Recherche Bay, on their voyage to Macquarie Harbour, Tasmania. Lieutenant Carew, 10 soldiers, and 13 prisoners were afterwards landed. August, 1829. The mutineers made their way to the Friendly Islands and Japan, thence to Canton, whence they took passages to England, and there three of them were arrested. Two (Watts and Davis) were condemned and executed; Captain Swallow was acquitted, 1830.

The "Frederick," 100 tons, seized by 10 prisoners at Macquarie Harbour; January 11, 1834. John Barker was chosen captain, and John Fair mate, and they escaped to Valdavau, where they landed, February 26, 1834. Some of them were arrested, and brought back to Tasmania, where they were tried, but acquitted on some technical points. 1837.

The "Louisa Maria," schooner, seized by the natives in Whitsunday Passage, and burnt. One of the crew was killed. August 11, 1878.

PITT TOWN, N.S.W., named December, 1810.

PITTWATER, near the mouth of the Hawkesbury, so named by Governor Phillip, who examined the coast from Port Jackson to Broken Bay.   March 2 to 9, 1788.

PLATINUM.   Mine discovered near Bendemeer, N.S.W., April 3, 1872.

PLOUGHING MATCHES.

First ploughing match, Bong Bong, Aug, 1828.

Great ploughing match—the fourth annual—at Mr. Waite's farm, Sutton Forest ; there were 19 ploughs in the field.   August 3, 1831.

The sixth annual ploughing match came off at Oldbury, near Sutton Forest ; 21 competitors. The Governor gave a silver medal, which was won by Gulmel Nicholl, overseer to Mr. Bowman.   July 9, 1833.

PLUNKETT, J. H., arrived by the ship "Southworth" from Cork, June 14, 1832.   Mr. Plunkett removed from the Chairmanship of the Board of National Education.   February, 1858. [This event was the subject of discussion among the colonists at large for some time.   The Board was appointed to superintend the formation and management of schools, to be " constituted under Lord Stanley's National System of Education " with power to make by-laws, rules, &c., directing such by-laws, rules, &c., to be published within a month of the date of making the same, in the *Government Gazette*.   At this time the Government aid was only extended to vested schools, but the Board, considering that the extension of grants to non-vested schools would advance education, drew up a set of rules to bring non-vested schools within the scope of their operations, and transmitted the same to the Chief Secretary, to be published in the *Gazette*, and also to be laid before Parliament.   The Board receiving no answer, and the rules not having been published, a correspondence took place between the Chairman of the Board and the Chief Secretary, when the latter replied that it was the deliberate opinion of the Government that the Board had no authority under the Act to make such rules and regulations, and that the Government was not pledged to find funds for the class of schools proposed to be established without express sanction of Parliament. Mr. Plunkett, in answer, said he did not attach much weight to the deliberate opinion of the Government, the office of Finance Minister being vacant, and the Attorney-General (Mr. Martin), being out of town, preparing for his election.   In consequence of this letter, and the publication by Mr. Plunkett of the correspondence and the regulations in one of the morning papers, while the correspondence was going on, a letter from the Chief Secretary was forwarded to Mr. Plunkett, in which Mr. Cowper informed him that the Executive Council considered the letter to the Government was in terms highly improper, and the publication of the correspondence they could not but consider unjustifiable in every respect ; it was therefore the duty of the Government, under the circumstances,

A VIEW OF PITTWATER
The Illustrated Sydney News, 1854

to dispense with his further services as a Commissioner of the Board of Education. On the same day Mr. Plunkett resigned all his other appointments, namely, President of the Upper House, with his seat in the Legislative Council, Justice of the Peace, and Manager of the Roman Catholic Orphan School. The matter of Mr. Plunkett's removal was afterwards brought before the House of Assembly, and resolutions were passed to the effect that the House desired to record its deep regret at the removal of Mr. Plunkett, and felt called upon to express a hope that the Government would take such steps as would enable it to restore him to a position in which he had already rendered such eminent services to the cause of education in the colony, and that the House desired to record its opinion that the Board, in drawing up the regulations, had not exceeded its power. Subsequently, it was announced that the Government were prepared to restore Mr. Plunkett, provided he withdrew the offensive part of the letter.]

POLICE.

A document was issued dated August 7, 1789, and signed by A. Phillip (Governor Phillip, who came out with the First Fleet), and David Collins (Judge-Advocate), contained regulations for a night watch of twelve persons that had been appointed for the more effectual preservation of public and private property, and for the prevention (or detection) of the commission of nightly depredations in the new settlement of Sydney. The names of the first watch were :—Herbert Keeling, Charles Peat, John Harris, John Coen Walsh, John Neal, John Massey Cox, William Bradbury, James Clark, Josh Marshall, Thomas Oldfield, George Robinson, and John Archer. Three of these were afterwards replaced by W. Hubbard, John Anderson, and Stephen Le Grove, Aug. 7, 1789.

First horse-patrol in N.S.W., consisting of 30 men, established 1825.

NUMBER OF POLICE IN AUSTRALASIA, 1879.

	Population.	No. of Police.
New South Wales	645,994	1,150
New Zealand..........	408,348	824
Queensland	195,002	520*
South Australia	231,383	320
Tasmania	106,294	340
Victoria	849,870	1,137
Western Australia	27,579	129

* And 201 native troopers.

POLICE MAGISTRATE. Mr. D'Arcy Wentworth retired from the office of police magistrate, which he had held for many years ; he was succeeded by Captain Rossi. 1825.

POPULATION.

The population of New South Wales (excluding Norfolk Island) was 3,500. Dec. 11, 1792.

The number of children in Sydney, born in the colony, was 300. 1796.

Population of New South Wales, 5,557. 1799.

MOUNTED POLICE
S. T. Gill. 1852

The population of the colony was 5,547 persons of all descriptions. Of these 776 were children ; at Norfolk Island 96 ; making a total under the authority of the Governor of 6,508 persons. June 30, 1801.

The population of New South Wales was 7,083 ; Hobart Town, 528 ; Norfolk Island, 1,084 ; and employed in fishing, 123. Total, 8,818. 1805.

First general muster of the colony, by order of Governor Macquarie, took place Feb. 1, 1810.

Census (a muster) taken, October, 1820.

Population of Sydney, 10,815. 1828.

Fifth census taken in New South Wales and Port Phillip, July 16, 1841.

First Queensland census taken, population, 30,059. April 7, 1861.

POPULATION OF AUSTRALASIA, JANUARY 1, 1878.

New South Wales	645,994
New Zealand........	408,348
Queensland	195,092
South Australia	231,383
Tasmania	106,294
Victoria	849,870
Western Australia	27,579
Total............	2,464,560

NOTE.—Statistics to December 31, 1878, show that the population of Victoria has increased to 879,386, and New South Wales to 693,743.

Estimated population of the principal cities in Australia and New Zealand (including suburbs of each), for 1878.

Sydney	200,000
Melbourne	260,678
Adelaide	60,000
Brisbane	35,000
Ballarat	47,156
Auckland	39,401
Dunedin	34,674
Christchurch	29,029
Sandhurst	26,929
Hobart Town	22,500
Wellington	21,005
Launceston	13,000
Rockhampton	9,650
Maitland	8,100
Newcastle	8,000
Perth	7,120
Bathurst	6,150
Goulburn	4,800
Grafton	3,900

PORT CURTIS.

Oxley anchored the "Mermaid" at Gatch Head, Port Curtis, November 6, 1823.

Lieutenant Colonel Barney anchored in Port Curtis, September, 1846.

Governor Fitzroy visited Port Curtis, 1854.

PORT DALRYMPLE.

Discovered by Bass, 1798.

Settled on by Colonel Paterson, 1809.

PORT DARWIN.

Captain Douglass, Government resident at Port Darwin, succeeded Goyder, and retired in May, 1874; Dr. Miller acted in that capacity until October, 1874, when G. B. Scott assumed the direction of affairs, a position which he still holds. 1878.

PORT DARWIN
J. Carr, Mitchell Library

PORT DENISON.

First sale at Brisbane of Port Denison land. September 7, 1861.

PORT ESSINGTON.

A committee of the Council (Dr. Charles Nicholson, Chairman) recommended the despatch of an overland expedition to Port Essington, 1843.

PORT JACKSON,

the principal harbour of New South Wales, the opening to which lies between two rocky promontories, known as North and South Heads. Sydney Harbour is said to be the most beautiful, and for shipping, one of the safest in the world. It has 900 miles of coast line, and a hundred and fifty bays and harbours within it. The shallowest depth of water at the entrance to Sydney Harbour, at low water, in the eastern channel is 26 feet, in the western channel 22 feet. The distances between the three headlands at the entrance to Sydney Harbour are as follows :—

Outer South Head to Outer North Head, 2¼ miles.
Inner South Head to Inner North Head, 1 mile 256 yds.
Inner South Head to Middle Head, 1,100 yards,

[See NEW SOUTH WALES, SETTLEMENT OF.]

PORT LINCOLN, S. A., discovered 1801.

PORT MACQUARIE.

Surveyed by Oxley, June 19, 1819.

Expedition for the formation of a settlement at Port Macquarie sailed from Sydney under command of Captain Allman, 48th Regiment, March 21, 1821.

Port Macquarie appointed a place to which offenders convicted in New South Wales, and being under sentence of transportation, should be sent, August 15, 1826.

PORT PHILLIP (*Now* VICTORIA.)

PORT PHILLIP BAY is over 30 geographical miles from north to south, and 35 miles from east to west ; area 700 square miles. In Port Phillip Bay there are two minor bays, viz. : Hobson's Bay, which is the anchorage of the Port of Melbourne, and the point at which the river Yarra Yarra, on which Melbourne is situated, empties itself, and Corio Bay, which is the anchorage of Geelong. Its width at the entrance is 3,900 yards.

First discovery of Port Phillip district made by Captain Cook, R.N., in his ship the *Endeavour*, 1770.

Mr. George Bass, Surgeon of H.M.S. *Reliance*, when on an exploring expedition in a whale boat, entered a harbour which he named Western Port, June 4, 1798.

Mr. Bass, with Lieutenant Matthew Flinders, R.N., in the *Norfolk*, discovered Bass's Straits, October, 1798.

Lieutenant Grant, R.N., in the *Lady Nelson*, passed through Bass's Straits on a voyage from England to Sydney, when he named Mount Gambier, Cape Banks, Cape Northumberland, Cape Bridgewater, Cape Nelson, the Lawrence Islands, Portland Bay, Lady Julia Percy's Island, Cape Otway, Cape Patton, Governor King's Bay (the curve in the land at the entrance of Port Phillip), Cape Liptrap, the Rodondo Rock, the Glennie Islands, the Hole in the Wall, Sir Roger Curtis Island, Moncur Island, and the Devil's Tower. December, 1800.

Lieutenant John Murray, R.N., in the *Lady Nelson*, examined the Bay now called Port Phillip Bay. He entered and named it Port King, in honor of Governor King, at whose request it was afterwards changed to Port Phillip, in honor of Governor Phillip. Lieutenant Murray also named Arthur's Seat and Point Nepean. February 18, 1801.

Lieutenant James Grant, R.N., made a survey of the coast from Wilson's Promontory, to, and including,

Western Port, March 21, 1801.
Lieutenant Matthew Flinders, R.N., in H.M.S. *Investigator* entered Port Phillip Bay, where he remained a week, and examined it, not knowing that Lieutenant Murray had already been there.   April 27, 1801.

Mr. Charles Grimes, Surveyor-General of New South Wales, was sent by Governor King, with Lieutenant Robbins, R.N., and Mr. James Meehan, a surveyor, to survey Port Phillip Bay, 1803. [Grimes' report of his explorations of Port Phillip have never been found in the colonial records, but in January, 1877, his original map was disinterred from an obscurity of 73 years, in the survey office, at Sydney, and, without doubt, gives the credit of the discovery of the river falling into the head of the bay to Grimes.]

H.M.S. *Calcutta*, 50 guns, Captain Woodriff, and the *Ocean*, transport, 500 tons, Captain Matthews, arrived in Port Phillip Bay.   The Calcutta had on board Lieutenant-Governor Collins, and the vessels contained free settlers and convicts, for the purpose of forming a settlement. October 9, 1803.

Mr. J. H. Tuckey, first Lieutenant of the *Calcutta*, published an account of this attempt to form a settlement, in which he says, "Though the vicinity of the harbour's mouth afforded no situation calculated for the establishment of the colony." 1803.

The *Ocean*, transport, left Port Phillip Bay for Port Jackson, November 16, 1803.

A marriage was solemnized at Sullivan's Bay Camp, Port Phillip, by the Rev. Robert Knopwood, between Richard Garrett and Hannah Harvey, 27th November, 1803.

The *Ocean*, transport, returned to Port Phillip Bay from Port Jackson, December 12, 1803.

The *Francis*, schooner, arrived from Port Jackson. She was sent by Governor King to assist at the removal of Lieutenant-Governor Collins's party to Van Diemen's Land. December 14, 1803.

H.M.S. *Calcutta* sailed for Sydney, December 18, 1803.

Four of the convicts, William Buckley, David Marmon, — Pye, and David Gibson, escaped from the settlement, December 27, 1803.

In consequence of the reports of Lieutenant Tuckey's explorations being unfavourable, the settlement was abandoned January 24, 1804.

Port Phillip abandoned, January 31, 1804.

Messrs. Hume and Hovell succeeded in travelling overland from Sydney to the shores of Port Phillip Bay, October, 1824.

In consequence of reports that the French had resolved to found settlements on some parts of the Australian coast, an expedition was sent from Sydney with that object, consisting of H.M.S. "Fly," Captain Wetherall, and the brigs "Dragon" and "Amity," with detachments from the 3rd Regiment (Buffs) and the 39th Regiment, under Colonel Stewart.   This expedition reached Western Port, and the officers and soldiers intended for that place disembarked on its eastern side, and erected a small fortification at the eastern end of Phillip Island, which lies across the entrance.   They found a French expedition had been there before them but that no steps had been taken to form a settlement. 1826.

Mr. Joseph Tice Gellibrand and Mr. John Batman made an application by letter soliciting a grant of land at Western Port, January 11, 1827.   Sir Richard Bourke replied to Messrs. Gellibrand and Batman's letter, refusing their request, March 17, 1827.

The cutter "Fairy," Wishart master, having been caught in a south-westerly gale, put into a bay which was named Port Fairy, 1828.

Mr. William Dutton visited Portland Bay in the schooner "Madeira Packet," on a sealing voyage, December, 1828.

Mr. Dutton visited Portland Bay in the schooner "Henry," Captain McLean, on a sealing voyage.   He was captain of a boat's crew which landed at the present site of Portland, where he remained sealing, and built a house and lived in it.   July, 1829.

Captain Charles Sturt, accompanied by Mr. George Macleay, reached a river which Messrs. Hume and Hovell had crossed in 1824, on their journey to Port Phillip, and called the Hume.   Captain Stuart gave it the name of the Murray, by which it has been since known.   January, 1830.

Mr. William Dutton again visited Portland Bay, and resided there until March, 1833.   He established a whaling station, and erected buildings and grew vegetables for his own use. 1832.

Mr. Edward Henty, in the schooner "Thistle," Captain

BATMAN SIGNS TREATY
Picturesque Atlas of Australia

Liddle, entered the bay, July, 1833.

Mr. Edward Henty landed at Portland Bay with stock, and also boats, &c., to form a whaling establishment. This was the first permanent settlement in Port Phillip. November 19, 1834.

Mr. John Batman returned to Port Phillip, in the *Caledonia*, accompanied by his wife and family and Miss Newcombe, his governess. Mr. James Simpson and the Rev. James Orton, a Wesleyan Minister, were passengers by the same vessel, as also Major Wellman and his son, who were on their way to India. Batman conducted the remainder of his party from Indented Head to the Yarra Yarra river, and fixed his abode on a hill at the western extremity of Collins-street, called from the circumstance Batman's Hill. He built a house there, and opened a general store. His first sheep station was the present site of St. James's Cathedral, in William-street, where he had a shepherd's hut. April, 1835.

It was on this occasion that Mr. Wedge named the Yarra Yarra from the following circumstance : On arriving in sight of it, the native boy who was with him, pointing to the river, called out "Yarra Yarra"; which at the time he imagined was the native name of the river, but he afterwards learnt that the words were those the natives used to designate a waterfall, as the boy afterwards used the same expression to denote a small fall in the river Werribee. 1835.

Mr. Wedge left Port Phillip by the vessel in which he came. 1835.

Batman went up the Yarra Yarra in a boat to the falls above the basin, June 8, 1835.

Batman determined to return to Van Diemen's Land, and proceeded in his vessel to Indented Head, near Swan Point, about twelve miles inside the Heads, where he left the three white men he had brought with him, and five of the aboriginal natives of Sydney, viz., Pigeon, Joe the Marine, Bungit, Bullet, and Old Bull ; also a supply of provisions for three months, a quantity of garden seeds, and six dogs, and gave directions to erect a hut and commence a garden, June 9, 1835.

Batman quitted Port Phillip and arrived at Launceston after a passage of thirty-six hours, June 14, 1835.

William Buckley, one of the prisoners who had escaped in 1803 from Governor Collins, came to Batman's camp at Indented Head, July 12, 1835.

Mr. John Helder Wedge landed at Indented Head in company with Henry Batman and his wife, August 7, 1835.

Mr. John Pascoe Fawkner purchased a schooner called the "Enterprise," and on July 18, 1835, he proceeded to purchase provisions, blankets, tomahawks, knives, handkerchiefs, a whale boat, horses, ploughs, grain for sowing, &c. He put to sea from George Town, having on board all the members of the party, July 27, 1835. Mr. Fawkner became ill from sea-sickness; in consequence he caused the vessel to put back to George Town, July 1835. She again put to sea and entered Western Port, August 8, 1835.

The "Enterprise" entered Port Phillip Heads, August 15, 1835.

The "Enterprise" proceeded to the mouth of the Yarra Yarra river, where she arrived August 20, 1835.

Sir Richard Bourke, Governor of New South Wales, issued a proclamation, notifying "that every treaty, bargain, and contract, with the aboriginal natives, for the possession, title, or claim to any Crown lands within New South Wales, is void, as against the rights of the Crown ; and that all persons found in possession of any such lands, without license or authority from Her Majesty's Government for such purpose, first had and obtained, would be considered as trespassers." August 26, 1835.

John Pascoe Fawkner's party first encamped on the site of Melbourne, August 29, 1835.

John H. Wedge left Indented Head in company with one white man, James Gumm, two Sydney blacks, and a Port Phillip aboriginal boy, and reached the present site of Melbourne, where, with no little surprise, he observed in the basin a vessel, the "Enterprise," moored. For a moment he fancied he had come upon an unknown settlement. Mr. Wedge says, "She was certainly the first vessel that had ever worked her way up to where the Queen's Wharf has since been built." September 2, 1835.

An Association was formed in Van Diemen's Land, consisting of Messrs. John Batman, Joseph Tice Gellibrand, James and William Robertson, Henry Arthur, John Sinclair, Charles Swanston, James Simpson, John Thomas Collicott, Anthony Cottrell, William George Sams, Michael Connolly, Thomas Bannister, and John Helder Wedge, to colonize Port Phillip. It was determined by the association that Batman should at once cross over to Port Phillip, with a view, as Batman states in his journal, "Of secretly ascertaining the general character and capabilities of Port Phillip as a grazing and agricultural district." Concerning this visit, there are two sources of information, viz., Batman's journal, and his letter of June 25, 1835, to Colonel Arthur, Lieutenant Governor of Van Diemen's Land, and the chart and copies of deeds accompanying it. Between these two accounts many grave discrepancies exist, concerning the details of the undertaking. 1835.

Captain Lancey, Mr. George Evans, his servant, Evan Evans, Charles Wise, James Gilbert and his wife, sowed with wheat five acres of land at the south-western extremity of Melbourne, and erected near Batman's hill some tents or huts, as well as a secure place for the stores, 1835.

The "Enterprise" again returned to Port Phillip, having on board Mr. John Pascoe Fawkner and his servant Thomas Morgan. Mr. Fawkner removed the tents or huts which had been erected near Batman's Hill to the rise opposite the falls, and formed a cultivation paddock of 80 acres, on the opposite, or south side of the river, October 10, 1835.

The "Endeavour," with Mr. John Aitken on board, followed Mr. Fawkner's vessel, and arrived at Melbourne a short time after it, October, 1835.

Mr. John Batman addressed a letter from Launceston to Mr. John Helder Wedge, in reference to Fawkner's intrusion upon the land, which he (Batman) had obtained from the natives of Port Phillip. Oct. 13, 1835.

Five hundred sheep were imported from Launceston, in the "Normal," Captain Coltish, for Batman's Association, and landed at Point Gellibrand. This vessel also brought fifty pure Hereford cows, belonging to Dr. Thompson. October 26, 1835.

The first publican's license was issued in Melbourne, October 31, 1835.

First house erected on the site of Melbourne, November 17, 1835.

The first newspaper was published in Melbourne by Mr. John Fawkner, and was called *The Melbourne Advertiser*. It consisted at first of a written sheet; was distributed weekly for nine weeks; and was afterwards continued in a printed form to the extent of 32 numbers. January 1, 1836.

Dr. Thompson arrived at Melbourne with his family, March, 1836.

Lord Glenelg, in a despatch to Governor Sir Richard Bourke, in reply to his letter of the 10th October ultimo, approved of the course he had pursued in reference to Batman's proceedings at Port Phillip, April 13, 1836.

Lord Glenelg, in a despatch in reply to Governor Arthur's despatch of July 4, 1835, on the subject of the negotiations which had been entered into by Batman for the acquisition of a large portion of land, consisting of 600,000 acres in the vicinity of Port Phillip stated, "That all schemes for making settlements by private individuals or companies in the unlocated districts of Australia, have of late years been discouraged by His Majesty's Government, as leading to fresh establishments, involving the mother country in an indefinite expense, and exposing both the natives and the new settlers to many dangers and calamities. And there is so much of prudence and of justice, and I think I may add of humanity in this policy, that I do not feel disposed to depart from it in the present instance." January 23, 1836.

A public meeting of the residents in Melbourne was held, at which seventy-seven persons were present. A resolution was passed, "That James Simpson be appointed to arbitrate between individuals disputing, on all questions excepting those relating to land, with power to name two assistants when he may deem fit." Other resolutions were also passed, including one, "That a

PORT PHILLIP HEADS
The Illustrated Sydney News, 1854

petition be prepared to Governor Bourke, praying him to appoint a resident magistrate at Port Phillip, as well as other magistrates from among the residents." June, 1836.

Messrs. Henry, Alexander, and James Brock imported sheep from Van Diemen's Land, and landed them at Gellibrand Point, near Williamstown, which they occupied for some few months as a station, removing afterwards to Emu Creek, beyond Sunbury.   July 8, 1836.

The brig " Chili," Captain Nixon, arrived at Port Phillip. This vessel had been chartered at Launceston by Messrs. Gellibrand, Swanston, Geo. Evans, and Messrs. S. and W. Jackson, to convey stock to Port Phillip. July 10, 1836.

Messrs. Jackson and Evans, upon landing, explored the Deep Creek, and reached a place afterwards called Jackson's Creek, now Sunbury, where they determined to form a station.   July, 1836.

Captain Lonsdale, police magistrate, arrived to take charge of Port Phillip, September 29, 1836.

Major (afterwards Sir) Thomas Mitchell, Surveyor-General of New South Wales, crossed the Murray river June 15, proceeded along its southern bank, and subsequently reached Portland Bay, where he saw a vessel, the *Elizabeth*, of Launceston, at anchor, and visited the establishment of the Messrs. Henty, 1836.

Major Mitchell surveyed Port Phillip.   September, 1836.

Mr. Russell and his assistants were instructed to survey the shores of Port Phillip Bay.   1836.

C. H. Ebden, Esq., formed a station on the Murray.   He first established a crossing place at Albury.   September, 1836.

Mr. Charles Franks and his shepherd were killed by blacks, supposed to be of the Goulburn tribe of aborigines, at Mr. Frank's station, at Mount Cottrell, near the River Exe or Werribee.   Their remains were brought to Melbourne and interred at the Flagstaff Hill, which had been already selected as a burial place where the child of a man named Goodman had been interred previously, the child being the first person buried by Europeans at Melbourne. · 1836.

Her Majesty's ship " Rattlesnake," Captain Hobson, R.N., arrived in Port Phillip Bay, having on board Captain William Lonsdale, late of the 4th Regiment of Foot, as resident magistrate.   September 29, 1836.

Captain Hobson surveyed the inlet at the head of the bay, which now bears his name.   Mounts Martha and Eliza were named by one of the Lieutenants of the " Rattlesnake," in compliment to Mrs. Lonsdale and Mrs. Batman, respectively.   1836.

The brig " Stirlingshire," which left Sydney September 24, arrived in Port Phillip Bay.   This vessel had on board Mr. Robert Saunders Webb, officer in charge of the customs ; Mr. Skene Craig, commissariat officer ; and Mr. Robert Russell and his assistants ; Mr. Fred. Robert Darcy and Mr. William Wedge Dark, of the survey department ; Ensign King, with a detachment of the 4th Regiment ; thirty prisoners, and Mr. Joseph Howson as chief constable.   October 5, 1836.

Cattle were brought to Port Fairy in the *Thistle*, by Captain Mills, 1836.

Messrs. Gellibrand and Swanston, accompanied by Mr. Dobson, a solicitor at Hobart Town, proceeded to Sydney, to urge upon the Government the claims of Batman's Association, and ultimately obtained for the association as compensation in respect of their claims, an allowance of £7,000, in the remission of the purchase of land at Port Phillip.   October, 1836.

Messrs. Joseph Hawdon and John Gardiner, on their way overland from New South Wales to Port Phillip with cattle, met at Mr. M'Arthur's station on the Murrumbidgee, called Nangus, Major Mitchell and his party, returning to Sydney from their exploration of Port Phillip.   Messrs. Hawdon and Gardiner reached Melbourne at the end of November or beginning of December.   October 27, 1836.

Mr. John Batman had a son born, who was subsequently drowned in the Yarra Yarra at the Melbourne Falls. November 5, 1836.

A census taken in Port Phillip showed the population to be 186 males and 38 females, November 8, 1836.

An aboriginal mission was established at Port Phillip, The station was on the banks of the Yarra, on the site of the present Botanical Gardens.   Mr. George Langhorne was appointed missionary to the aborigines, and was joined by Mr. John Thomas Smith, as his assistant.   December, 1836.

The *Francis Freeling*, Captain Pollock, arrived from Van Diemen's Land, having been chartered by Mr. Joseph Sutherland to convey to Port Phillip 800 sheep, which he had purchased at Hobart Town for two guineas a head.   The sheep were landed in Port Phillip Bay between Indented Head and Point Henry, 1836.

The revenue cutter *Prince George* arrived from Sydney, having on board George Stewart, Esq., who was a Territorial Magistrate, and also Police Magistrate at Goulburn, New South Wales.   He was the first to exercise magisterial authority in Port Phillip, and was ordered to report on the place, and on the condition of its inhabitants.   A meeting took place between Mr. Stewart, as representative of the Government, and the inhabitants, when it appeared that 177 persons from Van Diemen's Land had settled in the neighbourhood of Port Phillip Bay, and had imported live stock and other property to the value of £110,000.   1836.

Mr. Thomas Bates imported from Launceston, in the " Indemnity " and " Henry," some sheep which he landed at Point Henry.   Mr. Bates settled at Cowie's Creek, near the Bell Post Hill, so called in consequence of Messrs. Cowie and Stead having erected a bell on a high sapling, to give the alarm in case of an attack from the aborigines.   1837.

Henry Batman was appointed a district constable, February 7, 1837.

Mr. Taylor, with John Ewart, arrived in Melbourne with cattle.   This party was organized near Yass, by Mr. W. A. Brodribb, for Mr. John Gardiner and Mr. J. T. Gellibrand.   February 13, 1837.

Mr. Charles Bonney left Mr. Ebden's station on the Murray with about 9000 of Mr. Ebden's sheep, and took up a run which he had chosen, south of the Goulburn. They were the first sheep brought by land to Port Phillip.   March 2, 1837.

Governor Sir Richard Bourke arrived from Sydney at the settlement on the Yarra Yarra, in H.M. ship "Rattlesnake," Captain Hobson, R.N., March 4. He was accompanied by Captain Hunter, military secretary; George Kenyon Holden, Esq., his private secretary; Captain P. P. King, as his travelling companion; and Mr. Robert Hoddle, surveyor in charge. The object of this visit was to fix the site for a township. One morning, shortly after their arrival, and whilst they were in camp, the shock of an earthquake was felt. No repetition of the shock occurred, however, and the Town of Melbourne was laid out by Mr. Hoddle. The principal streets were marked to be 99 ft. wide. Governor Bourke named Melbourne after the then Prime Minister, Lord Melbourne; Collins-street, after Lieutenant Governor Collins; Flinders-street, after Captain Flinders; Bourke-street, after himself; Lonsdale-street, after Captain Lonsdale; Swanston-street, after Captain Swanston; and Russell-street, after Lord John (now Earl) Russell. March, 1837.

An address was presented to Sir Richard Bourke, by the inhabitants, to which he replied, and he subsequently made a trip into the interior under the guidance of Mr. Wm. Jackson and Wm. Buckley: he visited Mount Macedon and Geelong, the latter of which he named after the native name of the hill on which it stands.

Governor Sir Richard Bourke named Hobson's Bay after Captain Hobson, R.N., of H.M.S. "Rattlesnake," April 10, 1837.

First marriage solemnized in Melbourne, April 30, 1837.

The first child baptized at Melbourne was the son of James Gilbert, who arrived with Fawkner's party at Port Phillip on the first voyage of the "Enterprise." He was named John Melbourne Gilbert. April 30, 1837.

The first land sale took place at Melbourne, Robert Hoddle, Esq., surveyor in charge of the district, acting as auctioneer. The average price realised for each lot of about half an acre was £35. June 1, 1837.

Sir Richard Bourke landed and encamped on the site of Melbourne, March 4, 1837.

Messrs. John and Joseph Hawdon brought cattle from their station at Howlong on the Murray to Melbourne, and took them to a station at Dandenong called Bigning, which Mr. Alfred Langhorne had formed on Dandenong Creek for Captain Lonsdale and himself. July, 1837.

Foster Fyans, Esq., was appointed police magistrate at Geelong, September 5, 1837.

Patrick Cussen, Esq., was appointed colonial assistant-surgeon, September 12, 1837.

A second land sale was held at Melbourne. Mr. John Pascoe Fawkner purchased the allotment at the corner of Collins and Market-streets for £10. November 1, 1837.

Messrs. James Backhouse and George Washington Walker, Quaker missionaries, arrived at Port Phillip in the "Edora," Stephen Addison, master. They left Port Phillip on the 17th November of the same year. November 10, 1837.

Messrs. J. T. Gellibrand and Hesse were lost in the bush at the Cape Otway ranges. It is supposed that they were murdered by the aborigines. A skeleton, discovered some time after, was identified as that of Mr. Gellibrand, from the fact of one of the teeth being filled with gold. Two hills not far from Winchelsea were named after these explorers, November, 1837.

A fortnightly mail by land was established between Sydney and Melbourne. Mr. Joseph Hawdon contracted to convey it between Melbourne and Yass. It was carried on horseback by his stockman, John Bourke, who acted as mailman. December 30, 1837.

A bushranger, named Cummerford, having at Sydney confessed that he and a shoemaker, name unknown, and a man named Dignam, had murdered between Melbourne and Portland Bay six bushrangers, whilst asleep, Governor Sir Richard Bourke sent Cummerford to Port Phillip to point out the place where the murder had been committed. Upon Cummerford's arrival in Melbourne he was sent for this purpose in charge of a sergeant, one soldier, and two constables. On arriving at the spot indicated, 200 miles from Melbourne, the police found one or two bushels of calcined human bones, some human teeth, and hair

unburnt, and some shoe nails and buttons from the clothes of the murdered men. On their return they found the bones of a horse's head, which Cummerford stated had belonged to Mr. Ebden, and which he and Dignam had shot. One constable and the soldier turned back for some tea which they had left behind, whilst the sergeant, the remaining constable (Tompkins), and Cummerford went on. The party stopped to cook, the sergeant giving his musket to Tompkins whilst he made a fire. Tompkins having left the firearms, Cummerford seized a musket and shot him, and he died in three hours, the ball having entered the left side and passed out at the right breast. Cummerford then plundered the pack-horse and escaped, though pursued by the sergeant for some time. This took place on December 30, 1837, and on January 1, 1838, Cummerford, whilst trying to steal a horse, was taken into custody by three of Mr. Wedge's men.

Mr. Benjamin Baxter was appointed clerk of the bench of magistrates, January 16, 1838.

The Rev. James Forbes, Presbyterian minister, arrived in Melbourne, January 28, 1838.

Mr. Joseph Hawdon, in company with Mr. Charles Bonney and a party of nine men, started from his station on the River Murray (at that time known as the Hume), to drive to Adelaide about three hundred head of cattle, which he had, towards the end of the previous year, brought from New South Wales. January, 1838.

Peter Snodgrass, Esq., appointed commissioner of Crown Lands for the Port Phillip district, February 8, 1838.

Mr. John Pascoe Fawkner commenced the printing and publication of a newspaper, which was called The Melbourne Daily News and Port Phillip Patriot. It was some time after edited by Mr. George Darly Boursiquot, March, 1838.

A party of men in charge of Mr. William P. Faithful's sheep, travelling from New South Wales, were preparing to proceed from the Broken River to the Goulburn River, in the Port Phillip district, where it was understood good sheep stations might be had. Whilst the bullocks were being yoked, the men with the drays heard the shepherds shouting for help: these latter, who were a short distance from the encampment herding the sheep were presently seen running with great speed towards the drays, pursued by a body of blacks throwing spears at them. Their companions at the encampment, three of whom were armed with guns, immediately ran to their assistance, with the intention of driving off the blacks, who were at that time within three or four hundred yards of the encampment. One of these men, named Bentley, fired his gun into the air, thinking by this means to intimidate the blacks, but the shot had no effect; the blacks still pushed forward, cautiously sheltering themselves in their advance behind the trees. When very near the whites, one came forward, and was in the act of deliberately poising his spear when Bentley shot him dead, and was himself immediately afterwards pierced with three spears: the contest then became general, and Bentley was last seen wounded and fighting desperately with the butt end of his musket; the other men, at whom spears were hurled from all directions, fired several shots without effect, owing to the shelter of the trees of which the blacks had availed themselves. The blacks increased in numbers and pressed their advance, until the whites were in danger of complete massacre. Seven of the party of fifteen were killed, and one mortally wounded. The survivors joined in a final rush for escape: the blacks opened in two lines, and speared at the whites as they fled between them. John Campbell, who escaped, died of his wounds. Mr. Crossley, the overseer of the party (subsequently a butcher at Kilmore), was one of those who escaped. The attacking party appeared to the fugitives to be about 150 in number, as seen ranged up in the two lines through which they retreated. At about 100 yards distant another strong party of armed blacks was drawn up; but took no part in the contest. It is said there were not fewer than 300 fighting men present, and that not one old man was seen among them. The party in charge of the sheep and cattle had been awaiting from the Saturday previous the arrival of Mr.

George Faithful, who was only a day's stage behind, and was momentarily expected. The sheep were dispersed, but with the exception of 130 were all recovered ; some of the cattle were lost. Mr. George Faithful and Col. White were camped near the crossing place of the Ovens River, where one of the men who had escaped from the affray arrived some 28 hours after, reporting that he believed he was the only man of the party saved.   April 11, 1838.

Mr. Alfred Langhorne left Melbourne for Sydney, overland ; on his way he fell in with the remainder of Mr. Faithful's party, near the Broken River, on the morning after their affray with the blacks, and on the night of the same day camped with them near Ovens River. April, 1838.

Lady Franklin visited Port Phillip from Van Diemen's Land, of which colony Sir John Franklin, her husband, was Lieutenant-Governor, April, 1838.

The Rev. P. B. Geoghegan, a clergyman of the Church of Rome, arrived in Melbourne from Sydney, May 15, 1838.

The Rev. P. B. Geoghegan (subsequently Roman Catholic Bishop of Adelaide) celebrated mass in Melbourne, May 19, 1839.

William Wright was appointed chief constable at Melbourne, in place of Henry Batman, August 5, 1838.

A branch of the Bank of Australasia was opened at Melbourne, in a small brick building on the north side of Little Collins-street, near Elizabeth-street, with David C. M'Arthur, Esq., as manager, August 15, 1838.

Mr. David Kelsh was appointed by the Governor postmaster of Melbourne ; he opened a post office in a small brick building on the north side of Little Collins-street, a little to the westward of Temple Court. September, 1838.

An Act (2 Victoria, No. 20) was passed by the Legislative Council of New South Wales, to enable the printer and publisher of a newspaper to make the affidavit and enter into the recognisance required by law, before the police magistrate of the district in which such newspaper was to be printed and published. October 2, 1838.

A branch of the Union Bank of Australia was opened at Melbourne in a weatherboard building in Queen-street with William Highett, Esq., as manager, October 17, 1838.

A second newspaper, called *The Port Phillip Gazette*, was printed and published in Melbourne, by Messrs. Strode and Arden. It was issued twice a week. Mr. Strode had brought from Sydney, by the "Denmark Hill," the type, and a wooden press of very ancient construction, with which this paper was printed. October 27, 1838.

A general fast was kept in Port Phillip on account of the long-continued drought, November 2, 1838.

Captain Tobin commenced taking charge of vessels as a private pilot, and brought the schooner "Industry," drawing eight and a half feet of water, up to the Melbourne wharf, November, 1838.

Mr. George Augustus Robinson was appointed chief protector of Aborigines, and Messrs. Edward Stone Parker, William Thomas, Charles Wightman Sievwright, and James Dredge, assistant-protectors. December 11, 1838.

It appears from a memorandum of the chief protector of aborigines, that upon the establishment of the protectorate by the appointment of these gentlemen, Port Phillip was divided into districts as follows :—

"1. The Geelong or Western District, embracing the whole of the country bounded on the south by the coast extending from Indented Head to the Glenelg, or boundary of the South Australian Province ; on the north by a line running from a point 29 miles north of Melbourne to Nurniyong, the Mount Blackwood of Mitchell, thence to Mount Colo, Mount William, and the Glenelg ; the west boundary by the South Australian Province." This district was supposed to contain about 1000 aborigines, and was under C. W. Sievwright, Esq., assistant-protector, whose head-quarters were at Mount Rouse.

"2. The Mount Macedon, or North-Western District, bounded on the south by the district of Geelong ; on the west by the boundary of the South Australian Province ; on the east by a line running north from Tarerewait, or Mount Macedon ; the Northern boundary line undefined." This district was supposed to contain not more than 300 or 400 aborigines, and was under E. S. Parker, Esq., assistant-protector, whose head-quarters were on the Loddon River, at the foot of a volcanic hill, called Jim Crow, now Mount Franklin.

"3. The Goulburn River District, bounded upon the south by the Australian Alps ; on the west by the boundary of the Mount Macedon district ; northern and eastern boundaries undefined." This district was supposed to contain about 1000 aborigines, and was under W. Le Soueff, Esq., assistant-protector, whose head-quarters were on the Goulburn River.

"4. The Western Port, or Melbourne District, bounded on the south by the coast from Point Nepean, eastward ; on the north by the Australian Alps ; on the west by the Bay of Port Phillip ; the eastern boundary undefined." This district was supposed to contain 500 or 600 aborigines, and was under W. Thomas, Esq., assistant-protector, whose head-quarters were at Narre-Narre-Warren, about 20 miles from Melbourne.

The Chief Protector, Mr. G. A. Robinson, received a salary of £500 a year ; out of which he had to provide horses, travelling equipments, and attendants. He had the control of the assistant-protectors, had to travel, and also conduct the correspondence of the department. The salary to each assistant-protector was £250 a year, with an allowance of 10s. 6d. a day as commutation for forage and rations. The chief and assistant-protectors were also magistrates of New South Wales.

Prior to the establishment of the Protectorate, a Wesleyan Mission to the Aborigines was in operation at Buntingdale, on the Barwon river, in the County of Grant, on the reserve allotted to the Mission by the Government. The Rev. B Hurst was superintendent ; the Rev. F. Tuckfield, missionary ; and Mr. J. Dredge, secretary.

The Port Phillip Bank was established in Melbourne, with a capital of £120,000 ; John Gardiner, Esq., being the managing director. 1838.

First races held, 1838.

William Lonsdale was appointed police magistrate at Melbourne, January 1, 1839.

MELBOURNE, PORT PHILLIP, 1839
Mitchell Library

The Melbourne Club was instituted, January 1, 1839.

The barque "Hope," arrived from Sydney, with 130 immigrants, two officers, and 34 rank and file, 30 women, and 50 children ; Messrs. Parker, Thomas, Sievwright and Dredge, who had recently arrived from England with the appointments of Assistant-Protectors of Aboriginals were on board, January 3, 1839.

The minimum price of Crown Lands, which had heretofore been 5s. an acre, was raised to 12s. an acre, January 17, 1839.

The barque "Thomas Laurie," 300 tons, W. B. Price, master, sailed from Port Phillip, direct for London, taking the first mail, and 400 bales of wool, valued at £6,500. January, 1839.

The members of the association formed by Batman, called The Port Phillip Association, having, as already stated, obtained an allowance of £7,000, in the remission of the purchase of land, in consideration of the expenses they had incurred in the first formation of the settlement, exercised this concession in the purchase of 9,416 acres of land to the west of Geelong. February 13, 1839.

The petition of Mr. W. H. Burnard was printed by order of the House of Commons. In this petition reference was made to a correspondence which took place in October, 1838, and January, 1839, between Messrs. James Graham and Co., and Lord Glenelg, in which the former solicited permission to purchase 20,000 acres of land at or near the Glenelg River, Australia Felix, with the object of establishing a colony there. The petitioner was informed that Australia Felix was a part of New South Wales, and that it must rest with the local Government, in the first instance to determine the expediency of putting up for sale lands in that district. February 14, 1839.

Mr. Charles Bonney left Port Phillip, for Adelaide, with cattle ; he proceeded by way of the Glenelg, following the coast line near Mount Gambier. He was the first person who crossed to that colony by this route. Mr. Alfred Langhorne followed Mr. Bonney, keeping his track to the junction of Lake Alexandrina with the Murray River. February 26, 1839.

A stone jetty was completed at Williamstown, March 24, 1839.

Edward Jones Brewster, Esq., barrister-at-law, was appointed chairman of quarter sessions at Port Phillip, March 27, 1839.

The first pound was established at Port Phillip, March 31, 1839.

The ship "John Barry," J. Robson, master, arrived from Sydney with 200 immigrants ; E. J. Brewster, Esq., was a passenger. April 28, 1839.

The first Court of Quarter Sessions was held at Melbourne, E. J. Brewster, Esq., being chairman, and Mr. Horatio Nelson Carrington, Crown Prosecutor, May 13, 1839.

The barque "Midlothian," George Morrison, master, arrive from Leith. This was the first merchant vessel direct from a British port to Hobson's Bay. Mr. John Hunter Kerr, a relative of Governor Hunter, came to the colony in her, as also 31 cabin passengers. On the same day, the barque "William Bryan," Roman, master, from London, viâ Circular Head and Launceston, passed up the bay. Thomas Herbert Power, Esq., late M.L.C., was on board. Both vessels grounded on the passage up. June 17, 1839.

A branch of the Colonial Treasury at Sydney established at Melbourne, July 7, 1839.

Mr. Edward Curr, afterwards known as "the Father of separation," arrived from Circular Head, Van Diemen's Land, in the schooner Eagle, bringing with him, for sale, some cattle descended from some of the best herds in England, August, 1839.

The foundation stone of an Independent Chapel, in Collins-street east, Melbourne, laid September 6, 1839.

Robert Saunders Webb, Esq., appointed sub-treasurer at Port Phillip, September 10, 1839.

Three allotments in the town of Melbourne, Nos. 5, 6, and 7, of block 14, situate in Collins-street, near Queen-street, each containing about half an acre, and which had been purchased by Mr. Charles H. Ebden, at the Government land sale on the 1st June, 1837, for £136, were sold by auction, and realized £10,224. September 14, 1839.

Charles Joseph La Trobe, Esq., who had been appointed Superintendent of Port Phillip by the Home Government, with a salary of £800 a year, arrived in Melbourne by the "Pyramus," from Sydney, and landed under a salute of nine guns. September 30, 1839.

Mr. La Trobe met the inhabitants of Melbourne in the Auction Company's Rooms, Collins-street. His instructions were read to the public, and he was presented with addresses, to which he replied. October 2, 1839.

The Rev. James Coud Grylls, a clergyman of the Church of England, arrived in Melbourne from Sydney, in the "Denmark Hill." He had been appointed, on the 5th September, bishop's surrogate for granting marriage licenses. October 12, 1839.

James Montgomery, Esq., was appointed Clerk of the Peace at Port Phillip, October 20, 1839.

The foundation stone of St. James's Church, William-street, was laid by his Honor C. J. La Trobe, November 6 1839.

James Croke, Esq., who had been appointed by the Home Government Clerk of the Crown at Port Phillip, Mr. (now Sir) Redmond Barry, J. B. Brewer, Esq., barrister-at-law, James Montgomery, Esq., and Messrs. Edward Sewell, Robert Dean, and Richard O'Cock, solicitors, and Neil Black, Esq., arrived in Melbourne by the "Parkfield." November 13, 1839.

Great flood at Port Phillip, November 26, 1839.

Foster Fyans, Esq., was appointed police magistrate at Portland Bay, and Nicholas A. Fenwick, Esq., police magistrate at Geelong, December 22, 1839.

First Government sale of land in Portland Bay District, at the Auction Company's rooms, Melbourne, October 15, 1840.

Port Phillip Turf Club formed. Committee:—J. D. Lyon Campbell, C. H. Ebden, J. Hawdon, H. Jamieson, G. B. Smyth, and William Verner, December 12, 1840.

First race meeting commenced under the auspices of the Club, April 13, 1841.

Regulations promulgated for the sale of Crown Lands in Port Phillip, January 21, 1841.

Foundation stone of the first Presbyterian church laid in Melbourne, January 22, 1841.

The Supreme Court, Melbourne, opened for the first time, April 5, 1841.

A Water Police Magistrate appointed for Port Phillip, July 8, 1841.

Little Bourke, Little Collins, and Little Lonsdale streets, Melbourne, named, and width fixed at 33 feet, March 7, 1844.

Foundation stones of Prince's Bridge and Melbourne Hospital laid, March 20, 1846.

Public meeting held, and measures taken, for separating Port Phillip from New South Wales, December 30, 1840.

First Judge (Willis) appointed, February 5, 1841.

Judge Willis, Resident Judge at Port Phillip, removed from the Bench November 12, 1842. [See MEN OF THE TIMES (Willis Judge).]

Governor Gipps visited Port Phillip, October 25, 1843.

Certain returns were laid before the Legislative Council with respect to the Port Phillip district, which showed that from the foundation of that settlement 40 whites had been killed, and the Europeans had despatched 113 blacks. 1844.

Erected into the Colony of Victoria, July 1, 1851. [See VICTORIA.]

PORT PHILLIP HEADS. The distance between the heads of Port Phillip is 3,900 yards. The navigable channel is about 1,600 yards. 1879.

PORT STEPHENS. Mr. Charles Grimes, Deputy Surveyor-General, was sent to Port Stephens to examine its locality, and returning from his visit, reported that he saw nothing in the locality to recommend it to the colony. 1794.

POSTAL.

Isaac Nichols first Postmaster, N. S. W., 1815. [He died in 1819.]

The system of General Post Office communication established. The lowest postage was three pence, the highest one shilling, according to distance, on newspapers one penny was charged ; March 8, 1827.

Mr. Raymond appointed Postmaster, New South Wales, 1829. [He died during his term of office, May 29, 1851.]

The question of a regular postal communication between England and the Colonies first opened ; two routes were advocated—one by the way of the Red Sea, and the other by the way of the Cape of Good Hope, but neither plans were put into practice until the lapse of many years. July, 1834.

Mr. John Bateman elected by the settlers of Port Phillip as their Postmaster General, July, 1836.

generally five months old. March, 1846.

Intelligence first received that the Lords of the Admiralty had advertised for tenders for the conveyance of the mails between Sydney and Singapore, January 15, 1849. The colonists were without the mails which were despatched from London on the 1st September, in the previous year. During this year the contract for the conveyance of mails was entered into by way of Singapore and Torres Straits, with the Indian and Australian Steam Packet Company. January, 1849.

The Government brought forward a measure for the introduction of a uniform rate of postage, 1849.

"Chusan," first steamer from England, arrived at Melbourne, July 23 ; arrived at Sydney, August 3, 1852.

A measure was passed in the Legislative Council for a reduction of charge for books sent by post. It was intended to foster a taste for

LOWER GEORGE STREET, SITE OF THE COLONY'S FIRST
POST OFFICE
John Carmichael, A & R Archives

Fortnightly mail between Sydney and Port Phillip established, February 3, 1837. [John Hawdon, first contractor.]

Melbourne Post Office opened August 12, 1841.

The first mail from Melbourne to Mount Macedon, started February 17, 1844.

A public meeting was held in Sydney, to consider the question of steam communication between Sydney and England. A committee was appointed to collect information on the subject, and the result was the recommendation of a postal service between this colony and England, which was subsequently adopted by a Committee of the Legislature. The route by way of Singapore was adopted. At this time the latest intelligence from England was

literature and disseminate useful information throughout the colony. 1852.

The New South Wales Government offered a bonus varying from £6,000 to £20,000 for the establishment of a monthly line of steamers to England. 1852.

New General Post Office, Melbourne, opened 1867.

New Post Office, Adelaide, opened May 6, 1872.

The "Sun Foo," first mail steamer via Torres Straits, arrived off Cape Moreton, December 12, 1873.

New General Post Office, Brisbane, erected, 1873.

The "Macgregor" steamship—the first

Australian and American mail vessel—left Sydney for San Francisco, December 20, 1873.

The English mail service from Sydney *via* San Francisco, undertaken, temporarily, by the A. S. N. Company, August 31, 1874.

New General Post Office, Sydney, commenced in February, 1866; opened by Hon. Saul Samuel, Postmaster-General, September 1, 1874.

Postal cards first issued in Sydney, New South Wales, by Hon. J. F. Burns, Postmaster-General, the first day's issue being 12,000, October 1, 1875.

Ladies first employed in Electric Telegraph Department, at the General Post Office, Sydney, N. S. W., by the Hon. J. F. Burns, Postmaster-General, 1875.

The R. M. S. S. "Siam" delivered the mails which left London on October 26th (the mails, allowing for detentions, having been only 34 days, 22 hours at sea), December. 3, 1877

R. M. S. S. "Siam" delivered in Melbourne the mails from England *via* Brindisi, in 36 days, August 11, 1878.

THE TELEPHONE EXCHANGE
Picturesque Atlas of Australia

POUNDS.
First established and pound-keepers appointed throughout New South Wales. August 24, 1811.

The first pound at Port Phillip, established March 31, 1839.

PRATT, MAJOR-GENERAL SIR THOMAS SIMPSON, publicly invested by his Excellency Sir Henry Barkly, Governor of Victoria, with the ribbon and badge of a Knight Commander of the Most Honorable Order of the Bath, this being the first ceremony of the kind performed in Australia. April 15, 1862.

PRESENTATION. Presentation of a silver tea and coffee service and a purse of sovereigns (total value £2,000), to Hon. J. S. Farnell, M.L.A., by the people of New South Wales, January 22, 1876.

PRESS, LIBERTY OF THE.
The liberty of the Press in the colony was acknowledged by His Excellency Sir Thomas Brisbane, by an official letter addressed by the Colonial Secretary, Goulburn, to the editor of the *Gazette*, October 15, 1824.

Threatened by Governor Darling, who was, however, foiled by the firmness of Chief Justice Forbes, 1826.

The Press threatened with a censorship if not conducted in a more temperate manner, February 27, 1828.

Newspaper reporters first allowed in the Council Chambers, Sydney, June 6, 1838.

PRICE, JOHN, Superintendent of Prisons at Williamstown, Victoria, murdered by convicts, March 26, 1857.

PRIMOGENITURE, Law of, done away with in New South Wales by the Act 26 Victoria, No. 20. Reserved December 20, 1862. Assented to July 21, 1863.

PRINCESS CHARLOTTE BAY, CAVERNS AT. Remarkable caverns, showing a variety of native paintings on the wall, discovered here by Captain King. 1821.

PRINTING.
Government orders first printed by a lately arrived prisoner, with a printing press brought out by the. "first fleet." November, 1795.

"Acts and Orders of Governor King," first book, printed by Geo. Howe, the first printer in Australia. 1795.

PRISONS.
First public meeting held in the colony of New South Wales, to raise funds to build a gaol, June, 1799.

The sum of £10,000 voted by the Council for the erection of a gaol at Darlinghurst, Sydney, 1835.

Cockatoo Island, Parramatta River, near Sydney, first established as a place for convicts, February, 1839.

Darlinghurst gaol first occupied by prisoners, June 7, 1841.

Cockatoo Island constituted as the penal establishment of the colony of N.S.W., 1841.

Pentridge Stockade, near Melbourne, proclaimed a House of correction, April 20, 1852.

Cockatoo was proclaimed as a penal station under the Colonial Government in 1847. [Although used by the Imperial Government as a prison for many years previously, by an order from the Colonial Secretary, dated April 2, 1856, it was directed that after that date it should be the destination of all prisoners sentenced to work on the roads and other public works of the colony.]

ENTRANCE TO THE PRISON

WAITING FOR EXAMINATION

LIFE IN PENTRIDGE
The Australasian Sketcher, 1873

Berrima gaol constituted a model prison, March 23, 1865.

St. Helena penal establishment of Queensland situated on an island 500 acres in extent, in Moreton Bay, 22 miles from Brisbane. First detachment of prisoners landed there in charge of Mr. John McDonald, May 20, 1867.

Cockatoo Island abandoned as a prison and its name changed to Biloela, 1872.

The alleged maltreatment of prisoners in Berrima gaol discussed in the Legislative Assembly, May 7, 1878; Royal Commission appointed to enquire, July 2, 1878; reported November 26, 1878.

PRIZE ESSAYS.

On progress of New South Wales, offered by proprietor of *Evening News*, won by Mr. Edward Dowling, 1867.

On the "Abolition of Newspaper Postage," won by Mr. Edward Dowling, 1869.

On "The Future Land Policy of New South Wales," offered by proprietors of *Wagga Wagga Advertiser*, won by Mr. Samuel Cook of *S. M. Herald*; Mr. Charles St. Julian, second. Nov. 24, 1869.

"New South Wales," offered by Philadelphia Exhibition Commission, won by A. M. Cameron. 1876.

PRIZE POEMS.

W. Mackworth Praed gained Chancellor's Medal at Cambridge for poem on Australia, beating W. C. Wentworth (whose poem was placed second in the list) and 25 others, 1822.

S. Smith, a student at Hydnex Albery School, Winchester, awarded a prize for a Latin poem on Australia, June 12, 1829.

W. H. H. Yarrington gained University of Sydney prize for poem on Australia, 1859.

John Perry, M.A., won prize poem, subject "Australia," offered by proprietor, Sydney *Evening News*, 1867.

PRAED'S POEM.

AUSTRALASIA.

A Poem which obtained the Chancellor's Medal at the Cambridge Commencement, 1823. By WINTHORP MACKWORTH PRAED, Trinity College.

THE sun is high in heaven; a favouring breeze
Fills the white sail, and sweeps the rippling seas;
And the tall vessel walks her destin'd way,
And rocks and glitters in the curling spray;
Among the shrouds, all happiness and hope,
The busy seaman coils the rattling rope,
And tells his jest, and carols out his song,
And laughs his laughter vehement and long,
Or pauses on the deck to dream awhile
Of his babes' prattle, and their mother's smile,
And nods the head, and waves the welcome hand,
To those who weep upon the lessening strand.

His is the roving step and humour dry,
His the light laugh, and his the jocund eye;
And his the feeling which in guilt or grief,
Makes the sin venial and the sorrow brief:

But there are hearts, that merry deck below,
Of darker error, and of deeper woe,
Children of wrath and wretchedness, who grieve
Not for the country but the crimes they leave;
Who, while for them on many a sleepless bed
The prayer is murmured, and the prayer is shed,
In exile and in misery, lock within
Their dread despair, their unrepented sin,—
And in their madness dare to gaze on heaven,
Sullen and cold, unawed and unforgiven!
There the gaunt robber, stern in sin and shame,
Shows his dull features and his iron frame;
And tenderer pilferers creep in silence by,
With quivering lip, flush'd brow, and vacant eye.
And some there are, who in the close of day,
With dropping jaw, weak step, and temples grey,
Go tottering forth, to find, across the wave,
A short sad sojourn and a foreign grave:
And some, who look their last and long adieu
To the white cliffs which vanish from their view
While youth still blooms, and vigour nerves the arm,
The blood flows freely, and the pulse beats warm;
The hapless female stands in silence there,
So weak, so wan, and yet so sadly fair,
That those who gaze, a rude untutored tribe
Check the rude question, and the wounding gibe.
And look, and long to strike the fetter off,
And stay to pity, though they came to scoff;
Then o'er her cheek there runs a burning blush
And the hot tears of shame begin to rush
Forth from her swelling orbs;—she turns away,
And her white fingers o'er her eyelids stray;
And still the tears through those white fingers glide,
Which strive to check them, or at least to hide.
And there the stripling, led to plunder's school,
Ere passion slept, or reason learned to rule,
Clasps his young hands, and beats his throbbing brain,
And looks with marvel on his galling chain.
Oh! you may guess from that unconscious gaze
His soul hath dreamed of those far fading days,
When, rudely nurtured on the mountain brow,
He tended, day by day, his father's plough;
Blessed in his day of toil, his night of ease,
His life of purity, his soul of peace.
Oh, yes! to-day his soul hath backward been
To many a tender face and beauteous scene;
The verdant valley and the dark brown hill,
The small fair garden, and its tinkling rill,
His grandame's tale, believed at midnight hour,
His sister singing in her myrtle bower,
And she, the maid of every hope bereft
So fondly loved, alas! so falsely left,
The winding path, the dwelling in the grove
The look of welcome, and the kiss of love—
These are his dreams; but these are dreams of bliss!
Why do they blend with such a lot as this?

And is there nought for him but grief and gloom,
A lone existence, and an early tomb?
Is there no hope of comfort and of rest
To the seared conscience, and the troubled breast
Oh say not so! In some far distant clime
Where lives no witness of his early crime,
Benignant penitence may haply muse
On purer pleasures, and on brighter views,
And slumbering virtue wake at last to claim
Another being and a fairer frame.

Beautiful land! within whose quiet shore
Lost spirits may forget the stain they bore ;
Beautiful land! with all thy blended shades
Of waste and wood, rude rocks, and level glades,
On thee, on thee I gaze, as Moslems look
On the blest island of their prophet's book ;
And oft I deem that, linked by magic spell,
Pardon and peace upon thy valleys dwell,
Like two sweet Houris beckoning o'er the deep
The souls that tremble and the eyes that weep.
Therefore on thee undying sunbeams throw
Their clearest radiance, and their warmest glow,
And tranquil nights, cool gales, and gentle showers
Make bloom eternal in thy sinless bowers.
Green is thy turf ; stern winter doth not dare
To breathe his blast, and leave a ruin there.
And the charmed ocean roams thy rocks around,
With softer motion, and with sweeter sound :
Among thy blooming flowers and blushing fruit
The whispering of young birds is never mute,
And never doth the streamlet cease to swell
Through its old channel in the hidden dell.
Oh ! if the Muse of Greece had ever stray'd
In solemn twilight, through thy forest glade,
And swept her lyre, and walked thy meads along
The liquid echo of her ancient song—
Her fabling fancy in that hour had found
Voices of music, shapes of grace around ;
Among thy trees, with merry step and glance,
The Dyrad then had wound her wayward dance,
And the cold Naiad in thy waters fair,
Bath'd her white breast, and wrung her dripping hair.
Beautiful land ! upon so pure a plain
Shall superstition hold her hated reign ?
Must bigotry build up her cheerless shrine
In such an air, in such an earth as thine ?
Alas ! Religion from thy placid isles
Veils the warm splendour of her heavenly smiles,
And the wrapt gazer on the beauteous plan
Finds nothing dark except the soul of man.

Sweet are the links that bind us to our kind,
Meek, but unyielding, felt, but undefined ;
Sweet is the love of brethren ; sweet the joy
Of a young mother in her cradled boy ;
And sweet is childhood's deep and earnest glow
Of reverence for a father's head of snow !
Sweeter than all, ere our young hopes depart,
The quickening throb of an impassion'd heart,
Beating in silence, eloquently still,
For one lov'd soul that answers to its thrill,
But where thy smile, Religion, hath not shone,
The chain is riven, and the charm is gone,
And unawaken'd by thy wond'rous spell,
The Feelings slumber in their silent cell.

Hush'd is the voice of labour and of mirth,
The light of day is sinking from the earth,
And evening mantles in her dewy calm
The couch of one who cannot heed its balm*.
Lo ! where the Chieftain on his matted bed,
Leans the faint form, and hangs the feverish head ;
There is no lustre in his wandering eye,
His forehead hath no show of majesty,
His gasping lips, too weak for wail or prayer,
Scarce stirs the breeze, and leaves no echo there.

*This sketch of the death of a New Zealander, and of the super-
stition which prevents the offering of any consolation or assistance,
under the idea that a sick man is under the influence of the Deity,
is taken from the narrative of the death of Duaterra, friendly
Chieftain.

And his strong arm, so nobly wont to rear
The feather'd target, or the ashen spear,
Droops powerless and cold ! the pang of death
Locks the set teeth, and chokes the struggling breath,
And the last glimmering of departing day
Lingers around to herald life away.

Is there no duteous youth to sprinkle now
One drop of water on his lip and brow ?
No dark-eyed maid to bring with soundless foot
The lulling potion, and the healing root?
No tender look to meet his wandering gaze ?
No tone of fondness, heard in happier days,
To soothe the terrors of the spirit's flight,
And speak of mercy, and of hope to-night ?

All love, all leave him ! terrible and slow
Along the crowd the whispered murmurs grow—
" The hand of Heaven is on him ! is it our's
" To check the fleeting of his number'd hours ?
" Oh not to us, oh not to us is given
" To read the book, or thwart the will of Heaven !
" Away, away !" and each familiar face
Recoils in horror from his sad embrace ;
The turf on which he lies is hallowed ground,
The sullen priest stalks gloomily around,
And shuddering friends that dare not soothe or save,
Hear the last groan and dig the destined grave.
The frantic widow folds upon her breast
The glittering trinket, and the gorgeous vest,
Circles her neck with many a mystic charm,
Clasps the rich bracelet on her desperate arm,
Binds her black hair, and stains her eyelid's fringe
With the jet lustre of the Emu's tinge ;
Then on the spot where those dear ashes lie,
In sullen transport sits her down to die.
Her sorrowing kindred mark the wasted cheek,
The straining eye-ball, and the stifled shriek,
And sing the praises of her deathless name,
As the last flutter racks her tortured frame.
They sleep together o'er the natural tomb,
The lichen'd pine rears up it form of gloom,
And long acacias shed their shadows grey,
Bloomless and leafless o'er the buried clay ;
And often there, when calmly, coldly bright,
The midnight moon flings down her ghastly light,
With solemn murmur, and with silent tread,
The prayer is murmured and the verse is said,
And sights of wonder, sounds of spectral fear,
Scare the quick glance, and chill the startled ear.

Yet direr visions e'en than these remain ;
A fiercer guiltiness, a fouler stain !
Oh ; who shall sing the scene of savage strife,
Where hatred glories in the waste of life ?
The hurried march, the looks of grim delight,
The yell, the rush, the slaughter, and the flight,
The arms unwearied in the cruel toil,
The hoarded vengeance and the rifled spoil ;
And, last of all, the revel in the wood,
The feast of death, the banqueting of blood ;
When the wild warrior gazes on his foe,
Convuls'd beneath him in his painful throe,
And lifts the knife, and kneels him down to drain
The purple current from the quivering vein ?
Cease, cease the tale—and let the ocean's roll
Shut the dark horror from my wildered soul !

And are there none to succour ? none to speed
A fairer feeling and a holier creed ?

Alas ! for this, upon the ocean blue,
Lamented Cook, thy pennon hither flew ;
For this,* undaunted o'er the raging brine,
The venturous Frank upheld his Saviour's sign.
Unhappy Chief ! while fancy thus surveys
The scattered islets, and the sparkling bays,
Beneath whose cloudless sky nd gorgeous sun
Thy life was ended, and thy voyage done,
In shadowy mist thy form appears to glide,
Haunting the grove, or floating on the tide ;
Oh ! there was grief for thee, and bitter tears,
And racking doubts through long and joyless years ;
And tender tongues that babbled of the theme,
And lonely hearts that doated on the dream.
Pale memory deems she saw thy cherish'd form
Snatch'd from the foe, or rescued from the storm ;
And faithful love, unfailing and untir'd,
Clung to each hope, and sigh'd as each expir'd.
On the bleak desert, or the tombless sea,
No prayer was said, no requiem sung for thee ;
Affection knows not whether o'er thy grave
The ocean murmur, or the willow wave ;
But still the beacon of thy sacred name
Lights ardent souls to virtue and to fame ;
Still science mourns thee, and the grateful muse
Wreathes the green cypress for her own Perouse.
But not thy death shall mar the gracious plan,
Nor check the task thy pious toil began ;
O'er the wide waters of the bounding main
The book of life shall win its way again,
And, in the regions by thy fate endear'd,
The cross be lifted, and the altar rear'd.

With furrow'd brow, and cheek serenely fair,
The calm wind wandering o'er his silver hair,
His arm uplifted, and his moisten'd eye
Fix'd in deep rapture on the molten sky—
Upon the shore, through many a billow driven,
He kneels at last, the messenger of heaven !
Long years, that rank the mighty with the weak
Have dimm'd the flush upon his faded cheek,
And many a dew, and many a noxious damp,
The daily labour, and the nightly lamp :
Have reft away, for ever reft, from him
The liquid accent, and the buoyant limb :
Yet still within him aspirations swell
Which time corrupts not, sorrow cannot quell,
The changeless zeal, which on, from land to land,
Speeds the faint foot, and nerves the wither'd hand
And the mild charity which, day by day,
Weeps every wound and every stain away,
Rears the young bud on many a blighted stem,
And longs to comfort, where she must condemn ;
With these, through storms, and bitterness, and wrath,
In peace and power he holds his onward path,
Curbs the fierce soul, and sheathes the murd'rous steel,
And calms the passions he has ceased to feel.

Yes ! he hath triumph'd !—while his lips relate
The sacred story of his Saviour's fate,
While to the search of that tumultuous horde
He opens wide the everlasting word,
And bids the soul drink deep of wisdom there,
In fond devotion and in fervent prayer,
In speechless awe the wonder-stricken throng
Check their rude feasting and their barbarous song :
Around his steps the gathering myriads crowd,
The chief, the slave, the timid, and the proud ;

* From the coast of Australasia the last despatches of La Perouse
were dated.

Of various features, and of various dress,
Like their own forest-leaves, confus'd and numberless
Where shall your temples, where your worship be,
Gods of the air, and rulers of the sea ?
In the glad dawning of a kinder light,
Your blind adorer quits your gloomy rite,
And kneels in gladness on his native plain,
A happier votary at a holier fane.

Beautiful land ! farewell !—when toil and strife,
And all the sighs, and all the sins of life,
Shall come about me ; when the light of truth
Shall scatter the bright mists that dazzled youth,
And memory muse in sadness o'er the past,
And mourn for pleasures far too sweet to last,
How often shall I long for some dear spot,
Where, not remembering and remember'd not,
With no false verse to deck my lying bust
With no fond tear to vex my smouldering dust,
This busy brain may find its grassy shrine,
And sleep, untroubled, in a shade like thine !

WENTWORTH'S POEM.

AUSTRALASIA.

Land of my birth ! tho' now alas ! no more
Musing I wander on thy sea-girt shore,
Or climb with eager haste thy barrier cliff,
To catch a glimmer of the distant skiff,
That ever and anon breaks into light,
And then again eludes the aching sight,
Till, nearer seen, she bends her foaming way
Majestic onward to yon placid bay,
Where Sydney's infant turrets proudly rise,
The new-born glory of the southern skies :
Dear Australasia, can I e'er forget
Thee, Mother Earth ? Ah no, my heart e'en yet
With filial fondness loves to call to view
Scenes which, though oft remembered, still are new
Scenes where my playful childhood's thoughtless years,
Flew swift away, despite of childhood's tears ;
Where later, too, in manhood's op'ning bloom,
The tangled brake, th' eternal forest's gloom,
The wonted brook, where with some truant mate
I loved to plunge, or ply the treach'rous bait ;
The spacious harbour with its hundred coves,
And fairy islets—seats of savage loves,
Again beheld—restampt with decper dye
The fading image of my infancy :
And shall I now, by Cam's old classic stream,
Forbear to sing, and thou propos'd the theme ?
Thy native bard, though on a foreign strand,
Shall I be mute, and see a stranger's hand
Attune the lyre, and, prescient of thy fame,
Foretell the glories that shall grace thy name?
Forbid it, all ye Nine ! 'twere shame to thee,
My Austral parent : greater shame to me.

Proud Queen of Isles ! Thou sittest vast, alone,
A host of vassals bending round thy throne :
Like some fair swan that skims the silver tide,
Her silken cygnets strew'd on every side,
So floatest thou, thy Polynesian brood
Dispers'd around thee on thy Ocean flood,
While ev'ry surge that doth thy bosom lave,
Salutes thee " Empress of the Southern Wave."

WILLIAM CHARLES WENTWORTH
Government Printer. N.S.W.

Say, Muse, when first of Europe's roving train
Burst on De Quiros' sight this island main,
What golden visions rose to fancy's view,
The towns he plunder'd, and the hosts he slew ;
How on all sides the argent tripods shone,
And temples richer than Peruvia's sun ;
Till av'rice glowed, while busy thoughts unfurl'd
The imag'd treasures of the new-found world ;
'Twas then triumphant Hope thy power confess'd,
Hush'd the rude tongue, and calmed the mourning
      breast ;
Then still'd sedition's buzz, each contrite soul
With awe and gladness hail'd a chief's control,
And ev'ry peril, ev'ry hardship past,
Seem'd to have found full recompense at last.
Say, too, what terror fix'd the natives' eye,
When first they saw, emerging from the sky,
That stranger bark in sullen silence sweep,
A wrathful spirit o'er the troubled deep,
Treading with giant stride the subject wave,
The wind his herald, and the tide his slave;
While onward stalking in terrific state
He loom'd portenful of impending fate,
Yet vain the dream of those, the dread of these ;—
For lo ! at length arriv'd with fav'ring breeze,
De Quiros' self directs the straining oar,
And leaps the foremost on the untrod shore—
Follows his band ; but dark on ev'ry side
Repulsive forests frown with paths untried ;
While from the hidden foe the frequent spear
Sweeps through their ranks, and wakes unwonted fear ;
Till struck with awe they cease the hopeless chase,

And to the ship their sullen course retrace.
Ye primal tribes, lords of this old domain,
Swift-footed hunters of the pathless plain,
Unshackled wanderers, enthusiasts free,
Pure native sons of savage liberty,
Who hold all things in common—earth, sea, air,—
Or only occupy the nightly lair
Whereon each sleeps ; who own no chieftain's pow'r
Save his, that's mightiest at the passing hour ;
Say—whence your ancient lineage, what your name,
And from what shores your rough forefathers came?
Untutor'd children, fresh from Nature's mould,
No songs have ye to trace the times of old ;—
No hidden themes like these employ your care,
For you enough the knowledge that ye are :—
Let Learning's sons who would this secret scan,
Unlock its mystic casket if they can,—
To your unletter'd tastes are sweeter far,
The dance of battle, and the song of war.
'Mid hostile ranks the deadly spear to throw,
Or see the foeman stagg'ring 'neath your blow :—
To you, ye sable hunters, sweeter, too,
To spy the track of bounding kangaroo,
Or long-neck'd emu :—quick with eager gaze
His path you follow thro' the tangled maze,
O'er boundless wilds your panting game pursue,
And come, like trusty hounds, at last in view ;
Then creeping round her, soon the forest's pride
Is hemmed with bristly spears that pierce her side ;
And now, the labours of the chase being o'er,
And Nature's keen suggestions heard no more,
In uncouth numbers, seated in a ring,
Your ancient fathers' warlike feats ye sing,
Or striking each his shield, with clattering lance,
The early night exhaust in Pyrrhic dance.

Such, mountain sons of freedom, your delight ;
Such your rude sport by day, your mirth by night,
Nor would you these few savage joys forego,
For all the comforts all the arts bestow.
What, if at times the barren chase deny
The scanty fare your niggard wilds supply ?
What, if to-day ye miss your sylvan feast ?
To-morrow's meal shall then derive a zest,
Unknown to those who live in slothful ease,—
Child of the heath, the mountain, and the breeze.
What, if the wint'ry blast and pelting rain
Howl through the woods and inundate the plain ?
To some near cave ye fly, which, jutting o'er,
Wards from your naked limbs the drenching show'r :
While kindled fagots soon with crackling sound
Dispel the gloom and scatter warmth around,
And nestling close each to his sable love,
Ye sleep, regardless of the storm above.
Had'st thou, old cynic, seen this unclad crew,
Stretch their bare bodies in the nightly dew,
Like hairy Satyrs, 'midst their sylvan seats,
Endure both winter's frosts, and summer's heats ;
Thy cloak and tub away thou would'st have cast,
And tried, like them, to brave the piercing blast.

Illustrious Cook ! Columbus of our shore,
To whom was left this unknown world t' explore !
Its untrac'd bounds on faithful chart to mark,
And leave a light where all before was dark :—
And thou, the foremost in fair learning's ranks,
Patron of every art, departed Banks !

Who, wealth disdaining and inglorious ease,
The rocks and quicksands dar'd of unknown seas;
Immortal pair! when in yon spacious bay
Ye moor'd awhile its wonders to survey,
How little thought ye, that the name from you
Its graceful shrubs and beauteous wild flowers drew
Would serve, in after times, with lasting brand
To stamp the soil and designate the land,
And to ungenial climes reluctant scare
Full many a hive that else had settled there.

Ah why, Britannia's pride, Britannia's boast,
Searcher of ev'ry sea and ev'ry coast,
Lamented Cook! thou bravest, gentlest heart
Why didst thou fall beneath a savage dart?
Why were thy mangled reliques doomed to grace
The midnight orgies of a barb'rous race?
Why could'st thou not, thy weary wand'rings past
At home in honour'd ease recline at last,
And like the happier partner of thy way,
In cloudless glory close life's setting day?

And thou, fam'd Gallic captain, La Perouse!
When from this Bay thou led'st thy fated crews,
Did thy twin vessels sink beneath the shock
Of furious hurricane, or hidden rock?
Fell ye, o'erpowered on some barbarian strand,
As fell before De Langle's butcher'd band?
Linger'd the remnants of thy shipwreck'd host
On some parch'd coral isle, some torrid coast,—
Where no green tree, no cooling brook is seen,
Nought living is, or e'er before has been,
Save some lone mew, blown from the rocky nest,
Had lit, perchance, her homeward wing to rest;—
Till gnaw'd by want, with joy a comrade dead
They saw, and rav'nous on his body fed,
And soon, his bones pick'd bare, with famished eye
Each glar'd around, then drew who first should die;
Till of thy ghastly band the most unblest
Surviv'd,—sad sepulchre of all the rest;
And now his last meal gorg'd, with frenzy fir'd,
And raging thirst, the last lorn wretch expir'd!
Whate'er thy fate, thou saw'st the floating arks
That peopled this new world, the teeming barks
That ardent Phillip led to this far shore,
And seeing them, alas! wert seen no more.
Ah! could'st thou now behold what man has done,
Tho' sev'n revolving lustres scarce have run,
How would'st thou joy to see the savage earth
The smiling parent of so fair a birth!
Lo! thickly planted o'er the glassy bay.
Where Sydney loves her beauties to survey,
And ev'ry morn, delight'd sees the gleam
Of some fresh pennant dancing in her stream,
A masty forest, stranger vessels moor,
Charg'd with the fruits of every foreign shore;
While, landward,—the throng'd quay, the creaking crane,
The noisy workman, and the loaded wain,
The lengthen'd street, wide square, and column'd front,
Of stately mansions, and the gushing font,
The solemn church, the busy market throng,
And idle loungers saunt'ring slow among,—
The lofty windmills that with outspread sail
Thick line the hills, and court the rising gale,
Shew that the mournful genius of the plain,
Driv'n from his primal solitary reign,
Has backward fled, and fixed his drowsy throne
In untrod wilds, to muse and brood alone.
And thou, fair Port! whose triad sister coves

Peninsulate these walls; whose ancient groves
High tow'ring southward, rear their giant form
And break the fury of the polar storm;
Fairest of Ocean's daughters! who dost bend
Thy mournful steps to seek thy absent friend,
Whence she,—coy wild-rose, on her virgin couch
Fled loath from Parramatta's am'rous touch!
Skirting thy wat'ry path, lo! frequent stand
The cheerful villas 'midst their well-cropp'd land;
Here lowing kine, there bounding coursers graze,
Here waves the corn, and there the woody maze;
Here the tall peach puts forth its pinky bloom,
And there the orange scatters its perfume,
While, as the merry boatmen row along,
The woods are quicken'd with their lusty song—
Nor here alone hath labour's victor band
Subdued the glebe, and fertiliz'd the land;
For lo! from where at rocky Portland's head,
Reluctant Hawkesbury quits his sluggard bed,
Merging in Ocean—to young Windsor's tow'rs,
And Richmond's high green hills, and native bow'rs,—
Thence far along Nepean's pebbled way,
To those rich pastures where the wild herds stray,—
The crowded farm-house lines the winding stream
On either side, and many a plodding team
With shining ploughshare turns the neighb'ring soil,
Which crowns with double crop the lab'rer's toil.

Hail, mighty ridge! that from thy azure brow
Survey'st these fertile plains, that stretch below,
And look'st with careless, unobservant eye,
As round thy waste the forked lightnings ply,
And the loud thunders spring with hoarse rebound
From peak to peak, and fill the welkin round
With deaf'ning voice, till with their boist'rous play
Fatigued, in mutt'ring peals they stalk away;—
Parent of this deep stream, this awful flood,
That at thy feet its tributary mud,
Like the fam'd Indian, or Egyptian tide,
Doth pay, but direful scatters woe beside;—
Vast Austral Giant of these rugged steeps,
Within whose secret cells rich glitt'ring heaps
Thick piled are doom'd to sleep, till some one spy
The hidden key that opes thy treasury;
How mute, how desolate thy stunted woods,
How dread thy chasms, where many an eagle broods,
How dark thy caves, how lone thy torrents' roar,
As down thy cliffs precipitous they pour,
Broke on our hearts, when first with venturous tread,
We dar'd to rouse thee from thy mountain bed!
Till, gain'd with toilsome step thy rocky heath,
We spied the cheering smokes ascend beneath,
And, as a meteor shoots athwart the night,
The boundless champaign burst upon our sight,
Till, nearer seen, the beauteous landscape grew,
Opening like Canaan on rapt Israel's view.

Ye tranquil scenes! too long to man unknown,
Your hills remained uncropp'd, your dales unsown;
Yet lo! at last upon yon distant stream,
Increasing Bathurst's straggling honours beam,
While thick o'erspreading the fresh-cultur'd glade
The ripen'd harvest bends its heavy blade,
And flocks and herds, in thousands strewed around,
Awake the woodlands with their joyous sound.
Soon, Australasia, may thy inmost plains,
A new Arcadia, teem with simple swains;
Soon a Lycoris' scorn again inspire
A Gallus' song to moan his hopeless fire,

And, while he murmurs forth his plaintive tale,
The list'ning breezes waft it down the dale.

What, though no am'rous shepherd midst thy dells
E'er charm'd responsive Echo from her cells ;
What, though no liquid flute, nor shriller reed
E'er shot their wild notes o'er thy silent mead ;
Thy blue-eyed daughters, with the flaxen hair
And taper ankle, do they bloom less fair
Than those of Europe   do thy primal groves
Ne'er warble forth their feather'd inmates' love
Or, say, doth Ceres', or Pomona's reign
With scantier gifts repay thy lab'ring train ?
Ah ! no, 'tis slavery's badge, the felon's shame
That stills thy voice, and clouds thy op'ning fame ;
'Tis this that makes thy sorrowing Judah weep,
Restrains her song, and hangs her harp to sleep.

Land of my hope ! soon may this early blot,
Amid thy growing honours be forgot:
Soon may a freeman's soul, a freeman's blade,
Nerve ev'ry arm, and gleam thro' ev'ry glade—
No more the outcast convict's clanking chains
Deform thy wilds, and stigmatize thy plains :—
And tho' the fathers—these—of thy new race,
From whom each glorious feat, each deathless grace,
Must yet proceed,—by whom each radiant gem
Be won—to deck thy future diadem :—
Did not of old th' Imperial Eagle rise,
Unfurl his pinions, and astound the skies ?
Hatch'd in an eyrie fouler far than thine,
Did he not dart from Tiber to the Rhine ?
From Dacia's Forests to fair Calpe's height,
Fear'd not each cow'ring brood his circling flight ?
From Libya's sands to quiver'd Parthia's shore
Mark'd not the scatter'd fowl his victor soar ?
From swift Euphrates to bleak Thule's rock,
Did not opposing myriads feel the shock
Of his dread talons, and glad tribute pay,
To 'scape the havoc of his murd'rous way ?

Yet ne'er my country, roll thy battle-car
With deadly axle thro' the ranks of war :
Of foreign rule ne'er may the ceaseless thirst
Pollute thy sons, and render thee accurst
Amid the nations ; ne er may crouch before
Invading legions sallying from thy shore,
A distant people, that shall not on thee
Have first disgorg'd his hostile chivalry.
In other climes, Bellona's temples shine,
Ceres', Pomona's, Bacchus', Pan's, be thine,
And chaste Minerva's : from thy peaceful plains
May glory's star ne'er charm thy restless swains ;
Ne'er may the hope of plunder lure to roam
One Australasian from his happy home ;
But rustic arts their tranquil hours employ—
Arts crown'd with plenty, and replete with joy :
Be theirs the task to lay with lusty blow
The ancient giants of the forest low,
With frequent fires the cumber'd plain to clear,
To tame the steed, and yolk the stubborn steer,
With cautious plough to rip the virgin earth,
And watch her first-born harvest from its birth,
Till, tinged with summer suns the golden glade
Delight the hind and claim the reaper's blade ;—
Theirs too the task, with skilful hand to rear
The varied fruits that gild the ripen'd year ;
Whether the melting peach, or juicy pear,
Or golden orange, most engage their care :—

Theirs too round stakes or trellised bow'rs to twine

The pliant tendrils of the shooting vine ;
And, when beneath their blushing burdens grow
The yielding stems,—the generous juice to stow
In copious jar, which drain'd on festive day
May warm each heart, and chase its glooms away —
Theirs too on flow'ry mead or thymy steep
To tend with watchful dog the timid sheep ;
And, as their fleecy charge are lying round,
To wake the woodlands with their pipe's soft sound,
While the charm'd Fauns and Dryads skulking near,
Leave their lone haunts, and list with raptur'd ear.

Such be the labours of thy peaceful swains,
Thus may they till, and thus enrich thy plains ;
Thus the full flow of population's tide
Its swelling waters pour on every side :—
As, on the topmost boughs of some old wood,
When outcast rooks first hatch their infant brood,
The tufted nests, as buds each vernal year,
In growing groups, and thicker ranks appear,
Till soon the spacious grove, with clam'rous strife,
Resounds throughout, and teems with callow life ;—
So, Australasia, may thy exil'd band
Spread their young myriads o'er thy lonely land,
Till village spires, and crowded cities rise
In thick succession to the trav'llers' eyes,
And the grim wolf, chas'd from his secret hold,
No more with hungry howl alarm the fold.
Nor be the rustic arts alone thy pride :—
The ambient ocean half thy care divide ;
Whether thy roving sons on Tropic seas
Spread ev'ry sail to woo the sportive breeze ;—
Or with bare poles and dauntless bosoms brave
The icy horrors of the Antarctic wave ;
Till fruitful commerce in thy lap shall pour
The gifts of ev'ry sea and ev'ry shore.

And thou, fair Science ! pure ethereal light,
Beam on her hills, and chase her mental night ;
Direct her sons to seek the perfect day,
Where Bacon traced, and Newton led the way ;
Till bright Philosophy's full orb arise,
To gild her noon, and cheer her evening skies.
But 'mid the future treasure of their lore,
Still foremost rank the Greek and Latin ore ;
Still in the classic search the midnight oil
Be spent, nor deem'd that pleasing labour toil.
Till to their sight reveal'd all glorious shine
The hidden riches of this ancient mine !
Whether they follow with admiring view
The fam'd retreat of Xenophon's bold few ;
Or in Calypso's Isle, or Ida's grove,
And by Scamander's boiling eddies rove ;
Or see the pilferer of the empyrean fire
Chain'd to his rock, endure the Thunderer's ire ;
Or hear the caverns of the Lemnian shore
Ring with the raving hero's anguish'd roar ;
Or on Trozene's sands see Phædra's hate
Drawn on Hippolytus a guiltless fate !
Or with the glory of th' Augustan reign,
Enraptur'd drink the sweets of Maro's strain !
Or borne along by Tully's whelming flood
Feel all his anger kindling in their blood,
When to wide infamy and deathless shame,
He dooms the plund'rer's, or the traitor's name.

Celestial poesy ! whose genial sway
Earth's furthest habitable shores obey ;
Whose inspirations shed their sacred light,

Far as the regions of the Arctic night,
And to the Laplander his Boreal gleam
Endear not less than Phœbus' brighter beam—
Descend thou also on my native land,
And on some mountain summit take thy stand ;
Thence issuing soon a purer font be seen
Than charmed Castalia or fam'd Hippocrene ;
And there a richer, nobler fame arise,
Than on Parnassus met the adoring eyes.
And tho', bright Goddess, on the far blue hills,
That pour their thousand swift pellucid rills,
Where Warragamba's rage has rent in twain
Opposing mountains, thundering to the plain,
No child of song has yet invoked thy aid,
'Neath their primeval solitary shade,—
Still gracious Pow'r, some kindling soul inspire
To wake to life my country's unknown lyre,
That from creation's date has slumb'ring lain,
Or only breathed some savage uncouth strain,—
And grant that yet an Austral Milton's song
Pactolus-like flow deep and rich along,—
An Austral Shakespeare rise, whose living page
To Nature true may charm in ev'ry age ;—
And that an Austral Pindar daring soar,
Where not the Theban Eagle reach'd before.

And, oh Britannia ! should'st thou cease to ride
Despotic Empress of old Ocean's tide ;—
Should thy tam'd Lion—spent his former might—
No longer roar, the terror of the fight :—
Should e'er arrive that dark, disastrous hour,
When bow'd by luxury, thou yield'st to power ;
When thou, no longer freest of the free,
To some proud victor bend'st the vanquished knee :—
May all thy glories in another sphere
Relume, and shine more brightly still than here :
May this—thy last-born infant—then arise,
To glad thy heart, and greet thy parent eyes ;
And Australasia float, with flag unfurl'd,
A new Britannia in another world !

PROTECTION.

The owners and proprietors of land memorialised the Governor and Legislative Council for the prohibition of the use of sugar in brewing and to make use of grain as a substitute. They did not wish to see ardent spirits cheaper, but that by those means they would be enabled to transfer the wealth to the colony instead of its being drained by foreigners. They also memorialised for an import duty on corn, as their markets were destroyed by importations from countries that contributed nothing towards the revenue of the colonies. The result of these memorials was that the question of protective duties opened a discussion of more or less warmth for a considerable time, but without any definite results, 1831.

A petition for the protection and manufacture of colonial tobacco, in the shape of an import duty, presented to the Council, July 11, 1839.

Sir James M'Culloch introduced protective policy into Victoria, 1865.

PROUT, J. S., artist, died in London, 1876.

PUBLIC DEBT OF AUSTRALASIA.

Colony.	Estimated Population on Dec. 31, 1877.	Public Debt on Dec. 31, 1877.	Rate of Indebtedness per head of population, Dec. 31, 1877.
		£	£ s. d.
New South Wales	662,212	11,724,419	17 14 1
New Zealand	417,622	20,691,111	49 10 10¾
Queensland	203,084	7,685,350	37 16 10
South Australia	237,090	4,737,200	19 19 7½
Tasmania	107,104	1,589,405	14 16 10
Victoria	860,787	17,018,913	19 15 5
Western Australia	27,838	161,000	5 15 8
Total	2,515,737	63,607,698	25 5 8

QUEENSLAND.

Lieutenant Miller formed first settlement at Moreton Bay, August, 1824.

Queensland separated from New South Wales, December 10, 1859.

Toowoomba proclaimed a municipality, November 24, 1860.

Dalby proclaimed a municipality, Sept., 1863.

The foundation stone of the Town Hall, Brisbane, laid January, 1864.

The sod of the first railway turned at Ipswich, February, 1864.

The Bridge, and Brisbane Waterworks almost simultaneously inaugurated, August, 1864.

Wool, the principal export of Queensland, amounted to 33,901 bales, valued at £1,019,159 : wheat maize, coffee, tobacco, silks, preserved meat, tallow, cotton, Dugong oil, and copper, also appear in the lists of exports. 1866.

12,000lb. of arrowroot exported in 1866.

First Circuit Court opened at Townsville, January 12, 1875.

First sod of Toowoomba waterworks turned, September 4, 1876.

The Western Railway land sale realized £26,771, exclusive of deed and survey fees at Brisbane, November 20, 1877.

MARKET STREET, TOOWOOMBA
Picturesque Atlas of Australia

RACING.

Horse races at Parramatta (the first recorded in Australia). The first race was between a horse called Parramatta and another called Belfast. It was won by the former. The proceedings of the day were enlivened by cock-fighting, wheelbarrow racing, and jumping in sacks. A publican gave enough calico to make a chemise for a prize " to be run for by three vestals of the current order," and the race caused much amusement. April 30, 1810.

The first horse races held in Sydney, and established principally by the officers of the 73rd Regiment, a piece of ground being cleared for that purpose, to which the name of " race course " was applied, now called Hyde Park. The Subscribers' Plate was, on the first day's racing, won by a horse named Chase. The sports were continued for three days, and were followed by a ball. October 14, 1810.

Second Sydney races held at Hyde Park. The Subscription Plate of 50 guineas won by Mr. Bent's ch. g. Matchem ; the Two-year-old Sweep by Captain Ritchie's Cheviot. On second day the Ladies' Cup of 50 guineas was won by Colonel O'Connell's Carlo, and the trophy was presented to the winner by Mrs. Macquarie, the wife of the Governor. On the third day the Magistrates' Plate of 50 guineas was won by Mr. Williams's Strawberry. August 12, 14, and 16, 1811.

The third Sydney races were held at Hyde Park. Colonel O'Connell's bl. h. Carlo won Subscription Plate ; Mr. Lunden's roan h. Strawberry the Ladies' Cup ; and Mr. Birch's gr. c. Cheviot the Subscription Purse of 50 guineas. August 17, 19, 21, and 22, 1812.

The fourth Sydney annual races took place at Hyde Park. On first day, Colonel O'Connell's 3-year-old bay colt Little Pickles won the 50-Guinea Plate ; and on the second and third day Colonel O'Connell was again successful, winning, with Carlo, the Ladies' Cup and the 50-guinea Subscription Plate. Aug. 16, 18, and 19, 1813.

The fifth Sydney annual races took place at Hyde Park, May 31, 1819.

The sixth Sydney races at Hyde Park, September 11 and 12, 1820.

The seventh Sydney annual races, Aug. 14, 15, and 16, 1821.

Races on a course four miles from Sydney, March 17, 1825.

Meeting to organise a Turf Club at Sydney, March 18, 1825 ; a second meeting was held, and His Excellency Governor Sir Thomas Brisbane was announced as Patron and Sir John Jamison as President. March 23, 1825.

First races under the newly-formed Sydney Turf Club took place. Mr. Nash's horse Junius, which for long afterwards retained the championship of the colony, won his first race—Town Plate of £50, heats, twice round the course. April 25 and 26, 1825.

The Sydney Turf Club held their second race meeting, September 23, 24, and 25, 1825.

Parramatta Turf Club races, October 7 and 8, 1825.

Sydney Turf Club races on the new course, four miles from Sydney, on the Parramatta road, between Grose

Farm and a farm belonging to Mr. Johnston. 2,000 people present. Junius won the principal races. June 14 and 16, 1826.

Sydney Turf Club annual races took place. Junius again won the principal events. April 25, 27, 1827.

Races at Campbelltown; principal prize, £50. August 13, 1827.

Sydney Turf Club races. Junius beaten for the first time by Mr. Brown's bl. h. Scratch, in a race for the third Brisbane Cup, April 9 and 11, 1828.

Australian Jockey Club established in Sydney, April 23, 1828.

A second Racing Club established (in opposition to the old one) in Sydney, called the *Australian Racing and Jockey Club*, but better known as the Governor's (Darling) Club, 1828.

Great race for £100 aside, Sydney course, between the horses Scratch and Australian. Scratch won, July 28, 1828; the same horses again met. On each occasion Scratch won after a close contest. August 4 and 9, 1828.

First race meeting of the Governor's Club, held at Parramatta. October 1 and 3, 1828.

Sydney Annual Races; 5,000 persons present on first day. The fourth Brisbane Cup won by Mr. Lawson's 3-year-old colt, Spring Gun, in two heats, beating Crowcatcher, Scratcher, and Australian. Spring Gun won the Wentworth Purse, and the Town Plate of £50, at the same meeting, April 8 and 10, 1829.

Governor's Club races. Bennelong was the winner of the Challenge Cup. April 22 and 24, 1829.

Hawkesbury races took place July 22 and 24, 1829.

Match between Jamison's Bennelong and Lawson's Spring Gun, on the racecourse, Parramatta, £200 to £150, heats. Bennelong won the first heat by a head only, and in the second, Spring Gun who was lame, was distanced. September 24, 1829.

Governor's Club races, Parramatta, September 30, and October 2, 1829.

Mr. Potter's horse trotted in harness, 12 miles, under the hour, for a bet of £30; won by 15 secs. Dec. 8, 1829.

Sydney Turf Club Annual races took place. The fifth Brisbane Cup was won by Bennelong, beating Counsellor, Chase, Scratch, and Sir Hercules. Counsellor won the first heat, Bennelong who won the second, walked over for the third. Scratch and Spring Gun won the other principal events of the meeting. April 20 and 22, 1830.

Governor's Club races at Parramatta. Governor's Cup won by Mr. Icely's Counsellor, and the Town Plate and Turf Club Sweepstakes, by Mr. Bayley's 4-year-old colt, Chase. October 6 and 8, 1830.

Sydney Annual Turf Club races. The sixth Brisbane Cup of £50, heats, twice round the course, was the principal events of the meeting. Bennelong beat Counsellor and Bay Camerton the first heat, the second heat Bennelong won, and in the third he and Counsellor ran a dead heat, and the former was withdrawn. May 18 and 20, 1831.

Parramatta Subscription races. Principal events, won by Bayley's Tomboy, Hartley's Shamrock, and Sir J. Jamison's Bennelong. October 5 and 7, 1831.

The Hawkesbury races, on the Killarney course. Publicans' Purse, valued at 50 guineas, won by Bayley's Tomboy, beating Counsellor, Boshey, and Brutus. Ladies' Purse, by Flying Pieman; and the Scarvell Cup, by Sovereign. August 24, 26, and 27, 1831.

The Governor sanctioned a reserve on the Botany road for a new racecourse, and authorised the loan of twenty labourers to assist in its formation. January, 1832.

Mr. H. Bailey's imported colt, Whisker, won principal events at Hawkesbury races. August 1 and 3, 1832.

Turf Club races held at Parramatta. Mr. Icely's 3-year-old, Chancellor, by Steeltrap, won Governor Bourke's Cup; heats, beating Bennelong and Shamrock. The Wentworth Annual gift of £50, was won by Mr. Bailey's Lady Amelia. On the second day, the seventh Brisbane Cup was won by Chancellor; and the Parramatta Town Plate of £40, by Mr. Lawson's Belinda. April 11 and 13, 1832.

Turf Club, Parramatta. Principal events won by Mr. Bailey's b.f. Lady Emily, and Sir J. Jamison's Bennelong, October 3 and 5, 1832.

Liverpool races, (the first), took place on a course lent by Mr. Throsby. Members Purse, won by Mr. Roberts b. m. Selina; Ladies' Purse, by Mr. Throsby's Whitefoot. October, 12, 1832.

GRAND STEEPLECHASE AT NEWTOWN
The Illustrated Sydney News, 1854

Chancellor, a fine racehorse, owned by Mr. C. Smith which was bred by Mr. Icely, died, December 7, 1832.

At Sydney races Whisker won the principal event, the Governor's Cup, on the first day, and Mr. C. Smith's colt Emancipation won the Town Plate on the second day. April 17 and 19, 1833.

Mr. Simpson's colt, Pitch, won the Maitland Purse of £30, and Mr. Eales' Chance won the Governor's Purse of £55, at Maitland races, July 17 and 19, 1833.

The Hawkesbury races, Emancipation won the principal race, August 21 and 23, 1833.

Liverpool races. The winner of the principal event was Mr. C. Smith's Chester. September 11 and 13, 1833.

Parramatta races. Principal events won by Emancipation, Lady Emily or Emelia, and Chester. October 2 and 4, 1833.

Bathurst races. Principal events won by Mr. Grant's c. g. Lord Byron, and Mr. Piper's g.g. Earl Grey. October 11 and 13, 1833.

Steeltrap (property of Mr. C. Smith), celebrated old racehorse, died February, 1834.

Sydney Subscription races held on the new course, Botany Road. The Sydney Subscription Cup, value 50 guineas, heats, was won by Mr. Smith's Chester; and the Ladies' Purse, by Mr. Bayley's Whisker, beating Emancipation. On the second day, Whisker won the Town Plate of £50, again beating Emancipation, and the Ladies' Purse of £25, by again beating Chester. April 30 and May 2, 1834. [Whisker died a few days afterwards; his owner was offered £1,400 for him three days before.]

First race meeting of the Cumberland Turf Club held at Campbelltown, October 21 and 22, 1834.

Mr. Lawson's Spring Gun struck by lightning at Bathurst and killed, January, 1835.

First Illawarra (Wollongong) races, March 17, 1835.

Sydney Races. Mr. C. Smith's ch. h. Chester, 5 years, by Camerton, won the Melbourne Plate of £50, heats, twice round the course, defeating Roberts' Traveller and another; the Two-Year-Old Stakes by Captain Williams' President by Emigrant; the Ladies' Purse of £30, by Mr. C. Smith's Lady Godiva by Old Emigrant; on the second day Chester won the Town Plate, again beating Traveller. April 22 and 24, 1835.

Maitland Races. Horses named Pitch and Toss won the principal events, July 8 and 10, 1835.

Mr. Suttor's b. h. Slasher, 9st. 10lb. (M'Grath), beat Mr. Egan's b. g. Stranger, 9st. (Sickisson), £1,000, once round Sydney Racecourse, November 26, 1849.

Petrel, bred in N. S. Wales, and Bess o' Bedlam, by Cornbrough, out of Black Bess, contested for the Geelong Town Plate, 2 miles and a distance, heats, weight for age. Bess carried 9st. 7lb. as a four-year-old. 1st heat won by Bess in 4 min. 7 sec. 2nd heat won by Petrel by a nose, in 4 min 6 sec. 3rd heat won by Petrel by a head, in 4 min. 7 sec. The next day the two horses met again for the Publicans' Purse, over the same course, and Bess beat the horse in two heats, carrying the same weights. Time—1st heat, 4 min. 7 sec.; second heat, 4 min. 9 sec. 1849.

At the Autumn Races, Port Phillip, the New South Wales champion horses Emerald and Tally-ho, and the Tasmanian horses Coronet and Hollyoak, were beaten by the Victorian horse Bunyip, by Duke of Argyle. Bunyip won the same day the Town Plate, Publican's Purse, and Ladies' Purse; on the second day he won 2 two-mile and a distance heats races, 1849. [During this season he ran 14 principal races, winning them all.]

RAFFLE'S BAY.

Captain Barker founded settlement at Raffle's Bay in 1823, but it was abandoned, 1826.

Captain Sterling, in H.M.S. "Lucuss," arrived and formed a small settlement at Fort Wellington, on the north-east coast of Raffle's Bay, in lat. 11° 14′ S., long. 132° 24′ E., June 7, 1827.

[Those colonists who had located in Raffle's Bay (a few miles to the eastward of Port Essington, in Coburg Peninsula, North Australia) had a visit from one of the Malay vessels having a Dutch commander, with a crew of 14 men. She belonged to a fleet of 52 vessels which had left Macassar in company, with the object to fish for trepang. They annually visited the northern coast of New Holland for that purpose. 1827.]

RAILWAYS.

NEW SOUTH WALES. The question of railway construction first seriously occupied the attention of the colonists. A numerous and influential meeting was held in Sydney, when Mr. James Macarthur presided, and a committee of leading colonists was appointed to collect information on the subject of railways. Jan. 29, 1846.

The first official duty Governor Fitzroy was

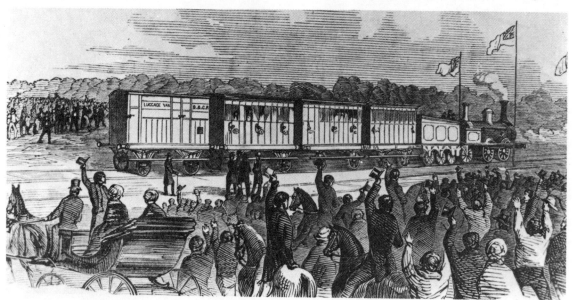

THE ARRIVAL OF THE FIRST TRAIN FROM PARRAMATTA
The Australian Picture Pleasure Book

called upon to perform was to receive a deputation on the subject of railways for the purpose of bringing certain recommendations relative to the same under the attention of the Ministers. August, 1846.

Sydney Tramroad and Railway Company established, capital £100,000. Sept. 11, 1846.

An important meeting held in connection with the contemplated railway, when a report was brought forward which set forth that the committee had collected subscriptions, that surveys had been effected for lines of railways, extending between Sydney and Goulburn and between Sydney and the Hawkesbury and Nepean Rivers. The survey embraced three several routes between Sydney and Bong Bong. January, 1848.

The first sod of the Sydney and Goulburn Railway turned at Redfern by the Hon. Mrs. Keith Stuart, daughter of the Governor, Sir C. Fitzroy, in the presence of His Excellency and about 10,000 people. July 3, 1850.

The first railway contract in the colony was accepted. The work to be executed was a portion of the line between Ashfield and Haslem's Creek at a cost of £10,000. March, 1851.

Railway from Sydney commenced. The "Concord" contract, 4½ miles; contractor, Mr. William Wallis; Mr. Shields and Mr. Mais, the first Engineers-in-Chief. May 1, 1851. [The works were in a few months discontinued for want of labour.]

Mr. Randle took a short contract between Sydney and Parramatta, August 9, 1851.

500 railway labourers arrived from England, August, 1852. Mr. Randle undertook the whole line from Sydney to Parramatta, August, 1852.

The question of railway communication taken up. A meeting was held in Sydney, at which all the wealthy and influential colonists attended, and a resolution to the effect that in consequence of the rapidly increasing prosperity of the colony, it became imperative on the inhabitants to adopt a comprehensive system in the construction of railways throughout the colony, was adopted. January, 1854.

Hunter River Railway projected for connection between Newcastle and Maitland. A company formed at Maitland; capital £100,000. April 20, 1853. Work commenced, but was continued only a year, when it was handed over to the Government on July 30, 1854.

Sydney and Goulburn Railway Company transferred to Government, September 3, 1854.

The carriages attached to a railway train ran off the line at Haslem's Creek; two passengers were killed (one being Mr. Randolph J. Want, solicitor) and two injured. January 10, 1858.

A collision occurred in Redfern tunnel, two persons being injured, September 10, 1863.

A collision occurred between Homebush and Haslem's Creek, between a goods train and a passenger train following; one passenger injured. October 25, 1864.

A collision occurred at Newtown; one passenger was killed and several injured. Jan., 1868.

A collision took place at Redfern, several per-

sons being injured, September, 1868.

A collision took place between a passenger and a coal truck at Newcastle; several persons slightly injured. January 12, 1874.

Two platelayers were run over and killed at Haslem's Creek, January 21, 1876.

Deniliquin and Moama Railway (private company) opened, July 4, 1876.

A collision took place at Redfern, when two women were injured, July 30, 1877.

A collision occurred at Redfern, in which five passengers were injured, November 5, 1877.

The Government of New South Wales accepted tenders for the railway from Wagga Wagga to Albury—Messrs. Cornell and Mixner, contractors—January 24, 1878.

Two trains collided at Emu Plains, near Penrith, N.S.W.; three people were killed, the engines thrown off the line, and the waggons destroyed by fire. January 30, 1878.

Railway opened to Bathurst by Sir Hercules Robinson: great demonstration by the people, and a public dinner given at the School of Arts. April 4, 1876.

The Great Northern Railway extension to Tamworth opened by Sir H. Robinson. October 15, 1878.

George Perdue found guilty of manslaughter, for the collision at Emu Plains, Feb. 19, 1878.

Date of opening to the principal stations in NEW SOUTH WALES :—

Parramatta (S.W.), September 26, 1855.
Liverpool (S.), September 26, 1856.
East Maitland (N.), April 5, 1857.
Newcastle (N.), March 19, 1858.
Campbelltown (S.), May 17, 1858.
West Maitland (N.), July 27, 1858.
Lochinvar (N.), July 2, 1860.
Blacktown (W.), July 4, 1860.
Rooty Hill (W.), December 12, 1861.
Branxton (N.), March 24, 1862.
South Creek (W.), May 1, 1862.
Penrith (W.), July 7, 1862.
Menangle (S.), September 1, 1862.
Singleton (N.), May 7, 1863.
Picton (S.), July 1, 1863.
Morpeth (N.), May 2, 1864.
Richmond (S.W.), December 1, 1864.
Mittagong (branch from Blacktown), March 1, 1867.
Weatherboard (W.), July 11, 1867.
Sutton Forest (S.), December 2, 1867.
Mount Victoria (W.), May 1, 1868.
Marulan (S.), Aug. st 6, 1868.
Muswellbrook (N.), May 19, 1869.
Goulburn (S.), May 27, 1869.
Bowenfels (W.), October 18, 1869.
Wallerawang (W.), March 1, 1870.
Rydal (W.), July 1, 1870.
Aberdeen (N.), October 20, 1870.
Scone (N.), April 17, 1871.
Wingen (S.), August 1, 1871.
Murrurundi (N.), April 5, 1872.
Locke's Platform (W.), April 22, 1872.
Macquarie Plains (W.), July 1, 1872.
Raglan (W.), March 4, 1873.
Kelso (W.), February 4, 1875.
Bathurst (W.), April 4, 1876.
Gunning (S.), November 9, 1875.
Bowning (S.), July 3, 1876.
Yass (S.), July 3, 1876.
Murrumburrah (S.), March 12, 1877.
Quirindi (N.), August 13, 1877.
Cootamundra (S.), November 1, 1877.
Orange (W.), April 19, 1877.
Junee (S.), July 6, 1878.

Wagga Wagga (S.), September 3, 1878.
Tamworth (N.), October 15, 1878.
Breeza (N.), March 26, 1879.

Mount Gambier and Rivoli Bay Railway, S.A., opened by Sir W. D. Jervois, May 19, 1879.

Geelong and Queenscliff Railway opened by the Marquis of Normanby, May 21, 1879.

NEW ZEALAND.

Auckland District, in the provincial district of Auckland. The General Government have completed 141 miles of railway, and have considerably more under construction. Also 2 miles 68 chains from the Kawakawa mine to the shipping place have been constructed, and 5 miles 31 chains more are under way. The Waikato railway, which runs from Auckland southwards, was opened for traffic as far as Newcastle (Ngaruawahia), at the junction of the Waikato and Waipa rivers, once the capital of the Maori King, but now the site of a pretty and thriving British township, 1877. The Waikato railway opened to Ohapu, 1878. [The whole southern part of Auckland, and a large portion of the North is thus brought directly into easy communication with the city by railway.] The Maories refused to allow Government surveyors to survey for the railway from Taranaki to Wanganui (the connecting branches between Auckland and Wellington), March 20, 1879.

Otago District—Lyttleton railway opened, December 1, 1863.

Railway to Manaaru opened, Feb. 21, 1870.

Railway from Christchurch to Dunedin completed and opened at Dunedin, October, 1878.

Railways in New Zealand are open between the following places :—*Northern Island*, Auckland to Ohaupo, passing through Newmarket, Remuera, Drury, Rangariri, Huntly, Taupiri, Newcastle, Hamilton, a distance of 94 miles ; Auckland to Onehunga, connecting Auckland harbour with the Manukau, a distance of 8 miles, with a branch line from Riverhead to Helensville, 16 miles. Napier (commencing at the Spit or Port) to Kopua, a distance of 65 miles, passing Hastings, Waipawa, and Waipakaru. New Plymouth to Inglewood and Waitara, 12 miles. Wanganui to Foxton, 88 miles. Wellington to Upper Hutt and Kaitoke, 27 miles. *Southern Island*—Bluff to Invercargill, 17 miles ; Invercargill to Dunedin, 13 miles ; Dunedin to Omaru, 38 miles ; Omaru to Timaru, 53 miles ; Timaru to Christchurch, 100 miles ; Christchurch to Port Lyttleton, 7 miles, with various branch lines on these routes. Greymouth (West Coast) to Brunner, 8 miles ; Nelson to Foxhill, 20 miles, with numerous short lines on the West Coast. The total length of railway opened in New Zealand, 1,068 miles : December 31, 1877.

QUEENSLAND.

First sod of Queensland railway turned at Ipswich, February 24, 1864.

First railway, Queensland opened July 31, 1865.

First sod of the Rockhampton railway turned by Governor Sir G. F. Bowen, at Rockhampton, September 26, 1865.

A train proceeding to Warwick was blown off the rails by a violent gale of wind (some passengers were injured), January 27, 1875.

First sod of the Dalby and Roma railway turned by Governor Cairns, June 6, 1876.

Mr. Gresley Lukin, proprietor of *The Queenslander*, organised an expedition to effect a flying survey of the proposed transcontinental railway from Blackall to Port Darwin, June 21, 1878.

Dates of Opening, and the Length in Miles, of the different Sections of Railway Lines opened for Traffic from the commencement to December 31, 1877.

To where opened.	S. & W. Line.	N. Line.	All Lines.	Date of Opening.
	M.	M.	M.	
Ipswich to Grandchester	21	...	21	July 31, 1865
Total for 1865 ..	21	..	21	
Grandchester to Gatton	17	..	17	June 1, 1866
Gatton to Helidon	11	..	11	July 30, 1866
Total for 1866 ..	49	..	49	
Helidon to Toowoomba	29	..	29	May 1, 1867
Rockhampton to Westwood ..	..	30	30	Sept. 17, 1867
Toowoomba to Jondaryan....	28	..	28	Nov. 18, 1867
Total for 1867 ..	106	30	136	
Jondaryan to Dalby	24	..	24	April 20, 1868
Total for 1868 ..	130	30	160	
Gowrie Junction to Allora	46	..	46	Mar. 8, 1869
Total for 1869-70	176	30	206	
Allora to Warwick	12	..	12	Jan. 9, 1871
Total for 1871-2-3	188	30	218	
Westwood to Gogango	..	8	8	May 25, 1874
Gogango to Rocky Creek	..	6	6	Oct. 1, 1874
Ipswich to Oxley West	18	..	18	Oct. 5, 1874
Total for 1874 ..	206	44	250	
Oxley West to Oxley Point ..	2	..	2	Feb. 4, 1875
Oxley Point to Brisbane	4	..	4	June 14, 1875
Rocky Creek to Herbert Creek	..	9	9	Nov. 9, 1875
Total for 1875 ..	212	53	265	
Herbert Creek to Boolburra..	..	5	5	Jan. 10, 1876
Boolburra to Duaringa	..	7	7	Mar. 28, 1876
Duaringa to Dingo	..	23	23	Sept. 1, 1876
Total for 1876 ..	212	88	300	
Dalby to Warra	28	..	28	Sept. 10, 1877
Dingo to Blackwater	..	31	31	July 19, 1877
Total for 1877 ..	240	119	359	

NOTE.—The opening of the Ipswich Deviation has shortened the distance between Ipswich and Toowoomba by two miles ; consequently the total length travelled over between Brisbane and the present terminal stations, S. and W. Railway, now stands at 238 miles.

SOUTH AUSTRALIA.

The railway from Adelaide to Gawler, a distance of 25 miles, completed October 5, 1857.

Railway opened to Kapunda, August 3, 1860.

Wallaroo railway commenced, Jan. 17, 1862.

The Victor Harbour railway opened, Aug. 4, 1862.

Railway to the Burra opened, Aug. 29, 1870.

Glenelg railway opened, July 14, 1873.

Sir W. D. Jervois turned the first sod of the Port Augusta Railway, being the first instalment of the transcontinental line, Jan. 28, 1878.

Port Augusta line, first section opened to Gordon's, May, 1879.

Dates of Opening of the different sections to the principal Stations from the commencement to December 31, 1877.

Name of Line.	Date when first portion of Line was opened.	Miles of Line Open at close of 1877.
Adelaide and Port Adelaide....	April 21, 1866	7½
Port Adelaide and Semaphore	Not opened	—
Adelaide and Kapunda	June 1, 1857	50½
Dry Creek and Port Adelaide ..	Feb. 1, 1868	5
Roseworthy and Tarlee........	July 5, 1869	24
Tarlee and Burra	Feb. 21, 1870	46½
Gawler Tramway.......... ..	Not opened	—
Strathalbyn, Goolwa, and Victor Harbour..................	May 18, 1854	32
Port Wakefield and Hoyleton ..	May 8, 1867	28
Hoyleton and Blyth	March, 1876	14
Port Wakefield and Blyth	As above	—
Port Pirie and Gladstone......	Dec. 10, 1875	32½
Gladstone and Jamestown	Not opened	—
Port Pirie and Gladstone	As above	—
Port Broughton and Barunga Range....................	March 11, 1876	10
Kingston and Naracoorte......	July 22, 1876	52½

[NOTE.—The total cost of the South Australian railways to Dec. 31, 1877, was £2,704,404. The maximum speed on the 5ft. 3in. gauge is 25 miles per hour ; and on the 3ft. 6in. gauge, 17½ miles per hour.]

The following lines were completed and opened for traffic during the year 1878 :—

Burra and Hallett .... 18½ miles.
Kapunda and North West Bend (River Murray)............................ 55¾ ,,
Port Wakefield and Kadina .... 34m. 44chns.
Gladstone and Jamestown .... 19 miles.

[The first two being extensions of the trunk line are constructed on the 5ft. 3in. gauge; the other two are constructed on the 3ft. 6in. gauge.]

The following contracts have been let and are in various stages of progress, viz. :—

Port Augusta to Government Gums ....198¾ miles.
Kadina & Barunga Gap, with its extension 33 ,,
Rivoli Bay and Mount Gambier.......... 51 ,,
Harnley Bridge and Balaklava .... 22½ ,,

Making a total of 305 miles. All these lines are being constructed on the 3ft. 6in. gauge.

The following railways have been authorised during the Parliamentary session, 1878-9:—

Hallett to Terowie .... 20m. 44chns.
Terowie to Pichi-Richi .... 93 miles with
Branch to Jamestown .... 21m. 76chns.
Adelaide to Nairne .... 33 miles.

TASMANIA.

First sod of Launceston and Western Railway turned by H.R.H. Prince Alfred, Jan. 15, 1868.

First train on the first Tasmanian railway started August 19, 1869.

The Mersey and Deloraine Railway opened January 1, 1871.

The L. & W. Railway opened Feb. 3, 1871.

VICTORIA.

Railway from Melbourne to Sandridge commenced, January, 1853.

Geelong and Melbourne Railway incorporated, February 8, 1853.

Melbourne and Geelong Railway works commenced, September 20, 1853.

Melbourne and Hobson's Bay Railway opened, September 14, 1854.

Melbourne and St. Kilda railway opened, May 13, 1857.

Geelong and Melbourne railway opened, June 25, 1857.

Melbourne and Suburban railway commenced, July 1, 1858.

The Melbourne and Williamstown, Hobson's Bay (private company) railway opened, January 17, 1859.

The Victorian Railway department took possession of the Melbourne and Geelong line from the original company, September 4, 1860.

St. Kilda and Brighton railway opened, December 21, 1861.

Railway extension to Castlemaine opened, October 15, 1862.

Victorian Government purchased the extension railway, June 27, 1867.

First sod of Castlemaine and Maryborough railway turned, September 7, 1872.

First colonial-made locomotive delivered to the Victorian Government, February 6, 1873.

Railway from Melbourne to Wodonga, on the Murray, opened, November 19, 1873.

Maryborough and Dunolly railway opened, October 6, 1874.

Geelong and Colac railway began, October 23, 1874.

First sod of the Gippsland railway turned, March 11, 1875.

First sod of the Perth and Hamilton railway, Victoria, turned by Governor Sir George F. Bowen, April 27, 1876.

Experiment of running railway trains with carriage doors unlocked first tried on Williamstown line, January 15, 1877.

A disastrous accident happened to a goods and passenger train on the Echuca line, near the Epsom racecourse. Flood waters had unsettled the ballast, and the engine ran off the line over the embankment ; 38 of the goods trucks were smashed, none of the passengers being seriously hurt. February 13, 1877.

Serious accident occurred at Spencer-street terminus; nine of the passengers received severe injuries. June 11, 1877.

Opening celebration of Portland and Hamilton railway, January 9, 1878.

The Government commenced the construction of the Oakleigh line without the sanction of the Legislature, February 19, 1878.

The Gippsland railway from Oakleigh to Sale, a distance of 119 miles, formally opened, March 1, 1878.

Messrs. Lyell and Munro, M.L.A's., arranged terms for the purchase by the Government of the Hobson's Bay railway, for the sum of £1,320,820, June 25, 1878.

The Government of Victoria obtained a majority of 42 in favour of the purchase of the Hobson's Bay railway. The Opposition voted with them. July 24, 1878.

Messrs. Topham, Angus, and Smith's tender of £58.977 accepted for the construction of the Geelong and Queenscliffe line, August 9, 1878.

Messrs. J. P. Higgins and Co.'s tender of £48,868, accepted for the South Yarra and Oakleigh line, September 13, 1878.

Sale (Gippsland) and Melbourne railway joined at Oakleigh, April 2, 1879.

Dates of Opening, and Length in Miles, of the different Sections of Lines opened to the Principal Stations of Victoria, from the commencement to December, 1878.

Date of opening.	Opened to	Miles opened.	Total Distance.
	Main Line.		
Feb. 10, 1859	Sunbury	23¾	23¾
July 8, 1861	Woodend	24¾	48½
April 25, 1862	Kyneton	8¼	56¾
Oct. 21, 1862	Sandhurst	44	100¾
Sept. 19, 1864	Echuca	55¼	156
	Williamstown Line.		
Jan. 17, 1859	Williamstown	9¼	9¼
	Ballarat Line.		
Sept. 4, 1860	Geelong	45	45
April 11, 1862	Ballarat	55¼	100¼
	North-eastern Line.		
Jan. 9, 1871	*Essendon	4¾	4¾
April 18, 1872	School-house Lane	54	58¾
Aug. 26, 1872	Seymour	2½	61¼
Nov. 20, 1872	Longwood	23½	84¾
March 20, 1873	Violet Town	20	104¾
Aug. 18, 1873	Benalla	16	120¾
Oct. 28, 1873	Wangaratta	24	144¾
Nov. 21, 1873	Wodonga	42¼	187
Nov. 30, 1867	Newmarket to Racecourse	1½	

* Note.—Essendon Line opened by Company on October 22, 1860.

	Ballarat and Ararat Line.		
Aug. 11, 1874	Beaufort	28½	28½
April 7, 1875	Ararat	28½	57
	Castlemaine and Dunolly Line.		
July 7, 1874	Maryborough	34	34
Oct. 6, 1874	Dunolly	13½	47½
	Ballarat and Maryborough Line.		
July 7, 1874	Creswick	11½	11½
Nov. 16, 1874	Clunes	11¼	22¾
Feb. 2, 1875	Maryborough	19¾	42½
	Wangaratta and Beechworth Line.		
July 7, 1875	Everton	12¾	*15¾
Sept. 30, 1876	Beechworth	10¼	26

* From Wangaratta.

	Ararat and Stawell Line.		
Feb. 15, 1876	Scallan's Hill	17¾	17¾
April 14, 1876	Stawell	1	18¾
	Maryborough and Avoca Line.		
Oct. 21, 1876	Avoca	15	15
	Sandhurst and Inglewood Line.		
Sept. 19, 1876	Bridgewater	25¾	25¾
Nov. 18, 1876	Inglewood	4¼	30
	Geelong and Colac Line.		
Nov. 25, 1876	Winchelsea	25¾	25¾
March 13, 1877	Birregurra	12¾	38½
July 27, 1877	Colac	12	50½
	Gippsland Line.		
June 1, 1877	Sale to Morwell	38¾	38¾
Oct. 8, 1877	Oakleigh to Bunyip	38¾	77½
Dec. 1, 1877	Moe to Morwell	8¾	86¼
March 1, 1878	Moe to Bunyip	32	118¼
	Ararat and Hamilton Line.		
April 24, 1877	Dunkeld	47½	47½
Oct. 29, 1877	Hamilton	19	66½
	Portland and Hamilton Line.		
Dec. 19, 1877	Hamilton	53	53
	Dunolly and St. Arnaud Line.		
Sept. 3, 1878	Bealiba	12¼	12¼
Dec. 23, 1878	St. Arnaud	20½	32¾
	Geelong Racecourse Line.		
Feb. 1, 1878	Racecourse Station	1¾	1¾
	Stawell and Horsham Line		
Dec. 17, 1878	Murtoa	35½	35½

Note.—The number of miles open in Victoria, up to December 31, 1878, was 931. The broad gauge used, viz., 5 feet 8 inches.

Western Australia.

First sod of the Geraldtown railway turned by Governor Weld, November 22, 1874.

Total Length of Railways Open and in course of Construction throughout Australasia.

	Miles of Railway Open Dec. 31, 1877.	Miles of Railway in course of Construction, Dec. 31, 1877.
New South Wales	643	217¾
New Zealand	954	219
Queensland	357	168
South Australia	327	404
Tasmania	172½	....
Victoria	931	193
Western Australia	68	25
Total	3452½	1226¾

Total Expenditure for, in Australasia, to December 31, 1877.

New South Wales	£8,570,000
New Zealand	6,675,781
Queensland	3,500,000
South Australia	2,500.000
Tasmania	700,000
Victoria	14,562,984
Western Australia	100,000
Total	£36,608,765

RAILWAY BRIDGES and VIADUCTS.

Over the Hunter at Singleton, N.S.W. (N.); length, 400 feet.

Over the Hunter at Aberdeen (N.); length 480 feet; cylinders sunk 20 feet below ordinary level of water; height, 41 feet above ordinary level of water; cost, £25,000.

Over the Macquarie at Bathurst (W.); 480 ft. in length; cast iron cylinders 9 ft. in diameter, sunk 14 ft. below ordinary level of water in river; height above ordinary water level, 35 ft.; cost £32,000.

Over the Nepean at Menangle (S.); 498 feet in length; height of bridge above level of water in the river, to under side of girders, 65 feet; length of approaches from Sydney side, 978 feet, and on southern side, 432 feet; cost, £100,000. Opened for traffic, July 11, 1867.

Over the River Nepean at Penrith (W.), 35 miles from Sydney, is constructed for a double line, and carries the Main Western Road and a single line of railway. It consists of three openings of 186 ft. clear span each, and one span of 127 ft. The larger

GRAND CEREMONY AT LONG COVE VIADUCT
The Illustrated Sydney News, 1855

openings have two main girders of the box form, each 594 ft. in length, of an extreme depth of 13 feet, and placed 25 ft. 6 in. apart in the clear. The roadway is carried on wrought-iron cross girders 18 in. deep, and placed 3 ft. apart centre and centre, and covered with 3 in. planking throughout. The span of 127 feet has also wrought-iron girders of the box form, 135 feet in length and 10 feet in depth. The rails are 49 feet above the ordinary level of the river. Cost, £110,000.

Over Murrumbidgee at Wagga Wagga (S.) ; total length over main channel, 636 feet ; cast iron cylinders, 9 feet in diameter, and sunk 34 feet below ordinary level of water in the river ; work commenced, 1878.

Over the Macquarie River at Wellington (W.) ; length, 477 feet, or, including abutments, 648 feet ; work commenced, 1878.

Wollondilly River, N.S.W., 122 miles from Sydney (S.) ; 616 feet in length.

Wollondilly River, 127 miles from Sydney (S.) ; 614 feet in length ; rails 46 feet above ordinary level of water.

Boxer's Creek viaduct, 133 miles from Sydney (S.) ; 206 feet in length ; 46 feet above ordinary water level.

Mulwarree Creek viaduct, near Goulburn (S.) ; 858 feet in length.

Barber's Creek viaduct, 111 miles from Sydney (S.) ; 340 feet in length.

Picton viaduct, (S.) 53 miles from Sydney ; 276 feet in length ; 78 feet in its extreme height from foundations to rail level.

Knapsack Gully viaduct, 38 miles from Sydney (W.) ; 388 feet in length ; greatest height, 126 feet, from foundation to level of rails.

Over the Murray River at Echuca ; cost, £40,000 ; opened, March, 1879.

Over Brisbane River at Oxley ; cost, £36,000 ; opened, 1875.

RAILWAY CURVES AND GRADIENTS.
The smallest curve on the New South Wales line is eight chains, on the Western Line. The steepest gradient, 1 in 30, is also on the Western Line. In Victoria the steepest gradient is 1 in 30, on the Wangaratta and Beechworth Line.

RAILWAY GAUGES. New South Wales, 4 ft. 8½ in. ; New Zealand, 5 ft. 3 in., 4 ft. 8 in., 3 ft. 6 in. ; Queensland, 3 ft. 6 in. ; South Australia, 5 ft. 3 in., 3 ft. 6 in. ; Tasmania, 5 ft. 3 in. ; Victoria, 5 ft. 3 in.

RAILWAY TUNNELS. The longest tunnels in New South Wales are :—The Mount Clarence tunnel, Western line (88¼ miles from Sydney), 539 yards in length ; Liverpool Range tunnel, 126 miles from Newcastle (Northern line), is 528 yards in length ; the Picton tunnel (Southern line, 54 miles from Sydney) 198 yards in length ; the Gibraltar tunnel (Southern line, 79 miles from Sydney), 572 yards in length. In Victoria, the longest tunnel is the Mount Elphinstone (Echuca line), 418 yards in length. The Big Hill tunnel, on the same line, is 413 yards in length. In Queensland, the Victoria tunnel, S. W. line, is 26 chains in length. [*See* ZIG ZAG.]

REBELS, IRISH. Arrival in the settlement of New South Wales of a large number of Irish rebels, amongst whom were the Rev. Henry Fulton, C.E. ; Rev. Father Harold, R.C. ; Capt. Wm. Henry Alcock ; Dr. O'Connor ; Joseph Holt (better known as General Holt), 1799-1800.

RECEVEUR, PERE LE, the naturalist of the "Astrolabe," Captain M. de la Perouse, arrived with French expedition at Botany Bay, January 24, 1788 ; died there of wounds received in an encounter with the natives at the Navigators' Islands, February 17, 1788.

REGISTRATION SYSTEM OF BIRTHS, DEATHS, AND MARRIAGES. Mr. W. H. Archer first put into operation in Victoria a system of registration for legal and statistical purposes more scientifically comprehensive and minute than had ever been adopted by any nation, July 1, 1853. [It has been imitated by other States and the Registrar-General of England and the International Statistical Congress of Brussels have republished Mr. Archer's schedules as models.]

RELIGION.
Four Church of England Bishops were consecrated at Westminster Abbey, three of them were for Australia, June 21, 1847.

STATE-AID TO.
The discontinuance of the system of State endowments for religious purposes was mooted in the Legislative Council, N.S.W. A numerously attended meeting was held in Sydney, when a petition was adopted to the Council, praying that it might refuse the proposal of the Governor-General to supplement the estimates by an additional grant of £17,000 for ecclesiastical purposes, and to take measures to abolish State endowments. The House, however, voted the additional sum, 1854.

A supplementary grant of £14,000 for the support of public worship was struck out of the estimates, N.S.W., 1858.

Abolition of State-aid to religion in New South Wales, July 21, 1863.

Abolition of State-aid Bill passed in Victoria, 1869.

RELIGIOUS DENOMINATIONS in Australasia, in 1871. (Population, about 2,000,000).

Religion.	N.S.W.	New Zealand.	Queensland.	S. Australia.	Tasmania.	Victoria.	W. Australia	Total.
Church of England	229,243	124,373	61,962	50,849	53,047	257,835	14,619	791,630
Roman Catholics	145,932	40,412	43,147	28,668	22,091	176,620	7,118	463,988
Presbyterians	49,122	72,477	18,947	13,371	6,644	112,983	529	274,073
Wesleyan Methodists	36,275	25,219	11,065	27,075	7,187	94,220	1,374	202,415
Congregationalists or Independents.....................	9,253	5,441	2,560	7,969	3,931	18,191	882	49,227
Baptists	4,151	6,353	5,344	8,731	931	16,311	54	40,875
Primitive Methodists	......	......	......	8,207	......	......	......	8,207
Other Methodists	3,291	......	......	......	......	......	......	3,291
Lutherans and German Protestants	......	3,914	12,174	15,412	......	10,559	......	42,059
Christians, — Brethren and Disciples	......	......	......	1,188	......	......	......	1,189
Calvinists, or Calvinistic Methodists	......	......	......	......	......	1,432	......	1,432
Friends......................	......	......	......	92	82	333	......	507
Unitarians	849	......	......	662	......	1,016	......	2,527
Catholic Apostolic Church ..	......	......	......	......	......	278	......	278
Greek Church................	......	......	......	......	......	332	......	332
Israelites & Christian Israelites	......	......	......	......	......	285	......	285
Mormons, or Latter Day Saints	......	......	......	......	......	97	......	97
Jews, or Hebrews	2,395	1,215	427	435	232	3,571	62	8,337
Moravians, or United Brethren	......	......	......	210	......	93	......	333
Pagans, Mahomedans, Chinese	7,455	4,764	10,047	......	4	18,392	4	40,666
New Jerusalem Church	......	......	......	137	......	......	......	137
Bible Christians.............	......	......	......	7,758	......	......	......	7,758
Methodists New Connection ..	......	......	......	363	......	......	......	363
Free Presbyterians	......	......	......	......	2,420	......	......	2,420
Church of Christ	......	......	......	......	......	3,540	......	3,540
No Sect......................	......	......	......	508	......	2,150	147	2,805
Unspecified	5,946	......	5,936	4,753	......	5,560	......	22,195
Other Protestants............	7,208	......	......	......	......	1,028	......	8,236
Other Catholics	1,695	......	......	......	......	......	......	1,695
Other Persuasions...........	1,166	......	1,674	3,802	2,759	......	......	9,401
Objected to State Religion....	......	......	......	5,436	......	9,965	......	15,401

Approximate Estimate in 1878. (Population, about 2,500,000.)

Religion.	Estimated Number.
Church of England	989,537
Roman Catholics	579,985
Presbyterians	342,591
Wesleyan Methodists	253,019
Congregationalists or Independents	61,534
Baptists	51,094
Primitive Methodists	10,258
Other Methodists	4,114
Lutherans and German Protestants	52,574
Christians,—Brethren and Disciples	1,486
Calvinists, or Calvinistic Methodists	1,790
Friends	634
Unitarians	3,159
Catholic Apostolic Church.............	347
Greek Church	415
Israelites or Christian Israelites	356
Mormons or Latter Day Saints..........	121
Jews or Hebrews	10,421
Moravians or United Brethren..........	416
Pagans, Mahomedans, Chinese..........	50,833
New Jerusalem Church	171
Bible Christians	9,697
Methodist New Connection	454
Free Presbyterians	3,025
Church of Christ	4,425
No sect	3,506
Unspecified..........................	27,744
Other Protestants	10,295
Other Catholics	2,119
Other Persuasions	11,751
Objected to state religion	19,251

RELIGIOUS FANATIC. Andrew Fisher, of Nunawading, Victoria, better known as the "Nunawading Messiah," at the head of 100 followers, declared himself the Messiah. He was a charcoal burner, and took—his sect being polygamous—three sisters as his wives, June 21, 1871.

REVENUE.

William MacPherson, Collector of Internal Revenue, New South Wales, arrived, October 11, 1829.

Revenue of Australasian Colonies for year ending December 31, 1877 :—

	Revenue. £	Population.
New South Wales	5,748,245	645,994
New Zealand	3,916,023	408,348
Queensland	1,436,581	195,092
South Australia	1,447,401	231,383
Tasmania	361,771	106,204
Victoria	4,723,877	849,870
Western Australia	165,413	27,579
Total	17,799,311	2,464,470

RICHMOND, N.S.W. Richmond and other places in the Hawkesbury district (Pitt Town, Wilberforce, and Castlereagh), received their present names December, 1810.

RICHMOND, River, discovered, August, 1828·

RIFLE ASSOCIATION OF NEW SOUTH WALES established, October 5, 1860; held first Meeting at Randwick, September 26, 27, 28, 1861.

RIOTS.

An insurrection of prisoners, 250 strong, and armed with muskets, broke out at Castle Hill, near Parramatta. They were defeated in 15 minutes by Major Johnston, of the N.S.W. corps, with 24 men. 67 insurgents fell in the field, and 10 were tried and hanged. March 4, 1804.

A serious disturbance took place between the military and the lower class of the inhabitants of Sydney, the former treating with disdain and insult the native youth of the colony and the prisoners; and a crisis was eventually brought about by a party of soldiers armed with bludgeons and bayonets rushing into the cottages of some of the citizens and dangerously wounding a number of persons. The consequence was that the soldiers were disarmed and not allowed to go abroad after sundown. 1825.

Another disturbance between the military and citizens occurred at Sydney, when one civilian was killed and two wounded. Three soldiers were tried, in connection with the occurrence, for manslaughter, and one of them was found guilty. 1828.

A collision between the police and some seamen of H.M.S. "Favourite," then in port, occurred in Sydney. About 50 of the sailors had leave of absence for 48 hours; a disturbance took place between them and some civilians in the theatre; after a severe struggle a great number of persons were taken to the lock-up, amongst whom were 10 of the man-of-war's men. Next morning all but two were dismissed. These were remanded to their ship, but instead of being conveyed there they were taken to the watch-house. Their mates, hearing of the circumstance, went with about 300 of the town mob, to the watch-house, in Cumberland-street, where they put to flight the officers and made a wreck of the building, releasing such prisoners as were confined there; they then proceeded to St. James's watch-house, where they acted in a similar manner, and attempted the same at the

chief lock-up, at the corner of George and Druitt streets, but without effect. The military were called out, the Riot Act was read, and the mob not dispersing, blank cartridges were fired, but no heed being taken of it, and an inclination to violence being manifested, the military fired some rounds of ball. The mob then dispersed, but not until one man was shot, who died the next day. September 6, 1841.

Capture of the Eureka Stockade, Ballarat, Victoria. In consequence of dissatisfaction among the diggers at the imposition of a heavy license fee, resistance was offered, and a serious riot took place. December 3, 1854. [The miners of Ballarat were headed by Peter Lalor, as commander-in-chief, Frederick Vern, a Hanoverian by birth, Carboni Raffaello, an Italian, Alfred Black, James H. M'Gill, Curtain, Lesman, Kenworthy, John Lynch, J. W. Esmond, and J. B. Humffray. The number of diggers who took part in defending the stockade was about 200. The military and police numbered 276. Of these there were 117 men of the 40th Regiment, under command of Captain Wise, Lieuts. Bowdler, Hall, and Gardyne; 65 men of the 12th Regiment, under command of Captain Queade and Lieutenant Paul; 70 mounted police under command of Sub-inspectors Furnley, Langley, Chomley, and Lieutenant Cossack; and 24 foot police, under Sub-inspector Carter. The attack was made at dawn on Sunday morning, and was led by Captain Thomas, assisted by Captain Pasley, R.E. The engagement lasted 25 minutes. The rebels fought well; 22 were killed, 12 wounded, and 125 taken prisoners. The loss of the Queen's forces was, one killed and 12 wounded. Captain Wise, who was severely wounded, died a few days afterwards. Lalor, who fought well, fell within the stockade, and lost his right arm in the engagement. He however, escaped, and Government offered £200 reward for his capture, £500 reward for the capture of Vern, and £200 reward for the capture of Black.]

Brutal onslaught on the Chinamen of Lambing Flat, and "roll-up" of the diggers, amounting to 3,000 strong. They perpetrated many acts of violence and robbery, as tearing the goods and tents and maiming the Chinese in a fearful manner; June, 1861. The police proceeded to the spot, and a collision took place between them and the diggers. Troops were sent from Sydney under Colonel Kempt. July, 1861.

W. Lupton, a digger, who was mortally wounded at Lambing Flat, during the affray with the police, was interred with military honours by his fellow diggers, July, 1861.

The military ordered to the place to quell the riot. Royal Artillery, 2 officers and 42 men; Infantry, 7 officers and 123 men; Police (mounted), 21. The Hon. Charles Cowper, Premier, proceeded to the Flat. July, 1861.

Ten of the Lambing Flat rioters were tried at the Goulburn Circuit Court, and acquitted. September, 1861. [William Spicer afterwards convicted and imprisoned in Berrima Gaol for taking part in the riot.]

THE FRACAS AT THE STOCKADE
A & R Archives

BRUTAL ONSLAUGHT ON THE CHINESE AT LAMBING FLAT

Riot amongst the female inmates of the (reformatory) Industrial School at Newcastle, January 7, 1871.

Rev. Mr. Portus lectured in the School of Arts, Ipswich, on *Martin Luther*. The Roman Catholics attacked the Hall, and Captain Townley, P.M., read the Riot Act; several persons were severely injured. November 12, 1874.

Riot between Custom House officials and employés of Stevenson and Sons (soft-goods merchants), Flinder's Lane, Melbourne, Apr. 15, 1876.

A disturbance created in Hyde Park, Sydney, on account of Pastor Allen's preaching, March 10, 1878.

The Hyde Park (Sydney) rioters committed for trial, April 4, 1878.

The Hyde Park riot case terminated by the conviction of two prisoners, the Attorney-General not praying for judgment. May 29, 1878.

A disturbance took place at the Association Cricket Ground, Sydney, on the occasion of the return match between the New South Wales eleven and the Gentlemen of England. The mob, objecting to the Umpire for the English team, refused to allow the play to proceed. Feb. 8, 1879. The play was stopped but resumed on the Monday following.

RIOU, Captain Edward. H.M.S. "Guardian," 44 guns, Captain Edward Riou, having on board a large stock of provisions for the colony of New South Wales, struck against an iceberg to the S. and E. of the Cape of Good Hope, and was so much injured that the greater part of her valuable cargo was thrown overboard; most of the passengers and crew left her in five boats, when they thought she was sinking. Riou remained with his ship but gave them despatches for the Admiralty, and entreated that the country would protect and provide for his sister. December 23, 1790. [Four of the boats were never heard of; the third, after great privation, reached the Mauritius, but, meanwhile, the "Guardian" was fallen in with by a French frigate, towed into Table Bay, and the gallant Riou was saved to perish by a more glorious death, having been afterwards killed at Copenhagen.]

RIVERS.

The *Hunter*, discovered by Lieutenant Shortland, 1797.

Lieutenant - Colonel Paterson, Lieutenant Grant, and Mr. Harris visited the Hunter River, landed, and named Coal Island, Colliers' Island,

Mangrove Creek, Green Hill, Schank's Forest Plains, Mount Anne, Mount Elizabeth, King's Ranges, Mount Harris, Mount Grant. Mr. Barralier surveyed portion of the Hunter River. June 14 to July 17, 1801.

The *Macquarie*, New South Wales, named by G. W. Evans, December, 1813.

The *Hastings*, New South Wales, discovered by Oxley, 1818.

Penal settlement formed on the Hastings at Port Macquarie, 1822.

The *Castlereagh* discovered by Oxley, July, 1818.

The *Alligator*, North Australia, explored by King, 1818.

The *Brisbane*, explored and named by Oxley, 1822.

The *Goulburn*, discovered by Lawson, 1823.

The *Murrumbidgee*, discovered by Captain Currie and Major Ovens, June 1, 1823.

The *Murray* crossed by Hamilton Hume and party, November 17, 1824. [A monument on the banks of the river, at Albury, has been erected "by the inhabitants of the Hume River, in honour of Hamilton Hume," in commemoration of the event.]

The *Goulburn* crossed by Hume and Hovell, December 3, 1824.

The *Bogan* discovered by Sturt, 1829.

The *Bogan* traced by Dixon, 1833.

The *Glenelg* discovered by Mitchell, July 31, 1835.

The *Richmond* discovered, 1842.

The *Dawson* explored by Leichhardt and party, 1844.

The *Albert* discovered by Wickham and Stokes, 1844.

The *Bogan* reached by Mitchell, 1845.

The *Burdekin* discovered by Leichhardt, 1845.

The *Mackenzie* discovered by Leichhardt, 1845.

The *Burdekin* reached by Leichhardt Search Expedition, under A. C. Gregory, 1856.

The *Murrumbidgee* ascended by Captain Francis Cadell, in the steamer "Albury," September, 1858.

The *Maitland* discovered by Mr. F. Gregory, 1861.

The *Lyons* discovered by Gregory, 1861.

The *Ashburton* discovered by Gregory, 1861.

The *Goulburn* navigated from Echuca to Seymour by the steamer "Bunyip," April 30, 1878.

The *Mary* named, in honour of Lady Mary Fitzroy, wife of Sir Charles Augustus Fitzroy. 1854.

LENGTH OF.

New South Wales.

	Miles.		Miles.
Darling, from Bourke to Murray Junction	1,000	M'Intyre	350
		Warrego	103
Lachlan	700	Macquarie ..	750
Murrumbidgee ..	1,350	Hawkesbury	330
Murray	2,400	Hunter ..	300
Namoi	600	Shoalhaven ..	260
Bogan	450	Clarence ..	240
Gwydir	445	Macleay ..	190
Barwon	510	Richmond	120
Castlereagh	365	Manning	100

Victoria.

Yarra Yarra.. ..	90	Avoca..	130
Goulburn	230	Hopkins	110
Glenelg	205	Wannon	105
Loddon	150	Ovens	100
Wimmera	135		

No records are obtainable of the lengths of the rivers in South Australia, West Australia, Queensland, Tasmania, or New Zealand, which are referred to in other portions of this work. [*See* EXPLORERS, LAND for discoverers and origin of names of rivers.]

TABLE of distances on the Murray.

	Miles.
Albury to Corowa..	73
Corowa to Collendina	33
Collendina to Ovens River	4
Ovens River to Hell's Gates	14
Hell's Gates to Mulwalla	6
Mulwalla to Boomonoomana	25
Boomonoomana to Tocumwall	39
Tocumwall to Edwards River	59
Edwards River to Bamah	17
Bamah to Goulburn River	20
Goulburn River to Moama	10
Moama to Echuca..	$1\frac{1}{2}$
Echuca to Perricoota	38
Perricoota to Toorannabby	$17\frac{1}{2}$
Toorannabby to Clump Bend	61
Clump Bend to Goon	25
Goon to Murray Downs	48
Murray Downs to Swan Hill	$2\frac{1}{2}$
Swan Hill to Tyntynder	20
Tyntynder to Piang Hill	28
Piang Hill to Tooleybuc..	$5\frac{1}{2}$
Tooleybuc to Bitch and Pups	$10\frac{1}{2}$
Bitch and Pups to Wakool Junction..	$11\frac{1}{2}$
Wakool Junction to Windomal..	$10\frac{1}{2}$
Windomal to Murrumbidgee Junction	$17\frac{1}{2}$
Murrumbidgee Junction to Meilman..	42
Meilman to Euston	33
Euston to Gell's Island	$26\frac{1}{2}$
Gell's Island to Ki	22
Ki to Brett's	$21\frac{1}{2}$
Brett's to Tapalen	$8\frac{1}{2}$
Tapalen to Carwarp	$23\frac{1}{2}$
Carwarp to Mallee Cliffs..	11
Mallee Cliffs to Mallee Cliffs Station ..	$13\frac{1}{2}$
Mallee Cliffs Station to Gol Gol Creek	$15\frac{1}{2}$
Gol Gol to Mildwra	$5\frac{1}{2}$
Mildwra to Cowarra	$20\frac{1}{2}$
Cowarra to Darling Junction	12
Darling Junction to Goolwa	500
Total—Albury to the sea mouth, at Lake Alexandrina, where the Murray empties itself into the sea	1352

The great river next in importance is the Murrumbidgee, 1350 miles in length. It enters the Murray 700 miles above the mouth of the latter. The Murrumbidgee is navigable, except in dry seasons, up to the township of Gundagai, 670 miles above its junction with the Murray.

TABLE of Distances on the Murrumbidgee.

	Miles.
Gundagai to Wagga Wagga	86
Wagga Wagga to Yarragundry	23
Yarragundry to Yiorkibitto	48
Yiorkibitto to Grong Grong	36
Grong Grong to Narrandera	13
Narrandera to Yanco or Bedithera	11
Yanco to Yanco Station..	18
Yanco to Gojelderie	13
Gojelderie to Tubbo	15
Tubbo to Cararbury	34
Cararbury to Currathool	41
Currathool to Burrabogie	35
Burrabogie to Illilliwa	26
Illilliwa to Hay	14
Hay to Toogambie..	39
Toogambie to Maude	25
Maude to Lachlan Junction	44
Lachlan Junction to Balranald..	85

Balranald to Canally	.. ..	26
Canally to Weimby, Murray Junction	..	38

Total distance from Gundagai to Murrumbidgee Junction..	670

The Darling joins the Murray 500 miles from the sea. The Darling is a very long river, and receives a very large number of streams in its course. Its length is estimated to be 2,200 miles. Steamers ply to Fort Bourke, nearly 1,000 miles from the junction with the Murray, and they frequently go to Brewarrina, and occasionally to Walgett.

TABLE of Distances on the Darling.

	Miles.
From Junction of Darling with Murray to Kinchega	305
Kinchega to Menindie	15
Menindie to Pammemeroo	22
Pammemeroo to Wilcannia	158
Wilcannia to Fort Bourke (nearly) ..	500

Total distance from Murray Junction to Fort Bourke	1000

ROADS.

A road was first made from Sydney to Liverpool, February 22, 1814. [Previous to this it was only a bush track for equestrians and pedestrians, but not for vehicles.]

A road was constructed and opened over the Blue Mountains, January 21, 1815. [It was constructed in the short space of 6 months, by convicts, who volunteered, on condition of receiving emancipation when the work was completed. Mr. Wm. Cox, J.P., of Windsor, superintended the construction of the road.]

A route from Richmond to the Bathurst road, over the Blue Mountains, discovered and subsequently surveyed, May, 1823.

ROCKHAMPTON, QUEENSLAND.

Made a port of entry, October 8, 1858.

The first sale of Rockhampton Town allotments took place November 17, 1858.

Rockhampton proclaimed Municipality, December 15, 1860.

First Circuit Court held April 6, 1863.

Lighted with gas, December 17, 1874.

"ROLL-UP," a term applied by the miners in the various Diggings in Australia, when summoned from labour, or amusement, to attend a mass meeting for a special purpose. The term is now more general in application.

ROMA, QUEENSLAND, proclaimed Municipality May 25, 1867.

COX'S PASS OVER THE MOUNTAINS
A French engraving of 1825

Colony.	Population.	No. of Scholars.
New South Wales	662,212	138,267
New Zealand	417,622	66,947
Queensland	203,084	41,500
South Australia	236,864	29,133
Tasmania	107,104	12,557
Victoria	860,787	223,416
Western Australia	27,838	7,125

SAFES, FIRE PROOF. Result of a trial of Milner's and Wearne's fireproof Safes (Wearne being a colonial manufacturer), given by the judges in favour of the latter. [The trial took place at the Haymarket, Sydney.] June 17, 1871.

SAILORS' HOME, SYDNEY, established, May 18, 1839.

SALMON.

Alexander Black reported on the feasibility of introducing salmon into Tasmania, 1860.

The first salmon caught in Tasmania, Dec. 4, 1873. [To Mr. J. A. Youl, C.M.G., and Sir Robert Officer, much credit is due for the introduction of salmon into Tasmania.]

The Californian salmon imported by Sir Samuel Wilson to Victoria, Nov. 19, 1877.

Upwards of 28,000 of the Californian salmon ova imported by Sir Samuel Wilson hatched out at Ercildoune, Nov. 29, 1877.

Salmon fry deposited in the head waters of Yarra, some having previously been placed in the streams in the Cape Otway Ranges, December 19, 1877.

SALT. First salt made in New South Wales from sea water at Point Maskelcyne (Dawes' Battery), May, 1790.

SAMOA. Colonel Steinberger, an American, arrested at Samoa by order of Captain Stevens of H.M.S. Barracouta. A fight with the Samoans, loss of life resulting. Feb. 28, 1876.

SANDHURST, VICTORIA, proclaimed a municipality, April, 1855.

SAXE-COBURG. Their Serene Highnesses Prince Phillip and Prince Augustus of Saxe-Coburg (cousins of Queen Victoria), visited Sydney, N.S.W., October 22, 1872.

SCHOLARS attending public and private schools in Australasia :—

SCHOOLS.

First school in Sydney, in Rev. Mr. Johnston's church, opened, Feb. 18, 1793. [When the church was burnt, the school was held in the Court-house. The first teachers were W. Webster, W. Richardson, and Susannah Hunt.] J. M'Queen, first school-master at Norfolk Island, 1793.

There were three schools in New South Wales, Dec., 1797.

Rev. Mr. Johnston had 200 children in attendance at his school, 1798.

School established on the Hawkesbury, and 2d. per acre levied by the Government on the landholders there to support the teacher, 1804.

Mr. Crook advertised the first boarding school in Australia in 1808.

A free school established in Sydney, February 24, 1810.

A school for the education of young aboriginals established at Parramatta, May, 1816. [Many of them were given up by their parents, and placed under tutors ; the school continued to be well attended until the aboriginals had so far decayed that few were left.]

The foundation of the Georgian School-house in Castlereagh-street, Sydney, was laid by Governor Macquarie, March 20, 1820. [It was designed for the education of the children of the poor, and built to accommodate 500 pupils.]

The National School system intro'uced to the Colony of N.S.W. by the Rev. T. Reddall, August 1, 1820.

First Roman Catholic school in New South Wales established, 1822.

Rev. Thomas Reddall appointed Director General Public Schools, New South Wales, August 18, 1824.

Sydney Free Grammar School founded, Dr. Halloran Head-master, November 17, 1824.

Infant School first established in New South Wales by Rev. Richard Hill, December 16, 1824. [This, the first infant school in Australia, was opened through the efforts of Saxe Bannister, the Attorney-General, and Mr. Hill.]

The School of Industry established by Lady Darling, March 9, 1826.

An infant school established at Parramatta under the care of Mr. and Mrs. J. F. Staff, December, 1827.

The King's School, Parramatta, was opened, January 16, 1832.

Normal Institution, founded 1835.

Australian School Society began operations in the colony, under the guardianship of Rev. Mr. Mansfield, 1836.

St. James's Grammar School, founded 1839.

The Governor in Council proposed a plan of public instruction for the Colony, and inserted a sum of £3,000 on the Estimates for carrying the same into effect, 1839. [A Public School was to be built in Sydney, and two others in two of the principal towns in the interior. The "Irish National System of Education" was proposed, and was shortly afterwards established in the Colony.]

Denominational School system in the Colony established, 1840.

The National School system adopted in New South Wales, there being 26,000 children in the Colony, 1844.

Denominational School Board appointed, under which all that related to religious teaching was entrusted to the resident clergyman of the Denomination to which each school belonged. There were 27 schools and 2,596 scholars. 1848.

The Model National School, now called the Fort-street School, near Fort Phillip, Sydney, founded, 1849.

The National School Board, under Lord Stanley's system of Education, constituted, 1851.

Sydney Grammar School re-opened, August 3, 1834.

BOYS' SCHOOL, SYDNEY
The Picture of Sydney and Strangers' Guide in New South Wales, 1838

Schools in New South Wales:—
Church of England ..... 104 ⎫
Presbyterian .... 18 ⎬ 15,013 scholars.
Wesleyan .... 11 ⎪
Roman Catholic .... 69 ⎭   1857.
Church of England Grammar School, Melbourne, opened,
    April, 1858.
Church of England Grammar School, Geelong, opened
    June, 1858.
Ipswich Grammar School opened, September 25, 1863.
Foundation stone of the Brisbane Grammar School
    laid by H.R.H. Prince Alfred, February 29, 1868.
Presbyterian Ladies' College, Melbourne, inaugurated ;
    head master, Professor Pearson, January 11, 1875.
Foundation stone of new Public School laid at Wagga
    Wagga, by Sir Alfred Stephen, C.J., October 2, 1871.
Grammar School for Girls opened at Brisbane, May 15,
    1875.

SCHOOLS IN AUSTRALASIA.—1878.

Colony.	Popula-tion.	No. of Schools.	Cost to State.
			£
New South Wales	662,212	1695	285,496
New Zealand	417,622	987	177,212
Queensland	203,084	346	87,074
South Australia	236,864	529	162,669
Tasmania	107,104	165	14,705
Victoria	860,787	2156	677,330
Western Australia	27,838	83	..

HIGH SCHOOLS. Many of these are called
colleges. The principal in New South Wales
are—the Sydney College (founded June 26, 1830)
formally opened by W. T. Cape, January 19,
1835 ; Sydney Grammar School since 1854 ;
the King's School, Parramatta (founded January
16, 1832); Moore College (C.E.), Liverpool ;
Wesley College, Newington. In Victoria the
principal are—the Melbourne Grammar School
(C.E.); St. Patrick's College (R.C.); Scotch
College (Presbyterian) ; Wesley College, and

Geelong Grammar School. In Queensland the
Ipswich Grammar School, the Brisbane Grammar
School, and the Toowoomba Grammar Schools
are the principal. In South Australia, St.
Peter's Collegiate School (C.E.), was established
in 1848 ; and Prince Alfred Wesleyan College
in 1867. In Tasmania the principal are Horton
College, High School, Hutchin's School, and
Church Grammar School. In New Zealand the
principal are the Auckland, Wellington, and
Otago High Schools.

SCHOOLS OF ART.

There are nearly 70 Schools of Art in New
South Wales, having property to the value of
£100,000, and a membership of over 6,000 .per-
sons, 1879.

SYDNEY MECHANICS' SCHOOL OF ARTS, founded
in 1833, was the first institution of the kind
in Australia. It was established by a band of
Scotch mechanics, assisted by Governor Bourke
and Revd. H. Carmichael, A.M. The first
secretary was Mr. Robert Band, and the first
treasurer Mr. Peter Gardner. Number of members on the roll in 1878 was 2365, and 350 students
attended the Classes. A motion for the founding
of a Technical or Working Men's College, proposed
by Mr. E. Dowling, was adopted at the annual
meeting, February 4, 1873, but its inauguration
did not take place until the new buildings, the
erection of which cost £8,000 (£2,000 of which
was given by Government), were completed,
1879. £1,000 is annually granted towards paying professors and lecturers for this part of the
institution. The principal branches of technical
education in which instruction is given are :—
Agriculture, architecture, chemistry, domestic
economy and cookery, engineering, geology,

LABORATORY AND LADIES' READING ROOM SCHOOL
OF ARTS, SYDNEY
Gibbs, Shallard, & Co.'s *Illustrated Guide to Sydney*, 1882

mineralogy, mining and metallurgy, navigation, physiology, and other applied sciences.

During the first 25 years of its existence the Rev. H. Carmichael, Dr. George Bennett, W. T. Cape, J. Rae, Dr. L. Leichhardt, Archibald Michie, Dr. Nicholson, Judge Therry, Arthur A'Beckett, Richard Windeyer, D. H. Deniehy, Dr. Woolley, Sir W. Denison, and a host of other able men occupied the platform of the School of Arts lecture hall.

The first apartments used for the School of Arts were in the Surveyor-General's Office on Church Hill, lent for that purpose by Major Mitchell, the president of the institution. 1833.

SCOTCH MARTYRS.

The so-called "Scotch Martyrs" were named Muir, Palmer, Skirving, Gerald, and Margarot; they were convicted in Edinburgh for "leasing-

THE SCOTTISH MARTYRS
A woodcut printed on linen, Mitchell Library

making " *i.e.* libelling the Government, August, 1793, and were sentenced to transportation to Botany Bay, January, 1794; they embarked Feb. 10, and arrived in Sydney, with the exception of Gerald (who arrived a few months afterwards), September, 1794; Mr. Gerald, a man of great ability, and of most amiable and refined manners, purchased a piece of land at Farm Cove, now part of the Sydney Botanic Gardens, one of the most beautiful spots in Australia; he cultivated this little plot of ground as a garden, and when he died was, in accordance with his expressed wish, buried there, in 1796. Mr. Skirving only survived Mr. Gerald three days. Mr. Margarot survived his period of exile, went home in 1810, gave important evidence on the state of the colony before a Select Committee of the House of Commons in 1812, and died in 1813.

SCULLING. [*See* also AQUATICS.]

E. C. Laycock beat M. Rush, champion course, Parramatta River, £200 aside, April 12, 1879.

SEAL, GREAT. ILLEGAL AFFIXING OF.

The escheated lands of John Tawell [*see* CRIMES] were restored to trustees for the benefit of his widow and children. George Cooper Turner, Civil Crown Solicitor, was appointed agent for the trustees of the lands, &c., in New South Wales; he sold the land in 1849 and absconded to San Francisco. The Governor of New South Wales, Sir William Denison, in opposition to the advice of his ministers (Hon. Charles Cowper being Premier), affixed the great seal of the colony to the grant of land to the trustees of Mrs. Tawell, January 21, 1861; Sir Charles Cowper and colleagues resigned on the same day, but at the request of Sir William recalled their resignation on the eve of the Governor's departure.

SEAL OF THE COLONY.

The war ship *Gorgon* arrived with the Seal of the Colony, Sept. 21, 1791. [On the obverse of this Seal are the King's Arms, and on the margins, the Royal titles; on the reverse a representation of convicts landing at Botany Bay, received by Industry, who, surrounded by her attributes, a bale of merchandise, a pickaxe and shovel, is releasing them from their fetters, and pointing to oxen ploughing, and a town rising on the summit of a hill, with a fort for its protection; the masts of a ship are seen in the bay; in the margin are the words "Sigillum Nov. Camb. Aust.," and for a motto " Sic fortis Etruria crevit ;" the Seal is of silver, and weighs 40 ounces."]

New Territorial Seal arrived in the Colony, November 14, 1817.

" SECOND FLEET."

[*See* NEW SOUTH WALES, SETTLEMENT OF.]

SEPARATION.

The Colony of New South Wales divided into three districts—the northern, comprising all the country in the vicinity of Moreton Bay; the middle, comprising New South Wales proper; and the southern, consisting of the newly-settled district of Port Phillip. 1840.

A meeting held in Sydney for two purposes— one to oppose the separation of Port Phillip into a separate colony, the other, to take measures to introduce uniformity into the system under which the public lands of the colony were appropriated, and a petition to the Queen was adopted for that purpose. 1841.

A counter-petition was adopted in support of the measure for separation of Port Phillip from New South Wales, by the inhabitants of Port Phillip, on the grounds that Port Phillip was discovered by a naval officer; that it had been twice abandoned after it had been colonised in connection with New South Wales; that it was the inhabitants of Van Diemen's land who formed a permanent settlement in that district; and that the discoveries of Hume and Hovell were followed by no particular result by New South Wales. 1841.

The subject of the separation of Port Phillip from New South Wales again mooted in that district, and at an anti-transportation meeting there, the petitioners hinted that if the land fund of Port Phillip were applied exclusively for the advantage of the district, there would be no lack of immigration, and, consequently, of labour. 1847.

A despatch received relative to the separation of Port Phillip from New South Wales with a view to its erection into a distinct colony; the despatch mentioned that New South Wales would be divided into two colonies, the northern part to retain its name, and the southern to be called Victoria. 1848.

Great rejoicings at Port Phillip in consequence of the intelligence of the separation of that district from New South Wales; the people of Melbourne suspended business for four days, during which time every demonstration of rejoicing, thanksgiving in churches, royal salutes, processions, illuminations, fireworks, and games, were indulged in. July 1, 1851.

First public meeting held in Brisbane in favour of separation, July 8, 1851.

Meeting held at Moreton Bay for the purpose of petitioning the Home Government for separation from New South Wales, 1853.

Despatch received from the Home Government announcing the intention of erecting Moreton Bay into a separate colony, September, 1857.

The London *Gazette* announced the separation of Moreton Bay and its erection into a separate colony under the name of Queensland, January 3, 1859.

SEPARATION AND FOUNDATION DAYS.

New South Wales foundation, Jan. 26, 1788.

New Zealand foundation, January 29, 1840.

South Australia foundation, Dec. 28, 1836.

Queensland separation from New South Wales, December 10, 1859.

Tasmania foundation, February 16, 1804.
Victoria separation from N.S.W., July 1, 1851.
Western Australia foundation, June 1, 1829.

SETTLEMENT. First settlement of Australind attempted, December 17, 1840.

SETTLERS. A term applied to those families who settled on the lands of the interior of Australia and New Zealand.

THE FIRST SETTLERS ON THE LAND IN AUSTRALIA. The following are the names of the first settlers on the land, the date of settlement, and the quantity of land granted to them in Australia. Many of their descendants are still in the neighbourhood of Parramatta :—

FREE SETTLERS. Phillip Schæffer, superintendent of convicts; date, 30th March, 1791; quantity of land granted, 140 acres; place, on the north side of the creek leading to Parramatta. Robert Webb and William Reid, marines; date, 30th March, 1791; quantity of of land, 60 acres each; place, on the north side of the creek leading to Parramatta.

On the 5th April, 1791, the following persons, sailors or marines, were granted 60 acres of land each at Norfolk Island, by the Governor of New South Wales. Many of the descendants of these original settlers also are still in the colony of New South Wales :—Robert Watson, John Drummond, James Proctor, Peter Hobbs, Owen Cavanough, James Painter, William Mitchell, William Hambly, Charles Heritage, Samuel King, William Mitchell, Thomas Bramwell, Thomas Bishop, John M'Carthy, Laurence Richards, John Munday, Thomas Chipp, William Strong, James M'Manis, Thomas O'Brien, Richard Knight, Abraham Hand, William Dempsey, Thomas Scully, John Barrisford, James Redmond, William Tunks, Thomas Halfpenny, William Standley, John Gowen, Thos. Dukes, James Williams, Daniel Stanfield, John Roberts, William Sims, John Foley, Patrick Connell, Thomas Spencer, and John Scott.

CONVICT SETTLERS. The first convict settler had 30 acres of land granted to him on the 30th March, 1791, on the south side of the creek leading to Parramatta, and opposite to Phillip Schæffer's. On the 18th July in the same year a number of other persons received grants of land from 20 to 60 acres each, at distances two miles to four miles west and north-east of Parramatta, and some had each 10 acres allotted them at Norfolk Island.

FIRST SETTLER IN PORT PHILLIP. In December, 1828, Mr. William Dutton visited Portland Bay in the schooner "Madeira Packet," on a sealing voyage. He was one of a boat's crew that landed at Blacknose Point, and remained in the neighbourhood until the middle of January, 1829. Again, in July, 1829, Mr. Dutton visited Portland Bay in the schooner "Henry," Captain M'Lean, on a sealing voyage. He was captain of a boat's crew which landed at Whaler's Point, or Single Corner (the present site of Portland),

where he remained sealing, and built a house and lived in it. The third time, in March, 1831, Mr. William Dutton again visited Portland Bay in the schooner "Henry," then commanded by Captain Griffiths. The vessel anchored off Blacknose Point. Mr. Dutton landed, and occupied for some months the house he built in 1829. He then left in the schooner "Elizabeth." And the fourth time, in November, 1832, Mr. William Dutton again visited Portland Bay, and resided there until March, 1833. He subsequently returned to Portland in command of the schooner "Henry," and established a whaling station. erected buildings, and grew vegetables for his own use.

SHEEP.
29 sheep arrived in Australia in the "First Fleet," January, 1788.
[See STOCK.]
Merino sheep imported into the Colony by Captain Kent, R.N., to the order of Mr. John Macarthur, from the Cape of Good Hope, to which place some of the pure breed had been sent by the Dutch, 1796.

SHEEP SHEARING
The Illustrated Sydney News, 1855

[Mr. Macarthur having quitted the military service, and become settler, purchased one ram and five ewes, and immediately began to cross fleeced sheep with the merino, and in ten years his stock, which originally consisted of 70 Bengal animals, was increased to 4,000, although the wethers were slaughtered for use as they became fit; the effect of the crossing was a decided improvement of the animals, the hairy coat of the progeny of the Cape and Bengal breeds being gradually converted into wool, whilst it appeared the influence of the climate on the fleece of sheep generally was decidedly favourable.]

At Parramatta fair £300 was offered for one ram of the Merino breed, or £500 for a pair descended from the pure Spanish Merinos originally introduced by Mr. Macarthur, 1822.

Richard Jones, Esq., M.C., brought with him to the Colony on his return from Europe a choice flock of 120 Saxon sheep, April 26, 1825.

Sheep first boiled down in Australia by Henry O'Brien, J.P., of Yass, January 9, 1843.

[Sheep otherwise not worth half-a-crown realized from 5s. to 8s. per head; tallow became one of the staple commodities of export.]

NOTE.—Frederick Ebsworth is said to have boiled down sheep for tallow in 1838, and found the speculation paid well.

SHIP, FIRST.

Keel of first ship (called the "Rosehill Packet") built in the colony laid, Dec. 30, 1788.

The "Rosehill Packet" launched, Sep., 1789.

SHIPPING.

The "Endeavour," Captain Cook, anchored in Botany Bay, April 28, 1770.

The "First Fleet," 11 sail, under command of Governor Phillip, arrived in Botany Bay, January 19, 1788.

The French ships "Astrolabe" and "Boussole" anchored in Botany Bay, January 24, 1788.

The store ship "Lady Juliana" from London arrived, June 3, 1790.

The first foreign trading vessel, the "Philadelphia," brigantine, Captain Patrickson, entered Port Jackson with a cargo from Philadelphia, which was soon disposed of at a high profit, November 1, 1792.

The colonial vessel "Francis," brought from England in frame, launched in Sydney, February 14, 1793.

The "Reliance," with Governor Captain John Hunter on board, arrived, September 7, 1795.

A vessel, the "Norfolk," belonging to Messrs. Campbell and Clarke of Calcutta, arrived from Bengal with a cargo of merchandise and live stock. One of the owners of the vessel, Mr. Robert Campbell, was a passenger. October 1, 1798.

The "Albion," Captain Bunker, 3 months 15 days from England, being the fastest passage on record, to date, arrived June, 1799.

Lieutenant-Governor King and family arrived from England in the "Speedy," April 16, 1800.

Governor Hunter embarked for England in the "Buffalo," September 27, 1800.

118 ships had arrived in the harbour of Port Jackson, from January 25, 1788, to June 7, 1800. [Of these vessels 37 were transports from the British Isles carrying 6,000 prisoners. Up to September 12, other vessels had sailed from England and Ireland with prisoners, of whom there were on board 1924.]

The colonial vessel "Nancy" launched from the Green Hills, September 17, 1803.

The "Integrity" launched in Sydney, January 13, 1804.

The first colonial ship, named the "King George," built by Mr. James Underwood, and launched, April 19, 1805.

Governor Bligh arrived in the "Lady Madeline Sinclair," August 15, 1806.

Departure of Governor King for England in the "Buffalo," August 13, 1806.

The "Perseverance," colonial brig, launched Jan. 24, 1807.

The "Perseverance" sailed for India, February 9, 1807.

The "Mercury," colonial schooner, launched, February 26, 1807.

The "Governor Bligh," colonial schooner, launched at the Hawkesbury, April 1, 1807.

H.M. Frigate "Cornwallis" arrived from India under command of Captain Johnson, April 12, 1807.

The "Cornwallis" sailed from Sydney, April 23, 1807.

A fine teak-built ship, named the "Elizabeth," which had been brought from India in frame, was launched from the yard of Messrs. Campbell and Co., Nov. 7, 1812.

The following resolutions were passed at a public meeting in Sydney, Sir John Jamieson in the chair:—"That the restrictions which prevent merchants from employing ships of less than three hundred and fifty tons burthen in the trade from the mother country to this colony, operate so as to amount almost to a prohibition; as few mercantile adventurers here are willing or able to employ the large capital necessarily required for the cargoes of vessels of this magnitude; and we are consequently left ill supplied with many articles of British manufactories, which habit has rendered necessary to our comfort. But it is therefore expedient that an application should be made, by petition, to His Majesty's Government, through His Excellency Governor Macquarie, praying that navigation between Great Britain and the colony may be opened (as to British manufacturers and colonial producers) through the medium of vessels of one hundred and fifty tons burthen, and upwards," January 19, 1819.

The schooner "Prince Regent," which had been built by the Government as a present to the King of the Sandwich Islands, from His Highness the Prince Regent of England, was launched in Sydney, April 7, 1819.

The ship "Almorah," with all her cargo of stores and 100,000 dollars on board, seized by Captain Mitchell of H.M.S. "Slaney" in February, and in defiance of the Colonial Government despatched her to Calcutta under charge of his first lieutenant,—Mr. Matthews. March 2, 1825.

The "Warspite," 74-gun ship, arrived in the colony, under the command of Sir James Brisbane, on her passage to South America, October 19, 1826.

H.M.S. "Rainbow," Captain Rous, returned to Sydney from a voyage to the north coast of New South Wales, September 2, 1828.

The "Surprise" was the first steamer ever run in the colony, and was introduced by Mr. Henry G. Smith, a director of the Commercial Bank of Sydney in London. She was placed on the Parramatta River trade. [After an unsuccessful and short career, the "Surprise" was sent to Hobart Town]. March 31, 1831.

The first steamer arrived from England, "Sophia Jane," 256 tons burden, 50-horse power; was brought out to Sydney by Lieutenant Biddulph, of the Royal Navy, who was part owner. [She plied between Sydney and Newcastle.] May 16, 1831.

The colonial steam packet, "William IV," launched at the Williams River. She was built by J. H. Grose. October 22, 1831.

The ship "Hercules," Captain Daniels, left Sydney with a large number of passengers for England, March 13, 1836. [On the voyage she was struck by a tremendous sea which carried away the whole of her poop with the captain, first and second officers, and six passengers.]

The "James Watt," first steamer in Hobson's Bay from Sydney, July 4, 1837.

The first vessel cleared from South Australia for Great Britain. Her name was the "Goshawk," a brig of 245 tons. Her cargo consisted entirely of oil and whalebone. November 3, 1838.

The "Fairy Queen," first steam vessel built in the province of Port Phillip (to the order of Mr. Manton), launched at Melbourne, April 3, 1841.

Steam communication between Brisbane and Sydney established, January 26, 1842.

H.M. war steamer "Driver," 4 guns, arrived in Sydney from Hong Kong, being the first vessel of this character seen in the colonies. January 7, 1846.

The double-decked ship "Ticonderoga" from Liverpool, with 811 souls on board, after a voyage of 91 days entered Port Phillip Heads November 4, 1852. [She reported 96 deaths from typhus fever. Nearly every soul on board of her, including her crew, was sick. She anchored off the black buoy at Williamstown, but was sent back to the then newly-established quarantine ground at Port Nepean, and during the six weeks of her quarantine 82 more deaths occurred. The sick began to improve immediately they were landed and housed under the tents sent from Melbourne, and shelter rigged from the spars and sails of the ship. Great exertions were made by the Government to afford them relief. There were two surgeons on board the "Ticonderoga," one of whom lost his wife and all his children.]

The "Great Britain," steamship, first anchored in Port Jackson. She was the largest vessel then afloat, her burthen being 3,500 tons. November 20, 1852.

The "Spitfire," the first gunboat built in Sydney, New South Wales, launched, 1854.

Six English ships of war, carrying altogether 96 guns, exclusive of the ships in the Australian division of the station, two French frigates and a steamer, one Russian corvette and a steam sloop, were in the Southern seas. 1854.

A.S.N. COMPANY'S STEAMSHIP, THE "WONGA WONGA"
The Illustrated Sydney News, 1865

First steamer arrived at Otago, New Zealand, August 21, 1858.

The "Nelson," a line-of-battle ship now owned by the Colony of Victoria, anchored in Hobson's Bay, 1867. [She was built in 1806, immediately after the death of the naval hero whose name she bears; but she was never at sea until her voyage to Melbourne. She was presented to the colony by the Imperial Government].

The "Flying Squadron" arrived in Sydney, December 12, 1869.

The "Cerberus," monitor, Captain Panton, arrived in Hobson's Bay, after a most eventful passage, April 7, 1871.

Two Imperial gunboats launched in Sydney for suppression of the island slave trade, November 29, 1872.

The first iron vessel ever built in Melbourne, Victoria, launched from the yards of Foreman and Co., December 5, 1874. [She was a steam yacht of 50 tons, 60-horse power, length 72 feet.]

Commodore Hoskins assumed command of the Australian Station, hoisting his pennant on board H.M.S. "Pearl," December 16, 1875.

The steamer "Arawata" made the passage from Hokitika to Melbourne in four days nine hours, the quickest yet recorded, December 30, 1875.

The screw-steamer "Lusitania" of the Orient line arrived at Adelaide from England *via* the Cape of Good Hope, in 40 days 6½ hours, inclusive of 1 day 7 hours detention at St. Vincent, August 8, 1877.

The "Aconcagua," Orient steamer, made the passage from Plymouth to Adelaide in 39 days 20 hours steaming, July 2, 1878.

Quickest passage from England to Australia *via* Brindisi, made by P. & O. steamer: 36 days 23 hours to Melbourne, 1878.

SHOPS.

The first shop opened in Sydney by the Captain of the "Justinian," June 1790.

First brick shop in Sydney opened, July 1790.

The first shop at Parramatta opened, February 26, 1791.

SHOOTING THROUGH MISTAKEN IDENTITY.

Father Healey, Roman Catholic priest, shot at Deepwater, Murrumbidgee River, New South Wales, by Sergeant Foley and Trooper Townshend, in mistake for a bushranger, August 6, 1876. [*See* HEALEY.]

SHORTHORNS, SALE OF.

Robertson Brothers sale of shorthorns realised £25,742 17s. Twelfth Duke of Derrimut purchased for 2450 guineas on account of Mr. J. R. Lomax, Wirrah Station, New South Wales, Jan. 4, 1878. [*See* STOCK.]

SILK.

The growth of silk began to attract attention, 1848.

The experiment which had been made to grow silk on an extensive scale in the Colony proved a failure in consequence of the want of the proper species of mulberry tree, 1849.

[Mr. Charles Brady and Mrs. Bladen Neil are the most active promoters of sericulture in Australia, and have done much to advance it in the colonies. 1868 to 1879.]

SILVER.

Ore discovered at Moruya, New South Wales, June 9, 1862. [*See* MINERALS.]

SMALL-POX.

A contagious disease, having every appearance of the small-pox, was prevalent amongst the natives of Port Jackson; hundreds died. April and May, 1789.

Small-pox made its appearance in Sydney, July 25, 1825.

SERICULTURE IN AUSTRALIA
The Australasian Sketcher, 1874

The ship "Bussorah Merchant," Captain Baigrie, from London, with 170 convicts, arrived in Sydney with the small-pox on board ; placed in quarantine in Neutral Bay and the "Alligator" appointed as hospital ship, July 26, 1878.

Small-pox made its appearance in Sydney. Four of the children of a man named Holden died there, December 15th, 1876.

Small-pox found to have been introduced into Sydney by the Torres Straits mail steamer "Brisbane." Several cases reported in the Naval Squadron, January 19, 1877.

Ship "Macduff" arrived in Port Phillip Heads from London with seven cases of small-pox on board, August 10, 1877.

Three cases of small-pox broke out on board the R.M.S.S. "Siam" which arrived at Williamstown, Victoria, May 20, 1878. The "Siam" was placed in quarantine at Point Nepean, May 30, 1878. [*See* EPIDEMICS.]

SMUGGLING. A seizure of contraband spirits was made at Broken Bay, New South Wales, by Mr. H. H. Brown, Superintendent of the Water Police, October 19, 1842. The seizure consisted of 4,000 gallons of brandy and rum, which had been run ashore from the "Fair Barbarian." The owners (a mercantile firm), besides forfeiting the spirits, valued at £3,000, were fined in penalties jointly amounting to £11,000 with costs £1,000, thus costing the proprietors £15,000. The information was given by a ticket-of-leave man residing on the banks of the Hawkesbury. [*See* GOVERNMENT ORDERS.]

SNAKES.

A black snake, 22 feet long, killed on the lower branch of the Hawkesbury by Mr. Fleming, a settler, January, 1826.

During the first year of Sir John Franklin's administration in Tasmania nearly 14,000 snakes were killed, and Lady Franklin paid nearly £700 for their destruction. 1838.

SNOW.

"On Tuesday morning, June 28, between the hours of eight and nine o'clock, there was a heavy fall of snow in Sydney, which lasted for half an hour, a thing unprecedented in the memory of the oldest inhabitants."—*Sydney Gazette*, June 30, 1836.

"Tuesday last, the 28th current, will be memorable in the annals of this good town as the day on which its inhabitants were favoured for the first time with snow. The fall was by no means considerable in Sydney, although we are told it was several inches deep towards Parramatta. It lay for an hour or two on the tops of houses, and in other similar situations, and the Sydney boys were seen for the first time in their lives making snow-balls. The day was very cold throughout. We never felt it so cold before in Sydney."—The *Colonist*, June 30, 1836.

"Snow.—Sydney was visited by this strange visitant again on Sunday morning, though in less abundance than on the Tuesday previous. There have been very severe frosts in the country, which cut up the grass and vegetables considerably."—The *Australian*, July 5, 1836.

Great fall of snow near Sydney, June 28, 1837.

A slight fall of snow, which melted as it touched the ground, the curreney lads and lasses appearing quite excited at it. Sept. 4, 1837.

SNOWSTORM. Heavy snowstorm within 30 miles of Sydney, August 10, 1872.

SOCIETIES.

The Benevolent Society first established in the Colony of New South Wales, June 4, 1818.

A Philosophical Society first formed in Sydney. The proceedings were initiated by placing a brass plate on a rock at Botany, in commemoration of the landing of Captain Cook. March 19, 1822.

The Royal Society of New South Wales originated in 1822 as the " Philosophical Society of Australia;" after an interval of inactivity it was resuscitated in 1850, under the name of the " Australian Philosophical Society," by which title it was known until 1856, when the name was changed to the "Philosophical Society of New South Wales ;" and finally, by the sanction of Her Most Gracious Majesty the Queen, it assumed its present title in May, 1866.

Sydney Bethel Union founded, Aug. 5, 1822.

The Agricultural Society of Sydney founded, 1822.

The first show of the Floral and Horticultural Society, Sydney, held September 19, 1838.

The Royal Society of Tasmania established, 1843. [*Patroness:* Her Majesty the Queen ; *President:* His Excellency the Governor ; *Vice-Presidents:* Ven. Archdeacon Davies, Hon. Sir Robert Officer, Hon. J. S. Agnew, M.D., M.L.C., Right. Rev. Bishop Bromby, D.D.; *Hon. Sec.:* Hon. J. W. Agnew, M.D., M.L.C.

The Pastoral Society of Australia Felix formed at a great squatting demonstration in Melbourne, October 1, 1844.

First recorded meeting in Sydney to establish the Australian Mutual Provident Society. Present : Messrs. T. S. Mort, Thomas Holt, W. Perry, C. Lowe, and Rev. W. H. Walsh (chairman). August 31, 1848.

The Melbourne Philharmonic Society established in 1853. [John Russell was first conductor, Mr. Patterson hon. secretary. The first concert was given in the Mechanics' Institute under the patronage of Governor La Trobe.]

Acclimatisation Society founded in Melbourne. Dr. Black first president. 1857.

Entomological (now Linnean) Society of New South Wales established, April 7, 1862.

Inauguration of the Royal Society, Victoria, May 7, 1863.

Microscopical Society of Victoria formed, 1873.

The Victorian Humane Society's first boat launched at Prince's Bridge, Melbourne, May 20, 1876.

Foundation stone of new office of Australian Mutual Provident Society, New South Wales, laid at Sydney by Professor James Smith, August 23, 1877.

Zoological Society of New South Wales formed, March 24, 1879.

There were in Victoria on December 31, 1877, 35 societies with 765 branches and 47,352 members.

THE SITE OF ADELAIDE
William Light, Dixson Galleries, Sydney

SOUTH AUSTRALIA.

First ship for South Australia left England, February 23, 1836.

The brig " Rapid " with Colonel Light and a surveying staff for the new Colony of South Australia, left England May 1, 1836.

First immigrants arrived in Adelaide, July 3, 1836.

Colonel Light arrived in South Australia, August 30, 1836.

Sir George Kingston left Rapid Bay in the brig "Rapid" with the greater part of the survey staff and immigrants who came from England in the "Cygnet ;" landed in Holdfast Bay, November 5, 1836.

Mr. Kingston and party discovered a river, since named the Torrens, November 6, 1836.

Captain John Hindmarsh, R.N., arrived in the " Buffalo " as first Governor of South Australia, which was proclaimed a British Colony, December 28, 1836.

The site of the City of Adelaide finally decided on by Colonel Light, December 31, 1836.

First sale of Crown lands in Adelaide, March 27, 1837.

South Australian Register, first newspaper published in Adelaide, June 1, 1837.

Rev. T. Q. Stow, first Independent minister, arrived in Adelaide, October, 1837.

Rev. C. B. Howard, first Church of England clergyman in South Australia, arrived January 26, 1838.

Foundation stone of first Anglican Church laid in Adelaide, February 26, 1838.

First Wesleyan Chapel opened in Adelaide, the Rev. William Longbottom officiated, March 5, 1838.

First German Immigrants arrived, September 18, 1844.

Act passed in South Australia making ingot gold a legal tender at £3 11s. per oz.; for one year, January 28, 1852.

The Bullion Act of South Australia, empowering the Governor to establish an assay office, passed in one day, 1853.

Tobacco manufactory started at Adelaide by Mr. Dixon, of Sydney and Melbourne, December 15, 1876.

The population of South Australia was 163,452, or nearly double that of 10 years previously. The imports and exports amounted to 6 millions. There were 634 churches, 384 Sunday schools with 23,739 scholars, 279 other schools with 13,680 children in the rolls. The revenue for the year amounted to £1,089,189, and the expenditure to £790,504. 1865.

Sailors' Home opened at Adelaide, January 16, 1875.

SPANISH PRIZE. Arrival of two whalers with a prize—a Spanish ship—which they had captured off the coast of Peru. A Vice-Admiralty Court having declared the seizure legal, the ship and cargo were disposed of accordingly, at Port Jackson, in May, 1799.

SPELLING BEE. First in New South Wales held in Maitland, September 1, 1875.

THE FIRST SPELLING BEE IN MELBOURNE
The Australasian Sketcher, 1875

SPIRITS. The distillation of spirits first permitted under ordinary restrictions in New South Wales, 1820.

SQUATTER.

The term " Squatter " first applied to persons in the territory of New South Wales, who, without reasonable means of obtaining an honest livelihood, had formed stations in the interior, and then carried on predatory warfare against the flocks and herds in the vicinity, 1835.

The term " Squatter " is now used to describe one of the most useful and important classes of the community, principally the large pastoral tenants, who rent the land from the Crown for grazing purposes. The present signification was first applied in 1842.

THE SQUATTER'S FIRST HOME
A lithograph from *Scenes from the Bush,* 1846

SQUATTING.

New South Wales Squatting Act passed, March 22, 1827.

The Squatting Act (2 Vic. No. 27) passed the legislature of New South Wales, March 22, 1839.

A large squatting demonstration held in Melbourne. The lessees of the Crown lands came into Melbourne on horseback, and marched to the place of meeting with flags flying, preceded by a Highland piper playing martial airs. At this meeting petitions were adopted to be transmitted to the several branches of the Home and Colonial Legislatures, praying for alterations in the law of Crown lands and a total separation from the middle district (New South Wales). A new association was formed at this meeting, and designated the " Pastoral Society of Australia Felix." 1844.

Intelligence received in Sydney that an Act had passed the Imperial Parliament giving the squatters fourteen years' leases, 1846. [The change in their position as tenants gave general satisfaction to the pastoral community.]

STATISTICS.

Conference of Colonial Statists held, 1861. [The members were :—For New South Wales, C. Rolleston ; for South Australia, Mr. J.

Boothby; for Victoria, Mr. W. H. Archer; for Queensland, Mr. F. O. Darvall. The vital statistics of the Colonies have, by the labours of these gentlemen, been settled on a basis at once comprehensive and exact.]

STATUES.

The statue of Sir Richard Bourke unveiled at Sydney, April 11, 1842. [The event was marked by a general holiday and a public demonstration. A procession was led by the military, accompanied by the Commander of the Forces and his staff, the several Masonic lodges and public societies, the Church of England and other Protestant and Roman Catholic clergymen, with the children of all the schools of that denomination, formed part of the procession. The assemblage was the largest that ever congregated in Sydney. The Governor, Sir George Gipps, addressed the assemblage on the occasion. This was the first statue unveiled in New South Wales (Westmacott, sculptor).]

The Wentworth Statue, unpacked under the supervision of Mr. Wentworth, at the University, and put up in the entrance hall, whence it was subsequently shifted to its present site in the great hall. There was no unveiling ceremony. The statue bears on the pedestal the name "William Charles Wentworth," and on the side "Pro Temerani Fᵛᵃ." 1861.

Statue erected in Hobart Town in memory of Sir John Franklin, 1863.

First bronze casting in Victoria, Burke and Wills statue (erected in Collins-street, Melbourne), by Mr. Charles Sumners, Sept. 16, 1864.

Unveiling, by Sir John Young, of the Prince Albert statue (Theed sculptor), in Hyde Park, Sydney, April 23, 1866.

Foundation stone of the pedestal for Captain Cook's statue, Hyde Park, Sydney, laid by H.R.H. Prince Alfred, Duke of Edinburgh, March 27, 1869.

The first statue of Captain Cook unveiled in Australia by Commodore Goodenough, October 27, 1874. [This statue is situated at Randwick, near Sydney, N.S.W., and was the gift of Captain Watson to the colony. The sculptor was Mr. Walter M'Gill, of Sydney.]

Bronze statue to the memory of Captain Cook, in Hyde Park, Sydney, executed by Woolner, of London, 13 feet 6 inches high, unveiled by his Excellency Sir Hercules Robinson, Governor of New South Wales, in the presence of a vast concourse of spectators, a general holiday being proclaimed for the occasion, February 25, 1879.

THE BOURKE STATUE
The Illustrated Sydney News, 1854

STEAM-ENGINE first erected in Sydney, imported by Mr. Dickson, in the "Earl Spencer," May 29, 1815.

STOCK.

In the colony mustered :—1 stallion, 3 mares, 3 colts, 2 bulls, 5 cows, 29 sheep, 19 goats, 74 pigs (49 hogs, 25 sows), 5 rabbits, 18 turkeys, 29 geese, 35 ducks, 142 fowls (87 of these chickens), May 1, 1788.

Horses 11, horned cattle 23, sheep 105, pigs 43, December 11, 1792.

The ship " Marquis Cornwallis," Captain M. Hogan, left Sydney for the Cape of Good Hope, under contract, to procure cattle for the Government. She returned to Port Jackson with 28 bulls and 158 cows. October 27, 1798.

Attempts made extensively to introduce horned cattle into the settlement, but were only partially successful, from the inexperience to import stock for such a distant market, and the animals not being able to endure the rigour of the voyage, and thus of 15 bulls and 119 cows purchased for the colony, shipped from England, Cape of Good Hope, and elsewhere, since 1788 to 1794, only 3 bulls, 28 cows, and 5 calves were landed in Sydney, December 31, 1794.

A report received that a herd of wild cattle was seen in the interior, September, 1795. [The Governor, Captain Hunter, with a party, after two days' travelling in the direction of S.S.W., fell in with a very fine lot of cattle, sixty in number, and a bull having been killed, on comparison it was found to be similar to those brought from the Cape by Governor Phillip, and were the produce of those cattle which had strayed away seven years before. They were left to propagate their species on the plains where they were discovered, and hence called the "Cowpastures." The young fellow who had brought the report, and who had previously been in disgrace, received an amnesty or free pardon.]

The following were the live stock in the colony :—84 horses, 327 head of horned cattle, 4,247 hogs, 2,457 sheep, and 2,276 goats, 1796.

Two vessels arrived from the Cape of Good Hope, bringing a considerable number of horses, horned cattle, and sheep, June and July. 1796.

There were 203 horses, 1,044 cattle, and 6,124 sheep in the colony, 1799.

438 horses, 3,264 head of cattle, 16,501 head of sheep, 2,900 goats, and 14,300 swine in the colony, 1805.

There was a superabundance of cattle and sheep, far beyond the demand in the colony, and no markets had been formed abroad for the surplus. Cattle, which formerly sold for £10 a head, were selling for as many shillings, to the ruin of the owners. The result of this surplus was, that a duty was placed on all beef and pork imported into the colony. Beef was shipped to England and elsewhere, and horses were exported, chiefly to India, which has since continued. 1830.

The "Cumberland disease" first made its appearance amongst the cattle in the county of Cumberland, N.S.W., July, 1851.

Sale of Walter Lamb's Greystanes herd of cattle, New South Wales, January 19, 1876.

"Roan Duchess," a pedigree heifer, realized 2,200 guineas (being the highest price ever obtained in the world for a heifer), at Messrs. Robertson, Brothers' annual sale at Colac, Victoria. Mr. S. W. Gardiner was the purchaser. January, 1876.

The tax on live stock imported into Victoria was carried in the Legislative Assembly of Victoria, by 38 votes to 22, October 4, 1877.

SALE DAY AT MELBOURNE SHEEP AND CATTLE YARDS
The Australasian Sketcher, 1873

STRIKES.

Temporary suspension of the publication of *The Australian*, in consequence of compositors' strike, November 30, 1829.

Compositors on strike, Sydney, November, 1829.

Strike of A. A. Company's men at the Bore, Newcastle, N.S.W., 1855.

Friendly Society of Operative Stonemasons of New South Wales (established in 1852), struck for the eight-hour system, instead of ten hours, February 13, 1856. [Some men were out for about a week. The point was gained at the loss of 2s. 6d. per day. Wages reduced from 15s. for ten hours to eight hours for 12s. 6d.]

Compositors' Strike, *Empire* Office, Sydney, 1856.

Strike of the Coal and Copper Company's men, 1858.

Aggregate meeting of the miners at St. John's Church, Newcastle, Mr. James Fletcher in the chair, February 23, 1861.

Miners' strike at the Coal and Copper Company on Joseph Holmes' account, March 8, 1861.

Great open-air meeting held at Randall's camp against the 20 per cent. reduction ; Mr. James Fletcher in the chair ; 650 miners present, August 21, 1861.

The manager of the Coal and Copper Company brought sailors to the works to fill small coal whilst the miners were on strike. The women all turned out and fought the sailors, who went back to Newcastle. October 5, 1861.

Strike took place in consequence of the miners receiving fourteen days' notice of 20 per cent. reduction from the coal proprietors, October 14, 1861.

Strike ended, October 16, 1861.

Meeting of delegates at Mr. John Smith's, Newcastle, when a motion was passed that the F pit men come out on strike with the men at the other pits, May 2, 1862.

Miners' open-air meeting at Waratah, Thomas Alnwick in the chair. John Macintosh one of the speakers on the occasion. May 24, 1862.

Waratah Coal Mine strike, 1870.

Strike of cabmen, Sydney, January 2, 1874.

A strike at copper mines, S. A. A party of women went through Moonta mines with sticks and knocked off all hands. April 7, 1874.

Compositors' strike in printing offices in Sydney, September, 1875.

The operative stonemasons of Sydney struck for a rise of 1s. per day in the wages of competent masons, August 19, 1877. [The men remained out a week, when they gained their point. At this time more than half the employers of Sydney were giving the advanced rate.]

The Anvil Creek miners locked out, February 27, 1878.

The A.S.N. Company's seamen struck in Sydney against the employment of Chinese on the Company's boats, November 18, 1878. Strike ended January 1, 1879.

Strike of the carpenters employed at the International Exhibition Building in the Domain, Sydney, demanding two shillings a day above the current rate of wages, on the ground that the work in the tower of the building was dangerous, April 22, 1879. Strike ended by the men returning to work, April 26, 1879.

STRZLECKI, COUNT PAUL E., started to explore the Snowy mountains and Gippsland, February 6, 1840.

STUART, MOUNT. Central Mount Stuart is about two miles from the centre of Australia, and was reached by Stuart, April 22, 1860.

SUDDS AND THOMPSON, CASE OF. Sudds and Thompson were two private soldiers in the 57th Regiment, doing duty in New South Wales in 1825, the second year of Sir Ralph Darling's reign. Thompson was a well-behaved man, who had saved some money; Sudds was a loose character. They both wished to remain in the colony. In New South Wales these two soldiers saw men who had arrived as convicts settled on snug farms, established in good shops, or become even wealthy merchants and stockowners. As to procure their discharge was out of the question, Sudds, the scamp, suggested to Thompson that they should qualify themselves for the good fortune of convicts, and procure their discharge by becoming felons. Accordingly, they went together to the shop of a Sydney tradesman, and openly stole a piece of cloth—were, as they intended, caught, tried, convicted, and sentenced to be transported to one of the auxiliary penal settlements for seven years. In the course of the trial the object of the crime was clearly elicited. It became evident that the discipline of the troops required

THE DEATH OF PRIVATE SUDDS, 1826
Mitchell Library

to keep guard over the large convict population would be seriously endangered if the commission of a crime enabled a soldier to obtain the superior food, condition, and prospects enjoyed by a criminal. Accordingly, Sir Ralph Darling issued an order under which the two soldiers, who had been tried and convicted, were taken from the hands of the civil power, and condemned to work in chains on the roads of the colony for the full term of their sentence, after which they were to return to service in the ranks. On an appointed day the garrison of Sydney were assembled and formed in a hollow square. The culprits were brought out, their uniforms stripped off and replaced by the convict dress; iron-spiked collars and heavy chains, made expressly for the purpose by order of the Governor, were riveted to their necks and legs [these instruments of torture are now in the Colonial Secretary's office, Sydney], and then they were drummed out of the Regiment, and marched back to gaol to the tune of "The Rogue's March." Sudds, who was in bad health at the time (from an affection of the liver), overcome with shame, grief, and disappointment—oppressed by his chains, and exhausted by the heat of the sun on the day of the exposure in the barrack-square—died in a few days. Thompson became insane. A great outcry was raised in the colony: the opposition paper attacked, the official paper defended, the action of the Governor. The colony became divided into two parties. Until the end of his administration, Sir Ralph Darling, whose whole system was a compound of military despotism and bureaucracy, was pertinaciously worried for this action towards Sudds and Thompson by a section which included some of the best and some of the worst men in the colony. 1825.

SUGAR, MANUFACTURE OF.

Sugar first manufactured from cane grown in the colony at Port Macquarie, under the superintendence of Mr. Scott; 600 acres were planted with cane, and it was stated that the sugar and rum produced repaid the Government for their outlay. 1824.

First ton of Queensland sugar made at Captain Hope's works, September 9, 1864.

First parcel of Queensland sugar sold at Ipswich, February 8, 1866.

Sixty-three sugar mills manufactured 150,744 cwt. sugar, beside 78,823 gallons and 1,667 tons molasses. The two sugar refineries turned out 259,650 cwt. of sugar ; 150,737 gallons of rum were distilled from molasses in New South Wales. 1878.

12,243½ tons of sugar manufactured in 73 mills in Queensland for year ending March 31, 1878.

SUICIDE, ATTEMPTED. A female convict, detected stealing a flat-iron, hung herself up to the ridge pole of her tent, but was cut down alive, shortly after the formation of the settlement at Sydney, N.S.W., April 6, 1788.

SUICIDES.

The first suicide in New South Wales was that of a man who hung himself in gaol, 1803.

The Spanish Consul in Sydney committed suicide by throwing himself from a window, May 28, 1869.

Mr. John De Haga, opera singer, committed suicide by shooting himself at Williamstown, near Melbourne, October 12, 1872.

SUICIDES IN AUSTRALASIA for year ending December 31, 1877 :—

	Population.	No.
New South Wales	662,212	66
New Zealand	417,622	38*
Queensland	203,084	†
South Australia	236,864	17
Tasmania	107,104	9
Victoria	860,787	92
Western Australia	27,838	†

  * There were in addition to this number inquests held on 22 persons found dead, 42 drowned, and 4 hanged.
  † Not given in the statistics of the Colony.

SURVEY. Geological survey of Victoria commenced, April, 1853.

SURVEYING SQUADRON. The "Porpoise," "Cato," and "Bridgewater," comprising the Surveying Squadron, sailed for England, August 10, 1803.

SURVEYOR-GENERALS, N.S.W., EARLY.

Augustus Alt, Surveyor-General of New South Wales, from April 13, 1801.

Charles Grimes, Surveyor-General of New South Wales, from March 5, 1804.

John Oxley, Surveyor-General of New South Wales, from January 1, 1812, to May, 1828.

Sir Thomas Mitchell, May 1828 to Oct. 5, 1855.

SWIMMING. Professor Cavill swam eighteen miles on the Yarra (Victoria) in 5 hours 58 minutes, March 1, 1879. First public performance at Sydney, May 17, 1879.

SWINDLERS, NOTORIOUS.

John Dow, alias *Lutterell* alias *Edward Lord Viscount Lascelles* was tried and convicted of forgery, and transported for life, May 5, 1833. [In his assumed title this impostor travelled through New South Wales several months as Her Majesty's Commissioner to make inquiry into the state of the prison population.]

John Thomas Wilson absconded from the colony in the brig "Venus," which vessel he had bought some time previously. He had shipped on board of her a full cargo, purchased from a great number of the Sydney merchants and tradesmen. His debts amounted to upwards of £30,000. He left the Commercial Wharf by the "Sophia Jane" steamer, proposing only to go down the harbour a little way, giving a porter his horse to hold until he returned ; he, however, proceeded to sea, and boarded the brig outside the Heads. October 19, 1839. [The great bulk of the property he left behind was claimed by Mr. A. Polack, but the conveyance being proved faulty, he agreed to pay all the creditors 75 per cent. off their respective claims.]

Francisco Miranda. This extraordinary individual, who victimized the Joint Stock Bank, Sydney, to a large amount, appears to have proceeded on a most methodical plan. In June, 1857, he stayed at the "Charing Cross Hotel," London, where his business-like habits and punctuality of payment obtained for him a favourable opinion from all who had any dealings with him. During the time he was there his correspondence was very voluminous, and the porter who posted some of his letters stated that he wrote to distinguished people in all parts of the world. Letters were received by the Joint Stock Bank in Sydney from Messrs. Baring Brothers, the wealthy bankers of London, mentioning that Mr. Miranda was likely to call in Sydney, on his tour, and asking the Bank to assist him in his transactions to the best of their power, at the same time enclosing letters of credit in his favour to the amount of £15,000, and bills on a house in Hongkong amounting to £5,000. On October 12, 1857, Don Antonio Anom de Ayala, Spanish Consul at Sydney, was called on by Miranda, who (in the absence of a Portuguese Consul) presented to him his passport, duly signed, sealed, and vizéd at several places, and asked him to introduce him to the bank manager, a request at once complied with. Francisco Miranda, having determined upon purchasing an estate in the colonies, decided upon one near Melbourne, and having instructed the bank to cash his bills drawn on Hongkong, he obtained a letter of credit from them upon the Bank of Australia, Melbourne, and left for that place ; where he drew the whole of the amount (upwards of £19,000) out of the bank in gold, and on January 30, 1858, sent his trunks to the Castlemaine coach-office ; but he arriving too late, his trunks were not sent on, and he applied at the office for permission to leave them there till next day. Of course this was granted, and the next day he called for them, and from that day Francisco

Miranda was amongst the missing. The Spanish Consul, who had formed a high opinion of him, was under the impression that he had been murdered for the sake of the large amount of gold he had in his possession; but the Melbourne police found out that a French gentleman, named Monsieur Le Prairie, had sailed for Callao in the "Good Intent" some few hours after Miranda had removed his boxes from the coach-office, and from the description of the gentleman there was no doubt that he and Francisco Miranda were one and the same person. Letters from England were soon afterwards received by the bank, stating that both the letters of credit and bills of exchange were forgeries. His swindling transactions were on the most magnificent scale, in Australia and Cape Colony, some of the most influential mercantile firms having been the victims of the impostor. The account of his doings, if read in a novel, would be deemed gross exaggeration, but it was far exceeded by the actual facts.

Charles Woodman Eastwood, accountant in the Railway Department, New South Wales, absconded. His embezzlements of Government money commenced in 1863, and continued until January, 1867. He used to falsify the daily bank vouchers. His total defalcations amounted to £6,652. 1867.

Count Von Attems. In December, 1867, a gentlemanly-looking young man, calling himself Count Von Attems, arrived at Morley's hotel, Trafalgar-square, London, where he remained until January 11, 1868, when he sailed in the ship "Northampton" for Sydney. Whilst at Morley's he engaged a valet (named Auguste Stelzer) to accompany him abroad; and the first day they were at sea, he told Auguste not to dare to talk English to any one on board, or he would shoot him. The "Northampton" arrived in Sydney April 19, 1868, when the Count took up his quarters at the "Royal Hotel," Sydney, remaining here for about a month, his bill during that time amounting to £200. He then removed to a house in Richmond-terrace, next door to that occupied by the Prussian Consul, and resided there until the beginning of June. Representing himself to be connected with the Royal family of Austria, by means of forged credentials he imposed upon the merchants and inhabitants of Sydney, fleecing the former to a large extent. He was followed about and made much of by a few tuft-hunters, who considered it laudable to be on familiar terms with a scion of royalty "travelling incognita on a special mission." He even borrowed twenty-seven pounds from his valet, the savings of the unfortunate young man in his previous situation. But everybody seemed ready to assist him with their cash, equipages, and houses; and for many months the "Count Von Attems" was a conspicuous figure in the public and private society of Sydney. Von Attems purchased the yacht "Hamlet's Ghost" in Sydney, and sailed in it for Melbourne, promising his creditors that he would speedily return. He left his valet Auguste

behind him, having victimized him to the amount of one hundred and seven pounds for wages and cash borrowed. In Queensland he continued a similar career, his swindles amounting to many thousands of pounds, and then sailed for Batavia, where the "Countship" exploded, and he was captured and sentenced to twenty-two years' imprisonment with hard labour. Three several times has he made most desperate efforts to escape, and in one instance was very nearly successful, having assumed the role of a Captain Stone of the U. S. Army, and provided himself with forged documents to prove his identity, and also letters of credit and bills of exchange. 1868.

Some extensive forgeries and frauds were discovered in the Real Property Office, Brisbane. S. L. Petersen confessed a guilty knowledge of them, and absconded. Petersen was arrested on October 13. It was proved that £900 of the funds of the South Brisbane Mechanics' Institute had been misappropriated. October 7, 1878.

SWORD MATCH, CHAMPION. Match between the champion swordsmen of New South Wales and Victoria, Winterbottom and Parker, for £50 aside, at the Lyceum Theatre, Sydney. The former was declared victor. July, 1861.

SYDNEY, NEW SOUTH WALES.

SYDNEY, the capital of New South Wales, situated on the shores of Port Jackson (named in honour of Thomas Townshend Viscount Sydney), has a population (1879) of 200,000 inhabitants. It possesses many fine shops, warehouses, government buildings, cathedrals, and educational establishments, and private residences. Amongst the many charming reserves for the recreation of the people are Hyde Park, area 40 acres; the Domain, 138 acres; Prince Alfred Park, 18 acres; Belmore Park, 10 acres; Moore Park, 600 acres, ; and more particularly the Botanic Gardens, area 38 acres.

An emu ran through Sydney and was shot. It stood 7 feet four inches high. March, 1788.

On the first celebration of the King's birthday in New South Wales the name of Sydney was proposed as Albion. June 4, 1878.

Rushcutters' Bay. So named because in early days, as indeed now, rushes were most plentiful there, and several persons obtained a living by cutting them to make beds for horses. Two persons were murdered who went to cut rushes there. 1788.

The Governor laid down the lines of a regular town, the principal street extending one mile in a westerly direction from the landing place called Sydney Cove, July, 1790.

Sydney tanks commenced to be hewn out, November, 1791. [These tanks supplied Sydney with water for many years.]

Fort Macquarie Battery, Sydney harbour, completed, October 24, 1803.

First visit of New Zealanders to Sydney, N.S.W., November 23, 1805.

The town of Sydney divided into five districts, with police and watchhouses for each and streets named and organized by regulation. Names of streets in Sydney proclaimed, October 6, 1810 :—

George-street, in honour of the King.

Pitt-street, in honour of Pitt.

Castlereagh-street, in honour of Lord Castlereagh.

York-street, in honour of Duke of.

Clarence-street, in honour of Duke of.
Kent-street, in honour of Duke of.
Sussex-street, in honour of Duke of.
Phillip-street, in honour of Governor.
Macquarie-street, in honour of Governor.
Hunter-street, in honour of Governor.
Bligh-street, in honour of Governor.
King-street, in honour of Governor.
Goulburn-street, in honour of first Colonial Secretary.
Elizabeth-street, in honour of Mrs. Macquarie.

After the deposition of Governor Bligh, his successor, Colonel Paterson (who was not in any way connected with Bligh's deposition), acceded to Bligh's request to allow him to return to England in the "Porpoise" on certain conditions. These were that Bligh should embark with his family, put to sea, and go straight to England without touching at any part of the territory until he received the instructions of the British Government, and that while he remained he would not interfere in the government of the colony. History informs us: "Having solemnly pledged his honour as an officer and a gentleman to the unequivocal observance of the stipulations made by Lieutenant-Governor Paterson, Bligh no sooner put his foot on the deck of the 'Porpoise' than he threw his promises to the winds. Lieutenant Kent was the commander of H.M.S. 'Porpoise,' and Bligh instantly ordered him to batter down the town of Sydney, and to direct his guns against the merchant ship 'Admiral Gambier,' then ready for sea, and in which Major Johnston and Captain Macarthur had taken passage for England, so as to be present at the inquiry which they knew would take place as to their conduct in deposing the Governor. Lieutenant Kent, however, refused to obey these shameful orders, and was placed by Bligh under arrest, ostensibly for having taken the 'Porpoise' to Hobart Town to fetch Paterson to Sydney. Kent was in confinement for two years before his trial by court martial took place in England, when he was acquitted." 1808.

The public markets, Sydney, opened, October 20, 1810.

A bridge built in Bridge-street to connect the east and west portions of Sydney, 1811.

Boatmen first licensed to ply in the harbour, and carts and carriages for burthen ordered to be numbered, March, 1813.

Mrs. Macquarie's road round the inside of the Government Domain, measuring 3 miles 377 yards, completed June 13, 1813.

The first public wharf, known as the Queen's Wharf, completed at the commencement of 1813.

Hyde Park Barracks first occupied, June 4, 1819.

Foundation stone of Supreme Court laid in Sydney, June 4, 1819.

St. James' Church opened, January 5, 1822.

The Sydney Bethel Institution started by a "well-wisher to seamen," September 5, 1822.

Mrs. Fry's Newgate prison women arrived in Sydney in the "Morley," 1822.

The well-known Riley Estate, purchased by Mrs. Ann Riley for £2,290. It was 100 acres in extent. 1822.

Rev. Dr. Lang arrived, May 8, 1823.

The foundation stone of the first Presbyterian Church in the colony was laid on Church Hill by His Excellency Sir Thomas Brisbane, July 1, 1824.

Campbell's (first private) wharf erected in Sydney, 1824.

The name of Darling Harbour substituted for Cockle Bay, April, 1826.

A tunnel commenced to convey water from swamps, Botany to Sydney, under direction of Mr. James Busby, Mineral Surveyor. The work was known as Busby's tunnel. September, 1827.

Australian Free Library established, December 1, 1827.

Mr. Humphreys, Chief Police Magistrate, died, June, 1828.

The Court-house in King-street finished, August, 1828.

Cattle and other live stock market removed from George-street to the Haymarket, July 2, 1829.

Opening of the Royal Hotel Concert-room, George-street, by Mr. Levey, proprietor, August 20, 1829.

The foundation stone of the Sydney College laid by his Honor Chief Justice Forbes. This institution was established by a company, the capital being £10,000 in 200 shares. January 26, 1830.

The Government Domain first thrown open to the public, September 13, 1831.

Rev. George Innes, M.A., appointed Head Master of the King's School, to be opened in Sydney, January 2, 1832.

The Australian College (Dr. Lang's) opened in Sydney, 1832.

The Mechanics' School of Arts first formed in Sydney, March 22, 1833.

The Australian Steam Navigation Board first formed, April 12, 1833.

A public meeting held to adopt a petition to the Governor and Council against the appropriation of any portion of the revenue to the payment of the salaries and pensions granted for services not performed in the colony. This was caused in consequence of the pension of £750 being paid from the

SYDNEY COVE, VIEW TO THE SOUTH
An engraving from *The Gentleman's Magazine*, 1824

Colonial revenue, which had been granted to Mr. Macleay by the Imperial Parliament for services rendered in England; and also for a further sum of £550 per annum to be paid to Mr. Busby, appointed by the Home Government to look after the interests of the inhabitants of New Zealand, particularly as regarded the rights of the natives of that island, which the petitioners declared were in direct contravention of the laws, and were equally opposed to those principles of equity upon which the law was founded. The adoption of this petition was moved by Mr. Wentworth, and seconded by E. S. Hall. 1833.

It was publicly observed that the accumulation of mud was carried into the head at Sydney Cove by the Tank Stream, and that it was endangering the efficiency of the harbour, and rendering the atmosphere unwholesome. 1833.

The Port of Sydney declared a free port by order of the Lords Commissioners of the Admiralty; under this privilege vessels of foreign nations were allowed to land and warehouse cargoes for exportation. 1833.

Sydney Streets—

Victoria-street
Brougham-street
Judge-street }—Woolloomooloo.
Duke-street
Dowling-street
Forbes-street

The above six streets were so named by the late Sir James Dowling. He first opened them in consequence of their being on his own land. Victoria-street was so named after Queen Victoria, Brougham-street after Lord Brougham, Dowling-street after himself, and Forbes-street after Sir Francis Forbes. 1834.

Some land sold in Sydney at the rate of £10,000 per acre, 1834.

Mr. John Stephen elected President of the Patriotic Association, 1835.

The Proprietary Sydney College opened under the superintendence of Mr. W. T. Cape, 1835.

Sydney Gas Light Company established April 13, 1836.

Australian Museum established 1836.

Bishop Broughton arrived June 2, 1836.

Great fall of snow near Sydney, known as "Snowy Monday," June 28, 1837.

The aqueduct from Botany to Sydney, which was commenced in 1827, was completed in 1837. [The length of the tunnel was 12,000 feet, its average depth five, and its width four feet. The total cost of the aqueduct was £22,000. The work was done entirely by convict labour, which was estimated to be two-thirds less than free labour.]

Victoria Theatre opened March 17, 1838.

The Sydney Botanic Gardens thrown open to the public April 30, 1838.

The first show of the Floral and Horticultural Society took place September 19, 1838.

Foundation stone of Christ Church laid January 1, 1840.

Foundation stone of Trinity Church laid June 23, 1840.

Gas first used for lighting the shops, and the Company gave a brilliant illumination on Church Hill on the occasion, May 24, 1841.

Government House first occupied and especially fitted up for the celebration of Her Majesty's birthday, May 24, 1843.

Prisoners for debt first removed from Carter's Barracks to Darlinghurst gaol, December 31, 1843.

The owner of an unlicensed still in Sydney fined £500, 1843.

Great distress prevailed in Sydney amongst the working classes for want of employment. £1,000 was voted by the Council for the purpose of sending a portion of the unemployed into the interior. 1843.

First peal of bells heard in Australia ushered in the new year from the tower of St. Mary's (R.C. Cathedral), January 1, 1844.

The foundation stone of the first Bethel Chapel was laid, April 24, 1844.

Street robberies prevalent in Sydney—Mr. Noble murdered in his own bed by three ruffians, who were afterwards executed for the crime. 1844.

The first meeting of the subscribers to the Sydney Dis-

pensary, after its extension as an infirmary, when Drs. Macfarlane and Fullerton were elected the first physicians, and Messrs. Nathan and M'Crie the first surgeons of that institution. March 26, 1845.

A great scarcity of water experienced, when it was suggested that water should be conveyed from the Nepean River by means of an aqueduct, 1850.

Port Jackson became a free port by an Act abolishing harbour dues, entry and clearance fees, and lighthouse and water police dues, 1852.

Foundation stone of Sydney Exchange laid by Governor Fitzroy, 1853.

The works for the defence of the harbour commenced at Pinchgut (now Fort Denison), Lady Macquarie's chair, and other places in the harbour, 1853.

The American steamer "Golden Age" arrived in Sydney, January 6, 1854.

Banquet in honour of St. Patrick's Day, March 17, 1854.

Sydney Exchange, costing £25,000, opened by Sir Thomas Denison, December 30, 1857.

Public Soup Kitchen established in Sydney, June 12, 1867.

Foundation stone of Sydney Town Hall laid by H.R.H. Duke of Edinburgh, April 4, 1868.

A number of ladies and gentlemen visit the foundry of Messrs. P. N. Russell and Co., to witness the casting of a large bell for the new Post Office, August 12, 1871.

Foundation stone of Protestant Hall laid by Bishop Barker, November 9, 1875.

The foundation stone of the new Crown Lands Offices laid by Hon. T. Garrett, Minister for Lands, October 7, 1878.

The Botany main burst and caused a water famine in Sydney for two days, 1878.

Parliamentary dinner given to Alderman Macarthur, M.P., of London, November 29, 1878.

VIEW FROM WOOLLOOMOOLOO HEIGHTS
The Illustrated Sydney News, 1855

TAMAR, RIVER, Tasmania, discovered and named by Admiral d'Entrecasteaux and Captain Huon Kermondee, April 20, 1792; traced and named by Colonel Patterson, 1806. [The whole of the Tamar river, as far as its junction with the North and South Esk rivers, was formerly called Port Dalrymple.] [*See* PORT DALRYMPLE.]

TARIFF. A despatch from Lord Kimberley, objecting to the complex tariff between the Australian colonies, received July 13, 1871.

TASMAN, CAPTAIN ABEL JANSEN, a skilful Dutch navigator, sailed from Batavia on a voyage of discovery, August 14, 1642.

TASMANIA (*originally* VAN DIEMEN'S LAND, until 1854,) discovered by Tasman, November 24, 1642. [Tasmania is situated between the parallels of 40° 30′ and 43° 33′ south latitude, and 144° and 148° meridians of east longitude, and divided from Australia by Bass's Straits: length 170 miles, breadth 160 miles, area 15,751,500 acres, or with lakes and islands, 16,778,000 acres, or 26,215 square miles.]

Frederick Hemskirk Bay, so named, by its discoverer, Tasman, in honour of a stadtholder (chief ruler) of the Netherlands, December 1, 1642.

Marion Du Fresne, in the "Mascarion," arrived off the west coast of Van Diemen's Land, March 3, 1772.

Captain Fobias Furneaux, in H.B.M. "Adventure," made the West Cape, and anchored in D'Entrecasteaux Channel, March 9, 1773.

Captain Cook, with H.M.S. "Resolution" and "Discovery," made the S.W. cape of Australia, and, after steering eastward, anchored in Adventure Bay, January 24, 1777.

Captain Bligh, in the "Bounty," anchored in Adventure Bay, and, having landed, planted there a number of European fruit-trees, 1788.

Admiral Bruni D'Entrecasteaux, in the "Recherche," and Huon Kermondee, in the "Esperance," visited Tasmania and discovered D'Entrecasteaux Channel and the Rivière du Nord. 1792.

The Huon River, named after Huon Kermondee a Frenchman, who commanded the "Esperance," 1792.

Captain Tobias Furneaux, in H.M.S. "Adventure," visited Tasmania, and gave it as his opinion that no strait existed between the island and New Holland, but "a very deep bay." 1793.

"The Duke and Duchess of Clarence" ship anchored in Adventure Bay under the command of Commodore John Hayes, who named the Derwent (Riviére du

Nord of D'Entrecasteaux,) 1794.

Bass and Flinders discovered the entrance of the river Tamar, November 3, 1798.

Flinders and Bass explored Tasmanian coast, and named Port Dalrymple in honor of Alex. Dalrymple, of the Admiralty, November, 1798.

Bass and Flinders entered the Derwent River on December 7, proceeding as far as Sullivan's Cove, the present site of Hobart Town, having established the fact of the insularity of Van Diemen's Land. December 23, 1798.

Bass anchored his sloop, the "Norfolk," in Port Jackson, having established the fact of the insularity of Tasmania, and the Governor of New South Wales named the passage "Bass's Straits," January 12, 1799.

Bass left the Derwent, and returned to Sydney, January 3, 1799.

His Majesty the King of England's right to Van Diemen's Land established by proclamation, and the directions given to Lieutenant John Bowen, of H.M.S. "Glatton," to form an establishment on the island, he assuming the title of Commandant and Superintendent, March 29, 1803.

Lieutenant Bowen sailed in the "Lady Nugent" to form a settlement in Van Diemen's Land, June 23, 1803.

First settlement formed in Van Diemen's land by Lieutenant Bowen, Surgeon, Jacob Mountgarret, three soldiers, and ten male and 6 female prisoners, who settled on the left bank of the Derwent, at Restdown or Risdon Cove, having left Sydney in the schooner "Lady Nelson" on June 23. August 10, 1803.

Arrival (in the "Ocean") at Sullivan's Cove (Hobart Town), Derwent River, of first detachment of Port Phillip settlers (who had abandoned that place as unfit for habitation) to form new settlement in Tasmania under charge of Colonel Collins, as Lieutenant-Governor. The site chosen by the party was Sullivan's Cove, called Hobart Town, in honour of Lord Hobart, head of the Colonial office. January 30, 1804.

OFFICERS OF THE NEW SETTLEMENT.

Rev. R. Knopwood, Chaplain.
E. Bromley, Surgeon Superintendent.
W. Anson, Colonial Surgeon.
M. Boden   } Assistant Surgeons.
W. Hopley }
P. H. Humphrey, Mineralogist.
Lieutenant Fosbrook, Deputy Commissary-General.
G. P. Harris, Deputy Surveyor.
John Clark   } Superintendents of Convicts.
Wm. Paterson }
Lieutenants Sladen, Johnson, and Lord, with 44 marines, in charge of 367 convicts.

Arrival of the second vessel at Hobart Town, February 16, 1804.

Launceston named by Colonel Paterson, October, 1804.

Yorktown, the second establishment in Van Diemen's Land, settled by a small party of prisoners who were despatched from Sydney, October, 1804.

Fight between soldiers and natives; 40 of the latter shot. 1805.

Arrival of the settlers who had abandoned Norfolk Island. They called the place they settled on New Norfolk and Norfolk Plains. 1805.

The Tamar River traced and named by Colonel Paterson, 1806.

Convict establishment removed from Yorktown to a new settlement named Launceston, 1806.

First communication opened in nine days between Launceston and Hobart Town, by Lieutenant Laycock and party 1807.

First post office established in Hobart Town, April 25, 1809.

The site of George Town (now Launceston) marked out by Governor Macquarie, November, 1811.

Governor Macquarie and Mrs. Macquarie arrived from Sydney on a visit to Hobart Town. The Governor travelled overland from Hobart Town to Launceston, and marked out the site of George Town, Port Dalrymple. November 23, 1811.

Lieutenant-Colonel Geils, 73rd Regiment, Commandant of Tasmania, February 7, 1812.

The temporary church at Hobart Town blown down, 1812.

First Supreme Court held in Hobart Town, January 23, 1814.

Major Abbot, one of the officers of the old N.S.W. corps, sent from Sydney to Van Diemen's Land as judge advocate, 1814.

Macquarie Harbour, Tasmania, discovered, June 14, 1816.

Lieutenant-Governor's Courts, consisting of the deputy judge-advocate and two other persons, opened, 1816.

Hobart Town *Gazette* published by Andrew Bent, 1816.

Foundation stone first permanent church, St. David's, laid by Lieutenant-Governor Thomas Davey, at Hobart Town, February 19, 1817.

First sale of cattle held in Van Diemen's Land, October 3, 1817.

Government House, Hobart Town, finished, October 4, 1817.

First Sunday-school opened, May, 1818.

The first circuit court in the colony was held in Hobart Town, Mr. Justice Field presiding, December, 1818.

Rev. John Youl arrived, 1818.

In the third year of Sorell's administration £20,000 was obtained for wheat, and £1,000 for salt meat exported to Sydney. At the end of 1871 there were 170,000 sheep, 550 horses, 35,000 head of cattle, and 5,000 swine in the colony. 1820-21.

The "Emerald," first emigrant vessel, arrived from England at Hobart Town, March 18, 1821.

Governor Macquarie visited Tasmania for the second time, April 24, 1821. He left Tasmania June 29, 1821.

Promissory notes issued *ad. lib.* in Tasmania, July 12, 1821.

Rev. Archibald Macarthur, first Presbyterian clergyman, preached first sermon at Hobart Town, January 12, 1823.

St. David's Church (named St. David's in honour of first Governor), Hobart Town, consecrated by Rev. S. Marsden, 1823.

Chief Justice J. L. Pedder arrived in Hobart Town with a charter, 1824.

An agitation for the separation of Tasmania from New South Wales, 1824.

Names of the first Executive Council :—Colonial Secretary, Dudley Montague Perceval; the Chief Justice, John Lewis Pedder, Adolanis ; W. H. Humphrey and Jocelyn Thomas. The members of the Legislative body : William Henry Hamilton Humphrey and Edward Curr. December 3, 1825.

Tasmania proclaimed independent of New South Wales, December 3, 1825.

A separate Government established. Governor Darling called at the island and formally proclaimed its independency. The Lieutenant-Governor of Van Diemen's Land being subordinate to the Governor of New South Wales, who retained the title of Governor in Chief : in all other respects the separation was complete. An Executive and Legislative Council were called into existence, January 9, 1826.

A settlement formed at Circular Head, under Mr. Edward Curr, for the "Van Diemen's Land Company." The Company received a grant of about 25,000 acres on the north-east coast of Tasmania from the Government of George IV. 1826.

Crown Lands leased January 5, 1828.

Proclamation issued proclaiming martial law against aboriginal natives, November 1, 1828.

The King's Orphan School, Newtown, near Hobart Town, formed under the management of Mr. R. W. Giblin, 1828.

Mr. Thomas Kent discovered the virtues of Mimosa bark extract, and received as a reward 10,000 acres of the richest land he could find in Tasmania, 1829.

"Cyprus," Government vessel, seized by convicts and taken to the South Seas, August 9, 1829.

Extraordinary attempt made by Governor Arthur of Tasmania, to catch and pen up in Tasman's peninsula the aboriginal population of the island. Upward of 3500 (including 300 soldiers) white persons turned out for the exciting operation of clearing Tasmania by means of a cordon across the island. The attempt proved a total failure ; only two natives were captured, and the total cost of the expedition amounted to £35,000. 1830.

The first conveyance between Hobart Town and Launceston started, June 19, 1832.

Tasmania appointed place of transportation for natives of New South Wales, and persons arriving in the colony free, after being convicted of a first offence, 1832.

First Independent Church opened by Rev. F. Miller, 1832.

HOBART TOWN
The Australasian Sketcher, 1879

LAUNCESTON FROM CATARACT BRIDGE
Picturesque Atlas of Australia

First Temperance Society established by Messrs. Backhouse and Walker, 1832.

Rev. Robert Knopwood, M.A., first Clergyman in Tasmania, died, November 8, 1836.

The last of the Tasmania aboriginals (300) transferred from the main land to Flinders Island, by the instrumentality of Mr. George Augustus Robinson, 1837.

CONVICT POPULATION.

1824	5,938	1832	12,706
1825	6,845	1833	14,990
1826	6,762	1834	15,538
1827	7,260	1835	16,968
1828	7,449	1836	17,661
1829	8,484	1837	17,593
1830	10,195	1838	18,133
1831	12,018		

Tasmania formed into a separate bishopric, August 27, 1842.

Dr. Nixon installed as first Bishop of Tasmania, June 27, 1843.

Christ's College, Van Diemen's Land, commenced October 10, 1846.

Heavy fall of snow at Hobart Town, November 22, 1849.

Cricket Match between Melbourne and Tasmania, won by the latter, February 22, 1851.

First election of Tasmanian Legislative Council, October 24, 1851.

Transportation ceased, February 10, 1853.

John Mitchel escaped, July 20, 1853.

Name of Van Diemen's Land altered to Tasmania on address of Legislative Council, 1854.

Gas first used in Hobart Town, March 12, 1857.

Tasmanian building stone used in building the Melbourne Post office, 1862.

Duke of Edinburgh visited Tasmania, December, 1869.

Public cemetery, Hobart Town, opened July 22, 1872.

Hobart Town waterworks opened February 23, 1876.

TASMANIAN PRISONS, EARLY.

Brickfield.	Marie Island.
Bridgewater.	Picton.
Brown's River, Oyster Cove.	Port Arthur.
Macquarie Harbour.	South Port.

TAXATION.

TABLE SHOWING THE TAXATION IN THE AUSTRALASIAN COLONIES.

Colony.	Proportion of Revenue of 1877, raised by Taxation.	Rate of Taxation per head of Population.
	£	£ s. d.
New South Wales	1,235,021	1 18 2¾
New Zealand	1,343,944	3 5 9¾
Queensland	609,860	3 2 6¼
South Australia	499,885	2 3 2½
Tasmania	236,777	2 4 6½
Victoria	1,770,685	2 2 2¼
Western Australia	81,268	2 18 11
Total	5,777,440	2 7 0¾

TELEGRAPHIC.

A proposal for the establishment of electric telegraph between Sydney and Melbourne started, 1845.

Telegraph first used in New South Wales, December 5, 1851.

Electric telegraph construction commenced in Victoria, November, 1853.

The first electric telegraph put in operation in Victoria was between Melbourne and Williamstown, March 3, 1854.

[It was opened in the presence of Lieutenant-Governor Latrobe, members of the Legislative Council, and others, at the telegraph office, William-street. Mr. McGowan was appointed Superintendent of Telegraphs.]

The first telegraph in South Australia was from Adelaide to Port Adelaide; distance about 9½ miles. Opened February 18, 1856.

The first line of telegraph between Melbourne and Adelaide opened, July 19, 1856.

Telegraphic communication established in Tasmania, August 2, 1857.

Telegraphic communication between Sydney and Liverpool, New South Wales, completed, December 30, 1857.

First telegraphic message, Sydney to Liverpool, in N.S.W., sent by Mr. E. C. Cracknell, January 26, 1858.

Telegraphic communication between Melbourne and Adelaide established, July 19, 1858.

Telegraphic communication established between Sydney, Melbourne, and Adelaide, October 29, 1858.

Telegraph to Kapunda, South Australia, opened, May 11, 1859.

First telegram between Tasmania and Victoria, September 30, 1859, but proved a failure.

Cable laid from Cape Otway to King's Island, and thence to Tasmania, 1859; proved a failure. 1860.

First New Zealand telegraph office opened, July 1, 1862.

Telegraph line opened from Brisbane to Rockhampton, Queensland, April 6, 1864.

Telegraph line opened to Townsville, March 15, 1869.

The new Electric cable from Tasmania to Victoria laid, April 27, 1869.

DANGERS OF LINE REPAIRING IN NORTH QUEENSLAND
Sydney Punch, 1870

First message through Bass' Straits cable, May 1, 1869.

Telegraphic communication established between Perth and Freemantle, West Australia, June 21, 1869.

Overland telegraph commenced in the Northern Territory, South Australia, September 15, 1870.

The shore end of the cable between Port Darwin and Banjoewangie laid at the former place, November 7, 1871.

The first telegram came through stating that communication with Java was complete, November 20, 1871.

Telegraph line between Normanton, Gulf of Carpentaria, and Brisbane opened, January 3, 1872.

Telegraph line to Normanton officially opened, June 4, 1872.

First cable message from England received in Melbourne, July 2, 1872.

Cable communication with England by the construction of the South Australian telegraph line to Port Darwin, October 22, 1872. [The contract for the construction of the overland line was let in three divisions. From Port Augusta in lat. $31\frac{1}{2}°$ S. to lat. 27°, the line is 512 miles in length, and Mr. E. M. Bagot was the contractor for this portion of the work, and he erected the first pole on October 1, 1870; the next portion, from lat. 27° to lat. 19·30, is 612 miles in length, and it was undertaken by the Government; and the third portion, extending from lat. 19·30 to its completion, 629 in length, was entrusted to Messrs. Darwent and Dalwood, who planted the first pole on September 15, 1870. The total length of the wire from Port Darwin to Adelaide is 1,976 miles. After encountering extraordinary difficulties, the work was completed through the ability and energy of Mr. Todd, Superintendent of Telegraphs, South Australia. The Overland Telegraph, which cost £370,000, was placed in connection with the cable laid by the British Australian Company, between Singapore via Java to Port Darwin, October 22, 1872.]

First through telegram received in Adelaide, S.A., by the overland wire, October 22, 1872.

[Intercolonial Conference held in Sydney, September, 1874. The Governments of New South Wales, Victoria, South Australia, Queensland, New Zealand, Tasmania, and Western Australia were represented. Various questions were considered but no agreement arrived at in reference to cable duplication, which was the principal subject for decision. The delegates were New South Wales, John Robertson, Alexander Stuart, and J. F. Burns; Victoria, J. S. Anderson and Robert Ramsay; Western Australia, A. Frazer; Queensland, S. W. Griffith and C. S. Mein; New Zealand, George Maclean.]

Cable from Sydney to New Zealand, shore end laid at La Perouse, Botany, N.S.W., Feb. 5, 1876.

Cable communication between Australia and New Zealand established, February 20, 1876.

Telegraph opened Sydney to Manly Beach, July 1, 1876.

Telegraphic communication between Adelaide and Eucla opened, July 13, 1877.

Completion of the overland telegraph to Eucla; 2,046 miles of line available between Adelaide, South Australia, and Perth, Western Australia, December 1, 1877.

5,163 miles opened, and 1,031 miles authorized and in progress in December, 1877.

Intercolonial Cable Conference commenced its sittings at Melbourne, May 9, 1878.

The London *Times* published first intelligence of the New Caledonia massacre simultaneously with the Sydney *Evening News*, through the agency of S. W. Silver and Co., July 12, 1878.

The Cable Conference adopted its report, May 18, 1878. [The principal resolution authorized New South Wales and Victoria to enter into an agreement for a second cable from Rangoon from Singapore direct to Banjoewangie, and thence to Port Darwin, avoiding the Java land line, for an annual subsidy not exceeding £32,400, payable for 20 years. Government messages to be issued to Port Darwin at a reduction of 50 per cent., and Press messages at a reduction of 75 per cent. The delegates consisted of Graham Berry for Victoria, J. F. Burns for New South Wales, J. P. Boucaut and Charles Todd for South Australia, and C. S. Mein for Queensland. The arrangements were made with Colonel Glover, of Eastern Telegraph Company, who was examined by the Conference.

The Hon. J. F. Burns paid a visit to New Zealand in relation to the second cable, and succeeded in inducing the Government of that colony to join in the contract, June, 1878.

The route and length of cable and land lines are as follows between London and Adelaide :

London to Land's End (overland)	320
Land's End to Gibraltar via Lisbon (cable)	1,250
Gibraltar to Malta (cable)	981
Malta to Alexandria (cable)	819
Alexandria to Suez (overland wire)	224
Suez to Aden (cable)	1,308
Aden to Bombay (cable)	1,664
Bombay to Madras (overland wire)	600
Madras to Penang (cable)	1,213
Penang to Singapore (cable)	381
Singapore to Batavia (cable)	560
Batavia to Banjoewangie (overland wire)	480
Banjoewangie to Port Darwin (cable)	970
Port Darwin to Port Augusta, South Australia (overland wire)	1,800
Port Augusta to Adelaide	196
Total length of cable	9,146
Total length of overland wire	3,424
Total	12,570

From Port Augusta the overland wire stretches to Sydney, N.S.W., a distance of 650 miles. The connection here takes place with New Zealand, the submarine cable commencing at Botany Bay, and terminating at Wakapuaka, a distance of 1,150 miles. From Wakapuaka the overland wire is carried to White's Bay (88 miles), thence by cable to Wellington (41 miles), from which centre all the towns and cities of New Zealand are communicated with.

OVERLAND TELEGRAPH LINE—STATIONS AND DISTANCES.

From Adelaide to Beltana	.. ..	..	355 miles
,,	,, Strangway's Springs	..	545 ,,
,,	,, Peake ..	..	636 ,,
,,	,, Charlotte Waters ..	..	804 ,,
,,	,, Alice Springs ..	..	1036 ,,
,,	,, Barrow's Creek ..	..	1207 ,,
,,	,, Tennant's Creek ..	..	1354 ,,
,,	,, Powell's Creek ..	..	1467 ,,
,,	,, Daly Waters ..	..	1605 ,,
,,	,, Katherine ..	..	1765 ,,
,,	,, Pine Creek	..	1822 ,,
,,	,, Shackle [7 miles from Yam Creek]	..	1852 ,,
,,	,, South Port ..	..	1932 ,,
,,	,, Port Darwin	..	1973 ,,

LENGTHS OPENED IN AUSTRALASIA.

Number of miles of Telegraph Lines opened December 31, 1877 :—

New South Wales ..	..	..	..	6,000
New Zealand	..	..	..	3,307
Queensland..	..	..	..	5,033
South Australia ..	..	..	..	4,061
Tasmania ..	...	..	..	621
Victoria ..	..	..	..	2,885
Western Australia..	..	..	..	1,567
Total		..		23,474

TEMPERANCE.

Grand festival given by Mr. George Allen, Mayor of Sydney, at the Victoria Theatre; it was attended by 1,000 members of the Total Abstinence Societies, and as many more of all classes of the community. 1845.

N.S.W. Alliance instituted, Feb. 26, 1857. Number of pledged members to date, 14,600.

Foundation stone of Temperance Hall laid by Miss Denison, July 15, 1858.

Sons of Temperance formed in N.S.W., May 31, 1864; accumulated funds, £25,280.

New Temperance Hall opened in Sydney, August 12, 1872.

It is calculated that there are 60,000 temperance members in Australia. 1879.

TEMPERATURE.

MEAN TEMPERATURE OF SOIL AND DEW-POINT AT MELBOURNE.

Seasons.	Mean Temperature of—					
	Surface Soil.	Bulb at Depth of—				Dew Point.
		14 inches	3 feet	6 feet	8 feet	
	°	°	°	°	°	°
Spring ..	62·0	53·9	57·3	57·3	56·6	46·4
Summer	76·5	65·2	67·6	66·3	65·7	52·2
Autumn	61·9	58·2	63·5	65·0	64·5	49·1
Winter ..	49·2	46·6	51·5	55·0	56·6	42·6
Year ..	62·4	56·0	60·0	60·9	60·4	47·6

The mean temperature of the soil in Melbourne, as derived from observations taken during a number of years by means of a thermometer on the surface slightly covered with earth, but fully exposed to the action of the sun and wind; also the mean temperature of the bulb at various depths, and the mean temperature of the dew-point, are given as follow for the four seasons and for the entire year.

TEMPLARS. The Independent Order of Good Templars established a lodge at Queensland, February 19, 1873, and in N.S.W., March, 1873.

THAKOMBAU (CACOBAU).

Ex-King of Fiji, arrived in Sydney, N.S.W., with his sons Ratu Timothy and Ratu Joseph Celau, November 29, 1874.

Thakombau left Sydney for Fiji, Dec. 21, 1874.

THANKSGIVING.

Public thanksgiving for the break-up of the drought, which was protracted and destructive, November 12, 1829.

Thanksgiving day in N.S.W. proclaimed for recovery of Prince of Wales, February 27, 1872.

THEATRES.

The debtor's room in the Sydney Gaol used as a theatre, 1826.

Victoria Theatre foundation stone laid with masonic honors, Sep. 7, 1836; opened March 26, 1838. [Mr. Arabin as Othello, and Mr. Spencer, Iago.]

Signor Dalle Case opened a temporary theatre in Hunter-street, Sydney—designated it the "Olympic." January 26, 1842.

City Theatre, Market-street, Sydney, opened by Messrs. Simmons and Belmore, May 20, 1843.

Queen's Theatre, Queen's-street, Melbourne, opened with the play of the Honeymoon, May 1, 1845.

Princess's Theatre, Melbourne, opened, 1854.

Olympic Theatre, Melbourne, opened, 1855.

Old Theatre Royal, Melbourne, opened, 1855.

Prince Bartolo-meo (first Fijian entertainment) appeared at Victoria Theatre, May 30, 1857.

Prince of Wales Theatre, Melbourne, opened, 1858.

Professor Bushell (first electro-biologist) appeared at Victoria Theatre, August 15, 1859.

Prince of Wales Theatre, Sydney, destroyed by fire, October 3, 1860.

Haymarket Theatre, Melbourne, opened, 1863, burnt, September, 1871.

Prince of Wales Opera House, Sydney, burnt, January 6, 1872.

New Theatre Royal, Bourke-street, Melbourne, burnt, March 20, re-opened, November 9, 1872.

Opera House, Melbourne, opened, 1872.

New Theatre Royal opened at Wellington, N.Z., February 13, 1873.

Theatre Royal (built on the site of the old Prince of Wales Theatre), Castlereagh-street, Sydney, opened December 11, 1875.

Academy of Music, Melbourne, opened, 1876.

Theatre Royal, Adelaide, opened April, 1878. [*See* DRAMA ; *also* MUSIC.]

THEATRICAL STARS.

Gustavus Vaughan Brooke born at Hardwick Place, Dublin, April, 25, 1818; was intended for the bar, but abandoned it for the stage, on which he made his first appearance, at the age of fifteen, during Easter week of 1833, performing the part of William Tell at the Theatre Royal, Dublin. After the usual dramatic educational career in the British provinces, he performed in London, at first principally at the Surrey and Sadler's Wells theatres, provoking much adverse criticism from the press, combined with sound advice, which he judiciously followed, at the same time devoting his attention to a close study of a large round of characters, till his style became so improved and matured as to stamp him as one of the leading actors of the day. He arrived in Melbourne in 1855, whither his reputation had preceded him, and played several engagements there as well as in Sydney, and the leading cities of Australia. He was considered to be the greatest Shakesperian actor of his day ; and in certain characters, as well as in Irish comedy, was without a rival. He was drowned when returning to pay another visit to Australia in the "London," in the Bay of Biscay, Jan. 10, 1866. Mr. Brooke was married to the no less celebrated actress Avonia Jones.

John Gordon Griffiths was born in Shropshire, England, in August, 1810, and shortly after leaving school joined a dramatic company. He became a member of the celebrated McKay's company, and was next with Mr. Alexander, of Glasgow. It was with these managers that he obtained that intimate knowledge of lowland manners and language which made him so successful in Scottish dialect parts. After leaving Scotland he played in London, where he met Mr. Joseph Wyatt, of the Victoria Theatre, Sydney, who induced him to come to Australia. He arrived in Sydney early in 1842, and opened in the character of Hamlet. He met with a most determined opposition, which almost drove him from the stage, but he secured the favour of his enemies by an extraordinary study and performance of Coriolanus. The management of the Victoria Theatre was entrusted to him, and in 1855 he became manager of the Prince of Wales Theatre. He retired after a short time, and took up his residence at the "Pier Hotel," Manly Beach, where he died, March 4, 1857. His representation of the characters of Iago and Falstaff are by many considered to have been unequalled in Australia.

Francis Nesbitt McCron, better known as Francis Nesbitt, was born in Manchester, England, in 1809. He was educated by a clergyman, near Cork, Ireland, and selected the profession of surgeon. Becoming weary of hospital experiences, he determined upon the stage as the scene of his future labours. After travelling through England, and filling a leading engagement with Mr. Alexander, of Glasgow, his friends persuaded him to leave the stage, and he returned to Ireland in 1840. At the end of that year he eloped with a young lady, the daughter of an old and respectable family, and married her. He arrived in Port Jackson, January 7, 1841, bringing letters of introduction to Governor Gipps and others. Unable to obtain employment in commercial houses, he applied to the manager of the Victoria Theatre, who refused an engagement ; he then joined the police, but never went on duty, for as soon as the circumstance became known to his friends they induced the manager of the Victoria Theatre to allow him to appear. His first character was Pizarro. From that time until his death he held undisputed sway. He left Sydney in 1843, and took a tour round the colonies, and in 1848 he sailed for San Francisco, where, after a successful season, he went to the gold diggings. He returned to Sydney in 1852, and after performing a short time went to Victoria, and whilst acting in Geelong in William Tell, was carried from the stage in an almost insensible condition, and conveyed to the hospital, where he died, in 1853, aged 44 years. He was buried in the cemetery at Geelong, where Mr. G. V. Brooke, in 1856, placed a monument over his grave.

Charles Horace Frisbee Young was born in the City of Doncaster, April 5, 1819. His parents followed the profession of the drama, and it was with them he studied until he made his first bow to a London audience in the character of Little Pickle in the Spoiled Child, and Young Norval, in the tragedy of Douglass, and subsequently in the character of Noah Claypole, in Oliver Twist. He spent four or five years at sea, on the coast of England, in the navy and mercantile marine. In 1843 he arrived in Australia as second officer of a ship, and meeting there his sister, Mrs. G. H. Rogers, wife of G. H. Rogers, comedian, this decided his future career, and he determined to remain and follow the fortunes of the drama. His first appearance was made at Hobart Town, at the Victoria Theatre, in the character of Michael, in William Tell. He became lessee of the Queen's

A MESMERIC FEAT
The Illustrated Sydney News, 1855

Theatre, Melbourne, in 1851, having for a partner Mr. J. P. Hydes. In 1857 he returned to England and performed at the Strand, Sadler's Wells, the Royal Lyceum, and finally at St. James' Theatre. He left England, May 28, 1861, and arrived in Melbourne, August 18, 1861, appearing at the Theatre Royal as Squire Wannop, in A Friend in Need. He performed also at the Prince of Wales Theatre, in Sydney, and was leading comedian when that theatre was destroyed by fire. He died at his residence, William-street, Sydney, January 29, 1874. As a "low comedian," he was one of the finest representatives that ever appeared on the stage, his Beppo and like characters being unrivalled.

TICHBORNE, SIR ROGER CHARLES DOUGHTY, alias ORTON.

As the history of this extraordinary character presents so many features of interest to the people of Australia, where he resided for many years of his life, the following narrative, from his own AFFIDAVIT, will be considered as useful for reference :—

"I resided with my parents at Paris from the date of my birth until the year 1845, when I was brought over to this country, and was shortly afterwards placed at Stoneyhurst College, Lancashire, where I received my English education.

"In the month of July, 1849, I was appointed cornet, and subsequently lieutenant, in Her Majesty's 6th Dragoon Guards (Carabineers). I joined that regiment in the month of October, 1849, at Dublin, where it was then quartered, and remained on duty with the regiment from the month of October, 1849 until the month of January, 1853 (except during temporary leave of absence). I retired from the regiment in the month of February, 1853.

"During my vacations from college, and while on leave of absence from my regiment, I usually resided, from the year 1845 until I left this country to travel in foreign parts, as hereinafter mentioned, with my uncle, the said Sir Edward Doughty, at Tichborne Park, the family seat of the Tichbornes; and I was in the habit of shooting over the Tichborne estates and hunting in that neighbourhood, and I gave up much of my time to field sports and the management of horses.

"I left my regiment with the object of travelling for some years in distant parts, and in the first instance I determined to proceed to South America. In the month of March, 1853, I took passage on board a ship bound for Valparaiso, where I arrived in due course, and from that time until the month of April, 1854, I travelled from place to place in various parts of South America.

"In the month of April, 1854, the ship 'Bella,' of Liverpool, Captain Birkett, master, was at the port of Rio de Janeiro, and learning that she was bound, and shortly intended to leave that port, for New York, I took my passage by the 'Bella' for that city. The 'Bella' left the port of Rio on the morning of the 20th day of April, 1854, with myself on board, and proceeded on her voyage. To the best of my recollection and belief, when she left Rio the crew of the 'Bella' (including the captain) consisted of about seventeen persons, I being the only passenger on board.

"All went well until the fourth day after the 'Bella' had left Rio, and was far out of sight of land, but on the morning of that day the mate reported to the captain that she had sprung a leak, and all hands were instantly set to work at the pumps, and every effort was made to save the ship, but without effect. Very shortly after the mate had reported the leak, it became apparent that the vessel was fast filling with water, and the captain announced that all further efforts to save the ship were useless, and that all on board must instantly take to the boats.

"The 'Bella' carried a longboat on deck, and two smaller boats, one of which was slung from the davits on each quarter. One of the small boats was stove in and rendered useless, but the crew succeeded in safely lowering upon the sea the long-boat and the other boat, which was the larger of the two small ones, hereinafter referred to as the 'second boat'; and, stowing some provisions and casks of water into the boats, I, and to the best of my recollection and belief, eight of the crew, got into the second boat, and the captain, and to the best of my recollection and belief, the rest of the crew, got into the longboat, and immediately pushed off from the 'Bella,' and the ship 'Bella' soon afterwards sank.

"The captain, who had in the longboat the ship's charts, ordered that the second boat should keep in sight of the longboat, which she did for two days, but in the night of the second day a high wind and storm came on, and the boats were soon out of sight of each other, and the longboat was not again seen by those in the second boat. The man who had the command of the second boat then determined to let her drift with the wind. On the morning of the fourth day, after the 'Bella' had sank, the crew of the second boat descried a ship in the distance, and used every means to reach her and to attract notice, and for that purpose a red flannel shirt, which one of the crew of the boat wore, was attached to an oar and hoisted as a signal. Ultimately a signal was made in reply, and the crew of that boat rowed to the ship, and I and the whole of the crew on board the second boat were thus saved after we had been three days and nights at sea in an open boat.

"I was in a very exhausted state when I was rescued, and I was for some time seriously ill on board the ship that saved me, but I was landed at the port of Melbourne, in Australia, about the end of July, 1854.

"I had saved nothing from the 'Bella,' except the clothes I wore, and when I landed at Melbourne I had no means whatever there for my support.

THE TICHBORNE CLAIMANT
Picturesque Atlas of Australia

" On the first day I landed the captain of the ship which brought me to Melbourne took me to an office, which I believe was the Custom-house, and had a conversation with some person there as to what should be done for me ; but nothing was arranged except that I should be allowed to sleep on board the ship that night, which I accordingly did. Before returning to the ship the captain and I together called at an office and made inquiries for the purpose of ascertaining how I could get a passage to England, but without any useful result. I learnt that Melbourne was then in a very unsettled state, in consequence of the gold mania ; that the crews of ships, as they arrived, very frequently deserted for the gold diggings ; and that there was, consequently, great difficulty in procuring a passage to England. There were a great number of ships then in the port unable to start for want of hands.

" On the day after I first landed at Melbourne I was strolling about the town, and went into a yard called Row's yard, situate in Bourke-street, Melbourne, where a large number of horses were being sold. I was much attracted by what was taking place, and a person, whom I afterwards discovered to be Mr. William Foster, an extensive stockkeeper, of Gippsland, spoke to me, and, after ascertaining that I was a good rider, offered to take me with him to Gippsland, where there was good hunting and shooting.

" I accepted such offer, and for family reasons I assumed the name of Thomas Castro (after that of a friend named Don Thomas Castro, whose acquaintance I had made at Mellipilla, in Chili), and I continued to use, and was known in Australia by, the name of Thomas Castro, until shortly prior to my return to England, as hereinafter mentioned.

" I immediately afterwards left Melbourne with Mr. Foster and his horses, and proceeded to Mr. Foster's station, at Boisdale, in Gippsland, on the Avon River, nearly 300 miles from Melbourne, where I remained about 19 months. Mr. Foster then gave me charge of the Dargo station, in the Australian Alps, about 115 miles further inland, where I remained for about 18 months, and then returned to Boisdale, when, after staying for about three months, I travelled about and remained at various places, as in the 38th paragraph of my said bill mentioned.

" On the 29th day of January, 1865, I intermarried with Mary Ann Bryant. spinster. I and my wife are both Roman Catholics, but, being then desirous of concealing my real name, which I could not have done if the marriage had been solemnized by a priest of the Church of Rome, inasmuch as I must, prior to my marriage, have attended the confessional, my said marriage was solemnized by the Rev. Frederick Thomas Brentnall, a minister of the Wesleyan Church, at the residence of Mrs. Robinson, of Wagga Wagga, I being then married under my assumed name of Thomas Castro.

" I and my wife thenceforth continued to be residents of Wagga Wagga, passing under the assumed name of Castro, until shortly prior to my return to England, as hereinafter mentioned.

" I have been informed by my mother, and believe, that after the death of my father, and in the year 1863, she caused advertisements for me in the English, French, and Spanish languages, to be inserted in the *Times* newspaper, and that she sometime subsequently communicated with Mr. Arthur Cubitt, of the Missing Friends Office, Bridge-street, Sydney, New South Wales, advertising agent, and that the said Mr. Cubitt, by her direction, caused advertisements to be inserted in various newspapers published at Melbourne, Sydney, and elsewhere, announcing the death of my father, and giving a description of me, and offering a reward for my discovery.

" Ultimately, and towards the end of the year 1865, I, for the first time, learnt, by means of such advertisements, of my father's death, and in the early part of January, 1866, I wrote and sent a letter to my mother, informing her that I had at last made up my mind to face the sea once more, and requesting that money might be sent out to enable me to return to England. I had been informed by my mother, and believe, that she received such letter in course of post, and that she wrote and sent to me a letter urging my immediate return, and I have been informed by my mother, and believe, that she subsequently remitted a draft for £400, to defray the expenses of the voyage.

"As soon as practicable, in the year 1866, I made arrangements to return home with my wife and child, without awaiting the receipt of the draft. I believe that such draft reached Australia after I had left for England, and I have been informed by my mother, and believe, that the said draft has since been returned to her through the post.

"Having determined to return to England, I, on the 9th day of July, 1866, again went through the ceremony of marriage with my wife under my proper name, at the Roman Catholic Church of St. Peter and St. Paul, at Goulburn, New South Wales, according to the rites of the Church of Rome, the ceremony on that occasion being solemnized by the Rev. Michael M'Alroy, a priest of that church. There has been issue of my said marriage, two children, and no more—namely, Teresa Mary Agnes, the before-mentioned child, who was born at Wagga Wagga aforesaid, on the 18th day of March, 1866, and the above-named defendant, Roger Joseph Doughty Tichborne, who was borne at Croydon, as aforesaid, on the 1st day of May, 1867.

"While remaining at Sydney, previous to my embarkation, I accidentally met there a person named Guilfoyle, who was for many years in the employ of my uncle, the said Sir Edward Doughty (deceased). When I was at Sydney, Guilfoyle was, and I believe that he is now, carrying on business as a nurseryman. Guilfoyle and his wife, who also saw me at Sydney, well knew me before I left Sydney in the year 1853, and upon seeing me at Sydney they recognized me as the eldest son of the said Sir James Francis Doughty Tichborne.

"I also met at Sydney Andrew Bogle, who also had for many years been in the employ of my uncle, the said Sir Edward Doughty, as valet, and to whom I was well known before I left England in the year 1853. The said Andrew Bogle, upon meeting me at Sydney, also recognized me as the eldest son of the said Sir James Francis Doughty Tichborne, and the said Andrew Bogle, at his own request, accompanied me to England.

"I have been informed by the said Andrew Bogle, and believe, that he, the said Andrew Bogle, acting in the full belief that my relatives would be glad to hear that I was alive and had been recognized by one who knew me well, shortly before his embarkation sent to my aunt, Dame Katherine Doughty, a letter informing her of the fact, and that I and himself were about to embark for England. I believe that such letter was received by the said Dame Katherine Doughty in course of post, and in or about the month of October, 1866, and that the said Dame Katherine Doughty at once communicated the contents of such letter to the abovenamed defendants Teresa Mary Josephine Doughty Tichborne, William Stourton, and Renfric Arundell.

"In the month of September, 1866, I, my wife, and child, embarked at the port of Sydney on board the 'Rakaia,' bound for Panama, and, having arrived there, proceeded across the Isthmus to Aspinwall, and from thence by way of New York, to England, and arrived on the 25th day of December, 1866, at the Victoria Docks, Limehouse, on board the steamship 'Cella.'

"Shortly afterwards, and in the same month of December, I visited Alresford, near to Tichborne, and found that Tichborne house was occupied by Colonel Lushington. Having remained at Alresford a few days, I returned to London, and subsequently stayed for a few days at the 'Clarendon Hotel,' at Gravesend. On or about the 5th of January, 1867, the defendant, Vincent Gosford, accompanied by Mr. Plowden, a distant relative of mine, and Mr. Cullington, of the firm of Messrs. Slaughter and Cullington, solicitors for several of the defendants hereto, visited Gravesend and saw me.

"On Tuesday, the 8th day of January, 1867, the said Vincent Gosford again called upon me, and had a prolonged interview with me at the said hotel, and accompanied me in the train to London. During such interviews I and the said Vincent Gosford discussed various matters and circumstances relating to the Tichborne and Doughty families, and the neighbourhoods of Tichborne and Upton, with which we were both familiar. The said Vincent Gosford has since had another interview with me, and I then again very fully discussed with the said Vincent Gosford such matters and circumstances, and recalled to the memory of the said Vincent Gosford various facts which occurred previously to my leaving England in the year 1853, some of which were only known to me and the said Vincent Gosford; and the said Vincent Gosford admitted that some of such facts had escaped his recollection until they were recalled to his memory by me, but that he then well remembered that such facts did occur as stated by me; and I proved to the said Vincent Gosford, beyond a shadow of doubt, that I was the eldest son of the said Sir James Francis Doughty Tichborne.

"I verily believe that no circumstance whatever has arisen to lead to or to justify the said Vincent Gosford in raising any doubt whatever as to my identity.—(Signed) ROGER DOUGHTY TICHBORNE." [He was sentenced to 14 years' imprisonment, Feb. 28, 1874.] [See TRIALS.]

TICKETS-OF-LEAVE.

Ticket-of-leave holders were prisoners, who, after serving a portion of their sentence, had the remaining portion remitted, on condition that they resided in a certain district, and reported themselves periodically to the authorities.

First granted to female convicts in New South Wales, March 19, 1829.

The Governor of New South Wales issued an order that all ticket-of-leave holders in the colony should be mustered regularly four times every year, and their tickets endorsed by the Principal Superintendent of Convicts, April 13, 1826.

The Governor ordered that all prisoners holding tickets-of-leave do attend church or some place of public worship at least once on every Sunday; and that prisoners who shall fail so to do are immediately to be deprived of their tickets-of-leave and turned into Government employ.   June 9, 1826.

TIDAL WAVES.

Tidal wave in Port Jackson, Sydney, August 16, 1868.

Remarkable tidal disturbances occurred on the coasts of New Zealand and New South Wales, May 11, 1877.

TIDES, HIGH.   An extraordinary tide occurred in Sydney harbour; it rose 3 feet higher than the ordinary Spring tide, a phenomenon which could not be accounted for.   Nov. 17, 1821.

TIN.

Tin discovered in the Ovens district, now Beechworth, Victoria, March 11, 1843.

The Rev. W. B. Clarke reported his discovery of tin on the Alps, along part of the Murrumbidgee, New South Wales, August 16, 1849.

Tin discovered at Broadwater, a tributary of the Severn river, by James Daw, who submitted samples to Mr. John Scott, a silver-smith and metallurgist, who declared it to be excellent tin.   1849.

Mr. Stover, geologist of the United States expedition, analysed some tin specimens given him at Melbourne, and described those from the Ovens river as "very rich ore of tin."   Jan., 1854.

Victoria, up to September 1, 1865, produced 2,380 tons of ore.

On October 5, 1871, Mr. George Milner Stephen, in a letter to Sir Roderick Murchison, announced the discovery of a rich tin-field 15 miles east of Inverell, New South Wales.

Tin discovered in Queensland, 1872.

Great discoveries of tin at Tenterfield, January 12, 1872.

Tin ore discovered at Mount Bischoff, north-west coast of Tasmania, by Mr. James Smith, better known as "Philosopher Smith," 1873.

Tin smelting at Mount Bischoff mines, Tasmania, successfully commenced, Jan. 5, 1875.   [See MINERAL STATISTICS.]

TOBACCO.

The first sale of Australian tobacco took place, August 8, 1822.

A TICKET-OF-LEAVE
A & R Archives

Colonial manufactured tobacco first advertised for sale at Sydney, 1824.

Tobacco first manufactured in New South Wales, 1842. [The manufacturer was an American. The importance of this new branch of industry was demonstrated by the fact that, in 1841 the duty on tobacco amounted to £36,188.]

TOLLEMACHE, GEORGE. The following incidents of an Australian life will, no doubt, prove interesting :—"An old friend—and an older colonist, passed through Dubbo," says the *Dispatch*, "this week, going down the Macquarie. George Tollemache—*clarem et venerabile nomen* —now between 70 and 80 years of age, is a colonist of 54 years standing. Attached in the old colonial days to the Commissariat department, in 1824 he formed one of the expedition under Sir John Gordon-Bremer, who took possession of Moreton Bay, Keppel Bay, Rockhampton, Bathurst, and Melville Islands, &c. With the party of Lieutenant Miller, of the 40th was ordered to St. George's Sound in 1827, Captain Barlow, commandant, and after two years there was relieved. In 1834 turned squatter and took up Guyalman and Geary runs—the only stations in these parts then were Gobolion, owned by Judge Wild, Chief Justice at the Cape, and Murrumbidgerie, owned by Mr. Palmer. Like many more he went down in the commercial wreck of 1839. Poor old gentleman, his life is a history of New South Wales, and some day or another, perhaps, we will be enabled to give chapters from his narrative. 'Fifty-four years! why,' said he to us on Wednesday, 'I never saw Sir John Robertson but once, and then he was only a boy ten or twelve years old, walking by the side of his father in George-street, Sydney.'" January, 1879.

TOLL-HOUSES, erected in N.S.W. to raise funds to keep the road in repair, March 24, 1810.

TOLLS.

Tolls on the South Head Road, Sydney, discontinued, July 1, 1828.

All Tolls in South Australia abolished, November 31, 1870.

Tolls, with a few exceptions, abolished in New South Wales, 1877.

TORRES STRAITS.

Discovered, August 30, 1606.

Captain Blackwood surveyed Torres Straits during the years 1842-5.

TORPEDO CORPS.

Established in New South Wales (Major Cracknell in command), January 1, 1878 ; in Queensland, April 15, 1878.

Three torpedo boats launched in Sydney, designed by Norman Selfe, C.E. 1878.

Successful trial of torpedo boat in Port Jackson, April, 1879.

TORRENS' LAND ACT, THE.

" A great measure of legal reform is the Real Property Act, devised by Mr. (now Sir) R. R. Torrens, a gentleman formerly holding a high public position in the colony of South Australia. Mr. Torrens has seen and felt, as many more have done, the scandalous delay and expense of transferring real property under the old law of England. This system of transferring real estate by deed was brought from England to Australia, where it was soon found to be productive of the evils which attended it in the old country. In every fresh transaction in real property a new deed was necessary, which recapitulated all the deeds that had gone before ; this was both cumbrous and costly. It was thought that it might be possible to invent a simpler, cheaper, and safer system ; and the method of thinking out and formulating this system belongs to Sir R. R. (then Mr.) Torrens. He had been collector of Customs at Port Adelaide, South Australia, and his official employment made him familiar with the laws relating to shipping, having, as he stated in a pamphlet published by him, " just such an acquaintance with the English Constitution and laws as ordinarily entered into the education of an English gentleman."

" His starting point was to apply to the transfer of land the principles which regulated the transfer of shipping property, by means of registration. The idea was a correct one, but between its conception and its formulation into a code of law there was a long and painful interval. He consulted the then Chief Justice, Sir Charles Cooper, and other legal gentlemen, and they gave him but little encouragement. He was not a lawyer. Many technical difficulties would arise which would need a lawyer's trained skill to surmount, and they warned him that he might expect no help or support from the profession. Mr. Torrens, however, was one of the few men who are not to be discouraged by want of sympathy, or beaten by opposition. The subject was near his heart, and he pondered over it night and day, until it assumed shape and form in his mind. He then drafted a bill, submitted it to some of his friends, listened to their suggestions, adopting them where he thought it wise to do so, and then brought it before Parliament. The bill was laughed to scorn by the profession, but it was eagerly and enthusiastically welcomed by the public. Most of the lawyers stood aloof. For a layman to attempt to alter the whole system of transferring real estate by deed which had the prestige of immemorial usage in its favour, and to deal with real estate as if it were a mere chattel, was as absurd as if a tailor were to invent a new method of cutting for fistula, or an illiterate ploughman a new method of calculating an eclipse. Mr. Torrens, however, made light of both opposition and ridicule. There was a crying evil to be remedied ; he had undertaken to remedy the evil, and, in spite of all opposition, he would do it.

" Mr. Torrens was returned to Parliament as one of the members for the city for the express purpose of carrying the bill through the Assembly. The legal members opposed him "tooth and nail," but he had a large majority of willing supporters at his back, and the bill was literally forced through the House by "the brute force of a tyrannical majority." There was greater opposition in the Legislative Council, which has always been found more conservative of old institutions. But public opinion and the sense of the community were too strong to be resisted, and the bill passed the Council, was assented to by the Governor, Jan. 27, 1858, and became law.

" At the request of his friends, Mr. Torrens resigned his seat in Parliament, and became the official head of the department. He suggested or superintended all the machinery required for practically working the new system. He laboured at it unceasingly, and when the Act came into operation on July 2, 1858, all the office machinery was ready to work it.

AN ADVERTISEMENT FOR A SALE OF LAND UNDER THE TORRENS TITLE

" The first great principle of this Act is the transferring of real property by registration of title instead of by deeds ; the second is absolute indefeasibility of title. The system is very simple and very inexpensive. The certificate of title is registered in the official registry at the Lands Titles' Office, the owner obtaining a duplicate certificate. All transactions under the land appear on the face of the certificate, so that at a glance it may be seen whether the property is encumbered, or any charges are made upon it. If an owner wishes to mortgage his land, he takes his certificate to the office, and has the transaction marked upon it. If he wants to sell, he passes over the certificate to the pur-

chaser, and the transaction is registered. Any man of ordinary intelligence can do all that is necessary for himself when once his property is brought under the Act. The only difficulty is in getting the title registered at first. After that it is all plain sailing. When a man holding property under deed wishes to have it placed under the Act he takes his deeds, which are his title to the property, to the office. The deeds are carefully examined by the solicitors to the Lands Titles' Commissioners ; and if there is no difficulty, and after all due publicity is given and precautions taken to prevent fraud or mistake a certificate is issued and the old deeds are cancelled. From the moment the land is brought under the Act and a certificate is granted, the title of the person holding the certificate becomes indefeasible, unless it has been fraudulently obtained ; and he can hold the property against the world.

" Provision is made for errors that may possibly occur, by which persons may be damnified or deprived of their property. Even though a wrong may have been done, yet an innocent holder of a certificate cannot be dispossessed of his property. But to compensate persons who may through error or fraud have been deprived of their property, an assurance fund has been created by a percentage of one half-penny in the pound being levied on all property brought under the Act. This fund now amounts to between £30,000 and £40,000, and all the claims that have been made upon it during the seventeen years the Act has been in operation do not amount to £300, which is a sufficient proof of the carefulness exercised in the examination of old titles before the certificate is issued in the first instance.

" Since this Act came into operation all land grants issued from the Crown have been registered under it, and a large amount of property formerly held under deed is now registered. Confidence in the Act has gradually grown up. The lawyers very soon withdrew active opposition, and the simplicity of the scheme commended it even to the legal mind. Up to the close of 1874 the value of the property brought under the operation of the Act, including land grants, was £9,260,186. The benefit to the community of having a cheap, simple, and expeditious method of dealing with land is incalculable. Mr. Dudley Field, the well-known American jurist, who was recently on a visit to his daughter, the wife of Governor Musgrave, of South Australia, expressed his great admiration at the simplicity of our Real Property Act, which was much in advance of any system of dealing with real estate with which he was acquainted. The Act has been amended more than once, to render it more workable, but its essential principles have been jealously guarded.

" Soon after it was set into healthy operation Mr. Torrens obtained leave from the Government of S.A. to visit the neighbouring colonies at their request to explain and help to initiate this Act, and now all the colonies have adopted the Torrens's Act of registration of title. The principle of the Act has also been accepted by the first jurists at home, where several attempts have been made to get it into legal operation. Lord Westbury's Act was a step towards it, but it had some serious defects which have prevented it being a success. There is no doubt that it is much easier to introduce the system into new colonies where titles are easily traced, than into old countries where, during the lapse of generations, they have become complicated."

TOWN HALL.

ADELAIDE. Foundation stone laid by the Governor, Sir Dominick Daly, May 4, 1864; opened June 20, 1865. Cost £25,000.

BRISBANE, cost £28,000; opened 1865.

MELBOURNE. Memorial stone laid by Prince Alfred, November 29, 1867; opened August 9, 1870. [Length of great hall, 175 feet; width, 5 feet; height of tower, 140 feet. Organ largest in Australia; 4,500 pipes; cost £7,000.—Total cost, £100,000.]

SYDNEY. Foundation stone of the Town Hall laid by Prince Alfred, 1868; opened July 1, 1875. Cost £80,000.

TRACTION ENGINE. The "Magæthon," traction engine, reached Goulburn, after a six months journey. January, 1861. [The bad state of the roads, owing to heavy and continuous rains, was said to have caused the delay. B. H. Palmer was the owner.]

TRADE. The "Philadelphia," Captain Patrickson, was the first trading brig which ever entered Port Jackson. She came from Philadelphia, North America, and carried a large stock of goods, which were quickly disposed of by the captain at a high profit. Nov. 1, 1792.

TRAFFIC IN HUMAN MAORI HEADS. A traffic in human heads from New Zealand was carried on so extensively that the Government felt called upon to issue an order for stopping the importation of this singular description of goods. 1831. [The heads were sought for as curiosities, and they were so preserved that the fanciful tattooing to which the Maoris subject themselves whilst living was preserved perfect.]

TRANSIT OF VENUS.

Captain Cook's party observed the transit of Venus in two places. The first at Otaheite, and the second at the island of Eirnayd, near Otaheite. June 3, 1768.

Four distinct parties, organised by Mr. H. C. Russell to observe the transit of Venus, Australia being especially favourable for such observations, 1874.

TRANSPORTATION.

Returning from transportation was punishable with death until by 5 Will. IV, c. 67, when an Act was passed making the offence punishable by transportation for life. January 20, 1788.

John Eyre, a man of fortune, sentenced to transportation from England to Australia for stealing a few quires of note paper, November 1, 1779.

The inquiry on the abolition of transportation lasted three years, and was conducted by Mr. John Thomas Bigge, Commissioner. 1819.

Van Diemen's Land appointed a place of transportation for natives of New South Wales, and persons arriving in the colony free when convicted of a first offence. 1832.

A political association formed in Sydney to watch over the affairs of the colony, and to correspond with Mr. Bulwer. 1835. [From this time may be dated the commencement of that struggle which was some years afterwards crowned with success by the final abolition of transportation.]

Public meeting held at Sydney in favor of transportation, February 9, 1839.

Transportation to New South Wales virtually ceased, August 20, 1840.

Sir George Gipps informed the Council, Sydney, that transportation ceased on August 1 preceding. October 20, 1840.

The ship "Eden" arrived in Port Jackson with convicts from England, November 18, 1840.

A petition was got up, praying for the revival of transportation, which excited very considerable discussion, and those who were in favour of its revival were opprobiously called the "banditti party." 1842.

CONTACT OBSERVATIONS ON THE TRANSIT OF VENUS AT MELBOURNE UNIVERSITY
The Australasian Sketcher, 1874

The question for the renewal of transportation was brought formally before the Council, in consequence of a despatch from the then Secretary of State (Mr. Gladstone) to the Governor. Mr. Wentworth obtained a select committee of the Council to inquire into and report on the despatch respecting the renewal of transportation. The result was, that it spoke favourably of the system, and its views were adopted and advocated by Messrs. Dangar, Macarthur, and others; it was, however, strenuously opposed out of the House, and several anti-transportation meetings held in the colony. The first meeting was held at the City Theatre Sydney, to petition against the renewal of transportation. Mr. Charles Cowper presided, and moved a resolution to the effect that the meeting had heard with the deepest feelings of alarm and regret that it was proposed to renew transportation to this colony, and that they could not conceive any circumstances under which such a measure would be desirable or justifiable. The resolution was seconded by the Rev. John M'Encroe, and petition to that effect presented to the Legislative Council. To this petition, in four days, 2000 signatures were attached. It was presented at the close of the session, and on the last day of the assembling of the House, before its prorogation, the motion for printing the petition was negatived, so much at variance was the opinion within the House and out of doors on the subject of transportation. October 22, 1846.

In consequence of the Council refusing to print the petition, and the report of the House, favourable to transportation, being about to be sent to England, a meeting of the anti-transportation committee was held, when a memorial to the Governor was adopted, for his Excellency to transmit to England the official copies of the petition, and to use his influence to prevent the colony from being again made a penal settlement. The Governor's reply was favourable, that he would forward the petition, but " he could use no influence in the matter, for he had none." October, 1846.

A determination evinced by the colonists in all quarters of New South Wales against the resumption of transportation and assignment. November, 1846.

The colonists being much averse to the revival of transportation, a grand anti-transportation meeting took place at the Victoria Theatre, the immediate object being to protest against the terms of the despatch. The principal speakers were Mr. Charles Cowper, Mr. Robert Lowe, and the Rev. Dean M'Encroe. The adoption of a petition against the revival of transportation was the next step taken, in which it stated that " They felt bound, humbly but firmly, to represent to Her Majesty that it was their duty and their determination, by every legal and constitutional means, to oppose the revival of transportation in any shape." Similar petitions were adopted in all the principal towns in the colony. During these proceedings, intelligence was received that a shipload of convicts was about to

be despatched to the colony from one of the ports of England, but was prevented by cholera breaking out on board. February 13, 1849.

Great anti-transportation meeting held in Melbourne, February 13, 1849.

Great anti-convict demonstration at the Victoria Theatre, Sydney. The Mayor presided, and the principal speakers were Charles Cowper, Robert Lowe, and Dean M'Encroe. March 9, 1849.

Indignation meeting held in Sydney, near Circular Quay, to protest against misrepresentations of Governor Fitzroy to the Home Government on the transportation question. 4000 persons present, Robert Campbell presiding, and Henry Parkes, G. A. Lloyd, Rev. Dr. Fullerton, J. R. Wilshire, J. M. Grant, Richard Peek, and E. Flood being principal speakers. June 11, 1849.

The Governor visited Port Phillip, and at Melbourne was importuned to ward off the evils of transportation to the southern district, when his Excellency promised he would do so, and that in case any prison-ship arrived, he had given the Superintendent authority to forward the prisoners to Sydney. 1849.

A despatch received from the Secretary of State for the Home Department, that transportation to New South Wales would be again adopted, but that it was not intended to send any convicts but such as were considered deserving tickets-of-leave on their arrival, and calculated to become useful labourers in the colony. 1849.

[See CONVICT SHIPS, LAST.]

Last convict ship arrived in Moreton Bay, May 12, 1850.

Great transportation meeting held at Launceston, V. D. L., August 9, 1850.

LIST OF THE Traitors,—Trimmers,—Rose-water Liberals,—and Political Tidewaiters, who voted for MR. WENTWORTH'S ARTFUL DODGE, the adjournment of the Question of NO TRANSPORTATION!!! in the Legislative Council of New South Wales, August 30th, 1850.

W. C. WENTWORTH
J. B. DARVALL
S. A. DONALDSON
COL. SNODGRASS
THE COLONIAL TREASURER
THE AUDITOR GENERAL
THE COLLECTOR OF CUSTOMS
MR. EBDEN
MR. ICELY
MR. MARTIN
MR. JAMES MACARTHUR
MR. WILLIAM MACARTHUR
MR. NICHOLS
C. NICHOLSON, SPEAKER.

A POSTER DENOUNCING THOSE WHO SUPPORTED CONTINUED TRANSPORTATION OF CONVICTS
Mitchell Library

A large anti-transportation meeting held in Sydney, in the old Barrack Square, for the purpose of once more entering a protest in the name and on behalf of the colonists at large, against the revival of transportation in any shape, or under any name. 6,000 persons were present on the occasion. The principal speakers were the Rev. Dr. Ross, G. K. Holden, Archdeacon M'Encroe, George Bowman, Captain Lamb, Rev. Joseph Beazley, Rev. W. B. Boyce, Rev. Mr. West, Messrs. Mort, Piddington, and Weekes. September 16, 1850. [A combination of men representing every class, grade, and section of the community was present. At this meeting was initiated the New South Wales Anti-Transportation Association.]

The Governor very unpopular with a large class of colonists, on account of a despatch sent by him to the Secretary of State, and in which he stated that the anti-transportation meeting held at the Circular Quay was attended only by a portion of idlers, attracted by curiosity, but with no intention of taking part in the proceedings, whilst amongst those who did take part in the business, there was, with scarcely an exception, no person who had any stake or influence in the community. As soon as this document became publicly known an "indignation meeting" was convened, when above 4,000 persons were present, and resolutions were embodied in a memorial to the Queen, in which it mentioned that the Governor had grossly misrepresented a series of facts, traduced a large majority of the colonists of all classes, and betrayed the interests of the colony; that no faith could be placed in the promises of the Secretary of State for the Colonies, and solemnly demanded a revocation of the Order of the Council making New South Wales a penal settlement; that the despatch of the Governor testified his incapacity to act as Governor, and earnestly prayed his instant removal; and that, in accordance with a resolution adopted at a meeting in 1849, responsible government according to the principles of the British Constitution, was necessary for the government of the colony. 1850.

Transportation to Western Australia commenced, 1850.

The subject of transportation again taken up very warmly by the colonists. The Home Government still continued to transport convicts to Van Diemen's Land, and a meeting was held, when it was proposed for the formation of a great league, a solemn covenant on the part of all colonists to carry out the object of for ever putting an end to transportation to any of the Australian colonies, and delegates were appointed from the other colonies for the purpose of incorporating the Anti-Transportation Association into the General League. The delegates went through the interior, attending meetings through the colony for a similar purpose at all the principal towns. The result was that a meeting of the League was convened, and amongst a series of resolutions, they stated "that as parents, they were bound by every obligation of duty and affection to protect their children from the dangers incident to the transportation of offenders to these colonies, and they united in a solemn appeal to the humanity and justice of the Sovereign and people of Great Britain on behalf of the rising generation." January, 1851.

The petition from New South Wales against transportation presented to Parliament by Sir W. Molesworth, February 8, 1851.

Great anti-transportation meeting held at Melbourne in St. Patrick's Hall, February 13, 1851.

Another meeting of the Australian League was called (Mr. C. Cowper presiding), in consequence of Earl Grey, the then Colonial Secretary, continuing transportation to the colony, and to carry out that object it was proposed that the Moreton Bay district should be made a separate colony from New South Wales. July 29, 1851. [The result of the meeting was to consider whether the time had not arrived for appealing to the Queen by petition, praying Her Majesty to dismiss Earl Grey from her Councils, and entreating Her Majesty to command her Ministers to redeem the honour of the British crown by fulfilling its pledge touching transportation, which had repeatedly been given to the colonists of New South Wales and Van Diemen's Land. This petition was adopted, in which it also stated that "the petitioners felt compelled, humbly but firmly, to represent to Her Majesty in person, that the subterfuges, evasions, equivocations, and breaches of faith practised towards these colonies by Earl Grey had unhappily destroyed all confidence in his Lordship's administration of colonial affairs." The principal speakers on this occasion were :— Mr. Cowper (chairman), Messrs. Norton, J. F. Josephson, H. Parkes, Gilbert Wright, Kemp, J. K. Holden, Captain Lamb, Robert Campbell, and Archdeacon M'Encroe.]

Another transportation movement was made in consequence of Earl Grey's determination to continue transportation to Van Diemen's Land, as avowed by him to the Victorian delegate, Mr. King, and to separate Moreton Bay from New South Wales for penal purposes. A conference of the transportation league was held in Van Diemen's Land, when eighteen representatives from the colonies attended, and a petition to Her Majesty was decided to be prepared, to be signed by the president, embodying the decision of the Legislative Assemblies of all the Australian colonies on the question of transportation. 1852.

Transportation to Tasmania ceased, February 10, 1853.

Cessation of transportation to Australia, to take place in three years, announced, amidst much rejoicing, January 26, 1865.

Last convict ship arrived in Western Australia, transportation thus finally ceasing in Australasia, January 10, 1868. [See CONVICTS.]

TREASURY.

The Colonial Treasury buildings, Sydney, New South Wales, commenced in 1849, completed about the end of 1851.

The Treasury buildings, Melbourne, commenced in 1858, opened, 1862. [This structure, which faces Collins street, cost £80,000.]

TREES.

The three large Norfolk Island Pine trees standing in the Botanic Gardens, Sydney, were planted in 1817. The present heights of these trees are 88 feet, 102 feet, 110 feet. 1879.

THE HIGHEST TREES IN AUSTRALIA.—On the Black Spur Range, Gippsland, Victoria, is a gum-tree—alive—measuring 420 feet in height, and another (prostrate) the almost incredible height of 480 feet. Baron Mueller is the authority for these measurements. Professor Whitney says that " it overtops the highest sequoia by 100 feet."

"Along the Huon Road, Tasmania may be seen hundreds of blue-gum trees ranging from 250 to 300 feet high, and there are several trees in the Otway Ranges and Tasmania equal to and surpassing the celebrated " Grizzly Giant" of California, in diameter of fair trunk."

The largest tree in Tasmania is situated within five miles of Hobart Town, on Commissary Hall's estate, near O'Bryen's bridge. Commissary Hall writes as follows :—"I have visited the tree. It is a trifle over 300 feet, and there are some 50 feet of the top blown off. I myself have seen 14 men on horseback in the hollow of it. A horse and dray has been turned in the hollow of the tree ; and I was informed during the time that myself and Mr. Tally, Inspector of Surveyors in Hobart Town, were on a prospecting expedition to the Frenchman's camp (for gold) in Tasmania ; that in 1854 Sir Wm. Denison, the Governor, and 78 of the Legislative Assembly and their friends, dined in the hollow of the tree." It is now over 56 years since its discovery.

Mr. W. G. Robinson, of Berwick, Victoria, in a journey from Gippsland to Mount Baw Baw overland, saw and measured a tree 500 feet high.

Mr. M. Alexander gives the height of one in West Australia, 420 feet, and one in Victoria, 480 feet. 1879.

TRIAL BY JURY.

Trial by Jury obtained at the Quarter Sessions Court, N.S.W., October 15, 1824.

The first trial by jury in the Supreme Court, N.S.W., took place, February 12, 1825.

Mr. Bulmer presented a petition to the Imperial Parliament from the colonists of New South Wales, praying for trial by jury in all cases, civil and criminal, and also for a Legislative Assembly for New South Wales, June 29, 1832.

TRIALS, REMARKABLE.

First Breach of Promise Case (Cox v. Payne) tried in Sydney, N.S.W., May 17, 1825.

Lieutenant Lowe, of the 40th Regiment, tried at the Supreme Court, Sydney, for directing four of the soldiers under his command to shoot a native black, who was charged with the murder of a settler's servant, which order was at once carried into effect. The credibility of the testimony was shaken by that of the witnesses for the defence, and he was acquitted. 1827.

A settler named Jamison, tried for the murder of a native black, when it was found to be justifiable homicide. 1827.

A trial in the Supreme Court, Mudie v. Kinchela, occupied much public attention. It was a case in which Major Mudie prosecuted Mr. Kinchela (a son of the late Judge) for an assault. The assault complained of, consisted of a severe horsewhipping inflicted on the Major by Kinchela, in retaliation for insults to which his father (the Judge) had been subjected in a work published by Mudie, under the title of "The Felonry of New South Wales." The jury, taking into consideration the provocation which the matter in the book afforded, gave the small damages of £50, being one pound for every blow the plaintiff was said to have received. 1840.

The great trial between the Bank of Australasia v. The Bank of Australia, took place March 26, 1845. [It lasted until April 8 following, when the jury being equal, no verdict was returned. The amount sought to be recovered was £169,000. The parties being dissatisfied with the result, the Court granted a trial at Bar, which commenced June 23 following, and lasted 20 days, but a verdict was returned which caused an appeal to be made to the Privy Council by the Bank of Australasia.]

The Queen v. Bell for embezzlement and conspiracy. The trial, in Sydney, lasted day by day from October 8, 1845, until December 12 (65 days), when it was adjourned until January following, on account of the illness of one of the jurors, who subsequently died. The trial was not proceeded with, and no further steps were taken.

Rev. W. F. X. Bailey v. Fairfax (S. M. Herald), for libel in publishing from "Modern State trials, 1850," an account of an extensive forgery in London. Verdict for plaintiff : £100 damages. August 11, 1864.

The Newtown Ejectment Case, known also as the celebrated Devine will case, tried in the Supreme Court, Sydney, a verdict for defendant, given after a trial extending over eight days. 1852. [The circumstances were that Nicholas Devine, an officer who arrived in the "first fleet," and who served the Government for 25 years as Superintendent of Convicts, received in recognition of his services a grant of 210 acres of land adjoining Sydney, and afterwards called Newtown. One Bernard Rochford, lived with Devine as an assigned servant, or rather as his guardian, for he became enfeebled in mind

READING THE WILL
The Illustrated Sydney News, 1854

and body, and in 1827 Devine executed a conveyance of the whole of his landed property, to Rochford. After the death of Devine, Rochford sold the whole of the property, which in a few years became very valuable, by reason of Sydney having extended its limits and Newtown having become one of the most populous, healthy, and highly improved suburbs of the city. Things having assumed this altered aspect, the whole history of the affair was not long reaching the ears of Devine's relatives in Ireland, and the grand nephew and heir-at-law of the original grantee came to the colony and claimed the whole estate, on the ground that the conveyance of 1827 was a forgery or a fraud, Devine having been at that time and for some years previously, generally insane ; or if this ground were not tenable that Rochford being a prisoner of the Crown could not lawfully acquire, hold, or dispose of property of this nature. Twenty-six gentlemen defended their homesteads in this law-suit. The case, was, however referred to the Privy Council, and a new trial granted, which was heard in the Supreme Court, Sydney, before Judge Dickinson, in 1857, and lasted 30 days, resulting again in favour of defendants. September 19, 1857. Further litigation was prevented by a compromise, the plaintiff receiving a sum of money in consideration of foregoing his claim.]

First Queensland State Trial (*Regina v. Pugh*,) tried August 21, 1861.

Urquhart v. Argus, libel, Melbourne Supreme Court, damages 40s. March, 1865.

Chisholm v. Macauley. The right of free selectors in New South Wales to impound, confirmed, September 8, 1868.

Mate v. Nugent. Crown grant *v.* Selection. [Before N.S.W. Courts several years, ultimately decided in favour of Mate.] March 25, 1869.

William Lorando Jones, a sculptor, tried at the Parramatta Quarter Sessions, before his Honor Judge Simpson, for blasphemy in reading passages from the Old Testament scripture and commenting on them, intending thereby to bring the Holy Scriptures and the Christian religion into disbelief and contempt. Defendant was found guilty, and sentenced to two years' imprisonment in Darlinghurst Gaol, and to pay a fine of £100 to Her Majesty the Queen. February 18, 1871. [The event created considerable sensation, and the case was brought before Parliament. The Governor and the Executive decided to release Jones and remit the fine after he had served a few weeks' imprisonment.]

Trial of *George Robert Nicholls*, a native of the colony, aged 30, and *Alfred Lyster* or Froude, a native of Dorsetshire, England, aged 20, at the Criminal Court, Sydney, before Mr. Justice Hargrave, for the Parramatta River murders. May 21–22, 1872. [The murder of John Bridger took place March 8, 1872, and of Wm. P. Walker, on March 13, 1872. The prisoners were convicted and afterwards executed for latter offence.]

Trial at Melbourne of *Mount* and *Morris* for the " Carl " murders. Verdict of manslaughter returned. December 21, 1872. [The prisoners were afterwards released on a point of law.]

Barton v. Muir, right to transfer free selection. Ended in favour of the squatter (Barton). July 10, 1873.

Tichborne v. Lushington. The plaintiff declared himself to be Sir Roger Charles Tichborne, supposed to have been lost at sea, and claimed the baronetcy and estates, worth about £24,000 a year. [*See* TICHBORNE.] Roger Charles Tichborne, son of Sir James, born 1829 ; educated in France till about 1843 ; entered the army 1849 ; proposed marriage to his cousin Kate Doughty, declined, January, 1852 ; sailed from Havre for Valparaiso (March), and arrived there June 10, 1853 ; sailed from Rio Janeiro in the " Bella," which foundered at sea, April 20, 1854. [A Chancery suit was instituted, and his death legally proved.] His mother advertised for her son, May 10, 1865 ; the claimant (found by Gibbes and Cubitt in Australia) asserted that he and eight of the crew were saved from the wreck of the " Bella "; that he went to Australia, and lived there, roughly, for 13 years under the name of Castro ; married as Castro, January, as Tichborne, July 3, 1866 ; he set up his claim, and was accepted by the dowager Lady Tichborne as her son at Paris, January, 1867. [No others of the family accepted him ; but Sir Clifford Constable and some brother officers did.] His claim was resisted on behalf of Sir Henry (a minor), son of Sir Alfred Tichborne, and after Chancery proceeding (begun March, 1867), a trial begun in the Court of Common Pleas, London, before Chief Justice Bovill, May 11, 1871 ; the claimant was examined 22 days ; the trial adjourned on 40th day, July 7th ; resumed, November 7th ; case for plaintiff closed, December 21st ; trial resumed, January 15, 1872 ; the Attorney-General, Sir J. D. Coleridge, spoke 26 days ; on March 4th the jury expressed themselves satisfied that the claimant was not Sir Roger ; on the 103rd day he was declared non-suited, March 6, 1872. [The law proceedings are said to have cost the estate nearly £92,000.] He was lodged in Newgate to be tried for perjury, March 7th ; indicted as Thomas Castro, otherwise Arthur Orton, for perjury and forgery, April 9th ; the Court of Queen's Bench decided that he be admitted to bail, April 23rd ; released, April 26th ; Lady Doughty, mother of Sir Henry Tichborne, died December 13th ; the trial of the claimant for perjury and forgery begun before Chief Justice Cockburn and Justices Mellor and Lush at Bar April 23, 1873 ; case for the prosecution closed, July 10th ; resumed (for defence) July 21th. [Up to June 27th (47th day of the trial), out of 150 witnesses above 100 had sworn that the claimant was not Tichborne, and about 40 that he was Arthur Orton.] The claimant forbidden to attend public meetings, September 10, 1873 ; case for the defence closed on the 124th day, October 27th ; adjourned from October 31st to November 17th, then to November 27th ; rebutting evidence heard, November 27–28 ; Dr. Kennealy's summing up, December 2–14, January 15–28, 1874. [Mr. Whalley, M.P., for contempt of court, fined £250, January 23rd.] The Chief Justice's summing up, from January 29th, to February 28th. *Verdict :—* That the claimant did falsely swear : That he was Roger Charles Tichborne ; that he seduced Catherine N. E. Doughty in 1851 ; and that he was not Arthur Orton. *Sentence :* 14 years imprisonment with hard labour, February 28, 1874. [Longest trial known in England.] New trial refused by the judges, April 20, 1874 ; Jean Luie (Lindgren) and "Capt." Brown convicted of perjury in the Tichborne case (7 years' and 5 years' penal servitude), April 9–10, 1874.

Charles Orton declared the claimant to be his brother, at the *Globe* Office, London, March 10, 1874.

Joachim v. O'Shanassy. Joachim took up eight selections of 320 acres each in the names of his children on O'Shanassy's Moira run, N.S.W., on February 20, 1873. The litigation lasted three years ; ultimately Privy Council decided in favour of Joachim, 1877.

Peter F. Macdonald v. Queensland Government, for losses through irregular issue of pastoral leases of runs to others which were rented to him ; tried at Rockhampton. Verdict for plaintiff (including interest, £7,000), £19,700, April 12-19, 1879.

J. V. Lavers v. Municipal Council, Sydney, for £3,000 damages, being £1,000 per month for non-completion of Town Hall, Sydney, according to Act of Parliament. He lost the case on a technical point, April, 1875.

Hugh James Vincent O'Ferrall, convicted in Melbourne of embezzlement in the Lands office, sentenced to 12 years' imprisonment, July 31, 1875. [His defalcations were supposed to have amounted to £30,000.]

Learmonth v. *Bailey,* Great Victorian mining case. Case cast for plaintiff, £10,000. 1876.

Raynes, Treeve, and Co., auctioneers, Sydney, failed. Raynes died in September, 1876, and his partner, Josiah Richard Treeve, who had previously announced his succession to the title of Lord Blayney, attempted to escape from the colony in the "Fanny Wright," which however, in sailing out of Port Jackson, came into collision with the steamer "City of Hobart," and was sunk. Treeve was arrested a few days afterwards, and tried at the Criminal Court, Sydney, before Mr. Justice Faucett, on November 11, 1876, and following days, for forging the name of Mr. (now Sir) G. Wigram Allen, and other directors of a Building Society, to eight pieces of paper, each of the value of £3,000 to £4,000. The prisoner found guilty and sentenced to thirteen years' imprisonment, November 24, 1876.

Robert Hancock, a rich old colonist, died in Sydney (leaving property worth about £40,000), February 26, 1876. He left a will dated August 4, 1870, bestowing his property on Hannah Hincksman, Mary Hincksman, and Mary Payne. A solicitor's clerk, named Marshall, produced a second will dated November 1, 1875, leaving some of the property to Mrs. Burton and £2,000 to the Randwick Asylum. The trial to prove the validity of the second will took place in Supreme Court, Sydney, March 2, 5, 6, 7, and 8, 1877, and ended in a verdict against its validity. Marshall was tried for forging the second will ; convicted and sentenced to seven years hard labour, February 29, 1878.

Important insurance case, *Manning* v. *New Zealand Co.,* for insurance on "Lord Ashley," tried at Sydney. Verdict for plaintiff, March 19, 1878.

The charge preferred against *Mr. G. Stevenson and others* of conspiring to defraud the Customs, Melbourne, terminated August 22, 1878. [Ten of the jury were for an acquittal and two held out for the conviction of the defendant Stevenson ; no verdict could be taken.]

Important judgment in the Supreme Court in the case of *Lloyd* v. *Vickery.* November 21, 1878. [This trial, involving large interests in stations on Liverpool Plains, N.S.W., has already extended over five years, and has not yet (May, 1879) concluded.]

TURTLES. A turtle weighing 6 cwt., hooked by a fisherman in Broken Bay, December, 1805.

TWOFOLD BAY.

Discovered by Bass, Dec. 19, 1797.

Twofold Bay surveyed by Mr. Bass, surgeon, of the "Reliance," January 11, 1798.

Twofold Bay settled, August 15, 1834.

Governor Bourke made a voyage to Twofold Bay, returning overland by way of Goulburn, February 14, 1835.

from which the report emanated, the original projector of the Institution, and the author of the document in which the scheme of its formation was laid down. An Act to incorporate the Senate of the University was shortly afterwards passed.]

The Sydney University (the first institution of the kind in Australia) inaugurated, October 11, 1852.

The first Chancellor of the Sydney University was Sir Charles Nicholson, 1854.

Degrees (B.A.), first issued by Sydney University, 1857 (A. Renwick, G. Salting, W. Salting). [The degree of M.A. was first conferred in 1859 (M. Burdekin, W. C. Curtis, R. M. Fitzgerald, E. Lee, D. S. Mitchell, W. C. Windeyer, T. W. Johnson, T. Kinloch). The degree of LL.D. was first conferred in 1866 (J. S. Patterson, G. H. Stanley). The degree of LL.B. was first conferred in 1867 (F. E. Rogers). The degree of M.B. was first conferred in 1867 (P. Smith), and the degree of M.D. in 1868 (C. F. Goldsborough). The selection of professors for the several chairs was entrusted to a committee of gentlemen in England, and the professors arrived in 1852. E. T. Hamilton, M.A., late Fellow of Trinity College, Cambridge, was the first Provost. By Royal charter, issued February 7th, 1858, the same rank, style, and precedence are granted to graduates of the University of

U

UNIVERSITIES.

UNIVERSITY OF SYDNEY.

A motion brought into the Sydney Legislative Council by Mr. W. C. Wentworth, for instituting a University in the colony for the promotion of literature and science, to be endowed at the public expense, September 5, 1849. To William Charles Wentworth belongs the right of being named as the founder of the University of Sydney. He was chairman of the committee

LADY STUDENTS AT UNIVERSITY
The Australasian Sketcher, 1880

Sydney as are enjoyed by graduates of Universities within the United Kingdom. A similar charter was issued to Melbourne University on March 14, 1859.]

Sydney University public examinations for pupils of any public or private school, or those educated by private tuition, and founded on the middle class examinations of Oxford and Cambridge Universities, November, 1869.

William Charles Windeyer, Esq., elected to the Legislative Assembly of New South Wales as first Member for the University of Sydney, according to the Electoral Act, the University having at length attained on its roll the requisite number of one hundred superior graduates, September 8, 1876.

Sir E. Deas-Thomson, Chancellor of Sydney University, 1865; retired, April, 1878.

Sir William M. Manning elected Chancellor of the University of Sydney, April, 1878.

COLLEGES AFFILIATED TO. St. Paul's (Church of England) College established, 1858; St. John's (Roman Catholic) College established, 1858; St. Andrew's (Presbyterian) College established, 1868; St. John's College re-organised, 1874. [These colleges are all within the University of Sydney.]

NEW ZEALAND.

Dunedin University, New Zealand, opened, July 5, 1871.

Canterbury College, Christchurch, N.Z., opened by Governor the Marquis of Normanby, June 7, 1877. [This forms one of the colleges attached to the New Zealand "Travelling University."]

SOUTH AUSTRALIA.

Adelaide University founded, 1874. [Two colonists, Mr. W. W. Hughes and Mr. Thomas Elder, each gave £20,000 towards founding the Adelaide University, 1874.]

The first to receive the honour of a degree (B.A.) at the Adelaide University was L. A. Caterer, April, 1879.

VICTORIA.

The University of Melbourne was established by Act 16 Victoria, No. 34, to which Governor La Trobe gave the Royal Assent, January 22, 1853.

Mr. Justice Barry elected first Chancellor of Melbourne University, May 7, 1853.

The foundation-stone of the permanent building of Melbourne University, which stands in grounds of 40 acres, in the suburb of Carlton, was laid by Sir Charles Hotham, July 3, 1854.

Melbourne University opened as an institution in the Exhibition Building, Melbourne, April 13, 1855.

The permanent building of Melbourne University was opened for use October 3, 1855. [It has power to grant degrees in arts, law, medicine and music.]

Degrees (B.A.), first issued by the Melbourne University, 1858 (J. C. Cole, J. M. Mac-Farland, and G. H. Greene). [The degree of M.A. was first conferred in 1860 (J. C. Cole, J. M. MacFarland). The degree of M.B. was first conferred in 1867 (W. C. Rees, Patrick Moloney). The degree of LL.B. was first conferred in 1865 (Robert Craig, John Madden, J. T. Smith, A. Gilchrist). The degree of LL.D. was first conferred 1869 (John Madden). The degree of M.D. was first conferred in 1872 (W. C. Rees). The selection of the first professors for the several chairs were entrusted to a committee of gentlemen in England, and the professors arrived in the colony in 1854-5.]

Mr. (now Sir) Samuel Wilson presented £30,000 for the building of the Great Hall, Melbourne University, December 5, 1874.

Mr. J. S. Elkington, M.A., appointed to the Professorship of History and Political Economy. He was educated at the Melbourne University, and took his degree of Bachelor of Arts in 1866. He is the first gentleman appointed to a professorship in the Melbourne University who has completed his education and taken his degree at that institution. May, 1879.

VACCINATION, first used in Sydney, May 10, 1804.

VENUS, Transit of. [*See* Transit of Venus.]

"VERNON" Training Ship. As a training school and reformatory for boys under a certain age, brought before the magistrates on various charges, inaugurated April 17, 1867, proclaimed in the *Government Gazette* May 6, 1867; boys first sent on board, May 20, 1867. Number of boys received was 668, of whom 572 have been apprenticed or have left, leaving on board 96, of that number 53 being Protestants, 42 Catholics, and 1 Hebrew, up to June 30, 1877. [This institution has been of great benefit to many who have been by its means reclaimed from a life of vice and crime, and have become useful members of society. *Officers of the " Vernon :"*—Superintendent, F. W. Neitenstein; mate and clerk, W. H. Mason; visiting surgeon, Dr. Evans; schoolmaster, Wm. Plummer.]

VICTORIA.

First Birth in—The first child of European parents was born at Port Phillip, November 5, 1803. [The boy received the name of Hobart. His father was Sergeant Thomas.]

Estimated number of blacks about the locality of Melbourne and Geelong, 7,000, 1835.

The first arbitrator in Victoria was Mr. James Simpson, 1836.

The first judicial decision given in Victoria was as follows :—"We award in the dispute between Mr. Henry Batman and Mr. John Pascoe Fawkner—on the first claim—thirty shillings; on the second nothing, although a strong presumption is on our minds that some hasty expressions of Mr. Batman may have led Mr. Bullett to destroy the rabbits; on the third claim, damages, five shillings, and a fine of twenty shillings in consideration of its being an act of unauthorised aggression; and in the fourth claim nothing, as it does not appear that Mr. Batman set the dogs on the calf. We cannot omit remarking that there has been a degree of forbearance on the part of Mr. Fawkner highly gratifying to us, and if generally practised, very conducive to the general good.—Signed, A. Thomson, John Aitken, James Simpson. May 2, 1836. The fines to be appropriated to some general purpose."

Police Magistrate and Police Establishment appointed for Geelong, September 25, 1837.

A branch of the Colonial Treasury of New South Wales established at Melbourne, July 1, 1839.

Foundation stone of the Wesleyan Chapel, Melbourne, laid, May 11, 1840.

Great floods in Melbourne and suburbs; all the low lands were inundated, November 28, 1849.

"An Act for the better government of Her Majesty's Australian Colonies" was passed in the Imperial Parliament; it provided for the separation of Victoria from New South Wales. August 5, 1850.

The boundaries of Victoria, as settled by the Imperial Parliament were :—" On the north and north-east by a straight line drawn from Cape Howe to the nearest source of the Murray River and thence by the course of that river to the eastern boundary of the colony of South Australia." 1850.

Princes' Bridge, Melbourne, opened, November 14, 1850.

The first despatch ever written to a Governor of Victoria, was dated January, 1851. [It was addressed by Earl Grey to Lieutenant-Governor Latrobe.]

HODGSON'S PUNT ON THE YARRA YARRA
The Illustrated Sydney News, 1855

The first despatch by a Governor of Victoria, dated July 22, 1851.

Appointment of the Chief Officers of the Government, subject to Her Majesty's approval, appeared in the *Government Gazette*, July 15, 1851.

Colonial Secretary	William Lonsdale.
Colonial Treasurer	Alastair Mackenzie.
Auditor General ..	Chas. Hot Ebden.
Postmaster General ..	Alex. M'Crae.
Attorney General	Wm. Foster Stawell.
Solicitor General	Redmond Barry.
Master-in-Equity	R. William Pohlman.
Surveyor General	Robert Hoddle.
Sheriff	James Simpson.
Crown Solicitor ..	Henry Field Gurner.

The Treasury, Melbourne, burglariously entered and an iron safe carried away, October 28, 1851.

The following return of the writs for the election of the representative members of the first Legislative Council of the Colony were published in the *Government Gazette* of October 29, 1851 :—

North Bourke	Charles Hilton Dight. / John Thomas Smith.
South Bourke, Evelyn, and Mornington ..	Henry Miller.
Grant	John Henry Mercer.
Normanby, Dundas, and Follet	James Frederick Palmer.
Villiers and Heytesbury	William Rutledge.
Ripon, Hampden. Grenville, and Polwarth ..	Adolphus Goldsmith.
Talbot, Dalhousie, and Anglesey ..	John Pascoe Fawkner.
Gipps Land	Robert Turnbull.
The Murray	Francis Murphy.
The Loddon	William Campbell.
The Wimmera	William Francis Splatt.
Melbourne	William Westgarth. / John O'Shanassy. / James Stewart Johnston.
Geelong	Robert Robinson. / James Ford Strachan.
Portland	Thomas Wilkinson.
Belfast and Warrnambool	Thomas Hamilton Osborne.
Kilmore, Kyneton, and Seymour	Peter Snodgrass.

Governor La Trobe appointed, subject to Her Majesty's confirmation, the following non-elective members to the Legislative Council, being one-third of the total number, November 3, 1851.

OFFICIAL.

William Foster Stawell ..	Attorney General.
William Lonsdale ..	Colonial Secretary.
Charles Hotson Ebden ..	Auditor General.
Redmond Barry ..	Solicitor General.
Robert William Pohlman...	Master-in-Equity.

NON-OFFICIAL.

Alexander Cunningham Wallace Dunlop.
Charles James Griffith.
William Clarke Haines.
James Hunter Ross.
Andrew Russell.

The first Legislative ·Council (elective) of Victoria :—

Central Province ...	John Hodgson. / John Pascoe Fawkner. / Henry Miller. / John Hood. / Nehemiah Guthridge.

South Province	Donald Kennedy. / Thomas Herbert Power. / Wm. John Turner Clarke. / Thomas M'Combie. / John Barter Bennett.
South-western Province	James Ford Strachan. / Robert Cuthbertson Hope. / James Henty. / William Roope. / James Cowie.
Western Province ..	Stephen George Henty. / Andrew Rose Cruikshank. / Daniel Joseph Tierney. / James Fredk. Palmer. / Charles Vaughan.
North-western Province	John Allan. / Dennis Patrick Keogh. / George Urquart. / John Hunter Patterson. / Wm. Hy. Fancourt Mitchell.
Eastern Province ..	Matthew Hervey. / James Stewart. / Robert Thompson. / William Kaye. / Benjamin Williams.

The first Legislative Assembly under responsible Government :—

Melbourne...	David Moore. / Archibald Michie. / Wm. Foster Stawell. / John Thomas Smith. / John O'Shanassy.
St. Kilda	Frederick James Sargood. / Thomas Howard Fellows.
Collingwood ..	George Harker. / Thomas Embling.
South Melbourne ..	Andrew Clarke.
Richmond	George Samuel Evans. / Daniel Stodhart Campbell.
Williamstown ..	John Leslie Vesey Fitzgerald Foster.
Brighton	Jonathan B. Were.
Geelong	Alexander Fyffe. / Charles Sladen. / Charles Read. / John Hy. Brooke.
Portland	Hugh C. Eardley Childers. / Daniel Abraham Hughes.
Belfast	Francis Edis Beavor.
Warrnambool	Geo. Samuel Wegge Horne.
Colac	Andrew Rutherford.
Kilmore	John O'Shanassy.
Kyneton Boroughs ..	Geo. Walter Johnson.
Murray do. ..	Francis Murphy.
Alberton	James Davis.
Castlemaine Boroughs ..	Alexander Stenson Palmer. / Vincent Pyke.
Sandhurst do. ..	Jas. Macpherson Grant.
North Grant ..	John Basson Humffray.
North Grenville ..	Peter Lalor.
Ovens	Daniel Cameron.
Rodney	John Dunstan Baragwanath.
Loddon	John Downes Owens. / Ebenezer Syme.
Talbot	Butler Cole Aspinall. / David Blair.
East Bourke ..	Robert Bennett. / Augustus Fred. Adolphus Greeves.
West Bourke ..	Patrick Phelan. / Robert M'Dougall.
South Bourke ..	Charles Pasley. / Patrick O'Brien.
South Grant ..	Wm. Clarke Haines. / Horatio Spencer Wills. / John Myles.
Evelyn and Mornington	Wm. Acland Douglas Anderson.
Anglesey	Peter Snodgrass.
Dundas and Follett ..	Charles James Griffith.
Normanby	Edward Henty.
Villiers and Heytesbury	Charles Gavan Duffy. / William Rutledge.

Polwarth, Ripon, Hampden, and South Grenville	{ Jeremiah Geo. Ware. { Colin Campbell.
The Murray	{ John Goodman. { Travers Adamson.
Gipps Land	John King.

Circuit Courts for the first time appointed to be holden at Geelong and Portland, March 18, 1852.

The "Nelson" boarded in Hobson's Bay and 8,183 ozs. of gold stolen, April 2, 1852.

The local Government determined to have a guard-ship stationed in Hobson's Bay, April 9, 1852.

£160 per ton paid for cartage of stores to Bendigo, 100 miles from Melbourne, June 16, 1852.

The "Chusan" (first steamship from England) arrived in Hobson's Bay, July 28, 1852.

Hugh Culling Eardley Childers nominated Auditor General of Victoria in place of C. H. Ebden, resigned, October 26, 1852.

H. C. E. Childers appointed Collector of Customs in Victoria in place of Mr. Cassells, resigned, December 14, 1853.

Registration of Births, Deaths, and Marriages Bill passed, January 11, 1853.

The Western Market, Melbourne, destroyed by fire, January 23, 1853.

New Registration system first put into operation by Mr. Archer, July 1, 1853.

The private escort between McIvor and Castlemaine attacked and the gold stolen, July 20, 1853. The robbers of the McIvor escort captured, three weeks after the robbery, August 11, 1853. Trial and conviction of the McIvor escort robbers, September 18, 1853.

The 40th Regiment (Colonel Valiant) ordered to Bendigo gold-field, September 2, 1853.

The marines from H.M.S. "Electric" landed to do duty at the gaol and Government offices, September 3, 1853.

The 99th Regiment arrived at Melbourne from Van Diemen's Land, September 15, 1853.

First bills of mortality for Melbourne published by Mr. Archer, acting Registrar-General, October 24, 1853.

Great fire in Collins-street, Melbourne, October 28, 1853.

According to the latest computation, the area of Victoria is 88,198 square miles, or 56,446,720 acres. The whole continent of Australia is estimated to contain 2,983,264 square miles, and therefore Victoria occupies about a thirty-fourth part of its surface. 1879.

[See CONSTITUTION, COURTS, PARLIAMENT, &c., &c.]

VINES.

First grape vines planted in Australia, at Parramatta, November, 1791.

The first vineyard in Australia was at Camden Park, belonging to Mr. Macarthur, the first importer of sheep, 1816.

FALLON'S VINEYARD, ALBURY
Picturesque Atlas of Australia

The Agricultural Society lent its aid to encourage the growth of the vine, which began to draw general attention in 1823.

Mr. Skene Craig introduced the grape vine into Victoria, 1836. [His vineyard was planted in Collins-street West, Melbourne.]

Six German vine-dressers brought to N.S.W. by Sir Wm. Macarthur, 1839.

[See WINE.]

VOLUNTEER, AND OTHER FORCES.

The first Volunteers in Australia were the Sydney and Parramatta Loyal Associate Corps; two Volunteer Corps of fifty men each, formed in consequence of rumoured outbreak amongst the political prisoners, December, 1800.

The services of the Loyal Association at Sydney and Parramatta were partially dispensed with. Captain Thomas Rowley, late of New South Wales Corps, had charge of the Sydney; James Thomson of the Parramatta; and Wm. Balmain was commandant of both. October 22, 1802.

Volunteer movement commenced in Queensland, February 15, 1860.

Great Volunteer Review at Geelong, Victoria, April, 1870.

The Highland Brigade Rifle Corps formed at Wellington, N.Z., April, 1871.

Volunteer encampment, New South Wales, April 10, 1873.

Intercolonial Rifle Match between New South Wales, Victoria, and New Zealand, won by New South Wales, November 12, 1873.

Sydney Grammar School Cadet encampment at Botany, 1874.

[A lad named Paxton, son of Mr. Joseph Paxton, was accidentally drowned whilst bathing, causing great regret and the immediate break up of the Cadet camp, 1874.]

Volunteer encampment of three days, Campbellfield, New South Wales, May 24, 1874.

Sydney Grammar School Cadet encampment of one week held at Parramatta, N.S.W., 1876.

The Volunteer Force of South Australia organised, May 4, 1877.

Sydney Grammar School Cadet encampment of one week held at Bowenfels, near Hartley, New South Wales, October, 1877.

The Queensland Volunteers comprised the following :—A Commandant, Principal Medical Officer, Sergeant-Major, two Batteries of Artillery, one Company of Engineers, twelve Companies of Rifles, one Cadet Corps and Drill Instructors, consisting in all of 1,244 officers and men.   December 31, 1877.

Sydney Grammar School Cadet encampment of one week at Bathurst, October, 1878.

The N.S.W. estimates make provision for 1,356 officers and men for the land forces, torpedo corps 27, a naval brigade of 102, in all 1,385.   1878-9.

Of all kinds, including cavalry, artillery, engineer, and torpedo corps, and rifles, there were in Victoria on Dec. 31, 1877, 3,553, men officered by 167 commissioned officers and 209 sergeants, &c.   There were 7 troops of cavalry, 9 corps of artillery, 1 engineer corps, 1 torpedo and signal corps, and 12 corps of riflemen.   The official return of the Victorian Naval Forces gives the turret-ship *Cerberus*, with officers and crew numbering 110, and the *Nelson*, with a complement of 9 officers and a number of seamen, independent of a large staff of boys in training.   The Naval reserve numbered 225.   The *Cerberus* is an ironclad of 2,107 tons, engines of 250 horsepower, carrying in each of her turrets a ten-inch 400-pounder gun.   The *Nelson* was one of the old wooden line-of-battle ships of 2,736 tons, mounting 48 guns of various calibre, the largest being 2 seven-inch, throwing projectiles of 116 lbs., but she has been cut down, and now carries fewer but much heavier guns.   The expenditure during the year 1877 was £49,655 7s. 8d. for the land Forces, and £19,423 17s. 10d. for the naval Forces, a total of £69,079 5s. 6d.   In connection with the visit of Sir William Jervois, steps have been taken to fortify Port Phillip Heads, and to place the sea approaches to Melbourne in a state of defence.

DRILL OF THE N.S.W VOLUNTEER ARTILLERY AT PORT MACQUARIE, SYDNEY
The Illustrated Sydney News, 1855

W

WALLSEND, N. S. W. (incorporated) ; first aldermanic elections, April 21, 1874.

WAR VESSELS. [*See* SHIPPING.]

WARWICK, QUEENSLAND, proclaimed a municipality, May 25, 1861.

WATER SUPPLY.

Mr. Busby commenced operations for conveying water by tunnel from Botany Swamp to Sydney, September, 1827.

Mr. Blackbourn, City Surveyor of Melbourne, planned the Yan Yean water supply, and was first consulting engineer. 1850.

First sod of the Yan Yean waterworks turned by Governor La Trobe. December 20, 1853.

Yan Yean waterworks (under a Board of Government Commissioners), constructed by M. B. Jackson, finished in 1857.

The "Coliban" scheme of water supply completed November 23, 1877. [*See* SYDNEY, BRISBANE, MELBOURNE.]

WELLINGTON, N. S. W., a settlement under Lieutenant Percy Simpson, as commandant, at Wellington Valley, 80 miles from Bathurst; founded, February, 1823.

WELLINGTON N. Z.

Founded, January 22, 1848.

Governor Sir H. Robinson, arrived, March 27, 1879. [*See* NEW ZEALAND.]

WESTERN AUSTRALIA.

Major Lockyer left Sydney with a gang of prisoners to found a settlement on the west coast of Australia, 1825.

Expedition under Colonel Stewart, in the "Fly," sloop of war, and brigs "Dragon" and "Amity," left Sydney, with soldiers from the 3rd and 39th Regiments, and a number of prisoners, for King George's Sound and Western Port, to take possession of these places, 1826. [Arrangements were made for Major Lockyer's expedition party to remain at King George's Sound, and Captain Wright and Lieutenant Burchill to remain at Western Port. W. H. Howell was also attached to the expedition to Western Port. Major Lockyer formed a settlement called Albany, and in 1830 this military post was transferred to Swan River.]

Memorial presented to Sir George Murray, Principal Secretary of State for the Colonies,

THE FLOURISHING STATE OF THE SWAN RIVER THING, 1830
A cartoonist's view of a free settler family in Western Australia

PERTH
Picturesque Atlas of Australia

from Thomas Pell, Sir Francis Vincent, Mr. Edward W. H. Schenley, and Mr. T. Potter Macqueen, to colonise Swan River within four years, with 10,000 men, women, and children from England, Ireland, and Scotland, on condition the Home Government would give them grants of land to the value of £300,000, at 1s. 6d. per acre, November 4, 1828. [The proposal was assented to, but afterwards modified. On December 6, 1828, one million acres were promised conditionally. On January 28th, 1829, the project was abandoned.]

Captain James Stirling accepted 100,000 acres of land from the Home Government as a gratuity for his services in exploring West Australia. The site he chose was Isle Buache, December 26, 1828.

Mr. Thomas Peel's proposal to the English Government accepted January 28, 1829. [The Government granted him a tract of one million acres in West Australia on certain conditions : 250,000 acres were to be given him on his landing 400 persons at Swan River.]

Captain James Stirling, R.N., of H.M.S. "Challenger," appointed first Governor, and G. Brown, Esq., Colonial Secretary, January 13, 1829.

West Australia proclaimed a British colony at Freemantle, June 1, 1829.

First Settlement at Swan River, August, 1829.

A river called the Murray discovered 25 miles south of Freemantle, November, 1829.

There were in West Australia, 850 inhabitants, owning 525,000 acres of land; also, 70 horses, 204 cattle, 598 sheep, 176 pigs, according to Census of January 17, 1830.

P. Brown, Colonial Secretary, January 17, 1830.

WHALING AT TWOFOLD BAY
Public Library of New South Wales

Major Lockyer abandoned Albany and removed the settlement to Swan River, 1831.

The colony contained about 1,600 people, who had cultivated nearly 1,000 acres of land, and owned about 4,000 sheep, 1834.

Legislative Council of West Australia extended, January, 1839.

Governor John Hutt proclaimed at Perth, January 2, 1839.

First steamship arrived, December 4, 1845.

Sandalwood first exported, June 13, 1845.

Arrival at Freemantle of Right Rev. Henry Hutton Parry, D.D., new Church of England Bishop of Perth, May 20, 1877.

WHALING.

The "Britannia," Captain Thomas Melville, which had brought convicts to New South Wales, was the first ship to fish for whales on the Australian coast. She returned to Port Jackson from a successful cruise (having left October 25, 1791), November 10, 1791. [The "Britannia" was owned by Samuel Enderley and Sons.]

Frederick Henry Bay, the first whaling ground, Tasmania, 1816. [There were two brigs, owned respectively by Captain Fane and a negro named Hagard.]

The largest take in the shortest time was by the "Grecian," Captain Watson, who "tried out" 39 tuns of oil, captured in three days, 1816.

Bay whaling died out in Tasmania, 1847.

£2,600,000 is the estimated value of whale oil exported from New South Wales, from 1825 to 1879. Tasmania, value of oil exported, £1,200,000, to 1878.

NOTE.—A midshipman and three sailors of the "Sirius" were returning up Sydney harbour in a boat, when a whale rose so near them as to almost swamp them. The whale rose a second time, underneath their boat, capsizing it; by this accident three of the occupants were drowned, 1790.

WHARFS. First public wharf in Sydney, called King's Wharf, completed, 1813.

WIFE, SALE OF. An occurrence took place in the settlement of New South Wales which caused much indignation to the colonists. A man at Windsor led his wife, with her own consent, into the highway, with a halter round her neck, and offering her for sale, found a purchaser for her for £16. The man was brought to trial and sentenced to receive 50 lashes and to hard labour in irons for three months; the woman was sent to Newcastle, on the Coal River, as it was then called, and the purchaser lost his money. This had the effect of nipping in the bud this species of contempt of law and religion. 1811.

WILBERFORCE, N.S.W., named, Dec., 1810.

WILSON'S PROMONTORY, VICTORIA. Mr. William Wilson was an officer on board H.M.S. "Reliance," Captain Flinders, of which Mr. Bass was surgeon. After passing through Bass's Straits, so called after the doctor, they sighted the headland; and left the ship, in the cockboat, in charge of Mr. Wilson. As they got to the small beach on the north side, he jumped ashore first, the point where he landed being thenceforward called "Wilson's Promontory." [Mr. Wilson was the first who planted the Norfolk Island pine in New South Wales, viz., on the shore of the Parramatta River. His son was the first man who left New South Wales to import draught horses from England.] 1798.

WINDMILLS.

The first windmill in New South Wales erected, September, 1796.

The last of the Sydney Windmills was levelled to the ground. It was situated on the South Head Road, near the Waverley toll-bar. October 1, 1878.

WINDMILL NEAR FORT PHILLIP, SYDNEY
Picturesque Atlas of Australia

WINDSOR, NEW SOUTH WALES.

Formerly the Green Hills, received its present name, December 8, 1810.

A wooden bridge completed over the South Creek, 1810. [This bridge was the largest that had hitherto been constructed in the Colony.]

Foundation stone of St. Matthew's Church laid by Governor Macquarie, October 11, 1817. St. Matthew's Church opened, Dec. 8, 1822.

First Circuit Court opened, with much ceremony, by Mr. Justice Stephen, August 10, 1829.

First execution in Windsor of a man named Thomas Beylic, for breaking into the house of James M'Cooly, at Mulgrave, October 31, 1829.

Bridge over the Hawkesbury opened, August 20, 1874. [*See* FIRES.]

PART OF WINDSOR TOWN
An engraving of 1813, Rex Nan Kivell Collection

WINE.

Gregory Blaxland presented (whilst on a visit to England) with the "Gold Ceres Medal" by the Society of Arts, London, for wine, the produce of his vineyard in New South Wales, June 2, 1828.

Some of the produce of the Messrs. Macarthur's vineyard was sold at Calcutta, being the first appearance, as remarked by the local Press, of that new Australian export in that market, March, 1846. [According to official returns for the year 1845, there were 648 acres of vineyard throughout New South Wales, including thirty-seven acres for the Port Phillip district; the produce of wine amounted to 54,996 gallons, and of brandy to 1,433 gallons ; 214 gallons of wine had been manufactured during that year at Port Phillip.]

Mr. Blake introduced New South Wales wine into Victoria, 1860.

First real Champagne made in Australia exhibited at the manufacturer's, J. T. Fallon's, wine cellars, Albury, N.S.W., Nov. 28, 1875.

Messrs. Moody and Lumsdaine report :— "The natural wines of the northern portion of Victoria develop more alcohol than natural wines have been generally considered to be capable of doing, and range much higher in this respect than the British Customs standard of 26 per cent. of proof. The highest percentage was Albury wine, 34·1 per cent." Oct., 1875.

Quantity of wine manufactured in Australia, 1,868,355 gallons. 1878.

WOOL.

The first sample of wool was sent to England by Mr. Macarthur, in 1803. [It was inspected by a committee of manufacturers, then in London,

and it was so much approved of that Mr. Macarthur appeared before the Privy Council, and laid before it his plans rendering England independent of foreign countries for the supply of the best wools. The Privy Council adopted Mr. Macarthur's views, and with its encouragement he purchased from the merino flock of George the Third two ewes and three rams, with which he returned to New South Wales in 1806, appropriately calling the vessel in which the sheep were embarked, the "Argo." Such was the origin of the rapidly increasing flocks of Australia, whose wool has brought as high as 10s. 4d. per lb. in the London market, and "which for fineness and strength is pronounced by the best judges to be equal to any Saxon or Spanish wool imported into Britain." A grant of 5,000 (afterwards increased to 10,000) acres of land was given to Mr. Macarthur by the Privy Council, as an encouragement to him to persevere in the accomplishment of his plans. The land selected by him is on the banks of the Nepean (Cowpasture) River, on which a herd of wild cattle had been found grazing a few years previously, and it was named *Camden* in honour of Lord Camden, one of the Lords of the Privy Council.]

524lbs. of wool exported from the Colony, 1807.

A small quantity of wool sent from Tasmania to England by Mr. Henry Hopkins ; did not pay its freight. 1819.

79,299lbs. of wool shipped to England, 1819.

112,616 lbs. exported, 1820. [Highest price ever obtained for Australian wool, 1 bale sold for 10s. 4d. per lb., belonging to Mr. John Macarthur.]

Mr. Macarthur presented with two large gold medals by H.R.H. the Duke of Sussex at a large meeting of the Society of Arts, for importing into England wool, the produce of his flocks in the Colony, equal to the finest Saxony, 1822.

First wool-ship sailed from Moreton Bay direct to London, February 16, 1851.

First cargo of wool sent down the Murray by steamer, October 1, 1853.

WRECKS AND SHIPPING DISASTERS.

The "Batavia," frigate, Francis Pelsart captain, wrecked on the western coast of New Holland, 200 miles north of Swan River, at a place known as Houtman's Abrolhos, in latitude 28 deg. south, June 4, 1629. [The "Batavia" was one of the Dutch fleet of eleven sail that left to take possession of New Holland. She had on board a crew of about 200 men, and 100 passengers—men, women, and children. The captain, after the wreck, sailed to Batavia for assistance. Whilst absent, the supercargo, Jerom Cornelis, assumed command of the shipwrecked people, and, with a band of mutineers, murdered 125 of them; and when Pelsart returned in the frigate "Saardam," Cornelis had formed a scheme to seize this vessel and murder the captain. Through timely warning to Pelsart, given by one Mr. Weybuthaps and his men, on his return, the conspiracy failed, the mutineers were killed or captured and executed; and after recovering some of the chests of silver from the wrecked vessel, the remainder of the crew sailed for Java at the end of September, where they arrived safely. Numerous attempts have since been made (one at least within the past fifty years) to recover a portion of the "vast quantity of silver" lost in the "Batavia."]

THE MASSACRE OF THE CREW AND PASSENGERS OF THE "BATAVIA"
A & R Archives

Wreck of the Dutch ship "Vergulde Drake" (Golden Drake), Captain Pieter Alberts, on the coast of Western Australia, April 28, 1656. [The ship had on board 78,600 gueldens. Of 195 persons on board, 115 were drowned, and 75 reached the shore; with the exception of seven of these latter, who reached Batavia in a boat, the others were never afterwards heard of, and though several attempts were made the money was never recovered.]

Wreck of the "Zeawick," near a group of islands now called Elvart's Group, March 5, 1727.

"Falmouth," man-of-war, of fifty guns, on her voyage home, ran aground on a mudbank on the coast of Batavia, 1762. [She was not much injured, but could not be got off. After a time some of her officers and crew quitted her in the vessel's launch, hoping to reach England, but were never again heard of. The remainder stayed by the ship for eight years before they were afforded an opportunity of being taken home. Five years after the wreck, Captain Wallis, of H.M.S. "Dolphin," discovered them, but to their entreaties to be taken away, told them they were in charge of the wreck, which was then rotting to pieces, and consequently must await orders from home, and for upwards of two years more these poor fellows, true to their duty, remained by the rotting hull of their ship, till the Dutch Government interfered, and sent them home in a Dutch ship.]

The "Sirius," driven on the rocks at Norfolk Island, where she was irrecoverably lost, March 19, 1790.

The "Sydney Cove," whilst on a voyage from India to New South Wales, was wrecked at Furneaux Island, in Bass's Strait, February, 1797. [Mr. Clarke, the supercargo, the chief mate, and fifteen men endeavoured to reach Sydney in the launch, but were driven on shore somewhere to the south of Cape Howe, and now a part of the coast of Victoria. These people were probably the first Europeans to land on Victorian shores.]

The "Cato" wrecked on the Barrier Reef, Aug. 17, 1803. [The "Cato" was bound for England, sailing in company with the "Porpoise," Captain Flinders. Both vessels were wrecked; Flinders made his way back to Sydney, and subsequently rescued his eighty companions, who were living on the Reef.]

The colonial cutter "Nancy" lost, April 18, 1805.

Governor King's private colonial schooner wrecked, April 22, 1806.

The "Britannia Goodspeed" wrecked near Middleton Shoals, August 15, 1806. Two boats, with the captain, arrived in "Cygnet," September 13. One boat-load perished.

"Contest," colonial schooner, wrecked at Port Stephens, February 28, 1807.

The brig "Fox" caught fire at Campbell's Wharf, now the premises of the A.S.N. Company, Sydney. She was scuttled and saved with much damage. July 20, 1808.

The "Dundee," Capt. Cummings, from India, lost at Hunter River, August 15, 1808.

The "Eliza," colonial vessel, belonging to Mr. Joseph Underwood, lost, July 14, 1811.

The colonial vessels "Sally" and "Boyd" wrecked, July 16, 1812.

The "Mercury," owned by Mrs. Mary Reilly, and "Endeavour," owned by Mr. Kable, junr., colonial schooners, lost at Shoalhaven, March, 1813.

News received in Sydney by the ship "Eliza" of the loss of the ship "Mangalore," Capt. Earl. She had sailed from India for Port Jackson, and founded off the coast of Sumatra. July, 1813.

Ten persons arrived by the "Governor Bligh" from an island about a mile and a half distant from the mainland of New Zealand, left there by the brig "Active." Capt Baden, in February, 1809. December 23, 1813. The vessel has never since been heard of.

The ship "Three B's," having on board thirty casks of powder, took fire and burnt to the water's edge in Sydney Harbour, May 20, 1814. [Fourteen pieces of cannon went off, to the great danger of the townspeople. Fortunately the wind shifted and drifted the ship to the North Shore.]

The "Woodlark," Capt. Leary, from Sydney to the Cape of Good Hope, wrecked in Torres Straits, six persons being drowned, April 18, 1828.

The "Herald" wrecked at Hokianga, New Zealand, May 4, 1828.

The "Enterprise," schooner, wrecked at Hokianga, New Zealand; all on board drowned. May 5, 1828.

The "Dove" wrecked at Port Stephens; seven lives lost. June 5, 1828.

The brig "Percenean," of Sydney, lost at Campbell's Island; crew saved. October, 1828.

Wreck of the "Columbine," on her voyage from England to Australia, on the coast of Africa, May, 1829. [She had on board large supplies of religious books, pamphlets, and tracts, belonging to the London Wesleyan Missionary Society, for the use of the missionaries in the Australian Colonies, New Zealand, and Tonga.]

The schooner "Hunter," of Sydney, lost at Entry Bay
Island, Cook's Straits ; crew saved. June, 1829.
The sloop "Fly" lost outside Sydney Heads, and three
persons drowned ; two saved. October, 1829.
The "Mermaid" colonial government cutter, Captain
Samuel Nolbrow, left Sydney for Raffles Bay, but on
entering Torres Straits she got on shore and was lost,
October, 1829. [All on board were saved upon a rock.
In three days the "Swifture," Captain Johnson,
which sailed from Tasmania, hove in sight, and took
on board Captain Nolbrow and his crew, but in a few
days she got on shore and was wrecked. Two days
afterwards the "Governor Ready," also from Tasmania,
April 2, passing within sight, took the shipwrecked
people belonging to the "Mermaid" and "Swifture"
on board, but was itself wrecked, May 18, at 3 p.m.,
but all the people were saved by taking refuge in the
long-boats. The ship "Comet," also from Tasmania,
soon afterwards took the whole of the collected crews
of the lost ships "Mermaid," "Swifture," and
"Governor Ready" on board, but was herself wrecked ;
all hands were, however, saved. At last the "Jupiter,"
from Tasmania, came in sight, and taking all on
board, steered for Port Raffles, at the entrance to
whch harbour she got on shore, and received so much
damage that it may be said she was also wrecked.]
Wreck of the "Marquis of Anglesea," from London, at
Swan River, W.A., November, 1829.
The "Amphitrite," with female convicts to N.S.W., lost
on Boulogne Sands ; out of 131 persons, only three
were saved. August 30, 1833.
At the King's (Queen's) Wharf, a vessel named the Ann
Jamieson, whilst discharging her cargo, suddenly blew
up, with an awful explosion, when she was burnt to
the water's edge and sunk, eight lives being lost,
November 30, 1833.
"Lady Munro," from Calcutta to Sydney ; of ninety
persons on board, not more than twenty were saved.
January 9, 1834.
The "Charles Eaton," from Sydney, wrecked on
detached reef, Torres Straits, August 15, 1834.
The ship "Edward Lombe," wrecked at Middle Head,
Sydney, August 25, 1834. [The vessel was from London, and the wreck occurred at night. Twelve persons,
including the captain, first and second mates, and
surgeon, were lost, and seventeen, including one lady,
were saved.]
The convict ship "George III." wrecked in D'Entrecasteaux's Channel, April, 1835. [There were 208 male
prisoners on board, of whom 120 lost their lives.
Several shots were fired amongst the prisoners, to
prevent them coming on deck.]
The "Enchantress," Captain Roxburgh, wrecked in
D'Entrecasteaux Channel ; one passenger and all the
crew, excepting the captain, chief officer, and surgeon,
were lost. June 17, 1835.
The "Hive," with prisoners from England, wrecked at
Jervis Bay, 1835.
The "Neva" wrecked on King's Island, Bass's Straits ;
300 lives lost. 1835.
The brig "Stirling Castle" wrecked on Eliza Reef, on the
northern coast, May 21, 1836. Mrs. Frazer, wife of
the master, and six of the crew were saved, but were
detained by the natives for three months, enduring all
the time the most dreadful sufferings. They were
rescued by Lieutenant Atto and a party from Moreton
Bay, and brought on to Sydney by the revenue cutter
"Prince George."
The "Ceres," colonial steamer, wrecked near Bungaree
North, August 20, 1836.
The "Gellibrand and Hessie" lost in Port Phillip, December 6, 1837.
The ship "Lucretia" destroyed by fire in Sydney harbour, June 23, 1839.
The steamer "King William" wrecked at Newcastle,
N.S.W., July 4, 1839.
The steamer "Clonmel," Captain Tollervey, trading between Sydney and Melbourne, totally wrecked at
Corner Inlet, in the district of Port Phillip, January 3,
1841. [She was 598 tons burden, had lately arrived
from England, and was intended for the Melbourne
trade. The wreck of this vessel led to the discovery of a
splendid grazing country adjacent to the scene of the
disaster, which was speedily occupied. She had 75 passengers on board, all saved. A passenger, Mr. W. C.

Robinson, of the Union Bank, had £3,000 in notes in his
charge, and on the occasion they were stolen or lost.]
The "Rebecca" lost on King's Island, Bass's Strait ; one
life lost. 1843.
The emigrant vessel the "Cataraqui," bound from
Liverpool to Port Phillip, wrecked off King's Island, in
Bass's Straits, when 414 lives were lost and 9 saved.
August 4, 1845.
The "Isabella" wrecked off King's Island, Bass's
Straits ; no lives lost. 1845.
The cutter "Domain" wrecked at Wilson's Promontory,
fourteen lives lost. April 11, 1846.
The steamer "Sovereign" wrecked on the voyage from
Moreton Bay to Sydney, and a large number of lives
lost, some of the chief colonists being amongst the
number drowned. March 11, 1847.
The "Thetis," schooner, wrecked on Point Nepean ; four
lives lost. May 26, 1848.
The "Sophia," brig, from Hobart Town, wrecked on
Point Nepean, May 31, 1848.
The "Birkenhead" sunk off Point Danger ; 438 lives
lost. February 25, 1852.
The "Earl of Cumberland" (435 passengers) wrecked on
Barwon Heads, June 18, 1852.
The "Sacramento" wrecked on Point Lonsdale, April
26, 1853.
Wreck of the "Schomberg," April 26, 1853.
The "Rebecca" lost on west coast of Van Diemen's
Land ; Captain Shephard and many others lost. April
29, 1853.
"Bourneuf," Australian emigrant ship, driven on shore
on the Barra Islands, on west coast of Scotland ; Cap-
lain Bibby and six lives lost. August 3, 1853.
The ship "Dalhousie," 800 tons (Captain Butterworth),
which left London for Sydney on October 13 with forty-
eight crew and twelve passengers, together with a cargo
valued at £100,000, wrecked westward of Dungeness, in
the English Channel ; all on board but one perished.
October 19, 1853.
The "Monumental City," an American steamer, wrecked
near Gabo Island, whilst on her passage from Sydney
to Melbourne, when thirty lives were lost. Charles
Plommer, by swimming ashore with a rope, saved nine
persons. 1853.
The "City of Melbourne" wrecked off King's Island,
Bass's Straits ; no lives lost. 1853.
The "Eclipse," brig, wrecked on the Richmond River
bar, January 8, 1854.
The "Chatham," brig, wrecked on Penhryn's Island,
January, 1854.

The "Sir Henry Hardinge," from Sydney for Singapore,

THE "TORCH" RESCUING PASSENGERS FROM THE
"NINGPO"
The Illustrated Sydney News, 1855

totally wrecked near Smoky Cape; all hands saved. June 20, 1854.

The "Ningpo" wrecked, and the survivors rescued by H.M.S. "Torch." 1854.

The "Brahmin" wrecked on King's Island, Bass's Straits; no lives lost, 1854.

The "Waterwitch" wrecked on King's Island, Bass's Straits, no lives lost. 1854.

The "West Wind" burnt in Hobson's Bay, February, 27, 1854. [The captain, William Joy South, tried, but acquitted on the charge of setting the vessel on fire.]

The "Robert Sayers" destroyed by fire in Darling Harbour, Port Jackson, 1854.

The "Maypole" wrecked on King's Island, Bass's Straits; three lives lost. 1855.

The "Whistler" wrecked on King's Island, Bass's Straits; no lives lost. 1855.

The "Sea Belle" left Rockhampton, with Mr. Norman Leith as a passenger; after calling and leaving Gladstone was never heard of. March 7, 1857.

The "Dunbar," Captain Green, from London, wrecked at the Gap, near South Head, Sydney. August 20-21, 1857. [The night was dark, and a heavy gale from S.E. was blowing; it was supposed the captain mistook the Gap (only a short distance from the Heads) for the entrance to the port. Only one man, Johnson, escaped to tell the people of the dreadful occurrence. The total number of persons on board was 120; many of the passengers were families and individuals returning to the Colony. A number of bodies were recovered, and received a public funeral. On that day business was suspended; the ships in harbour wore their flags at half-mast, and the obsequies were followed by many thousand citizens. Johnson, the survivor, was on the rocks for thirty hours before he could communicate the intelligence of the disaster. The cargo was valued at £22,000.]

The "Lady Bird" s. ran into the "Champion" s., off Cape Otway; the "Champion" sinking in five or six minutes after the collision. August, 1857.

The "Catherine Adamson" from London, wrecked near the Inner North Head; twenty-one lives lost. October 23, 1857.

The barque "Magda," Captain Osterbeerg, from Geelong to Batavia, wrecked on Melville Island, near Port Essington, June 1, 1858. [Nine men went away in a boat with four blacks, near Port Essington, and were not heard of afterwards. The captain and remainder of the crew were picked up by the "Shamrock" schooner, Captain Pimmels, from Timor, and brought to Sydney in the latter part of July.]

Wreck of "Pomona," emigrant ship, April 20, 1859.

The s.s. "Admella," Captain McEven, on a voyage between Adelaide and Melbourne, wrecked off Cape Northumberland, August 6, 1859. [Out of nearly a hundred people, twenty-four were rescued after a week's suffering.]

The "Royal Charter," s. s., Captain Taylor, from Australia, totally wrecked off Moefra, on the Anglesea coast. 446 lives lost. Night of Oct. 25 and 26, 1859. [The vessel contained gold valued between £700,000 and £800,000, much of which has been recovered.]

The "Melbourne" s.s. wrecked, November 10, 1859.

The "Blenvie Castle" sailed from London Docks for Adelaide, lost in the Channel, and all on board, 57 persons. Last seen on December 25, 1859.

The "Firefly" wrecked whilst going north to form a depot on the Albert River, 1860. [On board was Mr. Wm. Landsborough, in charge of a party who set out in search of Burke and Wills.]

The "Wanderer" wrecked at Cape Barren, July 17, 1861.

The "Ocean Chief," Captain T. Brown, set fire to and destroyed at Bluff Harbour, Invercargill, N.Z., January 23, 1862.

Steamer "City of Sydney" wrecked near Green Cape, November 5, 1862.

H.M.S. "Orpheus," steamer, new vessel, 1,700 tons, Commander Burnett, wrecked on Manakau bar, west coast of New Zealand. 70 persons saved: about 190 souls perished. February 7, 1863.

The "Princeza," brig, 141 tons, wrecked on South entrance to Moreton Bay, March 15, 1863.

The "Everton," 904 tons, with railway plant, driven ashore at Moreton Island, Queensland, and became total wreck, March 19, 1863.

The "Acacia," barque, of 218 tons burthen, wrecked on the south heads of Hokianga, N.Z., July 29, 1863.

The "Antagonist," with horses to the value of £1,000, and stores £2,500, wrecked on Green Islet Reef, May 14, 1863.

The "Mimosa," steamer, belonging to the I.S.N. Co., totally lost on her voyage from Merimbula to Sydney, October 15, 1863. [She was uninsured, and valued at £11,000; two lives were lost.]

The "T. S. Mort," steamer, timber laden, abandoned water-logged on her voyage from New Zealand, July, 1863.

The "Maori," barque, 288 tons burthen, laden with coals, sprang a leak and went down off Western Port, September 10, 1863.

The "Earl of Windsor," 738 tons, from Otago for Welshpool, totally lost on the middle bank of Corner Inlet; all hands saved. October 12, 1863.

The "Sarah Dent," ketch, from Newcastle to Port Stephens, capsized by a squall near Cabbage Tree Island, going down with all hands (5), October 17, 1863.

The "Sporting Lass," whaling brig, of Sydney, wrecked on reefs near New Caledonia, November 4, 1863. [All the boats reached Brisbane, except one with seven men on board; never afterwards heard of.]

The "Emma Colvin," of London, 560 tons, from Sydney to New Caledonia, with 202 head of cattle, totally lost 50 miles S.E. of Port de France; all hands saved. November 12, 1863.

The "Farway," 195 tons, from Maryborough for Sydney, lost on a reef near Lady Elliott's Island; three hands out of nine lost. February 9, 1864.

The "Augusta," steamer, from Lyttelton, N.Z., to Sydney, wrecked on Cave Island, N.Z.; all hands saved. February 10, 1864.

The "All Serene," Australian ship, from Vancouver's Island, capsized in heavy storm; twenty-one hands out of thirty-eight lost. February 21, 1864. [The survivors suffered much until they reached the Fiji Islands in a punt.]

The "Phœbe Dunbar" burnt in Newcastle harbour, March 7, 1864.

The schooner "Zone" lost whilst attempting to enter Newcastle harbour. The mate of the "Zone" and three of the crew of the lifeboat (which upset) were lost. March 19, 1864.

The "Mynora," steamer (I.S.N. Co.), from Moruya to Sydney, ran on shore off George's Head, and became a total wreck; all hands saved. April 6, 1864.

The "Panama," barque, 414 tons burthen, totally wrecked on the north of Frazer's Island; one hand out of twenty lost. March 18, 1864.

The "Viceroy," schooner, Melbourne, 150 tons, run down by the Wonga Wonga, steamer, April 6, 1864. [Value, £1,000.]

The "Macleay Packet," schooner, of Sydney, left Sydney for Richmond River, with ten hands on board, and never arrived, April 30, 1864.

The "Rainbow," steamer (C. & R. R. S. N. Co.), driven on shore during a gale in Seal Rock Bay, June 2, 1864. [Value, £2,000. Seven hands out of sixteen were lost.]

The "Waratah," schooner, of Sydney, 109 tons, with seven hands on board, vessel and cargo being worth £1,000, left Newcastle for Sydney, but never arrived, June 2, 1864.

The "Tyflee," barque, of Sydney, 271 tons, failed in getting in to Port Stephens, and became a total wreck; seven hands out of ten lost; value of vessel and cargo, £1800. August 30, 1864.

The "New Moon," steamer, of Sydney, with a cargo to the value of £2,000, from the Macleay, was driven on shore near Port Stephens, and eleven out of twelve hands lost, October 1, 1864.

The "Breadalbane," barque, 215 tons, driven from her anchors and wrecked near Bellambi, N.S.W., October 1, 1864.

The "Guiding Star," schooner, left Manning for Sydney with a crew of five hands, but never arrived, October 1, 1864.

The "Circassian," schooner, ran on shore, in thick weather, near Twofold Bay; three out of seven hands lost; value £1,700. October 6, 1864.

The "William Buchanan," barque, of Melbourne, struck

on an unknown rock near the Clarence Heads ; value £3,080. December 8, 1864.

The " Star of Australia," steamer (A.S.N. Co.), left Sydney with seventeen hands on board for Rockhampton ; fate never known ; insured for £6,000. January 24, 1865.

The " Boomerang," schooner, left Newcastle with five hands for the Clarence River, but never arrived. January 12, 1865.

The " Blackall," clipper ship, Captain Yule, with 2,041 bales of wool, &c., bound from Brisbane to London, totally destroyed by fire, April 19, 1865.

The " City of Dunedin," steamer, lost off Taranaki, N.Z., May 20, 1865.

The " Julia Heyne," 318 tons, barque, of Melbourne, founded 20 miles off Cape St. George, May 20, 1865.

The " Edward," cutter, of Sydney, left Newcastle for Sydney with four hands on board, but never arrived, June 30, 1865.

The " Lady Young," barque, 418 tons, lost near Rabbit Island, July 14, 1865.

The " Duncan Dunbar " wrecked on a reef at Las Rocas, South American coast ; no lives lost. October 7, 1865.

The " London," steamer, on her way to Melbourne, foundered in the Bay of Biscay. About 220 persons perished, including Captain Martin, Dr. Woolley, Principal of the University of Sydney, G. V. Brooke, the tragedian, and many others. January 11, 1865.

The " Arrow," wrecked on King's Island, Bass's Straits ; no lives lost. 1865.

" Victor," brig, 227 tons, lost on rocks outside Newcastle harbour, March 19, 1866.

" Urara," steamer, 241 tons (C. & R.R.S.N. Co.), value £14,000, lost on the Clarence River bar in fine weather, May 4, 1866.

The " Ellen Simpson," barque, of Melbourne, 310 tons, lost in gale off Cape Howe ; nine out of eleven hands lost. May 28, 1866.

The " General Grant," on a voyage from Melbourne to London, wrecked off Auckland Isles ; only thirteen out of 100 saved. May, 1866.

The " Slippery Charlie " stranded at the entrance of the Nambuccra River ; only one hand out of thirteen saved. July 12, 1866.

The "Eclipse," schooner, with a cargo of cattle, foundered off the old bar, Manning River ; all hands (8) perished. July 12, 1866.

The " Mary and Rose" beached near entrance to Port Stephens ; five out of seven lost. July 12, 1866.

The " Corio," steamer, of Sydney (insured for £7,500), with a crew of ten hands, supposed to have foundered during a gale, July 12, 1866.

The " Cawarra," steamer, 438 tons, Captain Chatfield, was wrecked on the Oyster Bank at the entrance to Newcastle ; fifty-nine people drowned ; only one man, Frederick W. Hedges, was saved, and he was rescued by the only survivor (Johnson) of the " Dunbar " ; total value lost, £21,850. July 12, 1866.

The " Arthur," ketch, of Sydney, foundered on entering Newcastle Heads ; all hands (5) lost. July 13, 1866.

The " Roderich Dhu," schooner, of Sydney ; the " Lydia," ketch, of Sydney ; the " Carnation," schooner, of Sydney ; the " Friends," schooner, of Melbourne,—all wrecked July 13, 1866.

The " Janet," ketch, of Sydney, supposed to have foundered during a gale ; all hands (4) lost. July 13, 1866.

The " Woodpecker," schooner, lost five miles north of Port Macquarie ; one sailor drowned. July 13, 1866.

The " Sea Gull," schooner, of Sydney, foundered off Newcastle ; all hands (5) lost. July 13, 1866.

The " William Watson," barque, 384 tons, stranded on North beach endeavouring to make Newcastle harbour ; two out of ten hands lost. July 13, 1866.

The " Tiger," schooner, Sydney, stranded at Bulli during gale ; 3 out of 6 hands lost. July 13, 1866.

The " Eagle," schooner, 125 tons, missed stays, went ashore, breaking up at North Head, Port Jackson, July 30, 1866.

The " Result " burnt in Hobson's Bay, October 11, 1866.

The " Adolphus," brigantine, drifted on the rocks during a light wind at Wollongong, and became a total wreck, November 29, 1866.

The " Netherby " wreked on King's Island, Bass's Straits ; no lives lost. 1866.

The " Albion," schooner, of Sydney, 170 tons, lost on a reef near the south head of Port Hacking ; five lost out of seven hands. March 30, 1867.

The " Matador," barque, of Melbourne, 249 tons, wrecked in a S.E. gale at Bulli, September 7, 1867.

The " Telegraph," steamer, Sydney (A.S.N. Co.), struck on rock near Camden Head, October 9, 1867. Ship value, £12,000 ; cargo, £3,000 ; no lives lost.

The " Victoria," schooner, of Auckland, supposed to have foundered between Sydney and Macleay River, with seven hands on board, October 25, 1867.

The " Europe," wrecked on King's Island, Bass's Straits ; no lives lost. 1867.

The " Wave," brig, 195 tons, with coals, stranded three miles north of Terrigal, during S.E. gale ; all hands (9) lost. February 8, 1868.

The " Cheetah," schooner, 120 tons ; the " Raven," schooner, 116 tons ; and the " Abbey," schooner, 90 tons,—all went on shore during a S.E. gale, within three miles of Crowdy Head ; all hands (7) belonging to the " Cheetah " were lost. February 15, 1868.

The " General Wool," barque, of Sydney, 171 tons, supposed to have foundered with all hands (7), February 15, 1868.

The " Gratia," brig, 186 tons, foundered five miles north of Cape Hawk ; all hands (7) lost. February 15, 1868.

The " Barwon," schooner, 56 tons, foundered with all hands (5) during the easterly gale, February 15, 1868.

The " Woodlark," brig, 237 tons, lost in S.E. gale, eight miles from Seal Rocks, February 16, 1868.

The " Kellermont," brigantine, 200 tons, wrecked in S.E. gale, in Broken Bay, February 16, 1868.

The " Chelydra," barque, of Swansea, 300 tons, ran on shore quarter of a mile from Port Stephens during S E. gale ; one life lost. February 16, 1868.

The " Esperanza," brig, of Melbourne, foundered during S.E. gale to the leeward of Bird Island ; ten out of eleven hands on board were lost. February 16, 1868.

The " Helen S. Page," 217 tons, lost in the Bight of Newcastle during easterly gale, March 30, 1868.

The " Black Swan," steamer, became a total wreck on the bar of Manning River, during moderate weather, June 4, 1868.

The s.s. " Taranaki " sunk in Tory Channel, August 19, 1868.

The " Annie D " schooner, left Sydney for Richmond River, and never afterwards heard of, August 27, 1868.

The " Chippewa." ketch, struck on a rock at Crookhaven Heads, and went down with all hands (4), November 20, 1868.

The " Traveller," ketch, went on shore at Brisbane Water ; all hands (3) lost. November 20, 1868.

The " Elizabeth," schooner, upset in squall near Bulli ; all hands (5) lost. November 24, 1868.

The " Omagh " wrecked on King's Island, Bass's Straits ; no lives lost. 1868.

The " Mary Ann " wrecked on King's Island, Bass's Straits ; no lives lost. 1868.

The " Ths. Formosa," from Glasgow, wrecked outside Port Phillip Heads, February 8, 1869.

The " Christopher George," schooner, foundered off Wollongong in S.E. gale ; all hands (5) lost. February 23, 1869.

The " Jessie," schooner, Sydney, foundered off Newcastle in S.E. gale ; three hands lost. May 9, 1869.

The " Nancy," schooner, Newcastle, foundered off Newcastle in S.E. gale ; all hands (6) lost. May 9, 1869.

The " Don Juan," schooner, Sydney, foundered off Newcastle in S.E. gale ; all hands (6) lost. May 9, 1869.

The " Eagleton," schooner, Sydney, foundered eight miles south of Hannah Bay in S.E. gale ; all hands (6) lost. May 9, 1869.

The " Martha," schooner, Sydney, foundered at sea during S.E. gale ; all hands (6) lost. May 9, 1869.

The " Secret," schooner, dragged her anchors and went ashore in Providence Bay during S.E. gale ; one hand lost. May 9, 1869.

The " Burnett," brig, Sydney, 137 tons, foundered in the bight at Newcastle, about a mile from lighthouse, during S.E. gale ; all hands (7) lost. May 9, 1869.

The ship " John Duthie " burnt in Sydney Harbour, December 1, 1869.

The " Prince Patrick," schooner, 150 tons, came into collision with the brig " Drover " inside the North

Head, Port Jackson, drifted on the rocks, and became a total wreck, during a calm, December 17, 1869.

The "Wainui," sunk, Port Chalmers, N.Z., January 22, 1870.

The "Camden," barque, 235 tons, insured for £3,500, lost on a reef to the south of Ulladulla. Jan. 30, 1870.

The "Trio," steamer, Sydney, 120 tons, drifted ashore during N.E. gale at Seal Rock Bay, March 5, 1870.

The "Rangoon," barque, 374 tons, driven ashore four miles N. of Kiama during heavy gale, March 22, 1870.

The "Perseverance," steamer, driven on to the rocks at Point Danger, April 14, 1870.

The "Walter Hood," ship, of Aberdeen, 918 tons, wrecked between Ulladulla and Jervis Bay; eleven lives lost. April 27, 1870

The "Storm Bird," schooner, Sydney, supposed to have foundered during S.E. gale; all hands (7) lost. May 6, 1870.

The "Amity," ketch, Sydney, supposed to have met the same fate, at the same time, off the Manning River; all hands (5) lost. May 6, 1870.

The "Francis George," schooner, supposed to have met similar fate, on same day, near the Brunswick River; all hands (6) lost. May 6, 1870.

The "Harbech Castle," Captain Davis, with a crew of twenty-three men, left Melbourne for Newcastle, and never afterwards heard of, June 25, 1870.

The barque "Dunkeld" left Newcastle bound south, and has never since been heard of, June, 1870.

The "Aurifera," barque, of Melbourne, 436 tons, foundered at sea, 300 miles from Lord Howe's Island, July 24, 1870.

The "Dashing Wave," on a voyage from Foochoo to Sydney, with a cargo of tea, ran on a reef, August 31, 1870. [The crew took to the boats, in which they were thirty-one days, and, with but scant subsistence, reached Strong's Island, October 1.]

The "Summer Cloud," barque, 335 tons, ran ashore in Wreck Bay, December 5, 1870.

The "Deva," brig, 244 tons, abandoned at sea, 35 miles east of Port Macquarie, December 5, 1870.

The "Rialto," barque, 303 tons, wrecked on breakwater at Newcastle during a S.E. gale, December 5, 1870.

The "Freak," brig, from Gulf of Carpentaria, for Sydney, wrecked in Providential Channel; twelve hands (South Sea Islanders) lost. December, 1870.

The "Caroline," brig, foundered at sea, 50 miles from Sydney, on a voyage from Sydney to Hokianga; one man lost. January 28, 1871.

The steamer "Queen of the Thames," Captain Macdonald, which left Melbourne for London, February 18, wrecked near Cape Agulhas, about 200 miles from Cape Town, four persons drowned, March 18, 1871. [The captain was censured.]

The "Dayspring," barque, 560 tons, foundered 70 miles west of Newcastle; crew saved by the "Wonga Wonga." March, 1871.

The "Helen," brigantine, 165 tons, wrecked on the North Spit, Richmond River, April 12, 1871.

The "Auckland," steamer, from Melbourne to Sydney, lost on the Ninety-mile Beach, May 25, 1871.

Collision on the N.S.W. coast between the "Nevada" and the "A. H. Badger," October 15, 1871.

The ship "Loch Leven," Captain Crowne, from Geelong, Victoria, for London, wrecked, October 24, 1871. [Her cargo consisted of wool, leather, and copper; all valued at £170,000.]

The "Rangoon," Peninsula and Oriental steamer, valued at £78,000, wrecked on Kadir Rocks, off Point de Galle; cargo lost, but no lives. November 2, 1871.

The ship "Sussex," from Plymouth to Melbourne, wrecked at Barwon Heads, Victoria; a boat crew of six persons lost their lives. December 31, 1871.

The "Ocean Bride" wrecked on King's Island, Bass's Straits; no lives lost. 1871.

The "Loch Leven" wrecked on King's Island, Bass's Straits; one life lost. 1871.

The "Waimea," steamer, 156 tons, wrecked on the Richmond Bar, January 16, 1872.

The "Indus," barque, 364 tons, sprung a leak, on a voyage from Newcastle to Dunedin, and went down 100 miles off the Dromedary; crew saved in boats. February 13, 1872. [Four sailors who had refused to proceed to sea in her prior to her departure, alleging she was unsea-

worthy, were sentenced each to eight weeks' imprisonment in Maitland Gaol.]

The "Maria," with New Guinea expedition, wrecked on the Barrier Reef, February 26, 1872.

The "Megæra," Government iron screw steamer, sailed, with about 400 persons on board, for Australia, February 7, 1871; sprung a leak, June 8, when it was discovered that her bottom was nearly worn away by corrosion. She was beached on St. Paul's Island, in the Indian Ocean, June 16; huts were erected, and the crew settled and stores landed; Lieutenant Jones was taken on board a Dutch vessel, July 16; the "Oberon" brought provisions, August 26; the crew was carried off during a storm by the "Malacca," the stores being left behind, September 3, 1871. [This vessel was reported unfit for service in 1867. Captain Thrupp was tried, and acquitted of blame, November 17; Sir Spencer Robinson and various Admiralty officials were censured by a Government Commission, March 6, 1872.]

The "Bengal," barque, 428 tons, sprung a leak and foundered latitude 30° 20′ S., longitude 156 E.; crew saved by passing vessel. April 5, 1872.

The steamer "Examiner" wrecked at Clarence Heads, N.S.W., May 7, 1872.

The "Young Australia" wrecked on Moreton Island, June 1, 1872.

Steamer "Paterson" foundered in the Port of Newcastle, N.S.W., June 6, 1872.

The "Clarence," steamer (C. & R.R.S.N. Co.), ran ashore in fog near Bald Hill, June 30, 1872. [Value of cargo, £12,000.]

The "Saxonia," s., foundered near Newcastle, N.S.W., July 17, 1872; successfully raised, August 20, 1872.

The "Restless," schooner, 258 tons, struck by lightning and sprung a leak during a hurricane, near Solitary Islands, August 24, 1872.

The "Providence," steamer, blown to pieces by the boilers bursting; four lives lost; on the Murray River. November 9, 1872.

The "Katherow" wrecked on King's Island, Bass's Straits; no lives lost. 1872.

The "Tamar," steamer, 130 tons, sprung a leak, and was beached, to save life, at Norah Point, January 11, 1873.

The "Matilda," schooner, supposed to have foundered between the Macleay River and Sydney during S.E. gale, with all hands (7), January 11, 1873.

The "Polly Hopkins," supposed to have foundered between Newcastle and Sydney during S.E. gale, with all hands (7), January 11, 1873.

The "Northfleet," laden with railway iron, for Van Diemen's Land, and railway navvies, run into by a foreign steamer (probably the "Murillo," a Spanish vessel), off Dungeness, about 10·30 p.m.; 300 lives lost, January 22, 1873. [The "Murillo" was captured near Dover, September 22, and condemned by the Court of Admiralty to be sold (the officers severely censured), November 4, 1873.]

The "Polonaise" wrecked off Mast Island; crew and passengers saved. February 4, 1873.

The "Ellsmere," barque, 179 tons, totally wrecked on leaving the Richmond River, March 26, 1873.

The "Fire King," steamer (C. & R.R.S.N. Co.), lost at the Manning Bar; all hands saved. April 30, 1873. [Cargo estimated at £7,000.]

The "Belle Isle," ship, 1,180 tons, sprung a leak and was abandoned, May 5, 1873. [Crew saved by barque "Velocidad."]

The "Rangitoto," steamer, Captain Mackie, wrecked on Jackson's Head, at the entrance to Queen Charlotte's Sound, New Zealand coast, July 31, 1873.

The "Oscar," barque, 306 tons, wrecked between Sydney Heads by missing stays and getting on to the rocks at Old Man's Hat; crew saved. Sept. 12, 1873.

The "Maafu," schooner, foundered with all hands (8), between Sydney and Manning River, Sept. 16, 1873.

The "Iron King" foundered off Troubridge Island, South Australia, December 11, 1873.

The immigrant ship "Surat" wrecked off coast of Otago, N.Z.; no lives lost. December 31, 1873.

The "Alma" wrecked on King's Island, Bass's Straits; no lives lost. 1873.

The "Alice Jane" supposed to have capsized, with all hands (6) lost, was found bottom up, on the beach, near Port Hacking, January 15, 1874.

WRECK OF THE "BRITISH ADMIRAL"
The Australasian Sketcher, 1874

The "Australia," brigantine, lost at Richmond River Bar, cargo worth £1,200, February 11, 1874.

The "Traveller," 116 tons, totally wrecked on Myall Beach, through cable parting, May 1, 1874.

The "Corsair," brigantine, 134 tons, valued at £9,700, beached, to save life, 8 miles north of Merimbula, May 13, 1874.

The "British Admiral" wrecked at King's Island ; 79 out of 88 lives lost. May 23, 1874.

The "Corsair," pilot cutter, wrecked off Point Nepean, May 24, 1874.

The "Chance," ketch, lost whilst crossing the Manning River Bar ; three hands drowned ; master saved. June 6, 1874.

The "Flintshire," steamer, wrecked on a rock off Cape Cleveland, June 22, 1874.

The "G. H. Peake," brig, collided with an American vessel, the "Sierra Nevada," 7 miles south of Newcastle, and went down ; all hands saved by the "Sierra Nevada." July 11, 1874.

The "Clara," schooner, 130 tons, in ballast, valued at £1,500, drifted on reefs outside Nobby's and became a total wreck. July 26, 1874.

The "Eleanor," barque, 396 tons, foundered with all hands (12) between Sydney and New Zealand, July 26, 1874.

The emigrant ship "Cospatrick," Captain Elmslie, which left London for New Zealand, on September 11, 1874, caught fire a few hundred miles from the Cape of Good Hope. November 19, 1874. [Out of about 480 people, only five persons were rescued, after eight days' sufferings, by the "British Sceptre". The captain, his wife and son, perished amongst the number.]

The "Windhover," brig, 207 tons, valued at £2,000, sprung a leak after leaving Newcastle, and foundered ; all hands saved. December 13, 1874.

Wreck of the brig "Centaur," of Melbourne, near Freemantle, W.A. ; crew saved. January 9, 1875.

The "Blencathra" wrecked on King's Island, February 3, 1875.

The "Helen Macgregor" steamer (C. & N.E.S.N. Co.), wrecked on Clarence Heads ; eight lives lost. February 12, 1875.

The "Sarah Nicol," schooner, foundered during a gale near Bellinger River ; all hands (5) lost. February 19, 1875.

The "Euroka," schooner, foundered with all hands (5) near Sander River, February 19, 1875.

The "Waikato," steamer, burnt and scuttled, February 23, 1875.

The steamer "Gothenburg," from Port Darwin for Adelaide, wrecked on the south of Cape Bowling Green, Perar Reef, Flinders Passage, February 24, 1875. [102 lives were lost, including some distinguished South Australian colonists.]

The steamer "Schiller," from America, with Australian mails, lost on the English coast ; 311 lives lost. May 8, 1875.

The "New England," steamer, went on shore at Clarence Heads. May 28, 1875.

The A.S.N. Co.'s steamer "Rangatira," 500 tons, Captain Wood, lost on Roquea Reef, New Caledonia, May 31, 1875.

The s.s. "Pioneer" lost in Curranulla Bay, N. S. W., June 27, 1875.

The emigrant ship "Strathmore," 1472 tons, from London to Otago, N.Z, wrecked on Apostle Island, Crozet Group, July 2, 1875. [Out of 400 passengers and crew only 38 were saved, who remained on the Island until January 22, 1876, when they were taken off by the American whaler "Phœnix."]

The "Ben Nevis" wrecked at Newcastle, N.S.W., July 3, 1875.

The "Susannah Cuthbert," steamer, ran on Long Reef in foggy weather, and became a total wreck, July 7, 1875. [Value of cargo, £6,300.]

The "Naval Brigade" wrecked at Bowen, Queensland, August 1, 1875.

The "Cambridgeshire," from Gravesend to Sydney, wrecked on Night Island, Banks Straits, Sept. 7, 1875.

The "Susannah Booth," 111 tons, totally lost on Richmond River Bar, April 23, 1876.

The "Teirpan", barque, 222 tons, from Newcastle to Brisbane, sprung a leak and foundered in 40 minutes ; crew saved in boats. June 6, 1876.

The "Lightning," emigrant ship, Captain Cameron, with 406 emigrants on board, went ashore off Trowbridge Island on her way to Adelaide, July 6, 1876. [She was afterwards got off.]

Discovery of the wreck of the barque "Giltwood" (a new iron vessel, on her first voyage, from Liverpool to Melbourne), near Rivoli Bay, S.A. ; all on board perished. July 6, 1876.

The "Ann," barque, 277 tons, foundered off Port Stephens, with all hands (10), July 25, 1876.

The E. and A. Co.'s steamer "Queensland," sunk off Wilson's Promontory, through a collision with the M. S. Company's s.s. "Barrabool" ; one life lost. August 3, 1876. [Estimated value of the lost steamer, £75,000.]

The ship "Great Queensland," 1700 tons register, left Gravesend, England, with thirty-five passengers and thirty-five crew, bound for Melbourne, August 6, 1876. She was last sighted, and has not since been heard of, August 23, 1876. [She had on board 2,300 tons of general cargo, besides 35 tons of gunpowder.]

Barque "Ellengrove," from Newcastle to Adelaide, lost with eight of the crew, September 8, 1876.

A disastrous collision, resulting in the loss of about 100 lives, occurred off Portland, English coast, between the ship "Avalanche," bound for New Zealand, and the barque "Forest," on the night of September 9, 1876.

The "William," brigantine, 188 tons, driven on to the beach, Cape Byron Bay, and became a total wreck, September 11, 1876.

Wreck of the "Dandenong," off Jervis Bay ; forty lives lost. September 11, 1876.

The "City of Melbourne," Captain Paddle, narrowly escaped in a dreadful gale which raged along the southern and eastern coasts of Australia ; nine valuable racehorses, worth £20,000, lost. September 11, 1876.

The schooner "Atlantic," which left Richmond River September 8, 1876, discovered capsized off Sydney ; all hands lost. September 20, 1876.

The "Urania," schooner, 101 tons, sailed from Newcastle, and never heard of again ; six hands, all on board, lost. December 3, 1876.

The "Hector," schooner, 115 tons, sailed from Sydney, for Richmond River, with six hands on board, and was never again heard of, December 3, 1876.

The "Otago," steamer, wrecked at the entrance of Foveaux Straits, December 4, 1876.

The schooner "Postboy," with six hands, wrecked on the South Australian coast ; all lost. December 16, 1876.

The "Flying Squirrel" wrecked on King's Island, Bass's Straits ; no lives lost. 1876.

The mail steamer "Singapore" wrecked on Lone Island, off Port Mackay, January 30, 1877.

The s.s. "Victorian" came into collision with the steam dredge "Willunga," belonging to the South Australian Government, and sank her in the channel of Port Adelaide, February 6, 1877.

The "Blue Bell" steamer, wrecked on Keppel Rock, February 11, 1877.

The "Ocean Mail," ship, Captain Watson, bound from Wellington, N.Z., to London, wrecked on French Reef, Chatham Islands, March 15, 1877. [She had on board for England, 4,892 bales of wool and other cargo, of a total value of £78,000.]

The "City of Foochow," bound from Sydney to Calcutta, wrecked on Flinders Island ; passengers and crew all rescued. March 7, 1877.

The brig "Emily Smith," from King George's Sound to Adelaide, wrecked near West Bay ; twenty-one persons drowned. May 21, 1877.

Schooner "Young Australian," trading between Brisbane and Adelaide, wrecked at Curdie's Inlet, near Warrnambool, May 28, 1877.

The brig "Edith Haviland" wrecked at Carpenter's Reef whilst on a voyage from Adelaide to Sydney ; the master's wife and three children lost. June 20, 1877.

The barque "Sylphide," 294 tons, came into collision with the steamer "Ballina" off Port Jackson and sank, June 27, 1877.

The s.s. "Bulli" wrecked on Kent's Group, Bass's

Straits, June 26, 1877.

The "City of Hobart"'s., 459 tons, valued at £6,500, lost through screw-shaft breaking, when she foundered 60 miles N.E. of Wilson's Promontory, July 26, 1877.

The s.s. "Yarra Yarra" lost with all hands outside Newcastle harbour, July 15, 1877.

The barque "Gloucester," 526 tons, sprung a leak and foundered 31 miles off Smoky Cape, July 29, 1877.

The barque "Peony," 388 tons, sprung a leak and was beached near Richmond River ; five lives out of ten on board lost. August 8, 1877.

The Torres Straits mail steamer "Normanby" struck on a rock off Percy Island, Queensland coast ; passengers and crew all saved. August 13, 1877.

The steamer "Lord Ashley" wrecked off Terrigal Harbour, N.S.W., September 7, 1877.

The ship "Consett" ran into and sank the ship "Tessore," bound for Melbourne, when 150 miles off Cape Clear ; no lives lost. October 10, 1877.

The steamer "Florence Irving" (A.S.N. Co.), valued at £23,000, lost through striking on a rock near Port Stephens ; one life lost. December 4, 1877.

The "Abeona" wrecked on King's Island, Bass's Straits ; no lives lost. 1877.

The steamer "Queensland" (A.S.N. Co.) stranded on Central Island, Fitzroy River, Jan. 18, 1878. She was floated off and towed to Rockhampton, Feb. 8, 1878.

The Orient steamer "Chimborazo," Captain J. V. Hall, jun., ran on rocks at Point Perpendicular, March 15, 1878. [She remained on the rocks for a short time and was eventually got off, brought to Sydney, and repaired.] The Marine Board, Sydney, found that the stranding of the "Chimborazo" was due to the default of the captain, J. V. Hall, April, 1878. [The captain's certificate was suspended for six months.]

The ship "Loch Ard," 623 tons, wrecked at the Caves, one mile east of Sherbrooke Creek, fourteen miles from Moonlight Head, Victoria Coast, June 1, 1878. [All the passengers and crew, except Miss Eva Carmichael, and Thomas R. Pearce, midshipman, were lost ; Pearce gallantly rescued Miss Carmichael.]

The steamer "Blackbird," wrecked on the Ninety-mile Beach, a little west of Kate Kearney Channel ; no lives lost. June 2, 1878.

The Orient steamer "Garonne" went ashore at Ras Hafoon ; two lives lost. June 6, 1878. [The vessel was got off without damage, June 9, 1878.]

The barque "James Service," from Calcutta to Melbourne, lost near Pinjarrah, 40 miles south of Freemantle, West Australia, twenty-four persons being drowned, July 23, 1878.

The H.R.S.N.S. Co.'s steamer "City of Newcastle," 247 tons, T. Summerbell, master, lost during a fog by the vessel running on the rocks, under Sheppard's Hill, two miles south of Newcastle, September 12, 1878 [The cargo was valued at £25,000.]

The ship "City of Auckland," Captain Rolls, from London to Napier, with 256 emigrants, wrecked near Otago, New Zealand ; no lives lost. October 22, 1878.

The steamer "Mecca" wrecked in Torres Straits, December, 24, 1878.

The "Bonnie Dundee," steamer, bound north 8 miles south of Newcastle, came into collision with the M.S.S. Co.'s s.s. "Barrabool," and foundered four minutes after the collision. Three ladies and the cabin boy were drowned. March, 1879.

XENOPHON, a sloop of war, put in commission under the command of Lieutenant Flinders, who completely refitted and had her renamed the "Investigator." The vessel sailed from England on July 18, 1801 ; and amongst those who sailed with Flinders in her on the voyage of discovery in southern latitudes were Mr. James Crossley, the astronomer, Mr. Robert Brown, naturalist, Mr. Westall, the famous landscape painter, Mr. Bauer, natural history painter, and midshipman John Franklin, afterwards Sir John Franklin, afterwards the celebrated arctic navigator. After doing some good work on the Australian coast, the "Xenophon," or "Investigator," was brought to Sydney by Flinders, where she was condemned as unseaworthy. June 9, 1803.

XYLOGRAPHY. The art of *wood engraving* has been extensively followed in Australia, commensurate with the progress of literature. Artists on woods, of whom we have many possessing the highest qualifications, find ample scope for their abilities. When *Sydney Punch* was first established, its illustrations were engraved only on wood, as are now those of *Melbourne Punch*. The Sydney *Town and Country Journal*, the *Melbourne Sketcher*, the *Australian News* (Melbourne), *Illustrated Sydney News*, the *Sydney Mail*, the *Adelaide News*, and other papers, give illustrations on wood worthy to be placed side by side with those of their London contemporaries. Many books issued from the Australian press contain admirable specimens of wood-engraving ; amongst these may be mentioned Garnet Walch's "Head over Heels," published in 1874 ; the same author's "On the Cards," published in 1875 ; and G. H. Gibson's (Ironbark) "Southerly Busters," published in 1887. For many years there was resident in Sydney one of the first wood-engravers of the time. As a draughtsman he was an artist in the true sense of the word ; as a wood-engraver his works were ranked with those of the two Delamattes, the Viztellys, and the Dalziel Brothers. Mr. Walter George Mason's name appears on the drawings of that splendid work the original edition of "Lockhart's¡ Spanish Ballads," published by John Murray, and other important works, as well as in the earlier numbers of *London Punch*. The pictures in the *Sydney Punch* of 1862 are also from the graver of Mr. Mason. He died in 1865, leaving a son who follows the art in Sydney. [The *Ake ake*, or hardwood of New Zealand, was used for wood-engraving in 1875, and found to produce good effects. If properly seasoned, this will prove a valuable substitute for the Turkey boxwood, or sandalwood, which is becoming scarce and expensive. The use of ake ake for engraving was first made known in 1874, by Mr. W. Gordon, of Wanganui, New Zealand.]

YOUNG MEN'S CHRISTIAN ASSOCIATION.
The first of the Australian institutions established in Sydney—Mr. John Fairfax, president. 1853.

THE ZIG ZAG
Picturesque Atlas of Australia

Z

ZIG ZAG. One of the greatest engineering works in Australia, and is said to rank among the boldest and most substantial railway constructions in the world. The railway line is across the Blue Mountains, N.S.W., and commences at Penrith, 34 miles from Sydney. The line then ascends 155 feet, and crosses Knapsack Gully by the Viaduct, which is 388 feet long, and has a maximum height of 126 feet. This crossing is 245 feet above Emu Plains, and the line reaches the lower point of the first zig-zag at an elevation of 414 feet above sea-level, and thence an elevation of 470 feet is attained in a distance of 30 chains. After this the line continues to ascend till it reaches the summit of Lapstone Hill, and then it follows the range dividing the tributaries of the Nepean and Cox Rivers from those of the Grose River, passing Springwood, Blue Mountain, Weatherboard, Pulpit Hill, Blackheath, 3,494 feet, to near Shepherd's Toll-bar and Mount Victoria, 3,422 feet above the sea. Here the line commences to diverge to the north along Darling's Causeway, which divides the waters of the Lett from the sources of the Grose River, to Bell's line of road, or the range dividing the river Lett and Grose River tributaries from those of the river Colo. Following this range to Dargan's Creek the line passes through Mount Clarence by a tunnel 539 yards in length, the rails at the entrance of which are 3,658 feet above sea-level. This is the summit level of the line, 88 miles from Sydney, and 52 miles from the commencement of the ascent of the Blue Mountain Ranges at Emu Plains. The line then descends on a gradient of 1 in 42 towards Lithgow Valley beyond, reaching the higher points of the Great Zig-zag 91 miles from Sydney, at an elevation of 3,362 feet. At this point the line runs nearly parallel with the main line, but in an opposite direction, for a distance of 67 chains. After passing two viaducts and through a short tunnel it reaches the lower points of the Zig-zag at an elevation of 3,261 feet, and thence further descends towards Bathurst, which is situated 145 miles from Sydney, at an elevation of 2,153 feet. Between Mount Clarence, 88 miles from

Sydney, and Wallerawang, 105 miles, there are seven viaducts, of 2,225 feet in length, averaging in height from 10 to 70 feet, and in span from 10 to 54 feet—the majority being 30 feet; also three tunnels—one at Lithgow Valley Zig-zag 77 yards in length, one at Morangaroo 267 yards in length, and one under the Mudgee Road 47 yards in length. The smallest radius of a curve in this section is 528 feet, the total length of such curves being 5 miles, including those upon the two Zig-zags. There are also 20 miles of curves ranging from 8 chains to 12 chains radius. In the whole work the number of viaducts is 8, of tunnels 4, of bridges 8, and of culverts 268. The total excavations amounted to about 3,040,000 cubic yards, of which 1,783,000 were through rock. The cost of construction alone was about £812,000.

FINIS.

[*A prophecy, written by* DR. ERASMUS DARWIN, *about* A.D. 1790.]

WHERE Sydney Cove her lucid bosom swells,
Courts her young navies, and the storm repels;
High on a rock amid the troubled air
HOPE stood sublime, and wav'd her golden hair;
Calm'd with her rosy smile the tossing deep,
And with sweet accents charm'd the winds to sleep;
To each wild plain she stretched her snowy hand,
High-waving wood, and sea-encircled strand.
" Hear me," she cried, " ye rising Realms! record
Time's opening scenes, and Truth's unerring word:—
There shall broad streets their stately walls extend,
The circus widen, and the crescent bend;
There, ray'd from cities o'er the cultur'd land,
Shall bright canals, and solid roads expand:
There, the proud arch, Colossus-like, bestride
Yon glittering streams, and bound the chasing tide;
Embellish'd villas crown the landscape scene,
Farms wave with gold, and orchards blush between.
There shall tall spires, and dome-capt towers ascend,
And piers and quays their massy structures blend;
While with each breeze approaching vessels glide,
And northern treasures dance on every tide!"—
Then ceas'd the nymph—tumultuous echoes roar,
And Joy's loud voice was heard from shore to shore—
Her graceful steps descending press'd the plain,
And PEACE, and ART, and LABOUR, join'd her train!